MATHEMATICAL AND ECONOMIC THEORY OF ROAD PRICING

Related Elsevier series

DRESNER (ed.)
Research in Transportation Economics

HENSHER & BUTTON (eds.)
Handbooks in Transport

Related Elsevier journals

Transport Policy
Editors: Moshe Ben-Akiva, Yoshitsugu Hayashi and John Preston

Transportation Research Part A: Policy and Practice
Editor: Phil Goodwin

Transportation Research Part B: Methodological
Editor: Fred Mannering

For full details of all transportation titles published under the Elsevier imprint please go to:
www.elsevier.com/transportation

MATHEMATICAL AND ECONOMIC THEORY OF ROAD PRICING

HAI YANG
Department of Civil Engineering
The Hong Kong University of Science and Technology
Hong Kong, P. R. China

HAI-JUN HUANG
School of Management
Beijing University of Aeronautics and Astronautics
Beijing 100083, P. R. China

2005

ELSEVIER

Amsterdam – Boston – Heidelberg – London – New York – Oxford – Paris
San Diego – San Francisco – Singapore – Sydney – Tokyo

ELSEVIER B.V.
Radarweg 29
P.O. Box 211, 1000 AE Amsterdam
The Netherlands

ELSEVIER Inc.
525 B Street, Suite 1900
San Diego, CA 92101-4495
USA

ELSEVIER Ltd.
The Boulevard, Langford Lane
Kidlington, Oxford OX5 1GB
UK

ELSEVIER Ltd.
84 Theobalds Road
London WC1X 8RR
UK

First edition 2005

Library of Congress Cataloging in Publication Data
A catalog record is available from the Library of Congress.

British Library Cataloguing in Publication Data
A catalogue record is available from the British Library.

ISBN: 0 08 044487 3

♾ The paper used in this publication meets the requirements of ANSI/NISO Z39.48-1992 (Permanence of Paper).
Printed in The Netherlands.

CONTENTS

[illegible]

ACRONYMS

AC	Average Cost
BLPP	Bi-Level Programming Problem
BOT	Build-Operate-Transfer
BPR	Bureau of Public Roads
BLVI	Bi-Level Variational Inequality
CN	Cournot-Nash
DUE	Deterministic User Equilibrium
EB	Economic Benefit
EPEC	Equilibrium Problem with Equilibrium Constraints
KKT	Karush-Kuhn-Tucker
LP	Linear Program
MC	Marginal Cost
MPEC	Mathematical Program with Equilibrium Constraints
OD	Origin -Destination
SC	Social Cost
SO	System Optimum
SW	Social Welfare
STEN	Space-Time Expanded Network
SUE	Stochastic User Equilibrium
UB	User Benefit
UE	User Equilibrium
VI	Variational Inequality
VOT	Value Of Time

GLOSSARY OF NOTATION

a	a link $a \in A$
A	the set of all links
$\bar{A}$	the subset of links subject to a toll charge
$\tilde{A}$	the subset of links with observed flows
$B_w(d_w)$	the benefit function between OD pair $w \in W$
$B_w^m(d_w^m)$	the benefit function of user class $m \in M$ between OD pair $w \in W$
c_{rw}	the travel cost on path r connecting OD pair $w \in W$
$\mathbf{c}$	the vector of path travel costs
c_{rw}^m	the travel cost on path r between OD pair w by users of class $m \in M$
C_a	the capacity of link $a \in A$
d_w	the travel demand between OD pair $w \in W$
$\mathbf{d}$	the vector of OD demands
$\hat{D}_w$	the potential demand or the upper-bound of demand between OD pair $w \in W$
d_w^m	the travel demand of user class m between OD pair $w \in W$
$\hat{D}_w^m$	the potential demand of user class m between OD pair $w \in W$
$D_w(\mu_w)$	the demand function between OD pair $w \in W$
$D_w^{-1}(d_w)$	the inversed demand function between OD pair $w \in W$
E_v^u	Elasticity of v to u, $E_v^u = (u/v)\mathrm{d}v(u)/\mathrm{d}u$
f_{rw}	the flow on path $r \in R_w$
$\mathbf{f}$	the vector of path flows
f_{rw}^m	the flow of user class $m \in M$ on path $r \in R_w$ between OD pair $w \in W$
G	(N, A) be a network with node set N and link set A
K	the set of Cournot-Nash (CN) players or the set of vehicle types
$I_a(y_a)$	the construction cost of link a as a function of link capacity y_a
m	a user class $m \in M$
M	the set of all user classes with different values of time
N	the set of all nodes
r	a path or a route $r \in R$
R_w	the set of all paths connecting OD pair $w \in W$

R	$=\bigcup_{w\in W} R_w$
t_a^0	the free-flow travel time (moving time on link $a\in A$
$t_a(v_a)$	the travel time on link $a\in A$ as a function of link flow v_a
$\tilde{t}_a(v_a)$	the marginal social travel time on link $a\in A$, including the congestion externality, $\tilde{t}_a(v_a)=t_a(v_a)+v_a\,\mathrm{d}t_a(v_a)/\mathrm{d}v_a$
$t_a(v_a, y_a)$	the link travel time as a function of both flow and capacity variables
$\mathbf{t}(\mathbf{v})$	the vector of link travel times
u_a	toll charge on link $a\in A$
$\mathbf{u}$	the vector of link tolls
v_a	the flow on link $a\in A$
$\mathbf{v}$	the vector of link flows
v_a^m	the flow of user class m on link $a\in A$
v_a^k	the link flow of vehicle type $k\in K$ or CN player $k\in K$
w	an OD pair $w\in W$
W	the set of all OD pairs
W^k	the set of OD pairs of which users are controlled by CN player $k\in K$
W^K	$=\bigcup_{k\in K} W^k$
W^m	the set of OD pairs of which users are controlled by UE class $m\in M$
W^M	$=\bigcup_{m\in M} W^m$
y_a	the capacity of a new link a or capacity increase of an existing link a
$\mathbf{y}$	the vector of link capacity variables
β	the users' value of time
β_m	the average value of time of user class $m\in M$
δ_{ar}	1, if link $a\in A$ is on path $r\in R$ and 0, otherwise
Δ	the link/path incidence matrix, $\Delta=[\delta_{ar}]$
ε	a predetermined tolerance for stopping iterative process
Λ_{rw}	1 if path $r\in R_w$ and 0, otherwise
Λ	the OD/path incidence matrix, $\Lambda=[\Lambda_{rw}]$
μ_w	the Lagrange multiplier associated with the demand conservation constraint of OD pair $w\in W$, or the generalized travel cost between OD pair $w\in W$ at equilibrium
μ_w^m	the generalized travel cost of user class $m\in M$ between OD pair $w\in W$
μ	the vector of generalized OD travel costs

Ω	the feasible region of link flows and OD flows
Ω_f	the feasible region of path flows
Ω_v	the feasible region of link flows
Ω^k	the feasible region of links flows of CN player $k \in K$
Ω^m	the feasible region of link flows of a UE class $m \in M$
Ω^U	the feasible region of link flows of UE player
$\nabla_{\mathbf{v}}\mathbf{t}(\mathbf{v})$	the Jacobian matrix of link travel time function $\mathbf{t}$ with respect to $\mathbf{v}$
$\in$	element membership
$\subset$	proper set inclusion
$\cup$	union of sets
∞	infinity
$\lvert \cdot \rvert$	the cardinality of a finite set
$\lVert \cdot \rVert$	the Euclidean norm
$\arg\min_x F(x)$	the set of x attaining the minimum of the function $F(x)$

PREFACE

Road pricing as an effective means of both managing road traffic demand and raising additional revenue for road construction has been studied extensively by both transportation researchers and economists. Practical implementation has been progressing rapidly and electronic road pricing schemes have been proposed and tested worldwide. It is likely that over the next few years, with increasing public acceptability, there will be greater use of road pricing. The incontestable fact is that there is a great need for the development of efficient road-use pricing models.

Despite a few monographs and journal special issues in the literature that have been devoted to the topic in recent years, most studies have focused on empirical studies, policy experience, environmental issue of road congestion and road pricing. There is still scope for methodological development of advanced road pricing systems, such as dynamic pricing, integrated road and transit pricing, as well as practical toll charging schemes in general road networks. This book is intended to deal with a number of timely topics including: fundamentals of user-equilibrium problems; principle of marginal-cost pricing applied to road pricing; existence of optimal link tolls for system optimum under multi-class, multi-criteria, multiple equilibrium behaviors; social and spatial equity issues in road pricing; optimal design of private toll roads; simultaneous determination of optimal toll levels and locations; trial-and-error implementation of marginal-cost pricing on networks with unknown demand functions; dynamic road pricing.

This book would appear to be the first book devoted exclusively to the mathematical and economic investigation of road-use pricing in general congested networks, which aims at alleviating traffic congestion, improving transport conditions and enhancing social welfare. It constitutes an update of the state of the art of the latest research, mainly by the authors and their colleagues. The book is targeted at students, professionals and scientists who are studying and working in relevant transportation fields.

We are most thankful to a number of individuals for their help during our work in this field. First and foremost we would like to acknowledge the contribution and continuing encouragement of Prof. M.G.H. Bell of Imperial College London (ICL). In fact, the manuscript was finalized during the first author's sabbatical leave at ICL in early 2005, and he is particularly grateful to Prof. Bell for his hospitality during a very fruitful and enjoyable stay in ICL. Thanks are also due to Prof. R. Lindsey of the University of Alberta, Prof. E.

Verhoef of the Free University of Amsterdam, Prof. W.H.K. Lam of the Hong Kong Polytechnic University and Prof. S.C. Wong of the University of Hong Kong throughout our study of the various road pricing problems and in the preparation of this book. We highly appreciate our research collaboration that produced some of the material included in the book. We also wish to greatly thank three former Ph.D students at the Hong Kong University of Science and Technology, Dr. Qiang Meng (currently at the National University of Singapore), Dr. Xiaoning Zhang (currently at the Tongji University of Shanghai) and Dr. Judith Wang (currently at the University of Auckland) for their contributions to various topics in the book. Thanks also go to Miss Wei Xu and Mr Xiaolei Guo (currently PhD students at the Hong Kong University of Science and Technology) who helped in discussions in earlier drafts of the book. Funding for the research was provided by the Research Grants Council of the Hong Kong Special Administrative Region (HKSAR) and the National Natural Science Foundation, P.R. China.

Hai Yang
Hai-Jun Huang

31 May 2005

1

INTRODUCTION

1.1 BACKGROUND

Roadway congestion is a source of enormous economic costs. In principle, many of these costs can be prevented, as they result from socially inefficient choices by individual drivers. A number of regions have considered alleviating roadway congestion by introducing congestion pricing. Indeed, road pricing has become one of the priorities on transport policy agendas throughout the world. It is increasingly believed that road pricing may offer an effective instrument to manage travel demand, and to raise revenue that may, for instance, be used for transport improvements. An increasing number of congestion pricing schemes have been proposed, tested or implemented worldwide. Examples include the US's value pricing scheme, recent EU green and white papers, Dutch initiatives, electronic road pricing schemes in Singapore and Hong Kong, and the London congestion charging scheme that was introduced in February 2003.

It is conceivable that a new generation of road-use pricing technologies will be widely considered for introduction on many congested road networks. All these emerging technologies offer efficient tools and challenges for implementation of road pricing for traffic management, and also generate a great need for the development of efficient pricing models that allow for the evaluation and perhaps design of innovative road pricing schemes. Some monographs and journal special issues have been devoted to these topics in recent years. However, the majority of studies have focused on the empirical aspects, policy experiences, and environmental issues of road congestion and road pricing. There is, however, still ample scope for methodological developments for the analysis of advanced road pricing systems, such as dynamic pricing, integrated road and transit pricing, as well as practical toll charging schemes in general road networks.

1.2 THEORETICAL DEVELOPMENTS

The initial idea of road pricing was put forward by Pigou (1920), who used the example of a congested road to make points on externalities and optimal congestion charges (see, also, Knight, 1924, for early interpretation of social cost and toll charge). The fundamental concept is easy: to apply a price mechanism in the same way as it applies elsewhere in a market economy. Prices should be higher under congestion conditions and lower at less congested times and locations in order to deter excessive uses. The key question is how to choose the appropriate price in a simple yet practical manner, under what is often a complex set of economic and technical circumstances. The key issue from a practical point of view is how to implement the concept, not only in terms of developing technically efficient charging mechanisms, but also in gaining political acceptance as a valid policy instrument (Button and Verhoef, 1998).

There have been both intellectual and practical developments after Pigou's idea of using road pricing measures to regulate road traffic congestion. Seminal works on road pricing that need to be mentioned include Wardrop (1952), Walters (1961), Beckmann (1965) and Vickrey (1969). The subject of road pricing has particularly rejuvenated interest extensively from both economists and transportation researchers in recent years, because of the growing prominence and changing nature of urban transportation problems facing a modern city. Here we do not intend to fully review the large body of literature (which will be done in individual chapters) but merely outline the various types of road pricing problems of interest and some relevant analytical studies. Readers are invited to refer to McDoland (1995), Lo and Hickman (1997), Button and Verhoef (1998), Verhoef (1996), McDonald et al. (1999), Levinson (2002), Yang and Verhoef (2004), and Santos (2004) for excellent reviews or monographs on the subject, from the economic perspective.

1.2.1 The First-best Pricing Problem

The theoretical background of road-use pricing has relied upon the fundamental economic principle of marginal-cost pricing, which states that road users using congested roads should pay a toll equal to the difference between the marginal-social cost and the marginal-private cost in order to maximize the social surplus. By so doing, each user will face the marginal social cost of road use other than the marginal private costs. For a congested road, this includes the value of time losses imposed on other road users, as well as the value of emissions, noise and accident risks created. The social surplus, defined as the difference between the total benefits and total costs, is often considered as an appropriate indicator for social welfare, and its maximization is a condition for economic efficiency to prevail (Verhoef, 1996).

The theory of the marginal-cost pricing or the first-best pricing in the literature by Pigou and followers (for example, Walters, 1961; Vickrey, 1963; Evans, 1992; Hills, 1993) was developed based on the demand-supply (or performance) curves for the standard case of a homogenous traffic stream moving along a given uniform stretch of road, such as an expressway, connecting given entry and exit points. There would be some decision on what the optimal traffic flow should be, essentially determined by estimating the traffic speed-flow relationship underlying the performance curve. The congestion charge would then be an efficient way of attaining the target flow of traffic.

In the case of homogeneous users, the first-best congestion pricing theory is established in general traffic networks. In line with this theory, a toll that is equal to the difference between the marginal social cost and the marginal private cost is charged on each link, so as to internalize the user externalities and thus achieve a system optimum flow pattern in the network (Beckmann, 1965; Dafermos and Sparrow, 1969, 1971). Investigations have been conducted on how this classical economic principle would work in a general congested road network with multiple vehicle types, such as trucks versus passenger cars (Dafermos, 1972, 1973), with both multiple vehicle types and link flow interactions (Smith, 1979b), with queuing (Yang and Huang, 1998), and in a congested network in a stochastic equilibrium (Yang, 1999). Moreover, Bellei et al. (2002) developed a variational inequality model for network pricing optimization in a multi-user and multi-modal context; Liu and Boyce (2002) presented a variational inequality formulation of the marginal-cost pricing problem for a general transportation network with multiple time periods. Recently, Yang, Zhang and Meng (2004) developed a trial-and-error implementation method for marginal-cost pricing on networks in the absence of demand functions.

1.2.2 The Second-best pricing problems

In spite of its perfect theoretical basis, the first-best or marginal-cost pricing scheme is of little practical interest. The problem stems from the fact that it is impractical to charge users on each network link in view of the operating cost and public acceptance. Note that a simple introduction of the "marginal-cost pricing tolls" over a *subset* of the links of a network based on a local link speed-flow relation may distort the allocation of the traffic over the entire network and may cause degradation instead of improvement in social welfare. Thus, setting the toll equal to the marginal cost of the trips may not be valid for the design of an optimal road pricing scheme in a more complex environment.

Due to the imperfection of the first-best pricing, the second-best pricing is, in fact, often the most relevant case from a practical perspective and has received ample attention in the recent literature (Lindsey and Verhoef, 2001). The key questions to be answered in a second-best pricing scheme in general include: where to levy the toll and how much? What different impacts would the pricing schemes bring to different users?

Most studies in the context of the second-best pricing problems are generally conducted with respect to the determination of toll levels for given charge locations. The simplest version of the problem concerns the two route problem, where an untolled alternative road is available parallel to a toll road. This problem was probably first analyzed by Levy-Lambert (1968) and Marchand (1968), and more recently by Braid (1996), Verhoef et al. (1996), and Liu and McDonald (1999). There are in general four alternative types of toll charging schemes in road networks that are of practical interest (May and Milne, 2000): travel-distance based charging, travel time or travel-delay based charging, link-based charging and cordon-based charging. In a travel distance or travel time based charging scheme, a toll is charged in proportion to the distance traveled or the time spent in the network and the optimal toll charge per unit distance or travel time for minimization of total travel time or maximization of social welfare can be easily determined using simple optimization search methods. In a link-based pricing scheme, tolls are charged only on a subset of selected links, especially where there is a bottleneck. In many cities, congestion tolls are collected on some urban bridges; tunnels or expressways, and tolls at different locations are coordinated for congestion mitigation (Yang and Lam, 1996). Furthermore, the link tolls are considered to act as some additional costs that prevent traffic flow becoming unstable and/or producing unacceptable environmental damage. This consideration is intimately related to the emerging issue of sustainable development and transportation facing most major cities. Road pricing and travel demand management are being considered to be the key instruments to deal with the environmental impacts of transportation. With this pivotal issue in mind, Ferrari (1995, 1997, 1999) and Yang and Bell (1997) developed various mathematical models for the traffic restraint and road pricing problem that have important implications for enhancement of environmental quality and traffic management.

Instead of charging on separate individual links, a cordon-based pricing scheme emerged in recent years in some countries or regions for reducing traffic demand in congested urban central areas (May et al., 2002; Santos et al., 2001; Santos, 2002; Mun et al., 2003). There are many rational aims of second-best congestion pricing. They could be minimizing the system cost, including operating cost, maximizing social welfare gain and maximizing revenue. In addition, simultaneous determination of toll locations and toll levels on a network is of practical importance (Hearn and Ramana, 1998; Verhoef, 2002; Yang and Zhang, 2002a).

1.2.3 Value of Time and Road Pricing

The concept of value of time (VOT) plays a pivotal role in road pricing analysis as it describes how users make tradeoffs between cost and time. In the presence of heterogeneous users with different VOTs, various network equilibrium models have been developed by assuming either a discrete set of VOTs for several distinct user classes or by a continuously distributed VOT across the whole population (Leurent, 1993, 1996 and 1998; Marcotte and Zhu, 2000; Mayet and Hansen, 2000; Nagurney, 2000).

The optimal pricing problems for users with discrete or continuous VOT distributions had been investigated by Dial (1999a, 1999b) and Florian (1998). Dial (1999a, 1999b) established a model and algorithm for determining a system-wide optimal set of tolls that induce traffic that is simultaneously user- and system-optimal. The model permits the VOT to be continuously distributed for each Origin-Destination (OD) pair. Assuming that each trip uses a path that minimizes its own particular perception of generalized cost, Dial demonstrates what economists have always known, that is to minimize the total perceived cost of time and the best toll for a link is its expected value of the social component of its marginal cost. Arnott and Kraus (also refer to Lindsey and Verhoef, 2001) have shown that first-best pricing remains possible using anonymous tolls with heterogeneous user groups, provided that the tolls can be varied freely over time and the system objective function is measured in conventional unit of dollars. The optimality of anonymous tolling is derived from the fact that the appropriate tolls depend only on the marginal externality costs that drivers impose and that the congestion externality is anonymous at any departure time. Recently, Mayet and Hansen (2000) investigated second-best congestion pricing with continuously distributed VOT for a highway with an unpriced substitute, where alterenative optimal tolls are found depending on whether the social welfare function is measured in money or in time, and whether toll revenue is or is not included as part of the benefit. Yang and Huang (2004) further investigated the relationship between the multi-class, multi-criteria traffic network equilibrium and system optimum problems. Using a product differentiation approach, Verhoef and Small (2004) examined the impacts of user heterogeneity (with a continuously distributed VOT) on the results of the first-best, second-best and the revenue-maximizing pricing policies. De Palma and Lindsey (2004) examined the effect of congestion pricing with heterogeneous travelers using a general-equilibrium welfare analysis.

1.2.4 Equity Issues and Revenue Redistribution in Road Pricing

In congestion pricing, the social equity issue is concerned with the unequivocally distributional impacts of road pricing between the poor and the rich users, because fixed charges represent a larger portion of income for a low-income drivers than for a high-income driver. This socially inequitable issue has often been used as an argument to justify the political unacceptability of road pricing and has been debated extensively in the literature (Foster, 1975; Small, 1983; Starkie, 1986; Hau, 1992; Johansson and Mattsson, 1995; Litman, 1996; Button and Verhoef, 1998; Richardson and Bae, 1998; Giuliano, 1992; Viegas, 2001; Paulley, 2002; Raux and Souche, 2004).

Apart from the conventional social equity issue between poor and rich drivers by paying the same toll charge, there exists a spatial equity issue in the sense that the changes of the generalized travel costs of drivers traveling between different OD pairs may be significantly different when tolls are charged at some selected links. Santos and Rojey (2004) assessed the potential distributional impacts of a road pricing scheme in three English towns and indeed found that impacts are town specific and depend on where people live, where people work and what mode of transport they use to go to work. Recently, Yang and Zhang (2002b) incorporated both the social and spatial equity issues in the analysis of the second-best network toll design problems.

Road pricing can raise large amounts of revenue and the alternative allocations of the revenue vary from investment in infrastructure, to compensation to losers and improvement of public transport. The way in which the government allocates revenues will determine both the equity and the political acceptability of a road pricing scheme. Several researchers have looked into various revenue distribution strategies. For examples, Small (1992c) proposed a travel allowance for all commuters. Parry and Bento (2001) recommended that income taxes be reduced to offset congestion pricing-related labor supply restrictions. Goodwin (1989) suggested a combination of revenue uses in order to offset several congestion pricing impacts. Poole (1992) added that it may be possible to introduce off-peak discounts and peak-hour surcharges on a toll road. DeCorla-Souza (1994) proposed a cashing out strategy to induce a shift of peak-period travelers to other modes, thus reducing the need for additional infrastructure. Recently, Kalmanje and Kockelman (2004) proposed a credit-based congestion pricing strategy where the term "credit" refers to a monetary cash-out. The method can help tackle the problem of congestion in an equitable and efficient fashion.

From a theoretical perspective, Bernstein (1993) examined the possibility of user-neutral congestion pricing with both positive and negative tolls (tolls and subsidies) in the bottleneck congestion model; Adler and Cetin, (2001) discussed a direct distribution approach to congestion pricing in which monies collected from users on a more desirable route are directly transferred to users on a less desirable route using a two parallel route example with bottleneck congestion. For a OD pair connected by a number of parallel routes, Elliasson (2001) showed that a tolling and refunding system that reduced aggregate travel time and refunded the toll revenues equally to all users will make everyone better off than before the toll reform; Yang, Meng and Hau (2004) developed an optimal integrated pricing model in a bi-modal transportation network with explicit consideration of subsidy to the transit mode from road congestion pricing revenue. Apart from economic efficiency, they also showed that transport pricing and subsidy policy can also be justified on the grounds of the equity issues.

1.2.5 The Road Pricing and Capacity Choice Problem

Even if road capacity can be adjusted to cope with congestion, capacity policies alone will typically not be sufficient to reach a socially optimal outcome, and the use of congestion pricing remains warranted. Given the reality of public ownership of most roads and the possibility of internalizing the congestion externality with corrective congestion charge, there have been a number of studies looking at the link between the optimal congestion charge and the road investment strategy (Mohring, 1970). An important result in transport economics, the self-financing result, was first established by Morning and Harwitz (1962) for a single road: Under certain technical conditions, the revenues from optimal congestion pricing, equal to the difference between the marginal social cost and marginal private cost at any level of traffic flow, will be just sufficient for financing the fixed costs associated with the optimal capacity supply. The conditions are satisfied when there are constant returns to scale in road construction and maintenance, and the capacity can be increased in continuous increments (Morning and Harwitz, 1962). This self-financing result was later expanded to include damage. In this sense, a road charge equal to the sum of the optimal congestion charge and the road damage charge, covers the fixed operating cost and the variable maintenance cost, provided there are constant returns to scale in construction and, maintenance and use of road capacity (Newbery, 1988; 1989). The theorem has been shown to extend to each road individually in a full network and consequently to the network in aggregate, provided each link is optimally priced and all capacities are optimized (Yang and Meng, 2002), to dynamic models (Arnott and Kraus, 1995).

The growing participation of the private sector in constructing, maintaining and operating road infrastructures has been justified for its positive effects on public budgets and cost efficiency in the provision of the required road capacity. Under the so-called Build-Operate-Transfer (BOT) schemes, the private sector builds and operates roads at its own expense and receives the revenue from road toll charges over a number of years, after which these roads are transferred to the government. Such commercial and private provision of public roads has attracted fast-growing interest in recent years and is being used to finance modern road systems worldwide (Tam, 1998).

Once road provision moves into the market economy, there are many intriguing issues to be addressed. From the viewpoint of private investors, the profitability of a road project is of a great concern; while from the government side, social welfare should be the main goal. It is thus imperative to assess whether or not the construction of a toll road will give a positive welfare increment if it is profitable, compared with the do-nothing alternative, and vice versa whether or not a toll road, which adds to welfare, will be profitable and hence can be provided privately. Obviously, answers to these issues crucially depend upon the supply decisions made by individual firms in terms of capacity choice and pricing, which directly affect the cost of the road project and its attractiveness to potential users. The choice of capacity and prices is more complex when two or more competing firms operate multiple toll roads, because their profits are interrelated due to demand inter-dependence in the network. Apart from the consideration of road user responses, each firm must consider what its competitors' choices are likely to be in making its capacity design and pricing decisions.

There has been mounting interest in how price and capacity should be chosen by private road operators. General arguments over the private provision of roads are given by, for example, Geltner and Moavenzadeh (1987); Gomez-Ibanez *et al.* (1991); Banister *et al.* (1993); David and Fernando (1995); Nijkamp and Rienstra (1995); and Roth (1996). Theoretical studies range from the use of an analytical approach for a single road or bottleneck or parallel roads (Viton, 1995; Mills, 1995, Verhoef, 1996, Braid, 1996; De Palma and Lindsey, 2000, 2002; Verhoef and Small, 2004; Tsai and Chu, 2003; De Rus and Romero, 2004) to the use of general traffic equilibrium approach for general networks (Yang and Meng, 2000, 2002; Verhoef and Rouwendal, 2004). Yang and Tang et al. (2002) developed multiclass network equilibrium models and studied the effect of users' value of time distributions on profitability and social welfare gain from private toll roads. Yang and Woo (2000) examined graphically the competitive Nash equilibrium by considering two toll roads provided and operated by two profit-maximizing private firms. Wang et al. (2004) examined a situation where both highway infrastructure and transportation (bus) services on the highway are provided commercially and privately, and examined the strategic interactions of such a bilateral monopoly.

1.2.6 Mathematical Programming Approach to Road Pricing

By explicitly incorporating the users' responses to the toll pricing into the analysis, the general network toll design problem can be studied in the context of the TNO-UEC (Transportation Network Optimization with User Equilibrium Constraints), which has received a long-standing interest in the transportation science community. The TNO-UEC problem is to determine the optimal values of a set of decision variables (toll charge in the case of congestion pricing) so that an appropriate measure of transportation system performance is optimized, while taking into account the route choice behavior of network users (for a recent review, see, Yang and Bell , 2001; Clegg et al., 2001). It is well known that the TNO-UEC problems can be well described as BLPP (Bilevel Programming Problem) (Shimizu et al., 1997; Dempe, 2002) and more generally as MPEC (Mathematical Program with Equilibrium Constraints) (Luo et al., 1996).

There has been a growing number of studies recently on the various network toll design problems, in particular in the case where only a subset of links in the network is subjected to toll charges. Optimal determination of tolls for a subset of links in a network by Yang and Lam (1996) for the case with fixed demand, by Zhang and Ge (2004) for the case with elastic demand and Yang and Bell (1997) when there are link flow restrictions. Labbe et al. (1998) and Brotcorne et al. (2001) developed a linear bi-level model for toll optimization in uncongested networks. Yang and Zhang (2002b) dealt with the equity-constrained network toll design problem with multiple user classes. Bergendorff et al. (1997) and Hearn and Ramana (1998) proposed various methodologies to extract congestion toll sets such that the tolled user equilibrium is system optimal. Dial (1999c, 2000) proposed efficient algorithms to find the minimal-revenue congestion tolls that can sustain a user-optimal flow pattern as a system optimum; Bai et al. (2004) proposed a decomposition technique for the minimum toll revenue problem. Lawphongpanich and Hearn (2004) recently proposed a cutting plane method for solving the bilevel second-best toll pricing problem. Chen and Bernstein (2004) and Chen et al. (2004) simplified formulations and solution methods of the network toll design problem with multiple user classes using restricted path sets; Yang, Zhang and Meng (2004) dealt with the network toll design problem with entry-exit based toll charges using the network equilibrium model with path-specific cost.

1.2.7 Dynamic Road Pricing Problem

There has been a vast accumulation of the literature that deals with the dynamic road pricing problem, ranging from a single highway bottleneck to a general transportation network following the bottleneck model developed by Vickrey (1969). In the standard bottleneck model, congestion is assumed to arise when vehicles queue behind a bottleneck. All commuters wish to arrive at work at a certain time but there is a bottleneck with finite capacity that will not allow all of them to arrive at their preferred time. There are costs associated with early and late arrival, which together with the toll, are added to the cost of the trip. Commuters try to minimize their generalized trip costs by choosing their departure time. Departure time evolves during the rush hour and hence forms a time pattern of departure. The evolution of congestion in the rush hour is thus endogenously determined. Arnott, de Palma and Lindsey (1988; 1990a,b; 1992; 1993a,b; 1994; 1998) have further extended the bottleneck model along the lines traced by Vickrey (1969) to include heterogeneous commuters, route choice, stochastic capacity, elastic demand, and time-varying tolls.

A second form of the dynamic congestion model, initially developed by Henserson (1974), considers hyper-congestion. The approach also involves the distribution of travel delays and scheduling of costs of the peak, and the duration of the peak in the un-tolled equilibrium and the social optimum, being determined endogenously. This type of generic model was further extended by Mun (1994), Chu (1995), Huang and Yang (1996), Yang and Huang (1997). It is found that the social optimum does not require complete elimination of travel delays. Verhoef (2003) further examined the occurrence of hyper-congestion and the optimal road pricing in a continuous-time-continuous-place dynamic economic model of traffic congestion.

A third form of the dynamic congestion model, initially developed by Tabuchi (1993), involves two travel modes, consisting of a road with a bottleneck and a railroad exhibiting economies of scale, in order to investigate the efficiency of several railroad fare and road toll regimes. Huang (2000, 2002) derived and compared the socially optimal combination of transit fare and road toll for the two-mode problem in the case of the logit-based mode choice and two groups of commuters. Danielis and Marcucci (2002) explored the consequences of price distortion in the railroad mode on road congestion pricing. Such distortion may take place when the railroad operator seeks to make a zero loss, when railroads are privatized or when the market for railroad services is assigned through franchise bidding.

1.3 Outline of The Book

The theoretical background of road-use pricing has relied upon the fundamental economic principle of marginal-cost pricing, which states that road users using congested roads should pay a toll equal to the difference between the marginal-social cost and the marginal-private cost in order to maximize the social net benefit. Up to date, however, most theoretical arguments about road-use pricing are entirely concerned with abstract demand-supply models with simplifying assumptions. There exists in the literature considerable confusion about the analysis of road congestion that needs to be clarified. There are also many interesting, yet important issues, to be explored when the detailed modeling of a network is involved, such as bounding the efficiency gain achieved from a marginal-cost pricing scheme and the self-financing in a general road network with general traffic equilibrium models. In addition, various difficulties raised from the practice of road pricing, for example how to ensure the social/spatial equity, how to handle road pricing revenue, and how to determine the optimal location of toll links, are in need of efficient solutions. Moreover, there has been a great need for the development of practical and efficient methods for the actual design and implementation. A fundamental question is how to choose the optimal congestion tolls in a simple yet practical manner.

This book addresses the important, essential and practical problems of road pricing by making use of advanced modeling techniques with rigorous mathematical and economic theories. Most studies presented in the book are carried out on the economic equilibrium analysis of general transportation networks and hence are quite different from traditional analytical methods of road pricing. This book consists of thirteen chapters that provide in-depth accounts of the state of the art, either by dealing with new problems or developing new solution methods.

Chapter 2 provides the fundamentals of the concepts, models and algorithms of the traffic equilibrium and system optimum problems on networks and their various extensions, which are essential to the road pricing analysis. This chapter also contains review materials of well-known solution methods for the various traffic equilibrium models.

In Chapter 3, we expound the fundamental principle of marginal-cost pricing that is used to consider road congestion pricing. We explain how this classical principle would work in a general congested network and how the principle holds when link flow interactions and link capacity constraints are built into the traffic equilibrium model. We examine the conditions for unique user equilibrium and system optimum solutions.

In Chapter 4 we illustrate the application of the bilevel programming approach to the various types of second-best alternative pricing problems when the stringent assumptions of the first-best or marginal-cost pricing conditions are not satisfied as indeed in the case in reality. We develop a simple and general gradient-based sensitivity analysis of network traffic equilibrium, and present its meaningful application to the general traffic restraint and road pricing problem.

Chapter 5 continues to investigate the general second-best pricing problems in networks. We introduce equivalent, continuously differentiable single-level reformulation of the general bilevel network toll design problems using differentiable gap functions. Both the gap function, by virtue of the marginal or value function of the convex UE program, and the general gap function of the variational inequality formulation of the generalized UE problem are described. An application of the gap function based approach is given to the network toll design problem with entry-exit based toll charges.

Chapter 6 examines the question of the existence of optimal link tolls for system optima under multi-class, multi-criteria and multiple equilibrium behaviors. We investigate the following questions: whether the user-optimal flows depends on the unit (time or money) used in measuring the travel disutility in the presence of a toll charge; whether there are any uniform link tolls across all individuals with different values of time that can support a multi-class user-optimal flow pattern as a system optimum, when the system objective function is measured by either money or time units. In the presence of multiple equilibrium behaviors, whether a system-optimum flow pattern remains attainable by meaningful link tolls.

Chapter 7 is concerned with the social and spatial equity issues in road pricing. The social equity refers to the different financial burden imposed between lower-income and higher-income drivers and the spatial equity represents the different changes in the generalized travel costs of drivers traveling between different OD pairs, when tolls are charged at some selected locations in the network. We develop interesting and meaningful pricing and revenue redistribution schemes that can make all users better off. We also incorporate both the social and spatial inequities as constraints in the network toll design models.

Chapter 8 analyzes the pricing problems in the context of private roads. We first consider the profitability and social welfare gain of toll roads in a network with either homogeneous or heterogeneous users. We establish the conditions for the self-financing theorem to hold in a first-best road pricing and capacity choice scheme in a general network and examine its consequence in a second-best environment. We move to the investigation of the competition and equilibria, based on a situation where there are two or more profit-maximizing private firms that operate multiple interrelated toll roads in a road network.

Chapter 9 investigates the problem of the simultaneous determination of optimal toll levels and locations on general networks encountered in the various second-best pricing problems. Specifically, we deal with the second-best link-based and cordon-based pricing schemes that involve simultaneous selection of both toll levels and toll locations. Optimization models with mixed (discrete and continuous) variables are developed and solved with the meta-heuristic methods.

In Chapter 10, we examine the technical difficulty in determining the toll charge and develop novel new methods for the actual implementation of congestion pricing. Specifically we propose trial-and-error implementation of the first-best and the second-best pricing problems on networks when the demand functions are unknown. We establish the convergence of the trial-and-error procedure for the first-best pricing problem and propose a heuristic sequential experimenting approach to the second-best pricing problems. The proposed procedure allows a traffic planner to easily estimate the socially optimal congestion tolls in networks without resort to the demand functions.

In Chapter 11, we attempt to find the maximum efficiency gain that can be achieved through a marginal-cost pricing scheme in a general network. An upper bound of the efficiency gain of a marginal-cost pricing scheme is established, using the latest concept of price of anarchy of atomic and non-atomic congestion games. We also try to bound the efficiency loss of a second-best pricing scheme in relation to the first-best one.

Chapter 12 is devoted to the dynamic road pricing problems with single or parallel bottlenecks. We present the basic single bottleneck model and then its extension to a network of parallel routes. The two mode problem is also discussed in which an alternative mass commuting mode, such as a railway or subway, exists in parallel to the road with a bottleneck. In all cases, we obtain analytical results and provide sensible economic or behavioral interpretations.

Finally, in Chapter 13, a general model simultaneously dealing with departure time, route choice and optimal congestion toll in a general network is developed, using the space-time extended approach. The model can deal with a general queuing network with elastic demand, and allow for treatment of commuter heterogeneity in their work start time and schedule delay cost, and hence make a significant advance over the previous simple bottleneck models of peak-period congestion.

2

Fundamentals of User-Equilibrium Problems

2.1 Introduction

Two central concepts pertaining to road pricing are User-Equilibrium (UE) and System Optimum (SO) of traffic flow distribution in networks. In this chapter, we provide a tutorial in the various formulations of the standard UE and SO problems and their extensions, which are frequently used in subsequent analysis of various road pricing issues. A brief outline of the well established solution concepts for the various UE and SO problems is provided as well. The background materials would be useful in understanding the developments in the main body of the book.

The fundamental aim of traffic assignment is to find link or path flow patterns, given the Origin-Destination (OD) trip rates, network topology, and link performance functions. The result of the assignment is an estimate of traffic volume on each link in the network, and the associated measures of system performance. To do so, we have to make some assumptions that describe how commuters make their travel decisions. A well received assumption in the literature is that all users have perfect information about traffic conditions over the entire network and make consistently correct decisions in route choice, leading to the deterministic (UE or SO) assignment models. The UE model assumes that all users minimize their own individual travel costs on transportation networks, while the SO model hypothesizes that all users cooperate to minimize total network cost. Incorporating uncertainty in travel choice analysis, as usually done in stochastic traffic assignment models, is important, but is not covered in this book.

The following terms and concepts are frequently used throughout this book. An urban road transportation system is described as a strongly connected, directed network (N, A) where N and A denote the sets of nodes and links, respectively. The assumption of a strongly connected network means that there exists at least one route from each origin to each destination. A link $a \in A$ represents a road segment and nodes may be origins, destinations or road intersections. Trips are generated from various origins and absorbed to all destinations. Let W be the set of such OD pairs and d_w be the number of trips made between OD pair $w \in W$. Users select paths (or routes) for traveling from their origins to destinations in the network. A path is defined as a connected sequence of links and R_w denotes the set of all simple paths connecting OD pair $w \in W$. Traffic volume or flow on a link is the sum of flows along the paths that go through this link. Let f_{rw} denote the flow on path $r \in R_w$ between OD pair $w \in W$ and v_a the flow on link $a \in A$. The relationship between link flows and path flows can be expressed by

$$v_a = \sum_{w \in W} \sum_{r \in R_w} f_{rw} \delta_{ar}, \quad a \in A \tag{2.1}$$

where δ_{ar} is equal to 1 if link a is on path r and 0 otherwise. Due to traffic congestion, travel time on a link $a \in A$ is assumed to be an increasing function of flow on that link. Let $t_a(v_a)$ be the (average) link travel time function for link $a \in A$. It is assumed to be a differentiable, monotonically increasing function of link flow. A typical link travel time function is shown in Figure 2.1, where free-flow travel time corresponds to zero flow. Theoretically, the traffic flow on a link can not exceed its physical capacity, but an approximate form of the function is adopted in most models for facilitating the solution techniques. Traffic assignment models with explicit link capacity constraints are given later. The travel time along a path, c_{rw}, $r \in R_w$, $w \in W$, is given as the sum of travel times on all links that constitute the path. We thus have

$$c_{rw} = \sum_{a \in A} t_a(v_a) \delta_{ar}, \quad r \in R_w, \; w \in W \tag{2.2}$$

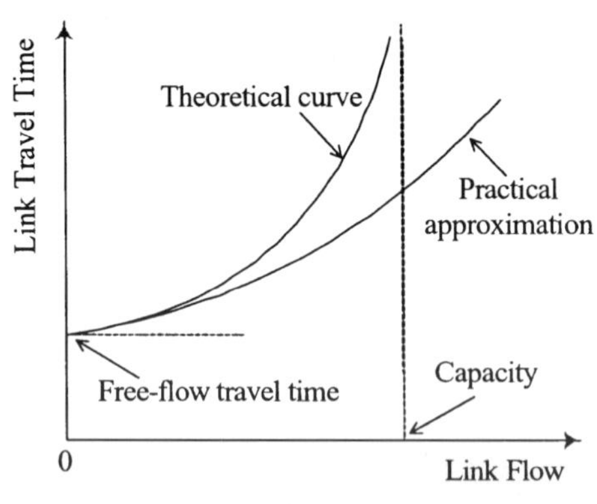

Figure 2.1 Typical form of a link travel time function

2.2 FORMULATION OF THE STANDARD USER-EQUILIBRIUM PROBLEMS

2.2.1 The UE Model with Fixed Demand

As mentioned above, in the UE assignment problems, all trips are assumed to select paths or routes independently that minimize their own individual travel costs. Under the resulting network flow pattern, all routes actually used for a specific OD pair have equal travel cost which is less than that on any of the unused paths. We call such a network being in a Wardrop UE state where no users can find a shorter path by unilaterally changing their routes. Here we provide formulation of the UE problem in the forms of mathematical programs.

It is well known that the link-flow pattern satisfying the UE conditions can be obtained through solving the following equivalent mathematical program

$$\min\ Z(\mathbf{v}) = \sum_{a\in A}\int_0^{v_a} t_a(\omega)\mathrm{d}\omega \tag{2.3}$$

subject to

$$\sum_{r\in R_w} f_{rw} = d_w,\ w\in W \tag{2.4}$$

$$f_{rw} \geq 0,\ r\in R_w,\ w\in W \tag{2.5}$$

where link flows, $\mathbf{v} = (v_a, a\in A)^{\mathrm{T}} = (\cdots, v_a, \cdots)^{\mathrm{T}}$ (arranged as a column vector), are given by (2.1). The objective function does not have any intuitive economical or behavioral interpretation. It can only be viewed as a mathematical construction for implementing the UE condition. Constraints (2.4) state that the sum of flows on all paths connecting each OD pair has to equal the OD demand. Constraints (2.5) are non-negativity requirements on all path flows. The relationships between link flows and path flows are expressed by (2.1).

Formulation (2.3)-(2.5) is called the Beckmann transformation. It is easy to prove that any flow pattern that solves (2.3)-(2.5) satisfies the Wardrop's UE conditions. View link flow $\mathbf{v}$ as a function of path flow vector $\mathbf{f}$ as defined by (2.1) and construct a Lagrangean function:

$$L(\mathbf{f},\mu) = Z(\mathbf{v}(\mathbf{f})) + \sum_{w\in W}\mu_w\left(d_w - \sum_{r\in R_w} f_{rw}\right) \tag{2.6}$$

where μ_w is the Lagrange multiplier associated with (2.4) for OD pair $w\in W$ and $\mu = (\mu_w, w\in W)^{\mathrm{T}}$. The first-order optimality conditions for an optimum solution $\mathbf{f}^* = (f_{rw}^*, r\in R_w, w\in W)^{\mathrm{T}}$ to the minimization problem (2.3)-(2.5) are

$$f_{rw}^{*}\frac{\partial L(\mathbf{f}^{*},\mu)}{\partial f_{rw}}=0 \text{ and } \frac{\partial L(\mathbf{f}^{*},\mu)}{\partial f_{rw}}\geq 0,\ r\in R_w, w\in W \tag{2.7}$$

$$\frac{\partial L(\mathbf{f}^{*},\mu)}{\partial \mu_w}=0,\ w\in W \tag{2.8}$$

together with the non-negativity condition (2.5) and the link-path incidence relationship (2.1). With use of eqn. (2.1), (2.7) and (2.8) can be expressed explicitly as

$$f_{rw}^{*}(c_{rw}-\mu_w)=0,\ r\in R_w, w\in W \tag{2.9}$$

$$c_{rw}-\mu_w\geq 0,\ r\in R_w, w\in W \tag{2.10}$$

$$\sum_{r\in R_w} f_{rw}^{*}-d_w=0,\ w\in W \tag{2.11}$$

where $c_{rw}=\sum_{a\in A}t_a\left(v_a^{*}\right)\delta_{ar},\ r\in R_w,\ w\in W$. It is readily verified that conditions (2.9) and (2.10) together yield the following results

$$c_{rw}=\mu_w \text{ if } f_{rw}^{*}>0;\ c_{rw}\geq\mu_w \text{ if } f_{rw}^{*}=0,\ r\in R_w, w\in W \tag{2.12}$$

These conditions imply that, at the optimum, the cost on any path with positive flow, i.e., $f_{rw}^{*}>0$, must equal a constant, μ_w, the OD specific Lagrange multiplier; otherwise it is greater than or equal to μ_w. This constant is the minimum among all possible path costs as stated by (2.10). Hence, the Lagrange multiplier associated with a specific OD pair can be regarded as the minimum path travel time between that OD pair. It is thus clear that the first-order conditions are equivalent to the Wardrop UE conditions: for each given OD pair, any actually used path has the same, minimum travel time.

Therefore, with the assumptions on link travel time functions, solving mathematical program (2.3)-(2.5) is equivalent to finding the UE link-flow pattern. It can be shown that (2.3)-(2.5) has only one stationary point in link flow, i.e., the optimal solution expressed by link flow. In fact, the objective function (2.3) is strictly convex with respect to $\mathbf{v}$, since its Hessian matrix,

$$\nabla^2 Z(\mathbf{v})=\begin{bmatrix} t_1'(v_1) & 0 & 0 & \cdots \\ 0 & t_2'(v_2) & & \cdots \\ 0 & 0 & \ddots & \\ \vdots & \vdots & & t_{|A|}'(v_{|A|}) \end{bmatrix} \tag{2.13}$$

is positive definite. In eqn. (2.13) the prime superscript denotes the derivative of the travel time function to link flow, i.e., $t_a'(v_a)=\mathrm{d}t_a(v_a)/\mathrm{d}v_a$, $a\in A$, and $|A|$ is the cardinality of the set A. Clearly, all entries in the diagonal matrix (2.13) are positive because the travel time of each link is assumed to be a monotonically increasing function of its own link flow. Note that in deriving (2.13) we employ

$$\frac{\partial^2 Z(\mathbf{v})}{\partial v_a \partial v_b} = \frac{\partial(\partial Z(\mathbf{v})/\partial v_a)}{\partial v_b} = \frac{\partial t_a(v_a)}{\partial v_b} = \{t'_a(v_a) \text{ for } b = a;\ 0, \text{otherwise}\} \tag{2.14}$$

This means the interactions of flows and travel times across links are temporarily not considered in UE problem (2.3)-(2.5). The right hand side of (2.13) is also called the Jacobian of link-travel-time vector, $\mathbf{t}$, with respect to link flow vector, $\mathbf{v}$.

The region of feasible solutions to mathematical program (2.3)-(2.5) is made by linear equalities and inequalities. This region is hence a convex set. So, problem (2.3)-(2.5) is a strictly convex mathematical programming problem which has only one link-flow pattern solution satisfying the UE requirements. However, it should be noted that this program is not *strictly* convex with respect to the path flow, hence there may exist more than one path-flow pattern solution, which generates the unique, optimal link-flow pattern solution.

2.2.2 Solution Method for the fixed Demand UE Problem

In the optimization theory, there are many algorithms suitable for solving the minimization problem (2.3)-(2.5). Among these, the convex combination method, which is based on feasible direction-searching, has been most widely employed. In this method, the direction-searching step which originally corresponds to solving a linear program (LP) is reduced to a shortest-path problem. The reason is that the gradient of the objective function, $Z(\mathbf{v})$, with respect to link flow at each iteration, *e.g.*, the nth iteration, equals the link travel time, i.e., $\partial Z(\mathbf{v}^{(n)})/\partial v_a = t_a(v_a^{(n)})$. The LP problem at the nth iteration thus becomes

$$\min\ Z^{(n)}(\overline{\mathbf{v}}) = \nabla Z(\mathbf{v}^{(n)})^{\mathrm{T}}\,\overline{\mathbf{v}} = \sum_{a\in A} \frac{\partial Z(\mathbf{v}^{(n)})}{\partial v_a}\overline{v}_a = \sum_{a\in A} t_a^{(n)}\overline{v}_a \tag{2.15}$$

subject to

$$\sum_{r\in R_w} \overline{f}_{rw} = d_w\,,\ w\in W \tag{2.16}$$

$$\overline{f}_{rw} \geq 0\,,\ r\in R_w,\ w\in W \tag{2.17}$$

where $\overline{v}_a = \sum_{w\in W}\sum_{r\in R_w} \overline{f}_{rw}\delta_{ar}$ is the auxiliary link flow on link a, and $\overline{f}_{rw}$ is the auxiliary path flow for path $r\in R_w$ connecting OD pair $w\in W$. The LP problem (2.15)-(2.17) minimizes the total network travel time with temporarily fixed link travel times, $t_a^{(n)} = t_a(v_a^{(n)})$, $a\in A$. Clearly, performing an all-or-nothing assignment just reaches this target, which assigns all trips on to the corresponding shortest paths. Consequently, solving the LP problem (2.15)-(2.17) is replaced by executing an all-or-nothing assignment. The step-by-step procedure of the convex combination algorithm for solving the problem (2.3)-(2.5) is given below.

Step 0. (*Initialization*) Perform all-or-nothing assignment based on link travel time $t_a = t_a(0)$, $a \in A$. This yields $\mathbf{v}^{(1)}$. Let iteration counter $n := 1$.

Step 1. (*Updating*) Update link travel times, $t_a^{(n)} = t_a\left(v_a^{(n)}\right)$, $a \in A$.

Step 2. (*Direction finding*) Execute all-or-nothing assignment to yield auxiliary link flows $\overline{\mathbf{v}}$.

Step 3. (*Line search*) Find an optimal step size $\alpha^{(n)}$ by solving

$$\min_{0 \le \alpha \le 1} \sum_{a \in A} \int_0^{v_a^{(n)} + \alpha\left(\overline{v}_a^{(n)} - v_a^{(n)}\right)} t_a(\omega) d\omega$$

Step 4. (*Updating*) Update link flows, $v_a^{(n+1)} = v_a^{(n)} + \alpha^{(n)}\left(\overline{v}_a^{(n)} - v_a^{(n)}\right)$, $a \in A$.

Step 5. (*Convergence check*) If a convergence criterion is met, then stop with $\mathbf{v}^{(n+1)}$ being the solution; otherwise, set $n := n + 1$ and go to Step 1.

Step 2 is about performing an all-or-nothing assignment by identifying the shortest paths for all OD pairs. Shortest-path finding is a well-researched problem in graph theory and various efficient algorithms are available in the operations research literature. The line search in Step 3 can be done by any of the interval reduction methods, such as the bisection method, Golden section method or Fibonacci method. The stopping criterion in Step 5 could be designed according to the reduction of objective function values or the change in link flows between two successive iterations. For example, the algorithm can terminate if

$$\frac{\sqrt{\sum_{a \in A}\left(v_a^{(n+1)} - v_a^{(n)}\right)^2}}{\sum_{a \in A} v_a^{(n)}} \le \varepsilon \tag{2.18}$$

where ε is a predetermined tolerance selected especially for our problem, based on the desired degree of accuracy. During the iterative process of the above algorithm, it is not required to store path flows, only the link flows. This follows from the observation that the value of the objective function (2.3) and all path costs are completely determined by link flows. Thus, considerable saving in the storage requirement is achieved. The convergence rate of the above Frank-Wolfe algorithm is sub-linear and the marginal contribution of each successive iteration becomes smaller and smaller as the algorithm proceeds. The algorithm converges rapidly in the first several iterations, but very slowly in the later stages, because the search direction $\left(\overline{\mathbf{v}}^{(n)} - \mathbf{v}^{(n)}\right)$ tends eventually to be orthogonal to the gradient of $Z\left(\mathbf{v}^{(n)}\right)$ at $\mathbf{v}^{(n)}$. The number of iterations required for convergence is significantly affected by the initial solution, the congestion level and the stopping criterion. In relatively un-congested networks, the flow pattern after a few iterations approaches the equilibrium state, since the updated link flows can not heavily change link travel times and then the set of shortest paths basically remains unchanged in the iterative process. As congestion builds up, more iterative works are required to equalize the costs on potentially possible-used paths. However, in most actual large-size applications with typical congestion levels, only six to ten iterations are usually sufficient to find the equilibrium link-flow pattern in terms of the tradeoffs among analytical accuracy, data limitations, and computer budget. All non-shortest paths are not assigned any flow.

2.2.3 The UE Model with Elastic Demand

The traffic assignment models presented so far have assumed that the traffic demand for each OD pair is given or fixed. Road pricing has in general long-term impact on traffic demand and thus a sound assessment of a pricing scheme requires consideration of price elasticity of travel demand. Here we briefly introduce the traffic assignment problem with elastic demand that is pertinent to road pricing analysis.

Suppose the OD demand in an OD pair is a function of the equilibrium OD travel time or cost between that OD pair (for simplicity and relevance in our subsequent studies, we consider separable demand functions unless mentioned specifically), namely $d_w = D_w(\mu_w)$ where μ_w is the shortest path time or cost between OD pair $w \in W$. We further assume that the demand function is a strictly monotone, invertible and decreasing function of travel time. Let $\mu_w = D_w^{-1}(d_w) = B_w(d_w)$, $w \in W$ denote the inverse or benefit function. The inverse or benefit function can be regarded as an amount that a user is willing to pay for his or her travel, or a benefit that he or she can obtain from this travel. The elastic demand traffic assignment problem is to determine a set of self-consistent link flows and an OD demand solution satisfying demand-performance relations. The convex optimization problem is expressed below

$$\min_{\mathbf{v},\mathbf{d}} \sum_{a\in A} \int_0^{v_a} t_a(\omega)\mathrm{d}\omega - \sum_{w\in W} \int_0^{d_w} B_w(\omega)\mathrm{d}\omega \tag{2.19}$$

subject to

$$\sum_{r\in R_w} f_{rw} = d_w,\ w\in W \tag{2.20}$$

$$f_{rw} \geq 0,\ r\in R_w,\ w\in W \tag{2.21}$$

where link flow v_a, $a\in A$ is given by (2.1).

Proceeding along the lines for obtaining (2.9)-(2.12) yields, for any optimum solution $(\mathbf{f}^*, \mathbf{v}^*, \mathbf{d}^*)$, the following relations

$$c_{rw} = \mu_w \text{ if } f_{rw}^* > 0;\ c_{rw} \geq \mu_w \text{ if } f_{rw}^* = 0,\ r \in R_w, w \in W \quad (2.22)$$

$$B_w(d_w^*) = \mu_w, \text{ if } d_w^* > 0;\ B_w(d_w^*) < \mu_w, \text{ if } d_w^* = 0,\ w \in W \quad (2.23)$$

again $c_{rw} = \sum_{a \in A} t_a(v_a^*)\delta_{ar}$, $r \in R_w$, $w \in W$ and $\mu_w = \min_{r \in R_w}\{c_{rw}\}$.

If the objective function is strictly convex, then the program (2.19) has a unique solution in terms of the OD demand and link flow. The first term in (2.19) is strictly convex if link time functions are monotonically increasing in link flows and the second term is strictly convex too if the benefit functions are monotonically decreasing in demands.

2.2.4 Solution Method for the Elastic Demand UE Problem

Note that the UE problem with elastic demand can be transferred into an equivalent UE problem with fixed demand by adding an auxiliary link between every OD pair, and all algorithms for the UE problem with fixed demand are applicable to the elastic demand case. Here we outline the convex combination method mentioned above for solving the convex program of the elastic-demand network equilibrium problem.

In terms of a set of auxiliary path flows $\bar{\mathbf{f}} = (\bar{f}_{rw}, r \in R_w, w \in W)^{\mathrm{T}}$, the counterpart of the auxiliary linear program at iteration n can be expressed as

$$\min\ Z^{(n)}(\bar{\mathbf{f}}) = \sum_{w \in W}\sum_{r \in R_w}\left[c_{rw}^{(n)} - B_w(d_w^{(n)})\right]\bar{f}_{rw} \quad (2.24)$$

subject to

$$\bar{f}_{rw} \geq 0 \quad r \in R_w, w \in W \quad (2.25)$$

$$\sum_{r \in R_w} \bar{f}_{rw} \leq \bar{D}_w \quad w \in W \quad (2.26)$$

where $c_{rw}^{(n)}$ is the travel time on path r between OD pair w at iteration n, $d_w^{(n)}$ is the value of the OD flow between OD pair w at iteration n, where $\bar{D}_w$ is an upper bound of the demand between OD pair $w \in W$. Clearly, the term in the bracket of (2.24) is constant with respect to $\bar{\mathbf{f}}$. In addition, constraint (2.26) applies to each OD pair independently. Thus, $Z^{(n)}(\bar{\mathbf{f}})$ can be minimized by each OD pair individually.

The problem for OD pair $w \in W$ is given by

$$\min\ Z^{(n)}\left(\overline{\mathbf{f}}_{rw}\right)=\sum_{r\in R_w}\left[c_{rw}^{(n)}-B_w\left(d_w^{(n)}\right)\right]\overline{f}_{rw} \tag{2.27}$$

subject to

$$\overline{f}_{rw}\geq 0\quad r\in R_w \tag{2.28}$$

$$\sum_{r\in R_w}\overline{f}_{rw}\leq \overline{D}_w \tag{2.29}$$

By inspection, the solution requires assignment of as much flow as possible (i.e., $\overline{D}_w$) for which $\left[c_{rw}^{(n)}-B_w\left(d_w^{(n)}\right)\right]$ is the smallest (most negative). One thus needs to determine the shortest path $c_{r'w}^{(n)}=\min_{r\in R_w}\left[c_{rw}^{(n)}-B_w\left(d_w^{(n)}\right)\right]$ and the value of $\left[c_{r'w}^{(n)}-B_w\left(d_w^{(n)}\right)\right]$ for each OD pair. If this term is positive, no flow should be assigned to any path in this OD pair. This procedure will result in the lowest value of objective function (2.27). In summary, for a given OD pair, the solution to the auxiliary linear program (2.27)-(2.29) can be simply obtained as

$$\overline{f}_{rw}^{(n)}=\begin{cases}\overline{D}_w,\ \text{if } c_{rw}^{(n)}\leq B_w\left(d_w^{(n)}\right)\\ 0,\ \text{otherwise}\end{cases},\quad r\in R_w,\ w\in W \tag{2.30}$$

$$\overline{v}_a^{(n)}=\sum_{w\in W}\sum_{r\in R_w}\overline{f}_{rw}^{(n)}\delta_{ar},\ a\in A;\quad \overline{d}_w^{(n)}=\sum_{r\in R_w}\overline{f}_{rw}^{(n)},\ w\in W \tag{2.31}$$

The Frank-Wolfe algorithm for solving the Elastic Demand UE problem is summarized below:

Step 0: (*Initialization*) Let $\{d_w^{(0)},\ w\in W\}$ be a set of initial OD demands and $\{v_a^{(0)},\ a\in A\}$ be the corresponding set of feasible link flows; Let $\varepsilon>0$ be a stop tolerance and set $n:=0$.

Step 1: (*Finding descent direction*) For each OD pair w, $w\in W$, compute the shortest path r' and the corresponding path cost $c_{r'w}^{(n)}$ based on the link travel costs $t_a\left(v_a^{(n)}\right)$, $a\in A$, obtain a set of auxiliary link flow and demand pattern $\{\overline{v}_a^{(n)},\ a\in A\}$ and $\{\overline{d}_w^{(n)}, w\in W\}$ by eqns. (2.30) and (2.31)

Step 2: (*Line search*) Find an optimal step size $\alpha^{(n)}$ by solving the following one-dimensional optimization problem

$$\min_{0\leq\alpha\leq 1}\sum_{a\in A}\int_0^{v_a^k+\alpha\left(\overline{v}_a^{(n)}-v_a^{(n)}\right)}t_a(\omega)d\omega-\sum_{w\in W}\int_0^{d_w^{(n)}+\alpha\left(\overline{d}_w^{(n)}-d_w^{(n)}\right)}B_w(\omega)d\omega$$

Step 3: (*Update link flows and OD demands*) Set

$$v_a^{(n+1)}=v_a^{(n)}+\alpha^{(n)}\left(\overline{v}_a^{(n)}-v_a^{(n)}\right),\ a\in A$$

$$d_w^{(n+1)}=d_w^{(n)}+\alpha^{(n)}\left(\overline{d}_w^{(n)}-d_w^{(n)}\right),\ w\in W$$

Step 4: (*Convergence check*) If

$$\frac{\sqrt{\sum_{a\in A}\left(v_a^{(n+1)}-v_a^{(n)}\right)^2}}{\sum_{a\in A} v_a^{(n)}}+\frac{\sqrt{\sum_{w\in W}\left(d_d^{(n+1)}-d_w^{(n)}\right)^2}}{\sum_{w\in W} d_w^{(n)}}\le \varepsilon$$

then terminate. Otherwise, let $n := n+1$ and go to Step 1.

2.3 TRAFFIC ASSIGNMENT WITH LINK CAPACITY CONSTRAINTS

On the theoretical and practical planes, the traffic flow on a link should not exceed its capacity. One method for capturing this idea is to introduce capacity constraints for links, if needed. Another method is to use an asymptotic travel time function that lets the travel time of a link become infinite when the flow approaches its upper bound. In this book, we introduce the former and show that the capacitated assignment model generates a flow-pattern still satisfying a modified Wardrop UE principle.

2.3.1 Model Formulation

Let C_a be the capacity of a link $a\in A$, C_a may be interpreted as saturation flow or exit capacity of the link. We presume that the capacitated assignment problem always has at least one feasible solution. This means that link capacities are large enough to allow all travel demands able to pass through the network. The capacitated UE traffic assignment is formulated as

$$\min\ Z(\mathbf{v})=\sum_{a\in A}\int_0^{v_a} t_a(\omega)\mathrm{d}\omega \tag{2.32}$$

subject to

$$\sum_{r\in R_w} f_{rw}=d_w,\ w\in W \tag{2.33}$$

$$v_a\le C_a,\ a\in A \tag{2.34}$$

$$f_{rw}\ge 0,\ r\in R_w, w\in W \tag{2.35}$$

where the link flow is given by (2.1).

Clearly, program (2.32)-(2.35) is strictly convex in link flows, hence has a unique optimal link-flow solution. Let μ_w and λ_a be the Lagrange multipliers associated with constraints (2.33) and (2.34), respectively. The first-order optimality conditions are given below:

$$f_{rw}\left(c_{rw}-\mu_w\right)=0,\ r\in R_w, w\in W \tag{2.36}$$

$$c_{rw} - \mu_w \geq 0,\ r \in R_w, w \in W \tag{2.37}$$

$$\sum_{r \in R_w} f_{rw} - d_w = 0,\ w \in W \tag{2.38}$$

$$f_{rw} \geq 0,\ r \in R_w,\ w \in W \tag{2.39}$$

$$v_a \leq C_a,\ a \in A \tag{2.40}$$

$$\lambda_a (v_a - C_a) = 0,\ a \in A \tag{2.41}$$

$$\lambda_a \geq 0,\ a \in A \tag{2.42}$$

where c_{rw} is given by

$$c_{rw} = \sum_{a \in A} \hat{t}_a (v_a) \delta_{ar},\ r \in R_w, w \in W \tag{2.43}$$

and

$$\hat{t}_a (v_a) = t_a (v_a) + \lambda_a,\ a \in A \tag{2.44}$$

We introduce a new definition about path travel time, i.e., the *generalized* path travel time given by (2.43). Then, a capacitated UE flow-pattern is expressed by (2.36)-(2.39), i.e., all paths actually used between an OD pair have equal and minimal generalized travel time, μ_w.

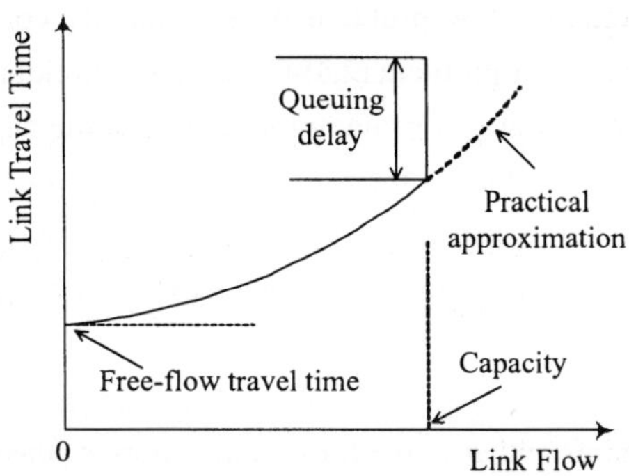

Figure 2.2 Equilibrium queuing delay or penalty when link capacity is reached

Equations (2.43) and (2.44) show that the generalized path travel time of a path is the sum of generalized link travel times on all links that belong to this path. The generalized link travel time consists of two components: $t_a(v_a)$ is the *moving time* on link $a \in A$, λ_a is the multiplier associated with constraint (2.34). From (2.40)-(2.42), it can be seen that $\lambda_a \geq 0$ only if $v_a = C_a$ and $\lambda_a = 0$ if $v_a < C_a$. We can naturally regard this multiplier, λ_a, as a equilibrium queuing delay time, i.e., an additional time penalty (besides the moving time) that users traveling on this saturated link are willing to wait for continuously using this link. Introduction of link queuing delays explore a way to create equal path travel times among all used paths (saturated or non-saturated ones). The queuing delay on a link exists only when the link flow reaches its capacity, see Figure 2.2.

It should be pointed out that although the equilibrium generalized path travel times, μ_w, $w \in W$, are unique, this is generally not true for the optimal multipliers, λ_a, $a \in A$. A necessary and sufficient condition for obtaining a unique equilibrium queuing delay is that all binding link capacity constraints (i.e., holding with strict equality) are linearly independent. The multiplier λ_a, can be interpreted as a toll charge imposed on all commuters who use link $a \in A$ for commuting, then an *un-queued* equilibrium flow pattern can be obtained. This toll charge produces no losses for network users if the toll is not beyond the queuing delay, because it simply substitutes the wasted queuing time.

2.3.2 Solution Algorithm

We now turn to study the solution methods for program (2.32)-(2.35). When applying the Frank-Wolfe algorithm to program (2.32)-(2.35), the direction searching step is required to solve a linear multi-commodity flow problem with inequality constraints, rather than the shortest path problem as done for problem (2.3)-(2.5). This is prohibitively expensive to solve repeatedly. Most algorithms employ a strategy that converts the capacitated problem into a sequence of un-capacitated problems through a penalization/dualization of the capacity constraints (2.34), so that various existing efficient approaches for program (2.3)-(2.5) can be applied for the solution of (2.32)-(2.35). Here, we present an augmented Lagrangean dual algorithm.

The penalty function methods, either in the form of an exterior penalty or an interior penalty, are often used to transform a constrained problem into an unconstrained or partially constrained problem. We set a penalty function for the link capacity constraint (2.34) as simple as

$$P_a(v_a) = \frac{1}{2}\max^2\{0,\ v_a - C_a\},\ a \in A \tag{2.45}$$

Then, the new objective function which contains all penalty components becomes

$$\tilde{Z}(\mathbf{v}) = Z(\mathbf{v}) + \rho \sum_{a \in A} P_a(v_a)$$

where ρ is a penalty parameter $(\rho > 0)$. For every specific ρ-value, an un-capacitated traffic assignment problem will be solved, i.e.,

$$\min_{\mathbf{v} \in \Omega_v} \tilde{Z}(\mathbf{v}) \tag{2.46}$$

where Ω_v is defined by

$$\Omega_v = \{\mathbf{v} \mid \mathbf{v} = \Delta\mathbf{f}, \Lambda\mathbf{f} = \mathbf{d}, \mathbf{f} \ge 0\} \tag{2.47}$$

where the link/path incidence matrix $\Delta = [\delta_{ar}]$, the OD pair/path incidence matrix $\Lambda = [\Lambda_{rw}]$ where Λ_{rw} =1 if $r \in R_w$ and 0, otherwise, and $\mathbf{d} = (d_w, w \in W)^{\mathrm{T}}$ is a column vector of all OD demands.

Denote $\mathbf{v}(\rho)$ as the solution of problem (2.46) for a specific ρ-value, $\mathbf{v}^*$ as the solution of the original problem (2.32)-(2.35), one can show that

$$Z(\mathbf{v}(\rho)) \le Z(\mathbf{v}^*) \text{ for all } \rho > 0 \tag{2.48}$$

$$\lim_{\rho \to +\infty} \mathbf{v}(\rho) = \mathbf{v}^* \tag{2.49}$$

The optimal multipliers associated with capacity constraints, or the link queuing delay at equilibrium, λ_a^*, $a \in A$, can be estimated below

$$\lim_{\rho \to +\infty} \rho \left. \frac{\mathrm{d}P_a(v_a)}{\mathrm{d}v_a} \right|_{v_a = v_a(\rho)} = \lambda_a^*,\ a \in A \tag{2.50}$$

It seems to us that now the original problem (2.32)-(2.35) can be efficiently solved by applying the Frank-Wolfe algorithm to a un-capacitated traffic assignment problem (2.46) with a *suitably large* ρ-value and the revised link travel time function $t_a(v_a) + \rho\,\mathrm{d}P_a(v_a)/\mathrm{d}v_a$, $a \in A$. However, such a *suitably large* ρ-value is not easy to find because of the numerical ill-conditioning inherent in penalty methods. In order to avoid this ill-conditioning, one may construct an *augmented Lagrangean function* as follows

$$L_\rho(\mathbf{v},\boldsymbol{\lambda}) = Z(\mathbf{v}) + \sum_{a \in A} \frac{1}{2\rho}\left[\max{}^2\{0,\ \lambda_a + \rho(v_a - C_a)\} - \lambda_a^2\right] \tag{2.51}$$

where λ is the vector of dual variables associated with capacity constraints.

For every specific ρ-value and λ vector, denote $\mathbf{v}(\rho,\lambda)$ as the solution of the problem: $\min L_\rho(\mathbf{v},\lambda)$ subject to $\mathbf{v} \in \Omega_v$, and $L_\rho(\lambda) = \min_{\mathbf{v}\in\Omega_v} L_\rho(\mathbf{v},\lambda)$ as its objective function value. It is true that, for any $\rho > 0$, there exists λ^* that

$$L_\rho(\lambda) \le L_\rho(\lambda^*) = Z(\mathbf{v}^*) \text{ for all } \lambda \ge 0 \tag{2.52}$$

$$\lim_{\lambda \to \lambda^*} \mathbf{v}(\rho,\lambda) = \mathbf{v}(\rho,\lambda^*) = \mathbf{v}^* \tag{2.53}$$

Hence, $L_\rho(\lambda)$, the so-called the augmented Lagrangean dual objective function, should be maximized subject to dual variables, λ, for any $\rho > 0$. All these are done for finite values of the penalty parameter, so the ill-conditioning is avoided.

The optimization problem $\{\max_{\lambda} L_{\rho}(\lambda)\}$ is concave and differentiable with

$$\frac{\partial L_{\rho}(\lambda)}{\partial \lambda_a} = \max\left\{\frac{-\lambda_a}{\rho},\ v_a(\rho,\lambda) - C_a\right\},\ a \in A \tag{2.54}$$

So, in iteratively solving the problem $\{\max_{\lambda} L_{\rho}(\lambda)\}$, λ can be updated as follows

$$\lambda_a = \max\left\{0,\ \lambda_a + \rho\left(v_a(\rho,\lambda) - C_a\right)\right\},\ a \in A \tag{2.55}$$

where a step length equal to ρ is used. We can see that, if $v_a > C_a$, λ_a will increase in the next iteration so as to reinforce the obstacle for traveling this link (i.e., let the equilibrium queuing delay increase); if $v_a < C_a - (\lambda_a/\rho)$, then $\lambda_a = 0$ in the next iteration which means there is no queue on link a and this link has redundant capacity. The iterative process adjusts the value of λ till it is sufficiently close to its optimal value and then correctly reflects the equilibrium queuing delay.

So far, the augmented Lagrangean dual algorithm can be summarized as below.

Step 0. (*Initialization*) Select the initial values for λ, *e.g.*, let $\lambda_a^{(0)} = t_a\left(v_a^{(0)}\right) - t(C_a)$ if $v_a^{(0)} > C_a$; and 0 otherwise for all links $a \in A$. Herein, $\mathbf{v}^{(0)}$ is the solution of the un-capacitated traffic assignment problem. Choose $\rho^1 > 0$ and set the iteration counter $n := 0$.

Step 1. (*Solving the sub-problem*) Solve the un-capacitated traffic assignment problem with link travel time function $t_a(v_a) + \max\left\{0,\ \lambda_a^{(n)} + \rho^{(n)}(v_a - C_a)\right\}$, $a \in A$, to get link flow pattern $\mathbf{v}^{(n)}$.

Step 2. (*Termination criterion*) If

$\max_{a\in A}\left\{\frac{\left|v_a^{(n)} - C_a\right|}{C_a}\lambda_a^{(n)}\right\} < \varepsilon$ (a small number), stop and accept $\left(\mathbf{v}^{(n)}, \lambda^{(n)}\right)$ as the solution; otherwise, continue.

Step 3. (*Updating multiplier and penalty*) Let

$$\lambda_a^{(n+1)} = \max\left\{0, \lambda_a^{(n)} + \rho^{(n)}\left(v_a^{(n)}\left(\rho, \lambda^{(n)}\right) - C_a\right)\right\},\ a \in A$$

$$\rho^{(n+1)} = \begin{cases} \kappa\rho^{(n)}, \text{ if } \sum_{a\in A}\max^2\left\{-\frac{\lambda_a^{(n)}}{\rho^{(n)}},\ v_a^{(n)} - C_a\right\} > \gamma^2 \sum_a \max^2\left\{-\frac{\lambda_a^{(n-1)}}{\rho^{(n-1)}},\ v_a^{(n-1)} - C_a\right\} \\ \rho^{(n)}, \text{ otherwise} \end{cases}$$

where $2 \le \kappa \le 10$ and $\gamma = 0.25$ can be chosen. Set $n := n+1$ and go to Step 1.

Since for every specific ρ-value and λ vector, the mathematical program: min $L_\rho(\mathbf{v},\lambda)$ subject to $\mathbf{v}\in\Omega_v$ is strictly convex, so all existing efficient algorithms for solving standard traffic assignment problems can be used in Step 1. Step 2 carries out a safe-guard termination check based on a measure of the infeasibility of link flows. In Step 3, the penalty parameter is increased if the total infeasibility does not decrease sufficiently. The convergence of the above algorithm can be established using the theory of dual sub-gradient schemes for convex programming, i.e., the algorithm generates such two sequences that $\{\lambda^{(n)}\}\to\lambda^*$ and $\{\mathbf{v}^{(n)}\}\to\mathbf{v}^*$.

2.4 TRAFFIC ASSIGNMENT WITH NON-SEPARABLE LINK TRAVEL TIME FUNCTIONS

The models presented so far assume that the link travel time functions are independent of each other, i.e., the travel time on a given link depends only on the flow through that link and not on the flow through other links. Such an assumption is not always valid. There are some cases where flow interaction must be considered, *e.g.*, the heavy traffic in two-way streets, the un-signalized intersections and the left-turning movements in signalized intersections, different types of flow share the same roadway, such as trucks and buses versus passenger cars. This subsection studies the equilibrium traffic assignment involving flow interaction.

2.4.1 Asymmetric Link Flow Interactions

Consider a general case in which the travel time for a given link is a function of flows on all links due to link flow interactions, i.e., $t_a(\mathbf{v})=t_a(\cdots,v_a,\cdots)$, $a\in A$. The vector of link travel time functions is arranged as a column vector: $\mathbf{t}(\mathbf{v})=\left(t_a(\mathbf{v}),\ a\in A\right)^{\mathrm{T}}=\left(\cdots,t_a(\mathbf{v}),\cdots\right)^{\mathrm{T}}$. The *Jacobian* of the vector of link travel time functions is a matrix $\nabla_v\mathbf{t}(\mathbf{v})$ of dimension $|A|\times|A|$ with a general element, $\partial t_a(\mathbf{v})/\partial v_b$, $a\in A$, $b\in A$. When this matrix is not symmetric, the problem is referred to as the traffic equilibrium problem with *asymmetric link flow interaction*. In this case, the UE conditions do not entail an equivalent mathematical program formulation, but can be formulated as Variational Inequalities (VI) as shown in the following theorem.

Theorem 2.1 *A link flow pattern* $\mathbf{v}^* \in \Omega_v$ *is in equilibrium if and only if it solve the the variational inequality problem:*

$$\mathbf{t}(\mathbf{v}^*)^{\mathrm{T}}(\mathbf{v}-\mathbf{v}^*) \geq 0 \text{ for all } \mathbf{v} \in \Omega_v \tag{2.56}$$

where Ω_v *is defined by (2.47).*

Proof. First we note that the traffic equilibrium conditions imply that

$$\left[c_{rw}(\mathbf{f}^*)-\mu_w\right]\cdot\left[f_{rw}-f_{rw}^*\right] \geq 0 \tag{2.57}$$

For any $f_{rw} \geq 0$. Indeed, if $f_{rw}^* > 0$ then $\left[c_{rw}(\mathbf{f}^*)-\mu_w\right]=0$ by letting $f_{rw}=0$ in (2.57). If $f_{rw}^*=0$ then $\left[c_{rw}(\mathbf{f}^*)-\mu_w\right] \geq 0$ since $f_{rw} \geq 0$. Thus (2.57) holds. Furthermore, observe that (2.57) holds for any path $r \in R_w$ and any OD pair $w \in W$, hence summarizing inequality over all paths and OD pairs yields:

$$\sum_{w \in W}\sum_{r \in R_w}\left[c_{rw}(\mathbf{f}^*)-\mu_w\right]\cdot\left[f_{rw}-f_{rw}^*\right] \geq 0$$

or

$$\sum_{w \in W}\sum_{r \in R_w} c_{rw}(\mathbf{f}^*)\left[f_{rw}-f_{rw}^*\right] \geq \sum_{w \in W}\sum_{r \in R_w}\mu_w\left[f_{rw}-f_{rw}^*\right] = \sum_{w \in W}\mu_w\left[d_w-d_w\right]=0$$

whereas

$$\begin{aligned}\sum_{w \in W}\sum_{r \in R_w} c_{rw}(\mathbf{f}^*)\left[f_{rw}-f_{rw}^*\right] &= \sum_{w \in W}\sum_{r \in R_w}\left[\sum_{a \in A} t_a(\mathbf{v}^*)\delta_{ar}\right]\left[f_{rw}-f_{rw}^*\right] \\ &= \sum_{a \in A} t_a(\mathbf{v}^*)\sum_{w \in W}\sum_{r \in R_w}\left[f_{rw}-f_{rw}^*\right]\delta_{ar} \\ &= \sum_{a \in A} t_a(\mathbf{v}^*)\left(v_a-v_a^*\right)\end{aligned} \tag{2.58}$$

which, in vector form, yields (2.56). ¦

We now show that any solution of (2.56) is an UE flow-pattern. From inequality (2.56) and the equivalence relation (2.58), we have

$$\mathbf{c}(\mathbf{f}^*)^{\mathrm{T}}\mathbf{f} \geq \mathbf{c}(\mathbf{f}^*)^{\mathrm{T}}\mathbf{f}^* \text{ for all } \mathbf{f} \in \Omega_f \tag{2.59}$$

where

$$\Omega_f = \left\{\mathbf{f} \mid \Lambda\mathbf{f} = \mathbf{d}, \mathbf{f} \geq 0\right\} \tag{2.60}$$

This implies

$$\min_{\mathbf{f} \in \Omega_f} \mathbf{c}(\mathbf{f}^*)^{\mathrm{T}}\mathbf{f} \geq \mathbf{c}(\mathbf{f}^*)^{\mathrm{T}}\mathbf{f}^* \tag{2.61}$$

The left-hand side is a linear program, while the right-hand side is a constant. From the inequality above it is clear that $\mathbf{f}^*$ solves this left-hand side linear program. Let μ and η be the vectors of multipliers associated with constraints $\Lambda \mathbf{f} = \mathbf{d}$ and $\mathbf{f} \geq 0$ in (2.60), respectively, for the linear program. If vector $\mathbf{f}^* \in \Omega_f$ is a solution to the linear program or equivalently VI (2.66), then there exist μ and η satisfying

$$\mathbf{c}(\mathbf{f}^*) - \eta - \Lambda^{\mathrm{T}}\mu = 0 \tag{2.62}$$

$$\eta^{\mathrm{T}}\mathbf{f}^* = 0 \tag{2.63}$$

$$\Lambda \mathbf{f}^* - \mathbf{d} = 0 \tag{2.64}$$

$$\eta \geq 0 \tag{2.65}$$

From (2.62) and (2.63), if $f^*_{rw} > 0$, then $c_{rw}(\mathbf{f}^*) = \mu_w$ for $r \in R_w$. Also, if $f^*_{rw} = 0$, then $c_{rw}(\mathbf{f}^*) = \mu_w + \eta_{rw}$ with $\eta_{rw} \geq 0$, for $r \in R_w$. Hence, $\mathbf{f}^*$ is an equilibrium flow pattern. ¦

As seen from the above proof, the VI formulation can also be written with the path-flow and path travel time variables, i.e., to find $\mathbf{f}^* \in \Omega_f$ such that

$$\mathbf{c}(\mathbf{f}^*)^{\mathrm{T}}(\mathbf{f} - \mathbf{f}^*) \geq 0 \tag{2.66}$$

for all $\mathbf{f} \in \Omega_f$ given in (2.60) and $\mathbf{c} = (c_{rw}, r \in R_w, w \in W)^{\mathrm{T}}$ with the following relation between link and path travel time:

$$\mathbf{c}(\mathbf{f}) = \Delta^{\mathrm{T}}\mathbf{t}(\mathbf{v}) = \Delta^{\mathrm{T}}\mathbf{t}(\Delta \mathbf{f})$$

It is easy to determine that solutions to VI problem (2.56) or (2.66) exist, because the function $\mathbf{t}(\mathbf{v})$ is continuous and the feasible solution set Ω_v in VI (2.56) is compact (closed and bounded).

Theorem 2.2 *If the link travel time function vector,* $\mathbf{t}(\mathbf{v})$, *is strictly monotone, namely,*

$$(\mathbf{t}(\mathbf{v}^1) - \mathbf{t}(\mathbf{v}^2))^{\mathrm{T}}(\mathbf{v}^1 - \mathbf{v}^2) > 0, \text{ for any } \mathbf{v}^1,\ \mathbf{v}^2 \in \Omega_v \text{ and } \mathbf{v}^1 \neq \mathbf{v}^2 \tag{2.67}$$

then problem (2.56) has a unique solution.

Proof. Consider any distinct $\mathbf{v}^1$, $\mathbf{v}^2 \in \Omega_v$, we have

$$(\mathbf{t}(\mathbf{v}^1) - \mathbf{t}(\mathbf{v}^2))^{\mathrm{T}}(\mathbf{v}^1 - \mathbf{v}^2) > 0 \tag{2.68}$$

Suppose $\mathbf{v}^1$ and $\mathbf{v}^2$ are two distinct equilibrium solutions. Then, from VI (2.56), we have

$$\mathbf{t}(\mathbf{v}^1)^{\mathrm{T}}(\mathbf{v}^2 - \mathbf{v}^1) \geq 0$$

$$\mathbf{t}(\mathbf{v}^2)^{\mathrm{T}}(\mathbf{v}^1 - \mathbf{v}^2) \geq 0$$

Adding the two inequalities yields

$$\left(\mathbf{t}\left(\mathbf{v}^1\right)-\mathbf{t}\left(\mathbf{v}^2\right)\right)^{\mathrm{T}}\left(\mathbf{v}^1-\mathbf{v}^2\right)\leq 0$$

Since $\mathbf{t}(\mathbf{v})$ is strictly monotone, we have $\mathbf{v}^1=\mathbf{v}^2$. ¦

Note that the strictly monotone condition is equivalent to the positive definiteness of the Jacobian, $\nabla_{\mathbf{v}}\mathbf{t}(\mathbf{v})$, of link cost functions. To see this, let $\mathbf{v}^1$, $\mathbf{v}^2\in\Omega_v$ be two distinct link flow patterns, then there exists $0\leq\alpha\leq 1.0$ such that

$$\mathbf{t}\left(\mathbf{v}^2\right)=\mathbf{t}\left(\mathbf{v}^1\right)+\nabla\mathbf{t}\left(\mathbf{v}^1+\alpha\left(\mathbf{v}^2-\mathbf{v}^1\right)\right)^{\mathrm{T}}\left(\mathbf{v}^2-\mathbf{v}^1\right) \tag{2.69}$$

and we have

$$\left(\mathbf{t}\left(\mathbf{v}^2\right)-\mathbf{t}\left(\mathbf{v}^1\right)\right)^{\mathrm{T}}\left(\mathbf{v}^2-\mathbf{v}^1\right)=\left(\mathbf{v}^2-\mathbf{v}^1\right)^{\mathrm{T}}\nabla\mathbf{t}\left(\mathbf{v}^1+\alpha\left(\mathbf{v}^2-\mathbf{v}^1\right)\right)\left(\mathbf{v}^2-\mathbf{v}^1\right)>0 \tag{2.70}$$

and vice versa.

2.4.2 Symmetric Link Flow Interactions

Mathematically, symmetric link flow interaction is stated as

$$\frac{\partial t_a(\mathbf{v})}{\partial v_b}=\frac{\partial t_b(\mathbf{v})}{\partial v_a},\ a\in A,\ b\in A,\ a\neq b \tag{2.71}$$

The above equation means that the marginal effect on one link's travel time inflicted by another link's flow is equal to the marginal effect on that link's travel time given by this link's flow. In other words, the Jacobian of the vector of link travel time functions is symmetric. In this case, an equivalent mathematical program that can generate a UE flow pattern can be constructed as follows

$$\min_{\mathbf{v}\in\Omega_v}\ Z(\mathbf{v})=\int_{\mathbf{0}}^{\mathbf{v}}\mathbf{t}(\omega)\mathrm{d}\omega \tag{2.72}$$

where Ω_v is defined by (2.47). The objective function (2.72) is defined by a line integral, which can be converted to the sum of a series of standard integrals, each with a single integrated parameter. To show this, we consider a well-used example with two-way streets where the travel time experienced by a user depends not only on the traffic volume in his direction (denoted by a) but also on the traffic volume in the opposite direction (denoted by a'). So, the travel times on link a and link a', respectively, can be written as

$$t_a(\mathbf{v})=t_a\left(v_a,v_{a'}\right),\quad t_{a'}(\mathbf{v})=t_{a'}\left(v_{a'},v_a\right),\ a\in A,\ a'\in A \tag{2.73}$$

After conversion, objective function (2.72) becomes

$$\min\ Z(\mathbf{v})=\frac{1}{2}\sum_{a\in A}\left[\int_0^{v_a}t_a(\omega,v_{a'})\mathrm{d}\omega+\int_0^{v_a}t_a(\omega,0)\mathrm{d}\omega\right] \tag{2.74}$$

with condition $\partial t_a(\mathbf{v})/\partial v_{a'} = \partial t_{a'}(\mathbf{v})/\partial v_a$, $a \in A$, $a' \in A$. It is easy to show that $\partial Z(\mathbf{v})/\partial v_a = t_a(v_a, v_{a'})$, which is important in deriving the first-order optimality conditions equivalent to the UE conditions. Furthermore, the fact that the Hessian of objective function $Z(\mathbf{v})$ is the Jacobian of link travel time functions, implies that program (2.72) will have a unique solution if the Jacobian is positive definite.

2.4.3 Flow Interactions between Multiple Types of Vehicles

The interaction between different types of flow (e.g, cars, trucks, buses) when sharing the same roadway induces non-separable and, in general, asymmetric link cost functions. Let K denote the set of flow types. Let v_a^k be the flow on link a associated with flow or vehicle type k and $t_a^i(\mathbf{v})$ be vehicle type-specific link travel cost function on link a, where $\mathbf{v} = (\mathbf{v}^k, k \in K)^{\mathrm{T}}$ and $\mathbf{v}^k = (v_a^k, a \in A)^{\mathrm{T}}$, $k \in K$. Note that the link cost function here includes interactions between different types of vehicles sharing the same links and between flows on different links examined in the previous sub-section. It is reasonable to assume that the demand by users of one type of vehicles depends only on its own price. Let $B_w^k(\mathbf{d})$ denote the OD benefit (inverse demand) functions where $\mathbf{d} = (\mathbf{d}^k, k \in K)^{\mathrm{T}}$ and $\mathbf{d}^k = (d_w^k, w \in W)^{\mathrm{T}}$. Likewise, the elastic demand UE problem with multi-class users in vehicle types can be formulated as the following VI: determine $(\mathbf{v}^*, \mathbf{d}^*)$ that satisfies

$$\sum_{k \in K} \sum_{a \in A} t_a^k(\mathbf{v}^*)(v_a^k - v_a^{k*}) - \sum_{k \in K} \sum_{w \in W} B_w^k(\mathbf{d}^*)(d_w^k - d_w^{k*}) \geq 0 \text{ for any } (\mathbf{v}, \mathbf{d}) \in \Omega \tag{2.75}$$

where

$$\Omega = \left\{ (\mathbf{v}^k, \mathbf{d}^k), k \in K \middle| \mathbf{v}^k = \Delta \mathbf{f}^k, \mathbf{d}^k = \Lambda \mathbf{f}^k, \mathbf{f}^k \geq 0, \mathbf{d}^k \geq 0 \right\} \tag{2.76}$$

with $\mathbf{f}^k = (f_{rw}^k, r \in R_w, w \in W)^{\mathrm{T}}$, $k \in K$.

Note that the multi-class traffic equilibrium model with several vehicle types can be reduced to a single user class model with link flow interactions by associating each class with a complete network copy. Then, the problem reduces to what we have discussed in the previous sub-section.

2.4.4 Positive Definiteness of Link Cost Functions with Flow Interactions

As shown above, positive definite Jacobian of link cost functions is sufficient to guarantee a unique link flow solution for both symmetric and asymmetric traffic equilibrium problems. A typical situation that gives rise to a positive definite Jacobian matrix $J_{\mathbf{v}} = \nabla_{\mathbf{v}}\mathbf{t}(\mathbf{v})$ is that both $J_{\mathbf{v}}$ and $J_{\mathbf{v}}^{\mathrm{T}}$ are diagonally dominant and each diagonal element is positive. Specifically, the positive definiteness of the Jacobian of link cost functions with all *nonnegative* elements is guaranteed if the following conditions hold:

(i) (Positive diagonal elements of the Jacobian) The travel time on each link is an increasing function of its own flow:

$$\frac{\partial t_a(\mathbf{v})}{\partial v_a} > 0, \ a \in A \tag{2.77}$$

(ii) (Row-diagonally dominant)

$$\frac{\partial t_a(\mathbf{v})}{\partial v_a} > \sum_{b(\neq a)} \frac{\partial t_a(\mathbf{v})}{\partial v_b}, \ a \in A \tag{2.78}$$

(iii) (Column-diagonally dominant)

$$\frac{\partial t_a(\mathbf{v})}{\partial v_a} > \sum_{b(\neq a)} \frac{\partial t_b(\mathbf{v})}{\partial v_a}, \ a \in A \tag{2.79}$$

Conditions (2.78) and (2.79) implied that the main dependence of a link's travel time is on its own flow, and the direct effect of flow of a link on its own travel time is much larger than its effect on any other link travel time:

$$\frac{\partial t_a(\mathbf{v})}{\partial v_a} >> \frac{\partial t_a(\mathbf{v})}{\partial v_b}, \ \frac{\partial t_a(\mathbf{v})}{\partial v_a} >> \frac{\partial t_b(\mathbf{v})}{\partial v_a}, \text{ for any } b \neq a \tag{2.80}$$

In the case of symmetric link flow interaction, conditions (2.78) and (2.79) are identical since $\partial t_a(\mathbf{v})/\partial v_b = \partial t_b(\mathbf{v})/\partial v_a$. The main dependence of a link's travel time on its own flow generally holds in the case of flow interaction between different links such as on a two-way street (a link and its opposite link examined above). Nevertheless, this assumption does not in general hold in modeling flow interaction between different types of vehicle sharing the same roadway such as between heavy and slow vehicles (trucks and buses) and light vehicles (passenger cars). It is thus critical to develop and use meaningful class-specific link cost functions with asymmetric flow interaction, which is important in traffic assignment as well as in examination of road self-financing with multiple types of vehicles (Section 8.5 of Chapter 8).

2.4.5 Practical Asymmetric Link Cost Functions

Here we introduce a vehicle type-specific, asymmetric link travel time function to characterize flow interaction between different types of vehicles, such as trucks versus cars. It is true that heavy and slow vehicles are generally confined to the outer slow lanes and cars use the inner faster lanes on a multi-lane road and they interact with each other due to lane changing. With reference to the popular and practical BPR (Bureau of Public Road) formula, the following form of vehicle type-specific link travel time function (without flow interaction between different links) is adopted:

$$t_{aT} = t_{aT}^0 \left\{ 1.0 + \alpha_T \left(\frac{v_{aT} + \eta v_{ac}}{C_{aT}} \right)^{\beta_T} \right\} \tag{2.81}$$

$$t_{ac} = t_{ac}^0 \left\{ 1.0 + \alpha_c \left(\frac{v_{ac} + \xi v_{aT}}{C_{ac}} \right)^{\beta_c} \right\} \tag{2.82}$$

where t_{aT}^0 and t_{ac}^0 are free-flow travel times of link $a \in A$ by heavy (e.g., truck) and light vehicles (e.g., cars); C_{aT} and C_{ac} are the link capacities measured in terms of heavy vehicles and cars respectively; η and ξ are positive parameters reflecting the degree of impacts of heavy and light vehicles on each other's moving speed; α_T, α_c, β_T, β_c are vehicle type-specific positive parameters of link travel time functions.

Clearly, t_{aT}^0 and t_{ac}^0 are differentiable in (v_{aT}, v_{ac}) and $0 < \partial t_{aT}/\partial v_{ac} \neq \partial t_{ac}/\partial v_{aT} > 0$ (asymmetric flow interaction). To ensure the above-mentioned positive definiteness of the Jacobian of link cost functions, it suffices to ensure the positive definiteness of each link-specific 2×2 diagonal sub-block given below:

$$\nabla_{ac,aT} = \begin{bmatrix} \dfrac{\partial t_{ac}}{\partial v_{ac}} & \dfrac{\partial t_{ac}}{\partial v_{aT}} \\ \dfrac{\partial t_{aT}}{\partial v_{ac}} & \dfrac{\partial t_{aT}}{\partial v_{aT}} \end{bmatrix} \tag{2.83}$$

In view of positive diagonal elements, we thus require that:

$$\frac{\partial t_{ac}}{\partial v_{ac}} \frac{\partial t_{aT}}{\partial v_{aT}} > \frac{\partial t_{ac}}{\partial v_{aT}} \frac{\partial t_{aT}}{\partial v_{ac}} \tag{2.84}$$

Now we consider the following specific partial derivatives:

$$\frac{\partial t_{ac}}{\partial v_{ac}} = \frac{\alpha_c \beta_c t_{ac}^0}{C_{ac}} \left(\frac{v_{ac} + \xi v_{aT}}{C_{ac}} \right)^{\beta_c - 1}, \qquad \frac{\partial t_{ac}}{\partial v_{aT}} = \xi \frac{\alpha_c \beta_c t_{ac}^0}{C_{ac}} \left(\frac{v_{ac} + \xi v_{aT}}{C_{ac}} \right)^{\beta_c - 1}$$

$$\frac{\partial t_{aT}}{\partial v_{ac}} = \eta \frac{\alpha_T \beta_T t_{aT}^0}{C_{aT}} \left(\frac{v_{aT} + \eta v_{ac}}{C_{aT}} \right)^{\beta_T - 1}, \qquad \frac{\partial t_{aT}}{\partial v_{aT}} = \frac{\alpha_T \beta_T t_{aT}^0}{C_{aT}} \left(\frac{v_{aT} + \eta v_{ac}}{C_{aT}} \right)^{\beta_T - 1}$$

Substituting the above results into (2.84) yields:

$$(1 - \xi\eta) \frac{\alpha_c \alpha_T \beta_c \beta_T t_{ac}^0 t_{aT}^0}{C_{ac} C_{aT}} \times \left(\frac{v_{ac} + \xi v_{aT}}{C_{ac}} \right)^{\beta_c - 1} \times \left(\frac{v_{aT} + \eta v_{ac}}{C_{aT}} \right)^{\beta_T - 1} > 0 \tag{2.85}$$

We thus require that $\xi\eta < 1.0$ to ensure the positive definiteness of the link cost functions. In view of $\xi > 1.0$ and $\eta < 1.0$, $\xi\eta < 1.0$ is in general satisfied in practice.

Furthermore, apart from the above mathematical requirement, the vehicle type-specific asymmetric link cost functions should produce behaviorally and physically coherent results in the sense that both heavy and light vehicles on the same road will move at different speeds under free-flow or less congested traffic conditions, and tend to travel at the same speed as the maximum practical flow density of the road is reached. Namely, for any combination (v_{aT}, v_{ac}) such that $v_{ac} + \xi v_{aT} = C_{ac}$ and / or $v_{aT} + \eta v_{ac} = C_{aT}$, we should have $t_{ac} = t_{aT}$, which requires that parameters (α_c, α_T) meet the condition: $(1+\alpha_c)t_{ac}^0 = (1+\alpha_T)t_{aT}^0$.

2.4.6 Diagonalization Solution Algorithm

The solution to the above traffic equilibrium problem with link flow interaction can be found by using the *diagonalization* algorithm described below

Step 0. (*Initialization*) Find a feasible link-flow vector $\mathbf{v}^{(1)}$. Set $n := 1$.

Step 1. (*Diagonalization*) Apply any standard UE-solving method to the following sub-problem, yielding a link-flow vector $\mathbf{v}^{(n+1)}$.

$$\min \; Z^{(n)}(\mathbf{v}) = \sum_{a\in A}\int_0^{v_a} t_a\left(v_1^{(n)},\ldots,v_{a-1}^{(n)},\omega,v_{a+1}^{(n)},\ldots,v_{|A|}^{(n)}\right)d\omega \text{ subject to } \mathbf{v}\in\Omega_v .$$

Step 2. (*Convergence check*) If $\mathbf{v}^{(n)} \cong \mathbf{v}^{(n+1)}$, then stop; otherwise, set $n := n+1$ and go to Step 1.

In Step 1, the objective function of the sub-problem includes only simple link travel time functions in one argument each (i.e., t_a is a function of v_a only), all other flows that may affect link a are fixed at their values in the previous iteration n. The formulation does *not* fix the flows themselves, but their cross-link effects. Accordingly, the sub-problem is known as *diagonalized* problem since its Hessian is now diagonal.

2.5 Traffic Assignment of Multi-class Users with Different Values of Time

Value of time (VOT) is a very important concept in transportation system modeling since each commuter (or user) has a different VOT, depending on his or her level of income and certainly affecting his or her travel decision-making behavior. Recent advanced network equilibrium models acknowledge this fact by incorporating user heterogeneity in route choice. These models simulate the way that users (commuters) select a route from among the competing paths that are differentiated on the basis of two cost criteria: journey time and monetary cost. For deeply examining the multi-class, multi-criteria network equilibrium problems with congestion pricing consideration, which will be presented in the following chapters of this book, this section briefly present a multi-class assignment model in a network, with a discrete set of VOTs for several user classes. Differing from the previous content, this section distinguishes travel time and monetary cost, two units used for measuring disutility.

2.5.1 Model Formulation

To distinguish the multiple user classes by types of vehicles, we use M to denote a set of all user classes corresponding to groups of users with different socio-economic characteristics (for example, income level). Let β_m $(\beta_m > 0)$ be the average VOT for users of class m, d_w^m be the demand for travel of class m between OD pair $w \in W$, and u_a be the exogenously given toll charged on link $a \in A$.

If each user of class m with a VOT of β_m is assumed to choose a route that minimizes his or her generalized travel time $c_{rw}^{m,\text{time}}$ defined below (money is transferred into equivalent travel time)

$$c_{rw}^{m,\text{time}} = \sum_{a \in A} \left\{ t_a(v_a) + \frac{u_a}{\beta_m} \right\} \delta_{ar},\ r \in R_w, w \in W, m \in M \tag{2.86}$$

then an equivalent minimization problem that leads to a time-based multi-class equilibrium assignment can be formulated as follows

$$\min_{\mathbf{f}} \sum_{a \in A} \int_0^{v_a} t_a(\omega) d\omega + \sum_{a \in A} \sum_{m \in M} \frac{1}{\beta_m} v_a^m u_a \tag{2.87}$$

subject to

$$\sum_{r \in R_w} f_{rw}^m = d_w^m,\ w \in W, m \in M \tag{2.88}$$

$$f_{rw}^m \geq 0,\ r \in R_w,\ w \in W, m \in M \tag{2.89}$$

where f_{rw}^m is the flow of user class m on path $r \in R_w, w \in W$, and v_a^m and v_a are defined as

$$v_a^m = \sum_{w \in W} \sum_{r \in R_w} f_{rw}^m \delta_{ar},\ a \in A, m \in M \tag{2.90}$$

$$v_a = \sum_{m \in M} v_a^m,\ a \in A \tag{2.91}$$

From the first-order optimality conditions of the convex optimization problem (2.87)-(2.91), we can easily establish the following equilibrium relations in terms of the minimization of travel disutility in time units:

$$\sum_{a\in A} t_a(v_a)\delta_{ar} + \sum_{a\in A}\frac{u_a}{\beta_m}\delta_{ar} = \mu_w^{m,\text{time}},\ \text{if } f_{rw}^m > 0,\ r\in R_w,\ w\in W,\ m\in M \tag{2.92}$$

$$\sum_{a\in A} t_a(v_a)\delta_{ar} + \sum_{a\in A}\frac{u_a}{\beta_m}\delta_{ar} \geq \mu_w^{m,\text{time}},\ \text{if } f_{rw}^m = 0,\ r\in R_w,\ w\in W,\ m\in M \tag{2.93}$$

where $\mu_w^{m,\text{time}}$ is the Lagrange multiplier associated with (2.88) and equals the minimum travel disutility in time units (inclusive of equivalent time of toll charge) between OD pair w by users of class m, i.e., $\mu_w^{m,\text{time}} = \min_{r\in R_w}\{c_{rw}^{m,\text{time}}\}$.

Finally, we note that the objective function (2.87) of the UE program is strictly convex in aggregate link flow if the link travel time function $t_a(v_a)$ is monotonically increasing, but linear in the class-specific link flow. Thus, the aggregate equilibrium link flows are unique, but the equilibrium link flows by user class are not unique.

2.5.2 Equivalence of the Time-based and Cost-based Multi-Class Traffic Equilibrium

The equivalence of the time-based and cost-based multi-class traffic equilibrium depends on users' trade-offs between time and money. The travel disutility of a path $r\in R_w$, $w\in W$ consists of two terms: travel time denoted by t_{rw} and travel cost (money) c_{rw}. We now define a general value of time function or simply VOT function, $g_m(t)$, that transforms a time of t units into equivalent amount of monetary cost for user class $m\in M$. Then the following assumption is generally true.

Assumption 2.1 The VOT function $g_m(t)$ for any $m\in M$ is a continuous and strictly increasing with respect to t for $t\geq 0$ and $g_m(0)=0$.

Assumption 2.1 implies that $t = g_m^{-1}(x)$ exists for $x\geq 0$. With this general VOT function, the travel disutility of path $r\in R_w$ is given by $c_{rw}^{m,\text{cost}} = u_{rw} + g_m(t_{rw})$ in cost unit, and is given by $c_{rw}^{m,\text{time}} = t_{rw} + g_m^{-1}(u_{rw})$ in time unit. Now we have the following equivalence theorem.

Theorem 2.3 *The time-based and the cost-based equilibrium solutions are identical in any general network if and only if $g_m(t)$ is a linear function of t for all $m\in M$.*

Proof: Note that, from the assumption that $g_m(t)$ is linear and strictly increasing with $g_m(0)=0$, the VOT of users of each class m must be a positive constant. Let $\beta_m>0$ denote this constant VOT for user class m as before. Each user in each class is assumed to choose a route that minimizes his or her generalized travel cost $c_{rw}^{m,\text{cost}}$ defined below (time is transferred into money according to VOT)

$$c_{rw}^{m,\text{cost}} = \sum_{a\in A} \{\beta_m t_a(v_a) + u_a\}\delta_{ar},\ r\in R_w,\ w\in W,\ m\in M \tag{2.94}$$

Multiplying both sides of the time-based equilibrium conditions (2.92) and (2.93) by β_m $(\beta_m > 0)$ for each user class $m\in M$ yields:

$$\sum_{a\in A} \beta_m t_a(v_a)\delta_{ar} + \sum_{a\in A} u_a\delta_{ar} = \mu_w^{m,\text{cost}},\ \text{if } f_{rw}^m > 0,\ r\in R_w,\ w\in W,\ m\in M \tag{2.95}$$

$$\sum_{a\in A} \beta_m t_a(v_a)\delta_{ar} + \sum_{a\in A} u_a\delta_{ar} \geq \mu_w^{m,\text{cost}},\ \text{if } f_{rw}^m = 0,\ r\in R_w,\ w\in W,\ m\in M \tag{2.96}$$

Clearly, $\mu_w^{m,\text{cost}} = \min_{r\in R_w}\{c_{rw}^{m,\text{cost}}\} = \beta_m \mu_w^{m,\text{time}}$ and (2.95) and (2.96) are the multi-class network equilibrium conditions on the basis of travel disutility defined in (2.94) in monetary units. We thus conclude that: the time-based and the money-based equilibrium problems are equivalent when users of each class have a constant VOT or the value of travel time changes linearly (but different VOTs for different user classes).

We now establish that the equivalence of the time-based and cost-based equilibrium solutions in a general network implies that $g_m(t)$ must be a linear function of t for all $m\in M$. Without loss of generality, we consider a special case with two paths and a single user class, for which the equivalence must hold, as it holds for a general network and any number of user classes. Suppose path 1 has a travel time t and monetary cost u, and path 2 has a travel time $t + g^{-1}(u)$ and no monetary cost. For path 1, the time-based travel disutility is $c_1^{\text{time}} = t + g^{-1}(u)$ and the money-based travel disutility is $c_1^{\text{cost}} = g(t) + u$; for path 2, the time-based travel disutility is $c_2^{\text{time}} = t + g^{-1}(u)$ and the money-based travel disutility is $c_2^{\text{cost}} = g(t + g^{-1}(u))$.

Suppose both paths are used and the time-based and cost-based equilibrium solutions are identical, then $c_1^{\text{time}} = c_2^{\text{time}}$ and $c_1^{\text{cost}} = c_2^{\text{cost}}$ must hold simultaneously. Namely,

$$g(t) + u = g(t + g^{-1}(u)) \tag{2.97}$$

Let $y = g^{-1}(u)$ and thus $u = g(y)$, eqn. (2.97) thus becomes

$$g(t) + g(y) = g(t + y) \tag{2.98}$$

Note that (2.98) holds for any positive t and y, it follows immediately that $g(t)$ is a linear function of t, because

$$g'(t) = \lim_{\delta\to 0}\frac{g(t+\delta) - g(t)}{\delta} = \lim_{\delta\to 0}\frac{g(t) + g(\delta) - g(t)}{\delta} = \lim_{\delta\to 0}\frac{g(\delta)}{\delta} = g'(0) = \text{constant}.$$

This completes the proof. ¦

An immediate consequence of Theorem 2.3 is that the optimization problem (2.87)-(2.91) with class-specific constant VOTs leads to a multi-class network equilibrium in terms of either generalized travel time given by (2.86) or generalized travel cost given by (2.94).

2.6 TRAFFIC ASSIGNMENT WITH NON-ADDITIVE PATH COSTS

In the multi-class UE model envisioned in the previous sub-section, route costs are assumed to be additive of link costs, and users value travel times differently but linearly. This additive assumption allows us to solve the traffic equilibrium problems without the need to handle individual routes explicitly. It is a significant advantage when one needs to solve large-scale network problems. However, the additive assumption is not appropriate in many situations. For example, the cost incurred on each route is made up of the sum of the link travel times plus a route-specific monetary cost for traveling on that route. It is generally true in practice that the toll charge for expressways depends on the entry and exit points of the user. Empirical studies indicate that the users' valuation of travel time savings is nonlinear rather than linear; small amounts of time are valued proportionately less than larger amounts of time. Here we describe the non-additive traffic assignment models for the situation with two basic route attributes: time and money, which is relevant to our road pricing studies in subsequent chapters. Like the previous section, we consider both cost-based and time-based route choices.

2.6.1 Model Formulation

In the cost-based model the generalized cost for a route is assumed to be

$$c_{rw}^{\text{cost}} = u_{rw} + g_{rw}\left(\sum_{a\in A}\delta_{ar}t_a\left(v_a\right)\right), r\in R_w, w\in W \tag{2.99}$$

where u_{rw} denotes the monetary costs (such as tolls) specific to route r in OD pair $w\in W$, g_{rw} is a nonnegative and increasing function that describes the value of time for route r in OD pair $w\in W$, which could be nonlinear, $v_a = v_a(\mathbf{f})$ is regarded as a function of the path flow vector as defined in (2.1). The second terms transfer travel times into an equivalent amount of money consistent with the first term. Typically, the general route cost function, c_{rw}^{cost}, like the link cost function $t_a(v_a)$, are assumed to be positive and continuous. In this case, it is difficult to convert the path-specific costs to equivalent additive link costs if common links exist among the used paths. Thus, we have to formulate and solve the traffic equilibrium problems in the path-flow domain.

The non-additive traffic equilibrium problem is to seek a path flow vector $\mathbf{f}^*$ and OD cost vector $\mu^{\text{cost}} = \left(\mu_w^{\text{cost}}, w \in W\right)^{\text{T}}$ (arranged as a column vector of path costs) such that, for every OD pair $w \in W$ and each path $r \in R_w$, the following Wardrop equilibrium conditions hold:

$$c_{rw}^{\text{cost}}\left(\mathbf{f}^*\right) - \mu_w^{\text{cost}} \begin{cases} = 0 & \text{if } f_{rw}^* > 0 \\ \geq 0 & \text{if } f_{rw}^* = 0 \end{cases} \tag{2.100}$$

where $c_{rw}^{\text{cost}}\left(\mathbf{f}^*\right)$ is regarded as a continuous function of the path flow vector as given in (2.99). The above equilibrium conditions are equivalent to the following VI of finding an $\mathbf{f}^* \in \Omega_{\text{f}}$ such that:

$$\mathbf{c}^{\text{cost}}\left(\mathbf{f}\right)^{\text{T}}\left(\mathbf{f} - \mathbf{f}^*\right) \geq 0, \text{ for any } \mathbf{f} \in \Omega_f \tag{2.101}$$

where $\mathbf{c}^{\text{cost}} = \left(c_{rw}^{\text{cost}}, r \in R_w, w \in W\right)^{\text{T}}$ and Ω_f is defined in (2.60). This NCP formulation offers the flexibility of relaxing the assumption of additive path costs. It allows many types of traffic assignment applications that could not be conveniently modeled previously. It includes the additive path cost function as a special case.

We now move on to consider the time-based model in which the generalized time for a route is given by

$$c_{rw}^{\text{time}} = \sum_{a \in A} \delta_{ar} t_a\left(v_a\right) + G_{rw}\left(u_{rw}\right), \; r \in R_w, w \in W \tag{2.102}$$

where $G_{rw} = g_{rw}^{-1}, \; r \in R_w, w \in W$, it is the inverse of the (linear or nonlinear) value of time function g_{rw} in (2.99) that transfers monetary cost into equivalent time. For a given constant monetary cost (toll charge) $u_{rw}, r \in R_w, w \in W$, an equivalent optimization model for this problem can be formulated as

$$\min_{\mathbf{f} \in \Omega_f} \sum_{a \in A} \int_0^{v_a} t_a(\omega) d\omega + \sum_{w \in W} \sum_{r \in R_w} G_{rw}\left(u_{rw}\right) f_{rw} \tag{2.103}$$

where $v_a, a \in A$ is given by (2.1). The only difference from the fixed-demand UE model (2.32) is the extra linear term in the objective function. Hence, problem (2.103) is a convex program, and its first-order optimality conditions lead to the following Wardrop equilibrium

$$c_{rw}^{\text{time}}\left(\mathbf{f}^*\right) - \mu_w^{\text{time}} \begin{cases} = 0 & \text{if } f_{rw}^* > 0 \\ \geq 0 & \text{if } f_{rw}^* = 0 \end{cases} \tag{2.104}$$

2.6.2 Solution Algorithm

Note that both the cost-based model (2.101) formulated as an VI and the time-based model (2.103) as an optimization problem involve path flow variables explicitly, and the path set is too large to be handled explicitly for networks of realistic size. Therefore, one has to generate profitable paths in a systematic and iterative manner. To this end, a column generation based solution method is effective and outlined briefly below.

Step 1. (*Initialization*) Use a path generation procedure to generate an initial set of working paths $R_w^{(n)}, w \in W$, set the main iteration counter: $n := 0$.

Step 2. (*Solving the master problem*) Solving the restricted master problems (2.101) or master problem (2.103) by replacing restricting R_w with $R_w^{(n)}$ for each $w \in W$. Denote the current solution by $\left(\mathbf{f}^{(n)}, \mathbf{v}^{(n)}\right)$.

Step 3. (*Path generation*) Checking whether some non-generated path $r \in R_w, w \in W$ has a cost less than the current minimum OD cost, i.e., to check whether

$$c_{rw}\left(\mathbf{v}^{(n)}\right) - \mu_w^{(n)} < 0 \tag{2.105}$$

where $\mu_w^{(n)} = \min_{r \in R_w^{(n)}} \left\{c_{rw}^{\text{time}}\left(\mathbf{v}^{(n)}\right)\right\}$ for the time-based UE problem or $\mu_w^{(n)} = \min_{r \in R_w^{(n)}} \left\{c_{rw}^{\text{cost}}\left(\mathbf{v}^{(n)}\right)\right\}$ for the cost-based problem. Updating the path set by adding path r for any that satisfies (2.105) to $R_w^{(n)}$. Let $n := n+1$.

Step 4. (*Convergence check*) If $R_w^{(n+1)} = R_w^{(n)}$ then stop. Otherwise go to Step 2.

Note that due to the nonlinear transformation of money to time or time to money, one cannot count on a shortest path algorithm to find the path that satisfies (2.105). One possible solution procedure is to determine the k–shortest paths based on the additive link travel time only, calculate the generalized non-additive time or cost for each of the k- shortest paths, and then check whether condition (2.105) is met for each path considered.

2.6.3 An Analytical Example

Example 2.1 Consider a simple network with a single OD pair connected by two parallel links. Let the OD demand $d = 1$ and $t_1(v) = t_2(v) = v$ be the link travel time function. The toll charge on the two links are $u_1 = 1/2$ and $u_2 = 0$ (in monetary unit).

If we assume that the (generalized) cost of path r ($r = a = 1$ or 2 in this simple network) is given by $c_r^{\text{cost}} = u_r + g_r(t_r)$ with $g_r(t_r) = (t_r)^2$ where g_r is the nonlinear value of time for path or link r ($r = 1$ or 2); and a generalized time $c_r^{\text{time}} = t_r(v_r) + g_r^{-1}(u_r) = t_r(v_r) + \sqrt{u_r}$. It is easy to verify that the cost-based equilibrium is

$$v_1^* = \frac{1}{4}, \quad v_2^* = \frac{3}{4}$$

and the time based equilibrium is

$$v_1^* = \frac{2-\sqrt{2}}{4}, \quad v_2^* = \frac{2+\sqrt{2}}{4}$$

Therefore, when travelers of any classes have a nonlinear VOT or the value of travel time changes nonlinearly, as in the current example, the time-based and the money-based equilibrium problems do not necessarily give the same equilibrium solution. As indeed shown in Theorem 2.3, the time-based and the cost-based equilibrium solutions are identical in any general network if and only if the VOT function is linear.

2.7 Traffic Assignment with Stochastic Route Choice

2.7.1 Utility Function and Discrete Route Choice Model

We now consider traffic assignment with stochastic route choice behavior of users in a congested network. Suppose that each user is a utility-maximizer, and each route, r, is an alternative associated with some random utility function U_{rw}. We suppose a given route's utility is primarily related to the route's travel time, then the utility, U_{rw}, received from one trip made between OD pair $w \in W$ is given by:

$$U_{rw} = V_{rw} + \xi_{rw} = -\theta c_{rw} + \xi_{rw}, r \in R_w, w \in W \tag{2.106}$$

where ξ_{rw} is a random term associated with the route under consideration and can be considered to represent the unobservable or unmeasurable factors of utility, $V_{rw} = -\theta c_{rw}$ is the measured utility, c_{rw} is the actual travel time on route $r \in R_w$ defined before and θ is a positive unit scaling parameter. Let P_{rw} denote the probability of users choosing route $r \in R_w$, $w \in W$. The utility maximization principle then implies that:

$$P_{rw} = \Pr\left(U_{rw} \geq U_{kw}, \forall\ k \in R_w\right), \ r \in R_w, \ w \in W \tag{2.107}$$

This probability has the following properties:

$$0 \leq P_{rw} \leq 1, \ r \in R_w \text{ and } \sum_{r \in R_w} P_{rw} = 1.0, \ w \in W$$

The expected indirect utility received by a randomly sampled individual traveling between OD pair $w \in W$ is defined by:

$$\tilde{S}_w = E\left[\max_{r \in R_w}\{U_{rw}\}\right] = E\left[\max_{r \in R_w}\{V_{rw} + \xi_{rw}\}\right],\ w \in W \tag{2.108}$$

The expected indirect utility has the following important property:

$$\frac{\partial \tilde{S}_w}{\partial V_{rw}} = P_{rw},\ r \in R_w, w \in W$$

In traffic assignment or route choice models, the emphasis is on cost or travel time minimization rather than utility maximization. With the definition of the indirect utility function (2.106) and the expected received indirect utility (2.108), the expected perceived travel time between an OD pair $w \in W$ can be obtained as:

$$S_w(\mathbf{c}_{rw}) = E\left[\min_{r \in R_w}(c_{rw} + \xi_{rw})\right] = -\frac{1}{\theta}E\left[\max_{r \in R_w}\{U_{rw}\}\right] = -\frac{1}{\theta}\tilde{S}_w \tag{2.109}$$

2.7.2 Model Formulation with Fixed Demand

An optimization formulation of the general stochastic user equilibrium (SUE) can be formulated as follows (Powell and Sheffi, 1982):

$$\min Z(\mathbf{v}) = -\sum_{w \in W} d_w S_w(\mathbf{c}_{rw}(\mathbf{v})) + \sum_{a \in A} t_a(v_a)v_a - \sum_{a \in A}\int_0^{v_a} t_a(\omega)d\omega \tag{2.110}$$

where $S_w(\mathbf{c}_{rw}(\mathbf{v}))$ is defined by (2.109) with $c_{rw} = c_{rw}(\mathbf{v})$, $r \in R_w$, $w \in W$.

If the random variables in (2.106) are assumed to be normally distributed, one would obtain the probit-based route choice model. However, our major concern here is about the analytically tractable logit-based route choice model. The logit-based route choice model assumes that the random variables in (2.106) are identically and independently distributed (i.i.d.) Gumbel variables, and have the following closed form of the route choice probabilities:

$$P_{rw} = \frac{\exp(-\theta c_{rw})}{\sum_{k \in R_w}\exp(-\theta c_{kw})},\ r \in R_w, w \in W \tag{2.111}$$

With the logit-based route choice probability (2.111), the expected indirect utility in (2.108) can be explicitly expressed as:

$$\tilde{S}_w = \ln \sum_{r \in R_w} \exp(-\theta c_{rw}) \tag{2.112}$$

and the expected perceived travel time between OD pair $w \in W$ becomes below:

$$S_w = E\left[\min_{r \in R_w}(c_r^w + \xi_r^w)\right] = -\frac{1}{\theta}\ln \sum_{r \in R_w}\exp(-\theta c_{rw}) \tag{2.113}$$

It is well-known the logit-based SUE can be formulated as the following equivalent minimization program (Fisk, 1980):

$$\min Z(\mathbf{f}) = \frac{1}{\theta} \sum_{w \in W} \sum_{r \in R_w} f_{rw} \ln f_{rw} + \sum_{a \in A} \int_0^{v_a} t_a(\omega) d\omega \tag{2.114}$$

subject to

$$\sum_{r \in R_w} f_{rw} = d_w, \; w \in W \tag{2.115}$$

$$f_{rw} \geq 0, \; r \in R_w, \; w \in W \tag{2.116}$$

where v_a, $a \in A$ is given by (2.1).

2.7.3 Model Formulation with Elastic Demand

We now extend the logit-based SUE model (7)-(9) with fixed-demand to the case when the demand is elastic. The demand between an O-D pair is given to be a continuous and monotonically decreasing function of the expected, perceived travel cost between that O-D pair. In other words,

$$d_w = D_w\left(S_w\left(c_w\right)\right), \; w \in W \tag{2.117}$$

where $S_w\left(c_w\right)$ is given by (2.113). It can be easily shown that the logit-based SUE model with elastic demand function (2.117) can be formulated as the following convex minimization program:

$$\min \; Z(\mathbf{f},\mathbf{d}) = \frac{1}{\theta}\left(\sum_{w \in W} \sum_{r \in R_w} f_{rw} \ln f_{rw} - \sum_{w \in W} d_w \ln d_w \right) + \sum_{a \in A} \int_0^{v_a} t_a(\omega) d\omega - \sum_{w \in W} \int_0^{d_w} D_w^{-1}(\omega) d\omega \tag{2.118}$$

$$\sum_{r \in R_w} f_{rw} = d_w, \; w \in W \tag{2.119}$$

$$f_{rw} \geq 0, \; r \in R_w, \; w \in W \tag{2.120}$$

where v_a, $a \in A$ is again given by (2.1).

2.8 SYSTEM OPTIMUM TRAFFIC ASSIGNMENT

The so-called Wardrop second principle is: all commuters select their routes so that the total network travel time (or cost) is minimized. This suggests that there is a central organization to completely coordinate all path choices, or the traffic allocation is dictated from a central authority to achieve a socially desirable flow pattern. We thus have the so called system optimum assignment models aiming at minimizing the total travel time spent in the network subject to the flow conservation conditions. The SO assignment model with fixed demand is given below

$$\min\ Z(\mathbf{v}) = \sum_{a\in A} v_a t_a(v_a) \tag{2.121}$$

subject to

$$\sum_{r\in R_w} f_{rw} = d_w,\ w\in W \tag{2.122}$$

$$f_{rw} \geq 0,\ r\in R_w, w\in W \tag{2.123}$$

where the link-flow $\mathbf{v}$ is given by (2.1).

In view of the following relation

$$\sum_{a\in A}\int_0^{v_a}\left(t_a(\omega)+\omega\frac{\mathrm{d}t_a(\omega)}{\mathrm{d}\omega}\right)\mathrm{d}\omega = \sum_{a\in A} v_a t_a(v_a) \tag{2.124}$$

The previously presented algorithm for solving the UE program (2.3)-(2.5) can be directly applied to solve the SO program (2.121)-(2.123) by replacing the link travel time function with

$$\tilde{t}_a(v_a) = t_a(v_a) + v_a\frac{\mathrm{d}t_a(v_a)}{\mathrm{d}v_a},\ a\in A \tag{2.125}$$

One should note that, without external influence such as congestion pricing, the SO and UE problems in general yield different solutions. Nevertheless, under some (unrealistic) extreme situations, solutions to the UE and SO problems may become identical. For instance, when the link cost function is homogeneous of degree κ (De Palma and Nesterov, 1998):

$$t_a(\phi v_a) = \phi^{\kappa} t_a(v_a),\ \kappa\geq 0,\ a\in A \tag{2.126}$$

In this case we have

$$\begin{aligned}\sum_{a\in A}\int_0^{v_a} t_a(\omega)\mathrm{d}\omega &= \sum_{a\in A}\int_0^1 v_a t_a(\phi v_a)\mathrm{d}\phi = \sum_{a\in A}\int_0^1 \phi^{\kappa} v_a t_a(v_a)\mathrm{d}\phi \\ &= \sum_{a\in A} v_a t_a(v_a)\int_0^1 \phi^{\kappa}\mathrm{d}\phi = \frac{1}{1+\kappa}\sum_{a\in A} v_a t_a(v_a)\end{aligned} \tag{2.127}$$

One immediately sees that the UE and SO objective functions obtain their respective minimum values at the same point or solution. For example, if

$$t_a(v_a) = \alpha_a(v_a)^{\kappa},\ \kappa\geq 0,\ a\in A \tag{2.128}$$

then the link cost function is homogeneous of degree κ, and as a result, the UE and SO problems result in identical solution. Function (2.128) includes the un-congested constant link travel time by setting $\kappa\equiv 0$, or a family of increasing convex link cost function if $\kappa > 1$ and increasing concave link cost function if $0 < \kappa \leq 1$, both emanating from the origin with a zero free-flow travel time. Clearly, this form of link cost function is unrealistic.

The UE and SO problems have, in general, different solutions, and the SO equilibrium cannot sustain itself, since some users may be able to decrease their travel time by unilaterally changing routes. In subsequent chapters we shall explore various pricing schemes to decentralize or support the above SO flow pattern as self-optimizing sustainable user equilibrium.

2.9 SOURCES AND NOTES

Since Wardrop (1952) put forward the two influential hypothesis of user equilibrium (Wardrop's First Principle) and system optimum (Wardrop's Second Principle) and Beckmann et al (1956) offered a nonlinear programming transformation of the UE concept, traffic assignment models and methods have become a subject of a substantial stream of research in transportation literature. Indeed, traffic assignment is a very rich subject and we have only touched upon some very basic models and algorithms well established in the literature. More details of traffic assignment methods can be found in excellent monographs by Sheffi (1985), Patriksson (1994), Bell and Iida (1997), Nagurney (1999), Hensher and Button (2000). In particular, the book by Sheffi (1985) makes good introductory reading of the materials presented in this chapter.

The application of the Frank-Wolfe convex combination method (Frank and Wolfe, 1956) to network equilibrium problems was first suggested by Bruynooghe *et al.* (1968), coded and tested by LeBlanc *et al.* (1975). The algorithm was further improved by Fukushima (1984) and LeBlanc *et al.* (1985) to enhance its computational efficiency. VI formulations of the generalized traffic equilibrium problem were given by Smith (1979a) and Dafermos (1980); relevant references for the diagonalization algorithm for the asymmetric traffic assignment problems are Dafermos (1982), Florian and Spiess (1982), Fisk and Nguyen, (1982). Application of the augmented Lagrangean dual algorithm to the capacity-constrained traffic assignment problem was reported in detail in Larsson and Patriksson (1995). An inner penalty function method that retains a similar sub-structure as the Frank-Wolfe algorithm was applied in Yang and Yagar (1994) for solving the link capacity constrained traffic assignment problem. Leurent (1993, 1996 and 1998), Dial (1997), Marcotte and Zhu (2000) and Nagurney (2000) developed various network equilibrium models with a discrete set of VOTs for several distinct user classes or a continuously distributed VOT across the whole population. The problem of non-additive traffic equilibrium problem is a relatively new research topic. Relevant recent references include Gabriel and Bernstein (1997) and Bernstein and Gabriel (1997) who proposed a first general formulation; Lo and Chen (2000a,b), Chen et al. (2001), Larsson et al. (2002) and Yang, Zhang and Meng (2004) studied various special cases of the traffic equilibrium problem with non-additive route cost. The concept of value of time plays an important role in theoretical and practical route choice analysis; an empirical finding of the nonlinear valuation of time saving underpinning the on-additive traffic assignment problem was given by Hensher and Truong (1985). In preparing this chapter, we have used the example in Larsson et al. (2002) to illustrate the non-equivalence of the time-based and money-based UE problem when users value time in a nonlinear manner. The vehicle type-specific link cost function is based on the Japanese paper by Kawakame, Hirobata and Xu (1989), and further discussion of the link cost function with flow interaction can be found in Toint and Wynter (1996), Marcotte and Wynter (2004).

Readers may refer to Bazaraa et al. (1993) and Bertsekas (1999) for general nonlinear programming theory and algorithms pertinent to traffic equilibrium analysis. Comprehensive treatment of the VI theory can be found in the classic book by Kinderlehrer and Stampacchia (1980) and in a recent excellent book by Facchinei and Pang (2003).

We conclude this chapter by pointing out that we have chosen to focus on those basic UE and SO models and algorithms which are relevant to our subsequent road pricing analysis. A very brief introduction is given to the logit-based stochastic traffic assignment; a number of variants of the traffic assignment problem are important but not covered in this chapter, such as the probit-based stochastic traffic assignment models, the combined trip distribution and assignment models. Readers are suggested to refer to Boyce et al. (1988) for an early excellent review of the combined trip distribution and assignment models, to Fisk (1980), Daganzo (1983), Akamatsu and Kuwahara (1989), Bell (1995), Huang (1995), Akamatsu (1997). In particular, there has been an ongoing growth in the body of literature dealing with dynamic traffic assignment, which is not mentioned at all in our review.

3

THE FIRST-BEST ROAD PRICING PROBLEMS

3.1 INTRODUCTION

Consider a road network in a given region. Such a network is sometimes described as a collective resource, since it represents a potential capacity that can be used simultaneously by firms and households in the region. On the other hand, a road network can also be assessed as a capacity that is actually consumed by particular individuals, and the utilization of road capacity can refer to collective consumption. When the roads are actually used for travel, the collective of the effect may cause congestion and pollution consequences during peak periods. It has long been recognized that marginal cost or the first-best pricing can reduce traffic congestion and, according to the theory, increase society's welfare. The principle tells us that the road users should pay for the additional congestion they create when entering a congested road. The optimal road price reflects the difference between the marginal social cost of trip-making and the average cost.

The standard theoretical arguments about marginal-cost road pricing are largely concerned with abstract demand-supply models for a single road link. In the case of general traffic networks with homogeneous users, the first-best congestion pricing theory still holds, which states that a toll that is equal to the difference between the marginal social cost and the marginal private cost is charged on each link, so as to internalize the user externalities and thus achieve a system optimum flow pattern in the network. The marginal cost pricing will minimize the total travel cost spent on the network by the whole population in the case of fixed demand, and maximize the total social welfare equal to the user benefit from trip-making minus total social cost in the case of elastic demand.

In this chapter, we describe the theoretical background of road pricing, namely, the fundamental economic principle of marginal-cost pricing. We show theoretically how the classical principle of marginal-cost pricing would work in a general congested network. The investigation will be extended to investigate the implications of marginal-cost pricing under different equilibrium conditions, including ones with link flow interaction and network physical or environmental capacity constraints. We examine the speed-flow relationship for formulating the appropriate congestion cost function used in congestion pricing by explicitly building link physical capacity constraint and queuing delay into the model. In view of the adverse environmental effects, such as air pollution from vehicular exhaust emissions, we also look into the pricing policy for sustainable transportation networks by explicitly taking into account the total emissions generated and quarantee that they do not exceed the imposed environmental quality standard. Further extension of the marginal-cost pricing is made to congested networks in stochastic user equilibrium. Throughout this chapter, the terms of travel time and travel cost are equally used for simplicity with an implicit assumption of a unit value of time.

3.2 MARGINAL-COST PRICING UNDER STANDARD USER-EQUILIBRIUM

3.2.1 Graphical Interpretation

Before we move to investigate marginal-cost pricing in general networks, we illustrate the underlying theory graphically. Consider a simplified but, in the literature, standard case of a homogenous traffic stream moving along a given uniform stretch of road, with fixed entry and exit points and no obstacles to the movement of traffic, apart from those arising from the limited capacity of the road. The standard analysis of congestion pricing could be presented in the form set out in Figure 3.1. The AC curve represents the average (private) cost of congestion at each level of traffic flow, and the MC curve represents the marginal (social) cost which includes the additional cost of adding one extra vehicle to the traffic stream. The MC may be seen as representing 'social costs' in the limited sense that they are the costs to the society of road users. However, any individual user entering the road will only consider the costs (AC) he personally bears. He will either be unaware of or unwilling to consider the external congestion costs he imposes on the other road users. Therefore, the MC curve relates to the marginal social cost for the new trip-maker and the existing road users of the traffic flow, while the AC curve is equivalent to the marginal private cost borne and perceived by the new trip-maker alone. The difference between the AC and MC curves at any traffic flow reflects the economic costs of congestion at that flow.

The optimal flow is, as we can see, equal to v_e where the marginal social cost and demand are equated, while the actual flow, when there is no toll, tends to be v_a, because road users ignore the congestion that they impose on others. From a social point of view the actual flow, v_a, is excessive because the v_a-th user is only enjoying a benefit of $\overline{\mathrm{ab}}$, but imposing costs of $\overline{\mathrm{ac}}$. The additional traffic beyond the optimal level v_e can be seen to be generating costs equal to the area $\overline{\text{ache}}$, but only enjoying a benefit equal to the area $\overline{\text{abhe}}$, a deadweight welfare loss of the area $\overline{\text{bch}}$ is apparent. A traffic flow lower than v_e is also sub-optimal because the potential consumer surplus gained from trip-making are not being fully exploited.

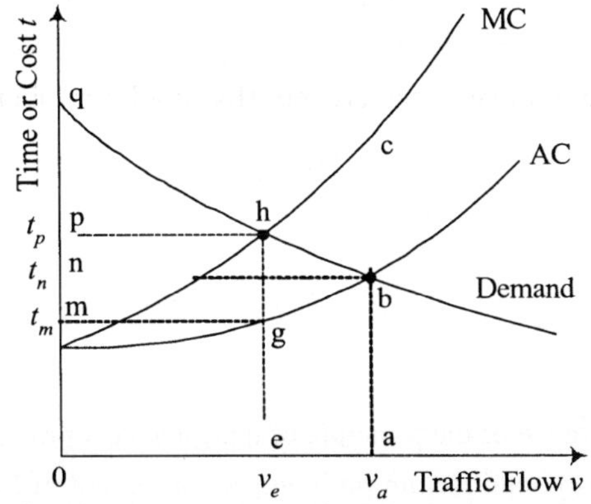

Figure 3.1 Graphical representation of marginal-cost pricing

Let the travel time-volume function or *AC* curve for the road be $t(v)$. The total cost $TC(v)$ associated with the flow v can be expressed as:

$$TC(v) = vt(v) \tag{3.1}$$

The marginal social cost, MC, is

$$MC(v) = \frac{\mathrm{d}TC(v)}{\mathrm{d}v} = t(v) + v\frac{\mathrm{d}t(v)}{\mathrm{d}v} \tag{3.2}$$

The first-term in (3.2) right hand side is the average cost AC. The toll that should be imposed in order to make an efficient use of the available capacity is equal to the second term

$$u(v) = v\frac{\mathrm{d}t(v)}{\mathrm{d}v} \tag{3.3}$$

which means that the optimal toll, u, equals the difference between the marginal social cost, MC, and the average cost, AC.

Note that the above result can be also derived by solving an economic benefit maximization problem at an aggregate level. In other words, under the marginal-cost pricing, the economic benefit (total trip benefit minus total social cost) will be maximized. Assuming the travel demand is given by a demand function

$$d = D(\mu) \tag{3.4}$$

where μ is the price or generalized cost of traveling through the road, and let $B(d)$ be the corresponding inverse or benefit function. Then the economic benefit (EB) is measured by

$$EB(v) = \int_0^v B(\omega)\mathrm{d}\omega - vt(v) \tag{3.5}$$

where $v = d$ since only a single link is involved. The economic benefit (EB) is given by the area $\overline{\text{ghqm}}$ in Figure 3.1. Evidently, EB is also equal to the sum of the consumers' surplus (area $\overline{\text{hqp}}$) and total government revenue (area $\overline{\text{ghpm}}$). Clearly, $\max EB(v)$ leads to the crossing of demand curve and MC curve, i.e., $B(v) = t(v) + v\left(\mathrm{d}t(v)/\mathrm{d}v\right)$, from which the optimal flow v_e is generated.

3.2.2 Fixed Demand Case

We now highlight the essence of the principle of marginal cost pricing by investigating how it would work in the network equilibrium problem. As presented in Chapter 2. the UE and SO models in general give rise to different link flow patterns, and our task is to determine a set of link tolls to decentralize the SO flow pattern into an UE flow pattern in a general network. This can be achieved by applying the marginal-cost pricing principle for the use of network resources. Namely, by levying a suitable flow-dependent congestion fee on each user using a particular link in the network, the traffic flow pattern which results from choosing cost-minimizing routes between any OD pair will be a system optimum. This particular fee level that will accomplish this aim is the additional travel cost an additional user on a link will inflict on each one of the users already using that link. To have a precise look at this proposal, we revisit the following SO model that minimize the total network travel time cost or disutility, TC, with fixed demand given in Chapter 2.

$$\min\ TC(\mathbf{v}) = \sum_{a\in A} v_a t_a(v_a) \tag{3.6}$$

subject to

$$\sum_{r\in R_w} f_{rw} = d_w,\quad w\in W \tag{3.7}$$

$$f_{rw} \geq 0,\quad r\in R_w, w\in W \tag{3.8}$$

where the link flows, $\mathbf{v} = \left(v_a, a\in A\right)^{\mathrm{T}}$, are defined by

$$v_a = \sum_{w\in W}\sum_{r\in R_w} f_{rw}\delta_{ar},\quad a\in A \tag{3.9}$$

From the first-order optimality conditions of program (3.6)-(3.8), we obtain for any optimum solution $\left(\mathbf{f}^*, \mathbf{v}^*\right)$ the following relations

$$c_{rw} = \mu_w \text{ if } f_{rw}^* > 0;\ c_{rw} \geq \mu_w \text{ if } f_{rw}^* = 0,\ r \in R_w, w \in W \tag{3.10}$$

where μ_w is the Lagrange multiplier associated with constraint (3.7), and

$$c_{rw} = \sum_{a \in A} \tilde{t}_a(v_a^*)\delta_{ar},\quad r \in R_w, w \in W \tag{3.11}$$

$$\tilde{t}_a(v_a^*) = t_a(v_a^*) + v_a^* \frac{\mathrm{d}t_a(v_a^*)}{\mathrm{d}v_a},\quad a \in A \tag{3.12}$$

We note that these optimality conditions are similar to those obtained for the UE program in Chapter 2 only excepting the definition on link travel time. The new link travel time given by (3.12) consists of two components: $t_a(v_a)$ is the travel time privately experienced or perceived by each individual user traveling on link a, and $v_a \mathrm{d}t_a(v_a)/\mathrm{d}v_a$ is the additional travel time imposed on all existing users by an additional user. The travel time defined by (3.12) can be interpreted as the *marginal contribution* of an additional user on link a to the total link travel time, i.e., $\tilde{t}_a(v_a) = \mathrm{d}(v_a t_a(v_a))/\mathrm{d}v_a$. With the assumptions of separable link travel time functions, $\tilde{t}_a(v_a)$ is also the marginal contribution to the total system travel time, *i.e,* $\tilde{t}_a(v_a) = \partial TC(\mathrm{v})/\partial v_a$. The term, $v_a \mathrm{d}t_a(v_a)/\mathrm{d}v_a$, in (3.12), is called *congestion externality* in pricing theory.

One thus observes that the SO flow pattern is decentralized as an user equilibrium stated by (3.10) if all users evaluate their link travel times according to eqn. (3.12). However, in deciding by which route to travel, each user normally considers his/her own travel time, $t_a(v_a)$, only, without including the congestion externality, $v_a \mathrm{d}t_a(v_a)/\mathrm{d}v_a$, that he or she imposes on others. If we introduce a congestion pricing scheme in which each user traveling on every link is charged a fee equivalent to the congestion externality evaluated at the SO solution with fixed demand denoted as $(v_a^{*,\mathrm{F}}, a \in A)$

$$u_a = v_a \left.\frac{\mathrm{d}t_a(v_a)}{\mathrm{d}v_a}\right|_{v_a = v_a^{*,\mathrm{F}}},\quad a \in A \tag{3.13}$$

then a user equilibrium state can be reached in which each user will face an actual travel cost inclusive of the additional term of congestion externality given by eqn. (3.12) on each link of the network. In other words, if the link cost perceived by an individual user has been modified, by charging a toll equal to the congestion externality, individual users' self-optimizing route choices are also socially optimal or the SO flow pattern is supported as an user equilibrium. This is the theoretical foundation of the well-known *marginal cost pricing principle*, stating that the road users using congested roads should pay a toll equal to the difference between the marginal social cost of trip making, $\tilde{t}(v_a)$, and the average private cost, $t_a(v_a)$, in order to achieve a system optimum flow pattern.

3.2.3 Elastic Demand Case

We can look at how the principle of marginal cost pricing works in the network equilibrium problem with elastic demand in a similar manner as in the case with fixed demand. Evidently, we cannot seek a toll pattern to minimize total network travel cost or achieve a SO whenever the demand is elastic. The reason is simple: the more the charge is, the less the realized demand, and thus the less the total travel cost becomes. An obviously unrealistic optimal solution would be the near zero traffic flow achieved through unacceptable high toll charges. The optimal tolls in the elastic demand case could, however, still be derived through corresponding SO formulation outlined in Chapter 2. The key point here is that the SO problem is defined in terms of maximization of the net economic benefit or social welfare. Recall that the total network user benefit (UB) from travel is evaluated as

$$UB = \sum_{w \in W} \int_0^{d_w} B_w(\omega) d\omega \tag{3.14}$$

where the benefit function, $B_w(d) = D_w^{-1}(d_w)$, is given as the inverse of demand function $D_w(\mu_w)$ between OD pair $w \in W$. The demand function $D_w(\mu_w)$ is assumed to be dependent on μ_w, the travel cost between that OD pair alone. The total social cost (SC) incurred by all network users is given by

$$SC = \sum_{a \in A} v_a t_a(v_a) \tag{3.15}$$

Therefore, the economic benefit (EB) is evaluated by

$$EB = UB - SC = \sum_{w \in W} \int_0^{d_w} B_w(\omega) d\omega - \sum_{a \in A} v_a t_a(v_a) \tag{3.16}$$

The optimal use of the transportation network requires that the economic benefit (EB) is maximized, an SO in this sense is achieved. The problem can be formulated as the following equivalent minimization problem

$$\min\ EB(\mathbf{v}, \mathbf{d}) = \sum_{a \in A} v_a t_a(v_a) - \sum_{w \in W} \int_0^{d_w} B_w(\omega) d\omega \tag{3.17}$$

subject to

$$\sum_{r \in R_w} f_{rw} = d_w,\ w \in W \tag{3.18}$$

$$f_{rw} \geq 0,\ r \in R_w, w \in W \tag{3.19}$$

$$d_w \geq 0,\ w \in W \tag{3.20}$$

where link flow $\mathbf{v}$ is given by (3.9) and $\mathbf{d}=(d_w, w\in W)^{\mathrm{T}}$.

Proceeding in a similar manner as in the fixed demand case, we obtain for an optimum solution $(\mathbf{f}^*,\mathbf{v}^*,\mathbf{d}^*)$ the following results

$$c_{rw}=\mu_w \text{ if } f_{rw}^*>0;\ c_{rw}\geq\mu_w \text{ if } f_{rw}^*=0,\ r\in R_w, w\in W,\quad r\in R_w, w\in W \tag{3.21}$$

$$B_w(d_w^*)=\mu_w, \text{ if } d_w^*>0;\ B_w(d_w^*)\leq\mu_w, \text{ if } d_w^*=0,\ w\in W \tag{3.22}$$

where μ_w is the Lagrange multiplier associated with OD demand constraint (3.18) and once again

$$c_{rw}=\sum_{a\in A}\tilde{t}_a(v_a^*)\delta_{ar},\quad r\in R_w, w\in W \tag{3.23}$$

$$\tilde{t}_a(v_a^*)=t_a(v_a^*)+v_a^*\frac{\mathrm{d}t_a(v_a^*)}{\mathrm{d}v_a},\quad a\in A \tag{3.24}$$

These optimality conditions are nothing but the network equilibrium conditions with elastic demand. The only difference from the elastic-demand equilibrium model in Chapter 2 is that the link cost governing the equilibrium is given by (3.24). As before, this new link cost function consists of two components: $t_a(v_a)$ is the cost experienced or perceived by an individual user traversing link $a\in A$; and $v_a\,\mathrm{d}t_a(v_a)/\mathrm{d}v_a$ is the externality which is the cost that a marginal user imposes on others already traveling on the link $a\in A$. In other words, congestion externality exists in the system optimality conditions, and the socially optimal pricing of road use with congestion effects is to charge a toll to internalize this externality so that the UE conditions coincide with the SO ones. Namely, if the link toll is given by

$$u_a=v_a\left.\frac{\mathrm{d}t_a(v_a)}{\mathrm{d}v_a}\right|_{v_a=v_a^{*,\mathrm{E}}},\quad a\in A \tag{3.25}$$

where $(v_a^{*,\mathrm{E}}, a\in A)$ denotes the optimum solution to the SO problem (3.17)-(3.20) with elastic demand, then a new network demand-performance equilibrium is established, and this new equilibrium is precisely an SO in the sense that the economic benefit is maximized.

It should be pointed out that although the marginal-cost toll in both fixed and elastic demand cases is expressed in a closed form, and is seemingly related to local link flow and congestion function, it also reflects implicitly the global marginal effects. Namely, when an additional user is added to the network, his or her global marginal effect will include the change in total travel cost due to redistribution of network flow, and the change in user benefit due to change in demand if the demand is elastic. These global effects are reflected in the models (3.6)-(3.8) or (3.17)-(3.20) by calculating all link tolls by (3.13) and (3.25) respectively at the point of network equilibrium that already embraces toll charge implicitly. In other words, link tolls are determined endogenously in the network equilibrium models. In addition, although the link toll formulae are identical for both fixed and elastic demand UE problems, the resulting link toll charge depends on the SO link flows obtained, which are different in different equilibrium models.

3.3 MARGINAL-COST PRICING WITH LINK CAPACITY CONSTRAINTS

The standard economic model of road congestion pricing relies on the assumption of monotone congestion cost and demand functions. However, most road-use pricing schemes are designated conceptually for removing vehicle queues that constitute a substantial part of travel delay in congested urban areas. A queue is caused by limited capacities on the links. It is thus desirable to develop pricing models that can consider link capacity constraints.

3.3.1 Pricing Model with Capacity Constraints

Again consider a single road connecting a given entry and exit point. The demand and average cost curves are depicted in Figure 3.2. In the absence of capacity constraint and toll charge, the equilibrium point will be a with a traffic flow v_a. Now suppose that the capacity of the road (hereinafter, capacity of a road is referred to its exit capacity) is C ($C < v_a$). Because the demand is greater than the capacity, a vehicle queue will occur. The queuing delay will grow so that the equilibrium between demand and capacity is attained. As shown in Figure 3.2, the equilibrium point without tolls will be b, at which the realized demand is equal to the capacity C and the resultant equilibrium queuing delay is equal to $\overline{t_2 t_4}$ $(= t_4 - t_2)$.

Now we consider marginal-cost pricing with a queue. If the marginal cost curve is MC_2, then the optimal congestion toll will be $\overline{t_1 t_5} = (t_5 - t_1)$ and the corresponding equilibrium point will be e. The marginal-cost toll is high enough to hold the demand below capacity and hence prevents a queue from occurring. However, if the marginal-cost curve is MC_1, the demand under marginal-cost pricing would be greater than the capacity, and hence a vehicle queue will still occur. The amount of delay is what is needed to choke off enough potential demand to match the realized demand at capacity, and thus the same equilibrium point b as that in the no toll case is reached. As we can see from Figure 3.2, the marginal-cost toll calculated at the flow equal to capacity is $\overline{t_2 t_3} = (t_3 - t_2)$, and the equilibrium queuing delay is $\overline{t_3t_4} = (t_4 - t_3)$. In this case, the theoretical marginal-cost toll is insufficient to prevent queue from occurring. Because queuing delay is a pure waste of time, it is desirable to remove the queue by toll charges. This means that the optimal toll charge should be $\overline{t_2t_4} = (t_4 - t_2)$ under which a queue is completely removed. Note that the additional toll charge $\overline{t_3t_4}$ (or even the total link charge $\overline{t_2t_4}$) produces no losses for road users, whenever the toll is not beyond the queuing delay, because it simply substitutes a charge for wasted time, between which road users are indifferent.

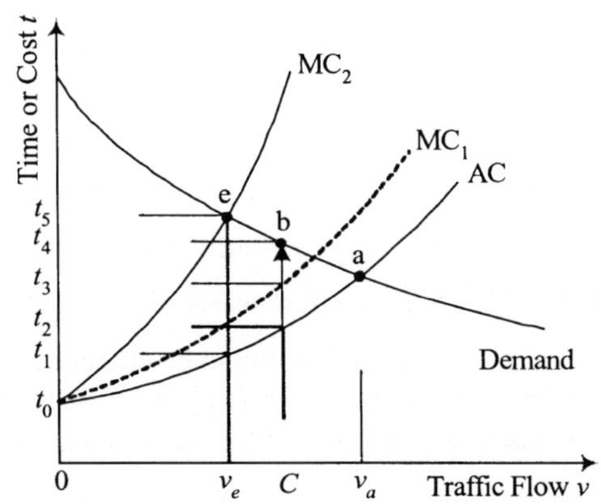

Figure 3.2 Optimal road pricing under congestion and queue

In general networks with elastic demands, the SO model for determining the optimal tolls under the aforementioned queue and congestion conditions can be formulated by simply adding the link capacity constraint to the problem (3.17)-(3.20).

$$\min_{(\mathbf{v},\mathbf{d})\in\Omega} \sum_{a\in A} v_a t_a(v_a) - \sum_{w\in W} \int_0^{d_w} B_w(\omega)d\omega \tag{3.26}$$

subject to

$$v_a \le C_a, \quad a \in A \tag{3.27}$$

where

$$\Omega = \{(\mathbf{v},\mathbf{d}) \,|\, \mathbf{v}{=}\Delta\mathbf{f},\ \mathbf{d}{=}\Lambda\mathbf{f},\ \mathbf{f} \ge 0, \mathbf{d} \ge 0\} \tag{3.28}$$

where the link/path incidence matrix $\Delta = [\delta_{ar}]$ and the OD pair/path incidence matrix $\Lambda = [\Lambda_{rw}]$ are defined before, and C_a is the capacity of link $a \in A$. We can easily show that the optimization problem (3.26)-(3.27) leads to the following relationships for an optimum solution $(\mathbf{f}^*, \mathbf{v}^*, \mathbf{d}^*)$.

$$c_{rw} = \mu_w \text{ if } f_{rw}^* > 0;\ c_{rw} \ge \mu_w \text{ if } f_{rw}^* = 0,\ r \in R_w, w \in W \tag{3.29}$$

$$B_w\left(d_w^*\right)=\mu_w, \text{ if } d_w^*>0;\ B_w\left(d_w^*\right)\leq \mu_w, \text{ if } d_w^*=0,\ w\in W \tag{3.30}$$

$$\lambda_a=0, \text{ if } v_a^*<C_a;\ \lambda_a\geq 0, \text{ if } v_a^*=C_a,\ a\in A \tag{3.31}$$

where $\lambda_a, a\in A$, is the Lagrange multiplier associated with capacity constraint (3.27) and

$$c_{rw}=\sum_{a\in A}\bar{t}_a\left(v_a\right)\delta_{ar} \tag{3.32}$$

$$\bar{t}_a\left(v_a\right)=\tilde{t}_a\left(v_a\right)+\lambda_a=t_a\left(v_a\right)+v_a\frac{\mathrm{d}t_a\left(v_a\right)}{\mathrm{d}v_a}+\lambda_a \tag{3.33}$$

Therefore, if the link cost function is modified to be $\bar{t}_a\left(v_a\right)$, then a queuing demand-performance equilibrium in the capacity-constrained network with elastic demand is established. From (3.31), queues only form ($\lambda_a>0$) when capacity is reached ($v_a=C_a$); below capacity, link costs will be solely given by $\tilde{t}_a\left(v_a\right)$.

In (3.33), $\left(v_a\,\mathrm{d}t_a\left(v_a\right)/\mathrm{d}v_a+\lambda_a\right)$ represents the marginal-cost toll evaluated at traffic flow $v_a, a\in A$. The queuing delay, $\lambda_a, a\in A$, is a pure waste of time and should be substituted by an additional toll. Consequently, the optimal link toll to be charged is given by

$$u_a=v_a\left.\frac{\mathrm{d}t_a\left(v_a\right)}{\mathrm{d}v_a}\right|_{v_a=v_a^{*,\mathrm{E\text{-}C}}}+\lambda_a,\ a\in A \tag{3.34}$$

where $\left(v_a^{*,\mathrm{E\text{-}C}}, a\in A\right)$ denotes the optimum solution to the SO problem (3.26)-(3.27) with elastic demand and capacity constraints; $\lambda_a=0$ if $v_a^{*,\mathrm{E\text{-}C}}<C_a$ and $\lambda_a\geq 0$ if $v_a^{*,\mathrm{E\text{-}C}}=C_a$, $a\in A$. Note that under this optimal toll charge, the economic benefit (EB) consists of three components: the consumer surplus, the revenue raised from congestion externality and the revenue generated by additional queuing charge.

3.3.2 Speed-flow Relationship for Congestion Pricing

In this subsection, we discuss the relationship between speed (or travel time) and flow which is fundamental to the understanding of congestion, and plays an important role in the standard economic model of road congestion pricing. Failure to correctly understanding this relation may result in incorrect conclusions and misconceptions.

Consider a standard case of a homogeneous traffic stream moving in a uniform road, with only one entry and one exit point. Conventional analysis for congestion pricing is based on a diagram of speed/flow relationship shown in Figure 3.3, which has a backward-bending branch going to the origin. Most analyses, in both road pricing and traffic assignment literature, are concerned with the normal speed/flow regime. Thus the marginal social curve could be shown by MSC_1 in the corresponding travel time/flow diagram (Figure 3.4). MSC_1 rises above the average cost curve, but goes asymptotically to infinity when flow reaches capacity C_{max}.

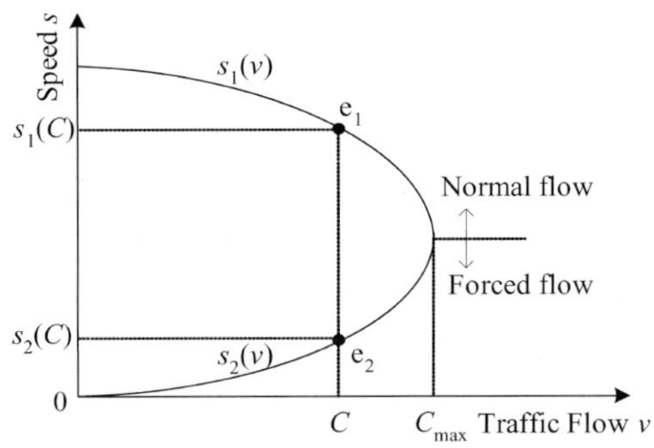

Figure 3.3 Speed-flow relationship

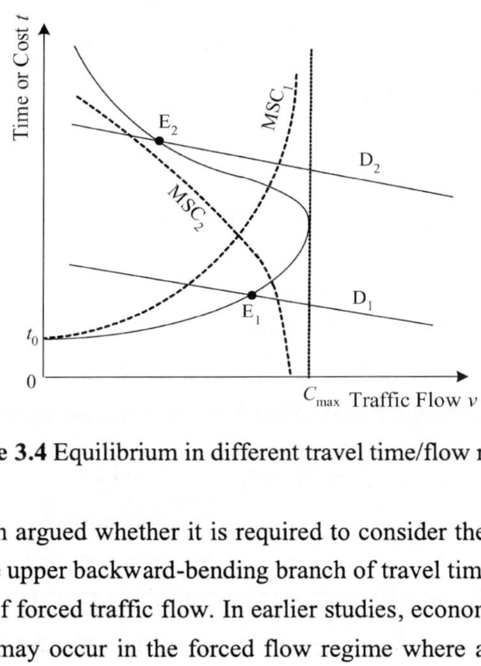

Figure 3.4 Equilibrium in different travel time/flow regime

However, it has long been argued whether it is required to consider the lower branch of the speed/flow diagram or the upper backward-bending branch of travel time/flow relation which describes the conditions of forced traffic flow. In earlier studies, economists pointed out that the equilibrium position may occur in the forced flow regime where a high demand curve (D_2) cuts the backward-bending section of the cost curve at point E_2. It is generally believed that a meaningful marginal social cost curve is non-existent in this backward-bending section because the change in output is negative (although an irrelevant downward-sloping marginal cost curve (MSC_2) could be derived mathematically).

Here we must point out that in reality, the backward-bending regime of speed/flow curve is never reached in a uniform roadway, which can be demonstrated from shock wave theory, and thus the aforementioned arguments are questionable. The whole curve including the backward-bending branch just describes the relationship between the local speed and local flow, though this relation should be satisfied at each point or a very short subsection of the roadway.

It is important to note that the cost curve used in road pricing should be defined for travel between two distant locations (a link with a certain length). The backward-bending section does not apply to the cost curve for the travel through the whole link even when a traffic jam or queue is present. The actual situation is that a traffic jam occurs in uninterrupted traffic flows when more vehicles enter the upstream end of a section of road than can get out of the downstream end. Hence, the link speeds concerned are actually in two distinctly different regimes represented by the two different branches of the parabola of Figure 3.3, a proportion of the link experiences the lower average speed characteristics of congestion, while the rest still flows freely. The cost consequence of this bimodal distribution of the speeds on the link should be dealt with in more detail.

We now use an example to show how to compute the travel time in a link with a queue and congestion. We assume that a queue, if it occurs, will start from the exit end of a link. If this link represents a freeway section, a queue may occur due to capacity reduction (lane drop) in its downstream section or because of the exit end being a merge or a diverge point with less capacity than the mainline section. If the link represents a street, a queue occurs from intersections where capacity is least. We also make a simplifying assumption that the link exit capacity is constant, although it may depend on the flows on adjacent links and queues.

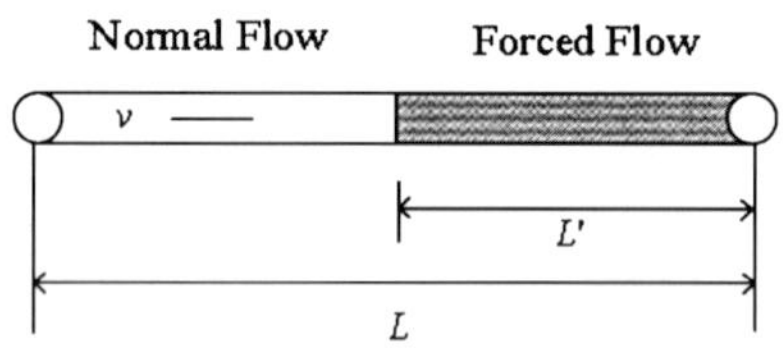

queuing delay will eventually approach certain values. This temporal steady-state could be assumed when considering daily recurring congestion during the peak commuting periods.

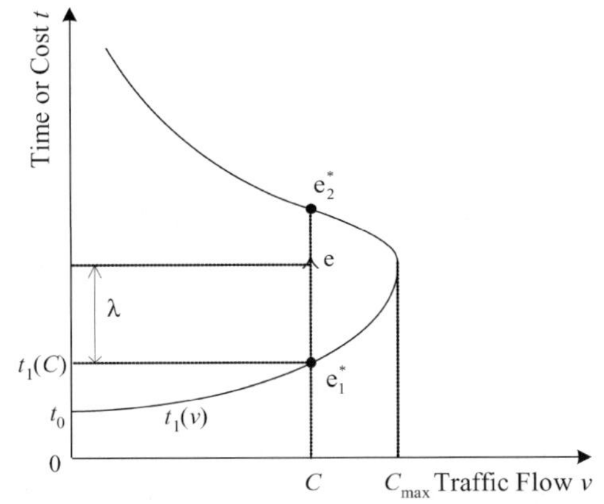

Figure 3.6 Flow-travel time relationship

Let the whole link length be L and the queuing length in the stationary state be L'. As shown in Figure 3.3, the relationship between speed, s, and traffic flow, v, is described by a monotonically decreasing function, $s_1(v)$, in the normal flow regime, and described by a monotonically increasing function, $s_2(v)$, in the forced flow regime (here for consistency with other parts, we have adopted different notation from those used in traffic flow analysis). Because the flow rate equals exit capacity in the steady-state, the moving speeds in the road subsections of normal flow and forced flow are $s_1(C)$ and $s_2(C)$, respectively, the travel time through the whole link is hence given by

$$t = \frac{L-L'}{s_1(C)} + \frac{L'}{s_2(C)} = \frac{L}{s_1(C)} + \left\{ \frac{L'}{s_2(C)} - \frac{L'}{s_1(C)} \right\} \tag{3.35}$$

The first term in the right hand side of (3.35) represents the travel time going through the whole link at a normal speed $s_1(C)$; the second term is the time delay due to the traffic jam and is treated as queuing delay. Therefore, the travel time on a link can be expressed as

$$t(v) = \begin{cases} t_1(v) & \text{for } 0 \le v < C \\ t_1(v) + \lambda & \text{for } v = C \end{cases} \tag{3.36}$$

where

$$t_1(v) = \frac{L}{s_1(v)}, \ \lambda = \frac{L'}{s_2(C)} - \frac{L'}{s_1(C)} \tag{3.37}$$

Since $0 \le L' \le L$, queuing delay, λ, should satisfy

$$0 \le \lambda \le \frac{L\left(s_1(C) - s_2(C)\right)}{s_1(C)s_2(C)} \tag{3.38}$$

and

$$\lambda = \frac{L\left(s_1(C) - s_2(C)\right)}{s_1(C)s_2(C)} \tag{3.39}$$

when the queue extends to the upstream node. Here, we do not consider the extreme situation where the queue grows to block the upstream links.

Figure 3.6 depicts the relationship between travel time and flow. The normal flow regime is described by a continuous, monotonically increasing function $t_1(v)$. This function is also what we have used in the equilibrium model. Once the link flow reaches its exit capacity ($v = C$), travel time will grow vertically. The vertical segment $\overline{e_1^* e}$ corresponds to the queuing delay when the queue arrives somewhere in the link as shown in Figure 3.5. Point e_2^* or the segment $\overline{e_1^* e_2^*}$ corresponds to the extreme case when the queue in the link grows up to its upstream node. From this analysis, we can see that the lower branch of the parabolic speed/flow relationship in Figure 3.3 (or the upper branch of the travel time/flow relationship in Figure 3.4 or Figure 3.6) does not apply to a street road. In addition, differing from the asymptotic travel time function which goes to infinity as the flow approaches capacity, the queuing delay will take a finite value at the stationary equilibrium state.

Hence, we have shown that there is no logical requirement for a backward-bending speed-flow relationship on a whole link to happen. However, a queuing delay, which reflects the delay to vehicles in the proportion of the link operating at that lower branch, is included. The queuing delay is due to limited capacity and takes a certain value which should be determined endogenously from network demand-performance equilibrium and flow equilibrium conditions. This is exactly what our model (3.26)-(3.27) with capacity constraint implies, in which the Lagrange multiplier associated with link capacity constraint (3.27) gives the queuing delay. Furthermore, from the above analysis, the physical length of queue has been implicitly reflected in our model.

3.4 Marginal-cost Pricing with a Total Environmental Quality Constraint

In this section we examine road pricing policy for sustainable transportation networks by taking into account environmental externality, from both a user-optimized and a system-optimized viewpoint. This is handled by incorporating the total emission generated or the total vehicle-km traveled in the network as a constraint in the SO model, thereby meeting the requirement for air quality and reduction of greenhouse gas emissions from road transport.

Suppose the emission from vehicles traveling on different links in the network to be proportional to flow volume. Let ρ_a denote the emission factor on link $a \in A$, which is assumed to be given for all links. Emission factors vary, depending on several factors, such as: vehicle type and age mix, vehicle speed and ambient temperature. Thus, the total environmental emission is given as $E = \sum_{a \in A} \rho_a v_a$, which is now constrained not to exceed a predetermined environmental quality standard, denoted by $\bar{E}$, that should be considered in setting the pricing policy.

Now consider the following SO problem with a single environmental quality constraint

$$\max_{(\mathbf{v},\mathbf{d}) \in \Omega} \sum_{w \in W} \int_0^{d_w} B_w(\omega) \mathrm{d}\omega - \sum_{a \in A} v_a t_a(v_a) \tag{3.40}$$

subject to

$$\sum_{a \in A} \rho_a v_a \le \bar{E} \tag{3.41}$$

where Ω is defined in (3.28). From the first-order optimality conditions, we have for an optimal solution $(\mathbf{f}^*, \mathbf{v}^*, \mathbf{d}^*)$

$$c_{rw} = \mu_w \text{ if } f_{rw}^* > 0;\ c_{rw} \ge \mu_w \text{ if } f_{rw}^* = 0,\ r \in R_w, w \in W \tag{3.42}$$

$$B_w(d_w^*) = \mu_w, \text{ if } d_w^* > 0;\ B_w(d_w^*) \le \mu_w, \text{ if } d_w^* = 0,\ w \in W \tag{3.43}$$

$$\lambda = 0, \text{ if } \sum_{a \in A} \rho_a v_a^* < \bar{E};\ \lambda \ge 0, \text{ if } \sum_{a \in A} \rho_a v_a^* = \bar{E},\ a \in A \tag{3.44}$$

where λ is the Lagrange multiplier associated with constraint (3.41) and

$$c_{rw} = \sum_{a \in A} \hat{t}_a(v_a^*) \delta_{ar} \tag{3.45}$$

$$\hat{t}_a(v_a^*) = \tilde{t}_a(v_a^*) + \rho_a \lambda = t_a(v_a^*) + v_a^* \frac{\mathrm{d}t_a(v_a^*)}{\mathrm{d}v_a} + \rho_a \lambda \tag{3.46}$$

Note that $\tilde{t}_a(v_a^*)$ in (3.46) denotes the generalized marginal cost associated with traveling on link $a \in A$, where the term: $\rho_a \lambda^*$, represents the marginal portion of the total cost due to the emission generated by traveling on link $a \in A$. In this case the link pricing policy is given by

$$u_a = v_a \left. \frac{\mathrm{d}t_a(v_a)}{\mathrm{d}v_a} \right|_{v_a = v_a^{*,\mathrm{EQ}}} + \rho_a \lambda \tag{3.47}$$

where $\left(v_a^{*,\mathrm{EQ}}, a \in A\right)$ denotes the optimum solution to the SO problem (3.40)-(3.41) with an environmental quality constraint, and $\lambda = 0$ if $\sum_{a \in A} \rho_a v_a^{*,\mathrm{EQ}} < \bar{E}$; $\lambda \geq 0$ if $\sum_{a \in A} \rho_a v_a^{*,\mathrm{EQ}} = \bar{E}$.

The combined emission and congestion tolls guarantee sustainability of the transportation network in the sense that the network flow pattern is optimal from both user and system perspectives, meanwhile satisfying the environmental quality standard. Note that if we only consider the environmental quality standard without pricing congestion externality, then the optimal link toll is given by $u_a = \rho_a \lambda$, $a \in A$ by dropping the congestion externality term. Furthermore, the emission control is carried out on individual links by imposing $\rho_a v_a \leq \bar{E}_a$, $a \in A$ or the total network allowable emission is allocated to individual links such that $\sum_{a \in A} \bar{E}_a = \bar{E}$. Then the problem in fact reduces to the SO problem with link environmental capacity constraints, and the individual link environmental capacity is given by $\bar{C}_a = \bar{E}_a / \rho_a$, $a \in A$. A formulation similar to (3.26)-(3.27) is available by superseding the link physical capacity C_a with its corresponding environmental capacity $\bar{C}_a$, $a \in A$.

3.5 Marginal-cost Pricing with Link Flow Interactions and Multiple Vehicle Types

3.5.1 The Case with Link Flow Interactions

In this section, we study traffic equilibrium, system optimum and marginal-cost pricing in a network with link flow interaction, where the travel cost on a link depends not only on its own flow but also the flows on other links. Relevant VI and optimization formulation of the UE problem in this case are presented in Subsection 2.3.2 in Chapter 2. Here we are interested in seeking a set of efficient link tolls to decentralize the corresponding SO flow pattern as user equilibrium. Consider link cost functions, $t_a(\mathbf{v}) = t_a(\cdots, v_a, \cdots)$, $a \in A$, and separable OD demand functions, $d_w = D_w(\mu_w)$ and OD benefit functions, $\mu_w = D_w^{-1}(d_w) = B_w(d_w)$, $w \in W$ where μ_w is the shortest path time or cost between OD pair $w \in W$. The SO problem is to maximize the economic benefit of the system that can be formulated as the following equivalent minimization problem

$$\min_{(\mathbf{v},\mathbf{d}) \in \Omega} \sum_{a \in A} v_a t_a(\mathbf{v}) - \sum_{w \in W} \int_0^{d_w} B_w(\omega) d\omega \tag{3.48}$$

where Ω is defined in (3.28). Similar to problem (3.17)-(3.20), it is straightforward to show that the first-order optimality conditions of problem (3.48) are given by (3.21)-(3.23), but the counterpart of the generalized link cost function (3.24) is replaced by

$$\tilde{t}_a\left(v_a^*\right)=t_a\left(v_a^*\right)+\sum_{b\in A}v_b^*\frac{\partial t_b(\mathbf{v}^*)}{\partial v_a},\quad a\in A \tag{3.49}$$

With the same argument as above, the desirable link tolls to be charged are equal to the congestion externality present in eqn. (3.49). Thus, the principle of marginal-cost pricing does still applies in this case and the link toll charge takes the following form

$$u_a=\sum_{b\in A}v_b\left.\frac{\partial t_b(\mathbf{v})}{\partial v_a}\right|_{\mathbf{v}=\mathbf{v}^{*,\mathrm{LFI}}}\quad a\in A \tag{3.50}$$

where $\left(v_a^{*,\mathrm{LFI}},a\in A\right)$ denotes the optimum solution to the SO problem (3.48) with link flow interaction.

3.5.2 The Case with Multiple Vehicle Types

We move on to study, in a similar manner, the equilibrium assignment and marginal-cost pricing in a network with several traffic flow types studied in sub-section 2.3.3 of Chapter 2. With the assumptions made in Chapter 2 and using the same notation, the SO problem of maximizing system economic benefit is given as the following minimization problem

$$\min_{(\mathbf{v},\mathbf{d})\in\Omega}\sum_{k\in K}\sum_{a\in A}v_a^k t_a^k(\mathbf{v})-\sum_{k\in K}\sum_{w\in W}\int_0^{d_w^k}B_w^k(\omega)\mathrm{d}\omega \tag{3.51}$$

where

$$\Omega=\left\{\left(\mathbf{v}^k,\mathbf{d}^k\right),k\in K\middle|\ \mathbf{v}^k=\Delta\mathbf{f}^k,\ \mathbf{d}^k=\Lambda\mathbf{f}^k,\ \mathbf{f}^k\geq 0,\mathbf{d}^k\geq 0\right\} \tag{3.52}$$

where $\mathbf{f}^k=\left(f_{rw}^k,r\in R_w,w\in W\right)^{\mathrm{T}}$, $k\in K$; $\mathbf{v}=\left(\mathbf{v}^k,k\in K\right)^{\mathrm{T}}$ and $\mathbf{v}^k=\left(v_a^k,a\in A\right)^{\mathrm{T}}$, $k\in K$; $\mathbf{d}=\left(\mathbf{d}^k,k\in K\right)^{\mathrm{T}}$ and $\mathbf{d}^k=\left(d_w^k,w\in W\right)^{\mathrm{T}}$, $B_w^k\left(d_w^k\right)$ is the benefit (inverse demand) function of flow type k between OD pair $w\in W$.

From the first-order optimality conditions, the following relations hold for an optimum solution $\left(\mathbf{f}^*,\mathbf{v}^*,\mathbf{d}^*\right)$

$$c_{rw}^k=\mu_w^k\ \text{if}\ f_{rw}^{k*}>0;\ c_{rw}^k\geq\mu_w^k\ \text{if}\ f_{rw}^{k*}=0,\ r\in R_w,w\in W \tag{3.53}$$

$$B_w^k\left(d_w^{k*}\right)=\mu_w^k,\ \text{if}\ d_w^{k*}>0;\ B_w^k\left(d_w^{k*}\right)\leq\mu_w^k,\ \text{if}\ d_w^{k*}=0,\ w\in W \tag{3.54}$$

where μ_w^k is the Lagrange multiplier associated with OD demand constraint for each type of flow and

$$c_{rw}^k = \sum_{a\in A} \tilde{t}_a^k\left(\mathbf{v}^*\right)\delta_{ar},\quad r\in R_w, w\in W \tag{3.55}$$

$$\tilde{t}_a^k\left(v_a^*\right) = t_a^k\left(\mathbf{v}^*\right) + \sum_{i\in K}\sum_{b\in A} v_b^i \frac{\partial t_b^i\left(\mathbf{v}^*\right)}{\partial v_a^k},\quad a\in A \tag{3.56}$$

Thus, the marginal cost pricing gives rise to the following vehicle type specific link toll

$$u_a^k = \sum_{i\in K}\sum_{b\in A} v_b^i \left.\frac{\partial t_b^i\left(\mathbf{v}\right)}{\partial v_a^k}\right|_{\mathbf{v}=\mathbf{v}^{*,\mathrm{MVT}}},\quad a\in A,\ k\in K \tag{3.57}$$

where $\left(v_a^{*,\mathrm{MVT}}, a\in A\right)$ denotes the optimum solution to the SO problem (3.51)-(3.52) with multi vehicle types. Therefore, the first-best pricing gives rise to a set of toll charges that are differentiated across flow or vehicle types. Indeed it is true in practice that different levels of toll charge are implemented for different types of vehicles on the basis of their observable differences.

3.6 Marginal-cost Pricing and Uniqueness of Social Optimum

3.6.1 Uniqueness of OD Demands

Now we revisit the objective functions of the UE problems presented in Chapter 2 and the SO problems examined in this Chapter. It is common that all the UE and SO objective functions in the case of elastic demand include a term, $-\sum_{w\in W}\int_0^{d_w} B_w(\omega)d\omega$ (class-specific demand function is adopted for the multi-class traffic equilibrium problems). This common term is convex if the benefit function is continuous and strictly decreasing, and hence all the relevant UE and SO problems have a unique solution in terms of OD demands. Note that we have assumed separable demand functions for simplicity. One can also use non-separable but invertible travel demand functions in the SO problem and employ a line integral to give an exact representation of the total social surplus. Such line integral can only be evaluated if the travel demand functions (or benefit functions) have a symmetric Jacobian. Namely, suppose $\mathbf{B}(\mathbf{d}) = \left(B_w(\mathbf{d}), w\in W\right)^{\mathrm{T}}$ and $\partial B_w(\mathbf{d})/\partial d_{w'} = \partial B_{w'}(\mathbf{d})/\partial d_w$, $w\in W, w'\in W, w\neq w'$. Then the second term in the SO problems can be written as $-\int_0^{\mathbf{d}} \mathbf{B}(?)\mathrm{d}?$. If we further assume that the symmetric Jacobin of the benefit functions is negative definite, then the above term is strictly convex and thus the solution of OD demands to the SO problem is unique. It should be pointed out that, for the UE problem with non-separable demand or benefit functions, a more general VI formulation can be applied without requiring the symmetry restriction like the SO problem. In this case the OD demand solution to the UE problem is unique if

$-\mathbf{B}(\mathbf{d})$, is strictly monotone. Namely for any distinct $\mathbf{d}^1, \mathbf{d}^2 \in \Omega_d = \left\{ \mathbf{d} \,|\, 0 \leq d_w \leq \hat{D}_w,\ w \in W \right\}$ where $\hat{D}_w$ is the upper bound of the demand function $D_w(\mu_w)$, we have

$$\left[-\mathbf{B}(\mathbf{d}^1) - \left(-\mathbf{B}(\mathbf{d}^2) \right) \right]^{\mathrm{T}} \left(\mathbf{d}^1 - \mathbf{d}^2 \right) > 0 \tag{3.58}$$

The symmetry assumption is not necessarily needed; it makes the conventional optimization formulation of the UE problem possible.

3.6.2 Uniqueness of Link Flows with Separable Link Cost Functions

Now we move on to look into the terms relating to the link flows and link cost functions in the SO problem. In the case of separable link cost functions, continuity and monotonicity are sufficient to ensure a unique link flow solution to the UE problem. Nevertheless, the SO problem requires one additional condition that each link travel time function is convex in order to ensure a unique link flow solution. To see this, we examine the Hessian matrix of the objective function. The Hessian matrix is a diagonal one for the separable link cost functions with entries as follows

$$2\frac{\mathrm{d}t_a(v_a)}{\mathrm{d}v_a} + v_a\frac{\mathrm{d}^2 t_a(v_a)}{\mathrm{d}v_a^2}, \quad a \in A \tag{3.59}$$

Clearly, the first term is positive since the link travel time function is assumed to be continuous and monotonically increasing. The second term is positive too if the link travel time function is convex. Then, the Hessian matrix is positive definitive and the SO programs presented in Section 3.2-3.5, involving separable link cost functions, have a unique link flow solution. Here one should particularly pay attention to the fact that, even in the simple case of separable link cost function, the term, $t_a(v_a)v_a$ or $\sum_{a \in A} t_a(v_a)v_a$ of the SO problems may not be convex if the link cost function is monotonically increasing but not convex, and hence the SO solutions may not be unique, as shown in the following example.

Example 3.1 (Unique UE but multiple SO solutions) Set the separable link cost functions

$$t_1(v_1) = 1 - e^{-av_1}, \quad t_2(v_2) = 1 - e^{-av_2}$$

where $a > 4$ is a constant. Note that both $t_1(v_1)$ and $t_2(v_2)$ are strictly increasing functions. Let the demand $d = 1$. The UE objective function is given by

$$Z^{\mathrm{UE}}(v_1, v_2) = Z^{\mathrm{UE}}(v_1, 1 - v_1) = \int_0^{v_1} \left(1 - e^{-a\omega}\right) \mathrm{d}\omega + \int_0^{1-v_1} \left(1 - e^{-a\omega}\right) \mathrm{d}\omega = 1 + \frac{1}{a}\left(e^{-av_1} + e^{-a(1-v_1)}\right)$$

Since the model is symmetric, we conclude that the equilibrium flow is given by $v_1^* = v_2^* = 1/2$. Now look at the derivative of the total social cost $Z^{SO}(v_1, v_2)$ at this point. Since $v_1 + v_2 = 1$, we can consider $Z^{SO}(v_1, v_2)$ as a function of one variable:

$$Z^{SO}(v_1, v_2) = Z(v_1, 1 - v_1) = v_1 t_1(v_1) + (1 - v_1) t_1(1 - v_1)$$

It is easy to see that

$$\left. \frac{dZ^{SO}(v_1, 1 - v_1)}{dv_1} \right|_{v_1 = \frac{1}{2}} = 0, \quad \left. \frac{d^2 Z^{SO}(v_1, 1 - v_1)}{dv_1^2} \right|_{v_1 = \frac{1}{2}} = (4a - a^2) e^{-a/2} < 0 \text{ since } a > 4$$

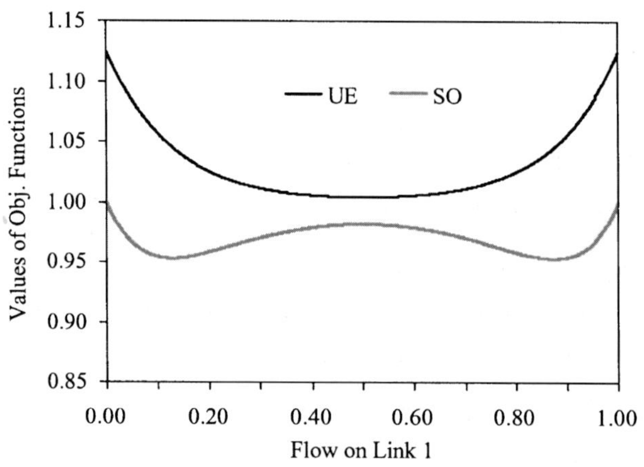

Figure 3.7 Curves of the UE and SO objective values versus link flow v_1 $(0 \le v_1 \le 1.0)$

Thus, we can see the UE in this network coincides with a local maximum of the total social cost. Moreover, it is easy to observe that the social optimum is not unique: there are two points with the same minimum value of the social cost. These points are symmetric with respect to $1/2$. Figure 3.7 shows the values of UE and SO objective functions when $a = 8$, where the SO objective value reaches its minimum at two points, i.e., $v_1 = 0.1265$ and $v_1 = 0.8735$. Clearly, the reason for the non-uniqueness of the SO result in this example is the non-convexity of the social cost, as shown in Figure 3.7. The non-convexity of the social cost is due to the fact that the link cost function is not convex.

This example confirms that even if the link travel cost functions are strictly monotone, the social cost, $TC(\mathbf{v})$, may not be convex.

3.6.3 Uniqueness of Link Flows with Non-separable Link Cost Functions

In the presence of non-separable link cost functions, $t_a(\mathbf{v})$, $a \in A$, the vector of link cost functions, $\mathbf{t}(\mathbf{v})$, is said to be convex if each $t_a(\mathbf{v})$, $a \in A$ is a convex function for $\mathbf{v} \geq 0$; $\mathbf{t}(\mathbf{v})$ is said to be strictly monotone if for any distinct $\mathbf{v}^1$, $\mathbf{v}^2 \in \Omega_v$, we have $\left(\mathbf{t}(\mathbf{v}^2)-\mathbf{t}(\mathbf{v}^1)\right)^{\mathrm{T}}\left(\mathbf{v}^2-\mathbf{v}^1\right)>0$, where $\Omega_v = \{\mathbf{v} \mid \mathbf{v} = \Delta\mathbf{f}, \Lambda\mathbf{f} = \mathbf{d}, \mathbf{f} \geq 0\}$. Alternatively, $\mathbf{t}(\mathbf{v})$ is strictly monotone if and only if its Jacobian $\nabla_{\mathbf{v}}\mathbf{t}(\mathbf{v})$ is positive definite. As mentioned in Chapter 2, the strictly monotone condition or positive definite Jacobian of link cost functions is sufficient to ensure a unique link flow solution to the UE problem.

In contrast, the social cost for the SO problem is given as $TC(\mathbf{v}) = \sum_{a \in A} t_a(\mathbf{v}) v_a = \mathbf{t}(\mathbf{v})^{\mathrm{T}} \mathbf{v}$ and its convexity, to ensure a unique SO link flow solution, is somewhat complicated. First, differing from the case of separable link cost functions, the convexity of the vector functions $\mathbf{t}(\mathbf{v})$, in the case of non-separable link cost functions, does not necessarily imply the convexity of $TC(\mathbf{v}) = \mathbf{t}(\mathbf{v})^{\mathrm{T}}\mathbf{v}$ for $\mathbf{v} \geq 0$. For example, linear (and hence convex, but not strictly convex) and non-separable link cost functions do not guarantee the convexity of $TC(\mathbf{v})$, as seen from Example 3.2 in the next subsection. Second, strict monotonicity of the vector functions $\mathbf{t}(\mathbf{v})$ does not imply the convexity of $TC(\mathbf{v})$ either. This is true even if the link cost functions are separable, as shown in the above Example 3.1. Nonetheless, let us consider the Hessian of $TC(\mathbf{v})$:

$$\frac{\partial TC(\mathbf{v})}{\partial v_a} = t_a(\mathbf{v}) + \sum_{b \in A} v_b \frac{\partial t_b(\mathbf{v})}{\partial v_a} \tag{3.60}$$

$$\frac{\partial^2 TC(\mathbf{v})}{\partial v_a^{\,2}} = 2\frac{\partial t_a(\mathbf{v})}{\partial v_a} + v_a \frac{\partial^2 t_a(\mathbf{v})}{\partial v_a^{\,2}} + \sum_{b \in A,\, b \neq a} v_b \frac{\partial^2 t_b(\mathbf{v})}{\partial v_a^{\,2}} \tag{3.61}$$

$$\frac{\partial^2 TC(\mathbf{v})}{\partial v_a \partial v_b} = \frac{\partial t_a(\mathbf{v})}{\partial v_b} + \frac{\partial t_b(\mathbf{v})}{\partial v_a} + \sum_{c \in A} v_c \frac{\partial^2 t_c(\mathbf{v})}{\partial v_a \partial v_b} \quad \text{for } a \neq b \tag{3.62}$$

Suppose the second-order cross partial derivatives can be omitted in relation to the rest of the terms, we have

$$\frac{\partial^2 TC(\mathbf{v})}{\partial v_a^{\,2}} \approx 2\frac{\partial t_a(\mathbf{v})}{\partial v_a} + v_a \frac{\partial^2 t_a(\mathbf{v})}{\partial v_a^{\,2}} \tag{3.63}$$

$$\frac{\partial^2 TC(\mathbf{v})}{\partial v_a \partial v_b} \approx \frac{\partial t_a(\mathbf{v})}{\partial v_b} + \frac{\partial t_b(\mathbf{v})}{\partial v_a} \quad \text{for } a \neq b \tag{3.64}$$

The conditions for having a unique SO link flow solution in the special case of symmetric link flow interactions can then be stated below.

(i) The travel time on each link is an increasing and convex function of the flow on that link, that is,

$$\frac{\partial t_a(\mathbf{v})}{\partial v_a} > 0, \quad \frac{\partial^2 t_a(\mathbf{v})}{\partial v_a^{\;2}} > 0, \quad a \in A \tag{3.65}$$

(ii) The main dependence of a link's travel time is on its own flow.

$$\frac{\partial t_a(\mathbf{v})}{\partial v_a} > \frac{1}{2} \sum_{b \in A, b \neq a} \left(\frac{\partial t_a(\mathbf{v})}{\partial v_b} + \frac{\partial t_b(\mathbf{v})}{\partial v_a} \right) = \sum_{b \in A, b \neq a} \frac{\partial t_a(\mathbf{v})}{\partial v_b} \tag{3.66}$$

Condition (3.66) together with (3.65) ensures $\partial^2 TC(\mathbf{v})/\partial v_a^{\;2} > \sum_{b \in A, b \neq a} \partial^2 TC(\mathbf{v})/\partial v_a \partial v_b$.

By comparing the above conditions for the SO problem with those for the UE problem in subsection 2.3.2 of Chapter 2, one can see that the additional condition for a unique SO link flow solution in the case of symmetric link interaction is that the travel time on each link is a convex function of its own flow. This observation is similar to that in the case of separable link cost functions.

As discussed in Chapter 2, one may expect that the symmetric situation may appear in the flow interactions between different links. Nonetheless, in the case of interaction between multiple types of vehicles sharing the roadway, as mentioned already, the Jacobian of link cost functions becomes asymmetric; their strict monotonicity or their positive definite Jacobian does not guarantee the positive definiteness of the Hessian or the convexity of the SO objective function $TC(\mathbf{v})$, and as a result, the SO link flow solutions may not be unique. It seems there is little hope to establish the general sufficient conditions for the convexity of $TC(\mathbf{v})$ in terms of the properties of asymmetric link cost functions $\mathbf{t}(\mathbf{v})$. Nonetheless, we now examine the convexity $TC(\mathbf{v})$ for the specific asymmetric link cost functions introduced in Section 2.4 of Chapter 2:

$$t_{aT} = t_{aT}^0 \left\{ 1.0 + \alpha_T \left(\frac{v_{aT} + \eta v_{ac}}{C_{aT}} \right)^{\beta_T} \right\}, \quad t_{ac} = t_{ac}^0 \left\{ 1.0 + \alpha_c \left(\frac{v_{ac} + \xi v_{aT}}{C_{ac}} \right)^{\beta_c} \right\} \tag{3.67}$$

where all variables and parameters are defined before. The Hessian of $TC(\mathbf{v})$ consists of 2×2 diagonal sub-blocks with each corresponding to one link. Hence it suffices to check the positive definiteness of each sub-block. In view of $T_a = t_{ac} v_{ac} + t_{aT} v_{aT}$, we have:

$$\nabla^2 T(v_{ac}, v_{aT}) = \begin{bmatrix} \dfrac{\partial T_a^2}{\partial v_{ac}^2} & \dfrac{\partial T_a^2}{\partial v_{ac} \partial v_{aT}} \\ \dfrac{\partial T_a^2}{\partial v_{aT} \partial v_{ac}} & \dfrac{\partial T_a^2}{\partial v_{aT}^2} \end{bmatrix}$$

$$= \begin{bmatrix} 2\dfrac{\partial t_{ac}}{\partial v_{ac}} + v_{ac}\dfrac{\partial^2 t_{ac}}{\partial v_{ac}^{\ 2}} + v_{aT}\dfrac{\partial^2 t_{aT}}{\partial v_{ac}^{\ 2}} & \dfrac{\partial t_{ac}}{\partial v_{aT}} + \dfrac{\partial t_{aT}}{\partial v_{ac}} + v_{ac}\dfrac{\partial^2 t_{ac}}{\partial v_{ac} \partial v_{aT}} + v_{aT}\dfrac{\partial^2 t_{aT}}{\partial v_{ac} \partial v_{aT}} \\ \dfrac{\partial t_{ac}}{\partial v_{aT}} + \dfrac{\partial t_{aT}}{\partial v_{ac}} + v_{ac}\dfrac{\partial^2 t_{ac}}{\partial v_{ac} \partial v_{aT}} + v_{aT}\dfrac{\partial^2 t_{aT}}{\partial v_{ac} \partial v_{aT}} & 2\dfrac{\partial t_{aT}}{\partial v_{aT}} + v_{ac}\dfrac{\partial^2 t_{ac}}{\partial v_{aT}^{\ 2}} + v_{aT}\dfrac{\partial^2 t_{aT}}{\partial v_{aT}^{\ 2}} \end{bmatrix}$$

where the specific partial derivatives can be obtained from (3.67) and are given below:

$$\frac{\partial t_{ac}}{\partial v_{ac}} = \frac{\alpha_c \beta_c t_{ac}^0}{C_{ac}} \left(\frac{v_{ac} + \xi v_{aT}}{C_{ac}} \right)^{\beta_c - 1}$$

$$\frac{\partial t_{ac}}{\partial v_{aT}} = \xi \frac{\alpha_c \beta_c t_{ac}^0}{C_{ac}} \left(\frac{v_{ac} + \xi v_{aT}}{C_{ac}} \right)^{\beta_c - 1}$$

$$\frac{\partial t_{aT}}{\partial v_{ac}} = \eta \frac{\alpha_T \beta_T t_{aT}^0}{C_{aT}} \left(\frac{v_{aT} + \eta v_{ac}}{C_{aT}} \right)^{\beta_T - 1}$$

$$\frac{\partial t_{aT}}{\partial v_{aT}} = \frac{\alpha_T \beta_T t_{aT}^0}{C_{aT}} \left(\frac{v_{aT} + \eta v_{ac}}{C_{aT}} \right)^{\beta_T - 1}$$

$$\frac{\partial^2 t_{ac}}{\partial v_{ac}^{\ 2}} = (\beta_c - 1) \frac{\alpha_c \beta_c t_{ac}^0}{C_{ac}^{\ 2}} \left(\frac{v_{ac} + \xi v_{aT}}{C_{ac}} \right)^{\beta_c - 2}$$

$$\frac{\partial^2 t_{ac}}{\partial v_{aT}^{\ 2}} = \xi^2 (\beta_c - 1) \frac{\alpha_c \beta_c t_{ac}^0}{C_{ac}^{\ 2}} \left(\frac{v_{ac} + \xi v_{aT}}{C_{ac}} \right)^{\beta_c - 2}$$

$$\frac{\partial^2 t_{ac}}{\partial v_{ac} \partial v_{aT}} = \xi (\beta_c - 1) \frac{\alpha_c \beta_c t_{ac}^0}{C_{ac}^{\ 2}} \left(\frac{v_{ac} + \xi v_{aT}}{C_{ac}} \right)^{\beta_c - 2}$$

$$\frac{\partial^2 t_{aT}}{\partial v_{ac}^{\ 2}} = \eta^2 (\beta_T - 1) \frac{\alpha_T \beta_T t_{aT}^0}{C_{aT}^{\ 2}} \left(\frac{v_{aT} + \eta v_{ac}}{C_{aT}} \right)^{\beta_T - 2}$$

$$\frac{\partial^2 t_{aT}}{\partial v_{aT}^{\ 2}} = (\beta_T - 1) \frac{\alpha_T \beta_T t_{aT}^0}{C_{aT}^{\ 2}} \left(\frac{v_{aT} + \eta v_{ac}}{C_{aT}} \right)^{\beta_T - 2}$$

$$\frac{\partial^2 t_{aT}}{\partial v_{ac} \partial v_{aT}} = \eta (\beta_T - 1) \frac{\alpha_T \beta_T t_{aT}^0}{C_{aT}^{\ 2}} \left(\frac{v_{aT} + \eta v_{ac}}{C_{aT}} \right)^{\beta_T - 2}$$

To ensure positive definiteness of the Hessian matrix, firstly it must hold that $\beta_c > 1$ and $\beta_T > 1$. In addition,

$$\det\left[\nabla^2 T(v_{ac},v_{aT})\right]=\left(2\frac{\partial t_{ac}}{\partial v_{ac}}+v_{ac}\frac{\partial^2 t_{ac}}{\partial v_{ac}{}^2}+v_{aT}\frac{\partial^2 t_{aT}}{\partial v_{ac}{}^2}\right)\left(2\frac{\partial t_{aT}}{\partial v_{aT}}+v_{ac}\frac{\partial^2 t_{ac}}{\partial v_{aT}{}^2}+v_{aT}\frac{\partial^2 t_{aT}}{\partial v_{aT}{}^2}\right)$$

$$-\left(\frac{\partial t_{ac}}{\partial v_{aT}}+\frac{\partial t_{aT}}{\partial v_{ac}}+v_{ac}\frac{\partial^2 t_{ac}}{\partial v_{ac}\partial v_{aT}}+v_{aT}\frac{\partial^2 t_{aT}}{\partial v_{ac}\partial v_{aT}}\right)^2$$

$$=4(1-\xi\eta)\frac{\alpha_c\beta_c t_{ac}^0}{C_{ac}}\left(\frac{v_{ac}+\xi v_{aT}}{C_{ac}}\right)^{\beta_c-1}\frac{\alpha_T\beta_T t_{aT}^0}{C_{aT}}\left(\frac{v_{aT}+\eta v_{ac}}{C_{aT}}\right)^{\beta_T-1}$$

$$-\left\{\xi\frac{\alpha_c\beta_c t_{ac}^0}{C_{ac}}\left(\frac{v_{ac}+\xi v_{aT}}{C_{ac}}\right)^{\beta_c-1}-\eta\frac{\alpha_T\beta_T t_{aT}^0}{C_{aT}}\left(\frac{v_{aT}+\eta v_{ac}}{C_{aT}}\right)^{\beta_T-1}\right\}^2$$

$$+(1-\xi\eta)^2 v_{ac}v_{aT}(\beta_c-1)(\beta_T-1)\frac{\alpha_c\beta_c t_{ac}^0}{C_{ac}{}^2}\frac{\alpha_T\beta_T t_{aT}^0}{C_{aT}{}^2}\left(\frac{v_{ac}+\xi v_{aT}}{C_{ac}}\right)^{\beta_c-2}\left(\frac{v_{aT}+\eta v_{ac}}{C_{aT}}\right)^{\beta_T-2}$$

$$+2(1-\xi\eta)\left\{v_{aT}(\beta_T-1)\frac{\alpha_c\beta_c t_{ac}^0}{C_{ac}}\frac{\alpha_T\beta_T t_{aT}^0}{C_{aT}{}^2}\left(\frac{v_{ac}+\xi v_{aT}}{C_{ac}}\right)^{\beta_c-1}\left(\frac{v_{aT}+\eta v_{ac}}{C_{aT}}\right)^{\beta_T-2}\right\}$$

$$+2(1-\xi\eta)\left\{v_{ac}(\beta_c-1)\frac{\alpha_T\beta_T t_{aT}^0}{C_{aT}}\frac{\alpha_c\beta_c t_{ac}^0}{C_{ac}{}^2}\left(\frac{v_{aT}+\eta v_{ac}}{C_{aT}}\right)^{\beta_T-1}\left(\frac{v_{ac}+\xi v_{aT}}{C_{ac}}\right)^{\beta_c-2}\right\}$$

Clearly, $1-\xi\eta>0$ is still necessary for positive definiteness just like that for UE. Furthermore, the second negative term cannot be too large in comparison with the rest positive terms. Namely,

$$\left|\xi\frac{\alpha_c\beta_c t_{ac}^0}{C_{ac}}\left(\frac{v_{ac}+\xi v_{aT}}{C_{ac}}\right)^{\beta_c-1}-\eta\frac{\alpha_T\beta_T t_{aT}^0}{C_{aT}}\left(\frac{v_{aT}+\eta v_{ac}}{C_{aT}}\right)^{\beta_T-1}\right|=\left|\frac{\partial t_{ac}}{\partial v_{aT}}-\frac{\partial t_{aT}}{\partial v_{ac}}\right| \tag{3.68}$$

should be small, which implies that the asymmetric effect between heavy and light vehicles should not be too significant.

As we can see from the discussions presented here and in Chapter 2, the conditions for a unique solution of link flows are different for the UE and SO problems, in particular, in the case of asymmetric link flow interactions. These conditions are summarized in Table 3.1 without further counting the common terms relating to the demand functions. The conditions in the table are important in the context of marginal cost pricing. It is self-evident that the SO problem is always given as a well-defined optimization program, but the UE problem may need to count on the VI formulation. The following three situations deserve our particular mention: 1) If both the UE and SO problems have a unique solution (in link flows) or there is an one-to one correspondence between the UE and SO solution, then there exists a unique set of link toll charges in line with the principle of marginal-cost pricing that drives the UE flow pattern toward a unique system optimum, or equivalently, a unique system optimum can be decentralized as one and only one UE flow pattern. 2) If only the SO problem has a unique solution, then all UE link flow solutions are driven to the same system optimum state through introducing marginal-cost pricing on each network link. 3) If the solution to the SO problem is not unique, then it becomes critical to identify the global system optimum that should be decentralized through marginal-cost pricing; otherwise applying marginal-cost pricing to a local SO solution may even make the situation worse (giving a UE flow pattern that actually corresponds to economic benefit lower than that in the do-nothing case).

Table 3.1 Summary of the sufficient conditions for a unique link flow solution of the UE and SO problems with and without link flow interactions

Type of Link Cost Function	Sufficient Conditions for a Unique UE Link Flow Solution	Sufficient Conditions for a Unique SO Link Flow Solution
Separable $t_a(v_a)$	Each $t_a(v_a)$ is monotonically increasing	Each $t_a(v_a)$ is monotonically increasing and convex
Non-separable with symmetric flow interaction, $\mathbf{t}(\mathbf{v})$, $\frac{\partial t_a(\mathbf{v})}{\partial v_b}=\frac{\partial t_b(\mathbf{v})}{\partial v_a}$, $a\in A,\ b\in A,\ a\neq b$	$\mathbf{t}(\mathbf{v})$ is strictly monotone or its Jacobian is positive definite	$\mathbf{t}(\mathbf{v})$ is strictly monotone or its Jacobian is positive definite. Furthermore, $t_a(\mathbf{v})$ is convex in v_a for each link $a\in A$
Non-separable with asymmetric flow interaction, $\mathbf{t}(\mathbf{v})$, $\frac{\partial t_a(\mathbf{v})}{\partial v_b}\neq\frac{\partial t_b(\mathbf{v})}{\partial v_a}$, $a\in A,\ b\in A,\ a\neq b$	$\mathbf{t}(\mathbf{v})$ is strictly monotone or its Jacobian is positive definite	Hessian of $TC(\mathbf{v})$ is positive definite, but its positive definiteness is difficult to establish in terms of the specific properties of $\mathbf{t}(\mathbf{v})$

3.6.4 Analytical Examples

All examples presented below are based on a simple network that has a single OD pair connected by two parallel links. We set different link cost functions and investigate the UE and SO solutions. Example 3.1 is for the case with separable link cost functions and the others for non-separable link cost functions.

Example 3.2 (Multiple UE and multiple SO Solutions) Set the non-separable link cost functions

$$t_1(v_1,v_2)=3+2v_1+3v_2,\quad t_2(v_1,v_2)=5+3v_1+2v_2$$

and let demand $d=5$. The Jacobian of link cost functions is given by

$$\nabla_v \mathbf{t}(\mathbf{v}) = \begin{bmatrix} 2 & 3 \\ 3 & 2 \end{bmatrix}$$

This matrix is symmetric but not positive-definite since $\det(\nabla_v \mathbf{t}(\mathbf{v})) = -5$. Obviously, $\mathbf{t}(\mathbf{v})$ is not strictly monotonic since for any distinct $\mathbf{v}^1 = (x_1, x_2)^T$, $\mathbf{v}^2 = (y_1, y_2)^T$, where $x_1 + x_2 = 5$ and $y_1 + y_2 = 5$, we have $(\mathbf{t}(\mathbf{v}^2) - \mathbf{t}(\mathbf{v}^1))^T (\mathbf{v}^2 - \mathbf{v}^1) = -2(y_1 - x_1)^2 < 0$. It can be easily found that there are three equilibrium flow solutions. The first equilibrium solution is: $v_1^* = 0$, $v_2^* = 5$, $t_1^* = 18$, $t_2^* = 15$; the second one is $v_1^* = 5$, $v_2^* = 0$, $t_1^* = 13$, $t_2^* = 20$; and the third one is $v_1^* = 1.5$, $v_2^* = 3.5$, $t_1^* = t_2^* = 16.5$. This example shows the existence of multiple equilibria in the cases where the Jacobian is not positive definite. We now check the SO for the same problem. The total travel cost is given by

$$TC(v_1, v_2) = (3 + 2v_1 + 3v_2)v_1 + (5 + 3v_1 + 2v_2)v_2 = 2(v_1)^2 + 2(v_2)^2 + 6v_1v_2 + 3v_1 + 5v_2$$

Since $v_1 = 5 - v_2$, we have $TC = -2(v_2)^2 + 12v_2 + 65$ which is a concave function. Solving $\min TC = -2(v_2)^2 + 12v_2 + 65$, subject to $0 \le v_2 \le 5$, we get a unique stationary point, $v_2 = 3$ which gives a maximum value for $TC = 83$. Two local optimal solutions of the SO problem are found at the boundary of the feasible region, which are $v_2^* = 0$ and $v_2^* = 5$, as shown in Figure 3.8. The former gives $TC = 65$ and the latter $TC = 75$.

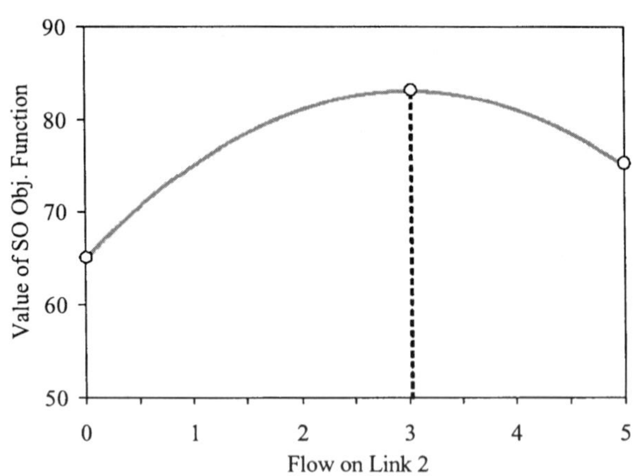

Figure 3.8 The SO objective value versus link flow v_2 $(0 \le v_2 \le 5)$

Example 3.3 (Multiple UE but unique SO) Set the non-separable link cost functions

$$t_1(v_1, v_2) = 8 + 4v_1, \quad t_2(v_1, v_2) = 2 + 5v_1 + v_1v_2$$

and let the demand $d=5$. It is easy to find two UE solutions: $v_1^*=3+\sqrt{3}$, $v_2^*=2-\sqrt{3}$, $t_1^*=t_2^*=20+4\sqrt{3}$; and $v_1^*=3-\sqrt{3}$, $v_2^*=2+\sqrt{3}$, $t_1^*=t_2^*=20-4\sqrt{3}$. The total travel cost is given by

$$TC=(v_1)^3-11(v_1)^2+56v_1+10,\ \text{where}\ 0\le v_1\le 5.$$

The above TC is a strictly increasing function of v_1 since

$$\mathrm{d}TC/\mathrm{d}v_1=3(v_1)^2-22v_1+56=\frac{(3v_1-11)^2+47}{3}>0$$

Therefore, there is only one SO solution: $v_1^*=0$, $v_2^*=5$, $TC=10$.

Example 3.4 (Unique UE but multiple SO) Set the non-separable link cost functions

$$t_1(v_1,v_2)=2+v_1v_2,\ \ t_2(v_1,v_2)=v_2$$

and let again the demand $d=5$. It is easy to find a unique UE solution: $v_1^*=3-\sqrt{6}$, $v_2^*=2+\sqrt{6}$, $t_1^*=t_2^*=2+\sqrt{6}$. The total travel cost is given by

$$TC=-(v_1)^3+6(v_1)^2-8v_1+25\ \text{where}\ 0\le v_1\le 5$$

As shown in Figure 3.9, there are two local optimal solutions for the SO problem: $v_1^*=2-2\sqrt{3}/3$, $v_2^*=3+2\sqrt{3}/3$, $TC=25-16\sqrt{3}/9=21.92$, and $v_1^*=5$, $v_2^*=0$, $TC=10$.

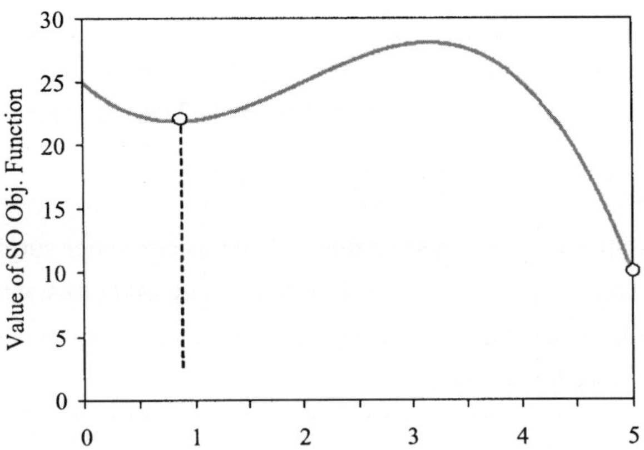

Figure 3.9 The SO objective value versus link flow v_1 $(0\le v_1\le 5)$

Example 3.5 (Unique UE and unique SO) Set the non-separable link cost functions

$$t_1(v_1,v_2)=2+5v_1+2v_2,\ \ t_2(v_1,v_2)=4+3v_1+4v_2$$

and let the demand $d=5$. The Jacobian is given by

$$\nabla_{\mathbf{v}}\mathbf{t}(\mathbf{v}) = \begin{bmatrix} 5 & 2 \\ 3 & 4 \end{bmatrix}$$

This matrix is asymmetric but positive-definite since $\det(\nabla_{\mathbf{v}}\mathbf{t}(\mathbf{v})) = 14$ and with positive diagonal elements. $\mathbf{t}(\mathbf{v})$ is of course strictly monotonic since for any distinct $\mathbf{v}^1 = (x_1, x_2)^{\mathrm{T}}$, $\mathbf{v}^2 = (y_1, y_2)^{\mathrm{T}}$, where $x_1 + x_2 = 5$ and $y_1 + y_2 = 5$, we have $\left(\mathbf{t}(\mathbf{v}^2) - \mathbf{t}(\mathbf{v}^1)\right)^{\mathrm{T}}(\mathbf{v}^2 - \mathbf{v}^1) = 4(y_2 - x_2)^2 > 0$. The unique UE solution is: $v_1^* = 3$, $v_2^* = 2$, $t_1^* = t_2^* = 21$. The total travel cost is given by

$$TC(v_1, v_2) = (2 + 5v_1 + 2v_2)v_1 + (4 + 3v_1 + 4v_2)v_2 = 5(v_1)^2 + 4(v_2)^2 + 5v_1v_2 + 2v_1 + 4v_2$$

Since $v_1 = 5 - v_2$, we have $TC = 4(v_2)^2 - 23v_2 + 135$ which is a convex function. The unique SO solution is: $v_1^* = 2.125$, $v_2^* = 2.875$, $TC = 101.94$.

3.7 MARGINAL-COST PRICING UNDER STOCHASTIC USER EQUILIBRIUM

3.7.1 Economic Benefit Measure and Maximization

As already mentioned in Chapter 2, with the logit-based route choice model, the expected indirect utility received by a randomly sampled individual can be expressed as

$$\tilde{S}_w = E\left[\max_{r \in R_w}(-\theta c_{rw} + \xi_{rw})\right] = \ln \sum_{r \in R_w} \exp(-\theta c_{rw}) \tag{3.69}$$

This measure has an economic interpretation related to consumer surplus. For example, in the absence of income effects, a change in price or any other characteristics of the travel environment results in an expected change in consumer's surplus which is equal to the change in the above welfare measure.

According to the representative consumer theory of the logit model (Oppenheim, 1995), the behavior of consumers with different tastes can be described by the choices made by a single individual who has a preference for diversity. The direct utility function of the representative consumer or user (i.e., the utility corresponding to the aggregate demand) can be expressed as follows:

$$U = \frac{1}{\theta} d_w \ln d_w - \frac{1}{\theta} \sum_{w \in W} \sum_{r \in R_w} f_{rw} \ln f_{rw} \tag{3.70}$$

The utility function (3.70) consistent with the logit model is an entropy-type function which has also been used as a benefit measure in terms of interactivity in trip distribution (Erlander and Stewart, 1990). On the other hand, the total social cost incurred by all users in the network is given by $\sum_{a\in A} t_a(v_a)v_a$. The net economic benefit could be measured as the traveler's benefit minus the total travel cost, and the socially optimal pricing requires that the net economic benefit is maximized. Observing that the problem can be transferred into a minimization problem by changing the sign of the objective function, thus, after deletion of the constant term, we have the following minimization program:

$$\min_{\mathbf{f}} \frac{1}{\theta}\sum_{w\in W}\sum_{r\in R_w} f_{rw}\ln f_{rw} + \sum_{a\in A} t_a(v_a)v_a - \frac{1}{\theta}\sum_{w\in W} d_w \ln d_w \tag{3.71}$$

$$\sum_{r\in R_w} f_r = d_w,\ w\in W \tag{3.72}$$

$$f_r \geq 0,\ r\in R_w,\ w\in W \tag{3.73}$$

where the demand d_w between OD pair $w\in W$ is fixed and given and the last term is constant (included for later use).

Note that the objective function (3.71) is strictly convex, thus the following Kuhn-Tucker conditions for any $f_{rw}^* > 0$ are also sufficient to obtain the unique optimal solution:

$$\sum_{a\in A} \tilde{t}_a(v_a^*)\delta_{ar} + \frac{1}{\theta}\left(\ln f_{rw}^* + 1\right) - \lambda_w = 0,\ r\in R_w,\ w\in W \tag{3.74}$$

where λ_w is the Lagrange multiplier associated with constraint (3.72), and

$$\tilde{t}_a(v_a^*) = t_a(v_a^*) + v_a^*\frac{\mathrm{d}t_a(v_a^*)}{\mathrm{d}v_a},\quad a\in A \tag{3.75}$$

Evidently, the first term of the right-hand side of (3.75) is the actual link travel time incurred by a traveler and the second term is the additional travel time that a traveler imposes on all other travelers in the link. It can thus be seen that user externality is present due to the effect of congestion on the network links.

Define

$$\tilde{c}_{rw}^* = \sum_{a\in A} \tilde{t}_a(v_a^*)\delta_{ar},\ r\in R_w,\ w\in W \tag{3.76}$$

as the generalized route travel time, we have from (3.74):

$$\ln f_{rw}^* = \theta\left(\lambda_w - \tilde{c}_{rw}^*\right) - 1 \tag{3.77}$$

Solving this equation and constraint (3.72) yields:

$$P_{rw} = \frac{f_{rw}^*}{d_w} = \frac{\exp\left(-\theta\tilde{c}_{rw}^*\right)}{\sum_{k\in R_w}\exp\left(-\theta\tilde{c}_{kw}^*\right)},\quad r\in R_w,\ w\in W \tag{3.78}$$

From the above derivation, we can observe that the optimality condition (3.74) for an optimum of the economic benefit maximization problem (3.71)-(3.73) is also the condition that governs the logit-based stochastic user equilibrium (SUE) model (3.78). The only requirement for this equivalence is that the link cost and the route cost should be given by (3.75) and (3.76) where the additional cost or user externality specified by the second term of eqn. (3.75) is included. This means that from the viewpoint of social welfare maximization, user externality exists in the system optimality conditions. Therefore, by imposing a toll at each link exactly equal to the externality, we can ensure that the users' optimal private choices will also be optimal social choices in terms of the maximization of net economic benefit. Consequently, the classical principle of traditional marginal-cost pricing is still applicable in the logit-based SUE situation.

3.7.2 Equivalence to the Minimization of Expected Perceived Travel Cost

In fact, maximization of the net economic benefit (3.71) is equivalent to the minimization of the total expected perceived user cost in the logit-based stochastic route choice model. To see this, we now change the objective function (3.71) as follows:

$$\begin{aligned} F(\mathbf{f}) &= \frac{1}{\theta}\sum_{w\in W}\sum_{r\in R_w} f_{rw}\ln f_{rw} + \sum_{a\in A} t_a(v_a)v_a - \frac{1}{\theta}\sum_{w\in W} d_w \ln d_w \\ &= \frac{1}{\theta}\sum_{w\in W}\sum_{r\in R_w} f_{rw}\ln f_{rw} + \sum_{w\in W}\sum_{r\in R_w} f_{rw}c_{rw}(\mathbf{f}) - \frac{1}{\theta}\sum_{w\in W} d_w \ln d_w \\ &= \frac{1}{\theta}\sum_{w\in W}\sum_{r\in R_w} f_{rw}\left[\ln f_{rw} + \theta c_{rw}(\mathbf{f})\right] - \frac{1}{\theta}\sum_{w\in W} d_w \ln d_w \end{aligned} \tag{3.79}$$

From the logit-model in Chapter 2: $f_{rw}/d_w = \exp(-\theta c_{rw})/\sum_{k\in R_w}\exp(-\theta c_{kw}),\ r\in R_w, w\in W$

we have

$$\ln f_{rw} + \theta c_{rw} = \ln d_w - \ln \sum_{k\in R_w}\exp(-\theta c_{kw}),\quad r\in R_w, w\in W \tag{3.80}$$

Substituting (3.80) into (3.79), we have

$$\begin{aligned} F(\mathbf{f}) &= \frac{1}{\theta}\sum_{w\in W}\sum_{r\in R_w} f_{rw}\left[\ln d_w - \ln\sum_{k\in R_w}\exp(-\theta c_{kw})\right] - \frac{1}{\theta}\sum_{w\in W} d_w\ln d_w \\ &= -\frac{1}{\theta}\sum_{w\in W} d_w \ln\sum_{k\in R_w}\exp(-\theta c_{kw}) = \sum_{w\in W} d_w S_w \end{aligned} \tag{3.81}$$

where

$$S_w = -\frac{1}{\theta}\ln\sum_{r\in R_w}\exp(-\theta c_{rw}) \tag{3.82}$$

is the expected perceived travel cost by an individual traveling between OD pair $w\in W$ (refer to Section 2.3.6 of Chapter 2). Since the first-term is a constant and the second-term the total expected perceived travel cost by all users in the network, we thus conclude that maximizing total net economic benefit in fact amounts to minimizing the expected total received cost by all users.

3.7.3 An Analytical Example

Example 3.6 Consider the network example shown in Figure 3.10 with the link cost function shown below the network. We investigate numerically the outcomes of marginal-cost pricing under SUE. The numerical results are plotted in Figures 3.11 and 3.12.

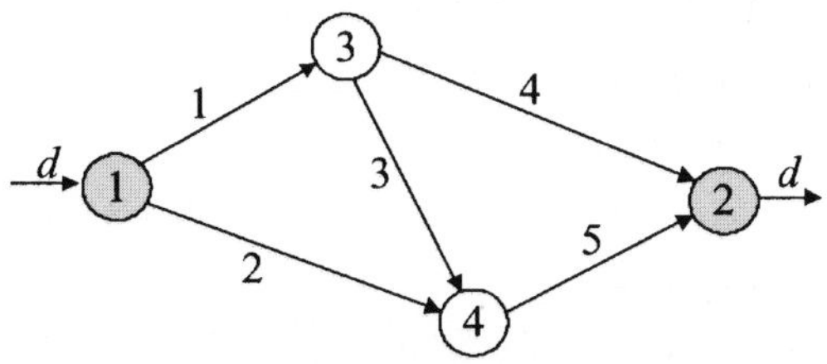

Link Cost Function:
$t_1(v_1) = 10 + 5v_1; \quad t_2(v_2) = 50 + v_2$
$t_3(v_3) = 20 + v_3; \quad t_4(v_4) = 50 + v_4$
$t_5(v_5) = 10 + 5v_5$

Figure 3.10 A simple network used in Example 3.6

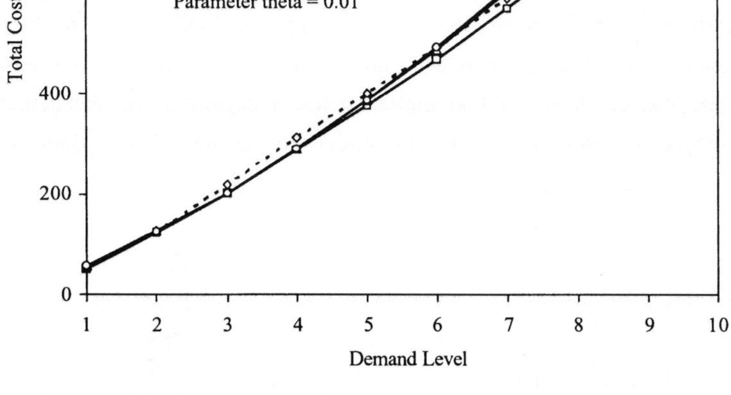

Figure 3.11 Changes of total network travel cost against demand

with and without marginal-cost pricing

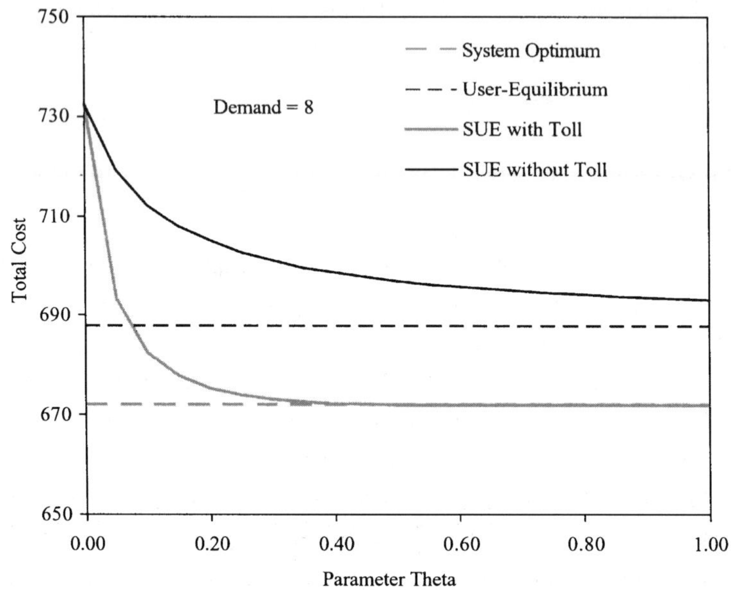

Figure 3.12 Change of total network travel cost against parameter theta with and without marginal-cost pricing

Figure 3.11 shows the changes of total network travel costs (corresponding respectively to system optimum, deterministic user-equilibrium, SUE with toll and SUE with no toll) against different levels of demand for a given value of parameter $\theta = 0.01$. From this figure, the following observations can be made. 1) In any case, the system optimum provides a lower limit of total network travel cost associated with a given demand. The marginal-cost pricing for a logit-based SUE cannot generally achieve the minimum total travel cost, although it does reduce the total cost to below that in the no toll case. 2) Compared to the total network travel cost under deterministic user-equilibrium, the total cost under the logit-based SUE with or with no toll charge may be either higher or lower depending on the demand level and network structure. 3) Marginal-cost pricing under the logit-based SUE does not necessarily reduce total network travel cost. It is found in Figure 3.11 that when the demand is smaller than 3, marginal-cost pricing actually increases total network travel cost.

Figure 3.12 shows the changes of total network travel cost against parameter θ for a given demand $d = 9$. It is well-known that in the logit-based model, if θ is very large, travelers will tend to select the minimum travel cost route, causing the flow pattern to approach the deterministic user-equilibrium flow pattern. This property is reflected in Figure 3.12: As parameter θ increases in SUE, the total cost for the SUE flow pattern with no toll charge approaches that for the deterministic user-equilibrium, and the total cost for the SUE flow pattern with toll charge approaches that for the Wardropian system optimum, while the latter has a much higher approaching speed.

3.8 SUMMARY

In this chapter, we have examined the classical principle of marginal-cost pricing in connection with the general network equilibrium problem, with or without link capacity constraints, link flow interactions, flow types and elastic demands. We have shown that the optimal tolls for both fixed- and variable-demand network equilibrium problems, with or without link flow interactions, take a unified form of the traditional marginal-cost pricing toll, and can be derived from system optimization models, but their meanings and objectives are somewhat different. In the presence of queues, due to limited capacity, the optimal toll consists of two components: one is the conventional marginal-cost term and the other is a equilibrium queuing delay. The former is predicted by an analytical formula from local link flow conditions, but the latter is determined endogenously from network equilibrium conditions. In addition, we revisited the widely discussed speed-flow relationship and showed that there is no logical requirement to embrace the backward-bending part of the speed-flow curve in designing appropriate congestion cost function. The combined emission and congestion tolls guarantee sustainability of the transportation network in the sense that the users, after the imposition of the emission and congestion tolls, still behave in a user-optimized fashion, but the generated flow patterns are also system-optimized and, hence, optimal from a societal perspective. We also extended the pricing policy by including the requirement for air quality and reduction of greenhouse gas emissions from road transport and the case of congested networks in stochastic user equilibrium.

3.9 SOURCES AND NOTES

Readers are recommended to consult the following references for the various first-best pricing policies: Hau (1992), Button (1993), Yang and Huang (1998) and Lindsey and Verhoef (2001). The two important terms "multi-class" and "link flow interaction" appear frequently in this chapter. There has been a long history in the study of multi-class traffic assignment and toll pricing problems. The marginal-cost pricing on a congested transportation network dates back to Beckmann (1956, 1965). Netter (1971) discussed marginal cost pricing on a road network with several vehicle (flow) types. Dafermos and Sparrow (1971) and Dafermos (1972, 1973), in a series of papers, examined the single class traffic equilibrium problem with (asymmetric) link flow interactions and the multi-class traffic equilibrium problem where user classes refer to different types of vehicles, such as truck versus passenger car. Each type of vehicle has an individual cost-flow function, and at the same time contributes to its own and other class's cost functions in an individual way. Dafermos (1971, 1972, 1973) particularly suggested that the multi-class traffic equilibrium model, with several vehicle types can be reduced to a single class user model with link flow interactions by associating each class with a complete network copy. Smith (1979b) also discussed marginal cost taxation of a transportation network with link flow interactions. Indeed, there are considerable confusing views and disputes in the literature concerning the appropriate use of the speed/flow relation to evaluate road pricing, which could be reflected in debates between Nash (1982) and Else (1981, 1982), and between Hills (1993) and Evens (1992, 1993). Walters (1961), Else (1981) and others pointed out that the equilibrium position may occur in the forced flow. Newell (1988) analyzed the impossibility of occurrence of the forced speed-flow regime from shock wave theory.

Several authors examined first-best or marginal-cost pricing on networks in a stochastic user equilibrium. Akamatsu and Kuwahara (1988, 1989) and Smith (1994) investigated the existence of optimal link tolls in deriving a stochastic user optimal flow pattern to a system optimum of total travel time minimization. Their studies use the notion of Wardropian system optima that focus entirely on *efficiency* with respect to cost considerations. In particular, Smith et al. (1994) showed that for any transportation network with regular link cost functions, and for any positive travel-demand, all fully positive system-optimal link-flows associated with a given demand are supportable as a logit-based SUE by non-negative link tolls if the route flows that induce the link flow pattern are strictly positive. From an economic and behavioral perspective, Yang (1999) proved that the traditional marginal-cost pricing remains applicable in terms of the maximization of net economic benefit derived from the logit-based discrete choice model, using the indirect and direct utility concepts (Williams, 1977; Small and Rosen, 1981). Maher et al. (2005) derived the marginal-cost pricing results by minimizing the total expected perceived travel time for networks in a general stochastic user equilibrium. Readers are suggested to further refer to Williams (1997), Ben-Akiva and Lerman (1985), Anderson et al. (1992), for discrete choice models and social welfare evaluation.

4

THE SECOND-BEST ROAD PRICING PROBLEMS: A SENSITIVITY ANALYSIS BASED APPROACH

4.1 INTRODUCTION

In spite of its apparently perfect theoretical basis, however, the marginal cost-pricing scheme is not practically appealing. The problems stem from the fact that we cannot charge on all links in view of the high operating cost and poor public acceptance. The cost of toll collection may actually justify the choice of not charging for an entire road network, but only some of its major congested links instead; the regulator may leave routes un-tolled for equity reasons, for instance, to protect low-income groups from having to pay fees, or to increase social feasibility of road pricing. As a result, the various second-best pricing regimes have received ample attention recently.

There are in general four alternative types of second-best toll charging schemes in road networks that are of practical interest: (*i*) travel-distance based charging; (*ii*) travel-time or travel-delay based charging; (*iii*) link-based charging; and (*iv*) cordon-based charging. In the travel-distance or travel-time based charging scheme, tolls are charged in proportion to the distance traveled or the time spent in the network, and the optimal toll charge per unit distance or travel time can be easily determined using simple optimization search methods for the minimization of total travel time or maximization of social welfare. In the link-based pricing scheme, tolls are charged only on a subset of selected links, especially where there are bottlenecks. In many cities, congestion tolls are collected on some urban bridges, tunnels or expressways, and tolls at different locations are coordinated for congestion mitigation. Instead of charging on separate individual links, the cordon-based pricing scheme has emerged in recent years in some cities to reduce the traffic demand in city centers, such as Singapore, Oslo, Trondheim and Bergen.

In this and the following chapters, we examine the second-best pricing problem when the assumptions of the first-best pricing conditions are not met in reality. We shall develop bi-level programming models for choosing the link-based tolls to optimize some specific system performance measures, meanwhile considering the equilibrium behavior in individuals' travel decisions. This Chapter is devoted to the development and application of the sensitivity analysis based approach for the second-best pricing problem.

4.2 FORMULATION AS MATHEMATICAL PROGRAMS WITH EQUILIBRIUM CONSTRAINTS

The general second-best road pricing problem is to choose a set of optimal values for toll charges to minimize (or maximize) an objective function while taking account of the route choice behavior of network users. Let $\bar{A} \subseteq A$ be a subset of links for which tolls are to be levied and $\mathbf{u} = (\cdots, u_a, \cdots)^{\mathrm{T}}$, $a \in \bar{A}$ denote the link tolls vector. Let $\mathbf{d}(\mathbf{u}) = (\cdots, d_w(\mathbf{u}), \cdots)^{\mathrm{T}}$, $w \in W$ and $\mathbf{v}(\mathbf{u}) = (\cdots, v_a(\mathbf{u}), \cdots)^{\mathrm{T}}$, $a \in A$ be the vectors of the deterministic equilibrium OD demands and link flows associated with link toll pattern $\mathbf{u}$, respectively. With the link based toll pricing, we redefine the link cost function as follows: $t_a(\mathbf{v}, \mathbf{u}) = t_a(\mathbf{v}) + u_a$ if $a \in \bar{A}$ and $t_a(\mathbf{v}, \mathbf{u}) = t_a(\mathbf{v})$ otherwise. The general second-best road pricing problems can be characterized as the following Mathematical Program with Equilibrium Constraints (MPEC):

$$\min_{\mathbf{u} \in U} F(\mathbf{u}, \mathbf{v}^*, \mathbf{d}^*) \tag{4.1}$$

subject to

$$\mathbf{g}(\mathbf{v}^*, \mathbf{d}^*) \le 0 \tag{4.2}$$

and $(\mathbf{v}^*, \mathbf{d}^*)$ is the solution of the following UE problem for given $\mathbf{u}$:

$$\mathbf{t}(\mathbf{v}^*, \mathbf{u})^{\mathrm{T}} (\mathbf{v} - \mathbf{v}^*) - \mathbf{B}(\mathbf{d}^*, \mathbf{u})^{\mathrm{T}} (\mathbf{d} - \mathbf{d}^*) \ge 0 \text{ for any } (\mathbf{v}, \mathbf{d}) \in \Omega \tag{4.3}$$

where

$$\Omega = \{(\mathbf{v}, \mathbf{d}) | \ \mathbf{v}{=}\Delta\mathbf{f},\ \mathbf{d}{=}\Lambda\mathbf{f},\ \mathbf{f} \ge 0,\ 0 \le \mathbf{d} \le \bar{\mathbf{D}}\} \tag{4.4}$$

where $\bar{\mathbf{D}} = (\cdots, \bar{D}_w, \cdots)^{\mathrm{T}}$, $w \in W$ and $\bar{D}_w$ is a sufficiently large upper bound of the O-D demand d_w between OD pair $w \in W$. Adding this (non-binding) upper bound will ensure that the constraint set is uniformly compact. Alternatively, when link cost and OD demand functions are symmetric or separable, the VI formulation of the traffic equilibrium problem can be replaced by an optimization formulation, leading to a nonlinear Bi-Level Programming Problem (BLPP). In this case $(\mathbf{v}^*, \mathbf{d}^*)$ is the solution of the following convex mathematical program

$$\left(\mathbf{v}^*,\mathbf{d}^*\right)=\arg\min_{(\mathbf{v},\mathbf{d})\in\Omega}\sum_{a\in A}\int_0^{v_a}t_a(\omega,\mathbf{u})d\omega-\sum_{w\in W}\int_0^{d_w}B_w(\omega,\mathbf{u})d\omega \tag{4.5}$$

In the above MPEC or BLPP formulations, U is the set of feasible link tolls. For example, U may be simply defined by the non-negative constraint and/or the upper bound of the toll decision variable, $U=\left\{\mathbf{u}\,|\,0\le u_a\le\bar{u}_a,\ a\in\bar{A}\right\}$, where $\bar{u}_a$ is the upper-bound of link toll u_a, $a\in\bar{A}$. $B_w(d_w)=D_w^{-1}(d_w)$ is the benefit function, or the inverse of demand function $D_w(\mu_w)$ between OD pair $w\in W$. $\mathbf{g}(\mathbf{v},\mathbf{d})$ denotes the vector of the upper-level constraints associated with the traffic flow variables $\mathbf{v}$ and $\mathbf{d}$. For example, as discussed later, in the traffic restraint and road pricing problem, it is desirable to reduce link flow within a certain threshold, such as link physical or environmental capacity, $v_a\le C_a$, $a\in A$. In addition, a minimum or a maximum revenue constraint might be imposed in determining an appropriate set of road tolls.

Note that, for generality, both VI (4.3) in the MPEC formulation and convex program (4.5) in the BLPP formulation allow for the decision variables $\mathbf{u}$ to appear in the benefit or inverse demand function, $B_w(\mathbf{d},\mathbf{u})$. One should remember that the elements of $\mathbf{u}$ that appear in $B_w(\mathbf{d},\mathbf{u})$ should be interpreted as the parameters of the demand functions, such as potential demands. It should not be interpreted as the additional trip- or OD-based toll charge, such as parking charge because, in this case, an appropriate redefinition of the benefit and inverse demand function is required for VI (4.3) and optimization formulation (4.5) of the traffic equilibrium problem. To avoid unnecessary confusion, hereinafter, unless specifically mentioned, our analysis is limited to link based toll charging problems and elements of $\mathbf{u}$ appearing in $B_w(\mathbf{d},\mathbf{u})$ represent non-toll related parameters of demand functions. Parking or destination-based charges can be easily modeled by introducing appropriate dummy links associated with individual destinations.

For any given set of link toll charges and with appropriate assumptions made on the link travel time and OD demand functions, a unique set of link flows and OD demands can be determined from the lower-level UE problem (4.3) or (4.5). The resulting net economic benefit or social welfare is well defined for the separable demand functions and the negative value of the economic benefit can be used as the upper-level objective function to minimize

$$F\left(\mathbf{u},\mathbf{v}^*(\mathbf{u}),\mathbf{d}^*(\mathbf{u})\right)=\sum_{w\in W}\int_0^{d_w}B_w(\omega)d\omega-\sum_{a\in A}t_a(v_a)v_a \tag{4.6}$$

4.3 SENSITIVITY ANALYSIS OF TRAFFIC EQUILIBRIA WITH PRICING

We consider a general situation where perturbation parameters exist in the link performance functions $\mathbf{t}(\mathbf{v},\varepsilon)$ and OD demand functions $\mathbf{D}(\mu,\varepsilon)$, where μ is a vector of generalized minimum OD travel costs between all OD pairs. In the case of link based road pricing the perturbation parameter ε can represent link toll and thus appear in the link performance function only. The perturbation parameter may also appear in the OD demand function as well when a trip-based road pricing is introduced. The general perturbed equilibrium network flow problem can be written as the following perturbed Variational Inequality (VI). Find $(\mathbf{v}^*,\mathbf{d}^*)\in\Omega$ such that

$$\mathbf{t}(\mathbf{v}^*,\varepsilon)^{\mathrm{T}}\cdot(\mathbf{v}-\mathbf{v}^*)-\mathbf{B}(\mathbf{d}^*,\varepsilon)^{\mathrm{T}}\cdot(\mathbf{d}-\mathbf{d}^*)\geq 0 \tag{4.7}$$

for all $(\mathbf{v},\mathbf{d})\in\Omega$ where Ω is defined in (4.4). It is assumed that $\mathbf{t}(\mathbf{v}^*,\varepsilon)$ and $\mathbf{B}(\mathbf{d}^*,\varepsilon)$ are once continuously differentiable in ε.

Typically, the development of sensitivity analysis for a traffic equilibrium problem involves several technical difficulties. Due to the special structure of the problem, its VI formulation usually includes path flow variables. However, the fact that the path flow pattern is usually not unique at equilibrium prohibits the direct application of the VI sensitivity analysis approach to the traffic equilibrium problem. Here we introduce a restriction approach in which an equivalent restricted problem for the network equilibrium problem is developed which has the desired properties required by the general *implicit function theorem*. The approach presented here is a rectified version of the original restrictive approach proposed by Tobin and Friesz (1988) that contains a few serious flaws. The approach is easily accessible by using a rather intuitive implicit function theorem and can be used as a popular tool for producing gradient information needed in traffic optimization analysis.

4.3.1 Sensitivity Analysis of the Restricted Network Equilibrium Problem

The restricted network equilibrium approach is intended to derive the derivative expressions and has the following advantages: 1) the information on traffic assignment results can be effectively utilized for calculation of derivative values; 2) the derivatives of link flows, O-D demands, O-D costs and other solution variables can be obtained and expressed explicitly in terms of the equilibrium flow solutions. Now we make the following assumption:

Assumptions 4.1 The functions $\mathbf{B}(\mathbf{d},\varepsilon)$ and $\mathbf{t}(\mathbf{v},\varepsilon)$ are positive and strictly monotone in $\mathbf{d}$ and $\mathbf{v}$ (decreasing and increasing) for $\mathbf{d} \geq 0$ and $\mathbf{v} \geq 0$, respectively, and once continuously differentiable in $(\mathbf{d}, \varepsilon)$ and $(\mathbf{v}, \varepsilon)$, respectively.

We assume that we already have a solution $\mathbf{d}^*(0)$, $\mathbf{v}^*(0)$ and $\mathbf{f}^*(0)$ to the above perturbed problem (4.7) for $\varepsilon = 0$. This solution is unique under assumption 4.1. In addition, under the strong monotone assumption, the equilibrium flows and OD costs vary continuously with perturbations of the link cost and OD demand functions (Hall, 1978; Dafermos and Nagurney, 1984). We also assume that at equilibrium the demand between each O-D pair is strictly positive, $d_w^* = D_w(\mu_w^*) > 0,\ w \in W$.

To overcome the difficulty of the non-uniqueness of the path flow in the network equilibrium problem, the equivalent restriction approach is to select a maximal set of *independent* paths in the feasible region of *equilibrium* path flows. Here we focus on the *equilibrated* paths or the paths with the minimum travel cost in relevant OD pairs only in the network. Let $\bar{\Delta}$ and $\bar{\Lambda}$ be the link/path and OD/path incidence matrices associated with the equilibrated paths only. Then any non-unique equilibrium path flows at $\varepsilon = 0$ must be contained in the following set:

$$\bar{\Omega}(0) = \bar{\Omega}(\varepsilon = 0) = \left\{ \bar{\mathbf{f}} \mid \bar{\Delta}\bar{\mathbf{f}} = \mathbf{v}^*(0),\ \bar{\Lambda}\bar{\mathbf{f}} = \mathbf{d}^*(0),\ \bar{\mathbf{f}} \geq 0 \right\} \tag{4.8}$$

where $\mathbf{v}^*(0)$ and $\mathbf{d}^*(0)$ are unique link flow and OD demand solutions at $\varepsilon = 0$. Then the linearly independent paths selected correspond to the linearly independent columns of the matrix $\begin{bmatrix} \bar{\Delta} \\ \bar{\Lambda} \end{bmatrix}$.

The linearly independent equilibrium paths can be obtained easily if the convex combination method (diagonalization algorithm in conjunction with the Frank-Wolfe method for the general asymmetric traffic equilibrium problems) is used to solve the network equilibrium problem. The Frank-Wolfe algorithm generates a unique set of minimum time paths between each O-D pair at each iteration. If the paths generated are saved from iteration to iteration, upon termination the algorithm provides an equilibrium path flow pattern and a link/path incidence matrix for the paths used, from which a maximal set of linearly independent paths can be identified (note that this is not always feasible, and a post-selection of equilibrated paths might be needed after executing an equilibrium traffic assignment).

At this point, we can assume that at equilibrium every link carries a positive flow, $v_a^* > 0,\ a \in A$ in the right-hand side of system (4.17). Otherwise, we can eliminate such links with zero flows in the sensitivity analysis, because, by Assumption 4.2 and uniqueness of link flow, any link with zero flow must be on the *non-equilibrated* paths only, which are already eliminated from our further analysis without effect on the derivation results. In this case, under Assumption 4.2, links with zero flows at $\varepsilon = 0$ will continue to have zero flows for ε near zero and the relevant derivatives in perturbations are equal to zero.

To proceed, we now introduce the following assumption.

Assumptions 4.2 There exists a set of strictly positive equilibrated path flows denoted as $\overline{\mathbf{f}}^{+}$, $\overline{\mathbf{f}}^{+} = \overline{\mathbf{f}}^{+}(0) \in \overline{\Omega}(0)$ at $\varepsilon = 0$.

Assumption 4.2 implies that, the path flows on the minimum cost paths are not unique, but we can at least find a set of positive flows from the set of equilibrium path flows on the equilibrated paths.

Now we look at the general necessary conditions for the perturbed network equilibrium problem (4.7) at $\varepsilon = 0$. The existence of equilibrium is that there exists a solution $\mathbf{f}^{*}$ of the full path flow vector to the following system equations:

$$\mathbf{c}\left(\mathbf{f}^{*},0\right) - \pi - \Lambda^{\mathrm{T}}\mu = 0 \tag{4.9}$$

$$\pi^{\mathrm{T}}\mathbf{f}^{*} = 0 \tag{4.10}$$

$$\Lambda\mathbf{f}^{*} - \mathbf{D}\left(\mu,0\right) = 0 \tag{4.11}$$

$$\mathbf{f}^{*} \geq 0 \tag{4.12}$$

$$\pi \geq 0 \tag{4.13}$$

where $\mathbf{c}$ in (4.9) is a full vector of all path cost functions, and π is a vector of multipliers associated with the non-negativity condition of path flows.

Under Assumption 4.1, the continuity of the equilibrium link flows and OD costs in perturbations of the link cost and OD demand functions is preserved. Thus, the nonbinding nonnegative constraints in (4.13) remain nonbinding near $\varepsilon = 0$, and can be eliminated without changing the solution near $\varepsilon = 0$, or the Lagrange multipliers, π, associated with the nonbinding constraints (*non-equilibrated* paths) at $\varepsilon = 0$ are strictly positive and remain strictly positive for ε near zero, and hence all *non-equilibrated* paths (non-shortest paths) are out of the question. Therefore, we have the following equivalent system of equations:

$$\overline{\mathbf{c}}\left(\mathbf{f}^{*},0\right) - \overline{\Lambda}^{\mathrm{T}}\mu = 0 \tag{4.14}$$

$$\overline{\Lambda}\overline{\mathbf{f}}^{*} - \mathbf{D}\left(\mu,0\right) = 0 \tag{4.15}$$

$$\overline{\mathbf{f}}^{*} \geq 0 \tag{4.16}$$

By our assumption 4.2 we have a strictly positive flow $\overline{\mathbf{f}} \in \overline{\Omega}$, or we have a strictly positive solution $\overline{\mathbf{f}} > 0$ to the following linear system of equations:

$$\begin{bmatrix} \overline{\Delta} \\ \overline{\Lambda} \end{bmatrix} \overline{\mathbf{f}} = \begin{bmatrix} \mathbf{v}^*(0) \\ \mathbf{d}^*(0) \end{bmatrix} \tag{4.17}$$

We now choose a maximum set of linearly independent columns or (*equilibrated*) paths in $\begin{bmatrix} \overline{\Delta} \\ \overline{\Lambda} \end{bmatrix}$. Denote the set of *equilibrated, linearly independent* paths as $\tilde{R}$ and the corresponding path variables as $\tilde{\mathbf{f}}$, and the further reduced link/path and OD/path incidence matrices as $\tilde{\Delta}$ and $\tilde{\Lambda}$. Equation (4.17) can be rewritten as:

$$\begin{bmatrix} \tilde{\Delta} & \tilde{\Delta}^c \\ \tilde{\Lambda} & \tilde{\Lambda}^c \end{bmatrix} \begin{bmatrix} \tilde{\mathbf{f}} \\ \tilde{\mathbf{f}}^c \end{bmatrix} = \begin{bmatrix} \mathbf{v}^*(0) \\ \mathbf{d}^*(0) \end{bmatrix} \tag{4.18}$$

where 'c' denotes the corresponding 'complementary' matrices and vector associated with the *equilibrated, but dependent* paths. For sufficiently small ε near zero, we can always fix the complementary or non-basic path flow variables as $\tilde{\mathbf{f}}^c = \tilde{\mathbf{f}}^{c+}$ and solve the following linear systems of equations for $\tilde{\mathbf{f}}$, for any ε near zero:

$$\begin{bmatrix} \tilde{\Delta} \\ \tilde{\Lambda} \end{bmatrix} \tilde{\mathbf{f}}(\varepsilon) = \begin{bmatrix} \mathbf{v}^*(\varepsilon) \\ \mathbf{d}^*(\varepsilon) \end{bmatrix} - \begin{bmatrix} \tilde{\Delta}^c \\ \tilde{\Lambda}^c \end{bmatrix} \tilde{\mathbf{f}}^{c+} \tag{4.19}$$

Note that the above system may generally contain linearly dependent equations (not of full row rank) in view of the fact that the network link flow vector must satisfy the flow conservation conditions at the nodes. Notwithstanding, because $\begin{bmatrix} \tilde{\Delta} \\ \tilde{\Lambda} \end{bmatrix}$ is of full column rank, for fixed $\tilde{\mathbf{f}}^c = \tilde{\mathbf{f}}^{c+}$, the solution $\tilde{\mathbf{f}}(\varepsilon)$ is uniquely determined and varies continuously with ε in view of the fact that both $\mathbf{v}^*(\varepsilon)$ and $\mathbf{d}^*(\varepsilon)$ are continuous functions of ε. By our Assumption (4.2), $\tilde{\mathbf{f}}(0) = \tilde{\mathbf{f}}^+ > 0$, we thus conclude that $\tilde{\mathbf{f}}(\varepsilon) > 0$ for ε near zero.

As we already show that, by fixing the flow of each equilibrated and dependent path (equal to a positive value) $\tilde{\mathbf{f}}^c = \tilde{\mathbf{f}}^{c+}$, flow variables $\tilde{\mathbf{f}}$ are positive in the reduced, linearly independent system (4.14)-(4.16) at $\varepsilon = 0$ and will remain so for perturbations of ε near zero. This means that the non-negative constraints (4.16) on $\tilde{\mathbf{f}}$ are not binding and can be eliminated without changing the solution in a neighborhood of $\varepsilon = 0$. Consequently, it is sufficient to consider the equilibrated and linearly independent working paths only, and the system (4.14)-(4.16) thus reduces to:

$$\tilde{\mathbf{c}}(\mathbf{f}^*, 0) - \tilde{\Lambda}^{\mathrm{T}} \mu = 0 \tag{4.20}$$

$$\tilde{\Lambda}\tilde{\mathbf{f}}^* - \mathbf{D}(\mu, 0) = 0 \tag{4.21}$$

where $\tilde{\mathbf{c}}(\mathbf{f}^*, 0)$ represents the corresponding reduced vectors (cost vector of the chosen linearly independent, equilibrated paths).

By our Assumption 4.1 of the differentiability of link cost and OD demand functions, differentiating both sides of the system of equations (4.20) and (4.21) with respect to perturbations ε yields:

$$\begin{bmatrix} \nabla_{\tilde{\mathbf{f}}}\tilde{\mathbf{c}}(\mathbf{f}^*, 0) & -\tilde{\Lambda}^{\mathrm{T}} \\ \tilde{\Lambda} & -\nabla_{\mu}\mathbf{D}(\mu, 0) \end{bmatrix} \begin{bmatrix} \nabla_{\varepsilon}\tilde{\mathbf{f}} \\ \nabla_{\varepsilon}\mu \end{bmatrix} = \begin{bmatrix} -\nabla_{\varepsilon}\tilde{\mathbf{c}}(\mathbf{f}^*, 0) \\ \nabla_{\varepsilon}\mathbf{D}(\mu, 0) \end{bmatrix} \tag{4.22}$$

where the Jacobian

$$\mathbf{J}_{\tilde{\mathbf{f}},\mu}(0) = \begin{bmatrix} \nabla_{\tilde{\mathbf{f}}}\tilde{\mathbf{c}}(\mathbf{f}^*, 0) & -\tilde{\Lambda}^{\mathrm{T}} \\ \tilde{\Lambda} & -\nabla_{\mu}\mathbf{D}(\mu, 0) \end{bmatrix} \tag{4.23}$$

is well defined and

$$\nabla_{\tilde{\mathbf{f}}}\tilde{\mathbf{c}}(\mathbf{f}^*, 0) = \tilde{\Delta}^{\mathrm{T}}\nabla_{\mathbf{v}}\mathbf{t}(\mathbf{v}^*, 0)\tilde{\Delta} \tag{4.24}$$

Theorem 4.1 *Under Assumptions 4.1 and 4.2 and the linear independence of the working path set* $\tilde{R}$*, the Jacobian,* $\mathbf{J}_{\tilde{\mathbf{f}},\mu}(0)$ *in (4.23) is nonsingular.*

Proof. To prove Theorem 4.1, it suffices to prove that all the columns of the Jacobian matrix are linearly independent. Consider a nonzero vector $\lambda = \left(\tilde{\lambda}^{\mathrm{T}}, \hat{\lambda}^{\mathrm{T}}\right)^{\mathrm{T}} \neq 0$, where $\tilde{\lambda}$ is a column vector with the same number of elements as that in $\tilde{\mathbf{f}}$ and $\hat{\lambda}$ is a column vector with the number of elements equal to the number of OD pairs (number of rows in Λ, $\bar{\Lambda}$ or $\tilde{\Lambda}$). Let $\left[\mathbf{J}_{\tilde{\mathbf{f}},\mu}\right]\lambda = 0$, and we have

$$\nabla_{\tilde{\mathbf{f}}}\tilde{\mathbf{c}}(\mathbf{f}^*, 0)\tilde{\lambda} - \tilde{\Lambda}^{\mathrm{T}}\hat{\lambda} = 0 \tag{4.25}$$

$$\tilde{\Lambda}\tilde{\lambda} - \nabla_{\mu}\mathbf{D}(\mu, 0)\hat{\lambda} = 0 \tag{4.26}$$

Multiplying both sides of eqn. (4.25) by $\tilde{\lambda}^{\mathrm{T}}$ (from the left side) and using eqn. (4.24) yields:

$$\left(\tilde{\Delta}\tilde{\lambda}\right)^{\mathrm{T}}\nabla_{\mathbf{v}}\mathbf{t}(\mathbf{v}^*, 0)\tilde{\Delta}\tilde{\lambda} - \left(\tilde{\Lambda}\tilde{\lambda}\right)^{\mathrm{T}}\hat{\lambda} = 0 \tag{4.27}$$

Substituting eqn. (4.26) into (4.27) yields:

$$\left(\tilde{\Delta}\tilde{\lambda}\right)^{\mathrm{T}}\nabla_{\mathbf{v}}\mathbf{t}(\mathbf{v}^*, 0)\tilde{\Delta}\tilde{\lambda} + \hat{\lambda}^{\mathrm{T}}\left[-\nabla_{\mu}\mathbf{D}(\mu, 0)\right]\hat{\lambda} = 0 \tag{4.28}$$

From Assumption 4.1, the link cost function vector $\mathbf{t}(\mathbf{v}, \varepsilon)$ and the demand function vector

$\mathbf{D}(\mu,\varepsilon)$ are strictly monotone (increasing and decreasing) in $\mathbf{v}$ and μ respectively, eqn. (4.28) thus implies that $\tilde{\Delta}\tilde{\lambda}=0$ and $\hat{\lambda}=0$. Here we still need to show that $\tilde{\lambda}$ must equal zero. Since $\hat{\lambda}=0$, we have $\tilde{\Lambda}\tilde{\lambda}=0$ from eqn, (4.26). By our early assumption that $\begin{bmatrix}\tilde{\Delta}\\ \tilde{\Lambda}\end{bmatrix}$ consists of only independent columns, we thus conclude that $\tilde{\lambda}=0$ from $\tilde{\Delta}\tilde{\lambda}=0$ and $\tilde{\Lambda}\hat{\lambda}=0$. These results contradict our assumption of the nonzero vector: $\lambda=\left(\tilde{\lambda}^{\mathrm{T}},\hat{\lambda}^{\mathrm{T}}\right)^{\mathrm{T}}\neq 0$. Therefore, the Jacobin matrix $\left[\mathbf{J}_{\tilde{\mathbf{f}},\mu}\right]$ in (4.23) is invertible. This is also true in the case of fixed OD demand where $\nabla_{\mu}\mathbf{D}(\mu,0)\equiv 0$. ¦

From the early assumptions and Theorem 4.1, the conditions for the *general implicit function theorem* are met, and from eqn. (4.22) we arrive at:

$$\begin{bmatrix}\nabla_{\varepsilon}\tilde{\mathbf{f}}\\ \nabla_{\varepsilon}\mu\end{bmatrix}=\left[\mathbf{J}_{\tilde{\mathbf{f}},\mu}(0)\right]^{-1}\begin{bmatrix}-\nabla_{\varepsilon}\tilde{\mathbf{c}}(\mathbf{f}^{*},0)\\ \nabla_{\varepsilon}\mathbf{D}(\mu,0)\end{bmatrix} \tag{4.29}$$

Let

$$\left[\mathbf{J}_{\tilde{\mathbf{f}},\mu}(0)\right]^{-1}=\begin{bmatrix}\mathbf{B}_{11} & \mathbf{B}_{12}\\ \mathbf{B}_{21} & \mathbf{B}_{22}\end{bmatrix} \tag{4.30}$$

Then the derivatives of the working path flows with respect to ε at $\varepsilon=0$ are

$$\nabla_{\varepsilon}\tilde{\mathbf{f}}=-\mathbf{B}_{11}\nabla_{\varepsilon}\tilde{\mathbf{c}}\left(\mathbf{f}^{*},0\right)+\mathbf{B}_{12}\nabla_{\varepsilon}\mathbf{D}(\mu,0) \tag{4.31}$$

In view of $\nabla_{\varepsilon}\mathbf{v}=\tilde{\Delta}\nabla_{\varepsilon}\tilde{\mathbf{f}}+\tilde{\Delta}^{c}\nabla_{\varepsilon}\tilde{\mathbf{f}}^{c}$ and $\nabla_{\varepsilon}\tilde{\mathbf{f}}^{c}\equiv 0$ as well as $\nabla_{\varepsilon}\tilde{\mathbf{c}}\left(\mathbf{f}^{*},0\right)=\tilde{\Delta}^{\mathrm{T}}\nabla_{\varepsilon}\mathbf{t}\left(\mathbf{v}^{*},0\right)$, the derivatives of link flows with respect to ε at $\varepsilon=0$ are obtained as:

$$\nabla_{\varepsilon}\mathbf{v}=-\tilde{\Delta}\mathbf{B}_{11}\tilde{\Delta}^{\mathrm{T}}\nabla_{\varepsilon}\mathbf{t}\left(\mathbf{v}^{*},0\right)+\tilde{\Delta}\mathbf{B}_{12}\nabla_{\varepsilon}\mathbf{D}(\mu,0) \tag{4.32}$$

Theorem 4.2 *The values of* $\nabla_{\varepsilon}\mathbf{v}$ *as calculated in (4.32) are independent of the choice of the equilibrated and linearly independent paths* $\tilde{R}$ *and the specific values of positive path flows* $\overline{\mathbf{f}}^{+}=\begin{pmatrix}\tilde{\mathbf{f}}^{+}\\ \tilde{\mathbf{f}}^{c+}\end{pmatrix}$.

Proof. The former independence of the choice of $\tilde{R}$ is implicitly due to the fact that the basic linear system of equations (4.19) holds at equilibrium for the values and small variations of link flows and OD demands, and path flows for any maximal number of linearly independent equilibrated paths $\tilde{R}$. The latter independence of the specific values of equilibrated positive path flows is self-evident from all the sensitivity analysis equations, the only term that involves the selected path flow values is the Jacobian of the path cost vector in

(4.24), which can be uniquely evaluated by the Jacobian of the link cost functions and the reduced link/path incidence matrix associated with the selected path set. To see this explicitly, like Tobin and Friesz (1988) we consider $\varepsilon=(\cdots,\varepsilon_i,\cdots)^{\mathrm{T}}$ and a unit vector e_i of the same dimension of ε, with unity in the i-th position and zeros elsewhere, and $\delta>0$ is a scalar. By definitions and assumptions, for any link $a\in A$ we have:

$$\begin{aligned} v_a^*(\varepsilon) &= \sum_{w\in W}\sum_{r\in R_w} f_{rw}(\varepsilon)\delta_{ar} \\ &= \sum_{w\in W}\sum_{r\in \bar{R}_w} \bar{f}_{rw}(\varepsilon)\delta_{ar} \quad \text{(Because non-equilibrated path has zero flow)} \\ &= \sum_{w\in W}\sum_{r\in \tilde{R}_w} \tilde{f}_{rw}(\varepsilon)\delta_{ar} + \sum_{w\in W}\sum_{r\in \tilde{R}_w^c} \tilde{f}_{rw}^c(\varepsilon)\delta_{ar} \quad \text{(by definition in (4.18))} \\ &= \sum_{w\in W}\sum_{r\in \tilde{R}_w} \tilde{f}_{rw}(\varepsilon)\delta_{ar} + \sum_{w\in W}\sum_{r\in \tilde{R}_w^c} \tilde{f}_{rw}^{c+}\delta_{ar} \quad \text{(by assumption } \tilde{\mathbf{f}}^c=\tilde{\mathbf{f}}^{c+}) \end{aligned}$$

The second-term is constant. Thus,

$$\begin{aligned} \frac{\partial v_a^*(\varepsilon)}{\partial \varepsilon_i} = \lim_{\delta\to 0}\frac{1}{\delta}\left[v_a^*(\delta e_i)-v_a^*(0)\right] &= \lim_{\delta\to 0}\frac{1}{\delta}\left[\sum_{w\in W}\sum_{r\in \tilde{R}_w}\tilde{f}_{rw}(\delta e_i)\delta_{ar}-\sum_{w\in W}\sum_{r\in \tilde{R}_w}\tilde{f}_{rw}^+(0)\delta_{ar}\right] \\ &= \sum_{w\in W}\sum_{r\in \tilde{R}_w}\left\{\lim_{\delta\to 0}\frac{1}{\delta}\left[\tilde{f}_{rw}(\delta e_i)-\tilde{f}_{rw}^+(0)\right]\right\}\delta_{ar} \\ &= \sum_{w\in W}\sum_{r\in \tilde{R}_w}\frac{\partial \tilde{f}_{rw}(\varepsilon)}{\partial \varepsilon_i}\delta_{ar} \end{aligned}$$

This completes the proof. ¦

Theorem 4.2 states that the value of $\nabla_\varepsilon \mathbf{v}$ is uniquely defined irrespective of the choice of the equilibrated, linearly independent paths and their specific positive values without perturbation. This means that link flows are differentiable with respect to a variety of perturbations of the link cost and OD demand functions and their well-defined derivatives are obtained in eqn. (4.32). Other derivatives, such as that of OD demand in perturbation parameters, can be obtained below. From eqn. (4.22) the derivatives of OD travel cost with respect to ε at $\varepsilon=0$ are:

$$\nabla_\varepsilon \mu = -\mathbf{B}_{21}\tilde{\Delta}^{\mathrm{T}}\nabla_\varepsilon \mathbf{t}(\mathbf{v}^*,0)+\mathbf{B}_{22}\nabla_\varepsilon \mathbf{D}(\mu,0) \tag{4.33}$$

We thus have

$$\nabla_\varepsilon \mathbf{d} = \nabla_\varepsilon \mathbf{D}(\mu,0)+\nabla_\mu \mathbf{D}(\mu,0)\nabla_\varepsilon \mu \tag{4.34}$$

where $\nabla_\varepsilon \mu$ is given by eqn. (4.33).

Note that, in the case of specific applications, the derivative expressions (4.32) and (4.34) can be considerably simplified. In particular, when the perturbation parameters are specified, the derivatives $\nabla_\varepsilon \mathbf{t}(\mathbf{v}^*,0)$ and $\nabla_\varepsilon \mathbf{D}(\mu,0)$ can be obtained in a straightforward manner. Of course, the sensitivity analysis formula presented so far does apply for the special case with fixed travel demand, but the perturbation parameter can then appear in the demand vector $\mathbf{d}(\varepsilon)$. In this case $\nabla_\varepsilon \mathbf{D}(\mu,0) \equiv \nabla_\varepsilon \mathbf{d}(0)$ in (4.22), (4.29), (4.32) and (4.33), and $\nabla_\mu \mathbf{D}(\mu,0) \equiv 0$ in (4.22), (4.36) and (4.34).

4.3.2 Relations to Other Gradient-based Sensitivity Analysis Methods

In the sensitivity analysis method by Tobin and Friesz (1988), an equilibrium path flow vector $\bar{\mathbf{f}}^*$ is chosen such that it is an extreme point of the polyhedron $\bar{\Omega}(0)$ in (4.8), which has exactly as many paths with a strictly positive flow as the rank of the matrix $\begin{bmatrix} \bar{\Delta} \\ \bar{\Lambda} \end{bmatrix}$ (such a path flow vector is called a non-degenerate extreme point of $\bar{\Omega}(0)$). An extreme point of the path flows at $\varepsilon = 0$ in this case correspond to the solution of our system (4.18) by setting $\tilde{\mathbf{f}}^c = 0$. Namely,

$$\begin{bmatrix} \tilde{\Delta} \\ \tilde{\Lambda} \end{bmatrix} \tilde{\mathbf{f}}(\varepsilon) = \begin{bmatrix} \mathbf{v}^*(\varepsilon) \\ \mathbf{d}^*(\varepsilon) \end{bmatrix} \tag{4.35}$$

Unfortunately, there is no guarantee that the solution to the above system is strictly positive (some are zeros) no matter which linearly independent columns in $\begin{bmatrix} \tilde{\Delta} \\ \tilde{\Lambda} \end{bmatrix}$ are selected from $\begin{bmatrix} \bar{\Delta} \\ \bar{\Lambda} \end{bmatrix}$. This exactly corresponds to the case where the number of paths with strictly positive flows at *any* extreme point of $\bar{\Omega}(0)$ cannot equal the rank of $\begin{bmatrix} \bar{\Delta} \\ \bar{\Lambda} \end{bmatrix}$. The latter observation was first shown by Josefsson and Patriksson (2003) through a simple example, which will be further presented later.

The Jacobian of the working path cost vector, $\nabla_{\tilde{\mathbf{f}}} \tilde{\mathbf{c}}(\mathbf{f}^*,0) = \tilde{\Delta}^{\mathrm{T}} \nabla_{\mathbf{v}} \mathbf{t}(\mathbf{v}^*,0) \tilde{\Delta}$, is in general not invertible, and we have to work directly with the inverting of the Jacobian in (4.23). The reason is simple. Let the number of (linearly independent) paths included in $\tilde{\Delta}$ be m and the number of links in the network with positive flow be n. Then $\tilde{\Delta}^{\mathrm{T}} \nabla_{\mathbf{v}} \mathbf{t}(\mathbf{v}^*,0) \tilde{\Delta}$ is an $n \times n$ matrix, but its rank is m if $m < n$ (as assumed, $\nabla_{\mathbf{v}} \mathbf{t}(\mathbf{v}^*,0)$ is non-singular), thus $\tilde{\Delta}^{\mathrm{T}} \nabla_{\mathbf{v}} \mathbf{t}(\mathbf{v}^*,0) \tilde{\Delta}$ is not invertible. If, otherwise, $\nabla_{\tilde{\mathbf{f}}} \tilde{\mathbf{c}}(\mathbf{f}^*,0)^{-1}$ does exist, then in (4.30) we can further obtain

$$\mathbf{B}_{22} = \left[-\nabla_{\mu}\mathbf{D}(\mu,0) + \tilde{\Lambda}\nabla_{\tilde{\mathbf{f}}}\tilde{\mathbf{c}}(\mathbf{f}^*,0)^{-1}\tilde{\Lambda}^{\mathrm{T}} \right]^{-1} \quad (4.36)$$

$$\mathbf{B}_{12} = \nabla_{\tilde{\mathbf{f}}}\tilde{\mathbf{c}}(\mathbf{f}^*,0)^{-1}\tilde{\Lambda}^{\mathrm{T}}\mathbf{B}_{22} \quad (4.37)$$

$$\mathbf{B}_{21} = -\mathbf{B}_{22}\tilde{\Lambda}\nabla_{\tilde{\mathbf{f}}}\tilde{\mathbf{c}}(\mathbf{f}^*,0)^{-1} \quad (4.38)$$

$$\mathbf{B}_{11} = \nabla_{\tilde{\mathbf{f}}}\tilde{\mathbf{c}}(\mathbf{f}^*,0)^{-1}\left[\mathbf{I} + \tilde{\Lambda}^{\mathrm{T}}\mathbf{B}_{21}\right] \quad (4.39)$$

where $\mathbf{I}$ is an identity matrix of appropriate dimension.

In the sensitivity analysis formulas developed by Tobin and Friesz (1988), the inverse of the Jacobian of the working path cost vector is indeed used. Albeit their working paths, as mentioned above, differ from ours , but correspond to the paths with strictly positive flows at a non-degenerate extreme point, and the invertibility is unfortunately not guaranteed in general, depending on the network topology. Indeed, as initially pointed out in Bell and Iida (1997) and cited recently in Patriksson (2004), there must be at least one possible path flow for each OD pair that carries a positive demand and in most realistic networks the number of used paths is far more than the number of links, and the non-invertibility problem is thus expected to be prevalent in networks of a practical size.

The original sensitivity approach by Tobin and Friesz (1988) and the corrected one developed here are in fact based on column (path) reduction. Cho, Smith and Friesz (2000) developed a row (or link)-based reduction method for sensitivity analyses of network equilibrium links flows under essentially the same conditions as required in this study. Their reduction method first works with the reduced polyhedron $\bar{\Omega}(0)$ by considering all minimum cost paths only. Then a maximum number of linearly independent equations from the system (4.17) is chosen to express dependent link flows (link flows that appear in the dependent equations) in terms of independent link flows and OD demand vector. Namely,

$$\begin{bmatrix} \bar{\Delta}_1 \\ \bar{\Delta}_2 \\ \bar{\Lambda} \end{bmatrix} \bar{\mathbf{f}} = \begin{bmatrix} \mathbf{v}_1^*(0) \\ \mathbf{v}_2^*(0) \\ \mathbf{d}^*(0) \end{bmatrix} \quad (4.40)$$

where $\bar{\Delta}_1$ is chosen to be a maximal set of rows of $\bar{\Delta}$ so that $\begin{bmatrix} \bar{\Delta}_1 \\ \bar{\Lambda} \end{bmatrix}$ is of full row rank (note that $\bar{\Lambda}$ contains linearly independent rows and is of full row rank equal to the number of OD pairs). Then, there exists matrices $\mathbf{M}_1$ and $\mathbf{M}_2$ such that

$$\bar{\Delta}_2 = \mathbf{M}_1\bar{\Delta}_1 + \mathbf{M}_2\bar{\Lambda}$$

and the dependent link flow vector can be expressed as:

$$\mathbf{v}_2^*(0) = \bar{\Delta}_2\bar{\mathbf{f}} = \mathbf{M}_1\bar{\Delta}_1\bar{\mathbf{f}} + \mathbf{M}_2\bar{\Lambda}\bar{\mathbf{f}} = \mathbf{M}_1\mathbf{v}_1^*(0) + \mathbf{M}_2\mathbf{d}^*(0)$$

To obtain an expression for $\mathbf{M}_1$ and $\mathbf{M}_2$ and preserve flow conservation conditions (to obtain feasible link flow set), they select a *unique* equilibrium path flow vector which is the 'least-distance' from an unperturbed positive path-flow vector $\bar{\mathbf{f}}^+$ by solving analytically the following minimum-distance or quadratic programming problem:

$$\min_{\bar{\mathbf{f}}} \left\|\bar{\mathbf{f}} - \bar{\mathbf{f}}^+\right\|^2 = \left(\bar{\mathbf{f}} - \bar{\mathbf{f}}^+\right)^{\mathrm{T}}\left(\bar{\mathbf{f}} - \bar{\mathbf{f}}^+\right)$$

subject to:

$$\begin{bmatrix} \bar{\Delta}_1 \\ \bar{\Lambda} \end{bmatrix} \bar{\mathbf{f}} = \begin{bmatrix} \mathbf{v}_1^*(0) \\ \mathbf{d}^*(0) \end{bmatrix} \tag{4.41}$$

A unique analytical positive solution of $\bar{\mathbf{f}}$ can be obtained but it involves complex operations (multiplication and inverse) of sub-matrices $\bar{\Delta}_1$ and $\bar{\Lambda}$ together with vectors $\bar{\mathbf{f}}^+$, $\mathbf{v}_1^*(0)$ and $\mathbf{d}^*(0)$, which makes the subsequent sensitivity analysis in the reduced version of the feasible link flow set free of path flow variables even more complicated.

In contrast, the column or path-based reduction approach requires only identification of a maximum set of equilibrated and linearly independent paths, as may exist, and is trivial to do by a simple linear algebra procedure for a given set of the minimum cost path set generated by a proper traffic assignment procedure. The actual positive values of the selected working paths, assumed to exist, are immaterial in our sensitivity analysis.

4.3.3 Dissection of Sensitivity Analysis with Analytical Examples

The sensitivity analysis method presented above is in fact a rectified one of the early sensitivity analysis approach developed by Tobin and Friesz (1988), which was found to contain a few serious flaws and was criticized recently by (Bell and Iida, 1997; Patriksson, 2004). Here we present a further dissection of the above sensitivity analysis method in connection with the early one proposed by Tobin and Friesz (1998).

i) The strict monotonicity conditions.

Assumption 4.1 of strictly monotone link cost and OD demand functions is a standard assumption used in traffic equilibrium modeling. One can always construct an example, for which strictly monotone condition is not met, but the equilibrium link flows and OD demand are unique, and we can readily find a trivial example, for which link flows and OD demands are differentiable in perturbations, but the strict monotonicity conditions are not needed. This means that Assumption 4.1 is standard but stronger than necessary in some special cases.

ii) Non-well-definedness of the strict complementrity conditions

Strict complementarity conditions are frequently alluded to in the literature, particularly in traffic equilibrium sensitivity analysis. The definition that is commonly used is the following: a path flow solution $\mathbf{f}^*$ is strictly complementary if and only if:

$$f_{rw}^* \geq 0,\quad c_{rw}\left(\mathbf{f}^*,\varepsilon\right)-\mu_w^* \geq 0,\quad f_{rw}^*\left(c_{rw}\left(\mathbf{f}^*,\varepsilon\right)-\mu_w^*\right)=0 \tag{4.42}$$

and furthermore,

$$f_{rw}^* + \left[c_{rw}\left(\mathbf{f}^*,\varepsilon\right)-\mu_w^*\right] > 0 \tag{4.43}$$

for all $r \in R_w, w \in W$. Condition (4.43) implies that $f_{rw}^* > 0$ if $c_{rw}\left(\mathbf{f}^*,\varepsilon\right)-\mu_w^* = 0$, and if $f_{rw}^* = 0$ then $c_{rw}\left(\mathbf{f}^*,\varepsilon\right)-\mu_w^* > 0$. This strictly complementarity condition is used together with the strict monotonicity condition as sufficient conditions for the differentiability of the traffic equilibrium link flows. Nevertheless, the above strict complementarity condition is not well defined for the traffic equilibrium problem, because of the non-uniqueness of the equilibrium path flows. Let us consider the following example network that often appears in the literature.

Example 4.1 Consider the following network shown in Figure 4.1, with a single OD pair from node 1 to node 3, with a fixed demand of $d_{1\to 3} = 2$ (flow units). The link cost functions are given by:

$$t_1 = 1 + v_1 + u_1,\quad t_2 = 1 + v_2,\quad t_3 = 1 + v_3,\quad t_4 = 1 + v_4 \tag{4.44}$$

with link 1 subjected to a toll charge.

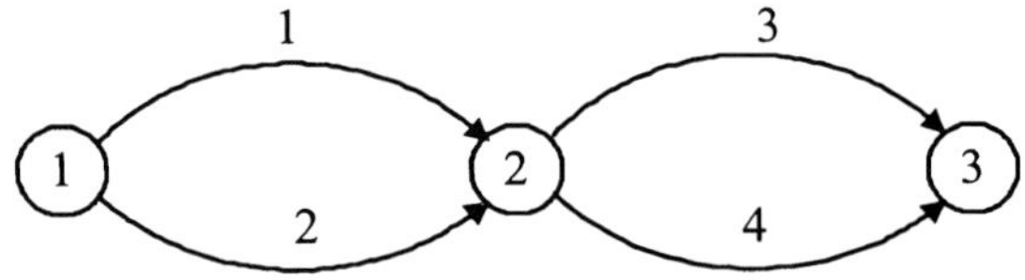

Figure 4.1 The network used in Example 4.1

There are four paths denoted by: $r_1 = \{1,3\}$, $r_2 = \{1,4\}$, $r_3 = \{2,3\}$, $r_4 = \{2,4\}$. Without toll charge $u_1^* = 0$, we have an obvious unique (unperturbed) equilibrium link flow solution: $\mathbf{v}^* = (1,1,1,1)^{\mathrm{T}}$. All four paths are the minimum cost path between the single OD pair and the equilibrium path flows are not unique but can be expressed as follows:

$$\bar{f}_1^* = \rho,\quad \bar{f}_2^* = 1-\rho,\quad \bar{f}_3^* = 1-\rho,\quad \bar{f}_4^* = \rho,\quad 0 \leq \rho \leq 1.0 \tag{4.45}$$

It becomes immediately clear that if $\rho = 0$ or $\rho = 1$ the strict complementarity conditions are not met, otherwise they hold for any $0<\rho<1$. From this simple example, we can see that the use of the conventional strict complementarity conditions in sensitivity analysis is misleading and sometimes makes it difficult to discern whether a traffic equilibrium solution is differentiable.

In connection with this example, we now recall our Assumption 4.2, which together with Assumption 4.1 ensures the existence of a nonsingular Jacobian (4.23) and thus the differentiability of equilibrium link flows and OD demands. Clearly, this assumption is satisfied because all path flows on the four equilibrated (or minimum cost) paths are strictly positive for any $0<\rho<1$.

iii) Non-differentiability at a degenerate equilibrium point

We have shown that Assumptions 4.1 and 4.2 are sufficient for the differentiability of equilibrium link flows and OD demand. We are naturally interested in the conditions under which the assumptions are not satisfied and as a result the traffic equilibrium solution may not be differentiable. We now introduce the following definition.

Definition 4.1 A path flow solution $\mathbf{f}^*$ is said to be a *degenerate* equilibrium point if there exists at least one *equilibrated* path on which path flow cannot be strictly positive or must be zero; otherwise it is said to be a non-degenerate equilibrium point. The *equilibrated* path(s) whose flow must be zero is called *degenerated* path(s).

By the above definition and our Assumption 4.1, equilibrium link flows and OD demands *may not be* differentiable in perturbations of link cost and OD demand functions at a degenerate equilibrium point, or the non-differentiability of link flows and OD demand may occur when one (or more) of the paths is exactly balancing between active and inactive states or when one or more paths have exactly travel cost equal to the minimum but are not used at all by users. In the current context of sensitivity analysis, this means that the perturbations, such as toll charge, change continuously to the point that just causes a used path to be abandoned or a new path to just come into use. One can thus see that there would be a 'zero' probability of finding or encountering cases where the equilibrium link flow is not differentiable in a continuous space of perturbations. To put it differently, in solving a bi-level network toll optimization problem, non-differentiability is hardly encountered when the solution by a sensitivity analysis based algorithm moves from one point to another within the feasible region of link tolls. Indeed, the equilibrium link flows are piecewise differentiable, and the non-differentiability corresponds to a set with a Lebesgue measure zero, such as an isolated point in the current example, a line (a plan) in a two (three) or higher dimensional space. To give further details on this observation, we now consider Example 4.1 again.

Example 4.2 Consider the same network example with the same input data in Example 4.1. The equilibrium link flows can be expressed in terms of link toll charge as follows:

$$v_1^*(u_1)=\begin{cases}1-\frac{u_1}{2}, & 0\le u_1\le 2\\ 0, & u_1>2\end{cases},\quad v_2^*(u_1)=\begin{cases}1+\frac{u_1}{2}, & 0\le u_1\le 2\\ 2, & u_1>2\end{cases},\quad v_3^*\equiv v_4^*\equiv 1 \tag{4.46}$$

One can readily see that there is one and only one degenerate equilibrium point corresponding to $u_1=2$ within the whole positive domain of toll charge. At $u_1=2$, $v_1^*(2)=0$ and hence $\bar{f}_1^*$ and $\bar{f}_2^*$ must be zero, but all four paths still have identical minimum cost. For any $u_1>2$, path r_1 and r_2 becomes non-equilibrated paths, r_3 and r_4 remain as equilibrated paths always able to have strictly positive flows. As indicated in Figure 4.2, the flows on links 1 and 2 are not differentiable at $u_1=2$. Indeed, the non-differentiability occurs at a point on a positive half line.

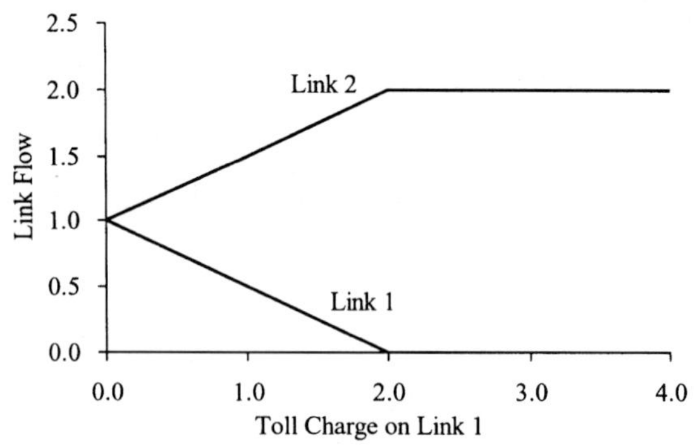

Figure 4.2 The equilibrium link flows as functions of toll charge on link 1 in Example 4.2

iv) Differentiability at a degenerate equilibrium point

One should be aware that the non-degenerate equilibrium is not a necessary condition for the differentiability of the traffic equilibrium solution. Here an example is provided to demonstrate that link flow is still differentiable in a link toll at the path switching or degenerate equilibrium point as the toll changes.

Example 4.3 (Differentiability of equilibrium link flow at a degenerate equilibrium point) We consider a network of two parallel links connecting a single OD pair, shown in Figure 4.3. Let the OD demand be fixed and given as $d=4$. The cost functions for the two links are given as $t_1(v_1) = v_1 + 2$ and $t_2(v_2) = 2\sqrt{v_2} + 7$, and link 1 is subjected to a toll charge $u_1 \geq 0$.

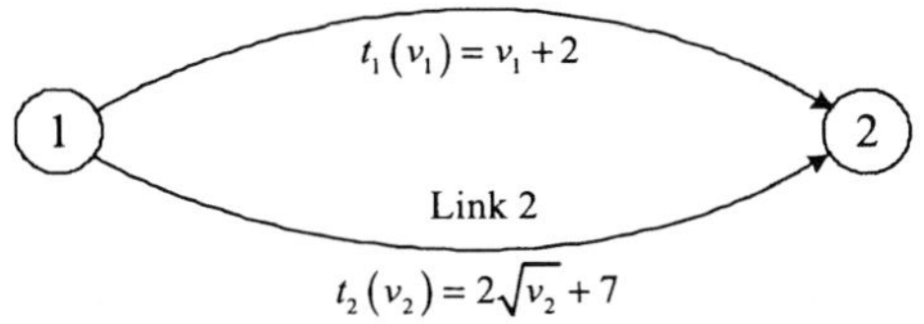

Figure 4.3 A simple network of two parallel links connecting a single OD

Note that the separable link cost functions are both strictly monotone in their respective link flows. It is straightforward to find the equilibrium link flows $v_1^*(u_1)$ and $v_2^*(u_1)$ as follows:

$$v_1^*(u_1) = \begin{cases} 4, & 0 \leq u_1 < 1 \\ 4 - \left(\sqrt{u_1} - 1\right)^2, & 1 \leq u_1 < 9, \\ 0, & u_1 \geq 9 \end{cases} \quad v_2^*(u_1) = \begin{cases} 0, & 0 \leq u_1 < 1 \\ \left(\sqrt{u_1} - 1\right)^2, & 1 \leq u_1 < 9 \\ 4, & u_1 \geq 9 \end{cases} \tag{4.47}$$

The curves of the above reaction functions are depicted in Figure 4.4. Obviously, the equilibrium point is degenerate at the following two points: $u_1 = 1$ where $v_1^* = 4$, $v_2^* = 0$, $t_1(v_1^*) + u_1 = t_1(v_2^*) = 7$ and $u_1 = 9$ where $v_1^* = 0$, $v_2^* = 4$, $t_1(v_1^*) + u_1 = t_1(v_2^*) = 11$.

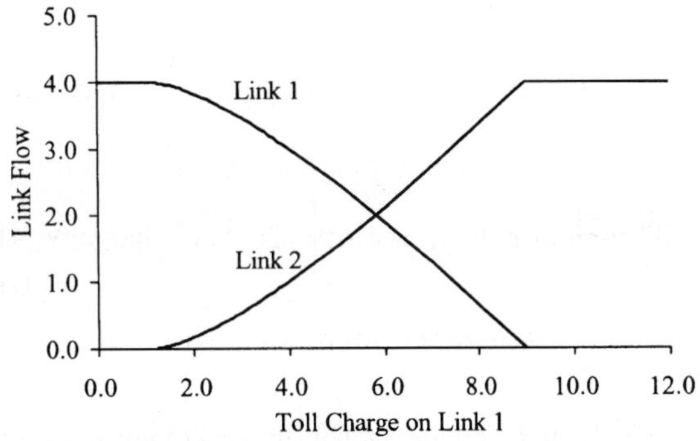

Figure 4.4 The equilibrium link flows as functions of toll charge on link 1 in Example 4.3

However, it can be straightforwardly checked that both $v_1^*(u_1)$ and $v_2^*(u_1)$ are differentiable at the first degenerate point $u_1 = 1$. Specifically,

$$\nabla_{u_1} \mathbf{v}(u_1)_{u_1=1.0} = \left(\frac{dv_1^*(u_1)}{du_1}, \frac{dv_2^*(u_1)}{du_1} \right)^{\mathrm{T}}_{u_1=1.0} = \left(\frac{1}{\sqrt{u_1}} - 1, 1 - \frac{1}{\sqrt{u_1}} \right)^{\mathrm{T}}_{u_1=1.0} = \begin{pmatrix} 0 \\ 0 \end{pmatrix}$$

However, $v_1^*(u_1)$ and $v_2^*(u_1)$ are not differentiable at the second degenerate point $u_1 = 9$, because their left and right derivatives are not identical. The left derivative (denoted by '$-$') and the right derivative (denoted by '+') are equal to:

$$\nabla_{u_1}^{-}\mathbf{v}(u_1) = \lim_{u_1 \to 9^-}\left(\frac{1}{\sqrt{u_1}} - 1,\ 1 - \frac{1}{\sqrt{u_1}}\right)^{\mathrm{T}} = \left(-\frac{2}{3}, \frac{2}{3}\right)^{\mathrm{T}},\quad \nabla_{u_1}^{+}\mathbf{v}(u_1) = (0,0)^{\mathrm{T}} \tag{4.48}$$

v) *Applicability at a degenerate equilibrium point*

We observed from Examples 4.2 and 4.3 that a degenerate equilibrium point can be either differentiable or non-differentiable. We next look at what happens when the sensitivity analysis formula is still applied at a degenerate equilibrium point where Assumption 4.2 is not met. Before we introduce specific analytical examples, we point out that the sensitivity analysis formula does work, because the invertibility of the Jacobian depends only on Assumption 4.1 and the linear independence of the equilibrated working paths, which is satisfied at the degenerate equilibrium point. What we need to do is to figure out the implication of the final results obtained.

Example 4.4 We apply the sensitivity analysis formula to the two degenerate equilibrium points at $u_1 = 1$ and $u_1 = 9$ in Example 4.3. For each degenerate point, we apply the formulas with and without including the degenerate path or link with zero flow, respectively.

We first consider the non-differentiable degenerate point: $u_1 = 9$, $v_1^* = 0$, and $v_2^* = 4$. When link 1 with zero flow is included in the sensitivity analysis formula, we have

$$\mathbf{J}_{\bar{\mathbf{f}},\mu}(0) = \begin{bmatrix} 1 & 0 & -1 \\ 0 & 1/2 & -1 \\ 1 & 1 & 0 \end{bmatrix},\quad \left[\mathbf{J}_{\bar{\mathbf{f}},\mu}(0)\right]^{-1} = \frac{1}{3}\begin{bmatrix} 2 & -2 & 1 \\ -2 & 2 & 2 \\ -1 & -2 & 1 \end{bmatrix},\quad \begin{bmatrix} -\nabla_{u_1}\mathbf{c}(\mathbf{f}^*,0) \\ \nabla_{u_1}\mathbf{D}(\mu,0) \end{bmatrix} = \begin{bmatrix} -1 \\ 0 \\ 0 \end{bmatrix}$$

Thus, from (4.29) we have

$$\nabla_{u_1}\mathbf{v} = \Delta\nabla_{u_1}\tilde{\mathbf{f}} = \frac{1}{3}\begin{bmatrix} 1 & 0 \\ 0 & 1 \end{bmatrix}\begin{bmatrix} 2 & -2 & 1 \\ -2 & 2 & 2 \end{bmatrix}\begin{bmatrix} -1 \\ 0 \\ 0 \end{bmatrix} = \begin{bmatrix} -2/3 \\ 2/3 \end{bmatrix} \tag{4.49}$$

Similarly, when link 1 with zero flow is not included in the sensitivity analysis formula, we have the following application results for the reduced path variables

$$\mathbf{J}_{\bar{\mathbf{f}},\mu}(0) = \begin{bmatrix} 1/2 & -1 \\ 1 & 0 \end{bmatrix},\quad \left[\mathbf{J}_{\bar{\mathbf{f}},\mu}(0)\right]^{-1} = \begin{bmatrix} 0 & 1 \\ -1 & 1/2 \end{bmatrix},\quad \begin{bmatrix} -\nabla_{u_1}\tilde{\mathbf{c}}(\mathbf{f}^*,0) \\ \nabla_{u_1}\mathbf{D}(\mu,0) \end{bmatrix} = \begin{bmatrix} 0 \\ 0 \end{bmatrix}$$

The final link flow derivatives can be readily obtained as:

$$\nabla_{u_1}\mathbf{v} = \begin{bmatrix} 0 \\ 0 \end{bmatrix} \tag{4.50}$$

It is interesting to observe that $\nabla_{u_1}\mathbf{v}$ in (4.49) and (4.50) with and without including the degenerate path, correspond, respectively, to the left and right derivatives of the scalar link flow functions $v_1^*(u_1)$ and $v_2^*(u_1)$ in u_1 at $u_1 = 9$, which is given in eqn. (4.48).

Next we consider the degenerate but differentiable point: $u_1 = 1$, $v_1^* = 4$, and $v_2^* = 0$. Application of the formula encounters a technical difficult in the sense that $\mathrm{d}t_2(v_2)/\mathrm{d}v_2 = 1/\sqrt{v_2} \to \infty$ as $v_2 \to 0$ (this is of course not due to any flaw of the sensitivity analysis method, only that Assumption 4.1 is not satisfied). If we let $\mathrm{d}t_2(v_2)/\mathrm{d}v_2\big|_{v_2=0} = \rho$ (a sufficiently large number) and then apply the sensitivity analysis formula, when both links are included, we have

$$\mathbf{J}_{\tilde{\mathbf{f}},\mu}(0) = \begin{bmatrix} 1 & 0 & -1 \\ 0 & \rho & -1 \\ 1 & 1 & 0 \end{bmatrix}, \quad \left[\mathbf{J}_{\tilde{\mathbf{f}},\mu}(0)\right]^{-1} = \frac{1}{\rho+1}\begin{bmatrix} 1 & -1 & \rho \\ -1 & 1 & 1 \\ -\rho & -1 & \rho \end{bmatrix}$$

and

$$\nabla_{u_1}\mathbf{v} = \left[-\frac{1}{\rho+1}, \frac{1}{\rho+1}\right]^{\mathrm{T}} = \begin{bmatrix} 0 \\ 0 \end{bmatrix} \text{ as } \rho \to +\infty$$

Likewise, when only link 1 with positive flow is included, applying the sensitivity analysis formula yields: $\nabla_{u_1}\mathbf{v} = (0,0)^{\mathrm{T}}$. These results are consistent with our earlier observation that the link flow is differentiable at $u_1 = 1$ (with identical left and right derivatives).

At this point it is still too early to say anything definite and the following example perhaps offers a further clue to the above observation.

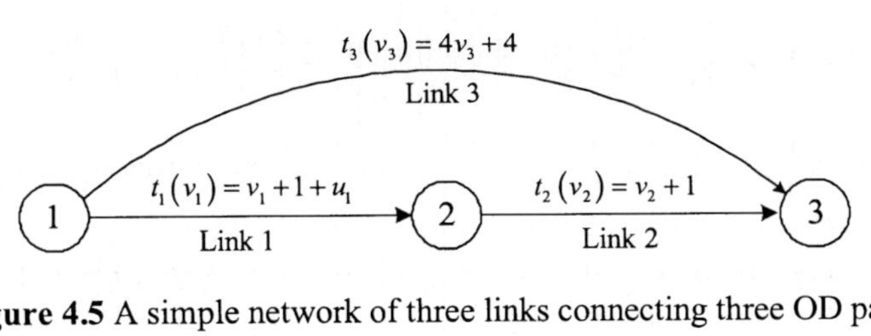

Figure 4.5 A simple network of three links connecting three OD pairs

Example 4.5 Consider a simple network again depicted in Figure 4.5 with 3 nodes, 3 links and 3 OD pairs: $1 \to 2$, $2 \to 3$ and $1 \to 3$. The link cost functions are shown in the network, with link 1 subjected to a toll charge u_1. The OD demands are fixed and given by $d_{1\to 2} = d_{2\to 3} = d_{1\to 3} = 2$. There are four paths denoted by: $r_1 = \{1\}$, $r_2 = \{2\}$, $r_3 = \{1,2\}$, $r_4 = \{3\}$.

The equilibrium link flows as a function of link toll u_1 is given below:

$$v_1^*(u_1) = v_2^*(u_2)\begin{cases} 3 - \dfrac{u_1}{6}, & 0 \le u_1 \le 6 \\ 2, & u_1 > 6 \end{cases}, \quad v_3^*(u_1) = \begin{cases} 1 + \dfrac{u_1}{6}, & 0 \le u_1 \le 6 \\ 2, & u_1 > 6 \end{cases}$$

Obviously, all three link flows are not differentiable at the point: $u_1 = 6$, $v_1^* = v_2^* = v_3^* = 2$. However, their left and right derivatives with respect to u_1 exist and are given as follows:

$$\nabla_{u_1}^{-}\mathbf{v}(u_1)_{u_1=6.0} = \left(-\frac{1}{6}, -\frac{1}{6}, \frac{1}{6}\right)^{\mathrm{T}}, \qquad \nabla_{u_1}^{+}\mathbf{v}(u_1)_{u_1=6.0} = (0,0,0)^{\mathrm{T}} \tag{4.51}$$

We can observe that this non-differentiable point is a *degenerate* equilibrium point, because travel costs on paths 3 and 4 in OD pair 3 are identical, but $\bar{f}_4^* = 2$ but $\bar{f}_3^*$ must be zero.

Now we consider application of the sensitivity analysis formula. By including the degenerate path 3, we have the following link/path and OD/path incidence matrices associated with the equilibrated paths:

$$\left[\tilde{\Delta}^{\mathrm{T}} \middle| \tilde{\Lambda}^{\mathrm{T}}\right] = \begin{bmatrix} 1 & 0 & 0 & 1 & 0 & 0 \\ 0 & 1 & 0 & 0 & 1 & 0 \\ 1 & 1 & 0 & 0 & 0 & 1 \\ 0 & 0 & 1 & 0 & 0 & 1 \end{bmatrix}$$

This matrix, with each row corresponding to a equilibrated path, has a rank 4, so we have to include all 4 linearly independent paths for further consideration. With all four paths we have

$$\nabla_{\tilde{\mathbf{f}}}\tilde{\mathbf{c}}(\mathbf{f}^*,0) = \tilde{\Delta}^{\mathrm{T}}\nabla_{\mathbf{v}}\mathbf{t}(\mathbf{v}^*,0)\tilde{\Delta} = \begin{bmatrix} 1 & 0 & 0 \\ 0 & 1 & 0 \\ 1 & 1 & 0 \\ 0 & 0 & 1 \end{bmatrix}\begin{bmatrix} 1 & 0 & 0 \\ 0 & 1 & 0 \\ 0 & 0 & 4 \end{bmatrix}\begin{bmatrix} 1 & 0 & 1 & 0 \\ 0 & 1 & 1 & 0 \\ 0 & 0 & 0 & 1 \end{bmatrix} = \begin{bmatrix} 1 & 0 & 1 & 0 \\ 0 & 1 & 1 & 0 \\ 1 & 1 & 2 & 0 \\ 0 & 0 & 0 & 4 \end{bmatrix} \tag{4.52}$$

$$\left[\mathbf{J}_{\tilde{\mathbf{f}},\boldsymbol{\mu}}\right]^{-1} = \begin{bmatrix} 1 & 0 & 1 & 0 & -1 & 0 & 0 \\ 0 & 1 & 1 & 0 & 0 & -1 & 0 \\ 1 & 1 & 2 & 0 & 0 & 0 & -1 \\ 0 & 0 & 0 & 4 & 0 & 0 & -1 \\ 1 & 0 & 0 & 0 & 0 & 0 & 0 \\ 0 & 1 & 0 & 0 & 0 & 0 & 0 \\ 0 & 0 & 1 & 1 & 0 & 0 & 0 \end{bmatrix}^{-1} = \begin{bmatrix} 0 & 0 & 0 & 0 & 1 & 0 & 0 \\ 0 & 0 & 0 & 0 & 0 & 1 & 0 \\ 0 & 0 & 1/6 & -1/6 & -1/6 & -1/6 & 2/3 \\ 0 & 0 & -1/6 & 1/6 & 1/6 & 1/6 & 1/3 \\ -1 & 0 & 1/6 & -1/6 & 5/6 & -1/6 & 2/3 \\ 0 & -1 & 1/6 & -1/6 & -1/6 & 5/6 & 2/3 \\ 0 & 0 & -2/3 & -1/3 & 2/3 & 2/3 & 4/3 \end{bmatrix}$$

Thus we obtain the following link flow derivatives:

$$\nabla_{u_1}\mathbf{v}(u_1)\big|_{u_1=0.0} = \tilde{\Delta}\nabla_\varepsilon\tilde{\mathbf{f}} = \begin{bmatrix}1&0&1&0\\0&1&1&0\\0&0&0&1\end{bmatrix}\begin{bmatrix}0&0&0&0\\0&0&0&0\\0&0&1/6&-1/6\\0&0&-1/6&1/6\end{bmatrix}\begin{bmatrix}-1\\0\\-1\\0\end{bmatrix} = \begin{bmatrix}-1/6\\-1/6\\1/6\end{bmatrix}$$

which is identical with the left derivatives of equilibrium link flows in (4.51).

Without including the degenerate path 3, we have the following link/path and OD/path incidence matrices associated with the equilibrated paths:

$$\left[\bar{\Delta}^{\mathrm{T}}\middle|\bar{\Lambda}^{\mathrm{T}}\right] = \begin{bmatrix}1&0&0&1&0&0\\0&1&0&0&1&0\\0&0&1&0&0&1\end{bmatrix}$$

This matrix has a rank 3, so we have to include all 3 linearly independent paths ($\tilde{\Delta} = \bar{\Delta}$ and $\tilde{\Lambda} = \bar{\Lambda}$) for further consideration as follows:

$$\nabla_{\tilde{\mathbf{f}}}\tilde{\mathbf{c}}\left(\mathbf{f}^*,0\right) = \tilde{\Delta}^{\mathrm{T}}\nabla_{\mathbf{v}}\mathbf{t}\left(\mathbf{v}^*,0\right)\tilde{\Delta}$$

$$= \begin{bmatrix}1&0&0\\0&1&0\\0&0&1\end{bmatrix}\begin{bmatrix}1&0&0\\0&1&0\\0&0&4\end{bmatrix}\begin{bmatrix}1&0&0\\0&1&0\\0&0&1\end{bmatrix} = \begin{bmatrix}1&0&0\\0&1&0\\0&0&4\end{bmatrix}$$

$$\left[\mathbf{J}_{\tilde{\mathbf{f}},\mu}\right]^{-1} = \begin{bmatrix}1&0&0&-1&0&0\\0&1&0&0&-1&0\\0&0&4&0&0&-1\\1&0&0&0&0&0\\0&1&0&0&0&0\\0&0&1&0&0&0\end{bmatrix}^{-1} = \begin{bmatrix}0&0&0&1&0&-1\\0&0&0&0&1&0\\0&0&0&0&0&1\\-1&0&0&1&0&-1\\0&-1&0&0&1&0\\0&0&-1&0&0&4\end{bmatrix}$$

$$\nabla_{u_1}\mathbf{v}(u_1)\big|_{u_1=0.0} = \tilde{\Delta}\nabla_\varepsilon\tilde{\mathbf{f}} = \begin{bmatrix}1&0&0\\0&1&0\\0&0&1\end{bmatrix}\begin{bmatrix}0&0&0\\0&0&0\\0&0&0\end{bmatrix}\begin{bmatrix}-1\\0\\0\end{bmatrix} = \begin{bmatrix}0\\0\\0\end{bmatrix}$$

which once again exactly agrees with the right derivatives of equilibrium link flows in (4.51).

From the above simple example, we do find that application of the gradient formula can still provide meaningful information. It provides the left and right derivatives of link flows (if not differentiable) and the desired derivatives (if differentiable) when including or not including the degenerate path. This is indeed true when there exist one degenerate path and one perturbation only, as in the above examples. An intuitive interpretation is given here. The equilibrium link flow is piecewise differentiable, and the left (or right) derivative with respect to a perturbation corresponds to the case that the perturbation just causes the degenerate path to be abandoned or to come into use. Therefore, the inclusion or exclusion of the degenerate path provides either the right or left derivative of equilibrium link flows.

Note that the above observation cannot be generalized to the cases where a degenerate equilibrium point contains two or more degenerate paths (this is very unlikely in practice). The reasons are as follows. When there are two or more degenerate paths, the left (or right) derivatives of equilibrium link flows correspond to a particular inclusion (or exclusion) of a subset of the degenerate paths, but not inclusion (or exclusion) of any subset of the degenerate paths can provide the desired results. It is thus necessary to identify appropriate or relevant degenerate paths for the analysis of the left and right derivatives.

vi) Non- Invertibility of the Jacobian of the cost vector of independent working paths

Here it is worthwhile to emphasize that the Jacobian of the cost vector of the *equilibrated, linearly independent* working paths: $\nabla_{\tilde{\mathbf{f}}}\tilde{\mathbf{c}}(\mathbf{f}^*,0)=\tilde{\Delta}^{\mathrm{T}}\nabla_{\mathbf{v}}\mathbf{t}(\mathbf{v}^*,0)\tilde{\Delta}$ that appears in the sensitivity analysis formulas is in general not invertible (and, of course, not invertible at the extreme point of the feasible region of the equilibrium path flows considered in Tobin and Friesz (1988)). The reason is clear. Let the number of (linearly independent) paths included in $\tilde{\Delta}$ be m and the number of links in the network with positive flow be n. Then $\tilde{\Delta}^{\mathrm{T}}\nabla_{\mathbf{v}}\mathbf{t}(\mathbf{v}^*,0)\tilde{\Delta}$ is an $n\times n$ matrix, but its rank is m if $m<n$ (as assumed, $\nabla_{\mathbf{v}}\mathbf{t}(\mathbf{v}^*,0)$ is non-singular), thus $\tilde{\Delta}^{\mathrm{T}}\nabla_{\mathbf{v}}\mathbf{t}(\mathbf{v}^*,0)\tilde{\Delta}$ is not invertible. Indeed, as initially pointed out in Bell and Iida (1997) and cited recently in Patriksson (2004), there must be at least one possible path flow for each OD pair that carries a positive demand and in most realistic networks the number of used paths is far more than the number of links, the non-invertibility problem is thus expected to be prevalent in networks of a practical size. In fact, we have already encountered the non-invertibility of the matrix $\nabla_{\tilde{\mathbf{f}}}\tilde{\mathbf{c}}(\mathbf{f}^*,0)$ in Example 4.5, where one can easily check that the (4×4) matrix $\nabla_{\tilde{\mathbf{f}}}\tilde{\mathbf{c}}(\mathbf{f}^*,0)$ in eqn. (4.52) has a rank of 3.

The non-invertibility of the matrix $\nabla_{\tilde{\mathbf{f}}}\tilde{\mathbf{c}}(\mathbf{f}^*,0)=\tilde{\Delta}^{\mathrm{T}}\nabla_{\mathbf{v}}\mathbf{t}(\mathbf{v}^*,0)\tilde{\Delta}$ simply implies that one should work directly with $\left[\mathbf{J}_{\mathbf{f}^0,\mu}\right]^{-1}$, which is proved to exist, rather than make use of the inverse of the partitioned matrix in calculation of the derivatives of equilibrium link flows, unless it is already known that $\nabla_{\tilde{\mathbf{f}}}\tilde{\mathbf{c}}(\mathbf{f}^*,0)^{-1}$ exists.

Example 4.6 Consider a simple network depicted in Figure 4.6, with 3 nodes connected by two links in series. The link cost functions for the two links are shown in the network. Suppose there are three OD pairs: $1\rightarrow 2$, $2\rightarrow 3$ and $1\rightarrow 3$, all having the same (fixed) demand $d_{1\rightarrow 2}=d_{2\rightarrow 3}=d_{1\rightarrow 3}=5$.

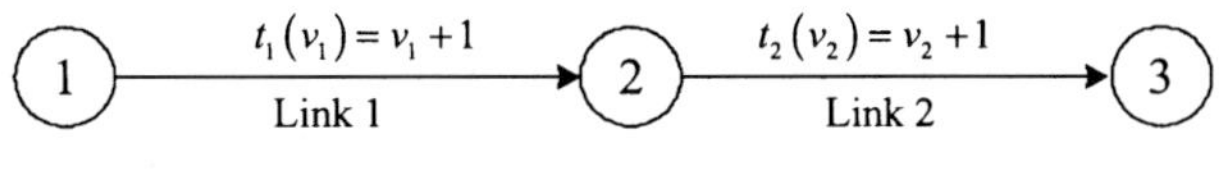

Figure 4.6 A simple network of two links in series connecting three OD pairs

Clearly, there are three paths denoted by $r_1 = \{1\}$, $r_2 = \{2\}$, and $r_3 = \{1,2\}$, one for each OD pair. The path costs in terms of path flows are given by:

$$c_1 = t_1(v_1) = f_1 + f_2 + 1,\ c_2 = t_2(v_2) = f_2 + f_3 + 1,\ c_3 = t_1(v_1) + t_2(v_2) = f_1 + f_2 + 2f_3 + 2$$

Since each OD pair is connected by a single path, all the three paths in the network must be included in the working path set. Let $\tilde{\mathbf{f}} = \mathbf{f} = (f_1, f_2, f_3)^{\mathrm{T}}$ and $\tilde{\mathbf{c}} = \mathbf{c} = (c_1, c_2, c_3)^{\mathrm{T}}$. In this case, the number of paths included for the sensitivity analysis is more than the number of links in the network and indeed $\nabla_{\tilde{\mathbf{f}}}\tilde{\mathbf{c}}(\mathbf{f}^*, 0)$ or $\tilde{\Delta}^{\mathrm{T}}\nabla_{\mathbf{v}}\mathbf{t}(\mathbf{v}^*, 0)\tilde{\Delta}$ ($\tilde{\Delta} = \Delta$ and $\tilde{\Lambda} = \Lambda$) is not invertible as we can see below:

$$\nabla_{\tilde{\mathbf{f}}}\tilde{\mathbf{c}}(\mathbf{f}^*, 0) = \begin{bmatrix} 1 & 0 & 1 \\ 0 & 1 & 1 \\ 1 & 1 & 2 \end{bmatrix} \quad \text{and} \quad \det\left[\nabla_{\tilde{\mathbf{f}}}\mathbf{c}(\mathbf{f}^*, 0)\right] = 0$$

Nevertheless, from (4.23) where $\nabla_{\mu}\mathbf{D}(\mu, 0) \equiv 0$ we have

$$\mathbf{J}_{\tilde{\mathbf{f}},\mu}(0) = \begin{bmatrix} 1 & 0 & 1 & -1 & 0 & 0 \\ 0 & 1 & 1 & 0 & -1 & 0 \\ 1 & 1 & 2 & 0 & 0 & -1 \\ 1 & 0 & 0 & 0 & 0 & 0 \\ 0 & 1 & 0 & 0 & 0 & 0 \\ 0 & 0 & 1 & 0 & 0 & 0 \end{bmatrix}$$

and its inverse exists and is given as follows

$$\left[\mathbf{J}_{\tilde{\mathbf{f}},\mu}\right]^{-1} = \begin{bmatrix} 0 & 0 & 0 & 1 & 0 & 0 \\ 0 & 0 & 0 & 0 & 1 & 0 \\ 0 & 0 & 0 & 0 & 0 & 1 \\ -1 & 0 & 0 & 1 & 0 & 1 \\ 0 & -1 & 0 & 0 & 1 & 1 \\ 0 & 0 & -1 & 1 & 1 & 2 \end{bmatrix}$$

If we assume a toll charge is introduced on link 1 and let $\varepsilon = u_1$, then $\nabla_{u_1}\mathbf{t}(\mathbf{v}^*, 0) = [1 \quad 0]^{\mathrm{T}}$ and $\nabla_{u_1}\mathbf{D}(\mu, 0) = [0 \quad 0 \quad 0]^{\mathrm{T}}$. All the derivatives of link flows in toll u_1 are intuitively zero because there is no route choice in this simple network with fixed demands. The derivatives at $\varepsilon = u_1 = 0$ can be readily found to be

$$\nabla_{u_1}\tilde{\mathbf{c}}(\mathbf{f}^*,0)=\tilde{\Delta}^{\mathrm{T}}\nabla_{u_1}\mathbf{t}(\mathbf{v}^*,0)=\begin{bmatrix}1&0&1\\0&1&1\end{bmatrix}^{\mathrm{T}}\begin{bmatrix}1\\0\end{bmatrix}=\begin{bmatrix}1\\0\\1\end{bmatrix}$$

Substituting the above results of $\left[\mathbf{J}_{\tilde{\mathbf{f}},\mu}\right]^{-1}$ and $\nabla_{\varepsilon}\tilde{\mathbf{c}}(\mathbf{f}^*,0)$ into (4.29) yields

$$\nabla_{\varepsilon}\tilde{\mathbf{f}}=\begin{bmatrix}0\\0\\0\end{bmatrix},\quad \nabla_{\varepsilon}\mathbf{v}=\tilde{\Delta}\nabla_{\varepsilon}\tilde{\mathbf{f}}=\begin{bmatrix}0\\0\end{bmatrix}$$

The result tells us that there is no change in path and link flows in all three OD pairs, as expected.

Next we assume that there is change in the fixed OD demand in OD pair $1\to3$ and let $\varepsilon=\delta d_{1\to3}$. Then in a similar manner, we have $\nabla_{\varepsilon}\mathbf{t}(\mathbf{v}^*,0)=[0\ \ 0]^{\mathrm{T}}$ and $\nabla_{\varepsilon}\mathbf{D}(\mu,0)=[0\ \ 0\ \ 1]^{\mathrm{T}}$. The derivatives at $\varepsilon=\delta d_{13}=0$ are given by

$$\nabla_{\varepsilon}\tilde{\mathbf{f}}=\begin{bmatrix}0\\0\\1\end{bmatrix},\quad \nabla_{\varepsilon}\mathbf{v}=\tilde{\Delta}\nabla_{\varepsilon}\tilde{\mathbf{f}}=\begin{bmatrix}1\\1\end{bmatrix},\quad \nabla_{\varepsilon}\mu=\begin{bmatrix}1\\0\\1\end{bmatrix}$$

Once again we obtain the expected derivative results.

Example 4.7 We consider the Network in Figure 4.1 with link cost functions (4.44) and OD demand $d_{1\to3}=2$ used in Example 4.1. Without toll charge $u_1^*=0$, we have the unique equilibrium link flow solution: $\mathbf{v}^*=(1,1,1,1)^{\mathrm{T}}$. The derivatives of equilibrium link flows with respect to u_1 at $u_1^*=0$ can be easily found from (4.46) in Example 4.2:

$$\nabla_{u_1}\mathbf{v}(u_1)_{u_1=0.0}=\left(-\frac{1}{2},\ \frac{1}{2},\ 0,\ 0\right)^{\mathrm{T}} \tag{4.53}$$

Now we consider application of the sensitivity analysis formula: Because all four paths are equilibrated paths, we have

$$\left[\bar{\Delta}^{\mathrm{T}}\middle|\bar{\Lambda}^{\mathrm{T}}\right]=\begin{bmatrix}1&0&1&0&1\\1&0&0&1&1\\0&1&1&0&1\\0&1&0&1&1\end{bmatrix} \tag{4.54}$$

This matrix, with each row corresponding to a path, has a rank 3, so we can choose three independent paths. It can be easily checked that paths r_1, r_2 and r_3 are linearly independent and are chosen here for further consideration. With this reduced set of paths we have

$$\nabla_{\tilde{\mathbf{f}}}\tilde{\mathbf{c}}\left(\mathbf{f}^*,0\right)=\tilde{\Delta}^{\mathrm{T}}\nabla_{\mathbf{v}}\mathbf{t}\left(\mathbf{v}^*,0\right)\tilde{\Delta}$$

$$=\begin{bmatrix}1&0&1&0\\1&0&0&1\\0&1&1&0\end{bmatrix}\begin{bmatrix}1&0&0&0\\0&1&0&0\\0&0&1&0\\0&0&0&1\end{bmatrix}\begin{bmatrix}1&1&0\\0&0&1\\1&0&1\\0&1&0\end{bmatrix}=\begin{bmatrix}2&1&1\\1&2&0\\1&0&2\end{bmatrix}$$

This matrix is invertible and hence the formulas for the inverse of a partitioned matrix can be applied. Here we use the following inverse of the Jacobian directly for our calculation:

$$\left[\mathbf{J}_{\tilde{\mathbf{f}},\mu}\right]^{-1}=\begin{bmatrix}2&1&1&-1\\1&2&0&-1\\1&0&2&-1\\1&1&1&0\end{bmatrix}^{-1}=\begin{bmatrix}1&-1/2&-1/2&0\\-1/2&1/2&0&1/2\\-1/2&0&1/2&1/2\\0&-1/2&-1/2&1\end{bmatrix}$$

Thus we obtain the following link flow derivatives:

$$\nabla_{u_1}\mathbf{v}\left(u_1\right)\Big|_{u_1^*=0.0}=\tilde{\Delta}\nabla_{\varepsilon}\tilde{\mathbf{f}}=\begin{bmatrix}1&1&0\\0&0&1\\1&0&1\\0&1&0\end{bmatrix}\begin{bmatrix}1&-1/2&-1/2&0\\-1/2&1/2&0&1/2\\-1/2&0&1/2&1/2\end{bmatrix}\begin{bmatrix}-1\\-1\\0\\0\end{bmatrix}=\begin{bmatrix}-1/2\\1/2\\0\\0\end{bmatrix}\qquad(4.55)$$

which is identical with the early solution in (4.53).

Example 4.8 We consider again the same network in Figure 4.1, but with the following link cost functions:

$$t_1=1+v_1+u_1,\ \ t_2=1+v_2,\ \ t_3=1+v_3+u_3,\ \ t_4=1+v_4$$

where both link 1 and link 3 are subjected to toll charge. In addition to the OD pair $1\rightarrow3$ considered earlier, we further add two OD pairs $1\rightarrow2$ and $2\rightarrow3$, and assume perturbations exist in all three OD demands given by $d_{1\rightarrow3}=2+\delta d_{1\rightarrow3}$, $d_{1\rightarrow2}=2+\delta d_{1\rightarrow2}$, $d_{2\rightarrow3}=2+\delta d_{2\rightarrow3}$. In this case we have five perturbation parameters denoted by

$$\varepsilon=\left(u_1,\ u_2,\ \delta d_{1\rightarrow3},\ \delta d_{1\rightarrow2},\ \delta d_{2\rightarrow3}\right)^{\mathrm{T}}$$

There are eight paths in the network denoted by: $r_1=\{1,3\}$, $r_2=\{1,4\}$, $r_3=\{2,3\}$, $r_4=\{2,4\}$, $r_5=\{1\}$, $r_6=\{2\}$, $r_7=\{3\}$, $r_8=\{4\}$. The number of paths is larger than the sum of the number of links and number of OD pairs.

Without toll charge and demand perturbation:

$$\varepsilon=\left(u_1,\ u_3,\ \delta d_{1\rightarrow3},\ \delta d_{1\rightarrow2},\ \delta d_{2\rightarrow3}\right)^{\mathrm{T}}=\left(0,0,0,0,0\right)^{\mathrm{T}}$$

We have an obvious unique (unperturbed) equilibrium link flow solution: $\mathbf{v}^*=\left(2,2,2,2\right)^{\mathrm{T}}$. Without difficulty, the derivatives of link flows with respect to ε at $\varepsilon=0$ can be found analytically as:

$$\nabla_{\varepsilon}\mathbf{v}(\varepsilon)\Big|_{\varepsilon=0.0}=\left[\nabla_{\mathbf{u}}\mathbf{v}(\varepsilon)\Big|_{\mathbf{u}=0.0},\ \nabla_{\delta\mathbf{d}}\mathbf{v}(\varepsilon)\Big|_{\delta\mathbf{d}=0.0}\right]=\begin{bmatrix}-1/2 & 0 & 1/2 & 1/2 & 0\\ 1/2 & 0 & 1/2 & 1/2 & 0\\ 0 & -1/2 & 1/2 & 0 & 1/2\\ 0 & 1/2 & 1/2 & 0 & 1/2\end{bmatrix} \tag{4.56}$$

Now we consider application of the sensitivity analysis formula. Again all four paths are equilibrated, and we have

$$\left[\bar{\Delta}^{\mathrm{T}}\,\middle|\,\bar{\Lambda}^{\mathrm{T}}\right]=\begin{bmatrix}1&0&1&0&1&0&0\\1&0&0&1&1&0&0\\0&1&1&0&1&0&0\\0&1&0&1&1&0&0\\1&0&0&0&0&1&0\\0&1&0&0&0&1&0\\0&0&1&0&0&0&1\\0&0&0&1&0&0&1\end{bmatrix} \tag{4.57}$$

This matrix, with each row corresponding to each equilibrated path, has a rank 5, so we can choose five independent paths out of the 8 equilibrated paths. It can be easily checked that paths r_1, r_2, r_3, r_5, r_7 are linearly independent and are chosen here for further consideration. With this reduced set of working paths, we have

$$\nabla_{\tilde{\mathbf{f}}}\tilde{\mathbf{c}}\left(\mathbf{f}^*,0\right)=\tilde{\Delta}^{\mathrm{T}}\nabla_{\mathbf{v}}\mathbf{t}\left(\mathbf{v}^*,0\right)\tilde{\Delta}$$

$$=\begin{bmatrix}1&0&1&0\\1&0&0&1\\0&1&1&0\\1&0&0&0\\0&0&1&0\end{bmatrix}\begin{bmatrix}1&0&0&0\\0&1&0&0\\0&0&1&0\\0&0&0&1\end{bmatrix}\begin{bmatrix}1&1&0&1&0\\0&0&1&0&0\\1&0&1&0&1\\0&1&0&0&0\end{bmatrix}=\begin{bmatrix}2&1&1&1&1\\1&2&0&1&0\\1&0&2&0&1\\1&1&0&1&0\\1&0&1&0&1\end{bmatrix}$$

The above Jacobian of the reduced path cost vector is singular (with a rank equal to 4). Nevertheless, the Jacobian $\mathbf{J}_{\tilde{\mathbf{f}},\mu}$ is invertible and its inverse is given by:

$$\left[\mathbf{J}_{\tilde{\mathbf{f}},\mu}\right]^{-1}=\begin{bmatrix}2&1&1&1&1&-1&0&0\\1&2&0&1&0&-1&0&0\\1&0&2&0&1&-1&0&0\\1&1&0&1&0&0&-1&0\\1&0&1&0&1&0&0&-1\\1&1&1&0&0&0&0&0\\0&0&0&1&0&0&0&0\\0&0&0&0&1&0&0&0\end{bmatrix}^{-1}=\begin{bmatrix}1&-1/2&-1/2&0&0&0&-1/2&-1/2\\-1/2&1/2&0&0&0&1/2&0&1/2\\-1/2&0&1/2&0&0&1/2&1/2&0\\0&0&0&0&0&0&1&0\\0&0&0&0&0&0&0&1\\0&-1/2&-1/2&0&0&1&1/2&1/2\\1/2&0&-1/2&-1&0&1/2&1/2&0\\1/2&-1/2&0&0&-1&1/2&0&1/2\end{bmatrix}$$

Then the link flow derivatives are given by:

$$\nabla_\varepsilon \mathbf{v}(\varepsilon)\big|_{\varepsilon=0.0} = \tilde{\Delta}\nabla_\varepsilon \tilde{\mathbf{f}}$$

$$= \begin{bmatrix} 1 & 1 & 0 & 1 & 0 \\ 0 & 0 & 1 & 0 & 0 \\ 1 & 0 & 1 & 0 & 1 \\ 0 & 1 & 0 & 0 & 0 \end{bmatrix} \begin{bmatrix} 1 & -1/2 & -1/2 & 0 & 0 & 0 & -1/2 & -1/2 \\ -1/2 & 1/2 & 0 & 0 & 0 & 1/2 & 0 & 1/2 \\ -1/2 & 0 & 1/2 & 0 & 0 & 1/2 & 1/2 & 0 \\ 0 & 0 & 0 & 0 & 0 & 0 & 1 & 0 \\ 0 & 0 & 0 & 0 & 0 & 0 & 0 & 1 \end{bmatrix} \begin{bmatrix} -1 & -1 & 0 & 0 & 0 \\ -1 & 0 & 0 & 0 & 0 \\ 0 & -1 & 0 & 0 & 0 \\ -1 & 0 & 0 & 0 & 0 \\ 0 & -1 & 0 & 0 & 0 \\ 0 & 0 & 1 & 0 & 0 \\ 0 & 0 & 0 & 1 & 0 \\ 0 & 0 & 0 & 0 & 1 \end{bmatrix}$$

$$= \begin{bmatrix} -1/2 & 0 & 1/2 & 1/2 & 0 \\ 1/2 & 0 & 1/2 & 1/2 & 0 \\ 0 & -1/2 & 1/2 & 0 & 1/2 \\ 0 & 1/2 & 1/2 & 0 & 1/2 \end{bmatrix}$$

The results are identical with those identified analytically.

vii) Infeasibility with an extreme point

As mentioned before, the sensitivity analysis formula developed by Tobin and Friesz (1988) is based on the choice of a non-degenerate extreme point $\bar{\mathbf{f}}^*$ of the polyhedron $\bar{\Omega}(0)$ which should have exactly as many paths with a strictly positive flow as the rank of the matrix $\begin{bmatrix} \bar{\Delta} \\ \hline \bar{\Lambda} \end{bmatrix}$. This condition cannot always be fulfilled as already demonstrated by an example in Josefsson and Patriksson (2003). To see this, we revisit Example 4.1 with the equilibrium path flows given by (4.45).

$$\bar{f}_1^* = \rho,\ \bar{f}_2^* = 1-\rho,\ \bar{f}_3^* = 1-\rho,\ \bar{f}_4^* = \rho,\ 0 \le \rho \le 1.0 \tag{4.58}$$

It is clear that there are two extreme points given by

$$\bar{\mathbf{f}}_1^* = (0,\ 1,\ 1,\ 0)^{\mathrm{T}} \ \text{ and } \ \bar{\mathbf{f}}_2^* = (1,\ 0,\ 0,\ 1)^{\mathrm{T}}$$

The equilibrium point is not degenerate and hence differentiable since we have $\bar{\mathbf{f}}^* > 0$ for any $0 < \rho < 1.0$. Indeed, the derivatives of equilibrium link flows with respect to u_1 at $u_1^* = 0$ are already obtained as given in (4.55) of Example 4.7. Nonetheless, either one of the two extreme points has and only has two paths with positive flows, which is not equal to the number of the rank 3 of the matrix $\begin{bmatrix} \bar{\Delta} \\ \hline \bar{\Lambda} \end{bmatrix}$ or $\left[\bar{\Delta}^{\mathrm{T}} \middle| \bar{\Lambda}^{\mathrm{T}}\right]$ given in (4.54).

Likewise, if we work with Example 4.8 with three OD pairs and eight equilibrated paths for the network in Figure 4.1, there are four extreme points given below:

$$\bar{\mathbf{f}}_1^* = (2,\ 0,\ 0,\ 0,\ 0,\ 2,\ 0,\ 2)^{\mathrm{T}},\quad \bar{\mathbf{f}}_2^* = (0,\ 2,\ 0,\ 0,\ 0,\ 2,\ 2,\ 0)^{\mathrm{T}}$$

$$\bar{\mathbf{f}}_3^* = (0,\ 0,\ 2,\ 0,\ 2,\ 0,\ 0,\ 2)^{\mathrm{T}}, \quad \bar{\mathbf{f}}_4^* = (0,\ 0,\ 0,\ 2,\ 2,\ 0,\ 2,\ 0)^{\mathrm{T}}$$

Once again, the number of paths with strictly positive flows at all four extreme points is 3, which is less than the number of rank 5 of the corresponding matrix $\left[\bar{\Delta}^{\mathrm{T}} \middle| \bar{\Lambda}^{\mathrm{T}}\right]$ given in (4.57) of Example 4.8.

4.3.4 A Sensitivity Analysis based Algorithm

In the application of the sensitivity analysis based algorithm for the second-best pricing problem formulated as an MPEC or BLPP in (4.1)-(4.5) presented in Section 4.2, the above sensitivity analysis for the elastic-demand network equilibrium problem is implemented to calculate the derivatives of equilibrium travel demand, $\mathbf{d}(\mathbf{u})$, and equilibrium link flow, $\mathbf{v}(\mathbf{u})$, with respect to link tolls, $\mathbf{u}$. With the derivative information, the upper-level objective function and capacity constraints, which are implicit, nonlinear functions of link tolls, $\mathbf{u}$, are linearly approximated using Taylor's formula. This algorithm is outlined below.

Sensitivity analysis based algorithm

Step 0. (*Initialization*) Determine an initial set of link toll pattern $\mathbf{u}^{(0)}$. Set $n := 0$.

Step 1. (*Traffic assignment*) Solve the lower-level elastic-demand network equilibrium problem for given $\mathbf{u}^{(n)}$ and hence get $\mathbf{d}^{(n)}$ and $\mathbf{v}^{(n)}$.

Step 2. (*Sensitivity analysis*) Calculate the derivatives, $\partial \mathbf{d}^{(n)} / \partial \mathbf{u}$ and $\partial \mathbf{v}^{(n)} / \partial \mathbf{u}$, using the sensitivity analysis method for the elastic-demand network equilibrium problem.

Step 3. (*Linear approximation*) Formulate local linear approximations of the upper-level objective function and capacity constraints using the derivative information, and solve the resulting linear programming problem to obtain an auxiliary solution $\tilde{\mathbf{u}}^{(n)}$.

Step 4. (*Updating*) Compute $\mathbf{u}^{(n+1)} = \mathbf{u}^{(n)} + \alpha^{(n)}\left(\tilde{\mathbf{u}}^{(n)} - \mathbf{u}^{(n)}\right)$ where $\alpha^{(n)}$ is a predetermined sequence of monotonically decreasing step sizes satisfying the conditions: $\sum_{n=1}^{\infty} \alpha^{(n)} = \infty$, $\sum_{n=1}^{\infty} \left(\alpha^{(n)}\right)^2 < \infty$. A simple sequence, $\alpha^{(n)} = \gamma/(1+n)$ $(\gamma > 0)$, can be used.

Step 5. (*Convergence check*) If $\left\|\mathbf{u}^{(n+1)} - \mathbf{u}^{(n)}\right\| \le \varepsilon$ for all $a \in \bar{A}$ then stop where ε is a predetermined tolerance. Otherwise, let $n := n+1$ and return to Step 1.

4.4 APPLICATIONS OF THE SENSITIVITY ANALYSIS METHOD

We now present a numerical example to illustrate how to use the sensitivity analysis method for obtaining the derivative information of interest. The road network, as shown in Figure 4.7, has 11 links and 7 nodes. The following link cost function, including a link toll, is the input, together with link free-flow travel time, t_a^0, link physical capacity, C_a, and link environmental capacity (to be used later), $\overline{C}_a$, given in Table 4.1.

$$t_a(v_a, u_a) = t_a^0\left(1+0.15\left(\frac{v_a}{C_a}\right)^4\right)+u_a \tag{4.59}$$

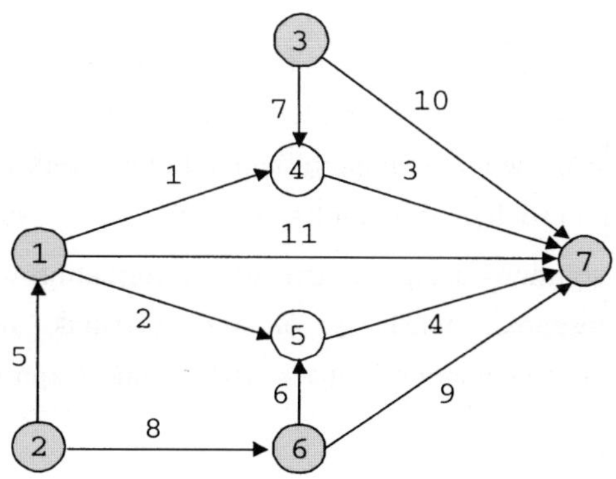

Figure 4.7 The network used for sensitivity analysis and application

Table 4.1 Input data for the example network

Link a	1	2	3	4	5	6	7	8	9	10	11
t_a^0	6	5	6	7	6	1	5	10	11	11	15
C_a	200	200	200	200	100	100	150	150	200	200	200
$\overline{C}_a$	160	150	200	150	100	100	150	100	160	160	150

It is assumed that there are 4 OD pairs (1→7, 2→7, 3→7 and 6→7) and the demand functions are given below:

$$D_{1\to7}(\mu_{1\to7}) = 600\exp(-0.04\mu_{1\to7});\quad D_{2\to7}(\mu_{2\to7}) = 500\exp(-0.03\mu_{2\to7})$$

$$D_{3\to7}(\mu_{3\to7}) = 500\exp(-0.05\mu_{3\to7});\quad D_{6\to7}(\mu_{6\to7}) = 400\exp(-0.05\mu_{6\to7})$$

where μ is the generalized travel costs between OD pairs.

Table 4.2 presents the derivatives of link flows $\mathbf{v}$ and OD demands $\mathbf{d}$ with respect to all link tolls at $u_a = 1.0$ for all $a \in A$ (note that link toll is measured in equivalent travel time units). From Table 4.2 it is interesting to note that

$$\frac{\partial v_b(\mathbf{u})}{\partial u_a} = \frac{\partial v_a(\mathbf{u})}{\partial u_b} \quad \text{for any } b \neq a,\ b \in A,\ a \in A \tag{4.60}$$

This means that the marginal impacts of link tolls on link flows are symmetric. In fact this symmetric effect can be easily confirmed from the theoretical sensitivity analysis formula (4.32) derived earlier.

The derivative information obtained is very useful in the design and operation of toll road systems. It produces the optimal 'direction' in which the flow pattern of the elastic-demand network equilibrium problem can move if the road tolls are changed, and thus the pricing strategies that should be sought for optimization of a system objective function. An important application of the sensitivity analysis results shown in Table 4.2 is the estimation of nearby solutions for any combination of link toll changes, once an equilibrium solution has been calculated. Table 4.3 presents the unperturbed solutions (link flows and OD demands) to the network equilibrium problem at link tolls $u_a = 1.0$, $a \in A$. Numerical comparisons of the estimated perturbed solutions using the derivative information with the actual perturbed solutions are also presented, when 3 of the 11 link tolls are changed by $\delta u_9 = \delta u_{10} = \delta u_{11} = 0.10$. The estimation is made using a linear approximation based on the derivative in Table 4.2.

One more important application of the sensitivity analysis results is the calculation of the elasticity of OD demand or link flows with respect to the toll charge levied on a particular link. This kind of elasticity is quite useful in road pricing analysis, but cannot be simply obtained with the conventional simplified technique that is based on explicit, abstract demand models. Given the values of the derivative of link flows in Table 4.2, the elasticity, $E_{v_b}^{u_a}$ of link flow, v_b, $b \in A$ with respect to link toll, u_a, $a \in A$ can be calculated as

$$E_{v_b}^{u_a} = \frac{\partial v_b(\mathbf{u})}{\partial u_a}\frac{u_a}{v_b},\quad b \in A,\ a \in A \tag{4.61}$$

where we have the direct toll elasticity of link flow when $a = b$ and cross toll elasticity of link flow when $a \neq b$. For example, from Table 4.2 and Table 4.3 we have

$$E_{v_1}^{u_1} = -26.61 \times \frac{1.0}{196.30} = -0.14,\quad E_{v_1}^{u_2} = 8.34 \times \frac{1.0}{196.30} = 0.04,\quad E_{v_1}^{u_3} = -13.16 \times \frac{1.0}{196.30} = -0.07$$

It is clear that the cross elasticity (or derivative) can be either positive or negative, indicating two substitutable or two complementary toll roads. Formally, toll road a and b are substitutes if $\partial v_b(\mathbf{u})/\partial u_a > 0$ (or equivalently $E_{v_b}^{u_a} > 0$) and complements if $\partial v_b(\mathbf{u})/\partial u_a < 0$

(or equivalently $E_{v_b}^{u_a} < 0$). The cross toll elasticity of the link flow given by (4.61) can be used to measure the degree of flow interdependence among toll roads, which depends on, among many factors, the network topology and OD demand pattern. Clearly, If $\partial v_b(\mathbf{u})/\partial u_a = 0,\ a \neq b$, then the two toll roads are said to be independent.

Likewise, given the values of the derivative of OD demands in Table 4.2, the elasticity, $E_{d_w}^{u_a}$ of demand between a specific O-D pair $w \in W$ with respect to toll u_a levied on a particular link $a \in A$ can be calculated as

$$E_{d_w}^{u_a} = \frac{\partial d_w(\mathbf{u})}{\partial u_a}\frac{u_a}{d_w},\quad w \in W,\ a \in A \tag{4.62}$$

Once again, as examples, we have

$$E_{d_{3\to7}}^{u_1} = 4.43 \times \frac{1.0}{246.86} = 0.018 \text{ and } E_{d_{3\to7}}^{u_3} = -3.86 \times \frac{1.0}{246.86} = -0.016$$

The toll elasticity or derivatives of OD demands can be either positive or negative.

Table 4.2 Derivatives of link flows, OD demands and objective functions with respect to link tolls at $u_a = 1.0$ for all links

Variable	$\partial(\cdot)/\partial u_1$	$\partial(\cdot)/\partial u_2$	$\partial(\cdot)/\partial u_3$	$\partial(\cdot)/\partial u_4$	$\partial(\cdot)/\partial u_5$	$\partial(\cdot)/\partial u_6$
v_1	-26.61	8.34	-13.16	4.41	-1.50	-3.92
v_2	8.34	-38.26	4.12	-17.54	-6.80	20.71
v_3	-13.16	4.12	-24.89	2.18	-0.74	-1.94
v_4	4.41	-17.54	2.18	-21.51	-0.89	-3.97
v_5	-1.50	-6.80	-0.74	-0.89	-12.44	5.91
v_6	-3.92	20.71	-1.94	-3.97	5.91	-24.68
v_7	13.45	-4.21	-11.73	-2.23	0.76	1.98
v_8	0.72	7.45	0.36	0.25	10.17	-7.20
v_9	3.69	-10.53	1.82	3.35	3.38	13.88
v_{10}	-9.02	2.83	7.87	1.50	-0.51	-1.33
v_{11}	14.47	19.94	7.16	10.56	-3.58	-9.39
$d_{1\to7}$	-2.31	-3.18	-1.14	-1.68	0.57	1.50
$d_{2\to7}$	-0.78	0.65	-0.38	-0.64	-2.27	-1.29
$d_{3\to7}$	4.43	-1.39	-3.86	-0.73	0.25	0.65
$d_{6\to7}$	-0.96	2.73	-0.47	-0.87	-0.88	-3.60

Table 4.2 Continued

Variables	$\partial(\cdot)/\partial u_7$	$\partial(\cdot)/\partial u_8$	$\partial(\cdot)/\partial u_9$	$\partial(\cdot)/\partial u_{10}$	$\partial(\cdot)/\partial u_{11}$
v_1	13.45	0.72	3.69	-9.02	14.47
v_2	-4.21	7.45	-10.53	2.83	19.94
v_3	-11.73	0.36	1.82	7.87	7.16
v_4	-2.23	0.25	3.35	1.50	10.56
v_5	0.76	10.17	3.38	-0.51	-3.58
v_6	1.98	-7.20	13.88	-1.33	-9.39
v_7	-25.18	-0.36	-1.86	16.89	-7.31
v_8	-0.36	-14.02	-5.42	0.24	1.72
v_9	-1.86	-5.42	-23.56	1.25	8.82
v_{10}	18.69	0.24	1.25	-19.61	4.91
v_{11}	-7.31	1.72	8.82	4.91	-43.50
$d_{1\to7}$	1.17	-0.27	-1.41	-0.78	-5.51
$d_{2\to7}$	0.39	-3.85	-2.03	-0.26	-1.85
$d_{3\to7}$	-8.29	-0.12	-0.61	-2.72	-2.41
$d_{6\to7}$	0.48	1.41	-4.26	-0.32	-2.29

Table 4.3 Estimated and exact solutions of link flows and OD demands for perturbed link tolls by $\delta u_9 = \delta u_{10} = \delta u_{11} = 0.1$ with respect to link tolls at $u_a = 1.0$ for all links

Solution Variable	Unperturbed Solution	Exact Solution	Estimated Solution
v_1	196.30	197.32	197.22
v_2	95.67	96.97	96.90
v_3	230.34	231.83	232.03
v_4	245.55	247.18	247.09
v_5	112.34	112.30	112.27
v_6	149.88	150.21	150.20
v_7	34.04	34.50	34.81
v_8	124.87	124.48	124.52
v_9	182.37	180.94	181.02
v_{10}	212.81	211.63	211.47
v_{11}	131.54	128.31	128.56
$d_{1\to7}$	311.17	310.30	310.40
$d_{2\to7}$	237.21	236.78	236.79
$d_{3\to7}$	246.86	246.13	246.28
$d_{6\to7}$	207.38	206.67	206.69

4.5 TRAFFIC RESTRAINT AND ROAD PRICING PROBLEM

Increasing levels of road traffic congestion have other important external costs, such as environmental effects, and as a result the need to find effective means of relieving congestion, such as congestion pricing, has become an issue of great and urgent social importance. Against this background, here we consider application of the bi-level programming model and the sensitivity analysis based approach presented in this chapter to a specialized, but meaningful second-best road pricing problem – the traffic restraint and road pricing problem. The problem is to seek a link toll pattern on a road network so as to hold traffic demand within a given threshold level, such as network environmental or physical capacity.

4.5.1 A Conceptual Framework

The general point of view here is that, when the potential traffic demand is high enough to cause congestion and queuing in the road networks, queuing delay at saturated links and thus travel cost between OD pairs affected will grow, causing the realized traffic demand to decrease to the capacity of the network. Finally, the resultant demand and travel cost will match each other, leading to a steady state queuing network equilibrium.

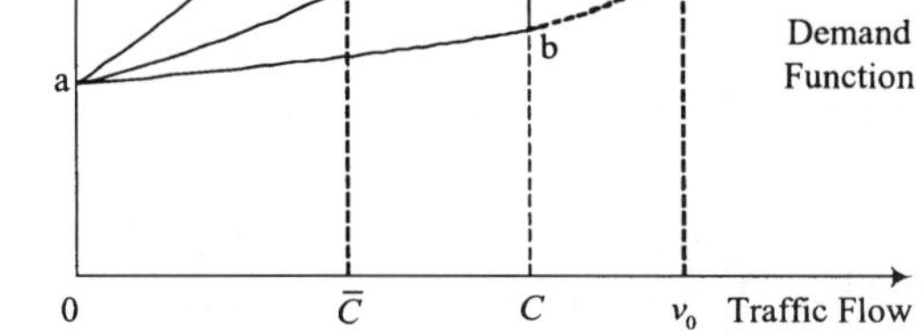

Figure 4.8 Demand-performance equilibrium with capacity constraints

Figure 4.8 depicts a performance curve showing how the generalized travel cost increases with the traffic flow, under different charging schemes as dictated by the various performance curves P. The figure also depicts a demand curve which shows the traffic flow, associated with any given generalized travel cost. From this figure, we can say that an equilibrium point e_0 with a level of flow v_0 would have been achieved if there was no capacity constraint on the network. The corresponding equilibrium demand without capacity constraint exceeds both physical capacity C and environment capacity $\bar{C}$ of the network ($v_0 > C$ and $v_0 > \bar{C}$). In reality, as traffic flow reaches network physical capacity $(v = C)$, vehicle queues will occur and drivers experience corresponding queuing delay. The actual supply performance curve will become a-b-e_0' where the vertical segment represents the queuing delay. The actual queuing delay will grow sufficiently to match the corresponding demand at network capacity, and thus the equilibrium point e_0' is reached, and the corresponding queuing delay is $\overline{be_0'}$.

Because queuing delay constitutes wasted time, it may be desirable to remove the queues by toll charges from the viewpoint of society. As stated earlier, this could be done by simply substituting the queuing delay $\overline{be_0'}$ with an equivalent amount of toll. However, in reality, it might be required to bring down the network demand to a level lower than its physical capacity. A typical situation is that the traffic volume through each street of the network or total amount of vehicle-kilometers over the network should not exceed a certain threshold for environmental damage, as discussed briefly in Chapter 3. From Figure 4.8, we can see that under road pricing scheme P_1, the equilibrium demand, v_1, corresponding to point e_1 is less than the network physical capacity, but greater than its environmental capacity ($\bar{C} < v_1 < C$). Under road pricing scheme P_2, the equilibrium demand, v_2, corresponding to point e_2 satisfies both physical and environmental capacity constraints. Therefore the problem of interest here is to find a road pricing scheme that holds the traffic flow within a given level such as below the network environment or physical capacity.

4.5.2 Direct Solution with the Queuing Network Equilibrium Model

Consider an elastic demand UE problem with link capacity constraints introduced in Chapter 2 as follows:

$$\min_{(\mathbf{v},\mathbf{d})\in\Omega} \sum_{a\in A}\int_0^{v_a} t_a(\omega)d\omega - \sum_{w\in W}\int_0^{d_w} B_w(\omega)d\omega \tag{4.63}$$

subject to

$$v_a \le C_a, \quad a\in A \tag{4.64}$$

where C_a is the capacity of link a and Ω is defined in (4.4). As discussed in Chapter 2 and Chapter 3, this minimization problem has following complementary slackness conditions at an optimum solution $(\mathbf{f}^*, \mathbf{v}^*, \mathbf{d}^*)$.

$$c_{rw} = \mu_w \text{ if } f_{rw}^* > 0;\ c_{rw} \geq \mu_w \text{ if } f_{rw}^* = 0,\ r \in R_w, w \in W \tag{4.65}$$

$$B_w\left(d_w^*\right) = \mu_w, \text{ if } d_w^* > 0;\ B_w\left(d_w^*\right) \leq \mu_w, \text{ if } d_w^* = 0,\ w \in W \tag{4.66}$$

$$\lambda_a = 0, \text{ if } v_a^* < C_a;\ \lambda_a \geq 0, \text{ if } v_a^* = C_a,\ a \in A \tag{4.67}$$

where μ_w is the minimum travel cost between OD pair $w \in W$, $\lambda_a, a \in A$ is the Lagrange multiplier associated with capacity constraint (4.64) and

$$c_{rw} = \sum_{a \in A} \bar{t}_a\left(v_a^*\right)\delta_{ar},\ \bar{t}_a\left(v_a^*\right) = t_a\left(v_a^*\right) + \lambda_a \tag{4.68}$$

and λ_a is the Lagrange multiplier associated with constraint (4.64) for link $a \in A$. The constraint set of problem (4.63)-(4.64) is linear and hence convex, and the objective function is strictly convex with respect to link flow and OD demand variables, and a feasible solution is guaranteed in which the equilibrium OD demands and link flows are determined uniquely.

Multiplying both sides of the equality $c_{rw} = \mu_w$ for $f_{rw}^* > 0$ and inequality $c_{rw} \geq \mu_w$ for $f_{rw}^* = 0$ by f_{rw}^* for each path $r \in R_w$ and for each OD pair $w \in W$ in (4.65), we have

$$\sum_{a \in A} t_a f_{rw}^* \delta_{ar} + \sum_{a \in A} \lambda_a f_{rw}^* \delta_{ar} = \mu_w f_{rw}^*,\ r \in R_w, w \in W \tag{4.69}$$

Clearly the equation holds for both $f_{rw}^* > 0$ and $f_{rw}^* = 0$. Taking the summation of both sides of (4.69) over all paths and all OD pair and using the flow conservation relations $v_a^* = \sum_{w \in W} \sum_{r \in R_w} f_{rw}^* \delta_{ar}$, $a \in A$, and $d_w = \sum_{r \in R_w} f_{rw}^*$, $w \in W$ we can easily obtain

$$\sum_{a \in A} \lambda_a v_a^* = \sum_{a \in A} \lambda_a C_a = \sum_{w \in W} \mu_w d_w - \sum_{a \in A} t_a\left(v_a^*\right) v_a^* \tag{4.70}$$

This interesting results tell us that the total queuing delay is unique since the link flow, OD demand and OD cost solutions are unique due to the convexity of the problem.

Consequently, by solving the above elastic-demand network equilibrium problem with capacity constraints, we can determine the queuing delays at bottleneck links. By charging a toll equivalent to the queuing delay, we can obtain an un-queued equilibrium network flow pattern that satisfies the network physical capacity constraints. Furthermore, if it is assumed that all users have an identical value of time, this toll charge produces no losses for road users, as long as the toll is not beyond the queuing delay, because it simply substitutes a charge for wasted time, for which road users are indifferent.

Note that constraint (4.64) in the elastic-demand network equilibrium model is not necessarily associated with link physical capacity. If we wish to restrain traffic flows through charging to satisfy the environmental capacity constraint, then at the equilibrium point of demand-supply, there should be no queue, because in general the environmental capacity of a link is less than its physical capacity, which means link flows are not allowed to reach their physical capacities. To this end, we can still use the above elastic-demand network equilibrium model (4.63)-(4.64) to obtain a particular link toll solution that could reduce travel demand to satisfy the environmental capacity constraint. In this case, what we need to do is just to replace C_a, $a \in A$ in (4.64) with the link environmental capacity $\bar{C}_a$ ($< C_a$), $a \in A$. Solving the corresponding elastic-demand network equilibrium problem, we can obtain an "imaginary queuing delay pattern", which provides a feasible solution of link tolls that could be used to hold network travel demand within environmental capacity. In addition, as we understand from (4.70), the total toll revenue generated from the proposed traffic restraint and road pricing scheme is constant for a given link flow constraint level.

4.5.3 Non-uniqueness of Link Tolls for Environmental Capacity Constraint

It is important to note that the aforementioned method just provides one possible solution of link tolls for traffic restraint. In general link tolls that could reduce realized travel demand to the capacity of the network are not unique; the solution obtained above may not represent the most desirable one. Now we employ a simple example to illustrate the non-uniqueness of the link toll solution for the traffic restraint problem. A simple linear network shown in Figure 4.9 with two links, denoted as 1 and 2, is used. There are two OD pairs from 1 to 3 and from 2 to 3, respectively. The demand functions are given by $d_{1\to3} = 15 - \mu_{1\to3}$ and $d_{2\to3} = 10 - \mu_{2\to3}$. The link cost functions including link toll are given by $t_1 = 2 + v_1 + u_1$ and $t_2 = 3 + v_2 + u_2$.

Without toll charge ($u_1 = u_2 = 0$) and without considering capacity constraint, we have the following equilibrium solution: $d_{1\to3} = 2.6$, $d_{2\to3} = 2.2$, $v_1 = 2.6$ and $v_2 = 4.8$.

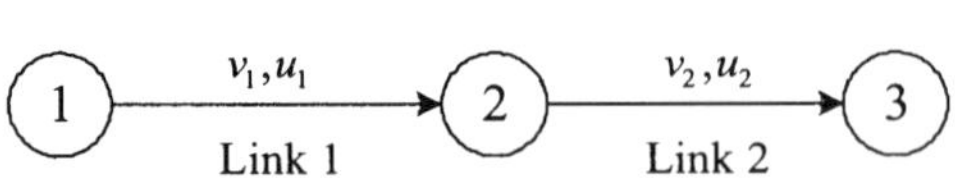

Figure 4.9 A simple linear network with elastic demand

Suppose the physical capacities of link 1 and 2 are $C_1 = 2.0$ and $C_2 = 4.0$, respectively (note that here the physical capacity of a link may be interpreted as saturation flow rate or exit capacity at the destination node of the link, because queues arise at intersections where capacity is least). Then we have the following queuing equilibrium solution: $d_{1\to3} = 2.0$, $d_{2\to3} = 2.0$, $v_1 = 2.0$, $v_2 = 4.0$, $\lambda_1 = 1.0$ and $\lambda_2 = 1.0$.

Both links become saturated, and queues occur, and queuing delays sufficient to match demand to the available capacity are generated. Note that the active capacity constraints in this case are linearly independent so the queuing delays are unique. If we only wish to eliminate the queues, we can replace the queuing delay (λ_1,λ_2) with an equivalent amount of tolls (u_1,u_2). In this case, link flow will be exactly equal to link exit capacity, but no queues occur. Of course, higher toll charges could achieve the same objective by reducing the link flow lower than its exit capacity, but the overcharging of users may give rise to socially non-optimal traffic demand realization.

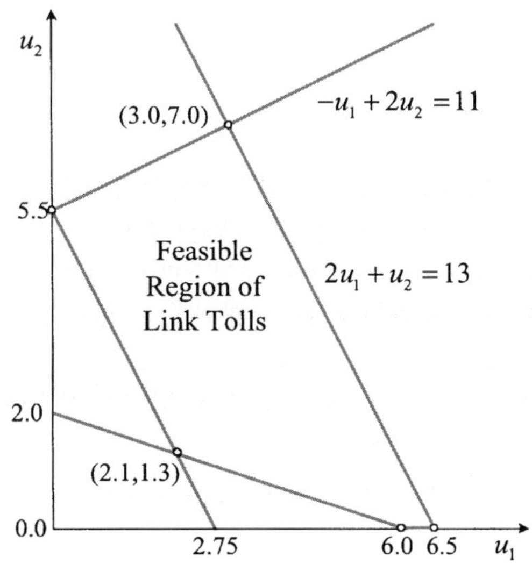

Figure 4.10 Feasible region of the link tolls satisfying environmental capacity constraints

Now suppose we wish to reduce the demand below environmental capacity (assumed to be lower than physical capacity) through road pricing, and the environmental capacities for the two links are assumed to be, $\bar{C}_1=1.5$, $\bar{C}_2=3.6$. It can be easily found that any combination of link tolls (u_1,u_2) in the shaded area of Figure 4.10 could hold the demand within the capacity constraint (here, upper limits of link tolls are imposed to ensure there would be positive demand given by the linear demand function). Therefore, the link toll pattern that could hold demand within a desirable level generally constitutes a feasible region rather than a unique point.

4.5.4 Selection of Optimal Tolls by Bi-level Programming

We have demonstrated that the link toll that could reduce demand to or below a given level is not unique, and the aforementioned method may not give the most desirable solution. Therefore, we must consider a second objective function to choose the best toll pattern from the set of feasible solutions. Many alternative system performance measures could be adopted for the selection of the optimal link tolls. Meaningful objectives would be the total realized travel demand or total revenue raised from toll charges. The total realized travel demand, denoted as F_1, is given by

$$F_1(\mathbf{u}, \mathbf{d}(\mathbf{u})) = \sum_{w \in W} d_w \tag{4.71}$$

where $\mathbf{u}$ is a vector of link tolls. The total revenue, denoted as F_2, arising from toll charges can be expressed as:

$$F_2(\mathbf{u}, \mathbf{v}(\mathbf{u})) = \sum_{a \in A} u_a v_a \tag{4.72}$$

The final results of link tolls are quite sensitive to the chosen objective function. In general, F_1 could be adopted if the road pricing is intended to restrain travel demand, while avoiding high charges on users. On the other hand, F_2 could be chosen if road pricing is to be used as a means of generating revenue for infrastructure investment. A weighted combination of these two objective functions could also be adopted.

The selection of a link toll pattern among all satisfying (physical or environmental) capacity constraints can thus be formulated as the following bi-level mathematical program:

$$\max_{\mathbf{u} \geq 0} F(\mathbf{u}, \mathbf{v}(\mathbf{u}), \mathbf{d}(\mathbf{u})) \tag{4.73}$$

subject to

$$v_a(\mathbf{u}) \leq C_a, \quad a \in A \tag{4.74}$$

where $\mathbf{v}(\mathbf{u})$ and $\mathbf{d}(\mathbf{u})$ for given $\mathbf{u}$, are obtained by solving:

$$\min_{(\mathbf{v},\mathbf{d}) \in \Omega} \sum_{a \in A} \int_0^{v_a} t_a(\omega, u_a) \mathrm{d}\omega - \sum_{w \in W} \int_0^{d_w} B_w(\omega) \mathrm{d}\omega \tag{4.75}$$

where Ω is again defined in (4.4), and the objective function may be selected either as F_1 or F_2 or their combination.

Note that in this model, the capacity constraint (4.74) is imposed at the upper-level rather than the lower-level as contrasted with the equilibrium model (4.63)-(4.64) with explicit capacity constraint (4.64). It is important to note this because impositions of capacity constraints in lower-level, or in upper-level or in both lower- and upper-level have different behavioral interpretations, and give rise to different solutions. Whereas here, the capacity constraint is imposed in the upper-level sub-problem only, no queuing is allowed on any link, because the lower-level sub-problem (which could be considered as a constraint of the upper-level problem) represents a standard elastic-demand network equilibrium model that admits of no queues. If the capacity constraint is imposed in the lower-level (or in both lower-level and upper-level) sub-problems, the problem would admit of queues at saturated links (links whose capacity constraints bind) in determining link tolls to optimize the system objective function because in this case the lower-level sub-problem would represent an elastic-demand network equilibrium model with queue.

Table 4.4 Numerical results for the traffic restraint and road pricing problem

Variable	Queuing Equilibrium Solution	Maximizing F_1	Maximizing F_2
u_1	0.00	7.74	21.55
u_2	0.00	5.50	21.75
u_3	8.39	0.60	7.61
u_4	10.24	3.53	24.03
u_5	2.56	9.32	17.69
u_6	0.00	6.97	22.69
u_7	0.00	1.60	16.38
u_8	1.61	8.58	20.40
u_9	8.04	6.83	27.24
u_{10}	5.67	2.16	20.57
u_{11}	5.27	5.63	26.30
F_1	818.83	<u>825.87</u>	348.01
F_2	6615.85	6386.02	<u>10282.23</u>

We now consider the determination of link tolls for satisfying capacity constraint by the proposed models. We consider the same example used in Section 4.4 with the network shown in Figure 4.7. By solving the elastic-demand network equilibrium problem (4.63)-(4.64) with the environmental capacity constraints given in Table 4.1, we can calculate the "queuing delays" at links whose capacity constraints bind. The queuing delays should be substituted by link tolls which present a particular link toll solution to the problem of interest. The calculated results are shown in the 2nd column of Table 4.4.

In order to select the best link toll patterns from all feasible solutions, the bi-level optimization model (4.73)-(4.75) is applied with both objective functions given by eqns. (4.71) and (4.72). The bi-level model is solved by the sensitivity analysis based algorithm presented in Section 4.3. It has been observed that the speed of convergence of the sensitivity analysis based algorithm is dependent upon the selected predetermined sequences in Step 4.

When the simple sequence, $\alpha^{(n)} = 1/(1+n)$ is used the convergence is achieved within about 50 major iterations in all cases for a convergence criteria of $\left|u_a^{(n+1)} - u_a^{(n)}\right| \le 0.1$ for all toll links $a \in A$.

Table 4.4 depicts the link toll patterns which have been selected from all feasible solutions, by maximizing the objective functions of total travel demand (4.71) and the total toll revenue (4.72). The following observations are ready from the numerical results. First, the elastic-demand network equilibrium model with capacity constraint provides a good approximate solution to the problem of the maximization of total realized demand. This solution might be considered to be an extreme one which merely removes queues at bottleneck links, while making full use of the network capacity. Second, as expected, maximization of revenue lead to a much higher level of link toll charges than the total demand objective function. In general, increasing link tolls leads to reduced realized travel demand. At lower levels of link tolls, increases in link tolls may outweigh the decrease in traffic, resulting in a pure increase in revenue. The maximum revenue will be achieved at a level of link tolls where the effect of link toll increases will be exactly canceled out by the reduced travel demand.

4.6 SUMMARY

In this chapter we formulated and solved the second-best road pricing problem as a bilevel programming problem with traffic equilibrium constraints. We then revisited the sensitivity analysis of network traffic equilibria and proposed a correct approach by applying the implicit function theorem for the equivalent restricted problem. In particular, we found that equilibrium link flows are differentiable in perturbation almost everywhere in the perturbation space, except degenerate equilibrium points. The sensitivity formula always functions independently of network topology. The sensitivity analysis method based on the traditional implicit function theorem has a useful role in road pricing analysis. As we have already showed, it can provide derivative information, if it exists, which can be used favorably for exploring the effect of link flows of small change in price and thus in demand, and hence for the analysis and design of a second road pricing scheme. As a specialized application of the bi-level programming and sensitivity analysis methods, we studied the traffic restraint and road pricing problem which is of great social importance due to increasing environmental concern.

It is meaningful to develop effective methods which able to identify the limited number of points or sets of Lebesgue measure zero where link flow is not differentiable (link flow is piecewise differentiable). Although the recent developments of sensitivity analysis of traffic equilibria provide a characterization of the existence and calculation of the directional derivatives (Qiu and Magnanti, 1989; Patriksson, 2004), the link flow directional derivative always exists due to its Lipschitz continuity. Nonetheless, application of the sensitivity analysis by directional derivatives is limited in practice. First, a full set of paths needs to be considered. Second, directional derivatives seem to be of less use in application, unless we know the direction is descending in solving an optimal second-best pricing problem. Third, in a desire to calculate the gradient of a link flow solution (if it exists) by the above method for calculating directional derivatives, then one has to try as many times as the number of perturbation variables.

4.7 SOURCES AND NOTES

The bilevel programming problem has been a subject of extensive study in mathematical programming literature. Readers may refer to the excellent monograph by Luo et al. (1996), Bard (1998) and Dempe (2000) for advanced treatments of the subject. Tobin and Friesz (1988) were the first to develop the gradient-based sensitivity analysis for the traffic equilibrium problem with fixed demand, although the approach was found to have a few flaws examined in this chapter. Cho et al. (2000) proposed a correct but complicated reduction method for sensitivity analyses of network equilibrium link flows. Sensitivity analysis of the traffic equilibrium problems with elastic demand or with link capacity constraints were considered in Yang (1997) and Yang (1995) respectively. The standard sensitivity analysis method for nonlinear programming problem is offered by Fiacco (1983). For more sensitivity analysis, authors may refer to Yin and Miyagi (2001), Clark and Watling (2002, 2000) and Ceylan and Bell (2004) in the case of stochastic traffic equilibrium, to Ying (2005) and Yin and Yang (2005) for bimodal traffic network equilibrium, and to Leurent (1998) for bicriteria traffic equilibrium problems. Meaningful applications of the gradient-based sensitivity analysis method can be found in, for example, Friesz et al. (1990), Yang and Yagar (1994) and Yang and Yagar et al. (1994) Readers may also further refer to Qui and Magnanti (1989) and Patriksson and Rockafellar (2003) and Patriksson (2004) for the development of sensitivity analysis by directional derivatives and its possible application in transportation network optimization problems. Part of the materials presented in this chapter is taken from Yang (1997) for sensitivity analysis of the elastic demand traffic equilibrium problem and Yang and Bell (1997) for the traffic restraint and road pricing problem. The new corrected sensitivity analysis method is recently developed (Yang and Bell, 2005).

5

THE SECOND-BEST ROAD PRICING PROBLEMS: A GAP FUNCTION BASED APPROACH

5.1 INTRODUCTION

In this chapter, we continue to investigate the second-best road pricing problem which is formulated as a Mathematical Program with Equilibrium Constraints (MPEC) or a Bi-Level Programming Problem (BLPP) in Chapter 4. With the same notation defined before, the MPEC/BLPP formulations are given below.

$$\min_{\mathbf{u}\in U} F\left(\mathbf{u},\mathbf{v}^*,\mathbf{d}^*\right) \tag{5.1}$$

subject to

$$\mathbf{g}\left(\mathbf{v}^*,\mathbf{d}^*\right)\leq 0 \tag{5.2}$$

where $\left(\mathbf{v}^*,\mathbf{d}^*\right)$ are the solution of the following VI for given $\mathbf{u}$:

$$\mathbf{t}\left(\mathbf{v}^*,\mathbf{u}\right)^{\mathrm{T}}\left(\mathbf{v}-\mathbf{v}^*\right)-\mathbf{B}\left(\mathbf{d}^*,\mathbf{u}\right)^{\mathrm{T}}\left(\mathbf{d}-\mathbf{d}^*\right)\geq 0 \text{ for any } \left(\mathbf{v},\mathbf{d}\right)\in\Omega \tag{5.3}$$

or alternatively $\left(\mathbf{v}^*,\mathbf{d}^*\right)$ are the solution of the following convex mathematical program

$$\left(\mathbf{v}^*,\mathbf{d}^*\right)=\arg\min_{(\mathbf{v},\mathbf{d})\in\Omega}\sum_{a\in A}\int_0^{v_a}t_a\left(\omega,\mathbf{u}\right)\mathrm{d}\omega-\sum_{w\in W}\int_0^{d_w}B_w\left(\omega,\mathbf{u}\right)\mathrm{d}\omega \tag{5.4}$$

where

$$\Omega=\left\{\left(\mathbf{v},\mathbf{d}\right)\middle|\ \mathbf{v}=\Delta\mathbf{f},\ \mathbf{d}=\Lambda\mathbf{f},\ \mathbf{f}\geq 0,\ 0\leq\mathbf{d}\leq\bar{\mathbf{D}}\right\} \tag{5.5}$$

Note that in this chapter we are limited to the link based toll charge, but again we allow $\mathbf{u}$ appearing in the benefit function, $\mathbf{B}\left(\mathbf{d},\mathbf{u}\right)$ for analysis of generality. As pointed out in Chapter 4, the corresponding elements in the benefit functions represent demand function parameters rather than OD-based toll charge.

We have developed and applied the sensitivity analysis based algorithm for solving the MPEC/BLPP models, in which the derivatives of the reaction functions, $\mathbf{v}\left(\mathbf{u}\right)$ and $\mathbf{d}\left(\mathbf{u}\right)$, are explicitly calculated. We have to admit that the reaction functions are not differentiable anywhere, although a case of such non-differentiability is very small or isolated. The sensitivity analysis based algorithm may fail to find the solution if indeed non-differentiability is encountered at an optimal or near-optimal solution.

To circumvent the non-differentiability issue of the sensitivity analysis based algorithm, we shall develop and apply a gap function based approach for solving the second-best road pricing problem in this chapter. With this approach we show that both the MPEC and the BLPP models in (5.1)-(5.5) can be reformulated as an equivalent, continuously differentiable single-level optimization problem, and can be solved effectively by the standard algorithms for nonlinear programming problems, such as the augmented Lagrangian algorithm, even for larger networks. The differentiable property of the gap function is elucidated with analytical examples. As a specialized application of the marginal function based approach, we deal with the second-best road pricing problem with entry-exit based toll charge encountered in most expressway network systems. In contrast with the pricing problems studied so far, where tolls are determined on individual links of the network and thus path costs are link additive if all users value travel times linearly, the entry-exit based second-best pricing problem does not have an additive toll structure. Such a non-additive toll structure leads to the network equilibrium problem with path-specific costs. We present a simple approach of network decomposition and transfer that allows for the application of the conventional optimization-based network equilibrium models and algorithms in dealing with the network toll design problem with the marginal function based method.

5.2 MARGINAL FUNCTION BASED APPROACH

5.2.1 Gap Function for the VI based Traffic Equilibrium Models

Consider the general MPEC formulation of the second-best road pricing problem. We associate with the VI (5.3), the following quadratic, differentiable gap or merit function introduced by Fukushima (1992):

$$G_{\alpha}(\mathbf{u},\mathbf{v},\mathbf{d}) = -\min_{(\tilde{\mathbf{v}},\tilde{\mathbf{d}})\in\Omega} \phi(\mathbf{u},\tilde{\mathbf{v}},\tilde{\mathbf{d}},\mathbf{v},\mathbf{d}) \tag{5.6}$$

where

$$\phi(\mathbf{u},\tilde{\mathbf{v}},\tilde{\mathbf{d}},\mathbf{v},\mathbf{d}) = \begin{pmatrix} \mathbf{t}(\mathbf{v},\mathbf{u}) \\ -\mathbf{B}(\mathbf{d},\mathbf{u}) \end{pmatrix}^{\mathrm{T}} \left(\begin{pmatrix} \tilde{\mathbf{v}} \\ \tilde{\mathbf{d}} \end{pmatrix} - \begin{pmatrix} \mathbf{v} \\ \mathbf{d} \end{pmatrix} \right) + \frac{1}{2\alpha} \left(\begin{pmatrix} \tilde{\mathbf{v}} \\ \tilde{\mathbf{d}} \end{pmatrix} - \begin{pmatrix} \mathbf{v} \\ \mathbf{d} \end{pmatrix} \right)^{\mathrm{T}} \mathbf{M} \left(\begin{pmatrix} \tilde{\mathbf{v}} \\ \tilde{\mathbf{d}} \end{pmatrix} - \begin{pmatrix} \mathbf{v} \\ \mathbf{d} \end{pmatrix} \right) \tag{5.7}$$

where α is a positive number and M can be any positive definite matrix. In the above problems Ω defined in (5.5) is a nonempty, closed convex and bounded set. Now, it is straightforward to obtain the following theorem due to Fukushima (1992).

Theorem 5.1 *$G_\alpha(\mathbf{u},\mathbf{v},\mathbf{d}) \geq 0$ and $G_\alpha(\mathbf{u},\mathbf{v},\mathbf{d}) = 0$ if and only if $(\mathbf{v},\mathbf{d})$ solves VI (5.3) (or satisfy the UE condition) for given toll vector $\mathbf{u}$.*

Let $\mathbf{M} = \begin{bmatrix} \mathbf{M}_A & 0 \\ 0 & \mathbf{M}_W \end{bmatrix}^{\mathrm{T}}$ where $\mathbf{M}_A$ is a proper $|A|\times|A|$ positive definite matrix and $\mathbf{M}_W$ is a proper $|W|\times|W|$ positive definite matrix, then (5.6) and (5.7) can be rewritten as following convex quadratic programming problem:

$$\min_{(\tilde{\mathbf{v}},\tilde{\mathbf{d}})\in\Omega} \phi(\mathbf{u},\tilde{\mathbf{v}},\tilde{\mathbf{d}},\mathbf{v},\mathbf{d}) = (\tilde{\mathbf{v}}-\mathbf{v})^{\mathrm{T}}\mathbf{t}(\mathbf{v},\mathbf{u}) + \frac{1}{2\alpha}(\tilde{\mathbf{v}}-\mathbf{v})^{\mathrm{T}}\mathbf{M}_A(\tilde{\mathbf{v}}-\mathbf{v})$$
$$-(\tilde{\mathbf{d}}-\mathbf{d})^{\mathrm{T}}\mathbf{B}(\mathbf{d},\mathbf{u}) + \frac{1}{2\alpha}(\tilde{\mathbf{d}}-\mathbf{d})^{\mathrm{T}}\mathbf{M}_W(\tilde{\mathbf{d}}-\mathbf{d}) \qquad (5.8)$$

Without losing generality, we can set $\mathbf{M}_A$ and $\mathbf{M}_W$ as two diagonal matrices with diagonal elements m_a, $a\in A$ and m_w, $w\in W$, then the parametric minimization problem (5.8) becomes the following quadratic network equilibrium problem, with separable linear link cost function and linear demand functions:

$$\min_{(\tilde{\mathbf{v}},\tilde{\mathbf{d}})\in\Omega} \phi(\mathbf{u},\tilde{\mathbf{v}},\tilde{\mathbf{d}},\mathbf{v},\mathbf{d}) = \sum_{a\in A}\int_0^{\tilde{v}_a} \tilde{t}_a(\omega,\mathbf{v},\mathbf{u})\,d\omega - \sum_{w\in W}\int_0^{\tilde{d}_w} \tilde{B}_w(\omega,\mathbf{d},\mathbf{u})\,d\omega \qquad (5.9)$$

where

$$\tilde{t}_a(\tilde{v}_a,\mathbf{v},\mathbf{u}) = \frac{\partial\phi(\mathbf{u},\tilde{\mathbf{v}},\tilde{\mathbf{d}},\mathbf{v},\mathbf{d})}{\partial\tilde{v}_a} = t_a(\mathbf{v},\mathbf{u}) + \frac{m_a}{\alpha}(\tilde{v}_a - v_a),\ a\in A \qquad (5.10)$$

$$\tilde{B}_w(\tilde{d}_w,\mathbf{d},\mathbf{u}) = \frac{\partial\phi(\mathbf{u},\tilde{\mathbf{v}},\tilde{\mathbf{d}},\mathbf{v},\mathbf{d})}{\partial\tilde{d}_w} = B_w(\mathbf{d},\mathbf{u}) + \frac{m_w}{\alpha}(\tilde{d}_w - d_w),\ w\in W \qquad (5.11)$$

Note that since $t_a(\mathbf{v},\mathbf{u}) > 0$ and $B_w(\mathbf{d},\mathbf{u}) > 0$ and $\tilde{v}_a$, v_a, $a\in A$ and $\tilde{d}_w$, d_w, $w\in W$ are bounded, we can always find appropriate small positive m_a, $a\in A$ and m_w, $w\in W$ together with appropriate positive α so that $\tilde{t}_a(\tilde{v}_a,\mathbf{v},\mathbf{u}) > 0$, $a\in A$ and $\tilde{B}_w(\tilde{d}_w,\mathbf{d},\mathbf{u}) > 0$, $w\in W$. This will ensure a straightforward use of the traditional Frank-Wolfe algorithm to solve the elastic demand traffic assignment problem (5.9)-(5.11) with normal link linear travel time and OD demand functions for fixed $(\mathbf{v},\mathbf{d},\mathbf{u})$.

Now we rewrite the problem (5.9) into the following equivalent form in terms of path flow variables $\tilde{\mathbf{f}} = \left(\cdots, \tilde{f}_{rw}, \cdots\right)^{\mathrm{T}}, r \in R_w, w \in W$ only:

$$\min_{\tilde{\mathbf{f}}} \phi\left(\mathbf{u}, \tilde{\mathbf{v}}\left(\tilde{\mathbf{f}}\right), \tilde{\mathbf{d}}\left(\tilde{\mathbf{f}}\right), \mathbf{v}, \mathbf{d}\right) = \sum_{a \in A} \int_0^{\tilde{v}_a(\tilde{\mathbf{f}})} \tilde{t}_a\left(\omega, \mathbf{v}, \mathbf{u}\right) d\omega - \sum_{w \in W} \int_0^{\tilde{d}_w(\tilde{\mathbf{f}})} \tilde{B}_w\left(\omega, \mathbf{d}, \mathbf{u}\right) d\omega \qquad (5.12)$$

subject to

$$\tilde{f}_{rw} \geq 0, r \in R_w, w \in W \qquad (5.13)$$

where $\tilde{v}_a\left(\tilde{\mathbf{f}}\right) = \sum_{w \in W} \sum_{r \in R_w} \tilde{f}_{rw} \delta_{ar}, a \in A$ and $\tilde{d}_w\left(\tilde{\mathbf{f}}\right) = \sum_{r \in R_w} \tilde{f}_{rw}, w \in W$. Of course, the optimal path flow solution, denoted as $\tilde{\mathbf{f}}^* = \left(\cdots, \tilde{f}_{rw}^*, \cdots\right)^{\mathrm{T}}$, to the problem (5.12)-(5.13) is not unique, but can be characterized by the following set

$$\Omega_{\tilde{f}}^*\left(\mathbf{u}, \mathbf{v}, \mathbf{d}\right) = \left\{\tilde{\mathbf{f}} \geq 0 \middle| \phi\left(\mathbf{u}, \tilde{\mathbf{v}}, \tilde{\mathbf{d}}, \mathbf{v}, \mathbf{d}\right) = G_\alpha\left(\mathbf{u}, \mathbf{v}, \mathbf{d}\right), \text{ where } \tilde{\mathbf{v}} = \Delta \tilde{\mathbf{f}} \text{ and } \tilde{\mathbf{d}} = \Lambda \tilde{\mathbf{f}}\right\} \qquad (5.14)$$

We then have the following Lemma immediately.

Lemma 5.1 *For given* $\mathbf{u} \in U$ *and* $\left(\mathbf{v}, \mathbf{d}\right) \in \Omega$ *let* $\tilde{\mathbf{f}}^* \in \Omega_{\tilde{f}}^*\left(\mathbf{u}, \mathbf{v}, \mathbf{d}\right)$ *be an optimal path flow solution associated with* $\left(\mathbf{u}, \mathbf{v}, \mathbf{d}\right)$ *to the problem (5.12)-(5.13), then* $\tilde{\mathbf{f}}^*$ *satisfies the Linear Independence Constraint Qualification (LICQ) for the problem (5.12)-(5.13).*

Lemma 5.1 is self-evident. For any active nonnegative path flow constraints in (5.13), the corresponding gradient is an unit vector with the element corresponding to the binding zero path flow equal to 1 and the rest are zeros. Because all path flows (within each OD pair or across different OD pairs) are independent variables for the elastic demand traffic equilibrium problems (5.12)-(5.13), all the gradients associated with the active nonnegative path flow constraints are thus linearly independent.

The LICQ property for any path flow solution of the problem (5.12)-(5.13) allows for the direct application of the sensitivty analysis results for parameterized nonlinear programming problems developed in Gauvin and Dubeau (1982). From Lemma 5.1 and the differentiability results of marginal function in nonlinear programming, the following theorem on the gap function $G_\alpha\left(\mathbf{u}, \mathbf{v}, \mathbf{d}\right)$ follows immediately.

Theorem 5.2 $G_\alpha\left(\mathbf{u}, \mathbf{v}, \mathbf{d}\right) \geq 0$ *is continuously differentiable in* $\mathbf{u} \in U$ *and* $\left(\mathbf{v}, \mathbf{d}\right) \in \Omega$ *and its gradient is given by*

$$\nabla_{\mathbf{u}} G_{\alpha}(\mathbf{u},\mathbf{v},\mathbf{d}) = \begin{bmatrix} \nabla_{\mathbf{u}}\mathbf{t}(\mathbf{v},\mathbf{u}) & 0 \\ 0 & -\nabla_{\mathbf{u}}\mathbf{B}(\mathbf{d},\mathbf{u}) \end{bmatrix} \begin{pmatrix} \tilde{\mathbf{v}}^* - \mathbf{v} \\ \tilde{\mathbf{d}}^* - \mathbf{d} \end{pmatrix} \tag{5.15}$$

$$\nabla_{(\mathbf{v},\mathbf{d})} G_{\alpha}(\mathbf{u},\mathbf{v},\mathbf{d}) = \begin{pmatrix} \mathbf{t}(\mathbf{v},\mathbf{u}) \\ -\mathbf{B}(\mathbf{d},\mathbf{u}) \end{pmatrix} - \left[\begin{pmatrix} \nabla_{\mathbf{v}}\mathbf{t}(\mathbf{v},\mathbf{u}) & 0 \\ 0 & -\nabla_{\mathbf{d}}\mathbf{B}(\mathbf{d},\mathbf{u}) \end{pmatrix} - \mathbf{M} \right] \begin{pmatrix} \tilde{\mathbf{v}}^* - \mathbf{v} \\ \tilde{\mathbf{d}}^* - \mathbf{d} \end{pmatrix} \tag{5.16}$$

where $\tilde{\mathbf{v}}^* = \tilde{\mathbf{v}}^*(\mathbf{u},\mathbf{v},\mathbf{d})$ *and* $\tilde{\mathbf{d}}^* = \tilde{\mathbf{d}}^*(\mathbf{u},\mathbf{v},\mathbf{d})$ *is the unique solution of the positive definite quadratic programming problem (5.8), or equivalently, the unique equilibrium link flow and O-D demand solution of the traffic assignment problem (5.9) for given* $(\mathbf{u},\mathbf{v},\mathbf{d})$.

In their detailed components, the expressions of the above derivatives are in fact simple, as given below (consider link based toll charge only and unit value of time or toll charge measured in equivalent time unit):

$$\frac{\partial G_{\alpha}(\mathbf{u},\mathbf{v},\mathbf{d})}{\partial u_a} = \left(\tilde{v}_a^* - v_a\right)\left(\frac{\partial t_a(\mathbf{v},\mathbf{u})}{\partial u_a}\right) = \begin{cases} \tilde{v}_a^* - v_a, & a \in \bar{A} \\ 0, & a \in A,\ a \notin \bar{A} \end{cases} \tag{5.17}$$

$$\frac{\partial G_{\alpha}(\mathbf{v},\mathbf{d},\mathbf{u})}{\partial u_w} = -\left(\tilde{d}_w^* - d_w\right)\left(\frac{\partial B_w(\mathbf{d},\mathbf{u})}{\partial u_w}\right) \tag{5.18}$$

$$\frac{\partial G_{\alpha}(\mathbf{u},\mathbf{v},\mathbf{d})}{\partial v_a} = \sum_{a' \in A}\left(\tilde{v}_{a'}^* - v_{a'}\right)\frac{\partial t_{a'}(\mathbf{v},\mathbf{u})}{\partial v_a} - \left(t_a(\mathbf{v},\mathbf{u}) + \frac{m_a}{\alpha}\left(\tilde{v}_a^* - v_a\right)\right),\ a \in A \tag{5.19}$$

$$\frac{\partial G_{\alpha}(\mathbf{u},\mathbf{v},\mathbf{d})}{\partial d_w} = -\sum_{w' \in W}\left(\tilde{d}_{w'}^* - d_{w'}\right)\frac{\partial B_{w'}(\mathbf{d},\mathbf{u})}{\partial d_w} + \left(B_w(\mathbf{d},\mathbf{u}) + \frac{m_w}{\alpha}\left(\tilde{d}_w^* - d_w\right)\right),\ w \in W \tag{5.20}$$

where $\tilde{v}_a^* = \tilde{v}_a^*(\mathbf{u},\mathbf{v},\mathbf{d})$, $a \in A$ and $\tilde{d}_w^* = \tilde{d}_w^*(\mathbf{u},\mathbf{v},\mathbf{d})$, $w \in W$ are again the unique link flow and O-D demand solution of the traffic equilibrium problem (5.9) for given $(\mathbf{u},\mathbf{v},\mathbf{d})$, $\partial B_w(\mathbf{d},\mathbf{u})/\partial u_w$ can be calculated once the role of $\mathbf{u}$ in the demand function is specified (e.g., potential demand or cost sensitivity parameter in the demand function).

5.2.2 Gap Function for the Optimization based Traffic Equilibrium Models

We first define the marginal or value function for the lower-level convex programming problem of the traffic equilibrium model (5.4)-(5.5) as follows

$$\varphi(\mathbf{u}) = \min_{(\mathbf{v},\mathbf{d}) \in \Omega} \sum_{a \in A} \int_0^{v_a} t_a(\omega,\mathbf{u})\,d\omega - \sum_{w \in W} \int_0^{d_w} B_w(\omega,\mathbf{u})\,d\omega \tag{5.21}$$

where Ω is defined by (5.5). Let $\mathbf{v}^*(\mathbf{u})$ and $\mathbf{d}^*(\mathbf{u})$ be an equilibrium solution, then, under the standard assumptions for the traffic equilibrium problem, $\mathbf{v}^*(\mathbf{u})$ and $\mathbf{d}^*(\mathbf{u})$ are continuous functions (although not differentiable anywhere as pointed out earlier) in $\mathbf{u}$. The value of the marginal function is thus equal to

$$\varphi(\mathbf{u}) = \sum_{a \in A} \int_0^{v_a^*(\mathbf{u})} t_a(\omega, \mathbf{u}) d\omega - \sum_{w \in W} \int_0^{d_w^*(\mathbf{u})} B_w(\omega, \mathbf{u}) d\omega \tag{5.22}$$

Although the equilibrium link flow $v_a^*(\mathbf{u}),\ a \in A$ and equilibrium OD demand $d_w^*(\mathbf{u}),\ w \in W$ that appear in the upper bound of the integral in (5.22) are functions of variable $\mathbf{u}$, the marginal function is differentiable and its partial derivative with respect to individual toll charge $u_b,\ b \in \overline{A}$ is determined by holding $v_a(\mathbf{u})$ and $d_w(\mathbf{u})$ fixed at their optimal value $v_a^*(\mathbf{u}),\ a \in A$ and $d_w^*(\mathbf{u}),\ w \in W$ respectively. Hence, $\varphi(\mathbf{u})$ is a differentiable function and its gradient is given by

$$\nabla\varphi(\mathbf{u}) = \left(\cdots, \frac{\partial\varphi(\mathbf{u})}{\partial u_a}, \cdots, \frac{\partial\varphi(\mathbf{u})}{\partial u_w}, \cdots\right)^{\mathrm{T}},\ a \in \overline{A},\ w \in W \tag{5.23}$$

$$\frac{\partial\varphi(\mathbf{u})}{\partial u_a} = \int_0^{v_a^*(\mathbf{u})} \frac{\partial t_a(\omega, \mathbf{u})}{\partial u_a} d\omega,\ a \in \overline{A} \tag{5.24}$$

$$\frac{\partial\varphi(\mathbf{u})}{\partial u_w} = -\int_0^{d_w^*(\mathbf{u})} \frac{\partial B_w(\omega, \mathbf{u})}{\partial u_w} d\omega,\ w \in W \tag{5.25}$$

For any given toll charge $\mathbf{u}$, the corresponding equilibrium OD demand $d_w^*(\mathbf{u}),\ w \in W$ and link flow, $v_a^*(\mathbf{u}),\ a \in A$ can be obtained easily by implementing an efficient traffic assignment procedure (see Chapter 2). Then the value and the derivative of the marginal function can be obtained straightforwardly through eqns. (5.23)-(5.25).

Now we are ready to define the following gap function for the convex programming formulation of the traffic equilibrium problem.

$$H(\mathbf{u}, \mathbf{v}, \mathbf{d}) = \sum_{a \in A} \int_0^{v_a} t_a(\omega, \mathbf{u}) d\omega - \sum_{w \in W} \int_0^{d_w} B_w(\omega, \mathbf{u}) d\omega - \varphi(\mathbf{u}) \tag{5.26}$$

Obviously, this function is nonnegative, continuously differentiable for any feasible flow pattern $(\mathbf{v}, \mathbf{d}) \in \Omega$ and toll vector $\mathbf{u} \in U$. Based on the differentiability established in (5.23) -(5.25) and in view of the fact that the traffic equilibrium problem is a strictly convex optimization problem in link flows and OD demands, it is straightforward to obtain the following theorem for this gap function (5.26) (consider separable link cost and OD demand functions and link based toll charges with unit value of time or toll charge measured in equivalent time unit).

Theorem 5.3 *The gap function (5.26) has the following properties*

(i) $H(\mathbf{u}, \mathbf{v}, \mathbf{d}) \geq 0$

(ii) $H(\mathbf{u},\mathbf{v},\mathbf{d})=0$ *if and only if* $(\mathbf{v},\mathbf{d})$ *is an equilibrium link flow pattern for given* $\mathbf{u}$.

(iii) $H(\mathbf{u},\mathbf{v},\mathbf{d})$ *is a continuously differentiable function with partial derivatives given by*

$$\frac{\partial H(\mathbf{u},\mathbf{v},\mathbf{d})}{\partial v_a}=t_a(v_a,\mathbf{u}),\ a\in A \tag{5.27}$$

$$\frac{\partial H(\mathbf{u},\mathbf{v},\mathbf{d})}{\partial d_w}=-B_w(d_w,\mathbf{u}),\ w\in W \tag{5.28}$$

$$\frac{\partial H(\mathbf{u},\mathbf{v},\mathbf{d})}{\partial u_a}=\int_0^{v_a}\left(\frac{\partial t_a(\omega,\mathrm{u})}{\partial u_a}\right)d\omega-\frac{\partial\varphi(\mathbf{u})}{\partial u_a}=v_a-\frac{\partial\varphi(\mathbf{u})}{\partial u_a},\ a\in\bar{A} \tag{5.29}$$

$$\frac{\partial H(\mathbf{u},\mathbf{v},\mathbf{d})}{\partial u_w}=\int_0^{d_w}\left(\frac{\partial B_w(\omega,\mathrm{u})}{\partial u_w}\right)d\omega-\frac{\partial\varphi(\mathbf{u})}{\partial u_w},\ w\in W \tag{5.30}$$

5.2.3 Reformulation as Continuously Differentiable Optimization Problems

From theorems 5.1-5.3, we can see the VI constraint (5.3) in the MPEC formulation and the lower-level optimization problem (5.4) in the BLPP formulation for the second-best pricing problems can be now replaced by their respective equivalent gap function constraints. Therefore, we have the following equivalent single-level continuously differentiable toll optimization model:

$$\min_{\mathbf{u}\in U,(\mathbf{v},\mathbf{d})\in\Omega} F(\mathbf{u},\mathbf{v},\mathbf{d}) \tag{5.31}$$

subject to

$$\mathbf{g}(\mathbf{v},\mathbf{d})\le 0 \tag{5.32}$$

$$G(\mathbf{u},\mathbf{v},\mathbf{d})=0\quad(\text{or } H(\mathbf{u},\mathbf{v},\mathbf{d})=0) \tag{5.33}$$

where Ω is again defined by (5.5) and U is the feasible set of link tolls.

In the equivalent model (5.31)-(5.33), the UE condition is expressed by the gap function constraint $G(\mathbf{u},\mathbf{v},\mathbf{d})=0$ or $H(\mathbf{u},\mathbf{v},\mathbf{d})=0$ together with the feasibility conditions $(\mathbf{v},\mathbf{d})\in\Omega$. Indeed, the complicated element in this formulation is constraint (5.33), in which the explicit formula of the gap function cannot be obtained. Fortunately, the value of the gap function and the value of its gradient can both be simply calculated by implementing a UE traffic assignment and the exact and explicit derivative formulas established above. These two values are key parameters in designing an efficient solution algorithm here. Consequently, we have reached a continuously differentiable nonlinear programming model for the general second-best road pricing problems.

5.2.4 A Scheme of the Augmented Lagrangian Algorithm

For a continuously differentiable minimization problem, a handful of methods can be applied to find a local minimum. Among these methods, the augmented Lagrangian algorithm is one of the efficient and locally convergent methods for the optimization problem with nonlinear constraints (Bertsekas, 1982). Here, we employ this type of algorithm to design a solution method for the second-best road pricing problem formulated in (5.31)-(5.33). One of the advantages of the method is that the nonlinear, implicit Constraint (5.33) can be incorporated into the objective function as a penalty term. The (partially) augmented Lagrangian function for the problem (5.31)-(5.33) is defined as

$$L(\mathbf{u},\mathbf{v},\mathbf{d},\lambda,\rho)=F(\mathbf{u},\mathbf{v},\mathbf{d})+\lambda G(\mathbf{u},\mathbf{v},\mathbf{d})+\frac{1}{2}\rho\left(G(\mathbf{u},\mathbf{v},\mathbf{d})\right)^2 \tag{5.34}$$

Here for brevity we omit the upper-level constraint (5.32), which, if existent, can be incorporated into the augmented Lagrangian function by a quadratic penalty function or remain kept as constraints. The framework of the augmented Lagrangian algorithm is given below.

Step 0. (*Initialization*) Select a feasible link flow pattern $v_a^{(0)}, a\in A$ and OD demand $d_w^{(0)}$, $w\in W$, link toll charge $u_a^{(0)}$, $a\in \overline{A}$ and a positive constant β. Choose a multiplier $\lambda^{(0)}\geq 0$ and a penalty parameter $\rho^{(0)}>0$. Let $n:=0$.

Step 1. (*Inner loop*) Solve the following sub-problem

$$\min_{\mathbf{u}\in U,(\mathbf{v},\mathbf{d})\in\Omega} L(\mathbf{u},\mathbf{v},\mathbf{d},\lambda,\rho) \tag{5.35}$$

Let $\mathbf{u}^{(n+1)}$ and $\left(\mathbf{v}^{(n+1)},\mathbf{d}^{(n+1)}\right)$ denote the solution and then the value $G\left(\mathbf{u}^{(n+1)},\mathbf{v}^{(n+1)},\mathbf{d}^{(n+1)}\right)$ can be obtained by executing a UE traffic assignment.

Step 2. (*Verify stopping criterion*) If $G\left(\mathbf{u}^{(n+1)},\mathbf{v}^{(n+1)},\mathbf{d}^{(n+1)}\right)\leq\kappa$, then terminate. Otherwise, go to Step 3.

Step 3. (*Update the Lagrangian multiplier*) If

$G\left(\mathbf{u}^{(n+1)},\mathbf{v}^{(n+1)},\mathbf{d}^{(n+1)}\right)\leq 0.25G\left(\mathbf{u}^{(n+1)},\mathbf{v}^{(n+1)},\mathbf{d}^{(n+1)}\right)$

then set

$$\lambda^{(n+1)}=\lambda^{(n)}+\rho^{(n)}G\left(\mathbf{u}^{(n+1)},\mathbf{v}^{(n+1)},\mathbf{d}^{(n+1)}\right) \tag{5.36}$$

let $n := n+1$ and go to Step 1. Otherwise, go to Step 4.

Step 4. (*Update penalty parameter*) Set $\rho^{(n+1)} = \beta\rho^{(n)}$, $\lambda^{(n+1)} = \lambda^{(n)}$, $n := n+1$, and go to Step 1.

In this algorithm, various penalty parameter-updating scenarios can be adopted for the problems considered here as long as the condition, $\sum_{n=0}^{+\infty}\rho^{(n)} = +\infty$, is satisfied. The sub-problem (5.35) can be solved by the Frank-Wolfe algorithm with a predetermined or optimized step size.

5.3 APPLICATIONS OF THE GAP FUNCTION APPROACH

Example 5.1 (Differentiability of VI gap function and toll optimization with the MPEC model) Consider a network with two parallel links connecting a single OD pair. Link cost functions are: $t_1(v_1) = 2v_1 + 2$ and $t_2(v_2) = v_2 + 4$, and a fixed OD demand is assumed to be $d = 5$. Link 1 is subjected to a toll charge u_1.

The equilibrium link flows $v_1^*(u_1)$ and $v_2^*(u_1)$ as a function of u_1 are given as follows

$$v_1^*(u_1) = \begin{cases} \frac{1}{3}(7-u_1), & 0 \le u_1 < 7 \\ 0, & u_1 \ge 7 \end{cases} \quad \text{and} \quad v_2^*(u_1) = \begin{cases} \frac{1}{3}(8+u_1), & 0 \le u_1 < 7 \\ 5, & u_1 \ge 7 \end{cases} \tag{5.37}$$

Suppose the MPEC problem (5.1)-(5.3) is to select u_1 to minimize total travel time cost: $F = v_1 t_1(v_1) + v_2 t_2(v_2)$, subject to (v_1, v_2) being equilibrium link flows given by (5.37). It is straightforward to find the following system optimal link toll charge and the corresponding link flows:

$$u_1^* = 1,\ v_1^* = 2,\ v_2^* = 3,\ F^* = 33$$

Now we consider solving the problem using the VI gap function approach. Let $\alpha = 1$, $m_1 = m_2 = 1.0$ for links 1 and 2 in the VI gap function (5.8). Then we have

$$G_\alpha(u_1, v_1, v_2) = -\min_{\tilde{v}_1+\tilde{v}_2=5,\tilde{v}_1\ge 0,\tilde{v}_2\ge 0} \phi(u_1, v_1, v_2, \tilde{v}_1, \tilde{v}_2) \tag{5.38}$$

where

$$\phi(u_1, v_1, v_2, \tilde{v}_1, \tilde{v}_2) = (\tilde{v}_1 - v_1)(2v_1 + 2 + u_1) + (\tilde{v}_2 - v_2)(v_2 + 4) + \frac{1}{2}(\tilde{v}_1 - v_1)^2 + \frac{1}{2}(\tilde{v}_2 - v_2)^2$$

Substituting $\tilde{v}_2 = 5 - \tilde{v}_1$ and $v_2 = 5 - v_1$ into the above expression yields

$$\phi(u_1, v_1, \tilde{v}_1) = \left(\tilde{v}_1 + \frac{1}{2}v_1 + \frac{1}{2}u_1 - \frac{7}{2}\right)^2 - \left(\frac{3}{2}v_1 + \frac{1}{2}u_1 - \frac{7}{2}\right)^2$$

One can thus readily obtain that

$$G_\alpha(u_1, v_1) = -\min_{0 \le \tilde{v}_1 \le 5} \phi(u_1, v_1, \tilde{v}_1) = \begin{cases} \frac{1}{4}(3v_1 + u_1 - 7)^2 & \text{if } u_1 + v_1 < 7 \\ v_1(2v_1 + u_1 - 7) & \text{if } u_1 + v_1 \ge 7 \end{cases} \tag{5.39}$$

One can easily verify that $G_\alpha(u_1, v_1)$ is continuously differentiable in both u_1 and v_1 and its derivatives are given below

$$\frac{\partial G_\alpha(u_1, v_1)}{\partial u_1} = \begin{cases} \frac{1}{2}(3v_1 + u_1 - 7), & \text{if } u_1 + v_1 < 7 \\ v_1, & \text{if } u_1 + v_1 \ge 7 \end{cases}$$

$$\frac{\partial G_\alpha(u_1, v_1)}{\partial v_1} = \begin{cases} \frac{3}{2}(3v_1 + u_1 - 7), & \text{if } u_1 + v_1 < 7 \\ 4v_1 + u_1 - 7, & \text{if } u_1 + v_1 \ge 7 \end{cases}$$

Let $G_\alpha(u_1, v_1) = 0$ in (5.39), we obtain the same equilibrium link flows, $v_1^*(u_1)$ (and $v_2^*(u_1)$ as well) as a function of u_1 as given in (5.37).

Next we consider the following penalized problem for finding a solution of minimizing total travel time cost

$$\begin{aligned} \min_{u_1 \ge 0, 0 \le v_1 \le 5} P_\rho(u_1, v_1) &= F(u_1, v_1) + \rho G_\alpha(u_1, v_1) \\ &= v_1 t_1(v_1) + (5 - v_1) t_2(5 - v_1) + \rho G_\alpha(u_1, v_1) \end{aligned} \tag{5.40}$$

where $\rho > 0$ is a positive penalty parameter. By eqn. (5.39), we can separate the above problem into two cases.

Case (a) When $u_1 + v_1 < 7$. Substituting the link cost functions and $G_\alpha(u_1, v_1)$ in (5.39) into (5.40) yields

$$\min_{\substack{u_1 \ge 0, 0 \le v_1 \le 5 \\ u_1 + v_1 < 7}} P_\rho(u_1, v_1) = 3v_1^2 - 12v_1 + 45 + \frac{\rho}{4}(3v_1 + u_1 - 7)^2$$

The optimal solution is reached at $(u_1, v_1) = (1,2)$ and $P_\rho(1,2) = F = 33$ or for any positive penalty parameter $\rho > 0$.

Case (b) When $u_1 + v_1 \ge 7$, similarly we have

$$\min_{\substack{u_1\geq 0, 0\leq v_1\leq 5\\ u_1+v_1\geq 7}} P_\rho(u_1,v_1)=3v_1^2-12v_1+45+\rho v_1(2v_1+u_1-7)$$

$$=(3+2\rho)\left\{\left(v_1+\frac{\rho u_1-7\rho-12}{2(3+2\rho)}\right)^2-\frac{1}{4}\left(\frac{\rho u_1-7\rho-12}{3+2\rho}\right)^2\right\}+45$$

The optimal solution is reached at

$$u_1(\rho)=\frac{15+7\rho}{3+\rho},\ v_1(\rho)=\frac{6}{3+\rho},\ v_2(\rho)=\frac{9+5\rho}{3+\rho},\ F(\rho)=45-\frac{36}{3+\rho}$$

Note that for any limited value of $\rho>0$, the solution of the penalized problem will not be exactly equal to the optimal solution (the UE condition is not satisfied or $G_\alpha(u_1,v_1)$ is not enforced to zero due to limited penalty value. However,

$$u_1(\rho)\to 7;\ v_1(\rho)\to 0;\ v_2(\rho)\to 5;\ P_\rho\to 45;\ F\to 45 \quad \text{as} \quad \rho\to\infty$$

The above solution meets the UE conditions but gives rise to a total travel time $F=45$, which is clearly inferior to the optimal solution identified in case (a).

To sum up, we conclude that the optimal solution is obtained when $u_1+v_1<7$ with an optimal solution $u_1^*=1,\ v_1^*=2,\ v_2^*=3$ and $F^*=33$, which is consistent with those obtained directly.

Example 5.2 (Differentiability of marginal function for the convex UE program and toll optimization with the BLPP model) Consider Example 4.1 in Chapter 4. There are two parallel links with link cost functions: $t_1(v_1)=2v_1+2$ and $t_2(v_2)=4v_2+8$, connecting a single OD pair with a fixed demand $d=3$. Link 1 is subjected to a toll charge u_1.

The equilibrium link flows $v_1^*(u_1)$ and $v_2^*(u_1)$ as a function of u_1 is given as follows

$$v_1^*(u_1)=\begin{cases}3-\frac{u_1}{6}, & 0\leq u_1\leq 18\\ 0, & u_1>18\end{cases} \quad \text{and} \quad v_2^*(u_1)=\begin{cases}\frac{u_1}{6}, & 0\leq u_1\leq 18\\ 3, & u_1>18\end{cases} \tag{5.41}$$

Given the above continuous reaction functions, $v_1^*(u_1)$ and $v_2^*(u_1)$ in the interval $u_1\in[0,+\infty)$ and by the definition of the marginal function (5.22), analytical expression of the marginal function for the example is readily obtained as follows

$$\varphi(v_1^*,v_2^*,u_1)=\int_0^{v_1^*}(2?+2+u_1)d\omega+\int_0^{v_2^*}(4?+8)d\omega=(v_1^*)^2+2v_1^*+u_1v_1^*+2(v_2^*)^2+8v_2^* \tag{5.42}$$

Substituting $v_1^*(u_1)$ and $v_2^*(u_1)$ in eqn. (5.41) into (5.42) yields

$$\varphi(u_1) = \begin{cases} 15 + 3u_1 - \dfrac{u_1^2}{12}, & 0 \le u_1 < 18 \\ 42, & u_1 \ge 18 \end{cases} \tag{5.43}$$

It is easy to verify that $\varphi(u_1)$ is differentiable in $u_1 \in [0, +\infty)$ and its derivative is directly given as

$$\varphi'(u_1) = \begin{cases} 3 - \dfrac{u_1}{6}, & 0 \le u_1 < 18 \\ 0, & u_1 > 18 \end{cases} \tag{5.44}$$

The gradient is a continuous function of u_1, and thus the marginal function is continuously differentiable. The values of both the marginal function and its gradient against toll charge u_1 are plotted in Figure 5.1.

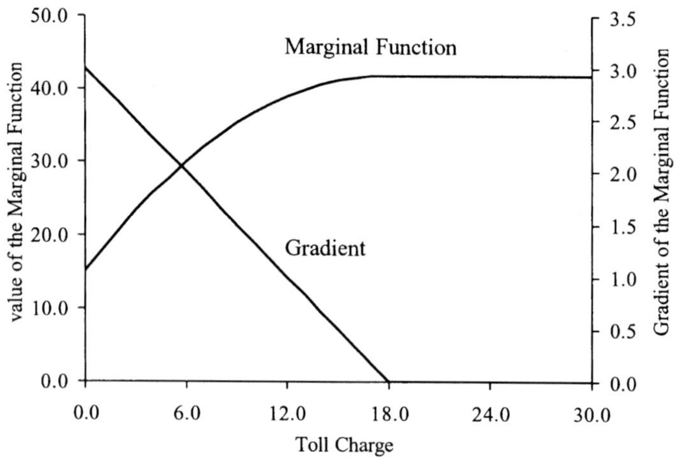

Figure 5.1 Values of marginal function φ and its gradient φ' against toll charge u_1

On the other hand,

$$\int_0^{v_1^*(u_1)} \frac{\partial t_1(\omega, u_1)}{\partial u_1} d\omega = v_1^*(u_1) = \begin{cases} 3 - \dfrac{u_1}{6}, & 0 \le u_1 \le 18 \\ 0, & u_1 > 18 \end{cases}$$

and

$$\int_0^{v_2^*(u_1)} \frac{\partial t_2(\omega, u_1)}{\partial u_1} d\omega = 0$$

This confirms that

$$\varphi'(u_1) = \int_0^{v_1^*(u_1)} \frac{\partial t_1(\omega, u_1)}{\partial u_1} \mathrm{d}\omega + \int_0^{v_2^*(u_1)} \frac{\partial t_2(\omega, u_1)}{\partial u_1} \mathrm{d}\omega$$

Next we suppose the road operator of the toll road in the network wishes to maximize the total revenue (*TR*) by choosing the toll charge u_1 levied on link 1. Namely, $\max_{u_1 \geq 0}\ F = u_1 v_1(u_1)$ subject to $v_1(u_1)$ and $v_2(u_1)$ being equilibrium link flows given by (5.41). This problem can be easily solved with the following optimal solution

$$u_1^* = 9,\ v_1^* = v_2^* = 1.5,\ F^* = 13.5$$

Now we consider solving the problem using the gap function approach for the convex UE program. We remove the constraint $v_1 + v_2 = 3$ by replacing v_2 with $3 - v_1$ and consider the penalized problem given below

$$\max_{u_1 \geq 0, 0 \leq v_1 \leq 3} P_\rho(u_1, v_1) = F(u_1, v_1) - \rho H(u_1, v_1) = u_1 v_1 - \rho H(u_1, v_1) \tag{5.45}$$

where $\rho > 0$ is a positive penalty parameter. From the definition of the gap function (5.26), $H(u_1, v_1)$ is given by

$$H(u_1, v_1) = \int_0^{v_1} (2? + 2 + u_1)\,\mathrm{d}? + \int_0^{3-v_1} (4? + 8)\,\mathrm{d}? - \varphi(u_1)$$

where the value function $\varphi(u_1)$ is given by (5.43). In view of the fact that the current objective function has different explicit expressions in different intervals of variable u_1, we can decompose the revenue maximization problem (5.45) into two sub-problems defined within the intervals of $0 \leq u_1 \leq 18$ and $u_1 > 18$ respectively.

Case (a) When $0 \leq u_1 \leq 18$, the partially penalized objective function is quadratic and the problem can be written as:

$$\max_{\substack{0 \leq v_1 \leq 3 \\ 0 \leq u_1 \leq 18}} A_1 \begin{pmatrix} v_1 \\ u_1 \end{pmatrix} + \frac{1}{2}(v_1, u_1) B_1 \begin{pmatrix} v_1 \\ u_1 \end{pmatrix} + C_1$$

where $A_1 = [18\rho,\ 3\rho]$, $B_1 = \begin{bmatrix} -6?, & 1-? \\ 1-?, & -?/6 \end{bmatrix}$, $C_1 = -27?$. In this case, B_1 is negative definite for any $? > 1/2$, which means the problem is a strictly concave maximization and the stationary point of the partially penalized problem is

$$v_1(?) = \frac{3?}{2? - 1},\quad u_1(?) = \frac{18?}{2? - 1}$$

which is feasible for the problem. Hence, the above $(v_1(?), u_1(?))$ is the optimal solution and we have

$$\lim_{?\to+\infty} v_1(?) = 1.5, \quad \lim_{?\to+\infty} u_1(?) = 9, \quad \lim_{\rho\to\infty} P_\rho(u_1, v_1) = 13.5$$

which is exactly the optimal solution identified earlier. Note that for any limited value of $\rho > 1/2$, the solution of the penalized problem will not be exactly equal to the solution of the example.

Case (b) When $u_1 > 18$, the problem can be written as

$$\max_{\substack{0\le v_1\le 3\\ u_1>18}} A_2\begin{pmatrix} v_1 \\ u_1 \end{pmatrix} + \frac{1}{2}(v_1, u_1) B_2 \begin{pmatrix} v_1 \\ u_1 \end{pmatrix} + C_2$$

where $A_2 = [18\rho,\ 0]$ $B_2 = \begin{bmatrix} -6\rho, & 1-\rho \\ 1-\rho, & 0 \end{bmatrix}$, $C_2 = 0$. The optimal solution of the problem here is not obvious for a limited positive parameter ρ. Nevertheless, it is straightforward to check the optimal solution as $\rho \to +\infty$. The problem can be rewritten below

$$\max_{0\le v_1\le 3, u_1>18} u_1 v_1 - \rho v_1 (3v_1 + u_1 - 18)$$

Clearly, $v_1(3v_1 + u_1 - 18) \ge 0$ for any feasible v_1 and u_1. Hence $v_1(3v_1 + u_1 - 18) = 0$ should hold as the penalty parameter ρ approaches infinity. This means that, as $\rho \to +\infty$, the optimal value of v_1 equals 0 but u_1 (>18) can be any limited positive value greater than 18. The solution can be interpreted as follows. As long as toll charge u_1 on link 1 is greater than 18, no one will use link 1. Hence the revenue is always 0, no matter how large the toll charge u_1 (>18) is. This observation coincides with the result of the reaction function (5.41).

Summarizing the discussion of the two cases, we can see clearly that the optimal solution of the whole problem is located in the first interval of $0 \le u_1 \le 18$, and given by $u_1^* = 9$, with the corresponding maximal revenue of $F^* = 13.5$.

Example. 5.3 (Toll selection for system optimal flow) We provide a larger numerical example to validate the marginal function based method and the augmented Lagrangian algorithm for the toll optimization problem.

The network, as depicted in Figure 5.2, consists of 9 nodes, 18 links and 4 O-D pairs with the following link cost function

$$t_a(v_a) = t_a^0\left(1 + 0.15\left(\frac{v_a}{C_a}\right)^4\right) \tag{5.46}$$

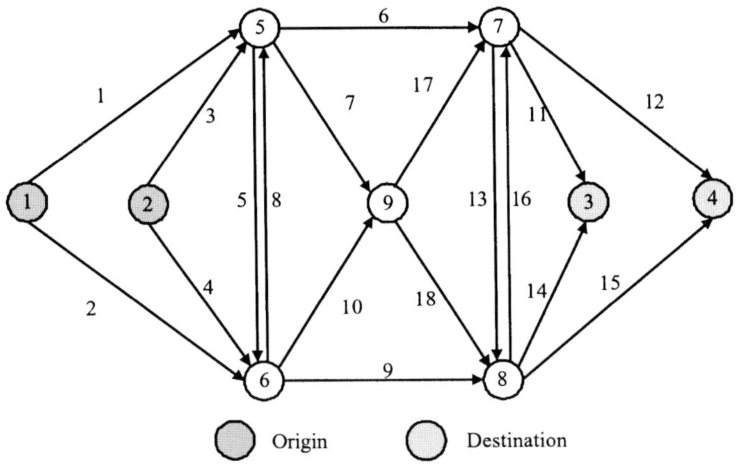

Figure 5.2 The network used for testing of the marginal function based solution method

OD Pair	$1 \rightarrow 3$	$1 \rightarrow 4$	$2 \rightarrow 3$	$2 \rightarrow 4$
Demand	10	20	30	40

The free-flow travel time t_a^0 and link capacity C_a for all links are presented in Table 5.1. The O-D demands are assumed to be fixed and given by

Table 5.1 The input data for the network in Figure 5.2

Link No.	t_a^0	C_a	Link No.	t_a^0	C_a
1	5	12	10	7	32
2	6	18	11	3	25
3	3	35	12	6	24
4	9	35	13	2	19
5	9	20	14	8	39
6	2	11	15	6	43
7	8	26	16	4	36
8	4	11	17	4	26
9	6	33	18	8	30

Suppose all links are subjected to toll charge $(\bar{A} = A)$ with an upper bound constraint for each link $0 \leq u_a \leq 20.0,\ a \in A$. We consider the toll pricing problem for minimizing the total equilibrium travel time with fixed OD demand. Then the detailed single-level continuously differentiable formulation with the gap function for the convex UE program is given below

$$\min_{\mathbf{u},\mathbf{v}} F(\mathbf{u},\mathbf{v}) = \sum_{a \in A} t_a(v_a) v_a \tag{5.47}$$

subject to

$$0 \le u_a \le 20.0,\ a \in A \tag{5.48}$$

$$H(\mathbf{u},\mathbf{v}) = \sum_{a\in A} \int_0^{v_a} \left(t_a(\omega) + u_a\right) d\omega - \varphi(\mathbf{u}) = 0 \tag{5.49}$$

$$v_a = \sum_{w\in W} \sum_{r\in R_w} f_{rw} \delta_{ar},\ a \in A \tag{5.50}$$

$$\sum_{r\in R_w} f_{rw} = d_w,\ w \in W \tag{5.51}$$

$$f_{rw} \ge 0,\ r \in R_w,\ w \in W \tag{5.52}$$

where the marginal function is given by

$$\varphi(\mathbf{u}) = \sum_{a\in A} \int_0^{v_a^*(\mathbf{u})} t_a(\omega, u_a)\, d\omega \tag{5.53}$$

where $v_a^*(\mathbf{u}),\ a \in A$ is the equilibrium link flow for any given toll charge $\mathbf{u}$.

The partially augmented Lagrangian function for the above formulation is given as

$$L(\mathbf{u},\mathbf{v},\lambda,\rho) = \sum_{a\in A} t_a(v_a) v_a + \lambda H(\mathbf{u},\mathbf{v}) + \frac{1}{2}\rho\left(H(\mathbf{u},\mathbf{v})\right)^2 \tag{5.54}$$

Let the values of the parameters for the augmented Lagrangian algorithm in Sub-section 5.2.4 be given as $\lambda^{(0)} = 0.0$ for the initial Lagrange multiplier and $\rho^{(0)} = 10.0$ for the penalty parameter associated with the gap function constraint, and the convergence tolerance be set to be $\kappa = 0.01$. The detailed results at each major iteration of the augmented Lagrangian algorithm are presented in Table 5.2. It is observed that the penalty is not enlarged at each iteration and the value of the gap function declines quickly below the desired threshold.

Table 5.2. Implementation results of the augmented Lagrangian algorithm

Iteration n	$\lambda^{(n)}$	$\rho^{(n)}$	$L\left(\mathbf{u}^{(n)},\mathbf{v}^{(n)},\lambda^{(n)},\rho^{(n)}\right)$	$H\left(\mathbf{u}^{(n)},\mathbf{v}^{(n)}\right)$
0	0.000	10.0	837,288,900.000	40,291.090
1	14.370	10.0	2332.800	1.437
2	14.404	10.0	2310.190	0.003

Table 5.3 summarizes and compares the optimal link tolls obtained by the augmented Lagrangian method, the direct marginal-cost pricing method and the MINSYS method (Bergendorff et al., 1997). Note that since a complete set of links are charged on the network, the marginal-cost pricing principle does apply here and gives the exact minimum total network travel time. As observed from the Table, the toll patterns in the table are quite different by different methods due to the well-known fact that the link tolls that support a system optimum as a user equilibrium, in the case of fixed demand, is not unique. We note

that the total travel time by the augmented Lagrangian method is marginally higher (2310.2 versus 2254.0 or 2.49%) than the exact optimum. This is not surprising because the augmented Lagrangian method proposed here is designed for the general BLPP second-best road pricing problem with UE constraints, whereas the MINSYS method optimizes a secondary objective of revenue minimization by restricting the problem to a predetermined convex system-optimal toll set (the minimum total travel time or exact system optimum is always kept in the minimization of total toll revenue).

Table 5.3. The optimal tolls and total travel time obtained by three alternative methods

Link No.	Marginal-cost pricing method	MINSYS method	Augmented Lagrangian method
1	1.135	0	10.400
2	6.162	0	9.600
3	2.590	4.00	12.680
4	3.618	0	7.320
5	0	0	11.640
6	16.880	11.200	16.800
7	5.135	0	7.880
8	0	0	0
9	7.370	7.200	12.040
10	0.107	0	8.480
11	3.541	4.000	10.040
12	2.014	0	7.400
13	0	0	20.000
14	0.024	0	9.960
15	2.497	0	12.600
16	0.000	0	15.000
17	3.746	3.200	2.880
18	0.063	0	20.000
Total cost	2254.0	2254.0	2310.2

5.4 ENTRY-EXIT BASED TOLL DESIGN PROBLEMS

In this section we provide an application of the gap function approach developed earlier in this chapter to a specialized second-best pricing problem in networks with entry-exit based toll charges (Yang, Zhang and Meng, 2004; Meng et al., 2004). A real expressway may consist of a sequence of road sections with multiple entry and exit points and the toll charge for a user depends on his or her entry and exit points. Thus, the toll charge is entry-exit specific, instead of section- or link-additive. The resulting traffic equilibrium problem for given toll charges thus becomes a special case of the general traffic equilibrium problems with non-additive path costs presented in Section 2.3 of Chapter 2, and can be solved by some path enumeration or generation. Our objective here is to develop a manageable BLPP model for toll optimization subject to traffic equilibrium constraints. In particular, we shall explore a convex programming formulation and solution of the traffic equilibrium problem without requiring path enumeration. This will greatly facilitate determination of optimal entry-exit tolls using the BLPP techniques such as the marginal function approach developed above.

We shall present a convex programming formulation of the traffic equilibrium problem with non-additive entry-exit tolls and adapt the Frank-Wolfe convex combination algorithm for its solution through an appropriate network transformation. Uniqueness of the entry-exit flows through the toll roads and the resulting revenue is investigated. We then discuss various alternative toll-pricing schemes, and propose a marginal function based BLPP model for toll optimization subject to traffic equilibrium constraints.

5.4.1 A UE Model with Entry-Exit Specific Tolls

We first configure a special network for formulating the problem, we define a tolling sub-network where users have to pay for entrance and a basic sub-network without tolling links. The tolling sub-network and the basic sub-network are connected by some controlling ramps (links). There are entry ramps from the basic sub-network to the tolling sub-network and exit ramps from the tolling sub-network to the basic sub-network. Figure 5.3 provides a schematic representation of the network system, where the basic and tolling sub-networks are connected by a number of entry and exit links. Note that there is only one block of tolling sub-network in Figure 5.3, but the subsequent model and algorithm apply for the general case with multiple tolling sub-networks. The toll charges for using the tolling sub-network are solely dependent upon the entry and exit points of the users regardless of how they have traveled within the sub-network.

With the basic notation used before, let E denote the set of entry-exit pairs in the tolling sub-network and q_e the traffic flow between entry-exit pair $e \in E$. Then we have:

$$q_e = \sum_{w \in W} \sum_{r \in R_w} f_{rw} \delta_{re}, \quad e \in E \tag{5.55}$$

where $\delta_{re} = 1$ if path $r \in R_w$ uses the tolling sub-network through entry-exit pair e, and 0 otherwise. Apart from the link additive path travel time through the whole network, a path may include monetary cost such as toll charges if this path goes trough the tolling sub-network. Let u_e be the toll charge for traveling between entry-exit pair $e \in E$, then the toll specific to path r for going through the tolling sub-network is given as:

$$u_{rw} = \sum_{e \in E} u_e \delta_{re}, \quad r \in R_w, w \in W \tag{5.56}$$

Assume users are homogeneous, each with an identical constant value of time. The generalized path cost function (in time unit) can be expressed as follows:

$$\tilde{c}_{rw} = \frac{1}{\beta} u_{rw} + c_{rw} = \frac{1}{\beta} \sum_{e \in E} u_e \delta_{re} + \sum_{a \in A} t_a(v_a) \delta_{ar}, \quad r \in R_w, w \in W \tag{5.57}$$

where β is the user's value of time. Thus, the path cost function (5.57) is a special case of the generalized non-additive path cost function introduced by Section 2.3 of Chapter 2, where a nonlinear (instead of constant) value of time is considered.

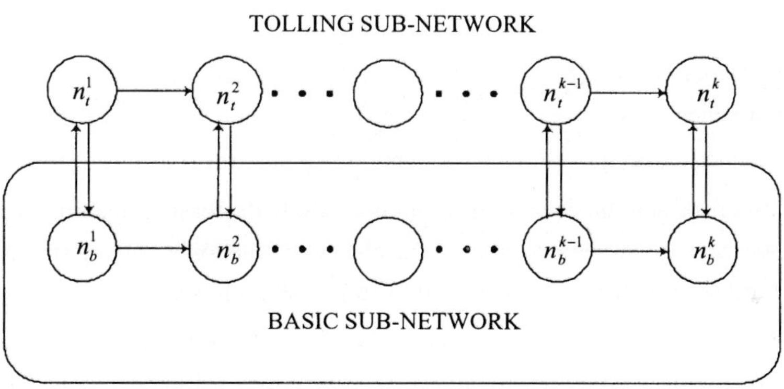

Figure 5.3 A schematic representation of the network system (n_b^i and n_t^i represent node i in the basic and tolling sub-networks, respectively)

Since a toll scheme influences the demand for travel, it is desirable to consider the elasticity of travel demand. We thus introduce the demand function $d_w = D_w(\mu_w)$ and $B_w = D_w^{-1}(d_w)$ (suppose separable OD demand function), which is a strictly decreasing function of the minimum generalized OD travel cost (in time unit) μ_w $\left(\mu_w = \min_{r \in R_w} \tilde{c}_{rw},\ w \in W\right)$. Furthermore, we assume that users have a free choice of whether to use the roads with or without toll charge and the route choice behavior of users satisfies the user equilibrium principle. In this case, a path-flow vector $\mathbf{f}^*$ with element f_{rw}^*, is said to be a user equilibrium if and only if

$$f_{rw}^* > 0, \text{ then } \tilde{c}_{rw}\left(\mathbf{f}^*\right) = \mu_w\left(\mathbf{f}^*\right) \text{ for all } r \in R_w,\ w \in W \tag{5.58}$$

$$f_{rw}^* = 0, \text{ then } \tilde{c}_{rw}\left(\mathbf{f}^*\right) \geq \mu_w\left(\mathbf{f}^*\right) \text{ for all } r \in R_w,\ w \in W \tag{5.59}$$

Together with the link flow vector $\mathbf{v}$ and OD demand vector $\mathbf{d}$, we also introduce vector $\mathbf{q} = (\cdots, q_e, \cdots)^{\mathrm{T}}$. With the above notation, we can construct the following minimization problem:

$$\min Z(\mathbf{v}, \mathbf{d}, \mathbf{q}) = \sum_{a \in A} \int_0^{v_a} t_a(\omega) \mathrm{d}\omega + \frac{1}{\beta} \sum_{e \in E} q_e u_e - \sum_{w \in W} \int_0^{d_w} B_w(\omega) \mathrm{d}\omega \tag{5.60}$$

subject to

$$\sum_{r \in R_w} f_{rw} = d_w, \quad w \in W \tag{5.61}$$

$$v_a = \sum_{w \in W} \sum_{r \in R_w} f_{rw} \delta_{ar}, \quad a \in A \tag{5.62}$$

$$q_e = \sum_{w \in W} \sum_{r \in R_w} f_{rw} \delta_{re}, \quad e \in E \tag{5.63}$$

$$f_{rw} \geq 0, \quad r \in R_w, w \in W \tag{5.64}$$

Note that constraints (5.61)-(5.64) are the conventional conditions of feasible flows, which are linear and hence define a convex set. The objective function (5.60) is separable with respect to variables $(\mathbf{v}, \mathbf{d}, \mathbf{q})$. With the assumption that link travel time is a strictly increasing function of link flow and the demand function is a strictly decreasing function of generalized travel cost, we can see that the first-term of the objective function (5.60) is strictly convex in $\mathbf{v}$ and the third term is strictly convex in $\mathbf{d}$. The second term is a linear function of $\mathbf{q}$ and hence also convex (but not strictly convex in $\mathbf{q}$). Thus the minimization problem (5.60)-(5.64) is a convex programming problem. It is straightforward to show that the first-order necessary conditions for the program are equivalent to the elastic demand network equilibrium conditions.

We now look into the uniqueness of the solutions of the problem (5.60)-(5.64) and the resulting revenue for given toll charges. This will be useful for defining the gap function and the upper-level objective function later. Due to strict convexity of the objective function in $\mathbf{d}$ and $\mathbf{v}$, OD demand and link flow solutions are thus unique. But the solution of entry-exit flow is not uniquely determined because the second-term of the objective function (5.60) is linear in $\mathbf{q}$. Nevertheless, the revenue collected from toll charges is uniquely defined for any given entry-exit based toll charge $\mathbf{u} = (\cdots, u_e, \cdots)^{\mathrm{T}}$ and given (non-unique) equilibrium solution $\mathbf{q}^*$. The reason is simple. For the given convex program, there is a unique optimal objective function value. Since the first and the third terms are strictly convex in $\mathbf{v}$ and $\mathbf{d}$, respectively, their values at optimal solutions $(\mathbf{v}^*, \mathbf{d}^*)$ are uniquely defined. This means that the value of the second term is also unique at equilibrium solution $\mathbf{q}^*$ for given toll charges. Because the second term of the objective function is exactly the total revenue multiplied by parameter β^{-1}, the total revenue at any equilibrium solution $(\mathbf{v}^*, \mathbf{d}^*, \mathbf{q}^*)$ is uniquely defined for any given toll charges $\mathbf{u}$.

Example 5.4 (Non-uniqueness of equilibrium entry-exit flows and uniqueness of revenue at equilibrium) Consider an example network shown in Figure 5.4 where links 1, 2 and 3 are the basic network and links 4, 5 and 6 are the road sections of a toll highway. Suppose the link travel time function is of the following linear form: $t = a + v/b$, where the values of parameters a and b are given in Table 5.4. There are 4 entry-exit pairs: pair 1 (nodes 1→4), pair 2 (nodes 1→3), pair 3 (nodes 2→4) and pair 4 (nodes 2→3), and the corresponding toll charges for these 4 pairs are supposed to be 4, 3, 3 and 2 (time units), respectively. There is only one OD pair from node 1 to node 4 with a demand of 100 (flow units).

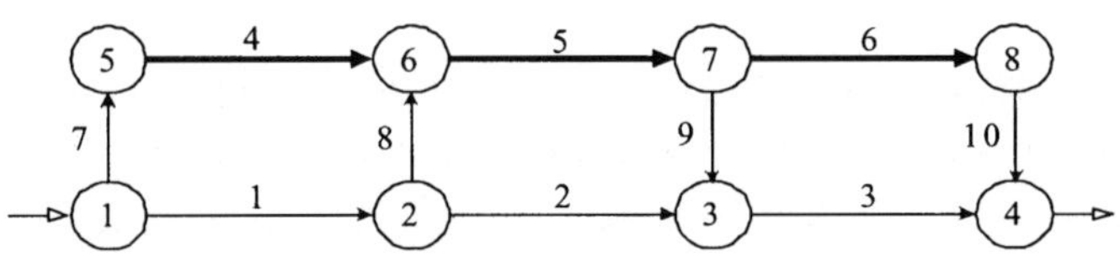

Figure 5.4 An example network with non-unique entry-exit flows but unique revenue at equilibrium solutions (4,5 & 6 = tolled links)

Table 5.4 value of parameters a and b for links of network in Figure 5.4

Link	1	2	3	4	5	6	7	8	9	10
a	3.0	9.0	3.0	2.0	2.0	2.0	0.5	0.5	0.5	0.5
b	50.0	50.0	50.0	50.0	50.0	50.0	100.0	100.0	100.0	100.0

Table 5.5 The equilibrium link flows on network in Figure 5.4

Link	1	2	3	4	5	6	7	8	9	10
Flow	50.0	0.0	50.0	50.0	100.0	50.0	50.0	50.0	50.0	50.0
Time	4.0	9.0	4.0	3.0	4.0	3.0	1.0	1.0	1.0	1.0

In equilibrium, the unique link flows obtained are given in Table 5.5. However, the entry-exit flows are non-unique. In fact, there are 4 paths with flows at equilibrium, they are (in link index): path 1 (7→4→5→6→10), path 2 (7→4→5→9→3), path 3 (1→8→5→6→10) and path 4 (1→8→5→9→3). Flows on the 4 paths are the entry-exit flows through the toll road. Suppose the flow on path (entry-exit pair) 1 is q $(0 \le q \le 50)$; then the flows along paths (entry-exit pairs) 2, 3 and 4 are $50 - q$, $50 - q$ and q, respectively. Obviously, for any

q $(0 \le q \le 50)$, the path flows are equilibrium flows. Thus the equilibrium entry-exit flow solution is not unique, but constitutes a convex set. However, for any q $(0 \le q \le 50)$, the total revenue at equilibrium is $4q + 3(50-q) + 3(50-q) + 2q \equiv 300$.

5.4.2 Solving the UE model with Entry-Exit Specific Tolls by Network Decomposition

We now consider how the standard convex combination method can be used to solve the convex programming problem of the traffic equilibrium model (5.60)-(5.64). As described in Chapter 2, the convex combination method consists of two major steps: finding a descent direction and implementing a line search. For problem (5.60)-(5.64), the descent direction can be found by solving the following linear program (LP) for a given current solution $(\mathbf{v}^{(n)}, \mathbf{d}^{(n)}, \mathbf{q}^{(n)})$:

$$\min_{\mathbf{f}} \sum_{w \in W} \sum_{r \in R_w} \left[\tilde{c}_{rw}^{(n)} - B_w\left(d_w^{(n)}\right) \right] \hat{f}_{rw} \tag{5.65}$$

subject to

$$\hat{f}_{rw} \ge 0, \ r \in R_w, \ w \in W \tag{5.66}$$

$$\sum_{r \in R_w} \hat{f}_{rw} \le \bar{D}_w, \ w \in W \tag{5.67}$$

where $\bar{D}_w$ is a fixed upper bound of the OD demand between OD pair $w \in W$; and the non-additive path cost $\tilde{c}_{rw}^{(n)}$ is defined by (5.57), where t_a is given to be $t_a^{(n)} = t_a\left(v_a^{(n)}\right)$ with current link flow solution $v_a^{(n)}$, $a \in A$. Finding the optimal solution of the LP problem (5.65)-(5.67) requires assignment of the demand $\bar{D}_w$ between each OD pair to the path r for which $\left[\tilde{c}_{rw}^{(n)} - B_w\left(d_w^{(n)}\right)\right]$ is the smallest, provided that $\left[\tilde{c}_{rw}^{(n)} - B_w\left(d_w^{(n)}\right)\right] \le 0$, and no flow should be assigned to any path if $\left[\tilde{c}_{rw}^{(n)} - B_w\left(d_w^{(n)}\right)\right]$ is positive. This allocation procedure requires finding the shortest path between each OD pair. Because the path cost defined in (5.57) is not link-additive, the standard shortest path algorithm, such as Dijkstra's labeling algorithm, is not directly applicable. Fortunately, the network with entry-exit toll charges considered here can be simply decomposed and transformed into a new network, for which a typical shortest path algorithm can be applied.

The whole network is decomposed into the basic sub-network and the tolling sub-network. Because travel time is link-additive, a conventional shortest path algorithm can be used to find the shortest travel time (exclusive of tolls) path between each entry-exit pair on the tolling sub-network. Each entry-exit pair is then connected by a hypothetical link, whose cost is the identified minimum travel time spent on the tolling sub-network, plus the corresponding entry-exit toll charge. We then have a new network consisting of the basic sub-network and all hypothetical links of the tolling sub-network. The path cost through the newly transformed network becomes link-additive, and thus the shortest uncongested path can be simply identified and the LP problem (5.65)-(5.67) can be solved without path enumeration. The same procedure is applied to each tolling sub-network when there are multiple disjoint tolling sub-networks.

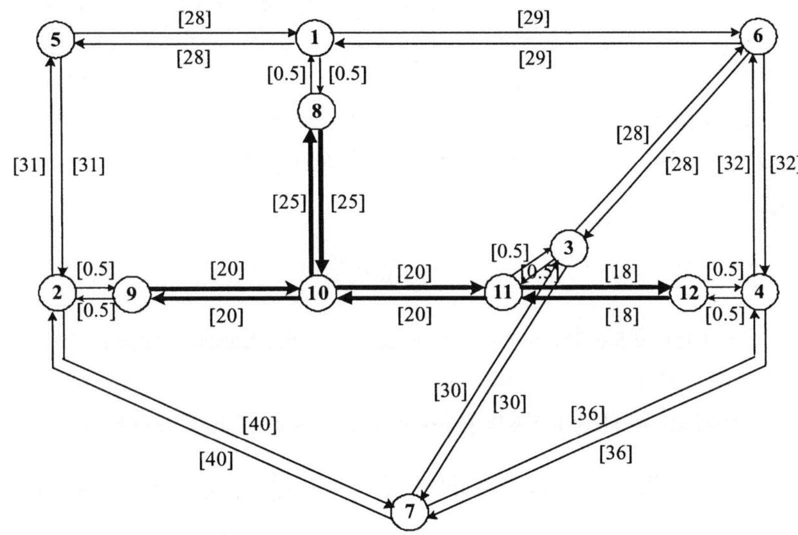

Figure 5.5 A network with fixed link travel times and tolls

Table 5.6 The entry-exit tolls on network in Figure 5.6

	Exit Node			
Entry Node	1	2	3	4
1		6	6	7
2	6		4	8
3	6	4		4
4	7	8	4	

Consider a network shown in Figure 5.5. The bold lines represent tolled road sections, the finer lines represent entry and exit ramps or links and all lines represent the basic sub-network links. Link travel times are given and indicated in brackets (all entry and exit links are assumed to have a short travel time of 0.5 time units), and the entry-exit tolls are given in Table 5.6. By network transformation, we have the new network depicted in Figure 5.6, where the costs (including travel times and toll charges) for hypothetical links are indicated in brackets.

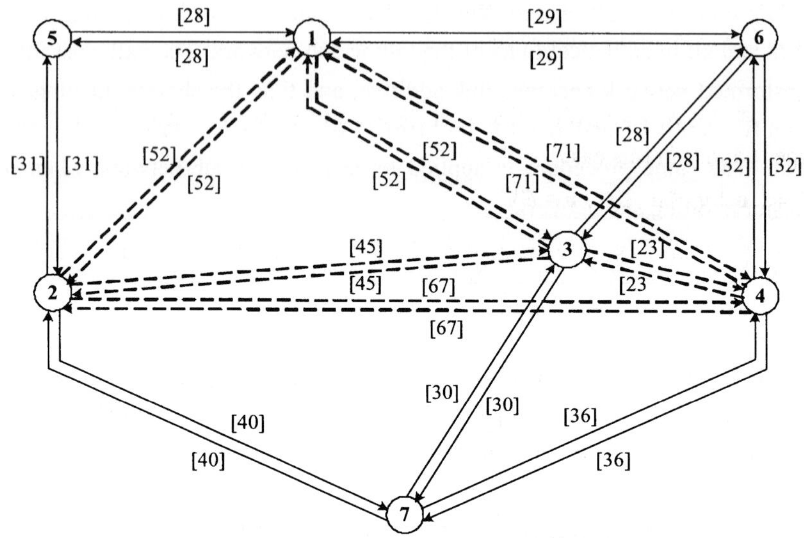

Figure 5.6 The network in Figure 5.5 after transformation

Solving the LP solution (5.65)-(5.67) gives rise to a set of link flows $\{\hat{v}_a^{(n)}, a \in A\}$, OD demands $\{\hat{d}_w^{(n)}, w \in W\}$ and entry-exit flows $\{\hat{q}_e^{(n)}, e \in E\}$. These flows, determined from the LP problem, are termed auxiliary flows that are used for the following line search of the convex combination algorithm:

$$\min_{0 \le \alpha \le 1} \sum_{a \in A} \int_0^{v_a^{(n)} + \alpha(\hat{v}_a^{(n)} - v_a^{(n)})} t_a(\omega)\,d\omega + \frac{1}{\beta} \sum_{e \in E} \left[q_e^{(n)} + \alpha\left(\hat{q}_e^{(n)} - q_e^{(n)}\right) \right] u_e - \sum_{w \in W} \int_0^{d_w^{(n)} + \alpha(\hat{d}_w^{(n)} - d_w^{(n)})} B_w(\omega)\,d\omega \tag{5.68}$$

where $0 \le \alpha \le 1$ is the step size. Note that the costs of the hypothetical links have to be updated at each iteration by calculating the shortest travel time between each entry-exit pair according to the current updated link travel time, and the assigned flows on the hypothetical links are the corresponding auxiliary entry-exit flows.

5.4.3 Alternative Tolling Schemes

We now consider how to design optimal tolling schemes for maximization of either total revenues or social welfare, while taking into account the routing behavior of users. Here we consider five realistically meaningful tolling schemes subject to different constraints. These constraints will constitute the feasible set of the entry-exit toll charges $\mathbf{u}=(\cdots,u_e,\cdots)^{\mathrm{T}}$ of the subsequent bi-level toll design models.

Scheme A. Toll charge is specific to individual entry-exit pairs, and subject to a lower bound and an upper bound. In this case,

$$U_1=\left\{\mathbf{u}\mid \underline{u}_e\le u_e\le \overline{u}_e,\ e\in E\right\} \tag{5.69}$$

where $\underline{u}_e$ and $\overline{u}_e$ are the lower and upper bounds of toll charge u_e between entry-exit pair $e\in E$.

Scheme B. Tolls charged are specific to individual entry-exit pairs, but longer distances traveled are subject to higher toll charges. Furthermore, if an entry-exit pair is made up of two or more sub entry-exit pairs, its toll charge should be less than or equal to the sum of the toll charges for these sub pairs. In this case,

$$U_2=\left\{\mathbf{u}\;\middle|\;\begin{array}{l}\underline{u}_e\le u_e\le \overline{u}_e,\ e\in E\\ l_{e'}\ge l_e\ \Rightarrow\ u_{e'}\ge u_e,\ \ e,e'\in E\\ e=e_1+e_2\ \Rightarrow\ u_e\le u_{e_1}+u_{e_2},\ \ e,e_1,e_2\in E\end{array}\right\} \tag{5.70}$$

where l_e is the shortest travel distance between entry-exit pair $e\in E$.

Scheme C. Toll charge is link-specific and thus additive. In this case, link-specific toll $u_a, a\in A$ is determined first and then the entry-exit based toll charge is obtained.

$$U_3=\left\{\mathbf{u}\;\middle|\;\underline{u}_e\le u_e\le \overline{u}_e \text{ and } u_e\ge 0,\ u_e=\sum_{a\in A}u_a\delta_{ae},\ e\in E\right\} \tag{5.71}$$

where $\overline{A}$ is the set of tolled links, $\delta_{ae}=1$ if entry-exit pair e uses link a and 0 otherwise.

Scheme D. Toll charge is proportional to the distance traveled, and a single variable u (a proportionality constant) is determined and then the entry-exit based toll charge is obtained.

$$U_4=\left\{\mathbf{u}\mid \underline{u}_e\le u_e\le \overline{u}_e \text{ and } u>0,\ u_e=ul_e,\ e\in E\right\} \tag{5.72}$$

where l_e is again the shortest travel distance between entry-exit pair $e\in E$.

Scheme E. Constant toll charge. In this case, the toll charge is independent of entry and exit points, and there is a single variable to be determined.

$$U_5=\left\{\mathbf{u}\mid \underline{u}_e\le u_e\le \overline{u}_e \text{ and } u_e=u,\ e\in E\right\} \tag{5.73}$$

5.4.4 BLPP Formulation and Gap Function Approach

We are now ready to introduce the BLPP formulation of the network toll design problem with entry-exit based toll charges as follows:

$$\max_{\mathbf{u}\in U} F\left(\mathbf{u}, \mathbf{v}(\mathbf{u}), \mathbf{d}(\mathbf{u}), \mathbf{q}(\mathbf{u})\right) \tag{5.74}$$

where $\mathbf{v}(\mathbf{u})$, $\mathbf{d}(\mathbf{u})$ and $\mathbf{q}(\mathbf{u})$ are the corresponding UE link flow, OD demand, and entry-exit flow through the toll roads, respectively, associated with a given toll pattern $\mathbf{u}$, and are determined by solving problem (5.60)-(5.64). The upper level objective function can be either total toll revenue or total social welfare, and are given below for a given entry-exit toll pattern $\mathbf{u}$:

$$F_1\left(\mathbf{q}(\mathbf{u}), \mathbf{u}\right) = \sum_{e\in E} u_e q_e(\mathbf{u}) \tag{5.75}$$

The social welfare is

$$F_2\left(\mathbf{v}(\mathbf{u}), \mathbf{d}(\mathbf{u}), \mathbf{u}\right) = \sum_{w\in W} \int_0^{d_w(\mathbf{u})} B_w(\omega)\mathrm{d}\omega - \sum_{a\in A} v_a(\mathbf{u}) t_a\left(v_a(\mathbf{u})\right) \tag{5.76}$$

The toll set U in (5.74) can be any $U_i, i = 1,2,\cdots,5$ defined by (5.69)-(5.73), respectively. As discussed earlier, the equilibrium link flow and OD demand are unique; hence, the social welfare is unique. Furthermore, the toll revenue is unique, although the equilibrium entry-exit flows are non-unique. Thus, the objective function (5.74) is uniquely defined with respect to the toll pattern.

We now consider applying the gap function based approach to solve the BLPP network toll design problem. Since the entry-exit flows are non-unique, the assumption of uniqueness like link flows and OD demands in the gap function introduced earlier does not hold, and, as a result, the optimal solution of entry-exit flow $\mathbf{q}^*(\mathbf{u})$ is not a continuous function of upper-level decision variable $\mathbf{u}$. We now consider the regularization approach proposed by Dempe (2000) for the BLPP with non-unique lower level solutions. The main idea is to regularize the lower level problem so that the objective function becomes strictly convex by adding an additional term relating to the non-unique variables. Then, the additional term is decreased gradually to a sufficiently small value, and the optimal solution of the regularized problem is uniquely determined. With this approach, we can circumvent the difficulties of non-uniqueness 0f the lower-level entry-exit flow solution by simply replacing the entry-exit toll u_e with $u_e + \eta q_e/2$ in objective function (5.60), where η is a small positive constant. By doing so, the second term of the objective function will become $\beta^{-1}\sum_{e\in E}\left(u_e q_e + \eta q_e^2/2\right)$, being a differentiable and strictly increasing function of entry-exit flows q_e. This term can be diminished by successively reducing η so that the resulting unique entry-exit flow solution belongs to the set of equilibrium entry-exit flows obtained from the original model (5.60)-(5.64) and the same unique OD demand and link flow solutions are generated. With this modification, the gap function based approach introduced in Section 5.2 now becomes applicable to the traffic equilibrium problem with non-additive path costs.

To make the notation compact, we define $\mathbf{x}=\left(\mathbf{v}^{\mathrm{T}},\mathbf{d}^{\mathrm{T}},\mathbf{q}^{\mathrm{T}}\right)^{\mathrm{T}}$. Let X denote the set of feasible solutions of the lower-level traffic equilibrium problem. Namely,

$$X=\left\{\mathbf{x}=\left(\mathbf{v}^{\mathrm{T}},\mathbf{d}^{\mathrm{T}},\mathbf{q}^{\mathrm{T}}\right)^{\mathrm{T}} \mid (\mathbf{v},\mathbf{d},\mathbf{q}) \text{ satisfies } (5.61)-(5.64)\right\} \tag{5.77}$$

The marginal function is defined as

$$\varphi(\mathbf{u})=\min_{\mathbf{x}\in X} \tilde{Z}(\mathbf{u},\mathbf{x}) \tag{5.78}$$

where $\tilde{Z}(\mathbf{u},\mathbf{x})$ is the regulated UE objective function given below:

$$\tilde{Z}(\mathbf{u},\mathbf{x})=\sum_{a\in A}\int_0^{v_a} t_a(\omega)\,d\omega+\frac{1}{\beta}\sum_{e\in E}\left(u_e q_e+\frac{1}{2}\eta q_e^{\,2}\right)-\sum_{w\in W}\int_0^{d_w} B_w(\omega)\,d\omega \tag{5.79}$$

Let $\mathbf{x}^*(\mathbf{u})=\operatorname*{argmin}_{\mathbf{x}\in X}\tilde{Z}(\mathbf{x},\mathbf{u})$ be the equilibrium solution, then $\mathbf{x}^*(\mathbf{u})$ is a continuous function of $\mathbf{u}$ and the marginal function is given by

$$\varphi(\mathbf{u})=\tilde{Z}\left(\mathbf{u},\mathbf{x}^*(\mathbf{u})\right) \tag{5.80}$$

As shown earlier, marginal function (5.80) is differentiable and its partial derivative with respect to $\mathbf{u}$ is given by

$$\nabla\varphi(\mathbf{u})=\left(\cdots,\frac{\partial\varphi(\mathbf{u})}{\partial u_e},\cdots\right)^{\mathrm{T}} \tag{5.81}$$

where

$$\frac{\partial\varphi(\mathbf{u})}{\partial u_e}=\frac{1}{\beta}q_e^*(\mathbf{u}),\quad e\in E \tag{5.82}$$

For any given toll pattern $\mathbf{u}$, the optimal solution $\mathbf{q}^*(\mathbf{u})$ (or $\mathbf{x}^*(\mathbf{u})$) is obtained by performing a traffic assignment; thus, the derivatives can be evaluated easily.

Now we define the gap function:

$$H(\mathbf{x},\mathbf{u})=\tilde{Z}(\mathbf{x},\mathbf{u})-\varphi(\mathbf{u}) \tag{5.83}$$

As stated earlier, this function is nonnegative, continuously differentiable for any feasible $\mathbf{x}$ and $\mathbf{u}$. Based on the uniqueness property of the regularized traffic equilibrium solution, the equation $H(\mathbf{u},\mathbf{x})=0$ implies that solution vector $\mathbf{x}$ satisfies the equilibrium conditions for a given toll pattern $\mathbf{u}$. Therefore, an equivalent, continuously differentiable formulation of the BLPP model (5.74) can be stated below:

$$\max_{\mathbf{u}\in U,\mathbf{x}\in X} F(\mathbf{u},\mathbf{x}) \tag{5.84}$$

subject to

$$H(\mathbf{x},\mathbf{u})=0 \tag{5.85}$$

In the above formulation the traffic equilibrium condition is enforced by constraint (5.85), in which the gap function $H(\mathbf{u},\mathbf{x})$ does not entail an explicit expression, but its value and gradient can be easily evaluated by performing a traffic assignment using the modified convex combination algorithm described in subsection 5.4.2. Note that the gap function $H(\mathbf{x},\mathbf{u})$ is generally non-convex. This means that the above formulation is still a non-convex minimization program and, theoretically, a standard decent-type algorithm can seek only a local minimum.

5.4.5 Solution by the Augmented Lagrangian Algorithm

Many methods are available in the existing literature to find a local exact solution for a continuously differentiable optimization problem. Here we apply the augmented Lagrangian algorithm, which is one of the efficient, locally convergent methods for the optimization problem with nonlinear constraints (Bertsekas, 1982). In this application for problem (5.84)-(5.85), the nonlinear, implicit constraint (5.85) is incorporated into the objective function as a penalty term. The partially augmented Lagrangian function for the problem (5.84)-(5.85) is defined below:

$$L_1(\mathbf{u},\mathbf{x},\lambda,\rho)=-F_1(\mathbf{u},\mathbf{x})+\lambda H(\mathbf{u},\mathbf{x})+\frac{1}{2}\rho\left(G(\mathbf{u},\mathbf{x})\right)^2 \tag{5.86}$$

$$L_2(\mathbf{u},\mathbf{x},\lambda,\rho)=-F_2(\mathbf{u},\mathbf{x})+\lambda H(\mathbf{u},\mathbf{x})+\frac{1}{2}\rho\left(G(\mathbf{u},\mathbf{x})\right)^2 \tag{5.87}$$

As described in subsection 5.2.4, the whole augmented Lagrangian scheme consists of three levels of iterative loops. The inner loop solves the following sub-problem:

$$\min_{\mathbf{u}\in U,\mathbf{x}\in X} L(\mathbf{u},\mathbf{x},\lambda,\rho) \tag{5.88}$$

where the Lagrangian function can be either (5.86) or (5.87). The middle loop updates the Lagrangian multiplier λ and the penalty parameter ρ. The outer loop is to diminish the regularization parameter η in the regularized objective function. The procedure will terminate when the optimal objective value obtained using the current η value is almost the same as that using the previous η value.

The major computational burden in the solution procedure of the augmented Lagrangian algorithm is to solve the sub-problem (5.88). Here we show in detail how the convex combination method can be used to find a solution of this sub-problem. Since the constraint set contains only simple bounds $\mathbf{u}\in U$ and flow conservation equations $\mathbf{x}\in X$, the LP problem for finding the descent direction in each iteration can be decomposed into two simple LP sub-problems as shown below.

Let n denote the iteration indicator. For any given feasible solution denoted by $(\mathbf{u}^{(n)},\mathbf{x}^{(n)})$, the multiplier λ, the penalty parameter ρ, the gradients at this point of the Lagrangian function (5.86) are as follows:

$$\left.\frac{\partial L_1}{\partial v_a}\right|_{(\mathbf{u},\mathbf{x})=(\mathbf{u}^{(n)},\mathbf{x}^{(n)})}=\left[\lambda+\rho H\left(\mathbf{u}^{(n)},\mathbf{x}^{(n)}\right)\right]t_a\left(v_a^{(n)}\right),\quad a\in A \tag{5.89}$$

$$\left.\frac{\partial L_1}{\partial q_e}\right|_{(\mathbf{u},\mathbf{x})=(\mathbf{u}^{(n)},\mathbf{x}^{(n)})}=-u_e^{(n)}+\frac{1}{\beta}\left[\lambda+\rho H\left(\mathbf{u}^{(n)},\mathbf{x}^{(n)}\right)\right]\left(u_e^{(n)}+\eta q_e^{(n)}\right),\quad e\in E \tag{5.90}$$

$$\left.\frac{\partial L_1}{\partial d_w}\right|_{(\mathbf{u},\mathbf{x})=(\mathbf{u}^{(n)},\mathbf{x}^{(n)})}=\left[\lambda+\rho H\left(\mathbf{u}^{(n)},\mathbf{x}^{(n)}\right)\right]\left[-B_w\left(d_w^{(n)}\right)\right],\quad w\in W \tag{5.91}$$

$$\left.\frac{\partial L_1}{\partial u_e}\right|_{(\mathbf{u},\mathbf{x})=(\mathbf{u}^{(n)},\mathbf{x}^{(n)})}=-q_e^{(n)}+\left[\lambda+\rho G\left(\mathbf{u}^{(n)},\mathbf{x}^{(n)}\right)\right]\left(\left.\frac{\partial G}{\partial u_e}\right|_{(\mathbf{u},\mathbf{x})=(\mathbf{u}^{(n)},\mathbf{x}^{(n)})}\right),\quad e\in E \tag{5.92}$$

The gradients at this point of the Lagrangian function (5.87) are as follows:

$$\left.\frac{\partial L_2}{\partial v_a}\right|_{(\mathbf{u},\mathbf{x})=(\mathbf{u}^{(n)},\mathbf{x}^{(n)})}=v_a^{(n)}\left.\frac{\partial t_a}{\partial v_a}\right|_{(\mathbf{u},\mathbf{x})=(\mathbf{u}^{(n)},\mathbf{x}^{(n)})}+\left[1+\lambda+\rho H\left(\mathbf{u}^{(n)},\mathbf{x}^{(n)}\right)\right]t_a\left(v_a^{(n)}\right) \tag{5.93}$$

$$\left.\frac{\partial L_2}{\partial q_e}\right|_{(\mathbf{u},\mathbf{x})=(\mathbf{u}^{(n)},\mathbf{x}^{(n)})}=\frac{1}{\beta}\left[\kappa+\rho H\left(\mathbf{u}^{(n)},\mathbf{x}^{(n)}\right)\right]\left(u_e^{(n)}+\eta q_e^{(n)}\right) \tag{5.94}$$

$$\left.\frac{\partial L_2}{\partial d_w}\right|_{(\mathbf{u},\mathbf{x})=(\mathbf{u}^{(n)},\mathbf{x}^{(n)})}=\left[1+\phi+\rho G\left(\mathbf{x}^{(n)},\mathbf{u}^{(n)}\right)\right]\left[-B_w\left(d_w^{(n)}\right)\right] \tag{5.95}$$

$$\left.\frac{\partial L_2}{\partial u_e}\right|_{(\mathbf{u},\mathbf{x})=(\mathbf{u}^{(n)},\mathbf{x}^{(n)})}=\left[\phi+\rho H\left(\mathbf{u}^{(n)},\mathbf{x}^{(n)}\right)\right]\left(\left.\frac{\partial G}{\partial u_e}\right|_{(\mathbf{u},\mathbf{x})=(\mathbf{u}^{(n)},\mathbf{x}^{(n)})}\right) \tag{5.96}$$

In (5.92) and (5.96), the partial derivative value of the gap function is

$$\left.\frac{\partial G}{\partial u_e}\right|_{(\mathbf{u},\mathbf{x})=(\mathbf{u}^{(n)},\mathbf{x}^{(n)})}=\frac{\partial\tilde{Z}\left(\mathbf{u}^{(n)},\mathbf{x}^{(n)}\right)}{\partial u_e}-\left.\frac{\partial\varphi}{\partial u_e}\right|_{\mathbf{u}=\mathbf{u}^{(n)}}=\frac{1}{\beta}q_e^{(n)}-\left.\frac{1}{\beta}q_e^{*}\right|_{\mathbf{u}=\mathbf{u}^{(n)}} \tag{5.97}$$

For the two Lagrangian functions, the algorithmic procedures are identical, and the following description is applicable for both cases. Denote the above four partial derivative values in each case as $\zeta_a^{(n)}$, $\xi_e^{(n)}$, $\kappa_w^{(n)}$ and $\gamma_e^{(n)}$ respectively, namely,

$$\zeta_a^{(n)} = \left.\frac{\partial L}{\partial v_a}\right|_{(\mathbf{u},\mathbf{x})=\left(\mathbf{u}^{(n)},\mathbf{x}^{(n)}\right)}, \quad a\in A \tag{5.98}$$

$$\xi_e^{(n)} = \left.\frac{\partial L}{\partial q_e}\right|_{(\mathbf{u},\mathbf{x})=\left(\mathbf{u}^{(n)},\mathbf{x}^{(n)}\right)}, \quad e\in E \tag{5.99}$$

$$\kappa_w^{(n)} = \left.\frac{\partial L}{\partial d_w}\right|_{(\mathbf{u},\mathbf{x})=\left(\mathbf{u}^{(n)},\mathbf{x}^{(n)}\right)}, \quad w\in W \tag{5.100}$$

$$\gamma_e^{(n)} = \left.\frac{\partial L}{\partial u_e}\right|_{(\mathbf{u},\mathbf{x})=\left(\mathbf{u}^{(n)},\mathbf{x}^{(n)}\right)}, \quad e\in E \tag{5.101}$$

Let $\bar{\mathbf{u}}=\left(\cdots,\bar{u}_e,\cdots\right)^{\mathrm{T}}$ and $\bar{\mathbf{x}}=\left(\bar{\mathbf{v}}^{\mathrm{T}},\bar{\mathbf{d}}^{\mathrm{T}},\bar{\mathbf{q}}^{\mathrm{T}}\right)^{\mathrm{T}}$, where $\bar{\mathbf{v}}=\left(\cdots,\bar{v}_a,\cdots\right)^{\mathrm{T}}$, $\bar{\mathbf{d}}=\left(\cdots,\bar{d}_w,\cdots\right)^{\mathrm{T}}$ and $\bar{\mathbf{q}}=\left(\cdots,\bar{q}_e,\cdots\right)^{\mathrm{T}}$, be the auxiliary. The descent direction $\left(\bar{\mathbf{u}}^{(n)}-\mathbf{u}^{(n)},\bar{\mathbf{x}}^{(n)}-\mathbf{x}^{(n)}\right)$ at the current solution $\left(\mathbf{u}^{(n)},\mathbf{x}^{(n)}\right)$ can be obtained by solving the following LP problem:

$$\min_{\bar{\mathbf{u}}\in U,\bar{\mathbf{x}}\in X} \sum_{a\in A}\zeta_a^{(n)}\bar{v}_a+\sum_{e\in E}\xi_e^{(n)}\bar{q}_e+\sum_{w\in W}\kappa_w^{(n)}\bar{d}_w+\sum_{e\in E}\gamma_e^{(n)}\bar{u}_e \tag{5.102}$$

subject to $\bar{d}_w\le\bar{D}_w$, where $\bar{D}_w$ is the upper bound of demand between OD pair $w\in W$ defined before.

In view of its structure, the above LP problem (5.102) can be decomposed into the following two independent LP sub-problems by partitioning the coefficients in the objective function and the constraints.

LP1:

$$\min_{\bar{\mathbf{x}}\in X} \sum_{a\in A}\zeta_a^{(n)}\bar{v}_a+\sum_{e\in E}\xi_e^{(n)}\bar{q}_e+\sum_{w\in W}\kappa_w^{(n)}\bar{d}_w \tag{5.103}$$

subject to $\bar{d}_w\le\bar{D}_w$, $w\in W$.

LP2:

$$\min_{\bar{\mathbf{u}}\in U} \sum_{e\in E}\gamma_e^{(n)}\bar{u}_e \tag{5.104}$$

Clearly, LP1 is an all-or-nothing traffic assignment problem where the OD demand $\bar{d}_w$, $w\in W$, is either zero or equal to its upper bound $\bar{D}_w$; and LP2 is a simple linear program where the solution is given by one of the vertices of the feasible toll set $U_i, i=1,2,\cdots,5$.

Once the decent direction is determined, an appropriate step size has to be determined. There are a couple of line search methods available to determine a step size, such as the exact line search method, Armijo's rule for inexact line search, and the method of successive averages (MSA). Since the exact line search involves too many equilibrium traffic assignments, and the MSA method converges slowly, here we suggest the Armijo's rule to solve the problem. The procedure of Armijo's rule is to find a step size $\alpha^{(n)} = \chi^k$, where k is the smallest non-negative integer satisfying

$$L\left(\mathbf{u}^{(n)} + \chi^k\left(\overline{\mathbf{u}}^{(n)} - \mathbf{u}^{(n)}\right), \mathbf{x}^{(n)} + \chi^k\left(\overline{\mathbf{x}}^{(n)} - \mathbf{x}^{(n)}\right), \lambda, \rho\right) - L\left(\mathbf{u}^{(n)}, \mathbf{x}^{(n)}, \lambda, \rho\right)$$
$$\le \upsilon\chi^k \cdot \left[\left(\nabla_{\mathbf{u}} L^{(n)}\right)^{\mathrm{T}} \cdot \left(\overline{\mathbf{u}}^{(n)} - \mathbf{u}^{(n)}\right) + \left(\nabla_{\mathbf{x}} L^{(n)}\right)^{\mathrm{T}} \cdot \left(\overline{\mathbf{x}}^{(n)} - \mathbf{x}^{(n)}\right)\right] \quad (5.105)$$

where $0 < \chi < 1$ and $0 < \upsilon < 0.5$, and $\nabla_{\mathbf{x}} L^{(n)}$ and $\nabla_{\mathbf{u}} L^{(n)}$ are the vectors of the gradients at current solution, namely $\nabla_{\mathbf{x}} L^{(n)} = \left(\cdots, \zeta_a^{(n)}, \cdots, \kappa_w^{(n)}, \cdots, \xi_e^{(n)}, \cdots\right)^{\mathrm{T}}$ and $\nabla_{\mathbf{u}} L^{(n)} = \left(\cdots, \gamma_e^{(n)}, \cdots\right)^{\mathrm{T}}$.

It is worth noting that for the aforementioned alternative toll pricing schemes $U_i, i = 1,2,\cdots,5$ defined by (5.69)-(5.73), the solution approaches are basically identical; the only difference lies in the linear program LP2 that should be subject to different feasible toll sets for different tolling schemes.

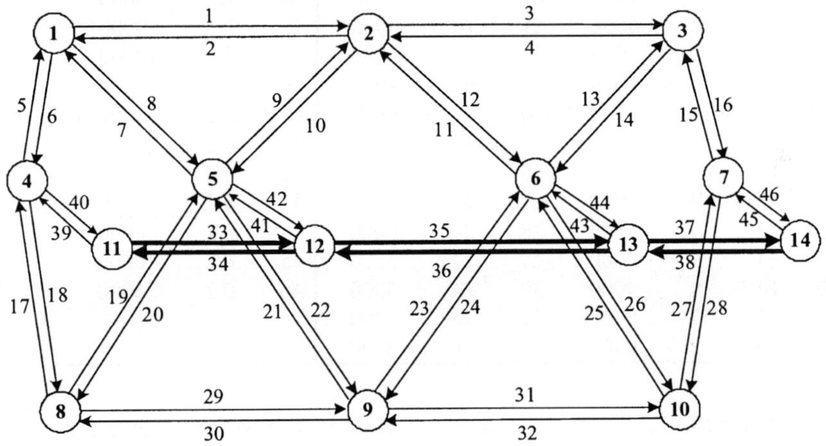

Figure 5.7 The network used for numerical experiment

5.4.6 Numerical Example and Discussion of Results

Consider a network depicted in Figure 5.7, consisting of 14 nodes and 46 links. The bold links {33, 34, 35, 36, 37, 38} are expressways subject to toll charge. The same link performance function in (5.46) is used, with free-flow travel time and capacity of each link given in Table 5.7. There are 8 OD pairs in the network with the following demand function:

$$d_w = \hat{D}_w \exp\left\{0.5\left(1.0 - \frac{\mu_w}{\mu_w^0}\right)\right\}, \quad w \in W$$

where μ_w and μ_w^0 are the equilibrium and free-flow travel costs, respectively, between OD pair w, and $\hat{D}_w$ is the corresponding potential demand having the value given in Table 5.8. Homogeneous users are considered with a single value of time equal to 120 (HK\$/h). The lower bounds for all entry-exit tolls are identical and are set to be 0, and the upper bounds are 100 (HK\$) for revenue maximization and 60 (HK\$) for social welfare maximization, respectively. The initial values of all toll charges for the inner loop iterations of solving the problem (5.88) are set to zero.

Table 5.7 Input data for network in Figure 5.7

Link No.	t_a^0 (min)	C_a (veh/h)	Link No.	t_a^0 (min)	C_a (veh/h)	Link No.	t_a^0 (min)	C_a (veh/h)
1	25	4000	17	2	6000	33	7	10000
2	25	4000	18	2	6000	34	7	10000
3	25	4000	19	9	4000	35	12	16000
4	25	4000	20	9	4000	36	12	16000
5	2	6000	21	10	4000	37	7	10000
6	2	6000	22	10	4000	38	7	10000
7	9	4000	23	9	4000	39	0.2	6000
8	9	4000	24	9	4000	40	0.2	6000
9	11	4000	25	10	4000	41	0.2	6000
10	11	4000	26	10	4000	42	0.2	6000
11	9	4000	27	2	6000	43	0.2	6000
12	9	4000	28	2	6000	44	0.2	6000
13	9	4000	29	24	3800	45	0.2	6000
14	9	4000	30	24	3800	46	0.2	6000
15	2	6000	31	26	4200			
16	2	6000	32	26	4200			

Table 5.8 Potential demand for each OD pair on network in Figure 5.7

OD Pair No.	1	2	3	4	5	6	7	8
O→D	1→3	1→10	3→1	3→8	8→3	8→10	10→1	10→8
Potential demand (10^3 veh/h)	10	10	9	11	10	10	12	8

As discussed previously, a regularization approach is utilized to determine a unique solution of the entry-exit flows. We choose an initial value of the regularization parameter $\eta^{(1)} = 0.04$ and reduce it by half after each iteration, $\eta^{(n+1)} = 0.5\eta^{(n)}$. In the augmented Lagrangian algorithm used in the example, we set the initial Lagrangian multiplier $\phi^{(1)} = 0.0$ and the initial penalty parameter $\rho^{(1)} = 10.0$, and employ the following updating procedure: If $H\left(\mathbf{u}^{(n+1)}, \mathbf{x}^{(n+1)}\right) \leq 0.25G\left(\mathbf{u}^{(n)}, \mathbf{x}^{(n)}\right)$, then set $\lambda^{(n+1)} = \lambda^{(n)} + \rho^{(n)} H\left(\mathbf{u}^{(n+1)}, \mathbf{x}^{(n+1)}\right)$ and $\rho^{(n+1)} = \rho^{(n)}$; Otherwise, set $\rho^{(n+1)} = 10.0\rho^{(n)}$ and $\lambda^{(n+1)} = \lambda^{(n)}$. In solving the sub-problem (5.88) by the convex combination method, the step size is determined by the Armijo's rule with parameters $\chi = 0.5$ and $\upsilon = 0.01$.

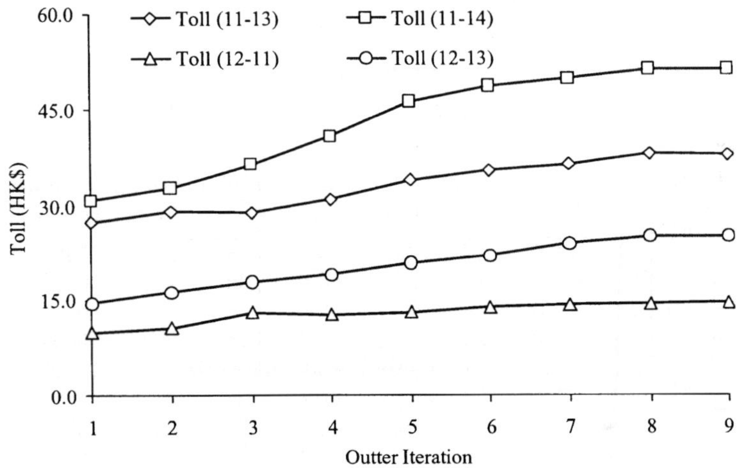

Figure 5.8 Change in entry-exit tolls versus number of outer-loop iterations

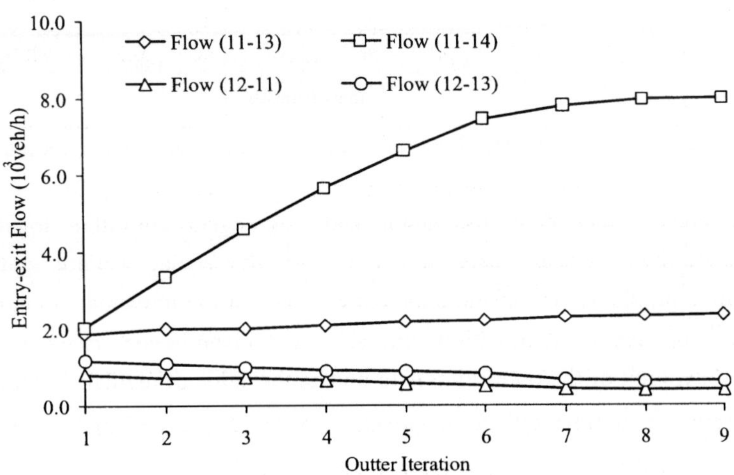

Figure 5.9 Change in entry-exit flows versus number of outer-loop iterations

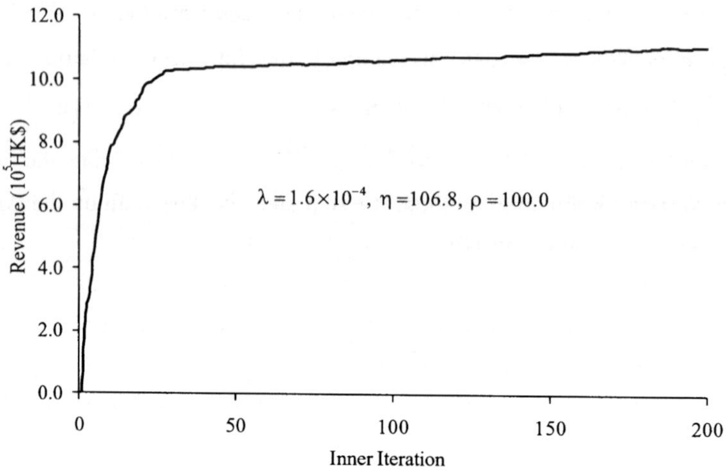

Figure 5.10 Change in revenue versus number of inner-loop iterations

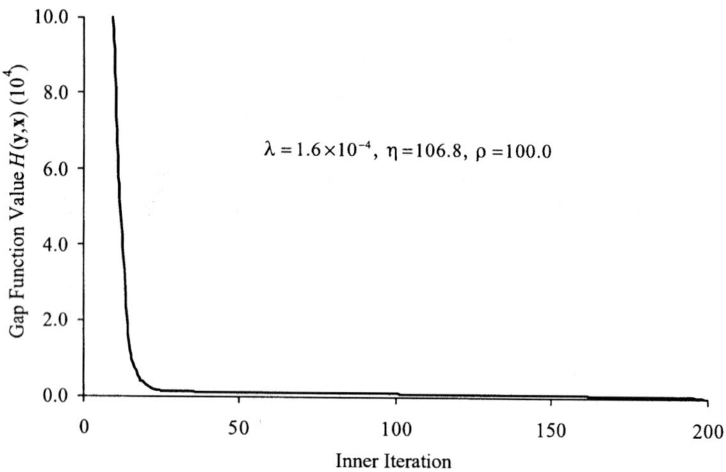

Figure 5.11 Change in gap function value versus number of inner-loop iterations

With the above input data, the augmented Lagrangian algorithm together with the regularization approach are used to solve both the social welfare and the revenue maximization problems. To illustrate the convergence of the implementation procedure, the case of revenue maximization with pricing Scheme A given in eqn. (5.69) is demonstrated. First, each iteration of the outer loop is to update the value of regulation parameter η and then determine the optimal tolls for the given η value. Figures 5.8 and 5.9 show the change of the optimal entry-exit tolls and the corresponding flows obtained versus the number of outer loop iterations. Here the solutions converge to certain values after the regularization parameter η is updated 9 times. Second, the middle loop is to solve the optimization problem (5.84)-(5.85) for a given parameter η by the augmented Lagrangian algorithm. In this example the program converges in 3 iterations for $\eta = 1.6\times10^{-4}$ with the following updating of multiplier λ and penalty parameter ρ:

$$\left(\lambda^{(1)}=0,\ \rho^{(1)}=10\right) \rightarrow \left(\lambda^{(2)}=106.8,\ \rho^{(2)}=10\right) \rightarrow \left(\lambda^{(3)}=106.8,\ \rho^{(3)}=100\right)$$

Finally, the inner loop is to solve the sub-problem (5.88) for given η, λ and ρ. Figures 5.10 and 5.11 plot the changes of revenue and the value of the gap function against the number of inner loop iterations, respectively, for given values of $\eta = 1.6\times10^{-4}$, $\lambda = 107.8$ and $\rho = 100.0$. Clearly, the inner loop exhibits an initial rapid convergence; the convergence rate slows down as the solution points move close to the optimum. It is generally found from our numerical experiments that Armijo's inexact line search is faster than the MSA.

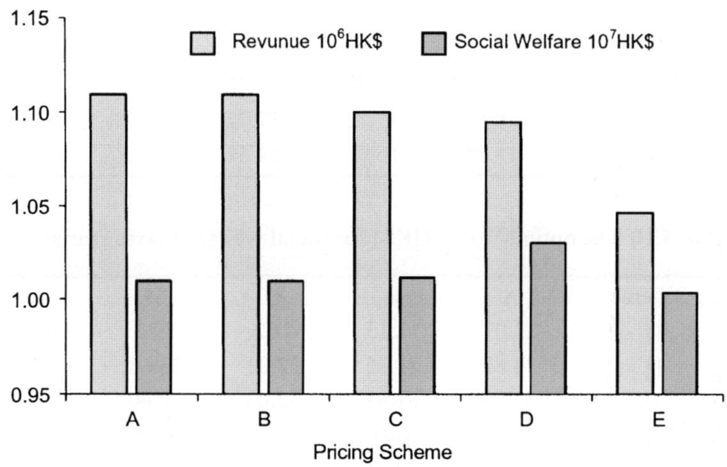

Figure 5.12 Maximum revenues and the corresponding social welfares

We now investigate the impacts of the five alternative pricing Schemes A to E, defined by eqns. (5.69)-(5.73), on social welfare and revenue maximizing solutions. In the case of revenue maximization, the solution of optimal entry-exit tolls for each scheme is given in Table 5.9. The maximal revenues collected under the five pricing schemes, together with the corresponding social welfares are presented in Figure 5.12. Evidently, the maximal revenues decrease from Scheme A to Scheme E, with decreasing freedom in choosing the tolls. Note that the upper bounds of tolls are set sufficiently large so that they are not binding at the final solutions. It is observed that the revenues collected in Schemes A and B are roughly identical, implying that the optimal tolls obtained in Scheme A also satisfy the toll constraint of Scheme B. This can be verified from the toll solutions presented in the first two columns of Table 5.9. We can further observe that there is a big drop in revenue associated with Scheme E in comparison with the other four schemes. This implies that the single, constant toll charge, although easily achieved, results in much lower revenue. In addition, among the five cases of revenue maximization, Scheme D gives rise to the highest social welfare.

Table 5.9 Optimal tolls (HK$) for revenue maximization

Pricing Scheme		A	B	C	D	E
u_1	11→12	15.42	15.61	12.42	13.37	48.66
u_2	11→13	37.82	37.78	35.74	37.30	48.66
u_3	11→14	51.21	51.91	50.16	49.67	48.66
u_4	12→11	14.52	14.26	13.03	13.37	48.66
u_5	12→13	25.13	24.31	23.32	22.92	48.66
u_6	12→14	38.71	39.39	37.74	37.30	48.66
u_7	13→11	37.56	37.33	37.44	37.30	48.66
u_8	13→12	23.59	23.31	23.41	22.92	48.66
u_9	13→14	15.71	15.82	14.42	13.37	48.66
u_{10}	14→11	51.47	51.82	50.75	49.67	48.66
u_{11}	14→12	38.54	37.72	37.72	37.30	48.66
u_{12}	14→13	15.08	15.61	14.31	13.37	48.66

Table 5.10 The optimal tolls (HK$) for social welfare maximization

Pricing Scheme		A	B	C	D	E
u_1	11→12	12.01	12.13	5.62	8.72	28.12
u_2	11→13	24.82	24.75	22.01	23.68	28.12
u_3	11→14	31.89	31.93	32.03	32.40	28.12
u_4	12→11	9.38	9.41	5.89	8.72	28.12
u_5	12→13	14.51	14.25	17.39	14.95	28.12
u_6	12→14	23.88	24.17	27.41	23.68	28.12
u_7	13→11	22.02	21.92	21.48	23.68	28.12
u_8	13→12	15.97	17.14	15.59	14.95	28.12
u_9	13→14	10.31	10.27	10.02	8.72	28.12
u_{10}	14→11	30.91	30.85	30.67	32.40	28.12
u_{11}	14→12	28.41	28.76	24.78	23.68	28.12
u_{12}	14→13	13.01	13.11	9.19	8.72	28.12

Table 5.10 and Figure 5.13 present the solutions for the case of social welfare maximization. Similar phenomena are observed, with declining maximal social welfare, from Scheme A to Scheme E. Again, Scheme A and Scheme B gives rise to nearly the same solutions. Moreover, Scheme E for uniform toll charge gives rise to the lowest social welfare and the lowest revenue. Scheme D for the distance based toll pricing scheme gives the highest revenue among the five cases of social welfare maximization.

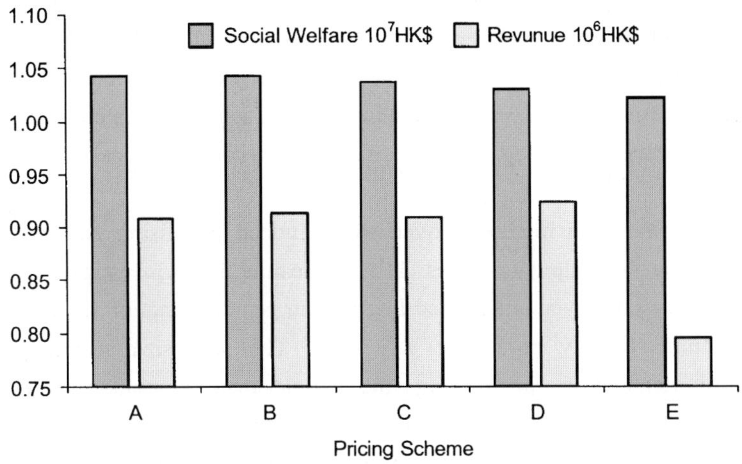

Figure 5.13 Maximum social welfares and the corresponding revenues

5.5 SUMMARY

In this chapter we developed a gap function based approach for the second best road pricing problems which are formulated as MPEC or BLPP. We proved that the gap function associated with the VI-based or optimization based lower-level UE problem is a continuously differentiable function and its value and gradient in flow and toll variables can be readily calculated via implementing an equilibrium traffic assignment only. The MPEC and BLPP are then transformed into a single-level continuously differentiable optimization program by treating the UE conditions as a nonlinear, implicit gap function constraint. By incorporating the gap function constraint into the objective function as a penalty term, the single-level differentiable problem was solved by the augmented Lagrangian algorithm, in which the critical sub-optimization problem is favorably solved by the conventional convex combination method. The gap function based approach was well illustrated with both simple analytical and larger numerical pricing examples with known solutions.

We have specifically addressed the application of the proposed gap function based approach for solving the optimal second-best pricing problem in a network with entry-exit based toll charges. Although the solution of equilibrium entry-exit flows using the toll roads is not uniquely determined, the resulting total toll revenue is found to be always unique. The Frank-Wolfe method is adapted to solve the traffic equilibrium model, where the descent-direction-finding sub-problem is solved by a conventional shortest path algorithm through an appropriate network transformation, and the network transformation avoids the difficulty of path information storage and enumeration. A regularization approach was used to address the non-uniqueness issue of the entry-exit flow on the tolling sub-network, thereby allowing for the application of the gap function approach to solve the optimal entry exit based toll design problem. The performance of the solution method is demonstrated and the solution properties of alternative toll pricing schemes are explored with a numerical example.

The proposed gap function method proved to be indeed promising and can be further extended to address the following issues: 1) It is meaningful to investigate the exact and inexact nature of the employed augmented Lagrangian penalty function to recover the local optimum for finite penalty parameter values; 2) The step size search procedure is computationally demanding in solving the single-level continuously differentiable optimization problem, and alternative algorithms, such as a trust region algorithm, can be explored to circumvent this difficulty; 3) A rigorous attempt for computing globally optimal solutions is presently out of the reach of existing methods, nevertheless, it is possible to further transform the single-level continuously differentiable program into a concave minimization problem subject to convex constraints, and then apply the well-established cutting plane algorithm to find the global optimum.

5.6 Sources and Notes

Value (or marginal) function is an important concept in nonlinear programming, and its differentiability property is well expounded in Gauvin and Dubeau (1982). In transportation literature, the value function for the convex UE program and its differentiability property was explored and applied for the traffic network design problem in Meng et al. (2001). Several gap functions are available for VIs, but not all of them are differentiable. The quadratic gap function used in this chapter for VI was proposed by Fukushima (1992) and has a desirable differentiable (in argument of VI itself) property. Further differentiability in upper-level decision variables in the context of MPEC for the second-best pricing problem was shown here. Readers may refer to Ye et al. (1997), Chen and Florian (1995) and Marcotte and Zhu (1996) for use of the gap function in the analysis of the general BLPP. Detailed description and discussion of the augmented Lagrangian algorithm can be found in the excellent textbook by Bazaraa et al. (1993) and Bertsekas (1982; 1999). Readers are recommended to consult the references: Meng et al. (2001) and Yang Zhang and Meng (2004), from which part of the materials presented in this chapter are drawn.

6

DISCRIMINATORY AND ANONYMOUS ROAD PRICING

6.1 INTRODUCTION

In this chapter, we move on to investigate the road pricing problem with extended multi-class equilibrium behaviors in the transportation networks introduced in Chapter 2. We begin our investigation by first recognizing that the terms of multi-class traffic equilibrium and pricing problems may refer to three distinct situations of observable and unobservable user heterogeneity, as summarized in Table 6.1.

The first situation is that the flows in a transportation network are divided into different classes of vehicles or modes, each of which has an individual cost-flow function, and at the same time contributes to its own and other class's cost functions in an individual way. As examined in Section 2.3 in Chapter 3, a classification of vehicle types could distinguish trucks and buses from cars; heavy vehicles from light ones; private transport from public transit. In this situation, applying the marginal cost pricing principle would burden each class with a different toll for social optimum, as shown in Section 3.5 in Chapter 3. This is economically meaningful and practically feasible. It is economically meaningful because the first-best discriminatory toll charges reflect the different congestion externalities brought about by different types of vehicles. It is practically feasible because toll charges can be differentiated across user classes on the basis of their *observable* differences. Differentiated toll pricing across vehicle types is indeed carried out in most pricing schemes.

The second and third situations are that all users or drivers are assumed to use the same type of vehicles and thus have identical congestion effects when using the same roadway, but users differ from one another in other, *unobservable* ways. In the second case, users differ from one another in the value they place on time; in the third case users differ in their routing behavior. In the latter two situations, users are *observationally indistinguishable* and then the congestion charge must be *anonymous* or *uniform* when they use the same road link.

In this chapter we deal with the multi-class, multi-criteria and multiple behavior equilibrium and system optimum problem. Here we refer the multi-class and multi-criteria to the situation that users have distinct values of time (VOT) and thus place different subjective weightings of two criteria, travel time versus travel cost, in route choice; we refer multiple behaviors to the situation that users make their route choices in different behavioral manners, such as the case when deterministic User equilibrium (UE) users and Cournot-Nash (CN) players share the same network resources. We establish the existence of meaningful anonymous link tolls in this case to decentralize a system optimum as a multi-class, multi-criteria and multiple behavior equilibrium, with resort to rigorous mathematical programming approach.

Table 6.1 Classification of multi-class traffic equilibrium problems

Single-class Traffic Equilibrium	**Multi-class Traffic Equilibrium**		
	By vehicle types	**By value of time**	**By routing behavior**
a) Traffic equilibrium without link flow interactions (standard traffic equilibrium formulated as a convex mathematical program) b) Traffic equilibrium with asymmetric link flow interactions (generalized traffic equilibrium formulated as a VI)	a) Each type of vehicle has an individual cost-flow function, and meanwhile contributes to its own and other class's cost functions in an individual way (*e.g.*, truck *vs* car). b) The resulting multi-class equilibrium problem can be reduced to a single class problem with asymmetric link flow interactions through multiple network copies (each class is associated with a network copy).	a) Discrete value of time distribution (finite number of user classes) b) Continuous value of time distribution (infinite number of user classes)	a) UE *vs* SUE b) UE *vs* CN controller or player (CN altruistic controller or CN private controller) c) UE *vs* SO player (SO player acts a leader in a Stackelberg game or SO player is capable of predicting the reaction of UE users)

Remark: UE: User Equilibrium; SUE: Stochastic User Equilibrium; CN: Cournot-Nash; SO: System Optimum

This chapter is organized as follows. After revisiting the single class traffic equilibrium and system optimum problem, we deal with the two criteria of cost versus time traffic equilibrium and system optimum problem, where system performance can be measured in either time or cost units. We then continue to examine the multiple behavior equilibrium and system optimum problem, followed by the combined multi-class, multi-criteria and multiple behavior equilibrium and system optimum problem.

6.2 TOLL PROPERTIES FOR THE SINGLE CLASS UE AND SO PROBLEMS

6.2.1 Characterization of Link Tolls for SO

As shown in Chapter 3, in the standard traffic network equilibrium model with homogeneous users, a so-called marginal-cost pricing toll can drive a user equilibrium flow pattern to a system optimum in the sense of total travel time minimization for the fixed demand case and social welfare maximization for the elastic demand case. The link toll according to the marginal-cost pricing principle equals the congestion externality given as the difference between marginal social cost and marginal private cost on each link.

As shown in Chapter 3, the SO problem with elastic demand can be formulated as:

$$\max_{(\mathbf{v},\mathbf{d})\in\Omega} \sum_{w\in W}\int_0^{d_w} B_w(\omega)\,d\omega - \sum_{a\in A} v_a t_a(v_a) \tag{6.1}$$

where

$$\Omega = \left\{(\mathbf{v},\mathbf{d}) \,\middle|\, v_a = \sum_{w\in W}\sum_{r\in R_w} f_{rw}\delta_{ar}, a\in A;\ f_{rw}\geq 0, r\in R_w, \sum_{r\in R_w} f_{rw} = d_w, w\in W\right\} \tag{6.2}$$

The same notation is used as before. Let $\bar{d}_w^{\mathrm{SO}}$, $w\in W$ and $\bar{v}_a^{\mathrm{SO}}$, $a\in A$ be the unique OD demand and link flow solution of the above SO problem (6.1)-(6.2). It is already shown in Chapter 3 that the marginal-cost pricing toll given by $u_a = \beta v_a \cdot dt_a(v_a)/dv_a\big|_{v_a=\bar{v}_a^{\mathrm{SO}}}$, $a\in A$, where β is the VOT of homogeneous users considered here, will support the SO flow pattern $(\bar{\mathbf{v}}^{\mathrm{SO}},\bar{\mathbf{d}}^{\mathrm{SO}})$, where $\bar{\mathbf{v}}^{\mathrm{SO}} = (\bar{v}_a^{\mathrm{SO}}, a\in A)^{\mathrm{T}}$ and $\bar{\mathbf{d}}^{\mathrm{SO}} = (\bar{d}_w^{\mathrm{SO}}, w\in W)^{\mathrm{T}}$, as an UE flow pattern that satisfies the following variational inequality (VI)

$$\sum_{a\in A}\left(t_a(\bar{v}_a^{\mathrm{SO}}) + \frac{u_a}{\beta}\right)(v_a - \bar{v}_a^{\mathrm{SO}}) - \sum_{w\in W} B_w(\bar{d}_w^{\mathrm{SO}})(d_w - \bar{d}_w^{\mathrm{SO}}) \geq 0, \text{ for all } (\mathbf{v},\mathbf{d})\in\Omega \tag{6.3}$$

It is known that the link tolls that can decentralize a given SO flow pattern as a UE is not unique; this observation is particularly prevalent in the traffic equilibrium problem with fixed demand. Our task here is how to identify all such valid link tolls including the economically meaningful marginal-cost pricing link toll. It is interesting to note that the desirable valid link tolls for a given SO flow pattern $(\bar{\mathbf{v}}^{\mathrm{SO}},\bar{\mathbf{d}}^{\mathrm{SO}})$ obtained from (6.1)-(6.2) is a polyhedron as shown in the following theorem.

Theorem 6.1 *Any link tolls* $\mathbf{u}=(u_a, a\in A)^{\mathrm{T}}$ *contained in the following polyhedron consisting of equalities and inequalities can support a SO flow pattern* $(\overline{\mathbf{v}}^{\mathrm{SO}}, \overline{\mathbf{d}}^{\mathrm{SO}})$ *obtained from problem (6.1)-(6.2) as an user equilibrium:*

$$\sum_{a\in A}\left(t_a(\overline{v}_a^{\mathrm{SO}})+\frac{u_a}{\beta}\right)\delta_{ar}\geq\mu_w,\ r\in R_w,\ w\in W \tag{6.4}$$

$$B_w(\overline{d}_w^{\mathrm{SO}})\leq\mu_w,\ w\in W \tag{6.5}$$

$$\sum_{a\in A}\left(t_a(\overline{v}_a^{\mathrm{SO}})+\frac{u_a}{\beta}\right)\overline{v}_a^{\mathrm{SO}}=\sum_{w\in W}B_w(\overline{d}_w^{\mathrm{SO}})\overline{d}_w^{\mathrm{SO}} \tag{6.6}$$

where μ_w *is the minimal travel cost between OD pair* $w\in W$.

Proof. We prove the above toll characterization for the standard single class elastic-demand traffic equilibrium problem using the duality theory in a linear program. Consider the UE problem with link cost $t_a(v_a)+u_a/\beta$, $a\in A$. Then, $(\overline{\mathbf{v}}^{\mathrm{SO}}, \overline{\mathbf{d}}^{\mathrm{SO}})$ is an UE flow pattern if and only if VI (6.3) holds. Equivalently,

$$\sum_{a\in A}\left(t_a(\overline{v}_a^{\mathrm{SO}})+\frac{u_a}{\beta}\right)v_a-\sum_{w\in W}B_w(\overline{d}_w^{\mathrm{SO}})d_w\geq\sum_{a\in A}\left(t_a(\overline{v}_a^{\mathrm{SO}})+\frac{u_a}{\beta}\right)\overline{v}_a^{\mathrm{SO}}-\sum_{w\in W}B_w(\overline{d}_w^{\mathrm{SO}})\overline{d}_w^{\mathrm{SO}},$$

$$\text{for all } (\mathbf{v},\mathbf{d})\in\Omega$$

This implies

$$\min_{(\mathbf{v},\mathbf{d})\in\Omega}\sum_{a\in A}\left(t_a(\overline{v}_a^{\mathrm{SO}})+\frac{u_a}{\beta}\right)v_a-\sum_{w\in W}B_w(\overline{d}_w^{\mathrm{SO}})d_w\geq\sum_{a\in A}\left(t_a(\overline{v}_a^{\mathrm{SO}})+\frac{u_a}{\beta}\right)\overline{v}_a^{\mathrm{SO}}-\sum_{w\in W}B_w(\overline{d}_w^{\mathrm{SO}})\overline{d}_w^{\mathrm{SO}}$$

The left-hand side is a linear program, while the right-hand side is a constant. From the inequality above it is clear that $(\overline{\mathbf{v}}^{\mathrm{SO}}, \overline{\mathbf{d}}^{\mathrm{SO}})$ solves this linear program, which can be equivalently written in terms of path flows and OD demands as

$$\min_{\mathbf{f},\mathbf{d}}\sum_{a\in A}\left(t_a(\overline{v}_a^{\mathrm{SO}})+\frac{u_a}{\beta}\right)\left(\sum_{w\in W}\sum_{r\in R_w}f_{rw}\delta_{ar}\right)-\sum_{w\in W}B_w(\overline{d}_w^{\mathrm{SO}})d_w \tag{6.7}$$

subject to

$$\sum_{r\in R_w}f_{rw}-d_w=0,\ w\in W \tag{6.8}$$

$$d_w\geq 0,\ w\in W \tag{6.9}$$

$$f_{rw}\geq 0,\ r\in R_w,\ w\in W \tag{6.10}$$

The dual formulation is given by

$$\max_{\eta,\mu}\sum_{w\in W}\sum_{r\in R_w}0\cdot\eta_{rw}+\sum_{w\in W}0\cdot\mu_w \tag{6.11}$$

subject to

$$\mu_w \leq \sum_{a\in A}\left(t_a\left(\bar{v}_a^{\mathrm{SO}}\right)+\frac{u_a}{\beta}\right)\delta_{ar},\ r\in R_w,\ w\in W \tag{6.12}$$

$$-\mu_w \leq -B_w\left(\bar{d}_w^{\mathrm{SO}}\right),\ w\in W \tag{6.13}$$

Since the dual linear program has the same optimal objective value, we arrive at

$$\sum_{a\in A}\left(t_a\left(\bar{v}_a^{\mathrm{SO}}\right)+\frac{u_a}{\beta}\right)\bar{v}_a^{\mathrm{SO}} - \sum_{w\in W} B_w\left(\bar{d}_w^{\mathrm{SO}}\right)\bar{d}_w^{\mathrm{SO}} = 0 \tag{6.14}$$

Therefore, by linear programming duality, there exists $\mu_w,\ w\in W$ (dual variables) such that conditions (6.12)-(6.14) or conditions (6.4)-(6.6) hold. ¦

The above proof shows that VI (6.3) and the system of linear equality and inequalities (6.4) -(6.6) are equivalent to each other. We thus conclude that the conditions (6.4)-(6.6) are both necessary and sufficient to characterize the set of valid link tolls that can decentralize a given SO flow pattern into a UE. Moreover, the valid toll set is clearly a convex polyhedron when the link cost function is strictly increasing and convex and it is nonempty, since the marginal-cost pricing toll is one of the valid solutions. In addition, the link tolls satisfying these conditions are free to be negative as well as positive; one can always consider the non-negative link tolls by adding the constraint $u_a \geq 0,\ a\in A$ to the above set of equations, the resulting toll set remains non-empty.

Corollary 6.1 *For a given* $\left(\bar{\mathbf{v}}^{\mathrm{SO}},\bar{\mathbf{d}}^{\mathrm{SO}}\right)$ *to the SO program (6.1)-(6.2), the total toll revenue generated from link tolls* $\mathbf{u}$ *satisfying linear system (6.4)-(6.6) is constant.*

Proof. It is obvious from eqn. (6.6) that the total toll revenue generated from valid link tolls $\mathbf{u}$ is given below:

$$\sum_{a\in A} u_a\bar{v}_a^{\mathrm{SO}} = \beta\sum_{w\in W} B_w\left(\bar{d}_w^{\mathrm{SO}}\right)\bar{d}_w^{\mathrm{SO}} - \beta\sum_{a\in A} t_a\left(\bar{v}_a^{\mathrm{SO}}\right)\bar{v}_a^{\mathrm{SO}} = \text{constant}$$

In the case with fixed OD demand $d_w,\ w\in W$, the SO problem is to minimize total travel time, $\max_{\mathbf{v}} \sum_{a\in A} v_a t_a(v_a)$ subject to flow conservation conditions. For a given unique SO link flow solution $\bar{\mathbf{v}}^{\mathrm{SO}}$, the valid link tolls to decentralize the SO as an UE is given by the following linear system:

$$\sum_{a\in A}\left(t_a\left(\bar{v}_a^{\mathrm{SO}}\right)+\frac{u_a}{\beta}\right)\delta_{ar} \geq \mu_w,\ r\in R_w,\ w\in W \tag{6.15}$$

$$\sum_{a\in A}\left(t_a\left(\bar{v}_a^{\mathrm{SO}}\right)+\frac{u_a}{\beta}\right)\bar{v}_a^{\mathrm{SO}} = \sum_{w\in W}\mu_w\bar{d}_w \tag{6.16}$$

Clearly in the fixed demand case, the total toll revenue is not constant. However, if μ_w is given (for example, as the unique minimum marginal route travel time at the SO solution) then $\sum_{a\in A} u_a \bar{v}_a^{so} = \beta \sum_{w\in W} \mu_w d_w - \beta \sum_{a\in A} t_a(\bar{v}_a^{so})\bar{v}_a^{so}$ is unique. ∎

In view of the non-uniqueness of the valid link tolls for decentralizing the SO flow pattern, one may introduce various secondary objectives such as toll revenue (for the fixed demand-case) or number of toll booths are optimized with respect to the feasible link tolls contained in the polyhedron developed above.

6.2.2 A Simple Example for the Valid Link Toll Set to Decentralize SO

Example 6.1 (Valid link toll set for the single-class UE and SO problem) Now we provide a simple example to explain the toll characterization results for the single class UE and SO problem discussed above. The network, shown in Figure 6.1, consists of 3 nodes and 4 directed links with one OD pair (origin node 1 and destination node 3). Suppose the VOT for all users is $\beta = 1.0$ and the link cost functions are given by

$$t_1 = 2 + v_1,\ \ t_2 = 3 + v_2,\ \ t_3 = 1 + v_3,\ \ t_4 = 2 + 2v_4$$

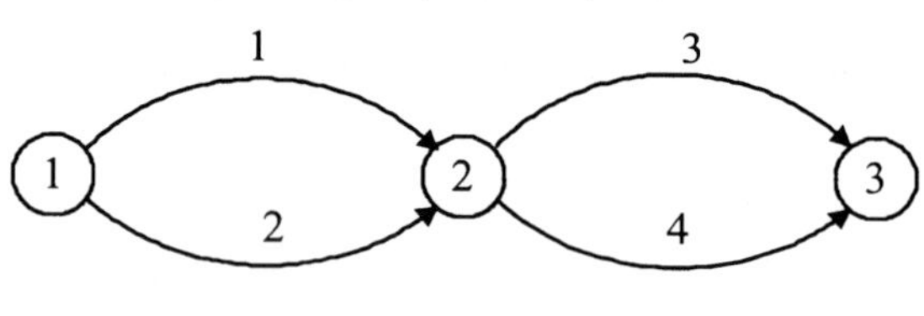

Figure 6.1 An example to explain the toll pricing for the single class UE and SO problem

1) *The elastic demand case.* Suppose the demand function between origin 1 and destination 3 is given by $d = 13 - \mu$ (omit the OD index for simplicity). The system optimal solution for the social welfare maximization is unique and is given by

$$\bar{\mathbf{v}}^{\mathrm{SO}} = \left(\bar{v}_1^{\mathrm{SO}}, \bar{v}_2^{\mathrm{SO}}, \bar{v}_3^{\mathrm{SO}}, \bar{v}_4^{\mathrm{SO}}\right)^{\mathrm{T}} = \left(\frac{13}{8}, \frac{9}{8}, 2, \frac{3}{4}\right)^{\mathrm{T}} \text{ and } \bar{d}^{\mathrm{SO}} = \frac{11}{4}$$

The corresponding link travel times are

$$\mathbf{t}(\bar{\mathbf{v}}^{\mathrm{SO}}) = \left(t_1(\bar{v}_1^{\mathrm{SO}}), t_2(\bar{v}_2^{\mathrm{SO}}), t_3(\bar{v}_3^{\mathrm{SO}}), t_4(\bar{v}_4^{\mathrm{SO}})\right)^{\mathrm{T}} = \left(\frac{29}{8}, \frac{33}{8}, 3, \frac{7}{2}\right)^{\mathrm{T}}$$

The set of valid tolls to decentralize the SO flow pattern is given below

$$\frac{29}{8} + 3 + u_1 + u_3 \geq \mu$$

$$\frac{29}{8} + \frac{7}{2} + u_1 + u_4 \geq \mu$$

$$\frac{33}{8}+3+u_2+u_3\geq\mu$$

$$\frac{33}{8}+\frac{7}{2}+u_2+u_4\geq\mu$$

$$\frac{41}{4}\leq\mu$$

$$\left(\frac{29}{8}+u_1\right)\times\frac{13}{8}+\left(\frac{33}{8}+u_2\right)\times\frac{9}{8}+(3+u_3)\times 2+\left(\frac{7}{2}+u_4\right)\times\frac{3}{4}=\frac{41}{4}\times\frac{11}{4}$$

which can be simplified into

$$u_1+u_3\geq\frac{29}{8}$$

$$u_1+u_4\geq\frac{25}{8}$$

$$u_2+u_3\geq\frac{25}{8}$$

$$u_2+u_4\geq\frac{21}{8}$$

$$\frac{13}{8}u_1+\frac{9}{8}u_2+2u_3+\frac{3}{4}u_4=\frac{289}{32}$$

The above system is simply equivalent to the linear equality systems:

$$u_1=u_2+\frac{1}{2},\quad u_3=u_4+\frac{1}{2},\quad u_2+u_4=\frac{21}{8}$$

It can be easily checked that the marginal-cost pricing toll: $\mathbf{u}=(13/8,9/8,2,3/2)^{\mathrm{T}}$, is included in the above system of equalities and inequalities. Clearly, the valid toll set is a convex polyhedron. The total toll revenue is $289/32$, and constant.

2) *The fixed demand case.* Suppose the demand between origin 1 and destination 3 is fixed to be $d=5$. The system optimal solution for total travel time minimization is unique and is given by

$$\overline{v}_1^{\mathrm{SO}}=\frac{11}{4},\quad \overline{v}_2^{\mathrm{SO}}=\frac{9}{4},\quad \overline{v}_3^{\mathrm{SO}}=\frac{7}{2},\quad \overline{v}_4^{\mathrm{SO}}=\frac{3}{2}$$

and

$$\overline{t}_1^{\mathrm{SO}}=\frac{19}{4},\quad \overline{t}_2^{\mathrm{SO}}=\frac{21}{4},\quad \overline{t}_3^{\mathrm{SO}}=\frac{9}{2},\quad \overline{t}_4^{\mathrm{SO}}=5.$$

The set of valid tolls decentralizing the system optimum is given below

$$\frac{19}{4}+\frac{9}{2}+u_1+u_3\geq\mu$$

$$\frac{19}{4}+5+u_1+u_4 \geq \mu$$

$$\frac{21}{4}+\frac{9}{2}+u_2+u_3 \geq \mu$$

$$\frac{21}{4}+5+u_2+u_4 \geq \mu$$

$$\left(\frac{19}{4}+u_1\right)\times\frac{11}{4}+\left(\frac{21}{4}+u_2\right)\times\frac{9}{4}+\left(\frac{9}{2}+u_3\right)\times\frac{7}{2}+(5+u_4)\times\frac{3}{2}=5\times\mu$$

The valid link toll set satisfying the above linear system can be further simplified into

$$u_1=u_2+\frac{1}{2},\quad u_3=u_4+\frac{1}{2}$$

The above valid toll set is a unbounded convex polyhedron which includes the marginal-cost pricing toll: $\mathbf{u}=(11/4,9/4,7/2,3)^{\mathrm{T}}$, the total toll revenue with the above valid link toll set is unbounded. Notwithstanding, if we set μ to be the unique minimal marginal OD travel cost cost of $31/2$, then the valid link toll set becomes:

$$u_1+u_3=\frac{25}{4},\quad u_2+u_4=\frac{21}{4},\quad u_1=u_2+\frac{1}{2},\quad u_3=u_4+\frac{1}{2}$$

which gives rise to a constant revenue of $238/3$.

6.3 Time-Based and Cost-Based Multi-Class UE and SO Problems

In Subsection 2.3.4 of Chapter 2, we introduced the multi-class bi-criteria UE models in which users select their routes to minimize total disutility measured either in time unit or cost unit, respectively, and concluded that both time-based and cost-based equilibria have identical link flows pattern that can be obtained from a convex minimization program. In this section, we examine the multi-class, bi-criteria or cost versus time network equilibrium and system optimum problem for several user classes in a network with a discrete set of VOTs, but with identical types of vehicles. We already know from Chapter 2 that the user-optimal link flow pattern is independent of the unit (time or money) used in measuring the travel disutility in the presence of road pricing when users value their travel times linearly. Here we are specifically interested in the following questions: are there any *anonymous* or *uniform* link tolls (link tolls that are identical for all user classes) that can drive a multi-class traffic network equilibrium into a system optimum? If yes, does such link toll pattern depend on the criterion or the unit (time or money) that defines the total travel disutility for the system optimum? What are the general properties of the valid toll set?

Recalling the following minimization problem with separable link cost functions and fixed class-specific OD demand introduced in Subsection 2.3.4

$$\min_{\mathbf{f}} \sum_{a\in A} \int_0^{v_a} t_a(\omega)d\omega + \sum_{a\in A} \sum_{m\in M} \frac{1}{\beta_m} v_a^m u_a \tag{6.17}$$

subject to

$$\sum_{r\in R_w} f_{rw}^m = d_w^m,\ w\in W,\ m\in M \tag{6.18}$$

$$f_{rw}^m \geq 0,\ r\in R_w,\ w\in W,\ m\in M \tag{6.19}$$

$$v_a^m = \sum_{w\in W} \sum_{r\in R_w} f_{rw}^m \delta_{ar},\ a\in A,\ m\in M \tag{6.20}$$

$$v_a = \sum_{m\in M} v_a^m,\ a\in A \tag{6.21}$$

This minimization problem leads to a multi-class network equilibrium in terms of either generalized path travel time given by

$$c_{rw}^{m,\text{time}} = \sum_{a\in A} \left\{ t_a(v_a) + \frac{u_a}{\beta_m} \right\} \delta_{ar},\ r\in R_w,\ w\in W,\ m\in M \tag{6.22}$$

or generalized path travel cost given by

$$c_{rw}^{m,\text{cost}} = \sum_{a\in A} \{\beta_m t_a(v_a) + u_a\} \delta_{ar},\ r\in R_w,\ w\in W,\ m\in M \tag{6.23}$$

In problem (6.17)-(6.21) and eqns. (6.22)-(6.23), M is the set of all user classes, β_m $(\beta_m > 0)$ is the average VOT for users of class m, f_{rw}^m is the flow of user class m on route $r\in R_w$ between OD pair $w\in W$, v_a^m is the flow of user class m on link $a\in A$, d_w^m is the demand for users of class m between OD pair $w\in W$, and u_a is the exogenously given toll levied on link $a\in A$. As assumed previously, all link travel time functions, $t_a(v_a)$, $a\in A$, are continuous, strictly increasing and convex.

For users with a single VOT, problem (6.17)-(6.21) collapses to a standard UE traffic assignment problem with fixed demand. It is well known that the marginal-cost pricing link toll, $u_a = \beta \bar{v}_a t_a'(\bar{v}_a)$, evaluated at the system optimum link flow, $\bar{v}_a$, $a\in A$, can support a SO flow pattern as a UE. The SO here refers to the minimization of total travel disutility that can be measured in terms of either time or monetary units.

6.3.1 System Optimum in Time Units and Pricing for Equilibrium

We next consider the following system optimum in time units and see how it leads to a different result:

$$\min_{\mathbf{f}} \sum_{a\in A} v_a t_a(v_a) \tag{6.24}$$

subject to (6.18)-(6.21).

Problem (6.24) is a strictly convex program in aggregate link flow $\mathbf{v}$ if the separable link travel time function is monotonically increasing and convex (see Chapter 2), and thus, the solution of aggregative link flow is unique. The link flow by user class is indeterminate, and any v_a^m, $a \in A$, $m \in M$ that leads to the unique aggregate link flow solution, $\sum_{m\in M} v_a^m = v_a$, $a \in A$, is optimal to the time-based SO program (6.24).

From the first-order necessary optimality conditions, for an optimum $\bar{v}_a$, $a \in A$ to the time-based SO program (6.24) we have

$$\sum_{a\in A}\left\{t_a(\bar{v}_a)+\bar{v}_a\frac{\mathrm{d}t_a(\bar{v}_a)}{\mathrm{d}v_a}\right\}\delta_{ar} = \mu_w^{m,\text{time}} \quad \text{if } \bar{f}_{rw}^m > 0,\ r\in R_w,\ w\in W,\ m\in M \tag{6.25}$$

$$\sum_{a\in A}\left\{t_a(\bar{v}_a)+\bar{v}_a\frac{\mathrm{d}t_a(\bar{v}_a)}{\mathrm{d}v_a}\right\}\delta_{ar} \ge \mu_w^{m,\text{time}} \quad \text{if } \bar{f}_{rw}^m = 0,\ r\in R_w,\ w\in W,\ m\in M \tag{6.26}$$

Similarly, the optimality conditions (6.25)-(6.26) for the time-based SO program (6.24) can be regarded as the network equilibrium conditions in time units, with $\mu_w^{m,\text{time}}$ being the corresponding minimum OD travel time. As seen from (6.25)-(6.26), $\mu_w^{m,\text{time}}$ is identical for all user classes $m \in M$ traveling between the same OD pair $w \in W$. The requirement for such equilibrium is that each user should face a marginal social travel time consisting of a private or experienced travel time and a travel time congestion externality common to all users, when using each link in the network.

As we can see, the above link travel time externality is anonymous, but can be internalized only when the toll charge for each link is differentiated according to each user's VOT:

$$u_{a,m}^{\text{SO}} = \beta_m v_a \left.\frac{\mathrm{d}t_a(v_a)}{\mathrm{d}v_a}\right|_{v_a=\bar{v}_a},\ a\in A,\ m\in M \tag{6.27}$$

This discriminatory link toll pattern is of course unrealistic and difficult, if not impossible, to implement in reality because, as mentioned earlier, users differ from one another in an *observationally indistinguishable* way.

Given the impossibility of introducing a discriminatory link toll pattern (6.27) for various user classes for achieving an exact time-based SO, we naturally wonder whether there exists an alternative uniform link toll pattern to decentralize a time-based SO flow pattern into a multi-class network equilibrium. In contrast to the single class case examined in Section 6.2, where the set of system-optimal link tolls can be characterized by a non-empty polyhedron, the answer to the existence of anonymous system-optimal link tolls to the present multi-class user equilibrium problem is not evident and straightforward.

Let $\overline{v}_a^{so}$, $a \in A$ be the link flow solution of the time-based SO program (6.24). Under our aforementioned assumption of increasing convex link travel time functions, the time-based SO link flows $\overline{v}_a^{SO}$ and hence link travel time $t_a\left(\overline{v}_a^{SO}\right)$, $a \in A$ are uniquely determined. We now begin to seek an anonymous link toll pattern to decentralize this unique time-based SO flow pattern as a multi-class bi-criteria UE.

Consider the following linear programming (LP) problem:

$$\min_{\mathbf{f}} \sum_{a\in A}\sum_{m\in M} \beta_m t_a\left(\overline{v}_a^{SO}\right) v_a^m \tag{6.28}$$

subject to

$$\sum_{w\in W}\sum_{m\in M}\sum_{r\in R_w} f_{rw}^m \delta_{ar} = \overline{v}_a^{SO},\ a \in A \tag{6.29}$$

$$\sum_{r\in R_w} f_{rw}^m = d_w^m,\ w\in W,\ m\in M \tag{6.30}$$

$$f_{rw}^m \geq 0, r\in R_w, w\in W,\ m\in M \tag{6.31}$$

where $v_a^m = \sum_{w\in W}\sum_{r\in R_w} f_{rw}^m \delta_{ar}$, $a\in A$, $m\in M$. The dual formulation of the above LP is given by

$$\max_{\lambda,\mu} \sum_{a\in A} \overline{v}_a^{SO} \lambda_a + \sum_{w\in W}\sum_{m\in M} d_w^m \mu_w^m \tag{6.32}$$

subject to

$$\mu_w^m + \sum_{a\in A} \lambda_a \delta_{ar} \leq \sum_{a\in A} \beta_m t_a\left(\overline{v}_a^{SO}\right)\delta_{ar},\ r\in R_w,\ w\in W,\ m\in M \tag{6.33}$$

where the dual variables, $\lambda = \left(\cdots,\lambda_a,\cdots\right)^{\mathrm{T}}$ and $\mu = \left(\cdots,\mu_w^m,\cdots\right)^{\mathrm{T}}$ are associated with the equality constraints (6.29) and (6.30), respectively, and λ_a and μ_w^m are unrestricted in sign. Note that the set of feasible solutions to the LP (6.28)-(6.31) is not empty, since the path flows corresponding to the link flow solutions, $\overline{v}_a^{SO}$, $a\in A$ of the time-based SO program (6.24) are at least feasible to this LP problem. Hence, both original and dual problems have solutions.

Let u_a replace $(-\lambda_a)$, $a\in A$ and rewrite (6.33) as

$$\sum_{a\in A}\left\{\beta_m t_a\left(\overline{v}_a^{SO}\right) + u_a\right\}\delta_{ar} \geq \mu_w^m,\ r\in R_w,\ w\in W,\ m\in M \tag{6.34}$$

Let $\bar{f}_{rw}^m$ and $\bar{v}_a^m$ be an optimal solution to the LP program (6.28)-(6.31). According to the duality theory, at the optimal points of the original and dual problems the following complementary slackness conditions hold:

$$\left\{\sum_{a\in A}\left(\beta_m t_a\left(\bar{v}_a^{\text{SO}}\right)+u_a\right)\delta_{ar}-\mu_w^m\right\}\bar{f}_{rw}^m=0,\ r\in R_w,\ w\in W,\ m\in M \tag{6.35}$$

$$\sum_{a\in A}\left(\beta_m t_a\left(\bar{v}_a^{\text{SO}}\right)+u_a\right)\delta_{ar}-\mu_w^m\geq 0,\ r\in R_w,\ w\in W,\ m\in M \tag{6.36}$$

The above conditions can be regarded as the multi-class user equilibrium conditions in cost units, with μ_w^m being the corresponding minimum OD travel cost. The dual variable, λ_a, can be interpreted as a shadow price, i.e., an additional cost implied by the need for consistency between the link flows generated by the time-based SO program (6.24) and used in the LP (6.28)-(6.31). If u_a is positive (or λ_a is negative), users traversing link $a\in A$ are charged by a toll equal to u_a, and otherwise subsidized with $-u_a$. Therefore, we conclude that if the link travel cost perceived by an individual user is modified by charging or subsidizing an amount of money, u_a, $a\in A$, given by the solution of the dual problem (6.32)-(6.33), then a new network equilibrium is established. This new equilibrium is precisely a time-based SO in the sense that the same system optimal link flows, $\bar{v}_a^{\text{SO}}$, $a\in A$, (and hence the same link travel times, $t_a\left(\bar{v}_a^{\text{SO}}\right)$, $a\in A$) are reproduced. In summary, we have the following finding:

Theorem 6.2 *A time-based SO for minimizing the system travel disutility measured in time unit can be supported as a multi-class network equilibrium by a uniform link toll pattern across user classes. The toll is given as the solution of the dual LP (6.32)-(6.33) and can be positive (charge) or negative (subsidy) to link users.*

Note that the Lagrange multipliers u_a $(\text{or } -\lambda_a)$ and μ_w^m satisfying (6.35)-(6.36) may not be unique. The valid feasible set of u_a, $a\in A$ and the corresponding OD cost μ_w^m, $w\in W$, $m\in M$ can be alternatively written as the following polyhedron consisting of a system of linear equalities and inequalities:

$$\sum_{a\in A}u_a\bar{v}_a^{\text{SO}}+\sum_{a\in A}\sum_{m\in M}\beta_m t_a\left(\bar{v}_a^{\text{SO}}\right)\bar{v}_a^m=\sum_{w\in W}\sum_{m\in M}\mu_w^m d_w^m \tag{6.37}$$

$$\sum_{a\in A}u_a\delta_{ar}+\sum_{a\in A}\beta_m t_a\left(\bar{v}_a^{\text{SO}}\right)\delta_{ar}\geq\mu_w^m,\ r\in R_w,\ w\in W,\ m\in M \tag{6.38}$$

where $\bar{v}_a^m$, $a\in A$, $m\in M$ solves the primal LP (6.28)-(6.31). Equation (6.37) follows directly from the duality theory that the dual LP has the same optimal objective value as the primal one, and (6.38) is simply an altered form of the dual feasibility constraint. Thus,

(6.37)-(6.38) are both necessary and sufficient to characterize the dual optimal solutions. Note that the first-term in the right-hand side of eqn. (6.37) is in fact the total revenue collected from the toll charge.

In reality, negative tolls or subsidies on road networks are difficult and seldom implemented by policy makers, and thus an optimal toll pattern with all link tolls being positive is more meaningful and acceptable to the policy makers. We note that the solution of a LP problem (including the dual problem) is not necessarily unique; this means that in certain cases, we are likely to obtain an anonymous positive link toll pattern from the set of feasible solutions of the dual LP (6.32)-(6.33). This is indeed possible by modifying the primal LP (6.28)-(6.31) slightly.

Consider a slightly modified version of the primal LP (6.28)-(6.31) with the equality constraints (6.29) replaced by the following inequality constraints:

$$\sum_{w\in W}\sum_{m\in M}\sum_{r\in R_w} f_{rw}^{m}\delta_{ar} = v_a \le \overline{v}_a^{\mathrm{SO}},\ a\in A \tag{6.39}$$

Because constraints (6.39) are a simple relaxation of constraints (6.29) and the other constraints remain unchanged, the feasible region of the new LP problem is expanded and hence nonempty. This means that the new LP problem and its dual problem have solutions. The dual formulation is given by (6.32)-(6.33) and the following additional constraints:

$$\lambda_a \le 0,\ a\in A \tag{6.40}$$

where the dual variables $\lambda_a,\ a\in A$ are associated with the inequality constraints (6.39). Thus, constraints (6.39) guarantee that the link tolls to be charged (i.e., $u_a = -\lambda_a,\ a\in A$) are always non-negative.

We still have to show that the modified LP also leads to a SO flow pattern at the optimum point. It suffices to prove that, at the optimum of the LP problem, constraints (6.39) are always binding or hold with strict equality for all $a\in A$. Suppose there is a link $b\in A$ for which $v_b < \overline{v}_b^{\mathrm{SO}}$, by monotonicity of link cost function we have $t_b(v_b) < t_b(\overline{v}_b^{\mathrm{SO}})$ and hence $t_b(v_b)v_b < t_b(\overline{v}_b^{\mathrm{SO}})\overline{v}_b^{\mathrm{SO}}$. For the same reason, from constraint (6.39), we have $t_a(v_a)v_a \le t_a(\overline{v}_a^{\mathrm{SO}})\overline{v}_a^{\mathrm{SO}}$ for all other links $a\in A,\ a\ne b$. Thus, we arrive at $\sum_{a\in A} t_a(v_a)v_a < \sum_{a\in A} t_a(\overline{v}_a^{\mathrm{SO}})\overline{v}_a^{\mathrm{SO}}$. This can never occur since $\overline{v}_a^{\mathrm{SO}},\ a\in A$ is the unique optimum solution of the total travel time minimization problem (6.24) for a given OD demand $d_w^m,\ w\in W,\ m\in M$. Therefore, at the optimum of the modified LP problem, $v_a = \overline{v}_a^{\mathrm{SO}},\ a\in A$ is always guaranteed.

From the above analysis, we can see that the new valid toll set for the system optimum is a subset of the original valid toll set, and is now given by the constraints (6.37)-(6.38) as well as the non-negativity condition $u_a \geq 0, a \in A$. The system-optimal toll set is a polyhedron made up of a finite number of linear equalities and inequalities, and the set is unbounded, since both u_a, $a \in A$ and μ_w, $w \in W$ can approach $+\infty$.

6.3.2 System Optimum in Cost Units and Pricing for Equilibrium

We now consider the SO in cost (monetary) units, allowing for multiple classes of users with distinct VOTs. The minimization of total system travel disutility measured in terms of monetary unit can be formulated as the following minimization problem:

$$\min_{\mathbf{f}} \sum_{a \in A} \sum_{m \in M} \beta_m v_a^m t_a(v_a) \tag{6.41}$$

subject to (6.18)-(6.21).

Note that the SO objective function is not necessarily convex in v_a^m, $a \in A$, $m \in M$, and hence there might be multiple local minima (multiple class-specific link flow solutions), and different local minimum may give rise to a different aggregate link flow v_a, $a \in A$. It is thus important to identify the global minimum targeted for meaningful pricing.

From the first-order optimality conditions, for an optimum $\tilde{v}_a$, $\tilde{v}_a^m$, $m \in M$, $a \in A$ to the cost-based program (6.41) we have:

$$\sum_{a \in A} \left\{ \beta_m t_a(\tilde{v}_a) + \sum_{k \in M} \beta_k \tilde{v}_a^k \frac{dt_a(\tilde{v}_a)}{dv_a} \right\} \delta_{ar} = \mu_w^{m,\text{cost}}, \text{ if } \tilde{f}_{rw}^m > 0, r \in R_w, w \in W, m \in M \tag{6.42}$$

$$\sum_{a \in A} \left\{ \beta_m t_a(\tilde{v}_a) + \sum_{k \in M} \beta_k \tilde{v}_a^k \frac{dt_a(\tilde{v}_a)}{dv_a} \right\} \delta_{ar} \geq \mu_w^{m,\text{cost}}, \text{ if } \tilde{f}_{rw}^m = 0, r \in R_w, w \in W, m \in M \tag{6.43}$$

Let

$$u_a^{\text{SO}} = \sum_{m \in M} \beta_m \tilde{v}_a^m \frac{dt_a(\tilde{v}_a)}{dv_a}, \quad a \in A$$

we then have

$$u_a^{\text{SO}} = \left(\sum_{m \in M} \frac{v_a^m}{v_a} \beta_m \right) \left(v_a \frac{dt_a(v_a)}{dv_a} \right) \Bigg|_{v_a = \tilde{v}_a, v_a^m = \tilde{v}_a^m}, \quad a \in A \tag{6.44}$$

Clearly, the optimality conditions (6.42)-(6.43) for the cost-based SO problem (6.41) can be regarded as the network equilibrium conditions in cost units and $\mu_w^{m,\text{cost}}$ is the corresponding minimum OD travel cost for user class $m \in M$. The only requirement for such an equilibrium is that, for each network link, each user of each class $m \in M$, traversing link $a \in A$ should be charged a toll given by (6.44) in addition to his/her actual experienced, class-dependent travel time cost, $\beta_m t_a(v_a)$ (in monetary units).

Note that, in link toll (6.44), $v_a \, \mathrm{d}t_a(v_a)/\mathrm{d}v_a$ is the congestion externality measured in time units which is the additional travel time that a marginal user imposes on others already traveling on link $a \in A$. This travel time externality is identical for all classes of users using identical vehicles. The resultant toll charge is uniform and equal to this common travel time externality multiplied by the average VOT of all users traversing the link:

$$\tilde{\beta}_a^{\mathrm{SO}} = \sum_{m \in M} \frac{\tilde{v}_a^m}{\tilde{v}_a} \beta_m, \quad a \in A \tag{6.45}$$

The mean VOT in (6.45) is link-specific and is the arithmetic mean of the VOTs of all classes of users using link $a \in A$. In summary, we have the following finding.

Theorem 6.3 *A cost-based SO for minimizing the system travel disutility measured in monetary units can be decentralized as a multi-class network equilibrium by a first-best link toll pattern anonymous to all classes of users. The link toll is equal to the user externality of travel time multiplied by the arithmetic mean of the VOTs of all users traversing that link.*

So far, we have only concerned ourselves with the first-best pricing link tolls which are anonymous. Like discussion in previous Sub-sections 6.31, there might be a set of valid link tolls including the first-best link tolls that can support the cost-based SO flow pattern as a multi-class traffic equilibrium. Proceeding in the same spirit as before, we have the following theorem.

Theorem 6.4 *A cost-based SO for minimizing the system travel disutility, measured in monetary units can be supported as a multi-class network equilibrium by link tolls anonymous to all user classes. The link toll is given as a polyhedron consisting of the following equalities and inequalities:*

$$\sum_{a \in A} u_a \tilde{v}_a^{\mathrm{SO}} + \sum_{a \in A} \sum_{m \in M} \beta_m t_a\left(\tilde{v}_a^{\mathrm{SO}}\right) \tilde{v}_a^m = \sum_{w \in W} \sum_{m \in M} \mu_w^m d_w^m \tag{6.46}$$

$$\sum_{a \in A} u_a \delta_{ar} + \sum_{a \in A} \beta_m t_a\left(\tilde{v}_a^{\mathrm{SO}}\right) \delta_{ar} \geq \mu_w^m, \; r \in R_w, \; w \in W, \; m \in M \tag{6.47}$$

The same procedure to prove Theorem 6.2 can be applied to establish the above theorem. The only difference is to replace the time-based SO solution $\bar{v}_a^{\mathrm{SO}}$ in (6.29) and (6.28)with the cost-based SO solution $\tilde{v}_a^{\mathrm{SO}}$ obtained from the cost-based SO program (6.41). Note that the class-specific link flow $\tilde{v}_a^m$, $a \in A$, $m \in M$ solves the LP (6.28)-(6.31) and of course solves the cost-based SO program (6.41).

6.3.3 Analytical Examples

Example 6.2 (Link toll set for the cost-based SO problem) Consider a simple network depicted in Figure 6.2, consisting of 2 parallel links connecting a single OD par. There are two classes of users, denoted by m and n, with equal travel demand $d^m = d^n = 4$ (flow unit, say in 10^3 veh/h) traveling from node 1 to node 2, their VOTs are assumed to be $\beta_m = 1.0$ and $\beta_n = 2.0$ (HK\$/min), respectively. Link travel time functions (in minute) are shown in the figure.

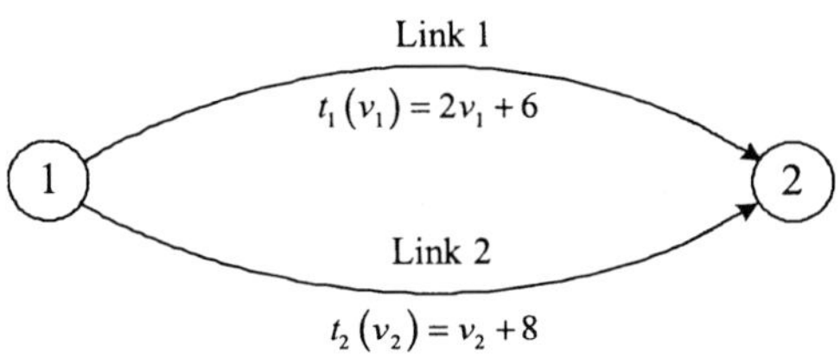

Figure 6.2 An Example to show the inequity problem in road pricing

We now consider the system optimum in terms of travel cost (denoted by TC) minimization (system disutility is measured in monetary unit) as given below:

$$\min_{v_1^m, v_2^m, v_1^n, v_2^n \geq 0} \quad TC = \left(\beta_m v_1^m + \beta_n v_1^n\right) t_1(v_1) + \left(\beta_m v_2^m + \beta_n v_2^n\right) t_2(v_2)$$

$$= \left(v_1^m + 2v_1^n\right)\left(2v_1^m + 2v_1^n + 6\right) + \left(v_2^m + 2v_2^n\right)\left(v_2^m + v_2^n + 8\right)$$

subject to

$$v_1^m + v_2^m = 4; \quad v_1^n + v_2^n = 4$$

This problem can be simplified into:

$$\min_{v_1^m, v_1^n} \; TC = 3\left(v_1^m\right)^2 + 6\left(v_1^n\right)^2 + 9v_1^m v_1^n - 22v_1^m - 32v_1^n + 192$$

subject to

$$0 \leq v_1^m \leq 4; \quad 0 \leq v_1^n \leq 4$$

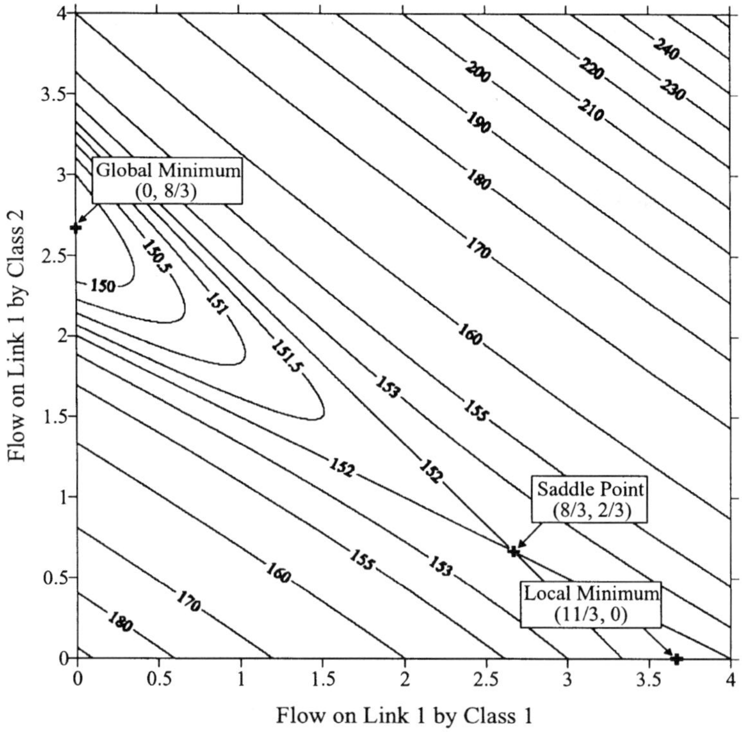

Figure 6.3 Contours of the system objective function in the two-dimensional space $\left(v_1^m, v_1^n\right)$.

Figure 6.3 displays the contours of the above cost-based system objective function in two-dimensional space $\left(v_1^m, v_1^n\right)$. Clearly, the objective function is non-convex in the feasible flow region. In fact, one can easily check that the Hessian matrix of TC is given by:

$$\frac{\partial^2 TC}{\partial v_1^m \partial v_1^n} = \begin{bmatrix} 6 & 9 \\ 9 & 12 \end{bmatrix}$$

which is not positive definite. There exist two minimum points. The first minimum point is a local minimizing point given by $v_1^m = 11/3$ and $v_1^n = 0$, yielding:

$$\mathbf{v}^m = \left(v_1^m, v_2^m\right)^{\mathrm{T}} = \left(\frac{11}{3}, \frac{1}{3}\right)^{\mathrm{T}}, \quad \mathbf{v}^n = \left(v_1^n, v_2^n\right)^{\mathrm{T}} = (0,4)^{\mathrm{T}}$$

$$\mathbf{v} = \left(v_1, v_2\right)^{\mathrm{T}} = \left(\frac{11}{3}, \frac{13}{3}\right)^{\mathrm{T}}, \quad TC = \frac{455}{3}$$

The second minimum point is a global minimizing point given by $v_1^m = 0$ and $v_1^n = 8/3$, yielding:

$$\mathbf{v}^m = \left(v_1^m, v_2^m\right)^{\mathrm{T}} = \left(0,4\right)^{\mathrm{T}}, \quad \mathbf{v}^n = \left(v_1^n, v_2^n\right)^{\mathrm{T}} = \left(\frac{8}{3}, \frac{4}{3}\right)^{\mathrm{T}}$$

$$\mathbf{v} = \left(v_1, v_2\right)^{\mathrm{T}} = \left(\frac{8}{3}, \frac{16}{3}\right)^{\mathrm{T}}, \quad TC = \frac{448}{3}$$

It is interesting to note that there is a saddle point located at $v_1^m = 8/3$ and $v_1^n = 2/3$ with $TC = 152$. This saddle point is a stationary point $\left(\partial TC/\partial v_1^m = 0,\ \partial TC/\partial v_1^n = 0\right)$, but it is neither a local maximum point nor a local minimum point. It can be easily checked this saddle point corresponds to an un-tolled multi-class equilibrium point with equal travel times on both links: $t_1(v_1) = t_1(10/3) = 38/3$, $t_2(v_2) = t_2(14/3) = 38/3$.

From the system (6.46)-(6.47), the valid toll set to decentralize the above global cost-minimizing point into multi-class traffic equilibrium can be expressed as:

$$8u_1 + 16u_2 + 448 = 12\mu^m + 12\mu^n$$

$$u_1 + \frac{34}{3} \geq \mu^m$$

$$u_2 + \frac{40}{3} \geq \mu^m$$

$$u_1 + \frac{68}{3} \geq \mu^n$$

$$u_2 + \frac{80}{3} \geq \mu^n$$

The valid toll set satisfying the above linear system can be simplified into:

$$u_1 - u_2 - 4 = 0$$

which includes the anonymous first-best link tolls $\mathbf{u} = \left(u_1, u_2\right)^{\mathrm{T}} = \left(32/3, 20/3\right)^{\mathrm{T}}$ (see Theorem 6.3: it is equal to the user externality of travel time multiplied by the arithmetic mean of the VOTs of all users traversing that link).

In a similar manner, one can also find that the valid toll set to decentralize the local cost-minimizing point can be expressed as

$$u_1 - u_2 + 1 = 0$$

Example 6.3 (Link toll set for the time-based SO problem) Now we present a simple example to further elaborate the results derived in Subsection 6.3.1. Figure 6.4 shows a network consisting of 4 nodes and 5 directed links. The link cost functions are given by

$$t_1 = 20 + 2v_1, \quad t_2 = v_2, \quad t_3 = v_3, \quad t_4 = 20 + v_4, \quad t_5 = 2v_5$$

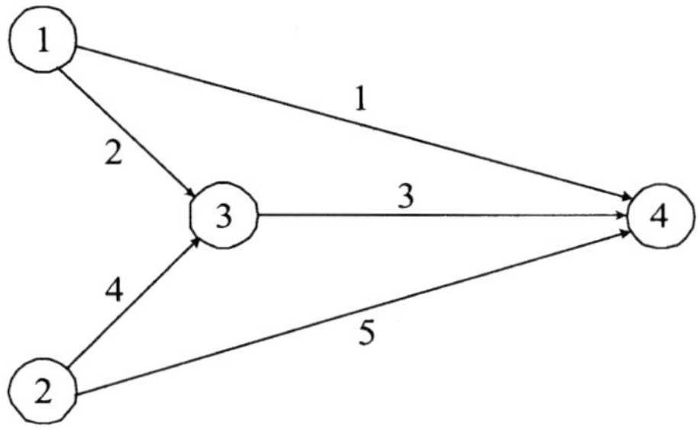

Figure 6.4 An example to explain the multi-class UE and SO problem

There are two classes of users with different values of time, class 1 consists of users with a lower value of time of $\beta_1 = 1.0$ (HK\$/min) (denoted by "m") and class 2 consists of users with a higher value of time of $\beta_2 = 2.0$ (HK\$/min) (denoted by "n"). There are two OD pairs for each class, one is from node 1 to node 4 (denoted by "a") and the other from node 2 to node 4 (denoted by "b"). The demand for each user class between each OD pair is $d_a^m = 10$, $d_a^n = 10$, $d_b^m = 20$ and $d_b^n = 10$. There are two paths connecting each OD pair. For OD pair a, path 1 (denoted by '$1,a$') includes link 1 only and path 2 (denoted by '$2,a$') includes links 2 and 3. For OD pair b, path 1 (denoted by '$1,b$') includes links 3 and 4 and path 2 (denoted by '$2,b$') includes link 5 only. Let $f_{j,k}^i$, $i = \{m,n\}$, $j = \{1,2\}$, $k = \{a,b\}$, denote the flow of class i on path j between OD pair k.

For a system optimum in terms of minimization of total travel time, the optimal link flows are given by:

$$\bar{\mathbf{v}}^{\mathrm{SO}} = \left(\bar{v}_1^{\mathrm{SO}}, \bar{v}_2^{\mathrm{SO}}, \bar{v}_3^{\mathrm{SO}}, \bar{v}_4^{\mathrm{SO}}, \bar{v}_5^{\mathrm{SO}}\right)^{\mathrm{T}} = (10,10,20,10,20)^{\mathrm{T}}$$

The corresponding link travel times are

$$\mathbf{t}\left(\bar{\mathbf{v}}^{\mathrm{SO}}\right) = \left(t_1\left(\bar{v}_1^{\mathrm{SO}}\right), t_2\left(\bar{v}_2^{\mathrm{SO}}\right), t_3\left(\bar{v}_3^{\mathrm{SO}}\right), t_4\left(\bar{v}_4^{\mathrm{SO}}\right), t_5\left(\bar{v}_5^{\mathrm{SO}}\right)\right)^{\mathrm{T}} = (40,10,20,30,40)^{\mathrm{T}}$$

The corresponding LP problem (6.28)-(6.31) is formulated as follows

$$\min\ 40\left(f_{1,a}^m + 2f_{1,a}^n\right) + 10\left(f_{2,a}^m + 2f_{2,a}^n\right) + 20\left(f_{2,a_1}^m + f_{1,b}^m + 2f_{2,a}^n + 2f_{1,b}^n\right)$$

$$+30\left(f_{1,b}^m + 2f_{1,b}^n\right) + 40\left(f_{2,b}^m + 2f_{2,b}^n\right)$$

subject to

$$f_{1,a}^m + f_{1,a}^n = 10$$

$$f_{2,a}^m + f_{2,a}^n = 10$$

$$f_{2,a}^m + f_{2a}^n + f_{1b}^m + f_{1,b}^n = 20$$

$$f^m_{1,b} + f^n_{1,b} = 10$$

$$f^m_{2,b} + f^n_{2,b} = 20$$

$$f^m_{1,a} + f^m_{2,a} = 10$$

$$f^n_{1,a} + f^n_{2,a} = 10$$

$$f^m_{1,b} + f^m_{2,b} = 20$$

$$f^n_{1,b} + f^n_{2,b} = 10$$

$$f^m_{1,a},\ f^n_{1,a},\ f^m_{2,a},\ f^n_{2a},\ f^m_{1b},\ f^n_{1,b},\ f^m_{2,b},\ f^n_{2,b} \geq 0$$

The optimal solution is $f^m_{1,a} = 10$, $f^n_{1,a} = 0$, $f^m_{2,a} = 0$, $f^n_{2,a} = 10$, $f^m_{1,b} = 10$, $f^n_{1,b} = 0$, $f^m_{2,b} = 10$, $f^n_{2,b} = 10$, with a corresponding minimal value of objective function equal to 2700.

The dual problem of the above LP is formulated as follows:

$$\max\ 10?_1 + 10?_2 + 20?_3 + 10?_4 + 20?_5 + 10\mu^m_a + 10\mu^n_a + 20\mu^m_b + 10\mu^n_b$$

subject to

$$\mu^m_a + ?_1 \leq 40$$

$$\mu^m_a + ?_2 + ?_3 \leq 30$$

$$\mu^n_a + ?_1 \leq 80$$

$$\mu^n_a + ?_2 + ?_3 \leq 60$$

$$\mu^m_b + ?_3 + ?_4 \leq 50$$

$$\mu^m_b + ?_5 \leq 40$$

$$\mu^n_b + ?_3 + ?_4 \leq 100$$

$$\mu^n_b + ?_5 \leq 80$$

The maximal value of the objective function is 2700, which is equal to the minimal value of the objective function in the primal problem. But the solution of the variables is not unique, and the solution set is made up of the following equations:

$$\mu^m_a + ?_1 = 40$$

$$\mu^m_a + ?_2 + ?_3 \leq 30$$

$$\mu^n_a + ?_1 \leq 80$$

$$\mu^n_a + ?_2 + ?_3 = 60$$

$$\mu^m_b + ?_3 + ?_4 = 50$$

$$\mu^m_b + ?_5 = 40$$

$$\mu^n_b + ?_3 + ?_4 \leq 100$$

$$\mu^n_b + ?_5 = 80$$

After simplification by eliminating μ and substituting $\mathbf{u}$ with $(-\lambda)$, the set of valid tolls to decentralize a system optimum as a multi-class, bi-criteria user equilibrium is given below:

$$10 \le u_2 + u_3 - u_1 \le 20$$

$$u_5 - u_3 - u_4 = 10$$

To seek a set of positive link tolls supporting a system optimum as a multi-class, bi-criteria user equilibrium, the first five equality constraints of the primal LP are replaced by the following five inequalities:

$$f_{1,a}^m + f_{1,a}^n \le 10$$

$$f_{2,a}^m + f_{2,a}^n \le 10$$

$$f_{2,a}^m + f_{2a}^n + f_{1,b}^m + f_{1,b}^n \le 20$$

$$f_{1,b}^m + f_{1,b}^n \le 10$$

$$f_{2,b}^m + f_{2,b}^n \le 20$$

Correspondingly, an additional constraint is imposed in the dual problem as below:

$$?_1,\ ?_2,\ ?_3,\ ?_4,\ ?_5 \le 0$$

Solving the revised primal LP problem, the same path flows for each class are obtained. Based on the revised dual problem, the set of positive valid link tolls is given by the linear equality and inequalities and nonnegative constraints:

$$10 \le u_2 + u_3 - u_1 \le 20$$

$$u_5 - u_3 - u_4 = 10$$

$$u_1,\ u_2,\ u_3,\ u_4,\ u_5 \ge 0$$

6.4 MULTIPLE EQUILIBRIUM BEHAVIORS AND SO PROBLEMS

The analyses presented so far assume that a UE flow pattern in a Wardropian sense always exists for any given toll pricing strategies in the network. The Wardrop UE principle can be characterized by a non-cooperative Nash game with many infinitesimal users, where each user is a game-player who aims to find his or her shortest path for given choices of other players. In other words, users are fully competitive under the UE principle. In the case of SO, one may assume that there is only one player in charge of all the users on the network, who attempts to minimize the total travel time of the system. In this case, users are fully cooperative under the control of a single player. Wardropian principles only consider two extreme cases, namely there exist either many infinitesimal players or only one central player.

In reality, however, users do not always behave in a UE manner, typically when there exist oligopoly Cournot-Nash (CN) firms. In this more general situation, where there exist some non-cooperative CN players on the network, users belonging to a common player are fully cooperative, and different players are fully competitive. If there is only one player, clearly the game reduces to the SO problem; and if there are an infinite number of infinitesimal players, the situation corresponds to the UE problem. When there exist both CN players (firms) and individual Wardropian UE users on a common network, we are led to a situation with multiple equilibrium behaviors. In this section, we examine whether an SO flow pattern on a network remains attainable by meaningful link tolls under the multiple equilibrium behaviors of UE and CN players. For simplicity, we assume that all users (UE users and users under a CN player) have *identical values of time*.

6.4.1 UE-CN Multiple Behavior Equilibrium and System Optimum

Suppose there are multiple classes of users by equilibrium behavior in a traffic network. Some individual users always seek the shortest paths based on the current flow pattern, and thus follow Wardropian user equilibrium. We assume that a single integrated *UE player* controls all the users who follow user equilibrium in their routing decisions. If the link cost function is separable as indeed assumed in our study, the UE player would have a well defined objective function, namely the Beckmann-type objective function (Chapter 2). In addition to the UE player in the network, there are some self-optimizing oligopoly Cournot firms. Each firm is referred to as a *CN player*, whose objective is to minimize the total cost of the users belonging to its firm. For instance, a shipping company may wish to minimize the travel expense by routing its own trucks.

Each player can control more than one OD pair, but for notational purpose, each OD pair is supposed to be controlled by only one player. If several players compete over the same physical OD pair, copies of this OD pair are made and treated as a set of OD pairs. Thus any ownership of the OD pairs can be represented. Apart from the common notation used in the book, the following additional symbols are needed:

U = the UE player on the network

K = the set of CN players on the network

W^U = the set of OD pairs of which users obey UE principle

W^k = the set of OD pairs of which users are controlled by CN player $k \in K$

$W \equiv W^U \cup W^K$ where $W^K = \cup_{k \in K} W^k$

v_a^U = the flow of link a arising out of the OD flows from the set W^U

$\mathbf{v}^U \equiv (\cdots, v_a^U, \cdots)^{\mathrm{T}}$, $a \in A$

v_a^k = the flow of link a arising out of the OD flows from the set W^k, $k \in K$

$\mathbf{v}^k \equiv \left(\cdots, v_a^k, \cdots\right)^{\mathrm{T}}$, $a \in A$

$v_a^K = \sum_{k \in K} v_a^k$

$v_a \equiv v_a^U + v_a^K$

$\mathbf{v} \equiv \left(\cdots, v_a, \cdots\right)^{\mathrm{T}}$, $a \in A$

Assume link cost function $t_a(v_a)$, $a \in A$ is separable, twice continuously differentiable and strictly increasing and convex in its flow; and further assume the OD demand d_w between each OD pair $w \in W$ is given and fixed. Then, the feasible sets for the UE player Ω^U, and for the CN players Ω^k, $k \in K$, are given below.

$$\Omega^U = \left\{ \mathbf{v}^U \middle| v_a^U = \sum_{w \in W^U} \sum_{r \in R_w} f_{rw} \delta_{ar}, a \in A; \sum_{r \in R_w} f_{rw} = d_w, f_{rw} \geq 0, r \in R_w, w \in W^U \right\} \tag{6.48}$$

$$\Omega^k = \left\{ \mathbf{v}^k \middle| v_a^k = \sum_{w \in W^k} \sum_{r \in R_w} f_{rw} \delta_{ar}, a \in A; \sum_{r \in R_w} f_{rw} = d_w, f_{rw} \geq 0, r \in R_w, w \in W^k \right\}, \quad k \in K \tag{6.49}$$

Note that the path flows appearing in the above equations are player-specific. Suppose each player aims to optimize its own objective function by routing flows under its control given knowledge of the other players' flows, but without realizing how the other players will react to its routing decision. In other words, each player treats the other players' flows as fixed when solving its flow optimization problem. Suppose the flows controlled by all players are already transformed into equivalent passenger car units, the optimization problem for each player is described below.

For the UE player, the behavior of UE-following users can be characterized by a minimization of the Beckmann-type objective function over the feasible set:

$$\min_{\mathbf{v}^U \in \Omega^U} \sum_{a \in A} \int_0^{v_a^U} t_a\left(v_a^K + \omega\right) d\omega \tag{6.50}$$

where variables $\mathbf{v}^K$ are taken as fixed. From the first-order optimality conditions for the UE problem (6.50), we have:

$$\sum_{a \in A} t_a\left(v_a^K + v_a^U\right)\delta_{ar} = \mu_w, \text{ if } f_{rw} > 0, \ r \in R_w, \ w \in W^U \tag{6.51}$$

$$\sum_{a \in A} t_a\left(v_a^K + v_a^U\right)\delta_{ar} \geq \mu_w, \text{ if } f_{rw} = 0, \ r \in R_w, \ w \in W^U \tag{6.52}$$

where μ_w, $w \in W^U$ is the Lagrange multipliers associated with OD flow constraint or the *actual* travel time between OD pair $w \in W^U$ by the UE users.

For a CN player $k \in K$, the total travel time of the users under this specific player is minimized, based on the current routing decisions of other players:

$$\min_{\mathbf{v}^k \in \Omega^k} \sum_{a \in A} v_a^k t_a\left(v_a^U + v_a^{-k} + v_a^k\right) \quad \left(= \sum_{a \in A} v_a^k t_a\left(v_a\right)\right), \quad k \in K \tag{6.53}$$

where $v_a^{-k} = \sum_{i \in K, i \neq k} v_a^i$, variables $\mathbf{v}^{-k} \equiv \left(\cdots, v_a^{-k}, \cdots\right)^{\mathrm{T}}$ and $\mathbf{v}^U$ are taken as fixed. From the first-order optimality conditions, for each CN player $k \in K$, we have:

$$\sum_{a \in A} \left\{t_a\left(v_a\right) + v_a^k t_a'\left(v_a\right)\right\} \delta_{ar} = \mu_w, \text{ if } f_{rw} > 0, r \in R_w, w \in W^k \tag{6.54}$$

$$\sum_{a \in A} \left\{t_a\left(v_a\right) + v_a^k t_a'\left(v_a\right)\right\} \delta_{ar} \geq \mu_w, \text{ if } f_{rw} = 0, r \in R_w, w \in W^k \tag{6.55}$$

where $t_a'\left(v_a\right) = \mathrm{d}t_a\left(v_a\right)/\mathrm{d}v_a$, $a \in A$ and μ_w, $w \in W^k$ is the Lagrange multipliers associated with OD flow constraint or the minimum *perceived* travel time between OD pair $w \in W^k$ by CN user $k \in K$. Note that we used notation μ_w in both (6.51)-(6.52) and (6.54)-(6.55), and one should distinguish the right-hand side expressions (actual travel time versus perceived travel time) of these equations according to the owner (UE player or CN player) of the concerned OD pair.

Under the assumption of strictly increasing and convex link cost functions, the above minimization problems (6.50) and (6.53) have unique solutions in their own arguments while other variables are fixed. The solution satisfying the simultaneous optimization of the problems (6.50) and (6.53) is called a UE-CN multiple behavior equilibrium. At equilibrium, the link cost perceived by the UE player is equal to the *marginal private cost* or actual cost $t_a\left(v_a\right)$, while the link cost perceived by a specific CN player $k \in K$ is the *'partial' marginal social cost* given by $t_a\left(v_a\right) + v_a^k t_a'\left(v_a\right)$. It is also straightforward to show that the vector $\left(\mathbf{v}^U, \mathbf{v}^k, k \in K\right)$ is a multiple behavior equilibrium if and only if it solves the following variational inequalities

$$\sum_{a \in A} \left\{t_a\left(v_a\right)\left(\tilde{v}_a^U - v_a^U\right) + \sum_{k \in K} \left(t_a\left(v_a\right) + v_a^k t_a'\left(v_a\right)\right)\left(\tilde{v}_a^k - v_a^k\right)\right\} \geq 0,$$
$$\text{for any } \tilde{\mathbf{v}}^U \in \Omega^U \text{ and any } \tilde{\mathbf{v}}^k \in \Omega^k, \ k \in K \tag{6.56}$$

Define

$$\mathbf{T}_a\left(v_a^U, v_a^k, k \in K\right) = \left[t_a\left(v_a\right), \ t_a\left(v_a\right) + v_a^k t_a'\left(v_a\right), \ k \in K\right]^{\mathrm{T}} \tag{6.57}$$

Clearly, if $\mathbf{T}_a\left(v_a, v_a^k, k \in K\right)$ is strictly monotone in $\left(v_a, v_a^k, k \in K\right)$ for each link $a \in A$, then there exist at most one solution to the multiple behaviour equilibrium model (6.56). It is desirable to establish a sufficient condition for uniqueness in term of the original link cost functions $t_a\left(v_a\right)$, $a \in A$. It is indeed true that, if the separable link cost functions

$t_a(v_a)$, $a \in A$ are linear and strictly increasing, then the multiple behavior equilibrium solution is unique. To see this, we write out the definition of strict monotonicity for $\mathbf{T}_a(v_a, v_a^k, k \in K)$ as follows:

$$\begin{aligned}
&\left[\mathbf{T}_a\left(v_a^U, v_a^k, k \in K\right) - \mathbf{T}_a\left(\tilde{v}_a^U, \tilde{v}_a^k, k \in K\right)\right]^{\mathrm{T}}\left[\left(v_a^U, v_a^k, k \in K\right) - \left(\tilde{v}_a^U, \tilde{v}_a^k, k \in K\right)\right] \\
&= \left[t_a(v_a) - t_a(\tilde{v}_a)\right]\left(v_a^U - \tilde{v}_a^U\right) + \sum_{k \in K}\left[t_a(v_a) - t_a(\tilde{v}_a)\right]\left(v_a^k - \tilde{v}_a^k\right) \\
&\qquad + \sum_{k \in K}\left[v_a^k t_a'(v_a) - \tilde{v}_a^k t_a'(\tilde{v}_a)\right]\left(v_a^k - \tilde{v}_a^k\right) \\
&= \left[t_a(v_a) - t_a(\tilde{v}_a)\right]\left(v_a - \tilde{v}_a\right) + t_a' \sum_{k \in K}\left(v_a^k - \tilde{v}_a^k\right)^2 > 0
\end{aligned}$$

where $t_a' = t_a'(v_a) = t_a'(\tilde{v}_a) =$ positive constant and $\left[t_a(v_a) - t_a(\tilde{v}_a)\right](v_a - \tilde{v}_a) > 0$ for linear and monotonically increasing link cost function $t_a(v_a)$, $a \in A$.

Now we consider the system optimum in terms of total travel time minimization. The SO problem is formulated below:

$$\min_{\mathbf{v}} \sum_{a \in A} v_a t_a(v_a) \tag{6.58}$$

subject to

$$v_a = v_a^U + \sum_{k \in K} v_a^k,\ a \in A,\ \mathbf{v}^U \in \Omega^U,\ \mathbf{v}^k \in \Omega^k,\ k \in K \tag{6.59}$$

From the first-order optimality conditions, we have:

$$\sum_{a \in A}\left\{t_a(v_a) + v_a t_a'(v_a)\right\}\delta_{ar} = \mu_w,\ \text{if } f_{rw} > 0,\ r \in R_w,\ w \in W \tag{6.60}$$

$$\sum_{a \in A}\left\{t_a(v_a) + v_a t_a'(v_a)\right\}\delta_{ar} \geq \mu_w,\ \text{if } f_{rw} = 0,\ r \in R_w,\ w \in W \tag{6.61}$$

With the assumption that the link cost function is strictly increasing and convex, the above SO problem has a unique solution in terms of aggregate link flows v_a, $a \in A$. Here we use $\overline{v}_a^{\mathrm{SO}}$ to denote the unique link flow solution of the SO problem. Note that the link flows v_a^U, v_a^k, $k \in K$, $a \in A$ at the SO solution by individual players may not be unique, but must satisfy the feasible conditions: $\mathbf{v}^U \in \Omega^U$ and $\mathbf{v}^k \in \Omega^k$, $k \in K$, together with the following equation: $v_a^U + \sum_{k \in K} v_a^k = \overline{v}_a^{\mathrm{SO}}$, $a \in A$. The SO conditions (6.60)-(6.61) imply that if the '*full' marginal social cost* equal to $t_a(v_a) + v_a t_a'(v_a)$ on each link $a \in A$ is perceived by all users of each player, a system optimum in terms of total travel time minimization is achieved.

Now we compare the UE conditions (6.51)-(6.52) and the CN equilibrium conditions (6.54)-(6.55) with the SO conditions (6.60)-(6.61), respectively. Clearly, in deciding by which route to travel, a UE user considers only his/her own private or actually experienced cost, and does not consider the congestion externality, $v_a t_a'(v_a)$, which he/she imposes on others. Thus the UE users should be charged with a system-optimal link toll equal to $v_a t_a'(v_a)$ to internalize their full externality or perceive their full social cost. On the other hand, a user under a CN player $k \in K$ will take account of private cost, as well as his/her partial externality, $v_a^k t_a'(v_a)$, which he/she imposes on the other users under the same player. Thus the users under a CN player $k \in K$ should be charged with a system-optimal link toll equal to $(v_a - v_a^k) t_a'(v_a)$ to internalize his/her additional congestion externality imposed on all UE users and users controlled by other players. Note that v_a^k is player-specific, this means that the system-optimal link tolls according to the marginal-cost pricing principle are different for users under different players, including the UE player. Certainly, such link toll differentiation across user classes is unrealistic and hardly implemented because users again differ from one another in an observationally indistinguishable way. Incidentally, the aggregate link flow v_a, $a \in A$ at the SO is unique but the player-specific link flow pattern $\mathbf{v}^k$, $k \in K$ may not be unique. This means that the UE-specific link toll pattern, $v_a t_a'(v_a)$, $a \in A$, is unique, but there might exist multiple player-specific link toll patterns, $(v_a - v_a^k) t_a'(v_a)$, $a \in A$, $k \in K$, for achieving a system optimum.

6.4.2 Anonymous Link Tolls to Decentralize a System Optimum

Given the impossibility of introducing a discriminatory link toll pattern for various user classes for achieving a system optimum, we now investigate whether there exists an alternative meaningful link toll pattern anonymous to all users to decentralize a system optimum as a UE-CN multiple behavior equilibrium.

As before, let $\bar{v}_a^{\mathrm{SO}}$, $a \in A$ denote the unique aggregate link flow at the system optimum, the corresponding link cost is $t_a(\bar{v}_a^{\mathrm{SO}})$, $a \in A$. Consider the following nonlinear (quadratic) programming problem:

$$\min_{\mathbf{v}^U, \mathbf{v}^k, k \in K} \sum_{a \in A} t_a(\bar{v}_a^{\mathrm{SO}}) \left(v_a^U + \sum_{k \in K} v_a^k \right) + \frac{1}{2} \sum_{a \in A} \sum_{k \in K} t_a'(\bar{v}_a^{\mathrm{SO}}) (v_a^k)^2 \tag{6.62}$$

subject to

$$v_a^U + \sum_{k \in K} v_a^k = \bar{v}_a^{\mathrm{SO}}, \; a \in A \tag{6.63}$$

$$v_a^U = \sum_{w \in W^U} \sum_{r \in R_w} f_{rw} \delta_{ar}, \; a \in A \tag{6.64}$$

$$v_a^k = \sum_{w \in W^k} \sum_{r \in R_w} f_{rw} \delta_{ar},\ a \in A,\ k \in K \tag{6.65}$$

$$d_w = \sum_{r \in R_w} f_{rw},\ w \in W \tag{6.66}$$

$$f_{rw} \geq 0,\ r \in R_w,\ w \in W \tag{6.67}$$

In this program, $\bar{v}_a^{\mathrm{SO}}$, $t_a\left(\bar{v}_a^{\mathrm{SO}}\right)$ and $t_a'\left(\bar{v}_a^{\mathrm{SO}}\right)$ are given and fixed. Clearly, the feasible solution set (6.63)-(6.67) of the program is nonempty, because the aggregate SO link flow solution $\bar{v}_a^{\mathrm{SO}}$, $a \in A$ is one of the feasible solutions satisfying flow conservation conditions. It can be easily observed that the program (6.62)-(6.67) is a convex program, since the objective function (6.62) is convex and all constraints (6.63)-(6.67) are linear. Furthermore, the first term of the objective function is a linear function in variables v_a^U, and the second term is strictly convex in variables v_a^k. Therefore, the solution of v_a^k is uniquely determined simply due to the strict convexity, and the solution of v_a^U is unique as well simply because $v_a^U = \bar{v}_a^{\mathrm{SO}} - \sum_{k \in K} v_a^k$. These observations mean that there exists one and only one global optimal solution of player-specific link flows to the program (6.62)-(6.67).

Since all the constraints are linear and therefore satisfy a constraint qualification, the first-order conditions are both sufficient and necessary for the optimality of the program. Thus for an optimal solution $\bar{v}_a^U$ and $\bar{v}_a^k$, $a \in A$, $k \in K$, following conditions are satisfied together with constraints (6.63)-(6.67):

$$\left\{\sum_{a \in A}\left(t_a\left(\bar{v}_a^{\mathrm{SO}}\right) + u_a\right)\delta_{ar} - \mu_w\right\}\bar{f}_{rw} = 0,\ r \in R_w,\ w \in W^U \tag{6.68}$$

$$\sum_{a \in A}\left(t_a\left(\bar{v}_a^{\mathrm{SO}}\right) + u_a\right)\delta_{ar} - \mu_w \geq 0,\ r \in R_w,\ w \in W^U \tag{6.69}$$

$$\left\{\sum_{a \in A}\left(t_a\left(\bar{v}_a^{\mathrm{SO}}\right) + \bar{v}_a^k t_a'\left(\bar{v}_a^{\mathrm{SO}}\right) + u_a\right)\delta_{ar} - \mu_w\right\}\bar{f}_{rw} = 0,\ r \in R_w,\ w \in W^k,\ k \in K \tag{6.70}$$

$$\sum_{a \in A}\left(t_a\left(\bar{v}_a^{\mathrm{SO}}\right) + \bar{v}_a^k t_a'\left(\bar{v}_a^{\mathrm{SO}}\right) + u_a\right)\delta_{ar} - \mu_w \geq 0,\ r \in R_w,\ w \in W^k,\ k \in K \tag{6.71}$$

In the above equations, u_a is the Lagrange multiplier associated with link flow constraint (6.63) and μ_w is the Lagrange multiplier associated with OD demand constraint (6.66). If u_a is viewed as the toll levied on link $a \in A$, regardless of user classes, and μ_w as the minimal perceived travel cost inclusive of link tolls between OD pair $w \in W$ controlled by a specific player, the above equations (6.68)-(6.71) together with the non-negativity constraint (6.67), imply the UE-CN multiple behavior equilibrium conditions. After u_a is embedded into the link cost, equations (6.68)-(6.69) together with (6.67) represent the UE conditions for the OD pairs controlled by the UE player as presented in (6.51)-(6.52); equations (6.70)-(6.71) together with (6.67) represent the CN equilibrium condition for the OD pairs controlled by the CN players as presented in (6.54)-(6.55).

In summary, the solution of the mathematical program (6.62)-(6.67) is in fact an assignment of the users or flows controlled by all players. This assignment generates an aggregate system-optimal link flow pattern as constraint (6.63) is imposed. The assignment also meets the UE-CN multiple behavior equilibrium conditions with a uniform toll charged on each link. Therefore, we conclude that there indeed exist link tolls anonymous to all users which drive the UE-CN multiple behavior equilibrium to a system optimum.

Note that the Lagrange multipliers u_a and μ_w satisfying (6.68)-(6.71) may not be unique. After manipulation of the optimality conditions (6.67) and (6.68)-(6.71), the valid link tolls are given by the following set:

$$\sum_{a\in A}\left\{\left(t_a\left(\bar{v}_a^{SO}\right)+u_a\right)\bar{v}_a^{SO}+\sum_{k\in K}t_a'\left(\bar{v}_a^{SO}\right)\left(\bar{v}_a^k\right)^2\right\}=\sum_{w\in W}\mu_w d_w \tag{6.72}$$

$$\sum_{a\in A}\left(t_a\left(\bar{v}_a^{SO}\right)+u_a\right)\delta_{ar}-\mu_w\geq 0,\ r\in R_w,\ w\in W^U \tag{6.73}$$

$$\sum_{a\in A}\left(t_a\left(\bar{v}_a^{SO}\right)+\bar{v}_a^k t_a'\left(\bar{v}_a^{SO}\right)+u_a\right)\delta_{ar}-\mu_w\geq 0,\ r\in R_w,\ w\in W^k,\ k\in K \tag{6.74}$$

Namely, the system of equalities and inequalities (6.72)-(6.74) and the system of equalities and inequalities (6.68)-(6.71) are equivalent to each other at the unique optimal solution, $v_a^U=\bar{v}_a^U$ and $v_a^k=\bar{v}_a^k$, $a\in A$, $k\in K$ of program (6.62)-(6.67), where $\bar{v}_a^{SO}$, $a\in A$ is again the given aggregate link flow at SO or the solution to the SO program (6.58)-(6.59). To show this equivalence, we note that inequalities (6.69) and (6.71) are still kept in (6.73) and (6.74), thus we only need to show eqns. (6.68) and (6.70) are equivalent to eqn. (6.72) under conditions (6.73)-(6.74). First, equations (6.68) and (6.70) imply eqn. (6.72) by summing them up directly over all $r\in R_w, w\in W^k, k\in K$ and $w\in W^U$, and then replacing v_a^k with $\bar{v}_a^k$. The reverse case that eqn. (6.72) under conditions (6.73)-(6.74) implies eqn. (6.68) and eqn. (6.70) can be easily proved by contradiction. From (6.67) and (6.69), we obtain

$$\left\{\sum_{a\in A}\left(t_a\left(\bar{v}_a^{SO}\right)+u_a\right)\delta_{ar}-\mu_w\right\}\bar{f}_{rw}\geq 0,\ r\in R_w,\ w\in W^U \tag{6.75}$$

Likewise from (6.67) and (6.71), we have

$$\left\{\sum_{a\in A}\left(t_a\left(\bar{v}_a^{SO}\right)+\bar{v}_a^k t_a'\left(\bar{v}_a^{SO}\right)+u_a\right)\delta_{ar}-\mu_w\right\}\bar{f}_{rw}\geq 0,\ r\in R_w,\ w\in W^k,\ k\in K \tag{6.76}$$

Supposed there exists a path $r\in R_w, w\in W$ for which either (6.68) or (6.70) is violated, so one strict inequality must hold in either (6.75) or (6.76). By summing up the two inequalities (6.75) and (6.76) for all paths and in view of the OD flow constraints (6.66), it follows that

$$\sum_{a\in A}\left\{\left(t_a\left(\bar{v}_a^{\mathrm{SO}}\right)+u_a\right)\bar{v}_a^{\mathrm{SO}}+\sum_{k\in K} t_a'\left(\bar{v}_a^{\mathrm{SO}}\right)\left(\bar{v}_a^k\right)^2\right\}>\sum_{w\in W}\mu_w d_w \tag{6.77}$$

This contradicts with (6.72). Thus, the equivalence is true.

To summarize the above analysis, we have the following key theorem derived in this section regarding the multiple behavior equilibrium and system optimum problem.

Theorem 6.5 *In a network with both UE users and CN players, a system optimum in terms of total travel time minimization can be decentralized into a UE-CN multiple behavior equilibrium by anonymous link tolls, which are characterized by a polyhedron consisting a system of linear equalities (6.72) and inequalities (6.73) and (6.74).*

Similar to the LP problem (6.28)-(6.31) in Section 6.3, constraints (6.63) are strict equality constraints, and the associated Lagrange multipliers $u_a, a\in A$ are unrestricted in sign. So, the link toll u_a can be either positive or negative. Proceeding along the same line of arguments as in Section 6.3, we can show that a set of positive uniform link toll patterns can be guaranteed and selected by replacing equality constraints (6.63) with inequality constraints $v_a^U+\sum_{k\in K} v_a^k \le \bar{v}_a^{\mathrm{SO}}$, $a\in A$. The corresponding Lagrange multipliers (link tolls) must be positive: $u_a \ge 0$, $a\in A$. In addition, at the optimum of the revised quadratic program, the inequality constraints are always binding and hence the system optimum link flows are always reproduced.

6.4.3 An Analytical Example

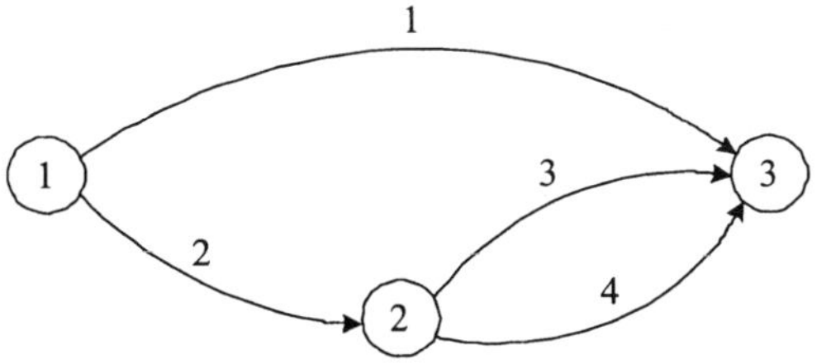

Figure 6.5 The simple network used in the example

Example 6.4 (Valid link toll set for the multiple behavior equilibrium and SO problem)
Consider a simple network shown in Figure 6.5, consisting of 3 nodes and 4 directed links.

Link cost functions are given by

$$t_1 = 6 + 2v_1, \quad t_2 = 20 + v_2, \quad t_3 = 8 + v_3, \quad t_4 = v_4$$

There are two OD pairs ($1 \to 3$ and $2 \to 3$) in the network, and the demands are fixed to be $d_{13} = 20$ and $d_{23} = 20$. There are three paths connecting the OD pair $1 \to 3$: path 1 with single link 1, path 2 with link 2 and link 3, and path 3 with link 2 and link 4. There are two paths connecting the OD pair $2 \to 3$: path 4 with single link 3, and path 5 with single link 4. Flows through the five paths are denoted by f_1, f_2, f_3, f_4 and f_5.

The unique link flows at the system optimum are obtained as:

$$\bar{\mathbf{v}}^{\mathrm{SO}} = \left(\bar{v}_1^{\mathrm{SO}}, \bar{v}_2^{\mathrm{SO}}, \bar{v}_3^{\mathrm{SO}}, \bar{v}_4^{\mathrm{SO}}\right)^{\mathrm{T}} = (14,6,11,15)^{\mathrm{T}}$$

The corresponding link travel times are given by:

$$\mathbf{t}\left(\bar{\mathbf{v}}^{\mathrm{SO}}\right) = \left(t_1\left(\bar{v}_1^{\mathrm{SO}}\right), t_2\left(\bar{v}_2^{\mathrm{SO}}\right), t_3\left(\bar{v}_3^{\mathrm{SO}}\right), t_4\left(\bar{v}_4^{\mathrm{SO}}\right)\right)^{\mathrm{T}} = (34,26,19,15)^{\mathrm{T}}$$

The total travel time at system optimum is 1066.

Now we seek anonymous link tolls to decentralize a system optimum to various multiple behavior equilibria. The following three cases are examined and compared.

Case A: OD pair $1 \to 3$ is controlled by a CN player (denoted by "C"), and the OD pair $2 \to 3$ is controlled by a UE player (denoted by "U").

Case B: The two OD pairs are controlled by two distinct CN players. OD pair $1 \to 3$ is controlled by player "$C1$", and the OD pair $2 \to 3$ is controlled by player "$C2$".

Case C: Both OD pairs are controlled by a UE player.

Case A. At the multiple behavior equilibrium without toll charge, the link flows routed by each player are:

$$\mathbf{v}^C = \left(v_1^C, v_2^C, v_3^C, v_4^C\right)^{\mathrm{T}} = \left(\frac{88}{7}, \frac{52}{7}, \frac{26}{7}, \frac{26}{7}\right)^{\mathrm{T}}, \quad \mathbf{v}^U = \left(v_1^U, v_2^U, v_3^U, v_4^U\right)^{\mathrm{T}} = (0,0,6,14)^{\mathrm{T}}$$

The total travel time is 7568/7. Now we apply program (6.62)-(6.67) to find the unique link flows routed by each player when anonymous link tolls are charged for system optimum. Substituting the above SO solution of link flows and link costs into the program, we have

$$\min_{\mathbf{v}^U, \mathbf{v}^C} 34\left(v_1^U + v_1^C\right) + 26\left(v_2^U + v_2^C\right) + 19\left(v_3^U + v_3^C\right) + 15\left(v_4^U + v_4^C\right)$$
$$+ \frac{1}{2}\left(2\left(v_1^C\right)^2 + \left(v_2^C\right)^2 + \left(v_3^C\right)^2 + \left(v_4^C\right)^2\right)$$

subject to

$$v_1^U + v_1^C = 14, \quad v_2^U + v_2^C = 6, \quad v_3^U + v_3^C = 11, \quad v_4^U + v_4^C = 15$$

$$v_1^U = 0,\ v_2^U = 0,\ v_3^U = f_4,\ v_4^U = f_5$$

$$v_1^C = f_1,\ v_2^C = f_2 + f_3,\ v_3^C = f_2,\ v_4^C = f_3$$

$$f_1 + f_2 + f_3 = 20,\ f_4 + f_5 = 20$$

$$f_1,\ f_2,\ f_3,\ f_4,\ f_5 \geq 0$$

This is a simple quadratic programming problem, to which the optimal solution can be easily identified. The link flows routed by each player at optimum are given by

$$\bar{\mathbf{v}}^U = \left(\bar{v}_1^U, \bar{v}_2^U, \bar{v}_3^U, \bar{v}_4^U\right)^{\mathrm{T}} = (0,0,8,12)^{\mathrm{T}},\quad \bar{\mathbf{v}}^C = \left(\bar{v}_1^C, \bar{v}_2^C, \bar{v}_3^C, \bar{v}_4^C\right)^{\mathrm{T}} = (14,6,3,3)^{\mathrm{T}}$$

Substituting the above solution into system (6.72)-(6.74) yields the following valid toll set:

$$14u_1 + 6u_2 + 11u_3 + 15u_4 + 1512 = 20\mu^U + 20\mu^C$$

$$19 + u_3 \geq \mu^U,\ 15 + u_4 \geq \mu^U$$

$$62 + u_1 \geq \mu^C,\ 54 + u_2 + u_3 \geq \mu^C,\ 50 + u_2 + u_4 \geq \mu^C$$

The valid toll set can be further simplified into:

$$u_1 = u_2 + u_3 - 8,\ u_4 = u_3 + 4$$

The resulting anonymous link tolls are unbounded. To seek positive toll patterns for supporting the system optimum as a UE-CN multiple behavior equilibrium, the aggregate link flow constraints are modified as:

$$v_1^U + v_1^C \leq 14,\ v_2^U + v_2^C \leq 6,\ v_3^U + v_3^C \leq 11,\ v_4^U + v_4^C \leq 15$$

It can be verified that the same player-specific link flows are obtained, and the valid positive anonymous link toll patterns are given by:

$$u_1 = u_2 + u_3 - 8,\ u_4 = u_3 + 4,\ u_1,\ u_2,\ u_3,\ u_4 \geq 0$$

Case B. At the multiple behavior equilibrium without toll charge, the link flows routed by each player at optimum are given by

$$\mathbf{v}^{C1} = \left(v_1^{C1}, v_2^{C1}, v_3^{C1}, v_4^{C1}\right)^{\mathrm{T}} = \left(\frac{88}{7}, \frac{52}{7}, \frac{50}{21}, \frac{106}{21}\right)^{\mathrm{T}}$$

$$\mathbf{v}^{C2} = \left(v_1^{C2}, v_2^{C2}, v_3^{C2}, v_4^{C2}\right)^{\mathrm{T}} = \left(0, 0, \frac{26}{3}, \frac{34}{3}\right)^{\mathrm{T}}$$

The total travel time is $67664/63$. Solving the program (6.62)-(6.67) gives rise to the following player-specific link flows:

$$\bar{\mathbf{v}}^{C1} = \left(\bar{v}_1^{C1}, \bar{v}_2^{C1}, \bar{v}_3^{C1}, \bar{v}_4^{C1}\right)^{\mathrm{T}} = (14,6,2,4)^{\mathrm{T}},\quad \bar{\mathbf{v}}^{C2} = \left(\bar{v}_1^{C2}, \bar{v}_2^{C2}, \bar{v}_3^{C2}, \bar{v}_4^{C2}\right)^{\mathrm{T}} = (0,0,9,11)^{\mathrm{T}}$$

The nonnegative valid toll set is given by:

$$u_1 = u_2 + u_3 - 9,\ u_4 = u_3 + 2,\ u_1,\ u_2,\ u_3,\ u_4 \geq 0$$

Case C. This is a simple UE problem corresponding to the standard case examined in Section

6.2. The UE link flows without toll charge are given by:

$$\mathbf{v}^U = \left(v_1^U, v_2^U, v_3^U, v_4^U\right)^{\mathrm{T}} = \left(\frac{116}{7}, \frac{24}{7}, \frac{54}{7}, \frac{110}{7}\right)^{\mathrm{T}}$$

The total travel time is $7680/7$. The valid nonnegative toll set to drive the unique UE flow pattern to the system optimum of total travel time minimization is given as:

$$u_1 = u_2 + u_3 + 11, \quad u_4 = u_3 + 4, \quad u_1, \ u_2, \ u_3, \ u_4 \geq 0$$

This toll set includes the following marginal-cost pricing link toll pattern as a special case:

$$\mathbf{u} = \left(u_1, u_2, u_3, u_4\right)^{\mathrm{T}} = (28, 6, 11, 15)^{\mathrm{T}}$$

Table 6.2 The perceived and actual experienced path costs for each player on the example network with anonymous link tolls for system optimum

Scenario		OD pair $1 \to 3$			OD pair $2 \to 3$	
		Path 1	Path 2	Path 3	Path 4	Path 5
Case A	Perceived cost	$62 + u_1$	$54 + u_2 + u_3$	$50 + u_2 + u_4$	$19 + u_3$	$15 + u_4$
	Experienced cost	$34 + u_1$	$45 + u_2 + u_3$	$41 + u_2 + u_4$	$19 + u_3$	$15 + u_4$
Case B	Perceived cost	$62 + u_1$	$53 + u_2 + u_3$	$51 + u_2 + u_4$	$28 + u_3$	$26 + u_4$
	Experienced cost	$34 + u_1$	$45 + u_2 + u_3$	$41 + u_2 + u_4$	$19 + u_3$	$15 + u_4$
Case C	Perceived cost	$34 + u_1$	$45 + u_2 + u_3$	$41 + u_2 + u_4$	$19 + u_3$	$15 + u_4$
	Experienced cost	$34 + u_1$	$45 + u_2 + u_3$	$41 + u_2 + u_4$	$19 + u_3$	$15 + u_4$

Evidently, the valid toll sets for the above three cases are different. For each case with any valid toll pattern $\mathbf{u}$, the perceived and experienced path costs of each OD pair controlled by each player with different equilibrium behavior are listed in Table 6.2. It is straightforward to confirm that the flows on the feasible paths between each OD pair are positive and the costs (perceived cost for CN players consisting of travel time cost, toll charge and partial user externality; actual or experienced cost for UE player consisting of travel time cost and toll charge) on the paths are identical in each of the three cases. Hence, the identified toll pattern in each case does support the system optimum as the corresponding multiple behavior equilibrium.

6.5 MULTI-UE-CLASS AND MULTI-CN-CLASS BEHAVIOR EQUILIBRIUM AND SO PROBLEM

In the same spirit as above, in this section we deal with the more general case of multi-class, multi-criteria behavior equilibrium and SO problems which include the models and methods presented Section 6.3 and 6.4 as special cases. All users in a network are divided into different classes, and different classes evaluate their travel disutility by different criteria. As before, let M and K be the set of UE classes and CN classes, respectively. Users in a specific UE class (or UE player) $m \in M$ will follow UE routing behavior based on their own evaluation criterion of travel disutility; users in a specific CN class (or CN player) $k \in K$ will minimize their own total generalized cost or follow their own criterion-based partial system optimum in their routing decisions. The criteria mentioned above refer to the weights used to value the impacts of link travel time and link travel cost. It is assumed that the disutility of traveling a link $a \in A$ is composed of travel time $t_a(v_a)$ and travel cost $c_a(v_a)$, and both the time and cost are continuously differentiable and increasing convex functions of the aggregate link flows v_a. Here, the travel cost can be regarded as the environmental cost raised due to vehicle gas emission. Hence, the travel disutility of a link is defined as $\beta_t t_a(v_a) + \beta_c c_a(v_a)$, where the weights β_t and β_c are different for different classes of users.

6.5.1 Multi-criteria and Multiple Behavior Equilibrium and System Optimum

Again suppose the demand d_w between OD pair $w \in W$ is given, where an OD pair is controlled by a specific player. Apart from the feasible flow set Ω^k of a CN player $k \in K$ defined by (6.49), we define the feasible link flow set of each UE player Ω^m, $m \in M$ as:

$$\Omega^m = \left\{ \mathbf{v}^m \middle| v_a^m = \sum_{w \in W^m} \sum_{r \in R_w} f_{rw} \delta_{ar}, \sum_{r \in R_w} f_{rw} = d_w, f_{rw} \geq 0, r \in R_w, w \in W^m, a \in A \right\},\ m \in M \quad (6.78)$$

where $\mathbf{v}^m \equiv \left(\cdots, v_a^m, \cdots\right)^{\mathrm{T}}$, $a \in A$ and v_a^m is the flow of link a arising out of the OD flows from the set W^m, W^m is the set of OD pairs of which users are controlled by UE player $m \in M$.

For a UE player $m \in M$, the route choice behavior of its UE-following users can be characterized by a minimization of the Beckmann-type objective function over its feasible set:

$$\min_{\mathbf{v}^m \in \Omega^m} \sum_{a \in A} \left\{ \beta_t^m \int_0^{v_a^m} t_a\left(v_a^{-m} + \omega\right) d\omega + \beta_c^m \int_0^{v_a^m} c_a\left(v_a^{-m} + \omega\right) d\omega \right\} \quad (6.79)$$

where $v_a^{-m} = v_a^K + \sum_{i \in M, i \neq m} v_a^i$ and $\mathbf{v}^{-m} \equiv \left(\cdots, v_a^{-m}, \cdots\right)^{\mathrm{T}}$, $a \in A$ is taken as fixed, β_t^m and β_c^m are the weighting factor of travel time and travel cost in the travel disutility evaluated by

UE user class $m \in M$. From the first-order optimality conditions for the UE program (6.79) of UE class $m \in M$, we have:

$$\sum_{a\in A}\left(\beta_t^m t_a\left(v_a\right)+\beta_c^m c_a\left(v_a\right)\right)\delta_{ar}=\mu_w^m,\ \text{if } f_{rw}>0,\ r\in R_w,\ w\in W^m \tag{6.80}$$

$$\sum_{a\in A}\left(\beta_t^m t_a\left(v_a\right)+\beta_c^m c_a\left(v_a\right)\right)\delta_{ar}\geq \mu_w,\ \text{if } f_{rw}=0,\ r\in R_w,\ w\in W^m \tag{6.81}$$

where $\mu_w^m,\ w\in W^m$ are the Lagrange multipliers associated with OD flow conservation constraints and equal the minimum travel disutility between OD pair $w\in W^m$ by users in UE class $m\in M$.

A CN player $k\in K$ is to minimize the total travel disutility of all users under its control based on the current routing decisions of other players:

$$\min_{\mathbf{v}^k\in\Omega^k}\ \sum_{a\in A}\left(\beta_t^k t_a\left(v_a^{-k}+v_a^k\right)+\beta_c^k c_a\left(v_a^{-k}+v_a^k\right)\right)v_a^k \tag{6.82}$$

where $v_a^{-k}=v_a^M+\sum_{j\in K, j\neq k} v_a^j$ and $v_a^M=\sum_{i\in M} v_a^i$, $\mathbf{v}^{-k}\equiv\left(\cdots,v_a^{-k},\cdots\right)^{\mathrm{T}}$, $a\in A$ is taken as fixed, β_t^k and β_c^k are the weighting factor of travel time and travel cost in the travel disutility evaluated by CN player $k\in K$. From the first-order optimality conditions for the partial SO program (6.82) of CN player $k\in K$ we have:

$$\sum_{a\in A}\left\{\beta_t^k\left(t_a\left(v_a\right)+v_a^k t_a'\left(v_a\right)\right)+\beta_c^k\left(c_a\left(v_a\right)+v_a^k c_a'\left(v_a\right)\right)\right\}\delta_{ar}=\mu_w^k,$$

$$\text{if } f_{rw}>0,\ r\in R_w,\ w\in W^k \tag{6.83}$$

$$\sum_{a\in A}\left\{\beta_t^k\left(t_a\left(v_a\right)+v_a^k t_a'\left(v_a\right)\right)+\beta_c^k\left(c_a\left(v_a\right)+v_a^k c_a'\left(v_a\right)\right)\right\}\delta_{ar}\geq\mu_w^k,$$

$$\text{if } f_{rw}=0,\ r\in R_w,\ w\in W^k \tag{6.84}$$

where $t_a'\left(v_a\right)=\mathrm{d}t_a\left(v_a\right)/\mathrm{d}v_a$ and $c_a'\left(v_a\right)=\mathrm{d}c_a\left(v_a\right)/\mathrm{d}v_a$, and μ_w^k is the Lagrange multiplier associated with OD flow constraints and equals the minimum perceived travel disutility between OD pair $w\in W^k$ by users under CN player $k\in K$. Again we should distinguish μ_w in (6.80)-(6.81) and (6.83)-(6.84) according to the owner of the concerned OD pair. Namely, μ_w represents the actual or experienced travel disutility if OD pair w is owned by a UE player and the perceived travel disutility if owned by a CN player.

Now we consider system optimum in terms of total travel disutility minimization. The SO player controls all the flows on the network and freely chooses individual weights β_t^{SO} for total travel time and β_c^{SO} for total travel cost, regardless of the weights taken by individual UE and CN players. The SO problem is formulated below:

$$\min_{\mathbf{v}} \beta_t^{\mathrm{SO}} \sum_{a \in A} t_a(v_a) v_a + \beta_c^{\mathrm{SO}} \sum_{a \in A} c_a(v_a) v_a \tag{6.85}$$

subject to

$$v_a = \sum_{m \in M} v_a^m + \sum_{k \in K} v_a^k,\ a \in A;\ \mathbf{v}^m \in \Omega^m,\ m \in M;\ \mathbf{v}^k \in \Omega^k,\ k \in K \tag{6.86}$$

From the first-order optimality condition for the strictly convex program (6.85), for an optimal solution $\overline{v}_a$, $a \in A$ we have:

$$\sum_{a \in A} \left\{ \beta_t^{\mathrm{SO}} \left(t_a(\overline{v}_a) + \overline{v}_a t'_a(\overline{v}_a) \right) + \beta_c^{\mathrm{SO}} \left(c_a(\overline{v}_a) + \overline{v}_a c'_a(\overline{v}_a) \right) \right\} \delta_{ar} = \mu_w^{\mathrm{SO}},$$
$$\text{if } \overline{f}_{rw} > 0,\ r \in R_w,\ w \in W \tag{6.87}$$

$$\sum_{a \in A} \left\{ \beta_t^{\mathrm{SO}} \left(t_a(\overline{v}_a) + \overline{v}_a t'_a(\overline{v}_a) \right) + \beta_c^{\mathrm{SO}} \left(c_a(\overline{v}_a) + \overline{v}_a c'_a(\overline{v}_a) \right) \right\} \delta_{ar} \geq \mu_w^{\mathrm{SO}},$$
$$\text{if } \overline{f}_{rw} = 0,\ r \in R_w,\ w \in W \tag{6.88}$$

where $W \equiv W^M \bigcup W^K$ where $W^M = \bigcup_{m \in M} W^m$ and $W^K = \bigcup_{k \in K} W^k$.

Again let $\overline{v}_a^{\mathrm{SO}}$, $a \in A$ denote the unique aggregate link flow solution to SO problem (6.85)-(6.86). The class-specific link flows v_a^m and v_a^k at the SO solution may not be unique, but must satisfy the feasible conditions: $\mathbf{v}^m \in \Omega^m$, $m \in M$ and $\mathbf{v}^k \in \Omega^k$, $k \in K$ together with: $\sum_{m \in M} v_a^m + \sum_{k \in K} v_a^k = \overline{v}_a^{\mathrm{SO}}$, $a \in A$.

Now we compare the SO optimality conditions (6.87)-(6.88) and the multi-class UE conditions (6.80)-(6.81), and also the multi-class CN equilibrium conditions (6.83)-(6.84). It is easy to observe that those SO optimality conditions and the individual player equilibrium conditions cannot be reconciled through the marginal-cost pricing even with toll differentiation. The reason is that the criteria (β_t^m, β_c^m) by UE user class $m \in M$ and (β_t^k, β_c^k) by CN player $k \in K$ are not consistent with the SO criteria $(\beta_t^{\mathrm{SO}}, \beta_c^{\mathrm{SO}})$, even if the *'full' marginal social travel time* equal to $t_a(v_a) + v_a t'_a(v_a)$ and the marginal social cost $c_a(v_a) + v_a c'_a(v_a)$ on each link $a \in A$ are perceived by all users of each player.

6.5.2 Anonymous Link Tolls to Decentralize a System Optimum

Along the same line to obtain an anonymous link toll pattern for the system optimum, we construct the following quadratic program for given unique SO link flow solution $\overline{v}_a^{\mathrm{SO}}$ as well as $t_a(\overline{v}_a^{\mathrm{SO}})$, $c_a(\overline{v}_a^{\mathrm{SO}})$, $t'_a(\overline{v}_a^{\mathrm{SO}})$ and $c'_a(\overline{v}_a^{\mathrm{SO}})$, $a \in A$.

$$\min_{v^m, m\in M; v^k, k\in K} \sum_{a\in A}\left\{\sum_{m\in M}\beta_t^m t_a\left(\bar{v}_a^{SO}\right)v_a^m + \sum_{k\in K}\beta_t^k t_a\left(\bar{v}_a^{SO}\right)v_a^k + \sum_{m\in M}\beta_c^m c_a\left(\bar{v}_a^{SO}\right)v_a^m + \sum_{k\in K}\beta_c^k c_a\left(\bar{v}_a^{SO}\right)v_a^k\right\}$$
$$+\frac{1}{2}\sum_{a\in A}\sum_{k\in K}\left\{\beta_t^k t_a'\left(\bar{v}_a^{SO}\right)\left(v_a^k\right)^2 + \beta_c^k c_a'\left(\bar{v}_a^{SO}\right)\left(v_a^k\right)^2\right\} \quad (6.89)$$

subject to

$$\sum_{m\in M} v_a^m + \sum_{k\in K} v_a^k = \bar{v}_a^{SO},\ a\in A \quad (6.90)$$

$$v_a^m = \sum_{w\in W^m}\sum_{r\in R_w} f_{rw}\delta_{ar},\ a\in A,\ m\in M \quad (6.91)$$

$$v_a^k = \sum_{w\in W^k}\sum_{r\in R_w} f_{rw}\delta_{ar},\ a\in A,\ m\in M \quad (6.92)$$

$$d_w = \sum_{r\in R_w} f_{rw},\ w\in W \quad (6.93)$$

$$f_{rw}\geq 0,\ r\in R_w,\ w\in W \quad (6.94)$$

Again in a similar argument as before, the set of feasible solutions to program (6.89)-(6.94) is nonempty, and for a class-specific optimal link flow solution, $\bar{v}_a^m$ and $\bar{v}_a^k$, $m\in M$, $k\in K$, $a\in A$, the following relationships come from the first-order optimality conditions of the convex program (6.89)-(6.94):

$$\left\{\sum_{a\in A}\left(\beta_t^m t_a\left(\bar{v}_a^{SO}\right)+\beta_c^m c_a\left(\bar{v}_a^{SO}\right)+u_a\right)\delta_{ar}-\mu_w\right\}\bar{f}_{rw}=0,\ r\in R_w,\ w\in W^m,\ m\in M \quad (6.95)$$

$$\sum_{a\in A}\left(\beta_t^m t_a\left(\bar{v}_a^{SO}\right)+\beta_c^m c_a\left(\bar{v}_a^{SO}\right)+u_a\right)\delta_{ar}-\mu_w\geq 0,\ r\in R_w,\ w\in W^m,\ m\in M \quad (6.96)$$

$$\left\{\sum_{a\in A}\left(\beta_t^k\left(t_a\left(\bar{v}_a^{SO}\right)+\bar{v}_a^k t_a'\left(\bar{v}_a^{SO}\right)\right)+\beta_c^k\left(c_a\left(\bar{v}_a^{SO}\right)+\bar{v}_a^k c_a'\left(\bar{v}_a^{SO}\right)\right)+u_a\right)\delta_{ar}-\mu_w\right\}\bar{f}_{rw}=0,$$
$$r\in R_w,\ w\in W^k,\ k\in K \quad (6.97)$$

$$\sum_{a\in A}\left(\beta_t^k\left(t_a\left(\bar{v}_a^{SO}\right)+\bar{v}_a^k t_a'\left(\bar{v}_a^{SO}\right)\right)+\beta_c^k\left(c_a\left(\bar{v}_a^{SO}\right)+\bar{v}_a^k c_a'\left(\bar{v}_a^{SO}\right)\right)+u_a\right)\delta_{ar}-\mu_w\geq 0,$$
$$r\in R_w,\ w\in W^k,\ k\in K \quad (6.98)$$

Once again, in the above equations, u_a is the Lagrange multiplier associated with the link flow constraint (6.90) and μ_w is the Lagrange multiplier associated with the OD demand constraint (6.93). If the travel disutility for all user classes is measured in monetary units, then u_a can be viewed as the anonymous toll levied on link $a\in A$ regardless of user classes, and μ_w as the minimal perceived travel disutility inclusive of link tolls between OD pair $w\in W$ controlled by a specific player (class), and the group of equations (6.95)-(6.98) together with the non-negativity path flow constraint (6.94) imply the multi-UE-class and multi-CN-class behavior equilibrium conditions.

Here we should note that it is required to measure the generalized travel disutility by each user class in monetary units in order to interpret u_a, $a \in A$ in (6.95)-(6.98) as the anonymous link tolls sought. In this case, the weighting factors, β_t^m, $m \in M$ and β_t^k, $k \in K$, attached to travel time in all the relevant equations, corresponds to the value of time of each UE class (player) and each CN player. The weighting factors, β_t^{so} and β_c^{so}, for the SO objective, although unrestricted, can be meaningfully chosen as the average of (β_t^m, β_t^k) and (β_c^m, β_c^k) of all user classes $m \in M$, $k \in K$, respectively, weighted by their OD demands.

By simplifying the system of equalities and inequalities (6.95)-(6.98) as before, we obtain the following polyhedron of valid links tolls:

$$\sum_{a \in A} \left\{ t_a\left(\bar{v}_a^{SO}\right)\left(\sum_{m \in M} \beta_t^m \bar{v}_a^m + \sum_{k \in K} \beta_t^k \bar{v}_a^k \right) + \sum_{k \in K} \beta_t^k t_a'\left(\bar{v}_a^{SO}\right)\left(\bar{v}_a^k\right)^2 \right.$$
$$\left. + c_a\left(\bar{v}_a^{SO}\right)\left(\sum_{m \in M} \beta_c^m \bar{v}_a^m + \sum_{k \in K} \beta_c^k \bar{v}_a^k \right) + \sum_{k \in K} \beta_c^k c_a'\left(\bar{v}_a^{SO}\right)\left(\bar{v}_a^k\right)^2 + u_a \bar{v}_a^{SO} \right\} = \sum_{w \in W} \mu_w d_w \qquad (6.99)$$

$$\sum_{a \in A} \left(\beta_t^m t_a\left(\bar{v}_a^{SO}\right) + \beta_c^m c_a\left(\bar{v}_a^{SO}\right) + u_a \right) \delta_{ar} - \mu_w \geq 0,\ r \in R_w,\ w \in W^m,\ m \in M \qquad (6.100)$$

$$\sum_{a \in A} \left(\beta_t^k \left(t_a\left(\bar{v}_a^{SO}\right) + \bar{v}_a^k t_a'\left(\bar{v}_a^{SO}\right)\right) + \beta_c^k \left(c_a\left(\bar{v}_a^{SO}\right) + \bar{v}_a^k c_a'\left(\bar{v}_a^{SO}\right)\right) + u_a \right) \delta_{ar} - \mu_w \geq 0,$$
$$r \in R_w,\ w \in W^k,\ k \in K \qquad (6.101)$$

where $\bar{v}_a^{SO}$, $a \in A$ is the given aggregate link flow at SO or the unique solution to the SO program (6.85)-(6.86), $\bar{v}_a^m$, $\bar{v}_a^k$, $m \in M$, $k \in K$, $a \in A$ are again the unique class-specific link flow solutions of convex program (6.89)-(6.94). As before, we can modify the program (6.89)-(6.94) with the equality constraints (6.90) replaced by relaxed inequality constraints and show the existence of anonymous positive link tolls to decentralize the system optimum into a multi-class multi-criteria behavior equilibrium.

6.5.3 An Analytical Example

Example 6.5 (Valid link toll set for the multi-criteria and multi-behavior equilibrium and SO problem)) Consider again a simple network shown in Figure 6.6, consisting of 3 nodes and 3 directed links. In addition to the in-vehicle travel time, users have to pay the environmental cost. The link travel time functions are given by

$$t_1 = 4v_1,\quad t_2 = 50 + v_2,\quad t_3 = 50 + v_3$$

The environmental cost functions are given by

$c_1 = 20 + 2v_1$, $c_2 = 30 + 2v_2$, $c_3 = 10 + 2v_3$

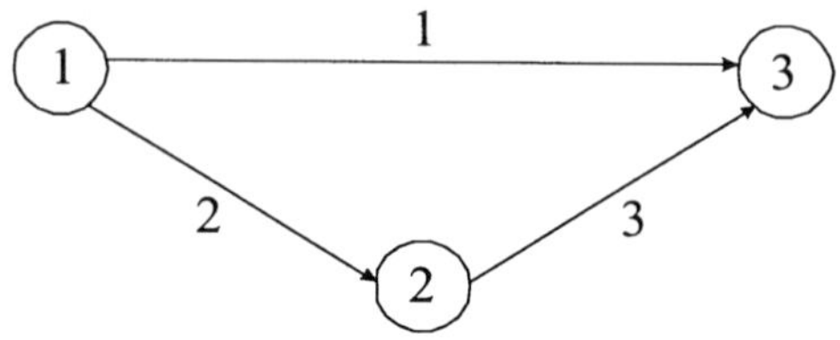

Figure 6.6 The small network used in the numerical example

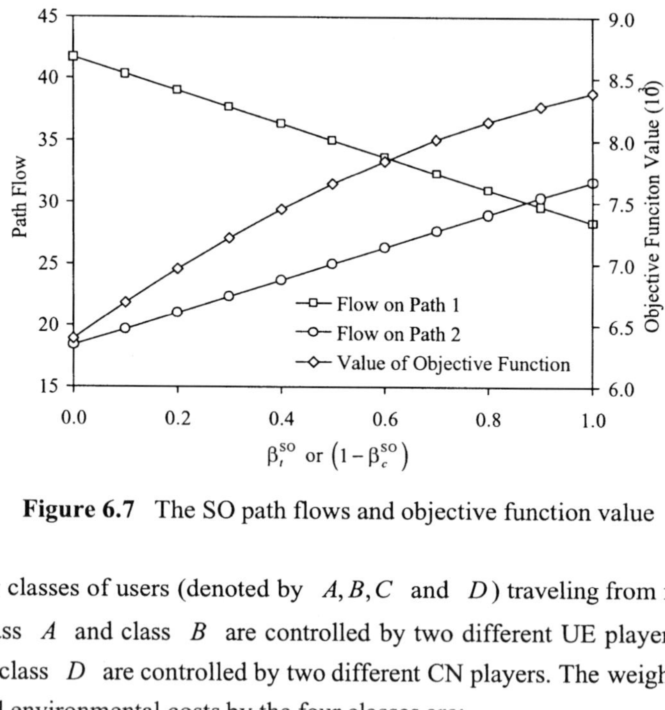

Figure 6.7 The SO path flows and objective function value

There are four classes of users (denoted by A, B, C and D) traveling from node 1 to node 3. Users in class A and class B are controlled by two different UE players, and users in class C and class D are controlled by two different CN players. The weighting factors for travel time and environmental costs by the four classes are:

$$\beta_t^A = 0.4,\ \beta_t^B = 0.5,\ \beta_t^C = 0.2,\ \beta_t^D = 0.6$$

$$\beta_c^A = 0.6,\ \beta_c^B = 0.5,\ \beta_c^C = 0.8,\ \beta_c^D = 0.4$$

The demands for the four classes in the single OD pair are $d^A = 10$, $d^B = 20$, $d^C = 20$ and $d^D = 10$, respectively. There are two paths connecting the OD pair $1 \to 3$: path 1 with single link 1 and path 2 with link 2 and link 3. The class-specific flows on these two paths are denoted by f_1^A, f_2^A, f_1^B, f_2^B, f_1^C, f_2^C, f_1^D, f_2^D.

The class-specific link flow solution of the multi-criteria, multi-class behavior equilibrium is:

$$\mathbf{v}^A = (10,0,0)^{\mathrm{T}},\ \mathbf{v}^B = (20,0,0)^{\mathrm{T}},\ \mathbf{v}^C = (9,11,11)^{\mathrm{T}},\ \mathbf{v}^D = (0,10,10)^{\mathrm{T}}$$

Consider the system optimum case with weighting factor $\beta_t^{\mathrm{SO}} + \beta_c^{\mathrm{SO}} = 1.0$. The path flow solutions and the SO objective values for the convex SO program (6.85)-(6.86) are plotted in Figure 6.7 for reference as β_t^{SO} changes from 0.0 to 1.0 (β_c^{SO} changes from 1.0 to 0.0).

Now we seek anonymous link tolls to decentralize the system optimum corresponding to SO weighting factors: $\beta_t^{\mathrm{SO}} = \beta_c^{\mathrm{SO}} = 0.5$, with the following aggregate link flow solutions, together with link travel time and environmental costs:

$$\bar{\mathbf{v}}^{\mathrm{SO}} = (35,25,25)^{\mathrm{T}},\ \mathbf{t}(\bar{\mathbf{v}}^{\mathrm{SO}}) = (140,75,75)^{\mathrm{T}},\ \mathbf{c}(\bar{\mathbf{v}}^{\mathrm{SO}}) = (90,80,60)^{\mathrm{T}}$$

The details of program (6.89)-(6.94) are written as follows:

$$\min_{\mathbf{v}^A,\mathbf{v}^B,\mathbf{v}^C,\mathbf{v}^D} 110v_1^A + 115v_1^B + 100v_1^C + 120v_1^D + 78v_2^A + 77.5v_2^B + 79v_2^C + 77v_2^D$$

$$+66v_3^A + 67.5v_3^B + 63v_3^C + 69v_3^D$$

$$+\frac{1}{2}\left(2.4\left(v_1^C\right)^2 + 3.2\left(v_1^D\right)^2 + 1.8\left(v_2^C\right)^2 + 1.4\left(v_2^D\right)^2 + 1.8\left(v_3^C\right)^2 + 1.4\left(v_3^D\right)^2\right)$$

subject to

$$v_1^A + v_1^B + v_1^C + v_1^D = 35,\quad v_2^A + v_2^B + v_2^C + v_2^D = 25,\quad v_3^A + v_3^B + v_3^C + v_3^D = 25$$

$$v_1^A = f_1^A,\ v_1^B = f_1^B,\ v_1^C = f_1^C,\ v_1^D = f_1^D,\ v_2^A = f_2^A,\ v_2^B = f_2^B,\ v_2^C = f_2^C$$

$$v_2^D = f_2^D,\ v_3^A = f_2^A,\ v_3^B = f_2^B,\ v_3^C = f_2^C,\ v_3^D = f_2^D$$

$$f_1^A + f_2^A = 10,\quad f_1^B + f_2^B = 20,\quad f_1^C + f_2^C = 20,\quad f_1^D + f_2^D = 10$$

$$f_1^A,\ f_2^A,\ f_1^B,\ f_2^B,\ f_1^C,\ f_2^C,\ f_1^D,\ f_2^D \geq 0$$

Solving the above simple quadratic program, we obtain the following optimal solution:

$$\bar{\mathbf{v}}^A = (10,0,0)^{\mathrm{T}},\ \bar{\mathbf{v}}^B = (7,13,13)^{\mathrm{T}},\ \bar{\mathbf{v}}^C = (14,6,6)^{\mathrm{T}},\ \bar{\mathbf{v}}^D = (4,6,6)^{\mathrm{T}}$$

Substituting the above results into (6.99)-(6.101) yields the following set of valid link tolls:

$$8150 + 35u_1 + 25u_2 + 25u_3 = 10\mu^A + 20\mu^B + 20\mu^C + 10\mu^D$$

$$110 + u_1 \geq \mu^A,\quad 144 + u_2 + u_3 \geq \mu^A$$

$$115 + u_1 \geq \mu^B,\quad 145 + u_2 + u_3 \geq \mu^B$$

$$133.6 + u_1 \geq \mu^C,\quad 163.6 + u_2 + u_3 \geq \mu^C$$

$$132.8 + u_1 \geq \mu^D,\quad 162.8 + u_2 + u_3 \geq \mu^D$$

This set can be further simplified into

$$u_1 = u_2 + u_3 + 30$$

One can, of course, further add nonnegative constraints to the above link toll set and the resulting nonnegative toll set remains nonempty and valid, as discussed before.

6.6 SUMMARY

In this chapter we examined the existence and properties of the valid link tolls that can decentralize a system optimal flow pattern into a standard user equilibrium or various multi-class, multi-criteria behavior equilibria. Our general point is that the toll charge must be anonymous or uniform in the case of unobservable user heterogeneity, such as users with different values of time or different routing behaviors but with the same type of vehicles.

In the case of single class or homogeneous users with identical VOTs, the relationship between UE and SO and the properties of valid tolls holds regardless of the cost (money) or time units that are used in expressing the objective function of the system optimum and the criterion for user equilibrium. The valid link toll set for SO is in fact a convex polyhedron in terms of a system of linear equalities and inequalities. All valid link tolls give rise to the same constant total toll revenue in the elastic-demand case.

In the case of multi-class users with a discrete set of VOTs, we showed that there exists an anonymous link toll pattern that supports a SO as a multi-class user equilibrium, whenever the system objective function is measured by either money (cost) or time units. For the cost-based SO, the anonymous link toll is equal to the user externality of travel time multiplied by the arithmetic mean of the values of time of all users traversing that link. For the time-based SO, the anonymous link toll is not based on the user externality, but can be determined from the solution to an artificially constructed linear dual problem.

With multiple equilibrium behaviors, such as the presence of both UE and CN users on a common network, we showed that, applying the traditional marginal-cost pricing for SO requires link tolls to be differentiated across user classes, because users of different classes have different *perceived* costs on each link in their route choice. By artificially constructing a convex quadratic program, we then showed that alternative meaningful, nonnegative, and anonymous link tolls identical to all user classes do exist to decentralize a SO flow pattern as a UE-CN multiple behavior equilibrium. The desirable link tolls are generally non-unique, but constitute a nonempty polyhedron, again expressed in terms of a linear system.

We further generalized our results to the multi-class, multi-criteria behavior equilibrium and system optimum problems. In fact, our findings from this chapter can be generalized as follows: *Any feasible link flow pattern can be supported by anonymous link tolls as a deterministic traffic equilibrium.* Here, feasibility of link flow patterns means that there exist path flows that satisfy the OD demand constraints and induce the given target link flows; the deterministic traffic equilibria herein comprise the standard user equilibrium, the equilibrium with multiple VOT user classes, the equilibrium with multiple UE-CN routing behaviors, and their combinations examined in this chapter. One should realize that the anonymous valid link tolls are not necessarily positive, depending on the nature of the chosen target link flow pattern. Finally, we point out that the explicit characterization of the valid link tolls set for decentralizing the SO flow patterns allows for further extraction of optimal link tolls with secondary objectives such as minimization of total revenue collected or minimization of number of toll booths.

6.7 SOURCES AND NOTES

The toll pricing framework in Section 6.2 for the single class traffic equilibrium and system optimum have been extensively developed by Bergendorf *et al.* (1997), Hearn and Ramana (1998), Hearn and Yildrim (2002), and recently by Yildirim and Hearn (2005). Selection of optimal link tolls with secondary objectives are also considered by Dial (1999c, 2000), Bai et al. (2004), Penchina (2004) and Lawphongpanich and Hearn (2004). The multi-class UE and SO problem in Section 6.3 is based on the recent work of Yang and Huang (2004), and further extension was made by Yin and Yang (2004). The SO and multiple equilibrium behaviors presented in Sections 6.4 and Section 6.5 was recently developed by Yang and Zhang (2003) and Yang, Zhang and Meng (2003), and details of the materials in the two sections are also available in the thesis of Zhang (2003). Reader may further refer to Haurie and Marcotte (1985) about the relation between Wardropian equilibrium and the Cournot-Nash game, to Harker (1988) about the multiple behavior equilibrium, and to Nagurney (2000) and Nagurney and Dong (2002) about multi-class, multi-criteria traffic equilibrium. Additional background on anonymous pricing can be found in Arnott and Kraus (1998) (also, Lindsey and Verhoef, 2001) in the case of bottleneck congestion models.

7

SOCIAL AND SPATIAL EQUITIES AND REVENUE REDISTRIBUTION

7.1 INTRODUCTION

Although congestion pricing is theoretically and technologically easy to implement, it has long been viewed as a political issue. A common criticism is that road use charges make unequivocally distributional impacts on users with different incomes. Generally speaking, the equity implications of congestion pricing are complex because of all the different options facing users under a congestion pricing scheme. People who continue to use the highway after a toll is imposed, pay the toll, but also have a lower travel time: the toll decreases traffic volume, which decreases travel time. Some users with very high values of time (VOT) would find that they become better off (the reduced congestion can more than compensate the users for the extra cost of toll charges). However, those with low values of time but still using the roads are generally made worse off than before. People who stop using the highway avoid the toll, but forgo the benefits associated with using the highway and experience the inconvenience of switching to another mode of transport. This inequitable issue among different social classes of users is termed the social equity issue and becomes the primary focus of road pricing arguments.

Apart from the social equity that is often measured with respect to income (and hence VOT), the spatial equity issue is directly applicable in the current context of road pricing. It is about accessibility to different points in space, or specifically about users traveling between different locations. It is evident that after introducing congestion pricing in a road network, the changes in travel costs (inclusive of toll charges) between different origin-destination (OD) pairs can be substantially different, depending on the amounts and locations of toll charges. Thus people traveling between different OD pairs will receive different effects from congestion pricing schemes, and this could result in another kind of unfairness on users and hence become a new obstruction on the implementation of pricing policy due to the public rejection.

It is very often the case that social and spatial segregation go hand in hand, their treatments thus requires explicit considerations of the various social groups (particularly the poorest social group on the basis of income) and the various (particularly the least well-served) geographical zones. One possible way to allay these equity concerns raised is to adopt a revenue neutrality policy, through a direct even or uneven redistribution of the revenue generated by the congestion charge, among users in different social and spatial groups. It is also desired to take explicit account of social and spatial equities in designing a road pricing scheme, even without direct revenue redistribution. In this chapter, we show that a congestion pricing scheme that reduces the total travel time and redistributes the toll revenue to all users can make everyone better off, and then we propose various Pareto refunding schemes. Without revenue redistribution, we explicitly incorporate the social and spatial equity constraints into the bi-level programming models for the second-best network toll design problem examined in Chapter 5. Social and spatial inequities are simply measured by the maximum relative increase of the generalized equilibrium OD travel costs between all OD pairs for various classes of drivers with different VOTs.

7.2 THE SOCIAL AND SPATIAL INEQUITY: AN EXAMPLE

Example 7.1 (Demonstration of the social inequity in road pricing) We begin with a simple example to demonstrate the aforementioned social and spatial inequity problem. The network depicted in Figure 7.1 consists of 2 parallel links connecting a single OD pair. There are two classes of users, denoted with equal travel demand $d^1 = d^2 = 5$ (flow unit, say in 10^3 veh/h) traveling from node 1 to node 2, and their VOTs are assumed to be $\beta_1 = 1.0$ and $\beta_2 = 2.0$ (HK\$/min), respectively. Link travel time functions (in minutes) are shown in the figure:

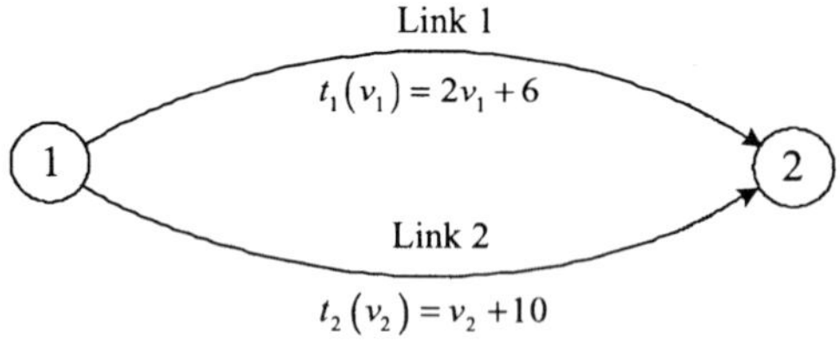

Figure 7.1 Network used for Example 7.1

Traffic equilibrium in the absence of toll pricing

In the absence of a toll charge, it is straightforward to obtain the unique aggregate equilibrium link flow, $\mathbf{v}$, corresponding equilibrium link travel time, $\mathbf{t}$, total system travel disutility, C in money units (veh-HK\$), and T in time units (veh-min), as follows:

$$\mathbf{v}=(v_1,v_2)^{\mathrm{T}}=\left(\frac{14}{3},\frac{16}{3}\right)^{\mathrm{T}},\ \mathbf{t}=(t_1,t_2)^{\mathrm{T}}=\left(\frac{46}{3},\frac{46}{3}\right)^{\mathrm{T}},\ C=230,\ T=\frac{460}{3}$$

The OD travel disutility by each class in time and money units is

$$\mu^1=\frac{46}{3}(\text{HK\$})=\frac{46}{3}(\text{min});\ \mu^2=\frac{92}{3}(\text{HK\$})=\frac{46}{3}(\text{min}) \tag{7.1}$$

As stated in Section 2.3 of Chapter 2, the time-based and the money-based equilibrium problems for multi-class users with distinct VOTs are equivalent to each other in the presence or absence of toll pricing given exogenously. The above aggregate equilibrium link flow is unique and independent of the unit (time or money) to measure OD travel disutility, but the class-specific link flow is not unique.

The cost-based system optimum and anonymous link tolls

As examined in Chapter 6, we now consider the system optimum in terms of travel cost minimization (system disutility is measured in monetary units and is denoted by C):

$$\min_{\mathbf{v}^1\geq 0,\mathbf{v}^2\geq 0}\quad C=\sum_{a=1,2}\sum_{m=1,2}\beta_m v_a^m t_a(v_a)=\left(v_1^1+2v_1^2\right)\left(2v_1^1+2v_1^2+6\right)+\left(v_2^1+2v_2^2\right)\left(v_2^1+v_2^2+10\right)$$

subject to

$$v_1^1+v_2^1=5;\ v_1^2+v_2^2=5$$

Like Example 6.2 in Chapter 6, the objective function is non-convex and there are minimizing points and one saddle point. The local mimimum is given by

$$\mathbf{v}^1=\left(v_1^1,v_2^1\right)^{\mathrm{T}}=\left(\frac{29}{6},\frac{1}{6}\right)^{\mathrm{T}},\ \mathbf{v}^2=\left(v_1^2,v_2^2\right)^{\mathrm{T}}=(0,5)^{\mathrm{T}}$$

$$\mathbf{v}=(v_1,v_2)^{\mathrm{T}}=\left(\frac{29}{6},\frac{31}{6}\right)^{\mathrm{T}},\ \mathbf{t}=(t_1,t_2)^{\mathrm{T}}=\left(\frac{47}{3},\frac{91}{6}\right)^{\mathrm{T}},\ C=\frac{2759}{12},\ T=\frac{1849}{12}$$

where T is the corresponding system disutility measured in time unit). The global minimum is given by

$$\mathbf{v}^1=\left(v_1^1,v_2^1\right)^{\mathrm{T}}=(0,5)^{\mathrm{T}},\ \mathbf{v}^2=\left(v_1^2,v_2^2\right)^{\mathrm{T}}=\left(\frac{43}{12},\frac{17}{12}\right)^{\mathrm{T}},$$

$$\mathbf{v}=(v_1,v_2)^{\mathrm{T}}=\left(\frac{43}{12},\frac{77}{12}\right)^{\mathrm{T}},\ \mathbf{t}=(t_1,t_2)^{\mathrm{T}}=\left(\frac{79}{6},\frac{197}{12}\right)^{\mathrm{T}},\ C=\frac{5351}{24},\ T=\frac{7321}{48}$$

The valid link tolls to decentralize the global cost-minimizing system optimum is given by

$$u_1=u_2+\frac{13}{2}$$

which includes anonymous first-best link tolls $\mathbf{u}=(u_1,u_2)^{\mathrm{T}}=(43/3,47/6)^{\mathrm{T}}$ for the cost-based system optimum. In this case, the OD travel disutility inclusive of equivalent toll charge by each class is

$$\mu^1 = \left(\frac{197}{12} + u_2\right)(\text{HK\$}) = \left(\frac{197}{12} + u_2\right)(\text{min}) \tag{7.2}$$

$$\mu^2 = \left(\frac{197}{6} + u_2\right)(\text{HK\$}) = \left(\frac{197}{12} + \frac{1}{2}u_2\right)(\text{min}) \tag{7.3}$$

The total revenue Π is given by $\Pi = 559/24 + 10u_2$, leading a revenue-neutral $(\Pi = 0)$ pricing $\mathbf{u} = (u_1, u_2)^{\mathrm{T}} = (1001/240, -559/240)^{\mathrm{T}}$.

The time-based system optimum and anonymous link tolls

Next we look at the system optimum in terms of travel time minimization (system disutility is measured in time unit):

$$\min_{\mathbf{v} \ge 0} \sum_{a=1,2} v_a t_a(v_a) = v_1(2v_1 + 6) + v_2(v_2 + 10)$$

subject to

$$v_1 + v_2 = 10$$

The time-based aggregate link flow SO solution is given by:

$$\mathbf{v} = (v_1, v_2)^{\mathrm{T}} = (4,6)^{\mathrm{T}},\ \mathbf{t} = (t_1, t_2)^{\mathrm{T}} = (14,16)^{\mathrm{T}},\ C = \text{indeterminate},\ T = 152$$

Note that the system disutility in monetary units is indeterminate, because the class-specific link flow is not unique at SO and travel times on the two links are not identical (different from the untolled UE case where both time-based and cost-based system disutilities are well defined). Again from Chapter 6, anonymous link tolls to decentralize the above time-based SO flow pattern can be obtained as

$$u_1 - u_2 - 4 = 0$$

With the above anonymous link toll charge, the class-specific equilibrium link flows together with total system disutility in monetary units are uniquely determined as

$$\mathbf{v}^1 = (v_1^1, v_2^1)^{\mathrm{T}} = (0,5)^{\mathrm{T}},\ \mathbf{v}^2 = (v_1^2, v_2^2)^{\mathrm{T}} = (4,1)^{\mathrm{T}},\ C = 224,\ T = 152$$

The OD travel disutility inclusive of equivalent toll charge by each class is

$$\mu^1 = (16 + u_2)(\text{HK\$}) = (16 + u_2)(\text{min}) \tag{7.4}$$

$$\mu^2 = (32 + u_2)(\text{HK\$}) = \left(16 + \frac{1}{2}u_2\right)(\text{min}) \tag{7.5}$$

The total revenue Π is given by $\Pi = 16 + 10u_2$, leading a revenue-neutral $(\Pi = 0)$ toll charge $\mathbf{u} = (u_1, u_2)^{\mathrm{T}} = (12/5, -8/5)^{\mathrm{T}}$.

System efficiency and inequity measure for alternative pricing schemes

Table 7.1 compares the system efficiency in terms of total system travel disutility in time and monetary units respectively for the alternative pricing schemes discussed above. Two points are worthwhile mentioning. First, the time-based and (global) cost-based SO enhances the system efficiency in terms of total system disutility, in both time and monetary units in comparison with un-tolled traffic equilibrium. The local cost-based SO actually worsens system performance in terms of total travel time. Therefore, it is critical to identify the global optimum solution for the cost-based SO program with a non-convex objective function.

Table 7.1 Comparison of system efficiency for alternative pricing schemes

	Total Cost-based System Disutility (veh-HK$)	Total Time-based System Disutility (veh-min)
Un-tolled Equilibrium	230.00	$460/3 = 153.33$
Local Cost-based SO	$2759/12 = 229.92$	$1849/12 = 154.08$
Global Cost-based SO	$5351/24 = 222.96$	$7321/48 = 152.52$
Time-based SO	224.00	152.00

Our attempt here is to look into the inequity impacts on the two user classes brought about by the above realistic nonnegative, anonymous link tolls to decentralize the time-based and cost-based system optimum into multi-class traffic equilibria. To do this, we now look at the ratios of the OD travel disutility or generalized O-D travel costs for each user class after and before introducing anonymous pricing. As noted previously, the time-based and the cost-based equilibrium problems for multi-class users with distinct VOTs are equivalent to each other, and the said ratio of OD travel disutility for a specific user class is independent of the unit (time or money) used to measure the travel disutility.

Now we provide the ratios of OD travel disutility of the two user classes in the case of cost-based SO with travel disutility given by (7.2)-(7.3) and time-based SO by (7.4)-(7.5) to the case of untolled equilibrium given by (7.1).

$$\eta_1^{\text{cost-SO}} = \left(\frac{197}{184} + \frac{3}{46}u_2\right); \quad \eta_2^{\text{cost-SO}} = \left(\frac{197}{184} + \frac{3}{92}u_2\right)$$

$$\eta_1^{\text{time-SO}} = \left(\frac{24}{23} + \frac{3}{46}u_2\right); \quad \eta_2^{\text{time-SO}} = \left(\frac{24}{23} + \frac{3}{92}u_2\right)$$

Figure 7.2 plots the change of the above ratios for the cost-based and time-based SO programs, respectively, against equilibrium link toll charge, u_2, starting from their revenue-neutral toll charges determined above: $\mathbf{u}^{\text{cost-SO}} = (u_1, u_2)^{\mathrm{T}} = (1001/240, -559/240)^{\mathrm{T}}$ and $\mathbf{u}^{\text{time-SO}} = (u_1, u_2)^{\mathrm{T}} = (12/5, -8/5)^{\mathrm{T}}$. From the two figures, the following observations are made.

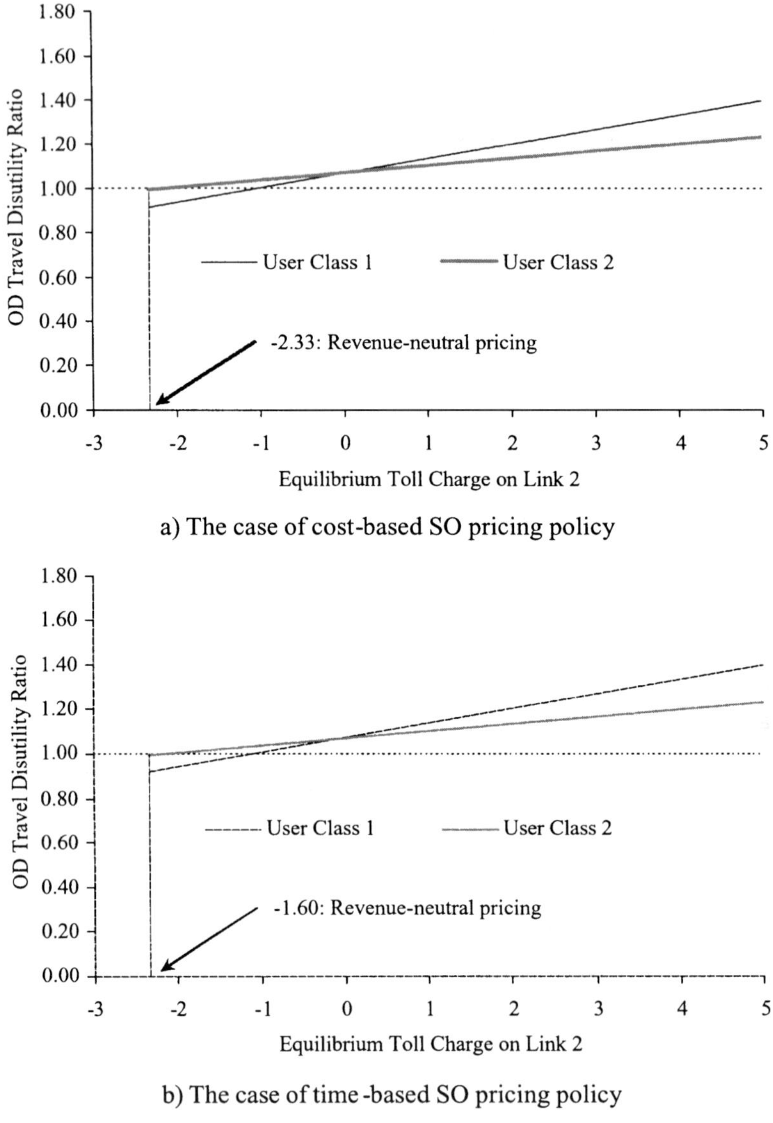

Figure 7.2 Change of travel disutility ratios between the SO-based pricing policy and the untolled traffic equilibrium against toll charge on link 2

First, the OD travel disutility ratios of course increase with toll charge, but the increasing rate for user class 1 is higher than that for user class 2 in both cost-based and time-based SO pricing policies. This indicates an inequitable impact of toll charge to the users with different VOTs, or lower-income users are more likely to be made worse off than before (social inequity). Second, ἰ is interesting to note that revenue-neutral toll pricing policy can bring good news to both classes of users and of course to the whole society. As observed in Figure 7.2, the revenue-neutral pricing policies for both cost-based and time-based SO programs are indeed Pareto-improving; the travel disutility change ratios are strictly less than unity for both user classes. This observation raised the possibility that an appropriate pricing and revenue refunding scheme may make all users better off.

Example 7.2 (Demonstration of the spatial inequity in road pricing) Consider a simple network example depicted in Figure 7.3, consisting of 3 nodes and 3 links. Link travel time functions are given below:

$$t_1(v_1) = 50 + v_1,\quad t_2(v_2) = 13 + v_2,\quad t_3(v_3) = 10 + \left(\frac{v_3}{5}\right)^2$$

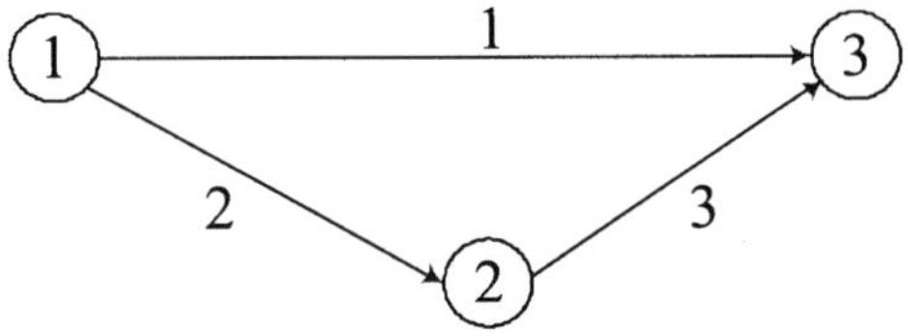

Figure 7.3 Network for Example 7.2

There are two OD pairs from node 1 to node 3 and from node 2 to node 3, with demand $d_{1\to 3} = 5$ and $d_{2\to 3} = 15$, respectively. For OD pair $1 \to 3$, there are two classes of users, with travel demand $d_{1\to 3}^1 = 1$ and $d_{1\to 3}^2 = 4$, VOT $\beta_1 = 2$ and $\beta_2 = 1$, respectively. For OD pair $2 \to 3$, there is only one single class of users with VOT $\beta = 1$.

In the absence of toll charge, traffic equilibrium solution is given by:

$$\tilde{v}_1 = 0,\ \tilde{v}_2 = 5,\ \tilde{v}_3 = 20;\ \tilde{t}_1 = 50,\ \tilde{t}_2 = 18,\ \tilde{t}_3 = 26$$

$$\tilde{\mu}_{1\to 3}^{\text{time}} = 44,\ \tilde{\mu}_{2\to 3}^{\text{time}} = 26,\ \tilde{T} = 610,\ \tilde{C} = 654$$

The time-based system optimum solution is given by:

$$\bar{v}_1 = \frac{110 - 5\sqrt{391}}{3} = 3.71,\quad \bar{v}_2 = \frac{5\sqrt{391} - 95}{3} = 1.29,\quad \bar{v}_3 = \frac{5\sqrt{391} - 50}{3} = 16.29$$

$$\bar{t}_1 = \frac{260 - 5\sqrt{391}}{3} = 53.71,\quad \bar{t}_2 = \frac{5\sqrt{391} - 56}{3} = 14.29,\quad \bar{t}_3 = \frac{581 - 20\sqrt{391}}{9} = 20.61$$

$$\bar{T} = \frac{92260 - 3910\sqrt{391}}{27} = 553.51,\ \bar{C} = \text{indeterminate..}$$

One of the simplest positive link toll schemes to decentralize this time-based SO is given by

$$\mathbf{u} = (u_1, u_2, u_3)^{\mathrm{T}} = \left(0, \frac{367 - 10\sqrt{391}}{9}, 0\right)^{\mathrm{T}} = (0, 18.81, 0)^{\mathrm{T}}$$

which gives rise to:

$$\bar{v}_1^1 = 0,\ \bar{v}_2^1 = 1,\ \bar{v}_1^2 = \frac{110 - 5\sqrt{391}}{3} = 3.71,\ \bar{v}_2^2 = \frac{5\sqrt{391} - 98}{3} = 0.29,$$

$$\bar{\mu}_{1\to 3,\,1}^{\text{time}} = \frac{1193 - 20\sqrt{391}}{18} = 44.31,\ \bar{\mu}_{1\to 3,\,2}^{\text{time}} = \frac{260 - 5\sqrt{391}}{3} = 53.71,$$

$$\bar{\mu}_{2\to 3}^{\text{time}} = \frac{581 - 20\sqrt{391}}{9} = 20.61$$

For OD pair $1 \to 3$,

$$\frac{\bar{\mu}_{1\to 3,\,1}^{\text{time}}}{\tilde{\mu}_{1\to 3}^{\text{time}}} = \frac{44.31}{44} = 1.01,\ \frac{\bar{\mu}_{1\to 3,\,2}^{\text{time}}}{\tilde{\mu}_{1\to 3}^{\text{time}}} = \frac{53.71}{44} = 1.22 \text{ (social inequity)}$$

which shows that the the relative changes of travel time costs are different for different user classes with different VOT, even if they are traveling between the same OD pair, and thus we encounter the social inequity issue associated with the road pricing considered here. In addition, we also have the following spatial inequity issues by furthering looking at the relative change of travel time cost between OD pair $2 \to 3$:

$$\frac{\bar{\mu}_{2\to 3}^{\text{time}}}{\tilde{\mu}_{2\to 3}^{\text{time}}} = \frac{20.61}{26} = 0.79 \text{ (spatial inequity)}$$

7.3 Redistribution of Congestion Pricing Revenue

The possible way to allay the equity concerns raised in the earlier section is to adopt a revenue neutrality policy through a direct redistribution of the revenue generated by the congestion charge among users in equal or unequal shares. In this section, we show that a congestion pricing scheme that reduces the total travel time for given OD travel demand and redistributes the toll revenue to all users can make everyone better off. We investigate the conditions under which this observation still holds with an *even redistribution* across users traveling in the same OD pair, regardless of their values of time and how this OD-specific even redistribution can be undertaken without cross-subsidization or wealth transfer among users traveling in different OD pairs.

7.3.1 Existence of a Pareto Refunding Scheme

Like Section 2.3 in Chapter 2 and Section 6.3 in Chapter 6, we consider a multi-class traffic equilibrium problem with a set of discrete VOTs. Let M denote the set of all user classes, β_m $(\beta_m > 0)$ be the average VOT for users of class $m \in M$ and d_w^m be the fixed demand for travel of class $m \in M$ between OD pair $w \in W$. Consider a network under a toll system $\mathbf{u} = (\ldots, u_a, \ldots)^{\mathrm{T}}$, $a \in \bar{A}$ where $\bar{A}$ is a subset of links subject to toll charge. Let

$\tilde{v}_a^m$, $a \in A$, $m \in M$ be the equilibrium flow distributions on the network in the absence of congestion charge $(\mathbf{u} = 0)$ and the corresponding travel times be $t_a(\tilde{\mathbf{v}})$, $a \in A$. Furthermore, the equilibrium flow pattern after the toll system is introduced is denoted by $\bar{v}_a^m$, $a \in A$, $m \in M$, with corresponding travel times $t_a(\bar{\mathbf{v}})$, $a \in A$. Here we consider a general travel time function $t_a(\mathbf{v})$ that allows interdependence among link flows $\mathbf{v} = (\cdots, v_a, \cdots)^{\mathrm{T}}$, $a \in A$.

We consider a general second-best pricing scheme, which means $\bar{A} \subset A$ or $\bar{A} = A$. The congestion pricing scheme is meaningful only if it reduces the total system disutility. As pointed out in Chapter 5, in the presence of multiple user classes with different VOTs, the total system disutility can be measured in either cost (monetary) or time units. This means that a congestion pricing scheme is desirable if either one (or both) of the following two conditions is met

$$\bar{T} = \sum_{a \in A} t_a(\bar{\mathbf{v}})\bar{v}_a < \tilde{T} = \sum_{a \in A} t_a(\tilde{\mathbf{v}})\tilde{v}_a \tag{7.6}$$

or

$$\bar{C} = \sum_{a \in A}\sum_{m \in M} \beta_m t_a(\bar{\mathbf{v}})\bar{v}_a^m < \tilde{C} = \sum_{a \in A}\sum_{m \in M} \beta_m t_a(\tilde{\mathbf{v}})\tilde{v}_a^m \tag{7.7}$$

Two points are worthwhile mentioning here. First, although class-specific equilibrium link flow v_a^m in a multi-class traffic equilibrium model is not unique, both T and C in (7.6) and (7.7) are unique with or without pricing. Uniqueness of T is self-evident because the aggregate equilibrium link flow is unique; uniqueness of C without and with pricing will become evident later in eqns. (7.15) and (7.19) in this section. Second, the cost-based system disutility can be regarded as a weighted sum of the time-based system disutilities of all user classes in the network.

As shown in Section 6.3 in Chapter 6, an anonymous link tolling scheme always exists to decentralize either a cost-based or a time-based system optimum (but not both) as a multi-class user equilibrium. We should also note that the two system disutility measures, T and C, may partially conflict with each other and no an anonymous link tolling scheme may exist that can reduce both measures simultaneously.

Example 7.3 (Non-existence of anonymousl link tolls to reduce both time-based and cost-based system disutilities) Consider again a simple network depicted in Figure 7.4 consisting of 2 parallel links with a single OD pair. There are two classes of users, denoted with equal travel demand $d^1 = d^2 = 1.0$ (flow unit, say in 10^3 veh/h) traveling from node 1 to node 2, their VOTs are assumed to be $\beta_1 = 1.0$ and $\beta_2 = 2.0$ (HK\$/min), respectively. Link travel time functions (in min) are shown in the figure:

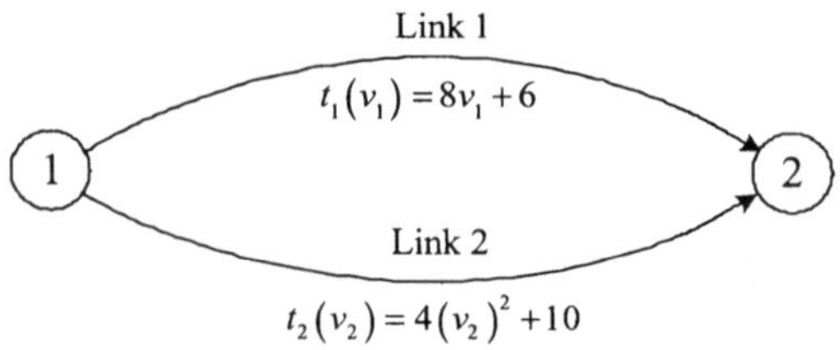

Figure 7.4 Network for Example 7.3

Without toll charge, the aggregate UE link flow and the aggregate time-based SO link flow are found to be identical as given below:

$$\mathbf{v}^{\mathrm{UE}}=\left(v_1^{\mathrm{UE}},v_2^{\mathrm{UE}}\right)^{\mathrm{T}}=(1,1)^{\mathrm{T}},\ \mathbf{v}^{\text{Time-SO}}=\left(v_1^{\text{Time-SO}},v_2^{\text{Time-SO}}\right)^{\mathrm{T}}=(1,1)^{\mathrm{T}}$$

giving rise to $T=28$ and $C=42$. Any link toll charges with $u_1\equiv u_2$ are both sufficient and necessary to decentralize the time-based SO into the same link flow pattern of traffic equilibrium.

The cost-based SO link flow solution is given by

$$\left(v_1^1,v_1^2,v_2^1,v_2^2\right)^{\mathrm{T}}=\left(0,\ \frac{15-\sqrt{93}}{6},\ 1,\ \frac{\sqrt{93}-9}{6}\right)^{\mathrm{T}}=(0.0,\ 0.893,\ 1.0,\ 0.107)^{\mathrm{T}}$$

giving rise to

$$T=\frac{582-34\sqrt{93}}{9}=28.235,\quad C=\frac{972-62\sqrt{93}}{9}=41.566$$

The anonymous link tolls to decentralize the above cost-based SO flow pattern is given by

$$u_1-u_2-\frac{12\sqrt{93}-84}{9}=0\ \text{ or }\ u_1-u_2-3.525=0$$

which includes the anonymous first-best link tolls

$$\mathbf{u}=\left(u_1,u_2\right)^{\mathrm{T}}=\left(\frac{120-8\sqrt{93}}{3},\ \frac{148-12\sqrt{93}}{3}\right)^{\mathrm{T}}=(14.284,\ 10.759)^{\mathrm{T}}$$

Here the first-best link toll is equal to the user externality of travel time multiplied by the arithmetic mean of the VOTs of all users traversing that link (see Theorem 6.3 in Chapter 6).

One can readily see that no link toll is available to reduce both T and C. The reason is simple. Any link tolls with $u_1\equiv u_2$, do not alter UE link flow patterns and hence do not alter T and C; Link tolls of reducing C below its current value $C=42$ exist (as shown above for the cost-based SO link flow solution and first-best link toll as an example), but must have $u_1\neq u_2$, which, unfortunately, must increase the value of T beyond its unique global minimum value of $T=28$.

Here we give a sufficient condition for the existence of anonymous link tolls to reduce both time-based and cost-based system disutilities, based on the theory established in Chapter 6.

Theorem 7.1 *Let $\bar{T}$ and $\bar{C}$ be the time- and cost-based system disutilities without toll charge. If there exists a link flow pattern* $\mathbf{v}$ *that satisfies*

$$T(\mathbf{v})=\sum_{a\in A}t_a(\mathbf{v})v_a<\bar{T}\,;\; C(\mathbf{v})=\sum_{a\in A}\beta_m t_a(\mathbf{v})v_a^{m*}<\bar{C} \tag{7.8}$$

where $\mathbf{v}^{m*}=\left(v_a^{m*},\, a\in A\right)^{\mathrm{T}},\, m\in M$ *is given by*

$$\left(\mathbf{v}^{m*},\, m\in M\right)=\arg\min_{\mathbf{v}^m\in\Omega_v^m,m\in M}\sum_{a\in A}\sum_{m\in M}\beta_m t_a(\mathbf{v})v_a^m \text{ subject to } \sum_{m\in M}v_a^m=v_a,\, a\in A \tag{7.9}$$

and

$$\Omega_v^m=\left\{\mathbf{v}^m=\left(v_a^m,a\in A\right)^{\mathrm{T}}\,\middle|\, v_a^m=\sum_{r\in R_w}f_{rw}^m\delta_{ar},\,\sum_{r\in R_w}f_{rw}^m=d_w^m,\, f_{rw}^m\geq 0,\, r\in R_w,\, w\in W\right\} \tag{7.10}$$

Then, there exists an anonymous link toll pattern $\mathbf{u}=\left(u_a,a\in A\right)^{\mathrm{T}}$ *to support* $\mathbf{v}^{m*},\, m\in M$ *and* $\mathbf{v}$ *as a multiclass traffic equilibrium and hence reduce both* T *and* C *below* $\bar{T}$ *and* $\bar{C}$ *respectively.*

Proof. The proof follows immediately from Theorem 6.2 and 6.3 in Chapter 6. Namely, any feasible link flow pattern can be supported as a multiclass traffic equilibrium with the class-specific equilibrium link flows solving the linear program (7.9). ¦

As we proved in Section 2.3 in Chapter 2, the same multi-class UE flow pattern arises regardless of the unit (cost or money) used to measure the travel disutility, with or without congestion charge. In the absence of toll charge $(\mathbf{u}=0)$, the following time-based UE conditions hold (Chapter 2, Section 2.3)

$$\sum_{a\in A}t_a(\tilde{\mathbf{v}})\delta_{ar}=\tilde{\mu}_{w,m}^{\text{time}},\text{ if } \tilde{f}_{rw}^m>0,\, r\in R_w,\, w\in W,\, m\in M \tag{7.11}$$

$$\sum_{a\in A}t_a(\tilde{\mathbf{v}})\delta_{ar}\geq\tilde{\mu}_{w,m}^{\text{time}},\text{ if } \tilde{f}_{rw}^m=0,\, r\in R_w,\, w\in W,\, m\in M \tag{7.12}$$

where $\tilde{\mu}_{w,m}^{\text{time}}$ is the equilibrium travel time between OD pair $w\in W$ for user class $m\in M$ in the absence of toll charge (in fact the equilibrium travel time is identical for all user classes in the absence of toll charge). Multiplying both sides of (7.11) and (7.12) by equilibrium path flow $\tilde{f}_{rw}^m$ and summing over all $r\in R_w,\, w\in W,\, m\in M,$ we have

$$\sum_{a\in A}\sum_{m\in M}\sum_{r\in R_w}t_a(\tilde{\mathbf{v}})\tilde{f}_{rw}^m\delta_{ar}=\sum_{w\in W}\sum_{m\in M}\sum_{r\in R_w}\tilde{\mu}_{w,m}^{\text{time}}\tilde{f}_{rw}^m \tag{7.13}$$

In view of $\sum_{r\in R_w}\tilde{f}_{rw}^m=d_w^m$, $\sum_{w\in W}\sum_{r\in R_w}\tilde{f}_{rw}^m\delta_{ar}=\tilde{v}_a^m$ and $\sum_{m\in M}\tilde{v}_a^m=\tilde{v}_a$, eqn. (7.13) becomes

$$\sum_{a\in A}t_a(\tilde{\mathbf{v}})\tilde{v}_a=\sum_{w\in W}\sum_{m\in M}\tilde{\mu}_{w,m}^{\text{time}}d_w^m \tag{7.14}$$

In the cost-based equilibrium, the following result can be obtained in a similar manner:

$$\sum_{a\in A}\sum_{m\in M}\beta_m t_a(\tilde{\mathbf{v}})\tilde{v}_a^m = \sum_{w\in W}\sum_{m\in M}\tilde{\mu}_{w,m}^{\text{cost}} d_w^m \tag{7.15}$$

where $\tilde{\mu}_{w,m}^{\text{cost}} = \beta_m \tilde{\mu}_{w,m}^{\text{time}}$, $w\in W$, $m\in M$ in the absence of toll charges. Since $\tilde{\mu}_{w,m}^{\text{cost}}$ is unique at equilibrium, eqn. (7.15) also means that the cost-based system disutility (the left-hand side) is unique at untolled traffic equilibrium.

After a toll scheme $\mathbf{u}$ is introduced, we have the following time-based UE condition

$$\sum_{a\in A} t_a(\bar{\mathbf{v}})\delta_{ar} + \sum_{a\in A}\frac{u_a}{\beta_m}\delta_{ar} = \bar{\mu}_{w,m}^{\text{time}}, \text{ if } \bar{f}_{rw}^m > 0,\ r\in R_w,\ w\in W,\ m\in M \tag{7.16}$$

$$\sum_{a\in A} t_a(\bar{\mathbf{v}})\delta_{ar} + \sum_{a\in A}\frac{u_a}{\beta_m}\delta_{ar} \geq \bar{\mu}_{w,m}^{\text{time}}, \text{ if } \bar{f}_{rw}^m = 0,\ r\in R_w,\ w\in W,\ m\in M \tag{7.17}$$

where $\bar{\mu}_{w,m}^{\text{time}}$ is the minimum travel disutility in time units (inclusive of equivalent time of toll charge) between OD pair w by user class m. Note that in this case $\bar{\mu}_{w,m}^{\text{time}}$ might be different for different user classes. One can readily observe that the above UE conditions mean

$$\sum_{a\in A} t_a(\bar{\mathbf{v}})\bar{v}_a + \sum_{m\in M}\frac{\Pi^m}{\beta_m} = \sum_{w\in W}\sum_{m\in M}\bar{\mu}_{w,m}^{\text{time}} d_w^m \tag{7.18}$$

where $\Pi^m = \sum_{a\in A} u_a \bar{v}_a^m$ is the total toll revenue collected from users of class $m\in M$ on the network. Or equivalently,

$$\sum_{a\in A}\sum_{m\in M}\beta_m t_a(\bar{\mathbf{v}})\bar{v}_a^m + \Pi = \sum_{w\in W}\sum_{m\in M}\bar{\mu}_{w,m}^{\text{cost}} d_w^m \tag{7.19}$$

where $\Pi = \sum_{a\in A} u_a \bar{v}_a$ is the unique (due to unique $\bar{v}_a$, $a\in A$) total toll revenue generated from all classes of users. Since $\bar{\mu}_{w,m}^{\text{cost}}$ and Π are unique at equilibrium, eqn. (7.19) also means that the cost-based system disutility (the first term of the left-hand side) is unique at the tolled traffic equilibrium.

In the case that the congestion pricing scheme aims to reduce total travel time and thus eqn. (7.6) holds, substituting (7.6) into (7.18) leads to

$$\sum_{w\in W}\sum_{m\in M}\bar{\mu}_{w,m}^{\text{time}} d_w^m - \sum_{m\in M}\frac{\Pi_m}{\beta_m} < \sum_{w\in W}\sum_{m\in M}\tilde{\mu}_{w,m}^{\text{time}} d_w^m \tag{7.20}$$

Furthermore, in the case that the congestion pricing aims to reduce total system disutility in monetary units and eqn. (7.7) holds, substituting (7.7) into (7.19) we arrive at

$$\sum_{w\in W}\sum_{m\in M}\bar{\mu}_{w,m}^{\text{cost}} d_w^m - \Pi < \sum_{w\in W}\sum_{m\in M}\tilde{\mu}_{w,m}^{\text{cost}} d_w^m \tag{7.21}$$

Lemma 7.1 *Suppose a pricing scheme reduces the total cost-based system disutility and the total toll revenue,* Π*, generated from the pricing scheme, is returned to all users, then there exists a refunding scheme:* $\Phi = \left\{\Phi_w^m,\ w \in W,\ m \in M\right\}$*, such that*

$$\sum_{w \in W} \sum_{m \in M} \Phi_w^m = \Pi \tag{7.22}$$

and

$$\bar{\mu}_{w,m}^{\text{cost}} d_w^m - \Phi_w^m < \tilde{\mu}_{w,m}^{\text{cost}} d_w^m \textit{ for any } w \in W,\ m \in M \tag{7.23}$$

Proof. Let

$$\Phi_w^m = \left(\bar{\mu}_{w,m}^{\text{cost}} d_w^m - \tilde{\mu}_{w,m}^{\text{cost}} d_w^m\right) + \alpha_w^m \left(\sum_{w \in W} \sum_{m \in M} \tilde{\mu}_{w,m}^{\text{cost}} d_w^m - \sum_{w \in W} \sum_{m \in M} \bar{\mu}_{w,m}^{\text{cost}} d_w^m + \Pi \right),\ w \in W,\ m \in M$$

where α_w^m is a positive number ($\alpha_w^m > 0$ for all $w \in W$, $m \in M$) and satisfies

$$\alpha_w^m > 0,\ w \in W,\ m \in M \text{ and } \sum_{m \in M} \sum_{w \in W} \alpha_w^m = 1$$

Then,

$$\sum_{m \in M} \sum_{w \in W} \Phi_w^m = \sum_{m \in M} \sum_{w \in W} \left(\bar{\mu}_{w,m}^{\text{cost}} d_w^m - \tilde{\mu}_{w,m}^{\text{cost}} d_w^m\right)$$
$$+ \left(\sum_{m \in M} \sum_{w \in W} \alpha_w^m \right) \left(\sum_{w \in W} \sum_{m \in M} \tilde{\mu}_{w,m}^{\text{cost}} d_w^m - \sum_{w \in W} \sum_{m \in M} \bar{\mu}_{w,m}^{\text{cost}} d_w^m + \Pi \right) = \Pi$$

and from (7.21) we have

$$\bar{\mu}_{w,m}^{\text{cost}} d_w^m - \Phi_w^m = \tilde{\mu}_{w,m}^{\text{cost}} d_w^m - \alpha_w^m \left(\sum_{w \in W} \sum_{m \in M} \tilde{\mu}_{w,m}^{\text{cost}} d_w^m - \sum_{w \in W} \sum_{m \in M} \bar{\mu}_{w,m}^{\text{cost}} d_w^m + \Pi \right) < \tilde{\mu}_{w,m}^{\text{cost}} d_w^m$$

This completes the proof. ¦

Lemma 1 states that eqn. (7.7), or equivalently eqn. (7.21) is a sufficient condition for the existence of a refunding scheme satisfying eqns. (7.22) and (7.23). In fact, it is also a necessary condition, which can be readily proved by summing eqn. (7.23) over all $w \in W$ and $m \in M$ and thus obtaining eqn. (7.21) or equivalent eqn. (7.7).

Equation (7.23) simply implies that

$$\bar{\mu}_{w,m}^{\text{cost}} - \Phi_w^m < \tilde{\mu}_{w,m}^{\text{cost}} \text{ for any } w \in W, m \in M \tag{7.24}$$

where $\phi_w^m = \Phi_w^m / d_w^m$ is the average amount of refund to each user in class $m \in M$ between OD pair $w \in W$. This means that each user in class $m \in M$ between OD pair $w \in W$ is made *better off* after toll charge and toll revenue redistribution. Since eqn. (7.24) holds for any $m \in M$ and $w \in W$, we thus have the following theorem.

Theorem 7.2 *A necessary and sufficient condition for the existence of a Pareto refunding scheme that redistributes the total toll revenue to all network users and makes everyone* *better off is that the congestion pricing scheme reduces the total system disutility measured in monetary units.*

We begin our further analysis of the refunding scheme by rationally assuming that $u_a \geq 0,\ a \in A$ or no direct subsidy is made for using individual links in the network, and hence $\Pi > 0$ in the tolling system. A practically meaningful (post-trip) refunding scheme would be such that $\phi_w^m \geq 0$ or $\Phi_w^m \geq 0$ for all $w \in W,\ m \in M$. This requires that a set of $\alpha_w^m,\ w \in W,\ m \in M$ be selected to satisfy:

$$\sum_{m \in M} \sum_{w \in W} \alpha_w^m = 1;\ \alpha_w^m \geq \max\{0,\ \hat{\alpha}_w^m\},\ w \in W,\ m \in M \tag{7.25}$$

where

$$\hat{\alpha}_w^m = \frac{\tilde{\mu}_{w,m}^{\text{cost}} d_w^m - \bar{\mu}_{w,m}^{\text{cost}} d_w^m}{\sum_{w \in W} \sum_{m \in M} \tilde{\mu}_{w,m}^{\text{cost}} d_w^m - \sum_{w \in W} \sum_{m \in M} \bar{\mu}_{w,m}^{\text{cost}} d_w^m + \Pi},\ w \in W,\ m \in M \tag{7.26}$$

Nonetheless, there may not exist a feasible $\alpha_w^m,\ w \in W,\ m \in M$ to meet the above requirement. As a result, the existence of such a Pareto refunding scheme may require some negative ϕ_w^m, which represents a *cross-subsidy* among the various classes of users traveling between various OD pairs. For example, if $\phi_w^m < 0$ occurs, users in class $m \in M$ between OD pair $w \in W$ cannot be subisidized from the toll revenue; on the contrary, they are required to pay an additional tax for their trip-making, which is certainly impractical. It is very likely to have negative ϕ_w^m when the tolling system reduces the total social costs for certain OD pairs but increases the rest. Even under a first-best marginal-cost pricing scheme, the total social costs for users in different OD pairs may either go up or down.

Example 7.4 (Non-existence of positive refunding scheme) Consider the same network, shown in Figure 7.3, used in Example 7.2, with the same link travel time function. For simplicity, suppose there is only one single class of users with a VOT $\beta = 1$ and thus $C = T$. There are two OD pairs from node 1 to node 3 and from node 2 to node 3, with demand $d_{1\to3} = 5$ and $d_{2\to3} = 15$, respectively. From this example, we show how the spatial inequity alone can lead to non-existence of a positive refunding scheme.

In the absence of toll charges, the traffic equilibrium solution is given by:

$$\tilde{v}_1 = 0,\ \tilde{v}_2 = 5,\ \tilde{v}_3 = 20;\ \tilde{t}_1 = 50,\ \tilde{t}_2 = 18,\ \tilde{t}_3 = 26$$

$$\tilde{\mu}_{1\to3} = 44,\ \tilde{\mu}_{2\to3} = 26,\ \tilde{C} = \tilde{T} = 610$$

Both time-based and cost-based system optimum solutions are given by:

$$\bar{v}_1 = \frac{110 - 5\sqrt{391}}{3} = 3.71,\quad \bar{v}_2 = \frac{5\sqrt{391} - 95}{3} = 1.29,\quad \bar{v}_3 = \frac{5\sqrt{391} - 50}{3} = 16.29$$

$$\bar{t}_1 = \frac{260-5\sqrt{391}}{3} = 53.71\,,\ \bar{t}_2 = \frac{5\sqrt{391}-56}{3} = 14.29\,,\ \bar{t}_3 = \frac{581-20\sqrt{391}}{9} = 20.61$$

$$\bar{C} = \bar{T} = \frac{92260-3910\sqrt{391}}{27} = 553.51$$

The valid link tolls to decentralize this SO flow pattern are given by

$$u_2 + u_3 - u_1 = \frac{367-10\sqrt{391}}{9} = 18.81$$

OD travel disutility are determined by link tolls as

$$\bar{\mu}_{1\to 3} = 53.71 + u_1\,,\ \bar{\mu}_{2\to 3} = 20.61 + u_3$$

Given that $\bar{C} < \tilde{C}$, according to Theorem 7.2, there exists a Pareto refunding scheme for any valid link tolls obtained above. However, even for positive link tolls, there is no guarantee for the existence of positive refunding schemes which meet conditions (7.26) and (7.25). For example, consider a valid positive toll scheme $\mathbf{u} = (u_1, u_2, u_3)^{\mathrm{T}} = (0, 18.81, 0)^{\mathrm{T}}$, which gives rise to: $\Pi = u_2\bar{v}_2 = 24.25$; $\bar{\mu}_{1\to 3} = 53.71$, $\bar{\mu}_{2\to 3} = 20.61$. Any feasible $(\alpha_{1\to 3}, \alpha_{2\to 3})$ for a positive refunding scheme must satisfy:

$$\alpha_{1\to 3} \geq \max\left\{0,\ \frac{\tilde{\mu}_{1\to 3}d_{1\to 3} - \bar{\mu}_{1\to 3}d_{1\to 3}}{\tilde{C} - \bar{C}}\right\} = \max\left\{0,\ -\frac{48.55}{56.49}\right\} = 0$$

$$\alpha_{2\to 3} \geq \max\left\{0,\ \frac{\tilde{\mu}_{2\to 3}d_{2\to 3} - \bar{\mu}_{2\to 3}d_{2\to 3}}{\tilde{C} - \bar{C}}\right\} = \max\left\{0,\ \frac{80.85}{56.49}\right\} = 1.43$$

$$\alpha_{1\to 3} + \alpha_{2\to 3} = 1$$

Obviously, the above system is not feasible and thus a positive refunding scheme does not exist.

Notwithstanding, it is possible to create a positive refunding scheme by better design and adjustments of a pricing scheme. First, for any pricing scheme, from (7.15) and (7.19) we have

$$\sum_{w\in W}\sum_{m\in M}\tilde{\mu}^{\text{cost}}_{w,m}d^m_w - \sum_{w\in W}\sum_{m\in M}\bar{\mu}^{\text{cost}}_{w,m}d^m_w + \Pi = \tilde{C} - \bar{C} = \text{constant}$$

In addition, $\tilde{\mu}^{\text{cost}}_{w,m}d^m_w$ in (7.26) is constant as well. Therefore, we can increase the toll charge within the valid link toll set, and hence increase $\bar{\mu}^{\text{cost}}_{w,m}$ so that $\hat{\alpha}^m_w$ in eqn. (7.26) becomes negative (in fact, it is sufficient that $\hat{\alpha}^m_w \leq 1/|W||M|$ for any $w\in W$, $m\in M$ where $|W|$ and $|M|$ denote the number of OD pairs and user classes). As a result, a feasible set of α^m_w, $w\in W$, $m\in M$ will exist to satisfy (7.25). Although this may not be achieved for an arbitrarily second-best pricing scheme with a restricted subset of tolling links, it is always possible for the valid link toll sets that decentralize the cost-based system optimum, because the valid link tolls and the resulting $\bar{\mu}_{w,m}^{\text{cost}}$ are unbounded for given OD demand, as examined in Chapter 6.

7.3.2 Design of Pareto Refunding Schemes

Now we continue our investigation of the existence and design of meaningful Pareto-improving revenue-refunding schemes. If we further assume that the toll system reduces the total social cost of each user class in each OD pair, then, along the same lines as in obtaining (7.21), we have the following inequalities by user class and OD pair:

$$\bar{\mu}_{w,m}^{\text{cost}} d_w^m - \Pi_w^m < \tilde{\mu}_{w,m}^{\text{cost}} d_w^m, \; w \in W, \; m \in M \tag{7.27}$$

where $\Pi_w^m = \sum_{a \in A} u_a \bar{v}_{a,w}^m$ is the total toll revenue and $\bar{v}_{a,w}^m$ is the link flow generated from user class m between OD pair $w \in W$. Clearly, eon. (7.27) in turn implies

$$\bar{\mu}_{w,m}^{\text{cost}} - \phi_w^m < \tilde{\mu}_{w,m}^{\text{cost}}, \; w \in W, \; m \in M \tag{7.28}$$

where $\phi_w^m = \Pi_w^m / d_w^m$ is the average amount of refund to each user in class $m \in M$ between OD pair $w \in W$. We thus lead to a simple OD-specific and class-specific Pareto refunding scheme that refunds the class-specific and OD-specific toll revenue *equally* to all users in the same OD pair and in the same user class. The refunding scheme can make everyone better off without requiring *cross-subsidization* among users in different classes and in different OD pairs. We thus have the following theorem.

Theorem 7.3 *If a congestion pricing scheme reduces the total social cost of each user class in each OD pair in the network, then there exists a Pareto refunding scheme that refunds the toll revenue equally to all users in the same OD pair and same user class, and makes everyone better off without requiring cross-subsidization among users in different classes and different OD pairs.*

As discussed in Chapter 6, the VOT of each user is in general unobservable and hence the above refunding scheme (7.27) and (7.28) by user classes is difficult to implement in practice. Thus, we explore an alternative *even* redistribution of the total toll revenue collected from all users traveling in a specific OD pair to all users in the same OD pair, regardless of their VOTs.

We look at a representative user class denoted by m with a VOT β_m. Without loss of generality, we can assume that users in this class prefer route $r^* \in R_w$ after introducing the tolling system. By the equilibrium, condition we have

$$\sum_{a \in A} u_a \delta_{ar^*} + \beta_m \sum_{a \in A} t_a(\bar{\mathbf{v}}) \delta_{ar^*} \le \sum_{a \in A} u_a \delta_{ar} + \beta_m \sum_{a \in A} t_a(\bar{\mathbf{v}}) \delta_{ar} \text{ for any } r \in R_w \tag{7.29}$$

Multiplying both sides by equilibrium path flow $\bar{f}_{rw}\ \left(=\sum_{m\in M}\bar{f}_{rw}^{m}\right)$, aggregated over user classes and summing over all $r\in R_w$, we have

$$\left(\sum_{a\in A}u_a\delta_{ar^{\cdot}}+\beta_m\sum_{a\in A}t_a(\bar{\mathbf{v}})\delta_{ar^{\cdot}}\right)\sum_{r\in R_w}\bar{f}_{rw}\le\sum_{a\in A}u_a\sum_{r\in R_w}\bar{f}_{rw}\delta_{ar}+\beta_m\sum_{a\in A}t_a(\bar{\mathbf{v}})\sum_{r\in R_w}\bar{f}_{rw}\delta_{ar}\qquad(7.30)$$

In view of $\sum_{a\in A}u_a\delta_{ar^{\cdot}}+\beta_m\sum_{a\in A}t_a(\bar{\mathbf{v}})\delta_{ar^{\cdot}}=\bar{\mu}_{w,m}^{\text{cost}}$, $\sum_{r\in R_w}\bar{f}_{rw}=d_w$ and $\sum_{r\in R_w}\bar{f}_{rw}\delta_{ar}=\bar{v}_{a,w}$ where $\bar{v}_{a,w}$ is the link flow by all users in OD pair $w\in W$, eqn. (7.30) becomes

$$\bar{\mu}_{w,m}^{\text{cost}}d_w\le\Pi_w+\beta_m\sum_{a\in A}t_a(\bar{\mathbf{v}})\bar{v}_{a,w},\ w\in W,\ m\in M$$

or

$$\bar{\mu}_{w,m}^{\text{cost}}-\frac{\Pi_w}{d_w}\le\beta_m\frac{\sum_{a\in A}t_a(\bar{\mathbf{v}})\bar{v}_{a,w}}{d_w},\ w\in W,\ m\in M\qquad(7.31)$$

where $\Pi_w=\sum_{a\in A}\sum_{m\in M}u_a\bar{v}_{a,w}$ is the total toll revenue generated from all user classes $m\in M$ between OD pair $w\in W$.

Suppose the tolling system reduces the *total travel time* for all users between each OD pair as given below

$$\sum_{a\in A}t_a(\bar{\mathbf{v}})\bar{v}_{a,w}-\sum_{a\in A}t_a(\tilde{\mathbf{v}})\tilde{v}_{a,w}<0,\ \text{for any } w\in W\qquad(7.32)$$

Furthermore, note that $\tilde{\mu}_{w,m}^{\text{time}}$ is identical for all user class $m\in M$ between OD pair $w\in W$ in the absence of toll charge, we have

$$\sum_{a\in A}t_a(\tilde{\mathbf{v}})\tilde{v}_{a,w}=\sum_{m\in M}\tilde{\mu}_{w,m}^{\text{time}}d_w^m=\tilde{\mu}_{w,m}^{\text{time}}d_w,\ w\in W,\ m\in M\qquad(7.33)$$

Thus, eqn. (7.31) becomes

$$\bar{\mu}_{w,m}^{\text{cost}}-\frac{\Pi_w}{d_w}<\beta_m\tilde{\mu}_{w,m}^{\text{time}},\ w\in W,\ m\in M\qquad(7.34)$$

Equation (7.34) simply means that

$$\bar{\mu}_{w,m}^{\text{cost}}-\phi_w<\tilde{\mu}_{w,m}^{\text{cost}},\ w\in W,\ m\in M\qquad(7.35)$$

where $\phi_w=\Pi_w/d_w$. Equation (7.35) states that all users between OD pair $w\in W$ regardless of their VOTs can be made better off after toll charges and an *even* redistribution of toll revenue. Since the representative user is randomly selected with an arbitrary VOT β_m, we can even conclude that this result holds for heterogeneous users with either a discrete or continuous VOT distribution. In addition, this OD-specific Pareto refunding scheme uses the revenue collected from users in the same OD pair only and refunds equally to all classes of user in the same OD pair. Thus, it does not require cross-subsidy among users traveling in different OD pairs as long as the total travel time between each OD pair in the network is reduced after introducing the tolling system. To sum up, we have the following theorem.

Theorem 7.4. *If a congestion pricing scheme reduces the total travel time of users in each OD pair in the network, then there exists a Pareto refunding scheme that refunds the toll revenue equally to all classes of users in the same OD pair regardless of their VOTs, and makes everyone better off without requiring cross-subsidization among users in different OD pairs.*

Theorem 7.4 needs a strong assumption that the travel time of users in each OD pair in the network is reduced. We now explore the possibility of a Pareto refunding scheme when a pricing scheme reduces the total system travel time, but allows increase in total travel times in certain OD pairs. To do this we now introduce additional notation. Let $T_w = \sum_{a\in A} t_a(\mathbf{v}) v_{a,w}$ be the total travel time of users between OD pair $w \in W$ and $\Delta T_w = \bar{T}_w - \tilde{T}_w,\ w \in W$ be the corresponding change after introducing the pricing scheme; similarly, let $\Delta T = \sum_{w\in W} \Delta T_w = \bar{T} - \tilde{T}$ be the change in total system travel time. By our assumption, $\Delta T < 0$; $\Delta T_w,\ w \in W$ can be either negative or positive.

Let Φ_w be the total amount of refund to be *evenly* returned to all classes of users in OD pair $w \in W$ and consider the following refunding scheme:

$$\Phi_w = \Pi_w + \Delta\Pi_w,\ w \in W \tag{7.36}$$

where $\Delta\Pi_w$ denotes the cross-subsidizations among different OD pairs, and is determined by:

$$\Delta\Pi_w = \begin{cases} \bar{\beta}\Delta T_w, & \text{if } \Delta T_w > 0 \\ \underline{\beta}\Delta T_w, & \text{if } \Delta T_w < 0 \\ 0, & \text{if } \Delta T_w = 0 \end{cases} \tag{7.37}$$

where $\bar{\beta} = \max\{\beta_m,\ m \in M\}$ and $\underline{\beta} = \min\{\beta_m,\ m \in M\}$. We say a refunding scheme $\Phi = \{\Phi_w,\ w \in W\}$ is feasible if the total amount of refund needed is less than or equal to the total revenue generated from the pricing scheme concerned, or if it satisfies:

$$\sum_{w\in W} \Phi_w \le \Pi \tag{7.38}$$

We also define the subsets of OD pairs in the network in which total OD travel time is increased or decreased after introducing the pricing scheme respectively as

$$W^+ = \{w \mid \Delta T_w > 0,\ w \in W\};\ W^- = \{w \mid \Delta T_w < 0,\ w \in W\} \tag{7.39}$$

Lemma 7.2 *Suppose $\Delta T = \bar{T} - \tilde{T} < 0$ for a pricing scheme, then a necessary and sufficient condition for the refunding scheme $\Phi = \{\Phi_w,\ w \in W\}$, defined by eqns. (7.36) and (7.37), to be feasible is*

$$\frac{\sum_{w\in W^+}\Delta T_w}{\tilde{T}-\bar{T}}=\frac{\sum_{w\in W^+}\Delta T_w}{|\Delta T|}\le\frac{\underline{\beta}}{\bar{\beta}-\underline{\beta}} \tag{7.40}$$

Proof.

$$\sum_{w\in W}\Delta\Pi_w=\bar{\beta}\sum_{w\in W^+}\Delta T_w+\underline{\beta}\sum_{w\in W^-}\Delta T_w=\left(\bar{\beta}-\underline{\beta}\right)\sum_{w\in W^+}\Delta T_w+\underline{\beta}\sum_{w\in W}\Delta T_w$$
$$=\left(\bar{\beta}-\underline{\beta}\right)\sum_{w\in W^+}\Delta T_w+\underline{\beta}\Delta T \tag{7.41}$$

Clearly, if eqn. (7.40) holds, then we have $\sum_{w\in W}\Delta\Pi_w\le 0$ and hence the proposed refunding scheme given by (7.36) and (7.37) is feasible. Conversely, if $\sum_{w\in W}\Delta\Pi_w\le 0$, then eqn. (7.41) leads to eqn (7.40) immediately. ¦

From (7.40) and (7.41) it is trivial to note that if

$$\frac{\sum_{w\in W^+}\Delta T_w}{\tilde{T}-\bar{T}}=\frac{\underline{\beta}}{\bar{\beta}-\underline{\beta}} \tag{7.42}$$

then we have

$$\sum_{w\in W}\Delta\Pi_w=0;\ \sum_{w\in W}\Phi_w=\Pi \tag{7.43}$$

and if

$$\frac{\sum_{w\in W^+}\Delta T_w}{\tilde{T}-\bar{T}}<\frac{\underline{\beta}}{\bar{\beta}-\underline{\beta}} \tag{7.44}$$

we have

$$\sum_{w\in W}\Delta\Pi_w<0;\ \sum_{w\in W}\Phi_w<\Pi \tag{7.45}$$

Equation (7.45) means that the feasib ility condition (7.38) of the refunding scheme is not binding, and thus the current refunding given by (7.36) and (7.37) can be further increased to an amount Φ_w^* such that $\Phi_w^*>\Phi_w$, $w\in W$ and $\sum_{w\in W}\Phi_w^*=\Pi$.

Lemma 7.3 *The refunding scheme given by eqns. (7.36) and (7.37), if feasible, satisfies the following equations:*

$$\bar{\mu}_{w,m}^{\text{cost}}-\frac{\Phi_w}{d_w}\le\tilde{\mu}_{w,m}^{\text{cost}},\ w\in W,\ m\in M \tag{7.46}$$

where "=" may hold for only three cases

$$\begin{aligned}&a)\ \Delta T_w=0\\&b)\ \Delta T_w>0,\ and\ \beta_m=\bar{\beta}\\&c)\ \Delta T_w<0,\ and\ \beta_m=\underline{\beta}\end{aligned} \tag{7.47}$$

Proof. From eqn. (7.31), which holds under traffic equilibrium conditions for any given pricing scheme, we have

$$\bar{\mu}_{w,m}^{\text{cost}} - \frac{\Pi_w}{d_w} \le \beta_m \frac{\bar{T}_w}{d_w}, \; w \in W, \; m \in M \tag{7.48}$$

It follows that

$$\bar{\mu}_{w,m}^{\text{cost}} - \frac{\Phi_w}{d_w} = \bar{\mu}_{w,m}^{\text{cost}} - \frac{\Pi_w}{d_w} - \frac{\Delta\Pi_w}{d_w}$$

$$\le \beta_m \frac{\bar{T}_w}{d_w} - \frac{\Delta\Pi_w}{d_w} \tag{7.49}$$

$$\le \beta_m \frac{\bar{T}_w}{d_w} - \beta_m \frac{\Delta T_w}{d_w} \tag{7.50}$$

$$= \beta_m \frac{\tilde{T}_w}{d_w}$$

$$= \tilde{\mu}_{w,m}^{\text{cost}}, \; w \in W, \; m \in M \tag{7.51}$$

where eqn. (7.49) follows from eqn. (7.48), eqn. (7.50) follows from (7.37) (or the definition of $\Delta\Pi_w$), and eqn. (7.51) follows from $\tilde{T}_w = \sum_{a \in A} t_a(\tilde{\mathbf{v}})\tilde{v}_a = \tilde{\mu}_{w,m}^{\text{time}} d_w$ or from eqn. (7.33). From the definition of $\Delta\Pi_w$ in (7.37), eqn. (7.50) takes "=" only for the three cases given by (7.47). This completes the proof. ¦

As mentioned earlier, if $\sum_{w \in W} \Phi_w < \Pi$ holds as stated in (7.45), then there exists a better refunding scheme such that $\Phi_w^* > \Phi_w$, $w \in W$ and $\sum_{w \in W} \Phi_w^* = \Pi$, and from eqn. (7.46) we obtain

$$\bar{\mu}_{w,m}^{\text{cost}} - \frac{\Phi_w^*}{d_w} < \tilde{\mu}_{w,m}^{\text{cost}}, \; w \in W, \; m \in M \tag{7.52}$$

To sum up, we have the following theorem.

Theorem 7.5 *For any pricing scheme that reduces the total system travel time, namely,* $\Delta T = \bar{T} - \tilde{T} < 0$,

1) *If eqn. (7.42) holds and hence* $\sum_{w \in W} \Phi_w = \Pi$, *then the uniform-refunding scheme for each OD pair,* Φ_w, $w \in W$, *given by eqns. (7.36) and (7.37) satisfies eqn. (7.46) or make everyone better off, where "=" may hold only for the three cases given by (7.47);*
2) *If eqn. (7.44) holds and hence* $\sum_{w \in W} \Phi_w < \Pi$, *then there exists a uniform-refunding scheme for each OD pair,* $\Phi_w^* > \Phi_w$, $w \in W$ *and* $\sum_{w \in W} \Phi_w^* = \Pi$, *that satisfies eqn. (7.52), or makes everyone in each OD pair strictly better off.*

Clearly, eqn. (7.44) is a sufficient condition for the existence of OD-specific uniform-refunding schemes that make everyone strictly better off, regardless of the VOT of individual users. In this case, cross-subsidization among different OD pairs is required. As stated by eqn. (7.37), the specific amount of subsidy allocated to an OD pair is positive if there is an increase in total travel time in that OD pair, and negative, if there is an decrease in its total travel time after introducing the pricing scheme. If $\Delta T_w < 0$ for all $w \in W$, then eqn. (7.44) must holds and thus we obtain Theorem 7.4, or Theorem 7.3 states a strictly Pareto-improving refunding scheme without cross-subsidization in a special case of Theorem 7.5, where total travel time in each OD pair is reduced.

So far we have investigated the existence of a simple and meaningful Pareto refunding scheme for various traffic flow conditions brought about by a pricing scheme. Given the existence of the Pareto refunding scheme in the general situation, characterized by eqns. (7.21)-(7.23), we now turn to the optimal design of a general Pareto refunding scheme. Suppose we wish to choose $\phi = \left(\phi_w^m, w \in W, m \in M\right)$ so that all users are equally better off irrespective of their VOTs and OD pairs, and suppose the better-off degree is measured by the percentage reduction of individualized travel cost after receiving the revenue redistribution, then this equitable Pareto refunding scheme can be simply obtained below. Let e be the uniform percentage reduction of travel cost for all user classes and OD pairs. From

$$e = \left(\bar{\mu}_{w,m}^{\text{cost}} - \phi_w^m\right)\left(\tilde{\mu}_{w,m}^{\text{cost}}\right)^{-1}, \quad w \in W,\ m \in M \tag{7.53}$$

we obtain

$$\phi_w^m = \bar{\mu}_{w,m}^{\text{cost}} - e\tilde{\mu}_{w,m}^{\text{cost}}, \quad w \in W,\ m \in M \tag{7.54}$$

From $\Phi_w^m = \phi_w^m d_w^m$ and eqn. (7.22), we have

$$e = \left(\sum_{w \in W}\sum_{m \in M} \bar{\mu}_{w,m}^{\text{cost}} d_w^m - \Pi\right)\left(\sum_{w \in W}\sum_{m \in M} \tilde{\mu}_{w,m}^{\text{cost}} d_w^m\right)^{-1} \tag{7.55}$$

From eqn. (7.19) and (7.15), eqn.(7.55) is equivalent to

$$e = \left(\sum_{a \in A}\sum_{m \in M} \beta_m t_a(\bar{\mathbf{v}})\bar{v}_a^m\right)\left(\sum_{a \in A}\sum_{m \in M} \beta_m t_a(\tilde{\mathbf{v}})\tilde{v}_a^m\right)^{-1} \tag{7.56}$$

which is the reduction ratio of the total cost-based system disutility after and before introducing the pricing scheme. Once e is calculated, ϕ_w^m is readily given by (7.54). Given that e is a measure of a uniform better-off degree across all users in the network, eqn. (7.56) simply implies that minimizing the cost-based system disutility C is equivalent to maximizing the average better-off degree of all users for a road pricing and revenue refunding scheme.

Note that the above refunding formulas (7.53)-(7.56) apply only if the various user classes can be identified and the cross-subsidizations among users in different classes and OD pairs are possible. Otherwise, one has to check whether the conditions for Theorems 7.3~7.5 are met and then apply the more plausible refunding schemes under the required conditions.

7.3.3 Remarks on the Pareto Refunding Schemes

Needless to say, the efficiency of a tolling system can be evaluated by the amount of total travel time savings, and the first-best pricing scheme induces a UE flow pattern to a system optimum and thus achieves the maximum efficiency gain which can be shown to be bounded in terms of the percentage reduction of total travel time for fixed OD demands. While everyone can be made better off, one intriguing question remains here as to how the system efficiency improvement and individual benefit gain are related under a pricing and revenue redistribution scheme. Specifically, it is not clear whether a pricing and refunding scheme that can bring a greater decrease in total travel time can nevertheless give rise to more positive individual benefit gain.

In the Pareto refunding scheme developed above, we assumed that the OD demand is fixed before and after introducing the tolling system. This is in some situations a restrictive assumption, because road pricing certainly has long-term impacts on travel demand. Furthermore, congestion pricing is in general introduced to ensure that users recognize the true social travel-time costs of their trip-making. It is thus immediately clear that refunding will indeed create distortions and the first-best conditions for the social-welfare maximization with elastic demand cannot be optimal, because users will not be able to perceive their real marginal social cost of trip-making. Nevertheless, the refunding scheme does report good news in that a socially optimal flow pattern for given demands can be accomplished by offering users compensation incentives for selecting socially optimal routes on a general network, while maintaining revenue neutrality. Incidentally, the refunding scheme does not discourage people from driving; this observation itself in turn justifies the assumption of fixed OD demands in the refunding model.

One may find that the constant travel demand is in fact a rather innocuous assumption and more good news can be shown if applying the above method and results to a multimodal transportation network. One may reasonably assume that commuting is a necessity to all users and users divide themselves among the various modes and routes based on their preferences for trading money for time saving, then the pricing and refunding scheme developed for fixed travel demand does make sense in developing a trans-modal integrated transport pricing and subsidy strategy that is both equitable and efficient. Under such a strategy, people tolled off the road often shift to transit, and road pricing revenues can be used to benefit users of more socially desirable modes, with lower social marginal cost like the transit mode. Indeed, the proposed refunding scheme does allow for both positive (subsidy) and negative (further charge) redistribution of congestion pricing revenues among socially and geographically diverse groups of users.

7.4 NETWORK TOLL DESIGN MODELS WITH EQUITY CONSTRAINTS

The refunding strategy proposed in the previous section to address the social and spatial equity issues is to maintain "revenue neutrality" by returning congestion pricing revenue to each class of users. If, for any reasons, a direct revenue redistribution to users cannot be adopted, it would then be necessary to address the impacts of congestion pricing on equities in designing an equitable and efficient network tolling scheme. In this section, we develop a network toll design model with explicit consideration of social and spatial equities.

7.4.1 Traffic Equilibrium and Social Welfare with Pricing

Differing from the previous sections, we consider demand elasticity in the multi-class network equilibrium model. This model adopts the discrete approach for VOT distribution, which is considered to be particularly suitable for congestion pricing modeling with elastic demand. The whole society is divided into a number of classes and each class is assumed to have an average VOT belonging to a certain interval, and can be characterized by class-specific demand functions. This treatment in certain cases can be regarded as a discrete approximation of the model using continuously distributed VOT and has some practical advantages. It is consistent with the conventional market segmentation approach for travel demand modeling and thus greatly facilitates model calibration with actual data.

Following the previous notation, let $\bar{A}$ be the subset of links with toll charge and $B_w^m\left(d_w^m\right)$ be the class-specific benefit function (inversed demand function) of user class $m \in M$ between OD pair $w \in W$. User classes are ordered according to their increasing VOTs, namely, $\underline{\beta} = \beta_1 < \beta_2 < \cdots < \beta_{|M|} = \bar{\beta}$. Let $\mathbf{v}^m = \left(v_a^m, a \in A\right)^{\mathrm{T}}$ and $\mathbf{d}^m = \left(d_w^m, w \in W\right)^{\mathrm{T}}$, and the equivalent convex program formulation for the elastic-demand multi-class network equilibrium problem is given below (Section 2.3, Chapter 2):

$$\min_{\left(\mathbf{v}^m, \mathbf{d}^m\right) \in \Omega^m, m \in M} \sum_{a \in A} \int_0^{v_a} t_a(\omega) \mathrm{d}\omega + \sum_{a \in \bar{A}} \sum_{m \in M} \frac{1}{\beta_m} v_a^m u_a - \sum_{w \in W} \sum_{m \in M} \int_0^{d_w^m} B_w^m(\omega) \mathrm{d}\omega \tag{7.57}$$

where

$$\Omega^m = \left\{ \left(\mathbf{v}^m, \mathbf{d}^m\right) \mid v_a^m = \sum_{r \in R_w} f_{rw}^m \delta_{ar},\ d_w^m = \sum_{r \in R_w} f_{rw}^m,\ f_{rw}^m \geq 0,\ r \in R_w,\ w \in W \right\},\ m \in M \tag{7.58}$$

Note that the travel disutility used here in characterizing the route choice behavior is measured in time units where the toll is converted into corresponding travel time by a given VOT of each class. All standard assumptions hold for the link travel time and OD benefit functions for the unique solution of aggregate link flows and class-specific OD demand.

For a given traffic equilibrium solution to program (7.57)-(7.58) associated with a pricing scheme $\mathbf{u}$, we can define the corresponding social welfare, $S(\mathbf{u})$, in time units as follows:

$$\begin{aligned} S\left(\mathbf{u},\mathbf{v}^m(\mathbf{u}),\mathbf{d}^m(\mathbf{u}),m\in M\right) &= \sum_{m\in M}\left\{\sum_{w\in W}\int_0^{d_w^m(\mathbf{u})} B_w^m(\omega)\,d\omega - \sum_{a\in A} v_a^m(\mathbf{u})\,t_a\left(v_a(\mathbf{u})\right)\right\} \\ &= \sum_{m\in M}\sum_{w\in W}\int_0^{d_w^m(\mathbf{u})} B_w^m(\omega)\,d\omega - \sum_{a\in A} v_a(\mathbf{u})\,t_a\left(v_a(\mathbf{u})\right) \end{aligned} \tag{7.59}$$

Here $\mathbf{v}^m(\mathbf{u})$ and $\mathbf{d}^m(\mathbf{u})$ are solutions to the UE program (7.57) for a given link toll $\mathbf{u}$. Although the class-specific equilibrium link flow, $\mathbf{v}^m(\mathbf{u})$, is not unique, the aggregate equilibrium link flow is unique and hence the social welfare, S, in (7.59) is well defined for given $\mathbf{u}$.

7.4.2 Specification of Equity Constraints

In reality, it is very difficult, if not impossible, to design a toll pattern that brings a completely equitable impact on all users traveling between different OD pairs. A simple yet practicable method is to prevent the percentage increase of travel cost of all network users from exceeding a certain threshold in designing a toll scheme. In this case, we can say that the relative inequity impact from a toll scheme is limited to a certain level. With this in mind, we deal with the equity issue by incorporating an equity constraint in the upper-level problem. The equity is measured as the relative change of the OD travel disutility (inclusive of toll charge) and thus the equity constraint can be specified as follows:

$$\frac{\mu_w^m(\mathbf{u})}{\tilde{\mu}_w} \le \chi_w,\ w\in W,\ m\in M \tag{7.60}$$

The term $\tilde{\mu}_w$ is the original equilibrium OD travel disutility in time units without pricing (which is commum to all user classes), and $\mu_w^m(\mathbf{u})$ is the equilibrium OD travel disutility in time units (inclusive of toll charge) for class m after introducing pricing scheme $\mathbf{u}$; χ_w is designated here as an equity index that dictates the degree of tolerance of the inequity associated with a pricing scheme. A sensible selection of the value of this index is given by:

$$\chi_w(\varphi) = \begin{cases} 1+\varphi\left(\dfrac{\hat{\mu}_w}{\tilde{\mu}_w}-1\right), & \text{if } \dfrac{\hat{\mu}_w}{\tilde{\mu}_w}>1 \\ 1, & \text{otherwise} \end{cases},\ 0\le\varphi\le 1 \tag{7.61}$$

Here the term $\hat{\mu}_w$ is the OD travel disutility after the first-best or marginal-cost pricing scheme is implemented; φ is a decision variable satisfying $0 \le \varphi \le 1$. Clearly, $1 \le \chi_w \le \hat{\mu}_w/\tilde{\mu}_w$, $w \in W$ for $0 \le \varphi \le 1$ if $\hat{\mu}_w > \tilde{\mu}_w$. It should be mentioned that for the marginal-cost pricing scheme used here, we assume that the same marginal time externality is internalized by differentiated tolls across user classes according to their respective VOTs. In this case, for a given OD pair $w \in W$, different classes have equal travel disutility $\hat{\mu}_w$ in time units inclusive of equivalent differentiated toll charge (see, Subsection 6.3.1 in Chapter 6).

In the general case of $\hat{\mu}_w > \tilde{\mu}_w$, we have $\chi_w(\varphi) = \hat{\mu}_w/\tilde{\mu}_w$ when φ equals 1. This means that χ_w takes its largest value equal to the ratio of the equilibrium OD travel cost after introducing marginal-cost pricing to the original OD travel time without pricing. In other words, the degree of inequity in a second-best pricing scheme is bounded by the first-best pricing case, or the travel disutility of each user class between each OD pair under a second-best pricing scheme cannot exceed that under the first-best pricing scheme. This specification of the upper bound of the equity parameter is quite justifiable and meaningful. The principle of marginal cost pricing states that road users using congested roads should pay a toll equal to the difference between the marginal social cost and the marginal private cost so as to maximize economic benefit. Thus, by requiring paying a marginal-cost toll, an individual driver will bear the full social cost generated by him or her in using a congested road. A toll charge higher than this amount seems to be economically irrational and unfair to users.

When φ is equal to 0, $\chi_w(\varphi)$ becomes 1. This means that the OD travel disutility cannot exceed the equilibrium OD travel disutility before introducing pricing. Namely, all the OD travel disutilities decrease or remain unchanged. Since in a real network, a congestion pricing scheme is very unlikely to lead to a decline in all OD travel disutilities inclusive of toll (note that this is not always impossible as, for example, in the Braess paradox network, introducing a toll charge on the paradoxical link may reduce the average OD travel cost.), the zero toll charge (do-nothing alternative) may become the only feasible solution when $\varphi = 0$.

In summary, φ is an appropriate measure that can be used by the system manager to adjust the level of social and spatial equity for consideration in establishing a fair and reasonable pricing scheme. A higher value of φ permits a greater negative inequity impact on users, and a lower value of φ sets a stricter inequity constraint. Note that, given the dispersion of gains or losses of travel disutilities among users with different VOTs and in different O-D pairs, one may measure network-wide inequities inflicted by a pricing scheme by using the so-called Gini coefficient, which is a well-established measurement of income inequality in the economic literature.

In eqn. (7.60), there are in total $|M|$ constraints associated with $|M|$ distinct classes of users for each given OD pair $w \in W$. In fact, only the equity constraint corresponding to class 1 with the lowest VOT is needed and the remaining $(|M|-1)$ constraints for each OD pair are redundant. Namely, imposition of the equity constraint for the lowest VOT user class automatically guarantees that the same equity constraints are satisfied for higher VOT user classes. This is due to the fact that the deterministic equilibrium OD travel disutilities (in time units) by the user class always satisfy $\mu_w^1(\mathbf{u}) \geq \mu_w^2(\mathbf{u}) \geq \cdots \geq \mu_w^{|M|}(\mathbf{u})$, $w \in W$, for any anonymous link pricing scheme with nonnegative tolls, where user classes are ordered according to increasing VOT. This is evident. Consider any two classes of users, class m and class n with $\beta_m < \beta_n$, traveling between a given OD pair $w \in W$. Let t_{rw} and u_{rw} $(u_{rw} \geq 0)$ be the travel time and total toll charge along any route $r \in R_w$. Clearly, we always have $c_{rw}^m = t_{rw} + u_{rw}/\beta_m > c_{rw}^n = t_{rw} + u_{rw}/\beta_n$ for any $r \in R_w, w \in W$, and thus $\mu_w^{m_1} > \mu_w^n$, $w \in W$ as long as $\beta_m < \beta_n$. In view of the fact that $\tilde{\mu}_w^m = \tilde{\mu}_w^n = \tilde{\mu}_w$ in the absence of pricing, the set of constraints (7.60) can now be replaced by

$$\frac{\mu_w^1(\mathbf{u})}{\tilde{\mu}_w} \leq \chi_w(\varphi), \ w \in W \tag{7.62}$$

Note that, as mentioned in Section 7.1, the equilibrium travel disutility ratio in (7.60) for a specific class is independent of its measurement unit (time or money) and hence eqn. (7.62) is always sufficient to ensure all equity constraints are met, despite the fact that $\mu_w^1(\mathbf{u}) \leq \mu_w^2(\mathbf{u}) \leq \cdots \leq \mu_w^{|M|}(\mathbf{u})$, $w \in W$, for $\beta_1 < \beta_2 < \cdots < \beta_{|M|}$, if the travel disutility is measured in monetary units $\left(c_{rw}^m = \beta_m t_{rw} + u_{rw}\right)$.

7.4.3 Network Toll Design with Equity Constraints

With the aforementioned social and spatial equity considerations, the network toll design problem with an equity constraint can now be formulated as the following bilevel programming problem:

$$\max_{\mathbf{u} \in U} F_1(\mathbf{u}) = \sum_{m \in M} \left\{ \sum_{w \in W} \int_0^{d_w^m(\mathbf{u})} B_w^m(\omega)\,\mathrm{d}\omega - \sum_{a \in A} v_a^m(\mathbf{u})\, t_a\left(v_a(\mathbf{u})\right) \right\} \tag{7.63}$$

subject to

$$\frac{\mu_w^1(\mathbf{u})}{\tilde{\mu}_w} \leq \chi_w(\varphi), \ w \in W \tag{7.64}$$

where $\mathbf{v}^m(\mathbf{u})$ and $\mathbf{d}^m(\mathbf{u})$ solves the equilibrium problem (7.57) with the time-based OD travel disutility $\mu_w^1(\mathbf{u})$, $w \in W$ associated with the lowest VOT user class. In the model, $\chi_w(\varphi)$, $w \in W$ is specified by eqn. (7.61) and U is the feasible set of link tolls defined by

$$U = \left\{ \mathbf{u} \,|\, u_a^{\min} \le u_a \le u_a^{\max},\ a \in \overline{A} \right\} \tag{7.65}$$

where $u_a^{\min}$ and $u_a^{\max}$ are the prespecified lower and upper bounds of link tolls u_a, $a \in A$.

As pointed out earlier, parameter φ $(0 \le \varphi \le 1.0)$ reflects the allowable degree of inequity in terms of the OD travel disutility ratios after and before implementing a pricing scheme. This parameter is selected by the decision-maker and can be, in fact, treated as a decision variable in the programming model. For each given φ, let $S^*(\varphi)$ be the maximum social welfare obtained by the bi-level model (7.63)-(7.64), $S^*(\varphi)$ can be regarded as an implicit function of parameter φ. By incorporating this equity decision parameter φ, we have the following tri-level programming model with dual top-level objective functions:

$$\min_{0 \le \varphi \le 1.0} F_2(\varphi) = \begin{pmatrix} F_2^1 = \dfrac{S^*(0) - S^*(\varphi)}{S^*(1) - S^*(0)} \\ F_2^2 = \varphi \end{pmatrix} \tag{7.66}$$

where, according to the specification and analysis of φ in Section 7.4.2, $S^*(0)$ with $\varphi = 0$ generally corresponds to the 'minimum' social welfare in the do-nothing or untolled situation; while $S^*(1)$ with $\varphi = 1.0$ corresponds to the 'maximum' social welfare in the differentiated first-best pricing situation (with inactive lower and upper toll bound in U).

In the bi-objective programming model (7.66), a considerate trade off is necessary to balance the need of increasing the total social welfare and the requirement of avoiding the great negative inequity impact. The problem thus becomes how to select a non-dominated efficient solution using an appropriate method. A widely used utility function approach is adopted here to transfer the two objectives into a single objective function as follows:

$$F_3(\varphi) = \omega F_2^1 + (1-\omega) F_2^2 = \omega \frac{S^*(0) - S^*(\varphi)}{S^*(1) - S^*(0)} + (1-\omega)\varphi \tag{7.67}$$

Here, ω is a weighting parameter with $0 < \omega < 1$. Consequently, the network toll design problem with an equity constraint becomes the following tri-level programming problem:

$$\min_{0 \le \varphi \le 1.0} F_3(\varphi) = \omega \left(\frac{S^*(0) - S^*(\varphi)}{S^*(1) - S^*(0)} \right) + (1-\omega)\varphi \tag{7.68}$$

where $S^*(\varphi)$ is again the optimal objective value of the bi-level model (7.63)-(7.64) for given φ.

7.5 ALTERNATIVE SOLUTION APPROACHES

We have proposed the bi-level programming model (7.63)-(7.64) to characterize the social-welfare maximizing pricing problem with social and spatial equity constraints, and the tri-level programming model (7.68) to treat the equity preference parameter as an endogenous decision variable. Although the bi-level model (7.63)-(7.64) can, in principle, be solved with the sensitivity analysis and gap function based approaches developed in Chapter 3 and Chapter 4 respectively, identification of the global or nearly global optimum solution is critical for meaningful and reliable policy parameter sensitivity analysis. Here we instead adopt the Simulated Annealing (SA) method, which is particularly suitable for the models proposed. It has the ability to obtain the global optimal solution without the requirement for differentiability.

7.5.1 Solution for Bi-level Model

We first consider how to solve the bilevel model (7.63)-(7.64). The nonlinear, implicit constraint (7.64) is incorporated into the objective function by using an inner penalty function approach in applying the SA method. The procedure is presented below.

The inner penalty function approach:

Step 0. (*Initialization*) Set a stop tolerance ε, an initial penalty multiplier ρ_0, a scale parameter ζ and an initial point $\mathbf{u}^{(0)} \in U$. Let $n := 0$.

Step 1. (*Finding an optimal solution*) Starting with $\mathbf{u}^{(0)}$, solving the following problem through the SA method and let $\mathbf{u}^{(n+1)}$ be the optimal solution

$$\min_{\mathbf{u}\in U} \bar{F}(\mathbf{u}) = -F_1(\mathbf{u}) + \rho_n \alpha(\mathbf{u}) \tag{7.69}$$

where

$$\alpha(\mathbf{u}) = \sum_{w\in W} \max\left\{ \frac{\mu_w^1(\mathbf{u})}{\tilde{\mu}_w} - \chi_w,\ 0 \right\} \tag{7.70}$$

Step 2. (*Verifying the stop criterion*) If $\rho_n \alpha\left(\mathbf{u}^{(n+1)}\right) < \varepsilon$, then stop. Otherwise, set $\rho_{n+1} = \zeta \rho_n$ and $n := n+1$, go to Step 1.

For any given toll vector $\mathbf{u}$, the equilibrium traffic assignment procedure is used to find the link flow $v_a^m(\mathbf{u})$, the OD demand for each class $d_w^m(\mathbf{u})$ and the generalized OD travel disutility $\mu_w^m(\mathbf{u})$, and so it is straightforward to calculate the objective function value $\bar{F}(\mathbf{u})$.

With this in mind, the procedure of the Simulated Annealing method for solving the bilevel problem (7.63)-(7.64) with any fixed penalty parameter ρ_n is given below.

Simulated Annealing method:

Step 0. (*Initialization*) Given an initial point $\mathbf{u}^{(0)} \in U$ and the parameter $0 < \upsilon_0 < 1.0$, $0 < \delta < 1.0$, $0 < t < 1.0$, integer L_0, J_0 and T_s (stop tolerance of temperature). Set $n = n_1 = 0$.

Step 1. (*Finding an initial temperature*) Uniformly generate at random J_0 points denoted by $\mathbf{z}^{(i)}$ $(i = 1, \cdots, J_0)$ over the feasible set U. For each $\mathbf{z}^{(i)}$, use equilibrium traffic assignment to obtain the equilibrium link flow and OD travel disutility and then calculate the corresponding function value $\bar{F}(\mathbf{z}^{(i)})$. Let J_2 denote the number of points $\mathbf{z}^{(i)}$ with $\bar{F}(\mathbf{z}^{(i)}) - \bar{F}(\mathbf{u}^{(0)}) \geq 0$ and $\overline{\Delta \bar{F}^+}$ the average value of those $\bar{F}(\mathbf{z}^{(i)}) - \bar{F}(\mathbf{u}^{(0)})$ (≥ 0). Then the initial temperature $T^{(0)}$ is calculated below

$$T^{(0)} = \begin{cases} \overline{\Delta \bar{F}^+} & \text{if } J_2 \leq \dfrac{1}{2} J_0 \\ \left(\ln \dfrac{J_2}{J_2 \upsilon_0 + (1 - \upsilon_0)(J_0 - J_2)} \right)^{-1} & \text{if } J_2 > \dfrac{1}{2} J_0 \\ +\infty & \text{if } J_2 = 0 \end{cases} \tag{7.71}$$

Step 2. (*Verifying the termination*) If $T^{(n)} < T_s$, then stop. Otherwise, go to Step 3.

Step 3. (*Checking the termination of a Markov chain*) If $n_1 > L_0 N$ (N represents the number of decision variables), go to Step 6; otherwise, go to Step 4.

Step 4. (*Generation of points*) Uniformly generate, at random, a number denoted by t_{random} from the internal [0, 1). If $t_{\text{random}} > t$, then use the method of Hooke and Jeeves with discrete steps from the point $\mathbf{u}^{(n_1)}$, as a local search procedure to find a local solution in the feasible set U for the problem denoted by $\mathbf{x}$. If $t_{\text{random}} > t$, then uniformly generate, at random, a point denoted by $\mathbf{x}$ over U.

Step 5. (*Metropolis' rule*) If $\bar{F}(\mathbf{x}) \leq \bar{F}(\mathbf{u}^{(n_1)})$ or if $\exp\left(-\left(\bar{F}(\mathbf{x}) - \bar{F}(\mathbf{u}^{(n_1)})\right)/T^{(n)}\right) >$ random $[0,1]$ when $\bar{F}(\mathbf{x}) > \bar{F}(\mathbf{u}^{(n_1)})$, set $\mathbf{u}^{(n_1+1)} = \mathbf{x}$, $n_1 := n_1 + 1$ and go to Step 3. Otherwise, let $\mathbf{u}^{(n_1+1)} = \mathbf{u}^{(n_1)}$, $n_1 := n_1 + 1$ and go to Step 3.

Step 6. (*Cooling schedules*) Calculate the standard derivation of the values of the objective function $\bar{F}\left(\mathbf{u}^{(n_1)}\right)$ $\left(n_1 = 0,1,\cdots,L_0N\right)$, denoted by $\sigma\left(T^{(n)}\right)$. Set the temperature as follows:

$$T^{(n+1)} = T^{(n)}\left(1+\frac{T^{(n)}\ln(1+\delta)}{3\sigma\left(T^{(n)}\right)}\right)^{-1} \tag{7.72}$$

Let $n := n+1$, $\mathbf{u}^{(0)} = \mathbf{u}^{(L_0N)}$, $n_1 = 0$ and go to Step 2.

Note that objective function evaluation is required in the Hooke-Jeeves direct search method in Step 4. This means that we need to perform the equilibrium traffic assignment procedure at each trial point in this local search method.

7.5.2 Solution for Tri-level Model

We first analyze how the two components F_2^1 and F_2^2 of the objective function F_3 vary with φ. When φ equals 0 or when no travel cost increase is allowed between any OD pair, the tolls have to be set equal to 0, and obviously $F_2^1 = 0.0$. When φ increases to a value greater than 0, non-zero tolls in U are charged on certain links, and the social welfare gain in the network must increase, otherwise the solution is not optimal. In other words, component F_2^1 will decrease to a number smaller than 0.0. When φ comes to 1.0, F_2^1 reaches its minimum value -1.0. Of course, the term $(1-\omega)F_2^2$ or the term $(1-\omega)\varphi$ linearly increases with φ. So, one component F_2^1 of F_3 decreases with φ and the other component F_2^2 of F_3 increases with φ.

In view of the fact that $S^*(0)$, $S^*(1)$, ω together with φ are constant for any given value of φ in the feasible interval $0 \le \varphi \le 1$, minimizing F_3 is equivalent to maximizing F_1. This means that model (7.68) reduces to (7.63)-(7.64) for a given value of φ. Based on this observation, we can use a one dimensional search method in conjunction with the algorithm for (7.63)-(7.64) to solve the tri-level optimization problem. At each new point of the one-dimensional search for φ, a sub-program (7.63)-(7.64), is solved to find the objective function value F_3, and the search is continued when both optimal φ and $\mathbf{u}$ are identified.

7.6 A NUMERICAL EXAMPLE

The road network shown in Figure 7.5 consists of 5 nodes and 8 links, of which link 4 and link 5 are subjected to toll charges (locations are predetermined). The link travel time function is:

$$t_a(v_a) = t_a^0 \left\{ 1.0 + 0.15 \left(\frac{v_a}{C_a} \right)^4 \right\} \tag{7.73}$$

The values of free-flow time t_a^0 and capacity C_a for each link are given in Table 7.2. There are 4 OD pairs with the following negative exponential demand function:

$$d_w^m = \hat{D}_w^m \exp\left(-\gamma \mu_w^m\right), \quad w \in W, \; m \in M \tag{7.74}$$

The potential demands are respectively $\hat{D}_{1\to5} = 5500$, $\hat{D}_{2\to5}$=2000, $\hat{D}_{3\to5}$=6000, $\hat{D}_{4\to5}$=2000 (veh/h) for the four OD pairs ($1 \to 5$, $2 \to 5$, $3 \to 5$, $4 \to 5$). Parameter γ is set to be 0.01 for all user classes.

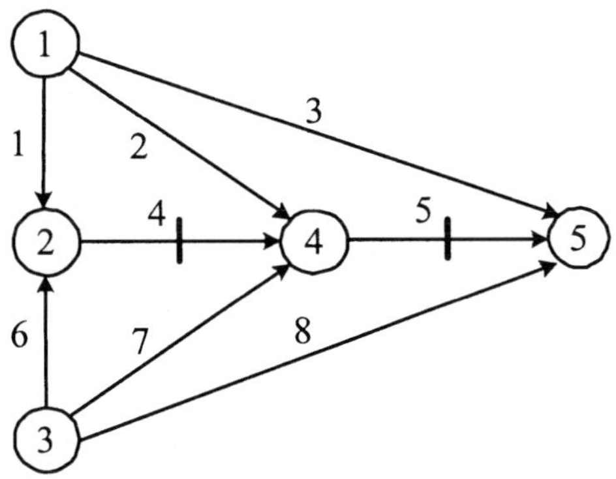

Figure 7.5 The network used in the numerical example

Table 7.2 Input data for test network in Figure 7.5

Link	1	2	3	4	5	6	7	8
t_a^0 (min)	10	23	42	10	15	10	23	42
C_a (veh/h)	1000	2000	3000	4000	6000	1000	2000	3000

Suppose there are 3 user classes with $m = 1, 2$ and 3 representing low, medium and high income user class, respectively. The potential market share of the three classes are assumed to be identical for all OD pairs and of values of 20%, 60% and 20%, and their VOTs are 75, 100 and 150 (HK\$/h), respectively.

Without implementation of a road-pricing scheme, the equilibrium OD travel disutility is presented in Table 7.3. The social welfare gain is 1.7701×10^4 (veh-h). When differentiated marginal-cost pricing link tolls are charged on each link, and the resulting generalized OD travel disutilities (in time units) are also listed in the same table, and the social welfare gain increases to a maximum value 1.7940×10^4 (veh-h). Table 7.3 also shows the ratios of the OD travel disutility after and before marginal-cost pricing is introduced, which are identical among different user classes in the same OD pair. It can be seen from the table that travel disutilities between all four OD pairs increase after the marginal-cost pricing link tolls are charged. In particular, the travel disutility between OD pair $4\rightarrow5$ increases most.

Table 7.3 Change in equilibrium OD travel disutility before and after road pricing

OD pair	1→5	2→5	3→5	4→5
Travel disutility without pricing (min)	42.631	30.587	42.779	19.544
Travel disutility with marginal-cost pricing (min)	48.651	37.120	49.084	25.408
Ratio of equilibrium OD travel disutility	1.141	1.214	1.147	1.300

Table 7.4 Numerical results for VOTs = 75, 100, 150 (HK$/h)

φ	0.0	0.2	0.4	0.6	0.8	1.0
u_1 (HK$)	0.00	0.30	1.35	2.91	4.22	5.21
u_2 (HK$)	0.00	2.90	4.35	5.01	5.68	5.81
Welfare (10^4 veh-h)	1.7701	1.7815	1.7866	1.7898	1.7908	1.7910
Revenue (10^4 HK$)	0.0000	2.0317	3.2232	4.0264	4.6898	5.0274
Binding OD pair	All	2→5	2→5	2→5	2→5	no

Now we consider a second-best pricing scheme with link 4 and link 5 subjected to toll charge for maximizing social welfare, while considering equity constraints with model (7.63)-(7.64). Table 7.4 shows the numerical results for 10 different values of the inequity threshold φ. The last row of the table lists the OD pairs, for which the constraint, $\bar{\mu}_w^1(\mathbf{u})/\tilde{\mu}_w \le \chi_w(\varphi)$, is binding. From the table, we can see that $\varphi = 0.0$ means that cost increase is not allowed for all OD pairs, and in this case no toll can be charged on both links and the equity constraints of all OD pairs are binding. As φ increases, the equity constraint is relaxed gradually, higher tolls can be charged on both links, and more revenue is generated, and as expected, the total social welfare increases. The binding equity constraint is always associated with OD pair $2\rightarrow5$ for $\varphi = 0.1 \sim 0.8$, this is clearly due to the fact that a free alternative route is not available for traveling from node 2 to 5 and low-income users from 2 to 5 suffer most from the pricing scheme. As $\varphi \ge 0.9$ relaxing the equity constraint does not lead to further increase in social welfare (objective function), and all equity constraints become inactive.

In fact, the dispersion of VOT distribution across user classes has significant impacts on the analysis result. Namely, as the VOT distribution is more dispersed, the inequity effect among user classes becomes more profound, and thus the equity constraints act more tightly. To verify this effect, Table 7.5 presents numerical results for another set of more dispersed VOT distribution given to be 50, 100 and 200 (HK$/h)), for the three classes. In comparison with the former case, optimal tolls for both links are smaller for the same φ value. Even when φ increases up to its maximal value of 1.0, the equity constraint is still binding. Thus the social welfare for $0 \leq \varphi \leq 1$ cannot reach its maximum value achieved in the case without equity constraints. This highlights the fact that both social and spatial equity issues deserve more attention as VOT differential across users becomes more remarkable.

Table 7.6 provides the numerical results for 5 different values of weighting factor ω. As ω increases, or as more emphasis is placed on maximization of social welfare than on the equity constraint, the value of φ, as expected, increases, and the toll charge on each link becomes higher. Meanwhile, the total revenue increases, and the total social welfare increases.

Table 7.5 Numerical results for VOT = 50,100, 200 (HK$/h)

φ	0.0	0.2	0.4	0.6	0.8	1.0
u_1 (HK$)	0.00	0.44	1.14	1.69	2.10	2.65
u_2 (HK$)	0.00	1.11	1.84	2.68	3.84	4.66
Welfare (10^4 veh-h)	1.7701	1.7760	1.7801	1.7839	1.7871	1.7895
Revenue (10^4 HK$)	0.0000	0.9298	1.6530	2.3587	3.1705	3.8562
Binding OD pair	All	2→5	2→5	2→5	2→5	2→5

Table 7.6 Numerical results for VOT = 75, 100, 150 (HK$/h)

ω	0.1	0.3	0.5	0.7	0.9
φ	0.00	0.14	0.40	0.63	0.74
u_1 (HK$)	0.00	0.22	1.35	3.04	3.89
u_2 (HK$)	0.00	2.08	4.35	5.29	5.59
Welfare (10^4 veh-h)	1.7701	1.7789	1.7866	1.7901	1.7908
Revenue (10^4 HK$)	0.0000	1.4905	3.2232	4.2024	4.5504
Binding OD pair	All	2→5	2→5	2→5	2→5

We now demonstrate how the two kinds of inequities examined here occur on the network and how the proposed models work. Figure 7.6 plots the percentage change in the average OD travel disutility (average over 3 classes weighted by their shares) for the 4 OD pairs.

From this figure, we can see that when φ is less than 0.4, the average OD travel cost of $4 \rightarrow 5$ increases most. As φ grows up, travel costs of $2 \rightarrow 5$ increases most.

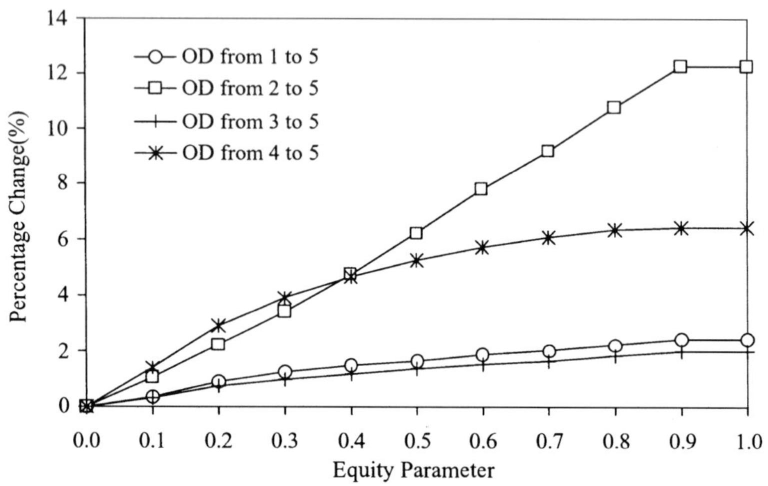

Figure 7.6 Percentage change in weighted average OD travel disutility

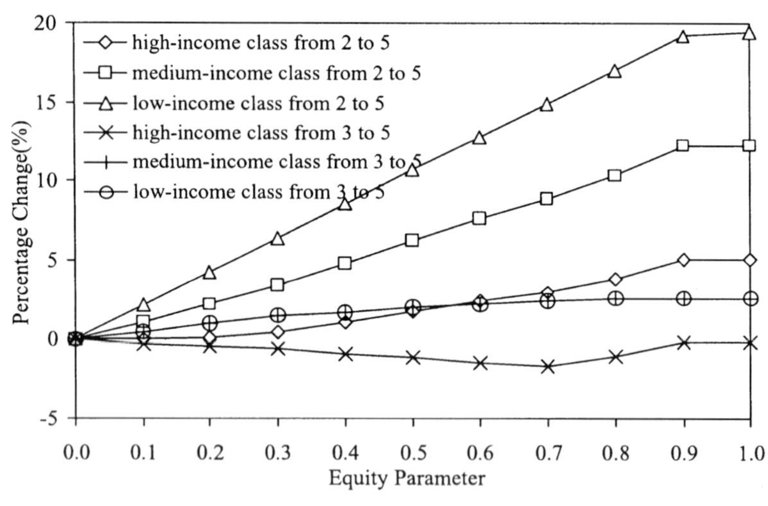

Figure 7.7 Percentage change in OD travel disutility by user class

Figure 7.7 depicts the percentage change in OD travel disutility by user class for two selected OD pairs $2 \rightarrow 5$ and $3 \rightarrow 5$. It is observed that for the OD pair $3 \rightarrow 5$, high-income class users actually benefit from the toll charge. As φ increases up to about 0.70, they enjoy more benefits, and as φ increases further beyond 0.70 they enjoy less benefits. In contrast, all other users suffer from the toll charge, and suffer more losses as φ increases. Note that for OD pair $3 \rightarrow 5$, the medium- and low-income class users have equal travel cost because they are both exclusively concentrated on the non-toll path (link 8). These results reveal that parameter φ plays an essential role in controlling the spatial and social equity impacts of a network-pricing scheme on heterogeneous users.

7.7 SUMMARY

After a general discussion of the social and spatial inequity issues in congestion pricing and a demonstration with a simple analytical example, this chapter first proved the existence of a Pareto refunding scheme that returns the congestion pricing revenues to all users to make everyone better off. More plausible refunding schemes are sought under specific conditions, such as whether aggregate travel times or costs by individual OD pairs are reduced, after introducing a tolling system. The Pareto refunding schemes developed in this chapter could be used as a basis for an acceptable implementation of congestion pricing in terms of both economic efficiency and equity. It holds promise as a way for invoking congestion pricing and using pricing revenue in a constructive manner that is viewed favourably by the public. With the advent of intelligent transportation systems, it is possible today to create complex systems capable of operating direct redistribution methods of congestion pricing.

Without direct redistribution of congestion pricing revenues to users, we then proposed and solved mathematical programming models that explicitly address the social and spatial equity concerns in designing a network-wide efficient pricing scheme. The impact of congestion charge on spatial equity is measured by the relative changes in the generalized O-D travel disutility in each O-D pair, whereas the impact on social equity is considered by examing the inequitable relative changes in travel disutilities of users of different social classes. Both equities are incorporated into the bilevel network toll design model as constraints. A penalty function approach, combined with a simulated annealing method, was applied for solving the equity-constrained network toll design problem. As demonstrated with numerical examples, the proposed models and algorithms allow for selection of a fair and reasonable link toll pattern that maximizes social welfare gain, and meanwhile attempts not to bring excessive negative impact on certain groups of users.

Finally, we should recognize the fact that, although the various equity issues and revenue allocations of congestion pricing have been argued extensively in the literature for more than a decade, only until recently, did their rigorous quantative analysis receive attention. There are many worthwhile topics for further studies. It remains an open question as to what extent the Pareto refunding scheme applies in the more realistic case of elastic demand. It is challenging to develop combined congestion pricing and revenue refunding models to create the best win-win situation, particularly under various social and economic constraints. Furthermore, instead of the change in travel disutility between individual OD pair used in the bilevel network toll design model, one may measure the impact of congestion pricing on social and spatial equities by the *accessibility* of different user classes from different zones. Accessibility aggregates the potential access from a zone to opportunities in different zones, each of which is weighted by a deterrence function of travel cost.

7.8 SOURCES AND NOTES

The Pareto refunding scheme for congestion pricing revenue presented in Sections 7.2 and 7.3 is a recent (unpublished) development by the authors. The network toll design models with equity constraints presented in Sections 7.4-7.6 are drawn from the work of Yang and Zhang (2002). There is substantial and extensive literature about social and spatial equity issues in road pricing, and readers are suggested to further refer to Foster (1975), Small (1983), Hau (1992), Giuliano (1992), Johansson and Mattsson (1995), Litman (1996), Button and Verhoef (1998), Richardson and Bae (1998), and, for most recent discussions, to Viegas (2001), Raux and Souche (2004) and Santos and Rojey (2004). A few research studies have looked at the revenue distribution strategies including: Small (1992a,b,c), Parry and Bento (2001), Eliasson (2001) and recently Kalmanje and Kockelman (2004). Readers may refer to Bernstein (1993), Adler and Cetin, (2001), Elliasson (2001) and Yang, Meng and Hau (2004) for theoretical developments of congestion pricing revenue redistribution strategies.

The simulated annealing method for solving the equity-constrained network toll design problem can be found in many reference books, such as Aarts and Korst (1989), Dekkers and Aarts (1991) and Romeijin and Smith (1994). Readers may also refer to Friesz *et al.* (1992), Huang and Bell (1998) and Meng and Yang (2002) for the successful applications of this method in solving the continuous equilibrium network design problems in transportation. Finally, the concept of accessibility is covered in many textbooks, such as Erlander and Stewart (1990).

8

PRICING, CAPACITY CHOICE AND FINANCING

8.1 INTRODUCTION

How should society go about expanding its road systems? Who would decide where to provide more road capacity, and how much more? Where would funds for expansion come from? The recent world-wide tendency toward the introduction of commercially and privately provided public roads proves to be an efficient answer to these questions. In a so-called Build-Operate-Transfer (BOT) project, the private sector would build and operate roads at its own expense and in turn should receive the revenue from road toll charge for some years, and then these roads will be transferred to the government. BOT projects use the market criterion of profitability for road development and rely on the voluntary participation of private investors, who hope to benefit financially or otherwise from their participation. This commercial and private provision of transport infrastructure has attracted fast-growing interest in recent years and is being employed to finance modern road systems.

Private provision of roads is driven by a number of factors. A primary motivation is a widespread belief that the private sector is inherently more efficient than the public sector, and therefore builds and operates facilities at less cost than the public sector. Also, the public sector, facing taxpayer resistance, may simply be unable to finance facilities that the private sector would be willing and able to undertake for a profit. In addition, if new road space is provided as an "add-on" to an existing network system, and if road users find it worthwhile to patronize this new road and pay charges, and if the charges cover all costs (including congestion and environmental costs), all may gain benefit, and there would be no obvious losers. Even those who do not use these new roads would benefit from reduced congestion on the old ones.

Once road provision moves to a market economy, there are many intriguing issues to be addressed. From the viewpoint of private investors, profitability of a project is of great concern because their private firms are put at risk. Specially, the paucity of experience with toll-charged roads and the long pay-back period after the initial investment make it more difficult to predict future revenues and thus makes the uncertainty and risks of investment in roads very high compared to alternative investment options. Therefore, careful project selection and a clear identification and assessment of the risks are important in order to guarantee that willing buyers are prepared to pay sufficiently to induce willing suppliers to provide it. From the viewpoint of society, it is meaningful to assess whether the construction of a road will give a positive welfare increment if it is profitable, compared with the do-nothing alternative, and vice versa whether any road which adds to welfare will be profitable, and hence can be provided privately. More importantly, under the commercial and private provision of roads, what roles can a government play? What government regulations concerning private toll roads should be imposed? For example, should the road charge level be controlled by the government to prevent private firms from abusing their monopoly over the road and for equity reasons (access to services for everyone)? It is obvious that these issues must be addressed carefully, because transport infrastructure has major strategic, economic, social, financial and environmental effects and because the interests of the private sector are different from those of the public sector.

In this chapter we look into the interrelations among pricing, capacity choice, financing and competition in simple and general networks. We begin with a description of traffic equilibrium models with heterogeneous users and alternative performance measures for a given pricing scheme. We elucidate the various possibilities of profitability and social welfare gain of a single toll road in a general network and then move to the analysis of the impacts of user heterogeneity on its profitability and social welfare gain. We investigate whether and under what conditions the classical self-financing principle holds in general transportation networks. Finally, we examine, both theoretically and numerically, the competition and equilibria based on a situation where there are two or more profit-maximizing private firms that operate some toll roads in a road network.

8.2. User Equilibrium and Performance Evaluation for Private Toll Roads

8.2.1 Multi-class UE Model with Elastic Demand

Suppose that the highway BOT project consists of a finite sequence of connected links (segments) and the location of the BOT project and the number of years of operations by the private sector are already determined. Let $\bar{A}$ denote a subset of these links and y_a, $a \in \bar{A}$ denote the capacity of a link if this link is a new link to be added to the network, or the capacity increase if this link is an existing link to be expanded, and furthermore let

$\mathbf{y} = \left(y_a, a \in \bar{A}\right)^{\mathrm{T}}$. Without loss of generality, here we consider new toll road links only and denote the toll to be charged on a new link $a \in \bar{A}$ by u_a and $\mathbf{u} = \left(u_a, a \in \bar{A}\right)^{\mathrm{T}}$. Like previous chapters, subdivide the demand for travel into a set M classes, corresponding to groups of user with different socio-economic characteristics (for example, income level). Because a BOT project generally involves long-term investment and cost-recovery made in a road network, and thus certainly influences the demand for travel, it is therefore desirable to consider the elasticity of travel demand. Let the demand, d_w^m, of user class m between OD pair w be a continuously decreasing function of the full price of travel incurred, including travel time plus toll, if toll roads are used. As discussed in Chapter 2, the discrete multi-class network equilibrium model with elastic demand is given below:

$$\min_{\mathbf{v},\mathbf{d}} \sum_{a \in A, a \notin \bar{A}} \int_0^{v_a} t_a(\omega)\mathrm{d}\omega + \sum_{a \in \bar{A}} \int_0^{v_a} t_a(\omega, y_a)\mathrm{d}\omega + \sum_{a \in \bar{A}} \sum_{m \in M} \frac{u_a}{\beta_m} v_a^m - \sum_{w \in W} \sum_{m \in M} \int_0^{d_w^m} B_w^m(\omega)\mathrm{d}\omega \tag{8.1}$$

subject to

$$\sum_{r \in R_w} f_{rw}^m = d_w^m, \; w \in W, \; m \in M \tag{8.2}$$

$$v_a = \sum_{w \in W} \sum_{m \in M} \sum_{r \in R_w} f_{rw}^m \delta_{ar}, \; a \in A \tag{8.3}$$

$$v_a^m = \sum_{w \in W} \sum_{r \in R_w} f_{rw}^m \delta_{ar}, \; a \in A, \; m \in M \tag{8.4}$$

$$f_{rw}^m \geq 0, \; d_w^m \geq 0, \; r \in R_w, \; w \in W, \; m \in M \tag{8.5}$$

Note that here A is the whole set of links in the entire network, including the newly introduced toll links $\left(\bar{A} \subset A\right)$, β_m is the average Value Of Time (VOT) of user class $m \in M$, $\mu_w^m = B_w^m\left(d_w^m\right)$ with $\mathrm{d}B_w^m / \mathrm{d}\mu_w^m < 0$, is the benefit function or the inverse of the demand function $d_w^m = D_w^m\left(\mu_w^m\right)$, for user class $m \in M$, and the other notations follow as before. As shown in Chapter 2, the above minimization model leads to a multi-class traffic equilibrium on the basis of travel disutility in time units. Users will minimize their individual travel disutility, and thus divide themselves among the various alternative routes that are differentiated on the basis of travel time and monetary cost. The equilibrium OD travel time μ_w^m (inclusive of equivalent time of toll charge if any) between OD pair w by users of class m is given by

$$\mu_w^m = \min_{r \in R_w}\left\{c_{rw}^m\right\} \text{ and } c_{rw}^m = \sum_{a \in A} t_a\left(v_a\right)\delta_{ar} + \sum_{a \in \bar{A}} \frac{u_a}{\beta_m}\delta_{ar}, \; w \in W, \; m \in M \tag{8.6}$$

8.2.2 Alternative Performance Measures

For a given combination of tolls and capacities of the private roads, the multi-class network equilibrium model will ascertain the realized demand between each OD pair and for each user class and determine the flows using the toll roads. Hence we are able to evaluate the benefit of the project to the different user classes, the private investor and the whole society.

Let $I_a(y_a)$ be the link construction cost function of link $a \in \bar{A}$, which is assumed to be a continuously increasing and differentiable function of y_a. The private firm intending to construct and operate the commercial road project is interested in the expected profit derived from a selected combination of toll and capacity, $\mathbf{u}$ and $\mathbf{y}$. The expected profit in dollars, $\Pi(\mathbf{u},\mathbf{y})$, is calculated by

$$\Pi(\mathbf{u},\mathbf{y}) = \sum_{a \in \bar{A}} \{v_a(\mathbf{u},\mathbf{y}) u_a - \eta I_a(y_a)\} \tag{8.7}$$

where $v_a, a \in \bar{A}$ is determined from the network equilibrium model (8.1)-(8.5) and η is a parameter that transfers the capital cost of the project into a unit period cost. It is assumed that the project cost ηI_a, $a \in \bar{A}$ does not vary with the level of traffic (variable operating cost is omitted here).

The social welfare in dollars, $W(\mathbf{u},\mathbf{y})$, per unit period generated from the BOT project is defined to be the sum of consumers' and producers' surplus, as given below:

$$W(\mathbf{u},\mathbf{y}) = \sum_{m \in M} \beta_m \left\{ \sum_{w \in W} \int_0^{d_w^m(\mathbf{u},\mathbf{y})} B_w^m(\omega)\, d\omega - \sum_{a \in A, a \notin \bar{A}} t_a(v_a) v_a^m(\mathbf{u},\mathbf{y}) - \sum_{a \in \bar{A}} t_a(v_a, y_a) v_a^m(\mathbf{u},\mathbf{y}) \right\} - \sum_{a \in \bar{A}} \eta I_a(y_a) \tag{8.8}$$

where v_a^m and d_w^m, $a \in A$, $w \in W$, $m \in M$, are again determined from the model (8.1)-(8.5). As already discussed in Chapter 7, the social welfare is well defined for given $\mathbf{u}$, even though the class-specific link flows may not be unique. The net social welfare gained from the BOT project can then be determined as $W(\mathbf{u},\mathbf{y}) - W(0,0)$, the difference of the social welfare between the BOT road case and the do-nothing alternative.

One favorable advantage of the multi-class network equilibrium approach is that the distribution of the benefit generated by the toll road across different user classes between each OD pair can be assessed. One direct meaningful measure of the benefit received by users of class m between OD pair w is the percentage change in their travel disutility before and after introducing the toll road:

$$\mu_w^m(\%) = \frac{\mu_w^{m,\text{after}} - \mu_w^{m,\text{before}}}{\mu_w^{m,\text{before}}} \times 100\ (\%),\ w \in W,\ m \in M \tag{8.9}$$

where $\mu_w^{m,\text{after}}$ and $\mu_w^{m,\text{before}}$ are, respectively, the origin to destination travel disutility (in time unit inclusive of toll charge) by users of class m between OD pair $w \in W$ after and before the toll roads are introduced to the network.

8.3 PROFITABILITY, SOCIAL WELFARE GAIN AND OPTIMAL PRICE-CAPACITY ADJUSTMENTS

As pointed out earlier, one of the major issues concerning a new private road through a BOT contract is the selection of its capacity and toll charge and the evaluation of the relevant benefits to the private investor, the road users and the whole society. Here we present a simple example with the model presented in Section 8.2 to elucidate this key issue in designing and tolling a private road.

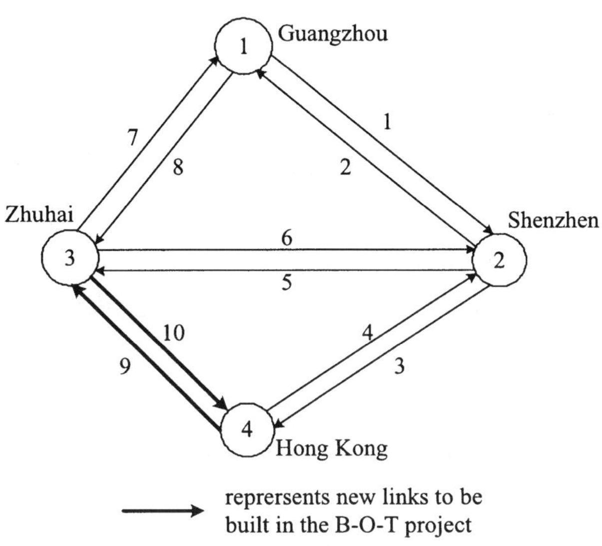

Figure 8.1 The network used for the numerical experiment

8.3.1 Experiment Setting

Consider a simplified version of the intercity expressway network in the Pearl River Delta Region of South China. The network is depicted in Figure 8.1 with 12 OD pairs. For simplicity, we consider homogeneous users with identical VOT, and this corresponds to the network equilibrium model (8.1)-(8.5) with a single class only (class index is thus omitted). The following negative exponential form of OD demand function is adopted

$$d_w = \hat{D}_w \exp(-\gamma\mu_w),\ w \in W \tag{8.10}$$

where $\hat{D}_w$ is the potential demand and μ_w is the travel disutility in time unit (inclusive of equivalent time of toll, if any) between OD pair w, γ is a scaling parameter which reflects the sensitivity of demand to full trip price. The link travel time function is:

$$t_a(v_a) = t_a^0 \left\{ 1.0 + 0.15 \left(\frac{v_a}{\text{cap}} \right)^4 \right\} \tag{8.11}$$

where t_a^0 is the free-flow travel time of link $a \in A$ and $\text{cap} = y_a$ if $a \in \bar{A}$, otherwise $\text{cap} = C_a$. The basic input date of the demand function and link travel time function are presented in Table 8.1 and Table 8.2, respectively.

Table 8.1 Input data for the link travel time function

Link No.	Free-flow travel time (h)	Link capacity (veh/h)	Link No.	Free-flow travel time (h)	Link capacity (veh/h)
1	1.5	9000	6	0.6	3400
2	1.5	9000	7	1.2	9000
3	0.4	7200	8	1.2	9000
4	0.4	7200	9	0.5	to be built
5	0.6	3400	10	0.5	to be built

Table 8.2 Potential demand between each OD pair (veh/h)

	D-1	D-2	D-3	D-4
O-1	0	9000	9000	6000
O-2	9000	0	3000	6000
O-3	9000	3000	0	6000
O-4	6000	6000	6000	0

The BOT project involves construction of an expressway between node 3 and node 4, leading to two new links, link 9 and 10 or $\bar{A} = (9,10)$, which are depicted in Figure 8.1. Because these two new links connect the same nodes in opposite directions, the same capacity and toll charge are assumed. Thus there are two variables only in the problem, toll u and capacity y in each direction associated with the new commercial road. Again for simplicity, the construction cost functions for the new links are assumed to take the following linear form with respect to capacity:

$$I_a(y_a) = \kappa t_a^0 y_a, \ a \in \bar{A} \tag{8.12}$$

where free-flow travel time t_a^0 is proportional to the length of the link and κ is a proportionality parameter. The following parameter values, selected without necessarily representing reasonable values for Pearl Delta Region, are assumed: $\eta = 3.4\times10^{-5}$ (1/h), β=120 (HK\$/h), γ=1.0 (1/h), $\kappa = 1.0\times10^{-6}$ (HK\$/(h · veh/h)).

8.3.2 Characterization and Analysis of Numerical Results

The changes in the profit and welfare gain generated by the new commercial road are calculated for the various combinations of toll and capacity. As shown in Figure 8.2, the positive and negative domains for the profit and social welfare gain are demarcated by the curves of zero welfare gain and zero profit contours in the two-dimensional capacity-toll space. The two curves together partition the capacity-toll space into three sub-areas. This graphical representation allows for intuitive characterization and discussion of the possibilities of profitability and welfare gain open to a road planner. Now we examine the divergence and convergence between welfare gain and profitability by checking the signs of profit and welfare increment in each of the three domains.

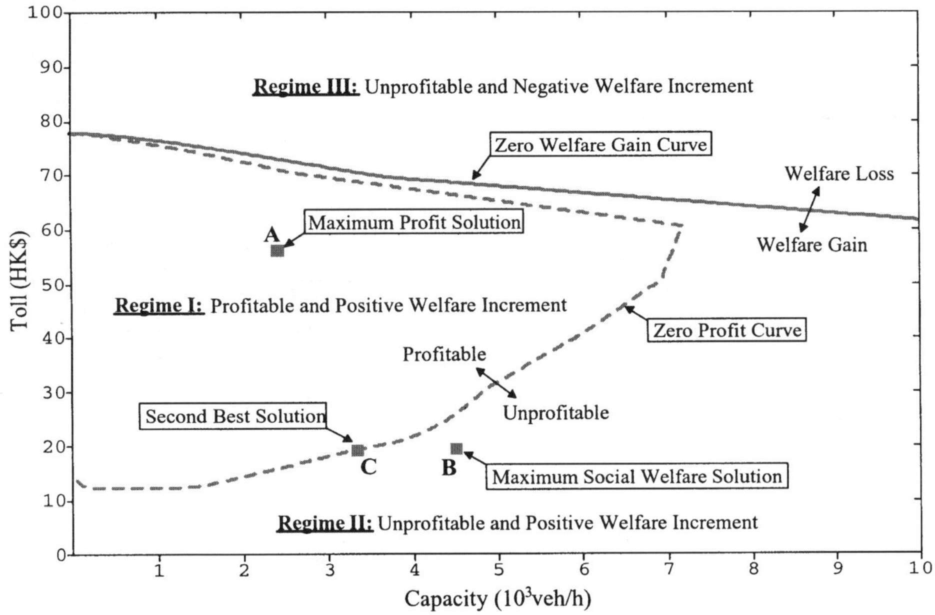

Figure 8.2 Economic regimes associated with the BOT road project in a capacity-toll space

Regime I. Profitable and positive welfare increment. This occurs within the half elliptical zero-profit curve where both profit and welfare gain are strictly positive. This result means that the BOT road project is profitable, and does add to social welfare as well, and hence the highway can be provided privately or an agreement of the BOT project between the government and the private sector can be reached.

Regime II. Unprofitable but positive welfare increment. This occurs in the area below the zero-welfare gain curve and outside the zero-profit elliptical curve. Within this range, the profit is negative but the welfare gain experienced by users is positive. Therefore, a subsidy from the government is essential to the successful implementation of the proposed commercial and private road if the selected capacity-toll combination is located in this domain.

Regime III. Unprofitable and negative welfare increment. This occurs in the area above both the zero-welfare gain curve and the zero-profit curve. This combined negative outcome results from the unrealistically high toll charge in the current example, and is certainly not desirable to both the investor and the users.

Regime IV. Profitable but negative welfare increment. This is not clearly observed in the current example but it is certainly possible in reality. A simple example can be easily constructed to show this case where profitability does not ensure positive welfare increment. For example, with the Braess' paradox network example (Braess, 1968), addition of a new link leads to increase in average travel cost and hence might not add to welfare, but this new link might be profitable since users are willing to patronize it. Therefore, profitability of a new road is not a sufficient ground for embarking upon construction since a new link that is profitable can nevertheless bring a negative welfare increment.

Table 8.3 Representative solutions of the BOT road design problem

Characteristic solution	Toll (HK$)	Capacity (veh/h)	Profit (10^3 HK$)	Welfare Gain (10^3 HK$)	Demand (veh/h)
Max welfare solution	19.0	4,400	-5.08	298.82	28,077
Max welfare solution with zero-profit constraint	20.0	3,900	-0.20	297.30	28,038
Max profit solution	57.0	2,500	160.83	212.39	26,745

Representative solutions. As seen from Figure 8.2 and Table 8.3, the maximum profit solution **A** $(u = 57.0 \text{ HK\$},\ y = 2500 \text{ veh/h})$ is located within *Regime* I representing a preferable win-win situation. The maximum profit that can be achieved is 160.83

$(10^3\ \text{HK\$/h})$. In a monopoly market, a single profit-maximizing firm will choose Point **A**. At the maximum profit solution, a positive welfare increment amounting to 212.39 $(10^3\ \text{HK\$/h})$ is achieved. The social welfare-maximizing Point **B** $(u = 19.0\ \text{HK\$},\ y = 4400\ \text{veh/h})$ is located in *Regime* II below the zero profit curve. Although located near the null-profit curve (see Figure 8.2 and Table 8.3), the welfare-maximizing solution does entail a small loss and cannot be achieved without a subsidy to the project from the government. A subsequent welfare-maximizing solution subject to a null profit constraint is shown by Point **C** $(u = 20.0\ \text{HK\$},\ y = 3900\ \text{veh/h})$ (with a negative but near zero profit due to rounding-up of toll and capacity). This point is of special interest from a government regulative perspective. Efficient toll charge and capacity regulation for the BOT project would require that toll and capacity be set at point **C** so that a feasible efficient solution is realizable. Under the zero-profit constraint, maximizing the social welfare in eqn. (8.8) is equivalent to maximizing net consumer surplus; one can thus expect that point **C** would approximately lead to the lowest generalized travel disutility (inclusive of toll) on the private road and a maximum realized demand throughout the network. It is also observed that the profit-maximizing point **A** is far away from points **C** and **B**, which indicates that the monopoly toll is much higher and the monopoly capacity is lower than those of the welfare-maximizing solutions, with and without zero-profit constraint.

We conclude this section by making two remarks. First, the welfare-maximizing point **B** does not correspond to the conventional first-best solution, which would otherwise optimize capacities and tolls of all links in the network, but involves the situation with un-priced congestion on the existing links of the network. One may thus term point **B** and **C** as the *quasi-first-best* and *quasi-second-best* solutions. Second, the occurrence of all the aforementioned possibilities of profitability and welfare gain in practice depends on the network structure, demand elasticity and the project cost. The question of profitability and the sign of change in social welfare must be examined case by case.

8.4 PROFITABILITY AND WELFARE GAIN OF PRIVATE TOLL ROADS WITH HETEROGENEOUS USERS

A major limitation in the analysis carried out in Section 8.3 is that a single (average) VOT for all road users is assumed in the network equilibrium model (8.1)-(8.5) for traffic forecasts. It is a fact that each user has a different VOT, depending on how much money or time he or she is willing or able to spend on a particular trip. The VOT of a user may greatly influence whether he or she will patronize a tolled road. Thus it is meaningful to incorporate user heterogeneity into private toll road modeling with the multi-class traffic equilibrium model presented in Section 8.2. To do so, we segment the entire population of users into a number of groups or classes according to their VOTs or income levels and then investigate the various possibilities of profitability and welfare gain of the private toll road under various combinations of road capacity and toll charge. In particular, we compare and contrast the outcomes with the case of a single average VOT, and investigate how VOT distribution affects traffic flow and profit forecasts of private toll roads.

8.4.1 Experiment Setting

The experiment setting is basically the same as that in Section 8.3 with the network shown in Figure 8.1 and basic input data in Table 8.1 and Table 8.2, except that the class-specific OD demand functions and VOTs are adopted. We use the following class-specific negative exponential demand functions:

$$d_w^m = \hat{D}_w^m \exp\left(-\gamma \mu_w^m\right),\ w \in W,\ m \in M \tag{8.13}$$

where $\hat{D}_w^m$ is the potential demand and μ_w^m is the travel time (inclusive of equivalent time of toll, if any) for users of class m between OD pair w, γ is again a scaling parameter. Note that in this case parameter γ in function (8.13) is fixed and common for all OD pairs and user classes for simplicity, as there is no way here to differentiate γ across user classes for comparative analysis, unless actual data are available for calibration.

Let $\hat{D}_w$ be the total potential number of users between OD pair $w \in W$ (identical to the single class UE model) and $f(\beta)$ be the continuous probability density function of the VOT β, for the whole population $\hat{D}_w$. Here for simplicity, $f(\beta)$ is assumed to be common for all OD pairs, although an OD pair-specific density function is allowed. Generally, $f(\beta)$ can be inferred from the income distribution of the population. Let $0 \le \beta \le \beta^{\max}$ where $\beta^{\max}$ is the maximum VOT in the population under consideration, and divide the whole interval $[0, \beta^{\max}]$ into $|M|$ intervals of equal length where $|M|$ is the number of user classes:

$$\left[\beta^{m-1}, \beta^m\right] = \left[\frac{m-1}{|M|}\beta^{\max}, \frac{m}{|M|}\beta^{\max}\right],\ m \in M \tag{8.14}$$

with $\beta^0 = 0$ and $\beta^{|M|} = \beta^{\max}$. Let $F(\beta)$ be the cumulative distribution function of $f(\beta)$, then the potential demand for class m is given by:

$$\hat{D}_w^m = \hat{D}_w\left[F\left(\beta^m\right) - F\left(\beta^{m-1}\right)\right],\ w \in W,\ m \in M \tag{8.15}$$

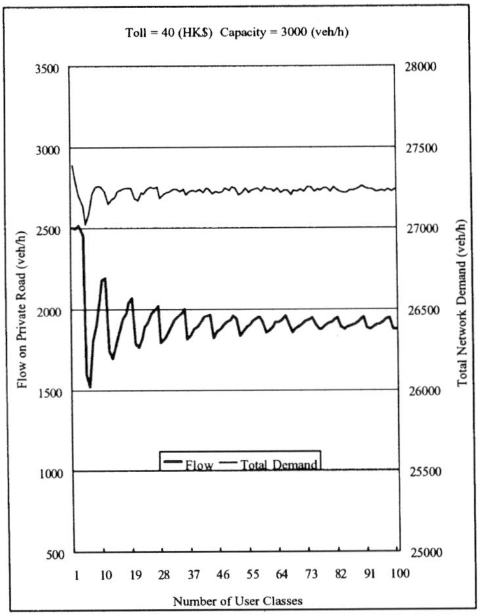

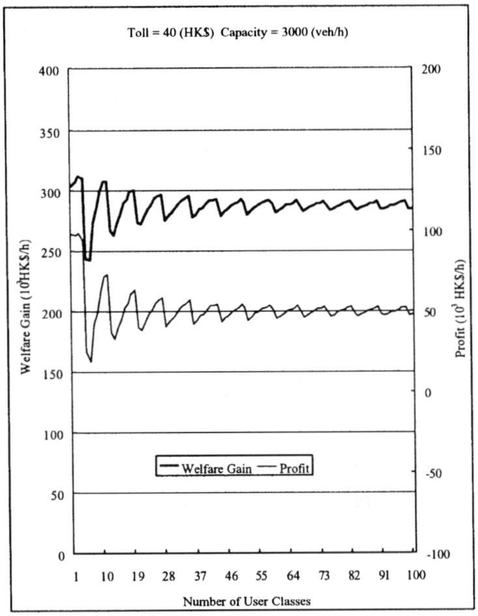

Figure 8.3 Change in flow, profit and welfare on the private road and total traffic demand on the network with the number of user classes for given toll and capacity of the private road

The average VOT for class m, which is used in the discrete multi-class network equilibrium model (8.1)-(8.5), is then determined by

$$\beta_m = \frac{\int_{\beta^{m-1}}^{\beta^m} \beta f(\omega)\,d\omega}{\int_{\beta^{m-1}}^{\beta^m} f(\omega)\,d\omega}, \quad m \in M \tag{8.16}$$

The income distribution of the population in a city can be well fitted by a log-normal distribution given below

$$f(x) = \frac{1}{(\mathrm{SD})\sqrt{2\pi}} x^{-1} \exp\left[-\frac{(\ln x - \mathrm{MV})^2}{2(\mathrm{SD})^2}\right] \tag{8.17}$$

From the income distribution data in Hong Kong, the actual log-normal distribution adopted here has the log-normal mean value of $\mathrm{MV} = 4.6041$ and the log-normal standard deviation value of $\mathrm{SD} = 0.6056$. These values correspond to a mean 120 (HK\$/h) (as used in the single class UE model in Section 8.3) and a standard deviation 79.87 (HK\$/h) of the VOT distribution. In the actual calculation a maximum VOT $\beta^{\max}$=600 (HK\$/h) is adopted. This will truncate 0.012% of the total potential demand with VOT higher than 600 (HK\$/h) in the distribution (the error from this truncation is negligible).

With the above setting, we are able to make a comparison of the numerical results between the single class and multi-class UE models and look into the impacts of user heterogeneity on the profitability and social welfare gain of the private toll road.

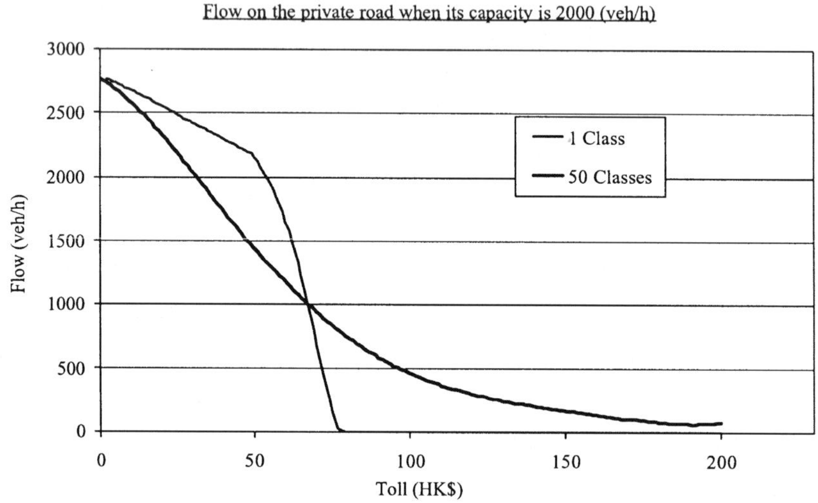

Figure 8.4 Change in flow on the private road with the level of toll charge for given capacity (2000 veh/h): the single class versus multi-class network equilibrium models

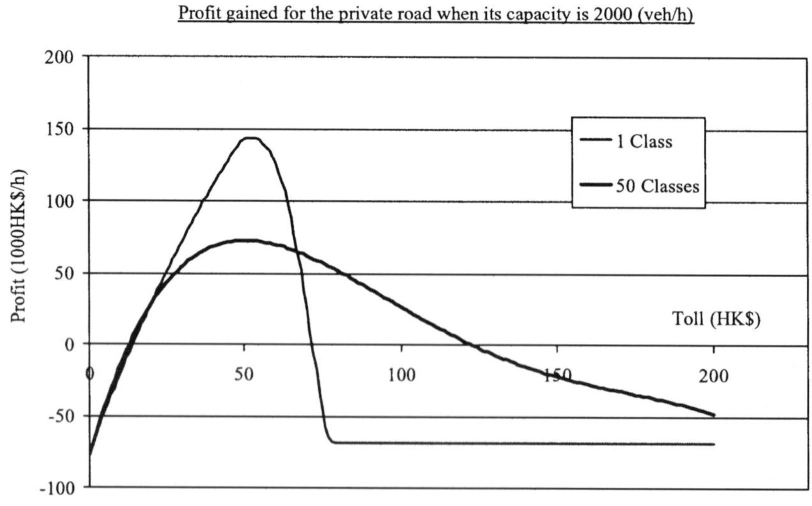

Figure 8.5 Change in profit for the private road with the level of toll charge for given capacity (2000 veh/h): the single class versus multi-class network equilibrium models

8.4.2 Characterization and Analysis of Numerical Results

Figure 8.3 depicts the change of the flow on the toll road, the total realized demand on the network, the profit and the total social welfare gain generated from the toll road, when the whole population of users is classified into different number of user classes. The patterns of change are generated for the case with a capacity of $y = 3000$ veh/h and a toll charge of $u = 40.0$ HK$ for the proposed private toll road. Note that "$m = 1$" corresponds to the standard single mean VOT equilibrium model used in Section 8.3. As the number of user classes used in the multi-class network equilibrium model increases, all the four measures (total social welfare gain, profit for the private road, flow through the private road and the total realized network demand) tend to stabilize. This is what we expect as a larger number $|M|$ of user classes in the multi-class equilibrium model will give a better approximation of the real network equilibrium solution with a continuous VOT distribution across the population. We acknowledge that the visualized convergence pattern depends on the vertical scales of the four measures. Nevertheless, value of $|M|$=50 is already a sufficiently good approximation of the continuous VOT distribution case. Thus all the following results for the multi-class case are generated with $|M|$=50.

Figures 8.4 and 8.5 depict the change in flow and profit of the private road with the amount of toll charge for a given capacity $y = 2000$ (veh/h) when the standard single class and multi-class network equilibrium models are respectively adopted. It is interesting to look at the discrepancy of the predicted results by the two types of model. In comparison with the more realistic multi-class case, the conventional single class model overestimates the flow and the resulting profit of the private road, when the toll charge is low (less than about 70 HK$). The reason is that the single class model assumes homogeneous users with an identical VOT, and all users with this common VOT may afford to use the toll road when the toll charge is low. However, in reality there is a certain segment of users who have lower VOT and may not wish to use the toll road even the toll charge is not high. The multi-class network equilibrium model, however, recognizes existence of such low-income users in flow prediction for the toll road. On the other hand, as the toll charge is high, the single class model underestimates the flow and the resulting profit of the toll road, because, in this case, the single class model assumes all users are homogeneous and may not be willing to pay a higher toll charge. Nevertheless, the multi-class model acknowledges the fact that there is a certain portion of high-income users in the whole population, who still wish to patronize the expensive, but fast toll road. Thus, the road investor can still extract greater profit from these time-sensitive users that demand faster service.

Figure 8.6 displays the change of net social welfare gain for the same case. The single class model underestimates the welfare gain generated from the toll road when its toll charge is either low or high, and overestimates the social welfare gain in a smaller interval of mediate toll charge around 50 HK$.

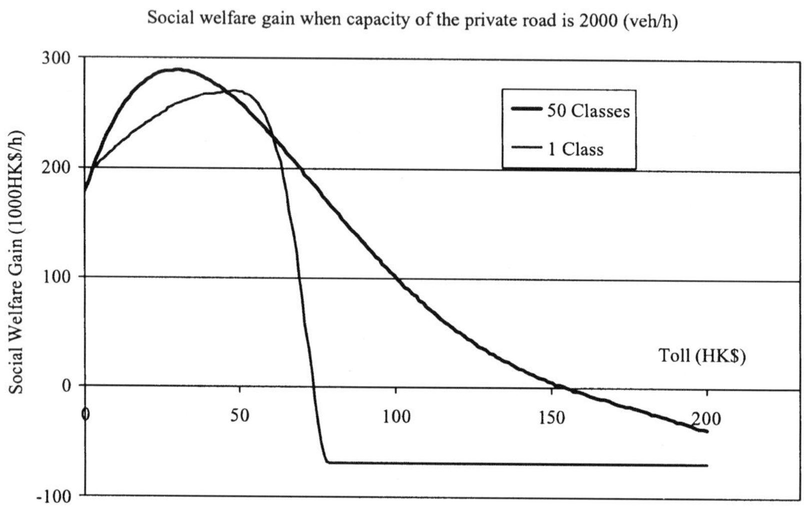

Figure 8.6 Change in social welfare for the private road with the level of toll charge for given capacity (2000 veh/h): the single class versus multi-class network equilibrium models

Figure 8.7 displays the profitable domains of the private toll road together with the profit-maximizing solution in the toll-capacity two dimensional space ascertained by the standard single mean VOT model and the multi-class equilibrium model, respectively. The multi-class model predicts a much wider range of toll charges and lower range of road capacity (investment level) that leads to a positive profit. In contrast, the single class model predicts a much wider range of capacity and a limited narrow range of toll charge that leads to a positive profit. The reason is exactly the same as mentioned above. The multi-class model acknowledges unwilling-to-pay users even at low toll charge, and willing-to-pay users even at high toll charge. The policy implication of this observation is that adoption of the conventional standard single class model may lead to over-investment in the BOT road project by a private potential investor, as demonstrated by the two patterns of profitable domain. Figure 8.8 depicts the domains with positive welfare gain together with the welfare-maximizing solutions in the toll-capacity space determined by the two types of model. Within the realistic road capacity level, the multi-class equilibrium model predicts a much higher toll level that gives rise to a positive welfare gain because of its recognition of the existence of high-income users. Finally, we point out that the domain of positive welfare gain generally embraces the profitable domain for each type of model applied to the current network case. This implies that a BOT road, if profitable, will generally add to the social welfare as well. In this case, the road can be provided privately.

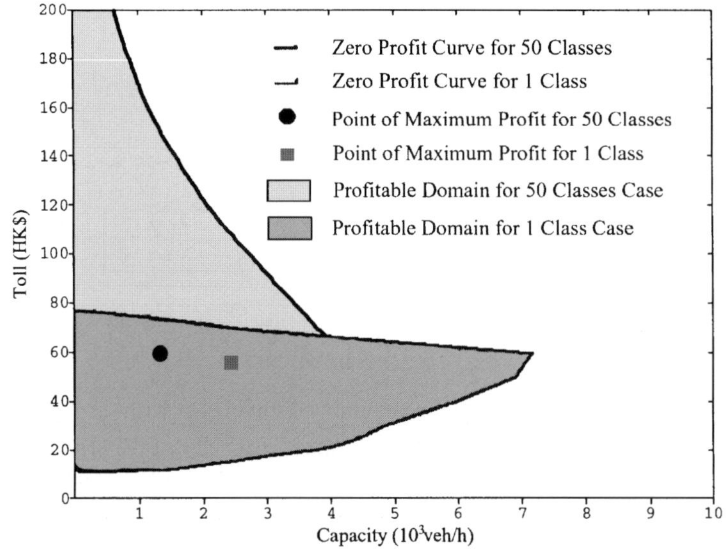

Figure 8.7 Profitable domain in the toll-capacity two dimensional space: the single class versus multi-class network equilibrium models

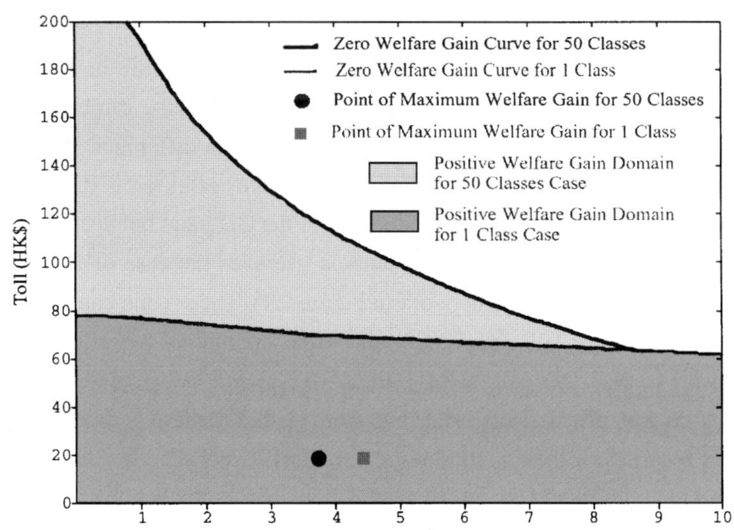

Figure 8.8 Positive welfare gain domain in the toll-capacity two dimensional space: the single class versus multi-class network equilibrium models

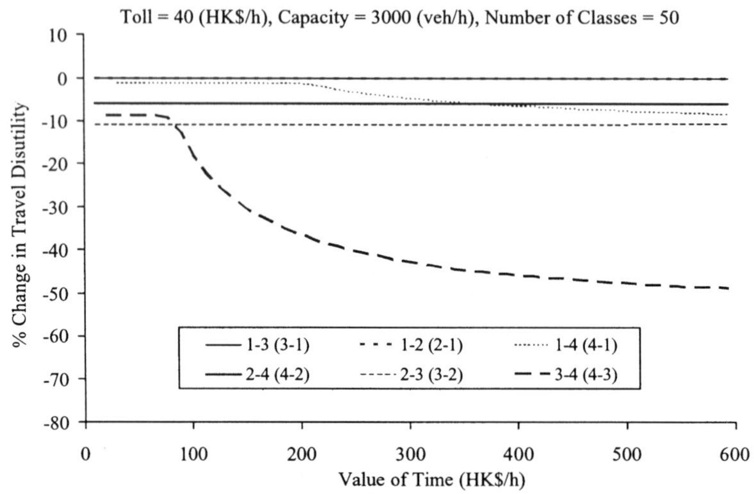

Figure 8.9 Percentage reduction of the generalized travel cost with respect to the users' VOT between each OD pair for given toll and capacity of the private road

One favorable advantage of the multi-class network equilibrium model is its capability to assess the distribution of the benefits generated by the toll road across different classes of user between each OD pair. Figure 8.9 plots the percentage reduction of origin to destination travel disutility (inclusive of equivalent time of toll) by users with different VOT for the case of $u = 40$ (HK\$/h) and $y = 3000$ (veh/h). Clearly, not all users benefit equally from construction of the new toll road, depending on the location of the new toll road and the individual OD pair in the network. As expected, even within the same OD pair, different classes of user enjoy different amounts of benefit due to the difference in their VOT. From the Figure, we can classify the OD pairs into three categories in terms of the benefit derived from the new toll road. The first category consists of the OD pairs between which travel costs do not change or the toll road has no impacts on users, as the case of OD pair: $1 \leftrightarrow 3$ and $1 \leftrightarrow 2$ (refer to this figure and the network in Figure 8.1). The second category consists of the OD pairs between which all users enjoy the same amount of benefit or travel disutility reduction, as the case of OD pair: $2 \leftrightarrow 4$ and $2 \leftrightarrow 3$. Users between these two OD pairs in this category do not use the toll road, but from it they benefit indirectly, because traffic congestion is reduced on their route due to some traffic attracted to the new toll road. The third category includes the OD pairs between which users enjoy benefit derived from the new toll roads, and the benefit or travel disutility reduction varies across user classes, depending on their VOTs. OD pairs, $1 \leftrightarrow 4$ and $3 \leftrightarrow 4$, belong to this category in the network. Users between OD pairs in this category may directly use the new toll roads and higher-income users enjoy more benefit because of their more willingness-to-pay, as can be seen from the figure.

8.5 SELF-FINANCIAL IN GENERAL NETWORKS

The pricing and self-financing problem is about whether the revenue from socially optimal pricing on a road can cover the capital cost for constructing and maintaining this road. The classic self-financing theorem is developed for a single road and holds under the following first-best conditions: (i) in addition to optimal tolling, the capacity of the road must be chosen optimally; (ii) there is a constant return to scale in road construction; and (iii) the trip cost (link travel time) function is homogeneous of degree zero in traffic volume and capacity. In this section, we deal thoroughly with the relationship between pricing, capacity choice and financing in a general network with a single or multiple types of vehicles under the first-best and second-best conditions.

8.5.1 Self-financing Rules with a Single Type of Vehicles

Assumption 8.1 (First-best conditions for pricing and capacity choice in networks) Network topology is given and pricing and capacity choice are unrestricted and apply for the entire set of links in the network.

Under Assumption 8.1, the problem of interest here is to set tolls and capacities for all links in the network to maximize the total social welfare. The problem with a single type of vehicle is formulated below:

$$\max_{\mathbf{y},\mathbf{v},\mathbf{d}} \sum_{w\in W}\int_0^{d_w} B_w(\omega)\,d\omega - \sum_{a\in A} t_a(v_a, y_a)v_a - \sum_{a\in A}\eta I_a(y_a) \tag{8.18}$$

subject to

$$\sum_{r\in R_w} f_{rw} = d_w,\ w\in W \tag{8.19}$$

$$v_a = \sum_{w\in W}\sum_{r\in R_w} f_{rw}\delta_{ar},\ a\in A \tag{8.20}$$

$$f_{rw} \geq 0,\ d_w \geq 0,\ r\in R_w,\ w\in W \tag{8.21}$$

where η is, as defined before, a parameter transferring the capital cost of the project into unit period cost, without loss of generality, VOT β is not explicitly included in the model by assuming a value of units for brevity throughout this section. From the first-order optimality conditions for the above minimization problem, we have

$$c_{rw} = \mu_w, \text{ if } f_{rw} > 0;\ c_{rw} \geq \mu_w, \text{ if } f_{rw} = 0,\ r \in R_w,\ w \in W \tag{8.22}$$

$$B_w(d_w) = \mu_w, \text{ if } d_w > 0;\ B_w(d_w) \leq \mu_w, \text{ if } d_w = 0,\ w \in W \tag{8.23}$$

where μ_w is the Lagrange multiplier associated with constraint (8.19) and

$$c_{rw} = \sum_{a \in A} \tilde{t}_a(v_a, y_a)\delta_{ar},\ r \in R_w,\ w \in W \tag{8.24}$$

$$\tilde{t}_a(v_a, y_a) = t_a(v_a, y_a) + v_a \frac{\partial t_a(v_a, y_a)}{\partial v_a},\ a \in A \tag{8.25}$$

It is clear that the optimality conditions (8.22)-(8.25) are the network equilibrium conditions with elastic demand if the link travel time governing the equilibrium is given by eqn. (8.25). For realizing eqn. (8.25), a toll equal to the congestion externality should be charged as given below:

$$u_a = v_a \frac{\partial t_a(v_a, y_a)}{\partial v_a},\ a \in A \tag{8.26}$$

Then, a new network demand-performance equilibrium is established (see, Chapter 2 and Chapter 3). This new equilibrium is precisely a system optimum in the sense that the social surplus is maximized. Furthermore, suppose an interior optimum or all $y_a > 0,\ a \in A$ at system optimum, then the first-order optimality condition with respect to link capacity is given by:

$$v_a \frac{\partial t_a(v_a, y_a)}{\partial y_a} + \eta \frac{\mathrm{d}I_a(y_a)}{\mathrm{d}y_a} = 0,\ a \in A \tag{8.27}$$

This states that the road capacity should be expanded to the point where the marginal cost of an extra unit of capacity is equal to the marginal value of user cost savings brought about by that investment.

With the optimally selected link tolls and capacities, we are now in a position to look into the relationship between the toll revenue and road construction cost, after the following assumption is made.

Assumption 8.2 (Homogeneous of degree zero link travel time function) The link travel time function $t_a(v_a, y_a)$, $a \in A$ is homogeneous of degree zero in both link flow v_a and link capacity y_a.

Note that a function, $f(\mathbf{x}) = f(x_1, x_2, \cdots, x_n)$, is homogeneous of degree k if $f(\phi x_1, \phi x_2, \cdots, \phi x_n) = \phi^k f(x_1, x_2, \cdots, x_n)$. Assumption 8.2 is equivalent to assuming that the speed of traffic on the road is dependent only on the volume-capacity ratio of the road, that is,

$t_a(v_a, y_a) = t_a(v_a/y_a)$, $a \in A$ such as the BPR type of function used before. Under this assumption, we readily obtain

$$y_a \frac{\partial t_a(v_a, y_a)}{\partial y_a} = -v_a \frac{\partial t_a(v_a, y_a)}{\partial v_a}, \ a \in A \tag{8.28}$$

Equations (8.26)-(8.28) together imply that

$$u_a v_a = \eta y_a \frac{\mathrm{d}I_a(y_a)}{\mathrm{d}y_a} = \eta I_a(y_a) E_{I_a}^{y_a}, \ a \in A \tag{8.29}$$

where $E_{I_a}^{y_a}$ denotes the elasticity of investment cost with respect to output capacity, defined as

$$E_{I_a}^{y_a} = \frac{\mathrm{d}I_a(y_a)}{\mathrm{d}y_a} \frac{y_a}{I_a(y_a)}, \ a \in A \tag{8.30}$$

Now we introduce the following additional assumption.

Assumption 8.3 (Constant return to scale in road construction) There is a constant return to scale in road construction, namely, $E_{I_a}^{y_a} = 1$ or $I_a(y_a) = \kappa_a y_a$, $a \in A$, where κ_a denotes the unit capital cost for link a and can be different for different links.

Under assumption 8.3, we then have from (8.29):

$$u_a v_a = \eta \kappa_a y_a = \eta I_a(y_a), \ a \in A \tag{8.31}$$

It now becomes clear that the left-hand side revenue generated from the optimum road user charge in a link just covers the right-hand side capital cost of road construction for this link. This observation is true for each individual link in the network. With increasing returns to scale, $E_{I_a}^{y_a} < 1$, the revenue will fail to cover the capacity costs and thus the road will have to be subsidized for efficient operation; and similarly, with decreasing returns to scale, $E_{I_a}^{y_a} > 1$, the revenue will exceed the capital costs and the road will earn a surplus. We thus have the following Self-financing theorem.

Theorem 8.1. *In a general network under Assumptions 8.1-8.3, the revenue from socially optimal pricing on a road just covers the capital cost for constructing the road. This break-even result holds for each road individually in the full network and consequently to the network in aggregate, provided that each link is optimally priced and all capacities are optimized.*

Note that the conditions for the above self-financing theorem to hold are rather ideal and restrictive. In the first place, it is impracticable to optimally design and construct a complete new network. A very frequent case is, after all, that one or more new roads are added to an existing network. Nevertheless, it can be found from its derivation that the self-financing theorem does throw light on the case when only a subset of new links is introduced to an existing network but all links (new and existing links) are optimally priced. Namely, if eqns (8.24) and (8.25) hold for all links, then the network traffic equilibrium conditions are maintained, but eqn. (8.28) is applied to individual links without direct relevance to the equilibrium conditions. Hence, the break-even result does hold for the subset of new links individually for given and fixed capacities of existing links in the network. We thus have the following theorem under this relaxed condition.

Theorem 8.2. *Suppose one or more new roads are introduced to an existing network and Assumptions 8.2-8.3 are satisfied, then the revenue from socially optimal pricing on a new road just covers the capital cost for constructing this road, as long as all existing and new links are optimally priced and the capacities of new links are optimally selected.*

Two points deserve our attention here. First, the break-even result applies for the new links only individually or in aggregate, the revenue from marginal-cost pricing on the rest of the network links is intact and hence the whole network makes a profit from the socially optimal pricing. Second, albeit the self-financing result holds for individual links in both Theorems 8.1 and 8.2, the resulting optimal toll setting and capacity choice are inter-twined because the tolls and capacities are calculated on the basis of link flows that are determined from the global network equilibrium conditions (see Section 3.2 in Chapter 3 for a prior discussion).

Theorem 6.1 and Theorem 6.2 are with respect to the situation under a first-best pricing environment, albeit capacity choice can apply for a subset of new links only. We naturally wonder what happens with financing road capacities when toll roads coexist with free roads in a common network. A general answer to this question proves to be difficult, as it depends on the network topology, the locations of toll roads as well as the OD demand and link performance functions. Nonetheless, some meaningful insight can be obtained from the following two styalized examples.

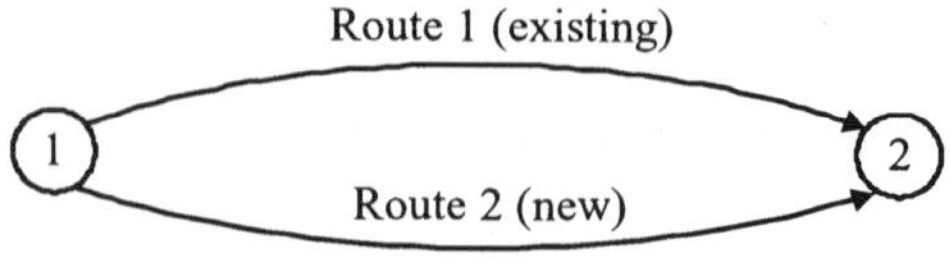

Figure 8.10 A two-parallel-route problem

Example 8.1 (The two parallel route problem) Consider a simple network in Figure 8.10, with two competing congested roads (or links) (the standard two-route problem in the literature). Route (or link) 1 already exists and remains free of toll and route 2 will be built and tolled.

Omitting the OD index for a single OD pair, we have the following equilibrium-constrained welfare-maximizing problem with respect to the toll and capacity of the new route 2 (suppose both routes are used at optimum, and unit capacity construction cost for route 2 is constant).

$$\max_{v_1, v_2, u_2, y_2} \int_0^d B(\omega)\mathrm{d}\omega - t_1(v_1)v_1 - t_2(v_2, y_2)v_2 - \eta\kappa_2 y_2 \tag{8.32}$$

subject to

$$B(d) = t_1(v_1) \tag{8.33}$$

$$B(d) = t_2(v_2, y_2) + u_2 \tag{8.34}$$

where $d = v_1 + v_2$ and constraints (8.33) and (8.34) characterize the UE conditions. Consider the following Lagrangian:

$$\begin{aligned} L(v_1, v_2, u_2, y_2, \lambda_1, \lambda_2) = & \int_0^{v_1+v_2} B(\omega)\mathrm{d}\omega - t_1(v_1)v_1 - t_2(v_2, y_2)v_2 - \eta I_2(y_2) \\ & + \lambda_1\left[t_1(v_1) - B(v_1 + v_2)\right] + \lambda_2\left[t_2(v_2, y_2) + u_2 - B(v_1 + v_2)\right] \end{aligned} \tag{8.35}$$

The first-order conditions are:

$$\frac{\partial L}{\partial v_1} = B(d) - t_1(v_1) - v_1 t_1'(v_1) + \lambda_1 t_1'(v_1) - (\lambda_1 + \lambda_2)B'(d) = 0 \tag{8.36}$$

$$\frac{\partial L}{\partial v_2} = B(d) - t_2(v_2, y_2) - v_2 t_2'(v_2, y_2) + \lambda_2 t_2'(v_2, y_2) - (\lambda_1 + \lambda_2)B'(d) = 0 \tag{8.37}$$

$$\frac{\partial L}{\partial \lambda_1} = t_1(v_1) - B(d) = 0 \tag{8.38}$$

$$\frac{\partial L}{\partial \lambda_2} = t_2(v_2, y_2) + u_2 - B(d) = 0 \tag{8.39}$$

$$\frac{\partial L}{\partial u_2} = \lambda_2 = 0 \tag{8.40}$$

$$\frac{\partial L}{\partial y_2} = (\lambda_2 - v_2)\frac{\partial t_2(v_2, y_2)}{\partial y_2} - \eta\kappa_2 = 0 \tag{8.41}$$

where $B'(\cdot) = \mathrm{d}B(\cdot)/\mathrm{d}(\cdot)$, $t_1'(\cdot) = \mathrm{d}t_1'(\cdot)/\mathrm{d}(\cdot)$ and $t_2'(\cdot,\#) = \partial t_2'(\cdot,\#)/\partial(\cdot)$. Substituting eqns. (8.40) and (8.38) into (8.36) and solving for λ_1 yields $\lambda_1 = v_1 t_1'(v_1)/\left(t_1'(v_1) - B'(d)\right)$. Substituting λ_1, λ_2 and (8.39) into (8.37) yields the optimal link toll

$$u_2 = v_2 t_2'(v_2, y_2) + \alpha v_1 t_1'(v_1) \tag{8.42}$$

where

$$\alpha = -\left(1 - \frac{t_1'(v_1)}{B'(d)}\right)^{-1} \tag{8.43}$$

Evidently, $-1 \le \alpha \le 0$ in view of $B'(d) < 0$ and $t_1'(v_1) \ge 0$. This equation shows that the optimal toll should be equal to the marginal external congestion costs on the new tolled road minus a (positive) term consisting of a fraction (between 1 and 0) of the marginal external congestion costs on the un-tolled route. This result reflects the fact that one should also take into account the flow "spill-over" effect on the un-tolled route in order to maximize the social welfare.

If the link travel time function $t_2(v_2, y_2)$ is homogeneous of degree zero, then eqn. (8.28) holds for link 2. In addition, from eqns. (8.42) and (8.41), we arrive at

$$u_2 v_2 = \eta \kappa_2 y_2 + \alpha v_1 t_1'(v_1) v_2 < \eta \kappa_2 y_2 = \eta I_2(y_2) \tag{8.44}$$

Equations (8.42) and (8.44) together tell us that: *in the presence of an un-tolled substitute to a new toll road, the second-best toll falls short of the marginal external congestion cost on the new route and the resulting revenue generated will fail to cover the capacity cost.*

Example 8.2 (The complementary two-serial-route problem) As depicted in Figure 8.11, the existing network comprises only one road (route 1), connecting nodes 1 and 2. Construction is contemplated of a road from node 2 to node 3. After the second new road is built, users make trips from node 1 to both nodes 2 and 3.

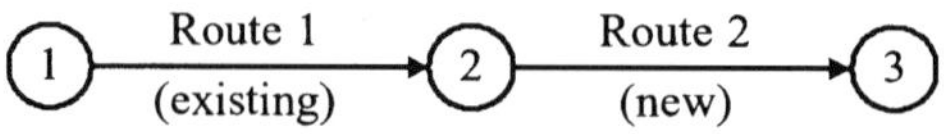

Figure 8.11 A two-serial-route problem

The equilibrium-constrained welfare-maximizing problem with respect to the toll and capacity of the new route 2 (suppose again both routes are used at optimum, and unit capacity construction cost for route 2 is constant) is given as:

$$\max_{u_2, y_2} \int_0^{d_{1\to 2}} B_{1\to 2}(\omega)d\omega + \int_0^{d_{1\to 3}} B_{1\to 3}(\omega)d\omega - t_1(v_1)v_1 - t_2(v_2, y_2)v_2 - \eta\kappa_2 y_2 \tag{8.45}$$

subject to

$$B_{1\to 2}(d_{1\to 2}) = t_1(v_1) \tag{8.46}$$

$$B_{1\to 3}(d_{1\to 3}) = t_1(v_1) + t_2(v_2, y_2) + u_2 \tag{8.47}$$

where $d_{1\to 2} + d_{1\to 3} = v_1$ and $d_{1\to 3} = v_2$ and constraints (8.46) and (8.47) characterize the demand-supply equilibrium.

Proceeding along lines similar to those which led to eqn. (8.42) yields

$$u_2 = v_2 t_2'(v_2, y_2) + \alpha v_1 t_1'(v_1) \tag{8.48}$$

where

$$\alpha = \left(1 - \frac{t_1'(v_1)}{B_{1\to 2}'(d_{1\to 2})}\right)^{-1} \text{ and } 0 \le \alpha \le 1.0 \tag{8.49}$$

This equation says, simply enough, that users who pay toll are charged in excess of their marginal external cost on the new tolled links. The extra toll charge (the second term) is a fraction of the marginal external congestion cost on the un-tolled link 1 and the fraction depends on the demand elasticity for the un-tolled users from node 1 to node 2. This is intuitively obvious because the external costs of users from 1 to 3 on link 1 are partly internalized through the charge on link 2.

If we further assume that users make trips from node 2 to node 3 as well, we also obtain the same toll expression given by (8.48), but α is given by

$$\alpha = \left(1 + \frac{B_{1\to 3}'}{B_{2\to 3}'} - \left(\frac{B_{1\to 2}' + B_{2\to 3}' + B_{1\to 3}'}{B_{1\to 2}' B_{2\to 3}'}\right) t_1'(v_1)\right)^{-1} \text{ and } 0 \le \alpha \le 1.0 \tag{8.50}$$

An immediate consequence of the charge on the new toll road 2 greater than the external congestion cost is

$$u_2 v_2 = \eta \kappa_2 y_2 + \alpha v_1 t_1'(v_1) v_2 > \eta \kappa_2 y_2 = \eta I_2(y_2) \tag{8.51}$$

where α is given by (8.49) or (8.50). The toll revenue on the new link 2 exceeds its capacity cost. This observation shows that: *in the presence of an un-tolled complement to a new toll road, the second-best toll is larger than the marginal external congestion cost on the new route and the resulting revenue generated will exceed the capacity cost.*

The above two examples, albeit involving perfectly substitutable and complementary routes, do show that the exact self-financing, a deficit or a surplus budget on a network with un-tolled links, would be possible under second-best optimal pricing and capacity choice. We now attempt to look at the issue in a general network. To keep the problem manageable, we suppose all paths in each OD pair are used (or alternatively all shortest (or active) paths in the network have strictly positive flows and the subset of active paths does not change in the relevant toll-capacity domain considered). With this simplifying assumption, the equilibrium conditions (8.22) and (8.23) become equality constraints for all relevant paths. The social-welfare maximizing problem with respect to the toll charge u_b of a single toll road $b \in A$ is given as the following standard nonlinear programming problem (here capacity choice is not considered).

$$\max_{u_b} \sum_{w\in W} \int_0^{d_w} B_w(\omega)\mathrm{d}\omega - \sum_{a\in A} t_a(v_a)v_a \tag{8.52}$$

subject to

$$\sum_{a\in A} t_a(v_a)\delta_{ar} + u_b\delta_{br} = B_w(d_w),\ r\in R_w,\ w\in W \tag{8.53}$$

$$f_{rw} \geq 0,\ r\in R_w,\ w\in W \tag{8.54}$$

where $v_a = \sum_{w\in W}\sum_{r\in R_w} f_{rw}\delta_{ar}$, $a\in A$ and $d_w = \sum_{r\in R_w} f_{rw}$, $w\in W$.

Now we consider the following Lagrangian in terms of path flow and Lagrange multipliers:

$$\begin{aligned} L(\mathbf{f},\lambda) = & \sum_{w\in W} \int_0^{\sum_{r\in R_w} f_{rw}} B_w(\omega)\mathrm{d}\omega - \sum_{a\in A}\left(\sum_{w\in W}\sum_{r\in R_w} f_{rw}\delta_{ar}\right) t_a\left(\sum_{w\in W}\sum_{r\in R_w} f_{rw}\delta_{ar}\right) \\ & + \sum_{w\in W}\sum_{r\in R_w}\lambda_{rw}\left[\sum_{a\in A} t_a\left(\sum_{w\in W}\sum_{r\in R_w} f_{rw}\delta_{ar}\right)\delta_{ar} + u_b\delta_{br} - B_w\left(\sum_{r\in R_w} f_{rw}\right)\right] \end{aligned} \tag{8.55}$$

where $\lambda_{rw}, r\in R_w, w\in W$ are the Lagrange multipliers associated with constraints (8.53). By our assumption that $f_{rw} > 0$ for any $r\in R_w, w\in W$, the first-order optimality conditions for the above minimization problem become

$$\frac{\partial L}{\partial f_{rw}} = B_w - \sum_{a\in A}(t_a + v_a t'_a)\delta_{ar} + \lambda_{rw}\sum_{a\in A} t'_a\delta_{ar} - B'_w\sum_{r\in R_w}\lambda_{rw} = 0 \tag{8.56}$$

$$\frac{\partial L}{\partial u_b} = \sum_{w\in W}\sum_{r\in R_w}\lambda_{rw}\delta_{br} = 0 \tag{8.57}$$

$$\frac{\partial L}{\partial \lambda_{rw}} = \sum_{a\in A} t_a\delta_{ar} + u_b\delta_{br} - B_w = 0 \tag{8.58}$$

Substituting eqn. (8.58) into eqn. (8.56) yields the following expression for the Lagrange multiplier

$$\lambda_{rw} = \frac{\sum_{a\in A} v_a t'_a\delta_{ar} - u_b\delta_{br}}{\sum_{a\in A}\delta_{ar}t'_a - B'_w\sum_{r\in R_w}\lambda_{rw}} \tag{8.59}$$

Substituting eqn. (8.59) into eqn. (8.57) yields, after rearrangement, the following expression of the link toll

$$u_b = v_b t'_b + \sum_{a\in A, a\neq b}\alpha_a v_a t'_a \tag{8.60}$$

where

$$\alpha_a = \left\{\sum_{w\in W}\sum_{r\in R_w}\frac{\delta_{ar}\delta_{br}}{\sum_{a\in A}\delta_{ar}t'_a - B'_w\sum_{r\in R_w}\lambda_{rw}}\left(\sum_{w\in W}\sum_{r\in R_w}\frac{\delta_{br}}{\sum_{a\in A}\delta_{ar}t'_a - B'_w\sum_{r\in R_w}\lambda_{rw}}\right)^{-1}\right\},\ a\in A,\ a\neq b \tag{8.61}$$

In view of $\delta_{ar} = 0$ or 1, we have

$$-\left|\sum_{w\in W}\sum_{r\in R_w}\frac{\delta_{br}}{\sum_{a\in A}\delta_{ar}t'_a - B'_w\sum_{r\in R_w}\lambda_{rw}}\right| \le \sum_{w\in W}\sum_{r\in R_w}\frac{\delta_{ar}\delta_{br}}{\sum_{a\in A}\delta_{ar}t'_a - B'_w\sum_{r\in R_w}\lambda_{rw}} \le \left|\sum_{w\in W}\sum_{r\in R_w}\frac{\delta_{br}}{\sum_{a\in A}\delta_{ar}t'_a - B'_w\sum_{r\in R_w}\lambda_{rw}}\right|$$

This means that in eqn. (8.61) we have

$$-1 \le \alpha_a \le 1.0,\, a\in A,\, a \ne b \tag{8.62}$$

The actual sign of α_a may well depend on whether link a is substitutable or complementary to the new toll road b which can be ascertained through the sensitivity analysis method of network traffic equilibrium described in Chapter 4.

Equations (8.60) and (8.62) generalize the early observation that the second-best efficient toll u_b on a new toll road b is equal to the marginal external cost on road b plus or minus a fraction of the marginal external cost on each of the un-tolled links in the network. Therefore, *the second-best toll on a new link can be either larger or smaller than or equal to the marginal external cost on that link, and as a result, the revenue generated will go either above or below or equal to the construction cost, for its optimally selected capacity.*

Occurrence of each possibility with an efficient toll road in a second-best environment depends on, among many others, the network topology, the OD demands and the location of the toll road in the network. With this observation in mind, we now recall our early numerical results shown in Figure 8.2 in Section 8.3. The efficient (*quasi-first-best*) point **B** in a second-best environment for the network in Figure 8.1 is associated with a *negative* profit or the self-financing does not hold for this new toll road. This is, as argued above, because there is *un-priced* congestion on the existing links of the network, only the toll revenue and construction cost of the new links are accounted for in the profit, and only the impact of the new links contributes to the change in social surplus. In this circumstance, it would be expected that, after compromising the substitutable and complementary impacts on the marginal external costs on the rest links of the network, the tolls on the new links may be set below the actual first-best levels, which would have been obtained if all existing and new links in the network were optimally priced.

8.5.2 Self-financing Rules with Multiple Types of Vehicles

We make a few extensions of the self-financing theory presented in the previous subsection by considering multiple types of vehicles on the network, such as buses versus cars, heavy versus light vehicles and including fixed and variable road maintenance costs. Such extensions will allow us to explicitly recognize the fact that different types of vehicles make different contributes to traffic congestion and road damage and thus should be subjected to different toll charges. The interaction between different types of flow when sharing the same roadway induces non-separable and, in general, asymmetric link cost functions, as discussed in Section 2.3 of Chapter 2.

To be distinguished from the multiple user classes by VOT, let K denote the set of weight-types of vehicles. It is reasonable to assume that the demand by users of one type of vehicles depends only on its own price. Let $B_w^k(d_w^k)$ denote the separable OD benefit (inverse demand) function by vehicle type $k \in K$. Let v_a^k be the flow on link a associated with vehicle type k and $t_a^k(\mathbf{v}_a)$ be vehicle type-specific link travel cost function on link $a \in A$, where $\mathbf{v}_a = \{v_a^k,\ k \in K\}^{\mathrm{T}}$, $a \in A$ and flow interaction between different links is not considered. We say the problem is asymmetric when the influence of one vehicle-type on another is not symmetric; that is, for $i \neq j$, there holds $\partial t_a^i(\mathbf{v}_a)/\partial v_a^j \neq \partial t_a^j(\mathbf{v}_a)/\partial v_a^i$. This is indeed true for a road where the influence of trucks and buses on the delay functions of cars is strong, but not the contrary. Note that it is of sufficient realism in the present context to consider the flow interactions across types of vehicles on the same link; interactions across different links on the network are negligible. The variable maintenance cost of a roadway link for a unit time period depends on the flow composition owing to the different degrees of road damage by different weight-type vehicles and is denoted by $M_a(\mathbf{v}_a)$. The fixed maintenance cost per unit period can be assumed to depend on the roadway width or capacity and can be absorbed into the construction cost function, $I_a(y_a)$, and thus is not explicitly considered in what follows. With these considerations, we now formally solve the following social welfare maximizing problem:

$$\max_{\mathbf{y},\mathbf{v},\mathbf{d}} \sum_{w \in W} \sum_{k \in K} \int_0^{d_w^k} B_w^k(\omega)\,\mathrm{d}\omega - \sum_{a \in A} \sum_{k \in K} t_a^k(\mathbf{v}_a, y_a) v_a^k - \sum_{a \in A} M_a(\mathbf{v}_a) - \sum_{a \in A} \eta I_a(y_a) \tag{8.63}$$

subject to

$$\sum_{r \in R_w} f_{rw}^k = d_w^k,\ k \in K,\ w \in W \tag{8.64}$$

$$v_a^k = \sum_{w \in W} \sum_{r \in R_w} f_{rw}^k \delta_{ar},\ k \in K,\ a \in A \tag{8.65}$$

$$f_{rw}^k \geq 0,\ d_w^k \geq 0,\ k \in K,\ r \in R_w,\ w \in W \tag{8.66}$$

Suppose the functions involved are differentiable and a unique optimum solution exists, then proceeding in a fashion analogous to that which led from the first-order optimality conditions to eqns. (8.26) and (8.27), leads to the vehicle-type-specific congestion toll on each link that can be written as:

$$u_a^k = \sum_{i \in K} v_a^i \frac{\partial t_a^i(\mathbf{v}_a, y_a)}{\partial v_a^k} + \frac{\partial M_a(\mathbf{v}_a)}{\partial v_a^k}, \; k \in K, \; a \in A \tag{8.67}$$

and the capacity of each link should be optimally chosen such that

$$\sum_{k \in K} v_a^k \frac{\partial t_a^k(\mathbf{v}_a, y_a)}{\partial y_a} + \eta \frac{\mathrm{d}I_a(y_a)}{\mathrm{d}y_a} = 0, \; a \in A \tag{8.68}$$

We further assume that the class-specific link travel time function is homogeneous of degree zero in class-specific traffic volume and capacity. By Euler's theorem, we have

$$\sum_{i \in K} v_a^i \frac{\partial t_a^k(\mathbf{v}_a, y_a)}{\partial v_a^i} + y_a \frac{\partial t_a^k(\mathbf{v}_a, y_a)}{\partial y_a} = 0, \; a \in A$$

Multiplying both side by v_a^k / y_a and summing over all $k \in K$ yields:

$$\frac{1}{y_a} \sum_{k \in K} v_a^k \sum_{i \in K} v_a^i \frac{\partial t_a^k(\mathbf{v}_a, y_a)}{\partial v_a^i} + \sum_{k \in K} v_a^k \frac{\partial t_a^k(\mathbf{v}_a, y_a)}{\partial y_a} = 0, \; a \in A \tag{8.69}$$

Substituting eqn. (8.69) into (8.68) yields:

$$\sum_{k \in K} v_a^k \sum_{i \in K} v_a^i \frac{\partial t_a^k(\mathbf{v}_a, y_a)}{\partial v_a^i} - \eta y_a \frac{\mathrm{d}I_a(y_a)}{\mathrm{d}y_a} = 0, \; a \in A \tag{8.70}$$

Combining (8.70) and (8.67) and rearranging the terms leads to

$$\sum_{k \in K} u_a^k v_a^k = \sum_{k \in K} v_a^k \frac{\partial M_a(\mathbf{v}_a)}{\partial v_a^k} + \eta y_a \frac{\mathrm{d}I_a(y_a)}{\mathrm{d}y_a}, \; a \in A \tag{8.71}$$

Again if we assume that there are constant returns to scale in both road maintenance (i.e., $\sum_{k \in K} E_{M_a}^{v_a^k} = 1.0$) and road construction $E_{I_a}^{y_a} = 1.0$, we arrive at the self-financing result for each individual link in the network again in this more general case.

Note that it is convenient, and indeed often the case in reality, to introduce a new aggregate traffic variable v_a defined as:

$$v_a = \sum_{k \in K} \phi_k v_a^k, \; a \in A \tag{8.72}$$

where ϕ_k is the conventional Passenger Car-equivalent Unit (PCU) for vehicle weight-type $k \in K$ and of course $\phi_1 = 1.0$ if vehicles in type 1 are passenger cars. The capacity, y, can be defined in terms of PCU as well. Note that this simplification does not necessarily reduce the multi-type dependences to single-type dependence as the travel time function on each link is still class-specific. It is generally true that heavy and slow vehicles are confined to the outer slow lanes and cars use the inner faster lanes on a multi-lane road and they interact with each other due to lane changing. This is captured in the model by adopting a vehicle type-specific link travel time function. With the definition of the aggregate traffic variable (8.72), the assumption that the class-specific link travel time function is homogeneous of degree zero in the aggregate traffic volume and capacity implies the following form of travel time function:

$$t_a^k\left(\mathbf{v}_a, y_a\right) = t_a^k\left(\frac{v_a}{y_a}\right) = t_a^k\left(\frac{\sum_{k\in K}\phi_k v_a^k}{y_a}\right), \; k\in K, \, a\in A \tag{8.73}$$

One should be aware that the PCU is a simple and practical concept used to reflect the consumption of road capacity and degree of damage to road surface by different vehicle weight-types. Nonetheless, the form of travel time function, albeit class-specific and indeed asymmetric (asymmetric Jacobian), does not always produce behaviorally and physically coherent results as discussed in Chapter 2; a sensible multi-type flow congestion function should reflect the fact that vehicles of different weight-types on the same road will move at different speeds under free-flow or less congested traffic conditions, and tend to travel at the same speed as the maximum practical flow density of the road is reached. In fact, the PCU equivalent ratio is not a constant but varies with the percentage of trucks (or buses) in the traffic stream. To put it differently, an increase in the percentage of heavy vehicles affects the flows on the link differently from an "equivalent" increase in cars.

In view of the observation that simple constant equivalence is not valid for accounting for the effect of heavy vehicles sharing the roadway space with cars, one may wish to explore alternative multi-type congestion functions other than the functional form (8.73). Fortunately, the homogeneous degree zero assumption required for the self-financing result allows for the use of a wide variety of class-specific link travel time functions. For example, one may presumably look into the following functional forms which are homogeneous of degree zero in class-specific traffic volume and capacity:

$$t_a^k\left(\mathbf{v}_a, y_a\right) = t_a^k\left(\frac{v_a^1}{y_a}, \frac{v_a^2}{y_a}, \ldots, \frac{v_a^{|K|}}{y_a}, \frac{v_a}{y_a}\right), \; k\in K, \, a\in A \tag{8.74}$$

where v_a, $a\in A$ is given by eqn. (8.72). Belonging to the above function category are the following functional forms:

$$t_a^k\left(\mathbf{v}_a, y_a\right) = \overline{t}_a^k\left(1+\xi_a\left(\frac{v_a}{y_a}\right)^{\gamma_a} + \sum_{i\in K}\xi_{ai}\left(\frac{v_a^i}{y_a}\right)^{\gamma_{ai}}\right), \; k\in K, \, a\in A \tag{8.75}$$

$$t_a^k\left(\mathbf{v}_a, y_a\right) = \overline{t}_a^k\left(1+\xi_a\left(\frac{v_a}{y_a}\right)^{\gamma_a} \prod_{i\in K}\left(\frac{v_a^i}{y_a}\right)^{\gamma_{ai}}\right), \; k\in K, \, a\in A \tag{8.76}$$

where $\overline{t}_a^k$, $k\in K$, $a\in A$ are vehicle-type-specific free flow travel time, $\left(\gamma_a, \xi_a, a\in A\right)$ are link-specific parameters and $\left(\gamma_{ai}, \xi_{ai}, a\in A, i\in K\right)$ are link-specific and vehicle-type-specific parameters.

8.6 COMPETITION AND EQUILIBRIA OF PRIVATE TOLL ROADS

The foregoing analyses involve only one operator of the private roads in a network. In reality, there might be more than one toll roads operated by different firms. Those toll roads (operators) are interrelated in demands and revenues, either as perfect or partial substitutes (*e.g.*, when two toll roads are in parallel) or perfect or partial complements (when two toll roads are in series). It is thus meaningful to examine the strategic interactions and market equilibria among the private firms. In this section, we study the equilibria based on a situation where there are two or more profit-maximizing private firms that operate multiple toll roads in a road network. We develop a competitive game model to analyze the strategic interactions among the private toll road operators in determining their supply (road capacity) and price (toll level) over the network.

8.6.1 Monopolistic Competition

Consider monopolistic competition among multiple private firms operating inter-related toll roads on a network. For simplicity, we suppose each firm provides a single toll road consisting of a single link on the network. Let J be the set of the competitive firms or toll roads on the network; clearly we have the private roads duopoly as a special case when there are only two competitive firms. We further assume that the locations of all the toll roads and the number of years of operations by the private firms are already determined. The road capacity and level of toll charge are the only two variables to be determined by each firm subject to the resulting traffic flow distribution in deterministic user equilibrium. Thus the decision problem of each firm $j \in J$ is to maximize its profit, given by the difference between revenue and cost, by choosing an appropriate level of capacity and toll charge of its operating toll road:

$$\max_{u_j, y_j} \pi_j(\mathbf{u}, \mathbf{y}) = v_j(\mathbf{u}, \mathbf{y}) u_j - \eta I_j(y_j), \; j \in J \tag{8.77}$$

where $v_j(\mathbf{u}, \mathbf{y}), j \in J$ is the equilibrium link flow that depends on the capacities and toll charges of all toll roads and can be determined by the traffic equilibrium model (8.1)-(8.5) (for simplicity, we consider homogeneous users and hence $m = 1$ in the traffic equilibrium model), it is assumed that parameter η is common to all toll roads or firms for simplicity and the unit period project cost $\eta I_j(y_j)$ does not vary with the level of traffic (variable cost of road use is omitted).

The monopolistic competitive equilibrium problem is to seek a vector of output $(u_j^*, y_j^*, j \in J)$ such that each firm's price-capacity choice is profit-maximizing given the output choices of the other firms. Such a vector of outputs is called a *Cournot-Nash* equilibrium. Assuming that the reaction functions $v_j(\mathbf{u},\mathbf{y}), j \in J$ is continuously differentiable (refer to the sensitivity analysis of network traffic equilibrium in Chapter 4) and an interior optimum emerges in the Cournot-Nash game (this is not a restrictive assumption for the simultaneous profitable case where toll and capacity must be strictly positive for all firms and thus the non-negativity constraints are not binding), we thus have the following first-order conditions for each active competitive firm $j \in J$:

$$\frac{\partial \pi_j(\mathbf{u},\mathbf{y})}{\partial u_j} = \frac{\partial v_j(\mathbf{u},\mathbf{y})}{\partial u_j} u_j + v_j(\mathbf{u},\mathbf{y}) = 0 \tag{8.78}$$

$$\frac{\partial \pi_j(\mathbf{u},\mathbf{y})}{\partial y_j} = \frac{\partial v_j(\mathbf{u},\mathbf{y})}{\partial y_j} u_j - \eta \frac{\mathrm{d}I_j(y_j)}{\mathrm{d}y_j} = 0 \tag{8.79}$$

Condition (8.78) can be alternatively rewritten as

$$E_{v_j}^{u_j} = \frac{\partial v_j(\mathbf{u},\mathbf{y})}{\partial u_j} \frac{u_j}{v_j(\mathbf{u},\mathbf{y})} = -1 \tag{8.80}$$

This simply says that the choice of toll level by each profit-maximizing firm occurs at the unit direct price elasticity of its flow or demand, at which the increase in the revenue with a higher fare is cancelled out with the loss due to reduced patronage. The intuition behind condition (8.79) is that the marginal cost of an extra unit of capacity is equal to the marginal pricing revenue brought about by that investment.

8.6.2 Alternative Formulation

The above monopolistic competitive equilibrium or Cournot-Nash game is subject to a network equilibrium constraint. Thus, the problem of interest is actually an *Equilibrium Problem with Equilibrium Constraint* (EPEC). The problem can be treated as two-level hierarchical problems or a *Multi-Leader-Follower Games*, which involve equilibria at both lower (Wardrop traffic equilibrium) and upper levels (Cournot-Nash Equilibrium), and can be regarded as an equilibrium counterpart (at the upper level) of Mathematical Programs with Equilibrium Constraints (MPEC) or the Bilevel Programming Problem (BLPP) studied in Chapters 4 and 5.

It is well known that both the traffic equilibrium problem and the Nash equilibrium problem can be formulated as a finite-dimensional Variational Inequality (VI). Thus the toll road competition problems can be in fact formulated as a *Bi-level VI* or BVI. To facilitate our formulation, define $\mathbf{u}_{-j} \equiv (u_i,\ i \in J,\ i \neq j)$ and $\mathbf{y}_{-j} \equiv (y_i,\ i \in J,\ i \neq j)$. Let $U_j \times Y_j$ denote the strategic set of firm or player j with respect to its toll charge and capacity choice. For example, $U_j \times Y_j = \{u_j : 0 \le u_j < \infty\} \times \{y_j : 0 \le y_j < \infty\}$. In this case, $U_j \times Y_j$ is a closed and convex subset and each player's strategy is independent of the rival players' strategies. Player j's problem is to determine, for each fixed $(\mathbf{u}_{-j}, \mathbf{y}_{-j})$ of other player's strategies, an optimal strategy $u_j^* \in U_j$, $y_j^* \in Y_j$ that solves the profit-maximizing problem (8.77), a set of $\mathbf{u}^* \equiv (u_j^*,\ j \in J)$ and $\mathbf{y}^* \equiv (y_j^*,\ j \in J)$ of strategies is said to be in equilibrium if no player is able to enhance its profit by unilaterally modifying its chosen strategy. That is,

$$\pi_j(\mathbf{u}^*, \mathbf{y}^*) \ge \pi_j(u_j, y_j, \mathbf{u}_{-j}^*, \mathbf{y}_{-j}^*),\ j \in J \tag{8.81}$$

Let us assume that each one of the profit functions π_j is convex on the set $U_j \times Y_j$ when viewed as a function of (u_j, y_j) alone and the other components are fixed. Using the optimality conditions for convex optimization, we see strategy set $\mathbf{u}^* \equiv (u_j^*,\ j \in J)$ and $\mathbf{y}^* \equiv (y_j^*,\ j \in J)$ is in equilibrium if and only if for any $(u_j, y_j) \in U_j \times Y_j$ and every $j \in J$:

$$-\frac{\partial \pi_j(\mathbf{u}^*, \mathbf{y}^*)}{\partial u_j}(u_j - u_j^*) \ge 0 \quad \text{and} \quad -\frac{\partial \pi_j(\mathbf{u}^*, \mathbf{y}^*)}{\partial y_j}(y_j - y_j^*) \ge 0$$

Adding these conditions, we conclude that $\mathbf{u}^* \equiv (u_j^*,\ j \in J)$ and $\mathbf{y}^* \equiv (\mathbf{y}_j^*,\ j \in J)$ must be a solution of the following VI:

$$(\mathbf{u} - \mathbf{u}^*)^{\mathrm{T}} \pi_{\mathbf{u}}(\mathbf{u}^*, \mathbf{y}^*) + (\mathbf{y} - \mathbf{y}^*)^{\mathrm{T}} \pi_{\mathbf{y}}(\mathbf{u}^*, \mathbf{y}^*) \ge 0 \text{ for any } \mathbf{u} \in U = \prod_{j \in J} U_j,\ \mathbf{y} \in Y = \prod_{j \in J} Y_j$$

where $\pi_{\mathbf{u}}(\mathbf{u}, \mathbf{y}) = (-\partial \pi_j(\mathbf{u}, \mathbf{y})/\partial u_j,\ j \in J)^{\mathrm{T}}$ and $\pi_{\mathbf{y}}(\mathbf{u}, \mathbf{y}) = (-\partial \pi_j(\mathbf{u}, \mathbf{y})/\partial y_j,\ j \in J)^{\mathrm{T}}$.

As shown in Chapter 2, for given $(\mathbf{u}, \mathbf{y})$ there will be a unique network equilibrium flow pattern, a vector of all OD demands, $\mathbf{d}(\mathbf{u}, \mathbf{y}) = (d_w(\mathbf{u}, \mathbf{y}),\ w \in W)^{\mathrm{T}}$ and a vector of all link flows, $\mathbf{v}(\mathbf{u}, \mathbf{y}) = (v_a(\mathbf{u}, \mathbf{y}),\ a \in A)^{\mathrm{T}}$. The unique equilibrium solution can be formulated as the VI of finding $\tilde{\mathbf{v}}$ and $\tilde{\mathbf{d}}$ such that

$$\mathbf{t}(\tilde{\mathbf{v}}, \mathbf{u}, \mathbf{y})^{\mathrm{T}}(\mathbf{v} - \tilde{\mathbf{v}}) - \mathbf{B}(\tilde{\mathbf{d}})^{\mathrm{T}}(\mathbf{d} - \tilde{\mathbf{d}}) \ge 0 \text{ for all } (\mathbf{v}, \mathbf{d}) \in \Omega \tag{8.82}$$

where, as defined before, $\Omega = \{(\mathbf{v}, \mathbf{d}) | \mathbf{v} = \Delta \mathbf{f}, \mathbf{d} = \Lambda \mathbf{f}, \mathbf{f} \ge 0, \mathbf{d} \ge 0\}$, $\mathbf{B}(\mathbf{d}) = (B_w(d_w),\ w \in W)^{\mathrm{T}}$ and $\mathbf{t}(\mathbf{v}, \mathbf{u}, \mathbf{y}) = (t_a(v_a, u_a, y_a), a \in \bar{A};\ t_a(v_a), a \in A, a \notin \bar{A})^{\mathrm{T}}$.

To sum up, we thus arrive at the following BVI formulation for the toll road competition problem that belongs to the class of EPEC:

Find $\mathbf{u}^* = (u_j, j \in J) \in U = \prod_{j \in J} U_j$ and $\mathbf{y}^* = (y_j, j \in J) \in Y = \prod_{j \in J} Y_j$ such that

$$(\mathbf{u}-\mathbf{u}^*)^{\mathrm{T}} \pi_{\mathbf{u}}(\mathbf{u}^*, \mathbf{y}^*, \tilde{\mathbf{v}}, \tilde{\mathbf{d}}) + (\mathbf{y}-\mathbf{y}^*)^{\mathrm{T}} \pi_{\mathbf{y}}(\mathbf{u}^*, \mathbf{y}^*, \tilde{\mathbf{v}}, \tilde{\mathbf{d}}) \geq 0 \text{ for any } \mathbf{u} \in U,\ \mathbf{y} \in Y \qquad (8.83)$$

where for each $\mathbf{u} \in U$ and $\mathbf{y} \in Y$, $(\tilde{\mathbf{v}}, \tilde{\mathbf{d}}) \in \Omega$ is the unique solution of the VI defined by

$$\mathbf{t}(\tilde{\mathbf{v}}, \mathbf{u}, \mathbf{y})^{\mathrm{T}} (\mathbf{v}-\tilde{\mathbf{v}}) - \mathbf{B}(\tilde{\mathbf{d}})^{\mathrm{T}} (\mathbf{d}-\tilde{\mathbf{d}}) \geq 0 \text{ for all } (\mathbf{v}, \mathbf{d}) \in \Omega \qquad (8.84)$$

8.6.3 Solution Methods

Although the EPEC problem is a sensible mathematical model with a well-defined solution concept, its complex bi-level VI structure makes it a computationally intractable problem. Any rigorous attempt to compute an EPEC solution (if it exists) is presently out of the reach of existing methods. Here we suggest two heuristic methods for the computation of EPEC solutions.

Diagonalization Method. Observe that the problem of a single dominant firm is an MPEC (or a Stackelberg leader-follower game) that chooses a simple pair of strategies $(u_j, y_j) \in U_j \times Y_j,\ j \in J$ subject to the UE constraint

$$\max_{u_j, y_j} \pi_j(u_j, y_j, \mathbf{u}_{-j}, \mathbf{y}_{-j}) = v_j(u_j, y_j, \mathbf{u}_{-j}, \mathbf{y}_{-j}) u_j - \eta I_j(y_j),\ j \in J \qquad (8.85)$$

where $v_j(u_j, y_j, \mathbf{u}_{-j}, \mathbf{y}_{-j})$ is obtained by solving VI (8.84). This is relatively a simple MPEC with two upper-level decision variables only, to which a host of computational methods is applicable such as the sensitivity analysis based or the gap function based methods developed previously in Chapters 4 and 5. One may as well employ a direct search method such as the Hooke-Jeeves method at the expense of iteratively solving the lower-level UE problem. The diagonalization method thus solves the individual MPECs of the firms separately and sequentially holds the decision variables of the other firms (or players) fixed in turn until the sequence converges.

Synchronous Iterative Method. The first-order conditions of each firms' MPEC is given by eqns. (8.78) and (8.79), which is in fact amenable to a decoupled simple solution adjustment. For a given current solution $(\mathbf{u}^{(n)}, \mathbf{y}^{(n)})$ at iteration n, one can find the corresponding link flow solution $\mathbf{v}^{(n)}$ and the necessary derivative information $\partial v_j^{(n)} / \partial u_j$ and $\partial v_j^{(n)} / \partial y_j$ for each

$j \in J$ by conducting a UE traffic assignment and its sensitivity analysis (see Chapter 3). Then, by virtue of eqn. (8.78), one can find an auxiliary toll $\bar{u}_j^{(n)}$ as given below:

$$\bar{u}_j^{(n)} = -v_j^{(n)} \left(\frac{\partial v_j^{(n)}}{\partial u_j} \right)^{-1}, \ j \in J \tag{8.86}$$

By substituting $\bar{u}_j^{(n)}$ into eqn. (8.79) and solving the resulting equation, one can obtain an auxiliary capacity $\bar{y}_j^{(n)}$ as well, if $\mathrm{d}I_j(y_j)/\mathrm{d}y_j$ is not a constant, but includes y_j, such as the case of nonlinear construction cost function: $I_j(y_j) = \kappa_j (y_j)^{\gamma_j}$ $(\gamma_j \neq 1)$, $j \in J$. In the case of constant return to scale construction cost function, $I_j(y_j) = \kappa_j y_j$, $j \in J$, then we have $\partial \pi_j(\mathbf{u}, \mathbf{y})/\partial y_j = u_j \partial v_j(\mathbf{u}, \mathbf{y})/\partial y_j - \eta \kappa_j$, which becomes a (positive or negative) constant and thus not solvable in terms of y_j. In this case, the auxiliary $\bar{y}_j^{(n)}$ is instead given by:

$$\bar{y}_j^{(n)} = \begin{cases} 0, \text{ if } u_j \dfrac{\partial v_j(\mathbf{u}, \mathbf{y})}{\partial y_j} - \eta \kappa_j > 0 \\ y_j^{(n)}, \text{ if } u_j \dfrac{\partial v_j(\mathbf{u}, \mathbf{y})}{\partial y_j} - \eta \kappa_j = 0 \\ y_j^{\max}, \text{ if } u_j \dfrac{\partial v_j(\mathbf{u}, \mathbf{y})}{\partial y_j} - \eta \kappa_j < 0 \end{cases}, \ j \in J \tag{8.87}$$

where $y_j^{\max}$ is the predetermined upper bound of capacity for toll road $j \in J$. After obtaining the auxiliary link toll and link capacity, the solution $\left(\mathbf{u}^{(n+1)}, \mathbf{y}^{(n+1)}\right)$ at iteration $n+1$ can be updated by the Method of Successive Average (MSA) as follows:

$$\begin{cases} u_j^{(n+1)} = u_j^{(n)} + \dfrac{1}{n+1}\left(\bar{u}_j^{(n)} - u_j^{(n)}\right) \\ y_j^{(n+1)} = y_j^{(n)} + \dfrac{1}{n+1}\left(\bar{y}_j^{(n)} - y_j^{(n)}\right) \end{cases}, \ j \in J \tag{8.88}$$

Consequently, the method simply iterates between the synchronous toll-capacity adjustment for all firms and the equilibrium traffic assignment together with its sensitivity analysis, and this process is repeated until an acceptable convergence is achieved.

We conclude this section by pointing out that the study of EPEC and/or BVI is still in its infancy, the computation of global solutions even to MPECs remains elusive, if not impossible, and hence efficient convergent methods for computing equilibrium solutions to the general EPEC are to date not available. Though we set forth two appealing computational methods for the specific EPEC of toll competition, the issue of convergence of the heuristic methods is not easily resolved.

8.6.4 Two Analytical Examples

Example 8.3 (Toll competition between two substitutable roads) We consider a simple network of two parallel links shown in Figure 8.10 and used in Example 8.1 to illustrate the synchronous iterative method. For simplicity, we suppose both firms already make their long-term choices of capacities and face short-term toll competition only. We further assume that both links are used $(v_1 > 0,\ v_2 > 0)$ throughout the iterative adjustment of tolls by the two firms. Thus, the following equilibrium conditions are always satisfied

$$B(v_1 + v_2) = t_1(v_1) + u_1 \tag{8.89}$$

$$B(v_1 + v_2) = t_2(v_2) + u_2 \tag{8.90}$$

Differentiating both sides of each equation with respect to toll and capacity respectively yields:

$$B'\left(\frac{\partial v_1}{\partial u_1} + \frac{\partial v_2}{\partial u_1}\right) = t_1' \frac{\partial v_1}{\partial u_1} + 1,\quad B'\left(\frac{\partial v_1}{\partial u_2} + \frac{\partial v_2}{\partial u_2}\right) = t_1' \frac{\partial v_1}{\partial u_2}$$

$$B'\left(\frac{\partial v_1}{\partial u_2} + \frac{\partial v_2}{\partial u_2}\right) = t_2' \frac{\partial v_2}{\partial u_2} + 1,\quad B'\left(\frac{\partial v_1}{\partial u_1} + \frac{\partial v_2}{\partial u_1}\right) = t_2' \frac{\partial v_2}{\partial u_1}$$

Solving the above equations for $\partial v_1/\partial u_1$ and $\partial v_2/\partial u_2$ yields:

$$\frac{\partial v_1}{\partial u_1} = \frac{t_2' - B'}{(t_1' + t_2')B' - t_1't_2'},\quad \frac{\partial v_2}{\partial u_2} = \frac{t_1' - B'}{(t_1' + t_2')B' - t_1't_2'}$$

Substituting these derivatives into (8.86) leads to the following auxiliary solution:

$$\bar{u}_1^{(n)} = v_1^{(n)}\left(t_1' + \frac{t_2'B'}{B' - t_2'}\right),\quad \bar{u}_2^{(n)} = v_2^{(n)}\left(t_2' + \frac{t_1'B'}{B' - t_1'}\right)$$

Now let $B = \bar{\varphi} - \varphi(v_1 + v_2)$, $t_1 = \bar{\alpha}_1 + \alpha_1 v_1$, $t_2 = \bar{\alpha}_2 + \alpha_2 v_2$ with the following parameter values: $\bar{\varphi} = 50$, $\varphi = 0.01$, $\bar{\alpha}_1 = \bar{\alpha}_2 = 20$, and $\alpha_1 = 0.02$, $\alpha_2 = 0.03$. For given u_1 and u_2 the equilibrium link flows are obtained (suppose both links are used) as:

$$v_1 = \frac{10}{11}(90 + u_2 - 4u_1),\quad v_2 = \frac{10}{11}(60 + u_1 - 4u_2)$$

Combining these equations with the following optimality conditions for tolls

$$\frac{\partial v_1}{\partial u_1}u_1 + v_1 = 0,\quad \frac{\partial v_2}{\partial u_2}u_2 + v_2 = 0$$

we obtain the optimal link tolls analytically as:

$$u_1^* = \frac{600}{47} \approx 12.766,\quad u_2^* = \frac{570}{47} \approx 12.128$$

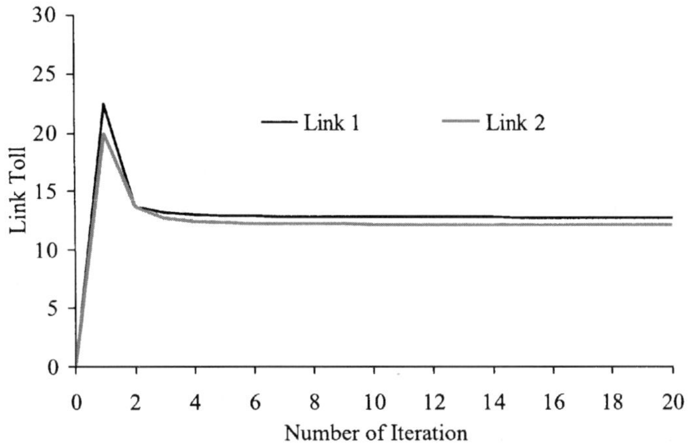

Figure 8.12 Change in the link toll rates versus number of iterations for Example 8.3

We now use the synchronous iterative method to find the solution. Figure 8.12 plots the change of the toll rates of the two roads versus the number of iterations, where the initial tolls are set as $u_1^{(0)} = u_2^{(0)} = 0$. It can be observed that the synchronous iterative method does converge to the optimal solution quickly.

Example 8.4 (Toll competition between two complementary roads) Next we consider the network in Figure 8.11 with two OD pairs and two toll links in series, used in Example 8.2. Proceeding in a similar manner as in Example 8.3, we obtain:

$$\frac{\partial v_1}{\partial u_1} = \frac{B'_{1\to 2} + B'_{1\to 3} - t'_2}{\left(B'_{1\to 2} - t'_1\right)\left(B'_{1\to 3} - t'_2\right) - B'_{1\to 2}t'_1}, \quad \frac{\partial v_2}{\partial u_2} = \frac{B'_{1\to 2} - t'_1}{\left(B'_{1\to 2} - t'_1\right)\left(B'_{1\to 3} - t'_2\right) - B'_{1\to 2}t'_1}$$

which leads to the following auxiliary link toll solution:

$$\bar{u}_1^{(n)} = v_1^{(n)}\left(t'_1 + \frac{B'_{1\to 2}\left(t'_2 - B'_{1\to 3}\right)}{B'_{1\to 2} + B'_{1\to 3} - t'_2}\right), \quad \bar{u}_2^{(n)} = v_2^{(n)}\left(t'_2 - B'_{1\to 3} + \frac{t'_1 B'_{1\to 2}}{B'_{1\to 2} - t'_1}\right)$$

In view of $d_{1\to 2} = v_1 - v_2$ and $d_{1\to 3} = v_2$ we let $B_{1\to 2} = \bar{\varphi}_{1\to 2} - \varphi_{1\to 2}(v_1 - v_2)$, $B_{1\to 3} = \bar{\varphi}_{1\to 3} - \varphi_{1\to 3}(v_2)$, $t_1 = \bar{\alpha}_1 + \alpha_1 v_1$, $t_2 = \bar{\alpha}_2 + \alpha_2 v_2$ with the following parameter values: $\bar{\varphi}_{1\to 2} = 50$, $\bar{\varphi}_{1\to 3} = 100$, $\varphi_{1\to 2} = \varphi_{1\to 3} = 0.01$, $\bar{\alpha}_1 = \bar{\alpha}_2 = 20$, and $\alpha_1 = 0.02$, $\alpha_2 = 0.03$. For given u_1 and u_2 the equilibrium link flows are obtained (suppose positive flows in two OD pairs) as:

$$v_1 = \frac{50}{7}\left(180 - 5u_1 - u_2\right), \quad v_2 = \frac{50}{7}\left(120 - u_1 - 3u_2\right)$$

The optimal tolls are obtained as:

$$u_1^* = \frac{960}{59} \approx 16.271, \quad u_2^* = \frac{1020}{59} \approx 17.288$$

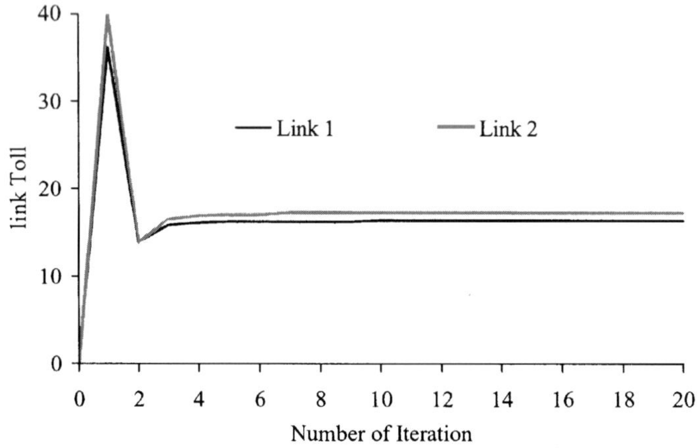

Figure 8.13 Change of the toll rates versus number of iterations for Example 8.4

As in Example 8.3, we again apply the synchronous iterative method to find the solution. Figure 8.13 plots the change in the toll rates of the two roads versus the number of iterations, where the initial tolls are set as $u_1^{(0)} = u_2^{(0)} = 0$. Once again, the synchronous iterative method converges quickly to the optimal solution.

8.6.5 Graphical Characterization of Toll Competition

In this section we provide a graphical characterization of toll road competition using a simple but representative case of two competitive firms (private road duopoly), each providing a single toll road (corresponding to a single link) in the network. The two toll roads are either substitutable or complementary in terms of the impacts of capacity supply and toll charge of one toll road on the demand of the other toll road. The basic network is depicted in Figure 8.14(a) with 2 OD pairs ($1 \rightarrow 3$ and $2 \rightarrow 3$). The following form of the OD demand function is adopted:

$$d_{1\rightarrow 3}(\mu_{1\rightarrow 3}) = 8.0\times 10^3 \exp(-0.20\mu_{1\rightarrow 3}),\ d_{2\rightarrow 3}(\mu_{2\rightarrow 3}) = 2.0\times 10^3 \exp(-0.20\mu_{2\rightarrow 3})$$

We consider two scenarios of the two competitive toll roads. The first scenario involves construction of a toll road m_1 from node 1 and node 3, and the second toll road n_1 from node 2 to 3, as depicted in Figure 8.14(b). The second scenario involves construction of two toll roads m_2 from node 1 to node 2 and n_2 from node 2 to node 3, respectively, as depicted in Figure 8.14(c). Clearly, scenario 1 involves two (partially) substitutable toll roads. Namely, the opening up (or decrease in toll and/or increase in capacity) of toll road m_1 will reduce demand for toll road n_1 and thus negatively affect the rival firm n_1's total profit. Scenario 2 involves two (partially) complementary toll roads. Namely, the opening up of toll road m_2 (or decrease in toll and/or increase in capacity) will stimulate (rather than depress) demand in toll road n_2 and thus positively affect firm n_2's profit.

For simplicity, the construction cost functions for the new links are assumed to take the following linear form with respect to capacity:

$$I_a(y_a) = \kappa t_a^0 y_a, \quad a = m_1,\ n_1,\ m_2 \text{ or } n_2$$

where κ is a proportionality parameter with value 1.0×10^6 $(\text{HK\$/(h}\cdot\text{veh/h))}$. The link travel time function (8.11) is used, with $\text{cap}_a = y_a$ for $a \in \{m_1, n_1, m_2, n_2\}$. The basic input data of link travel time function are presented in Table 8.4. Other parameters are: $\eta = 1.14\times10^{-5}$ $(1/h)$, $\beta = 100$ $(\text{HK\$/h})$ (average VOT to transfer toll in HK\$ into equivalent time in h).

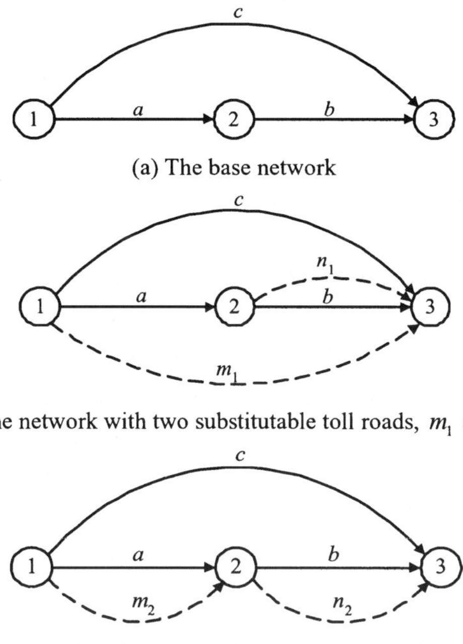

(a) The base network

(b) The network with two substitutable toll roads, m_1 and n_1

(c) The network with two complementary toll road, m_2 and n_2

Figure 8.14 The base network and the proposed private roll roads

Table 8.4 Input data for the link travel time function

Link No.	Free-flow Time (h)	Capacity (veh/h)
a	0.4	3000
b	0.6	3000
c	1.0	4000
m_1	0.8	to be determined
n_1	0.4	ditto
m_2	0.3	ditto
n_2	0.4	ditto

Two representative games. In view of the fact that road provision is inflexible in the short run (capacity cannot be changed frequently), while tolls are flexible, we will focus on the following two possib le competitive games.

Game A. This game is defined as a one-shot game where all decisions are made at the same time by both firms. Namely, two firms choose their capacities and tolls simultaneously when two new private toll roads are introduced at the same time.

Game B. In this game we suppose both firms have chosen their capacity and both capacity supplies are known to each other, the two firms simultaneously choose their toll levels (toll adjustment is flexible in the short run).

For each of the games under the aforementioned demand conditions (demand substitutes or complements), we determine and compare the solutions of the mixed supply and price competitions, including the total social welfare gain and the private firms' profits.

Representative results. For each of the networks, the results of both Game A and Game B are presented here. Table 8.5 shows the results associated with Game A, as well as the social optimum solution (welfare maximization) for both substitutable and complementary cases. Note that the social optimum solution can not be implemented because at least one firm receives negative profit. We note that for Game A, both firms are free to select their capacity and toll level in order to maximize their own profits simultaneously, and we find that a Nash equilibrium can always be achieved by the end of the game. We also find that there may be more than one equilibrium solution, depending on the initial combination of the decision variables. The results in Table 8.5 are just some that we believe to be practically meaningful.

Table 8.5 Representative results

		Substitutable Network (b)		Complementary Network (c)	
		Competitive Solution	Social Optimum Solution	Competitive Solution	Social Optimum Solution
Capacity	Firm *m*	6401.00	6212.50	3798.10	9388.16
	Firm *n*	5000.10	5509.00	7301.00	11947.57
Toll	Firm *m*	17.00	9.91	9.20	2.360
	Firm *n*	17.90	10.08	18.70	8.890
Profit	Firm *m*	18907.85	-12220.16	12908.96	-16198.34
	Firm *n*	39463.99	14628.97	62711.04	21623.16
Welfare Gain		229904.30	291813.20	296352.00	302840.70

Graphical interpretation

As the road capacity is more likely to be fixed, and toll is flexible to change in the short term, here we are more interested in examining the competitive characteristics of the toll roads with respect to toll charges only. This is the case of Game B, where the capacities are pre-selected and fixed, and we find there is only one toll charge solution for each case. By varying the combinations of the tolls by the two firms, the variations of social welfare and profit can be represented by the iso-welfare and iso-profit contours in Figure 8.15 to 8.19.

In scenario 1, for the network in Figure 8.14(b), the two firms compete with each other to attract traffic flow to their road. When the toll is set too low, even if a large amount of flow is attracted to the toll roads, the revenue received is not enough to cover the cost. On the other hand, if the toll is set too high, no one will use that road which will result in negative profit again. As shown in Figure 8.15, the profit increases from negative to its maximum, and then falls as the toll further increases. It is also interesting to notice that there is no contour at the right side for firm m_1, as does firm n_1 at the top of the graph, because the toll charge of either firm is too high. Two reaction lines of the firms can also be plotted on the graph. They represent the optimal selection of toll by one firm once the other firm has already selected its toll. Starting from any point on the graph, the firms will select their new tolls on these lines and finally they will converge to the intersection of these lines and reach the *Nash equilibrium* there.

In Figure 8.16 for the substitutable case, we can identify the corresponding social welfare gain in each combination of toll charges by the two competitive firms. As shown in the figure, the point of *Nash Equilibrium* has a positive welfare gain in this example, and the point of maximum social welfare gain also occurs inside the region of positive profits. Both toll roads have benefit for the whole society and the private firms. However, this is not always true; there are also cases where only one firm enjoys positive profit. Figure 8.17 depicts the profits for the complementary case, with the network in Figure 8.14(c). This graph is more or less the same as that in Figure 8.15 except that the maximum profit of one firm occurs at where the other firm has zero toll. This result stems from the fact that in this case the two toll roads are complementary. Figure 8.18 represents the corresponding social welfare gain for different toll combinations for the complementary case. Similar to Figure 8.16, we can find that both *Nash Equilibrium* and maximum social welfare gain occur in the positive profit and welfare region. Thus both toll roads benefit the private firms and the whole society. In Figure 8.19, we focus on the three curves for the substitutable case (the graph for the complementary case is similar), the *zero profit curves* and the *zero welfare gain curve*. These curves divide the space into a number of regimes that have different economic meanings. Regime I is bounded by the two *zero profit curves* within the positive welfare gain region. Thus in this regime, both firms enjoy positive profits and introduction of the two competitive roads is socially desirable. In Regime II, one firm is profitable and the other is unprofitable. Firm *n* is unprofitable within Regime II-b and Regime II-d, while firm *m* is unprofitable within Regime II-a and Regime II-c. In playing the competitive game, the unprofitable firm will always try to alter its toll charge and move toward profitable Regime I. Note that neither firm will choose regime III since both of them are unprofitable, unless being subsidized by the government. Finally, Regime IV is not preferred to both private firms and the whole society because it generates negative social welfare gain and negative profits.

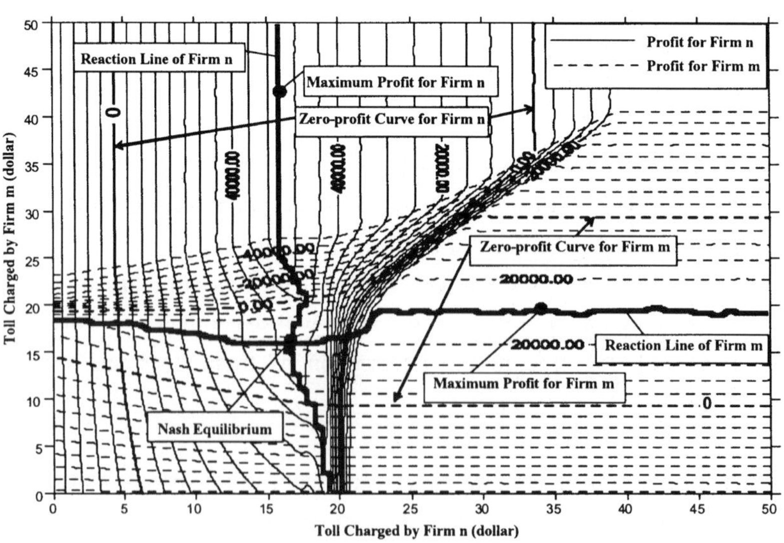

Figure 8.15 Profits for the substitutable case with capacity fixed

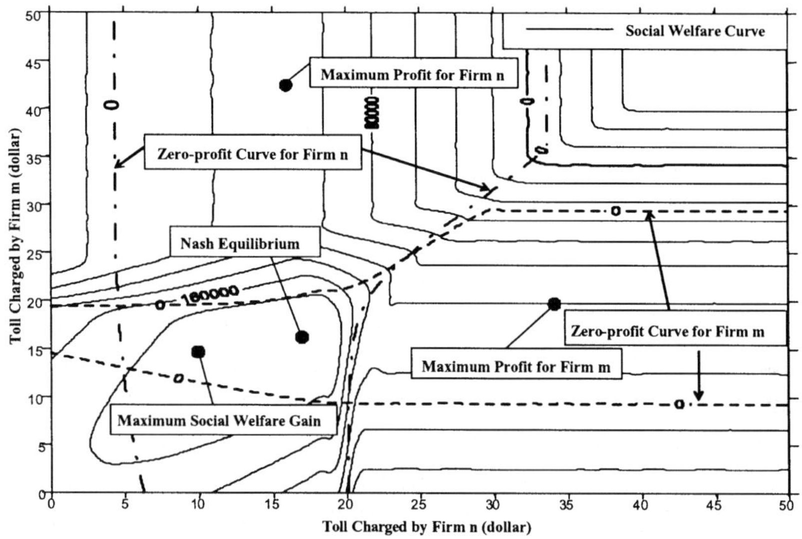

Figure 8.16 Social welfare gain for the substitutable case with capacity fixed

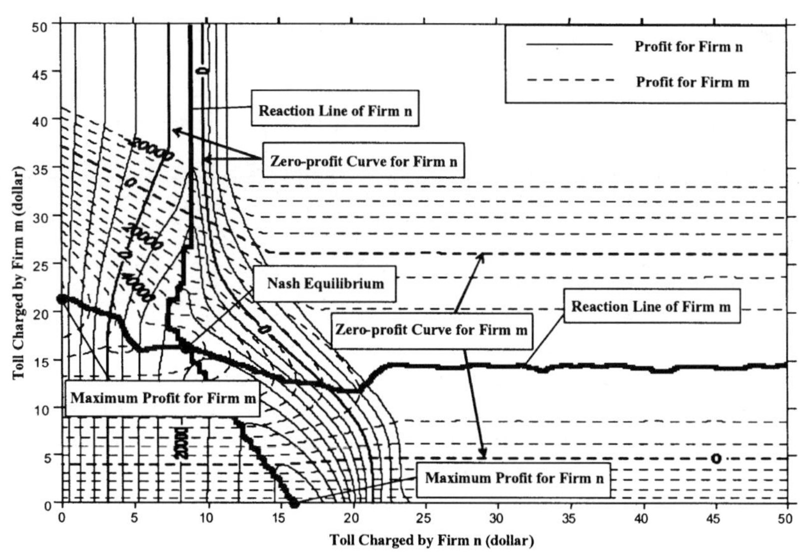

Figure 8.17 Profits for the complementary case with capacity fixed

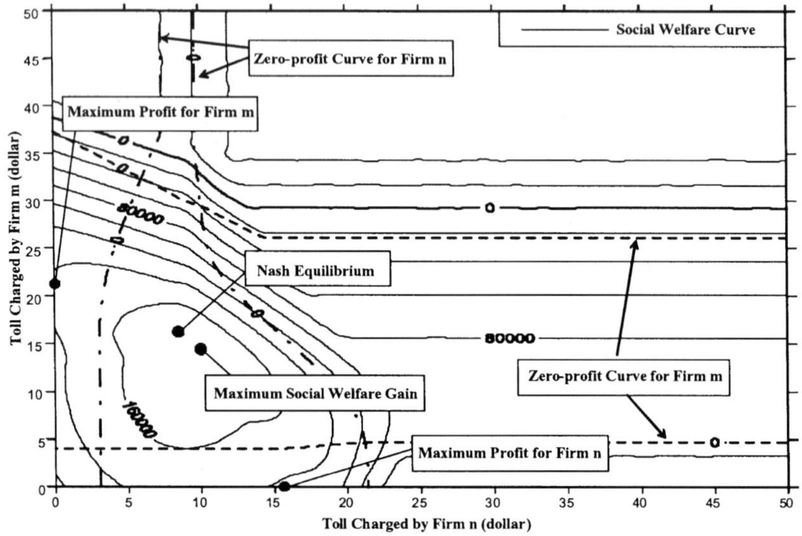

Figure 8.18 Social welfare gain for the complementary case with capacity fixed

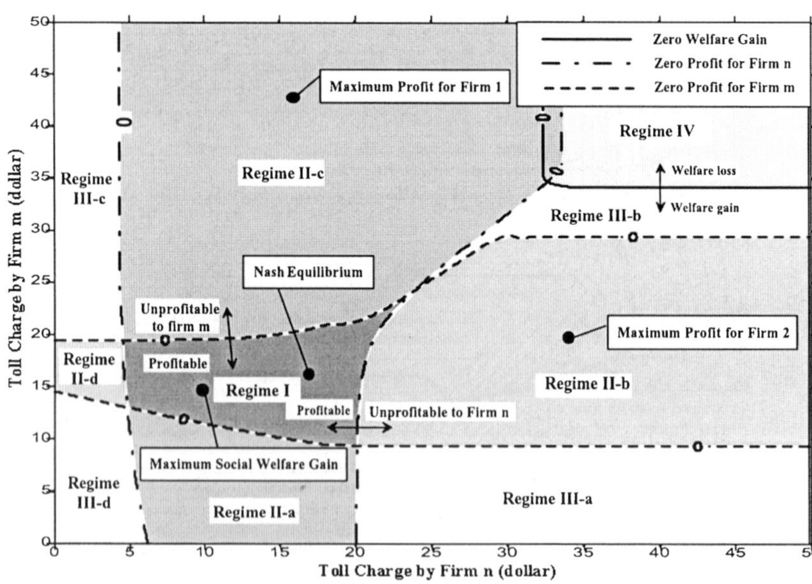

Figure 8.19 Economic regimes for the possibilities of profitability and welfare again

8.7 SUMMARY

In this chapter we made a thorough investigation of road pricing, capacity choice and self-financing in networks. With the use of the traffic equilibrium models developed in previous chapters, we investigate, through numerical experiments, the profitability and social welfare gain of a private road and the effects of user heterogeneity. Our graphical representation can help potential private investors identify how and under what circumstances, a BOT road project is feasible and profitable, and assist the public sector in understanding how the proposed project will benefit the private investor and the road users. Our numerical results from a simplified network example did highlight the importance of incorporating user heterogeneity in toll road modeling. Otherwise, the assumption of homogeneous users may give rise to either overestimation at lower toll or underestimation at higher toll of both the flow and profit, and may possibly lead to over-investment on a toll road.

We generalized the classic self-financing theorem to a general network with single or multiple vehicle types. We proved that the self-financing theorem holds for individual links and hence for the whole network under essentially the same first-best conditions for pricing and capacity choice, homogeneous of degree zero link travel time functions and constant return to scale link construction cost functions. In a more realistic case, with only a subset of new roads to be introduced into a network, the self-financing principle is still preserved, as long as all new and existing links are optimally priced and the capacities for the new roads are optimally selected. If, as is the more usual case, some if not all roads are un-tolled or priced at zero, then the rules derivable from "second-best" considerations become relevant. In these cases, traffic diverted to or from other roadways does matter. In particular, we have shown that the second-best efficient toll on a new toll road is equal to the marginal external cost on this road plus or minus a fraction of the marginal external cost on each of the un-tolled links in the network. As a result, the second-best toll on a new link can be larger, smaller than or equal to the marginal external cost on that link, and, the revenue generated will go beyond, below or equal to the construction cost for its optimally selected capacity.

Toll road competition is not an issue of mere academic interest, but one that is being encountered nowadays in many cities. We developed game-theoretic approaches to the study of the road network that involves multiple toll roads operated by competitive private firms. The toll road competition problems in general traffic equilibrium networks are formulated as equilibrium programs with equilibrium constraints or bi-level variational inequalities. We proposed heuristic solution methods which proved to be convergent with simple network examples. Finally, we investigated the strategic interactions and possible market equilibria among the private firms in a duopoly situation through graphical representation. Interesting insights are obtained from two experimental scenarios of two toll roads being either strategic substitutes or strategic complements in a network.

Our analyses have shown that private pricing and competition can be welfare-improving, but it is much imperative to develop efficient solution methods applicable to large networks. More investigations need to be done to understand what types of regulation by the government have to be imposed to the private oligopoly or the monopoly in order to avoid inefficient outcomes in a market economy.

8.8 Sources and Notes

This chapter is mainly drawn from a few selection of previous studies by the first author and his ex-students. Section 8.3 is taken from Yang and Meng (2000), and Section 8.4 from Yang and Tang et al. (2002). The material of self-financing in a general network was initially developed in Yang and Meng (2002), and the extension to the network traffic equilibrium with multiple vehicle types and discussion of self-financing in the more general second-best situation are newly developed and not yet published. The source of the numerical experiment results in Section 8.6 is Yang and Woo (2000), and mathematical formulations and solution heuristics of toll road competition in this section are newly developed.

Readers may refer to Mohring and Harwitz (1962), Strotz (1964), Mohrning (1976) and Keeler and Small (1977) on the early notable development of self-financing results. The subject of road pricing and financing has continued to attract interest by transportation economists. Henderson (1985) showed that self-financing is obtained in a case where users have a choice between two "modes"—which could either be driving on a road *vs.* taking transit, or choosing between two roads. Oum and Zhang (1990) examined the relationship between congestion tolls and capacity expansion costs when capacity expansion is indivisible. Arnott and Kraus (1995) showed that the first-best pricing and investment rule applies in Vickrey's bottleneck model of morning rush-hour congestion with heterogeneous users, provided that time variation of the toll is unconstrained. Small (1999) examined the conditions under which a congestible facility is self-financing in the presence of non-competitive factor markets; i.e. when the price of an input, such as land, varies with the quantity purchased. For surveys on congestion tolls and optimal investment, the reader may refer to, for example, Small (1992) and Hau (1998). Readers may also refer to De vany and Saving (1980), De Palma (1992), De Palma and Lindsey (2002) for toll road competition.

9

Simultaneous Determination of Optimal Toll Levels and Locations

9.1 Introduction

In the preceding chapters, we have examined various first-best and second-best pricing schemes, with exclusive focus on the existence and determination of desirable optimal link tolls for social optimum. We remarked that the first-best pricing scheme is purely a theoretical construct due to its unrealistic requirement for a perfect pricing environmental, but the second-best pricing scheme has received ample attention in the literature due to its practical relevance. Notwithstanding, a key question associated with a second-best pricing scheme remains open: how to determine the number and locations of tolling points, together with their charge levels, for a second-best pricing scheme in a general network? In connection with this question, two pricing schemes come into play; the individual link-based and the cordon-based pricing schemes. In a link-based pricing scheme, tolls are charged in a coordinated manner only on a subset of selected links in a network, especially where there are bottlenecks such as bridges, tunnels or expressways. In contrast, the cordon-based pricing scheme has emerged quickly in recent years in some cities to reduce traffic demand towards city centers.

This chapter is fully devoted to the second-best link-based and cordon-based pricing schemes that involve simultaneous optimization of toll levels and toll locations. Methods are drawn from mixed integer-discrete-continuous programming to maximize social welfare, subject to the elastic-demand traffic equilibrium in general networks. For a link-based second-best pricing scheme, we investigate how to search the optimal toll levels on given toll links, and then apply a widely used genetic algorithm to determine the optimal toll locations and toll levels simultaneously. The minimal number of toll links in a network is then sought to achieve system optimum with or without inclusion of pricing implementation cost. To deal with the cordon-based pricing scheme, we employ the concept of cutset in graph theory to describe the mathematical properties of a tolling cordon, and then search for the optimal cordon again with a genetic algorithm. Numerical examples are provided to demonstrate the two second-best pricing schemes considered.

9.2 THE LINK-BASED PRICING: METHODOLOGY

Since our emphasis in this chapter is placed on the determination of charging locations, we apply the bi-level second-best pricing model, subject to the standard traffic equilibrium problem, to find the optimal toll levels on a given set of toll links. Namely, we consider homogeneous users with identical values of time (VOT), and a single vehicle type, without flow interaction between links. The upper level problem aims to maximize social welfare and the lower level is an elastic demand traffic equilibrium model in terms of travel disutility in time units inclusive of equivalent time of toll charge, if any. The bi-level second-best pricing model for given charging locations is given as follows:

$$\max_{\mathbf{u}\in U} S(\mathbf{u}) = \sum_{w\in W} \int_0^{d_w(\mathbf{u})} B_w(\omega)\,d\omega - \sum_{a\in A} t_a(v_a(\mathbf{u}))v_a(\mathbf{u}) \tag{9.1}$$

where $v_a(\mathbf{u})$, $a \in A$ and $d_w(\mathbf{u})$, $w \in W$ are the solutions of the following lower-level traffic equilibrium program for a given toll pattern $\mathbf{u}$:

$$\min_{\mathbf{v},\mathbf{d}} \sum_{a\in A} \int_0^{v_a} t_a(\omega, u_a)\,d\omega - \sum_{w\in W} \int_0^{d_w} B_w(\omega)\,d\omega \tag{9.2}$$

subject to

$$\sum_{r\in R_w} f_{rw} = d_w,\ w \in W \tag{9.3}$$

$$v_a = \sum_{w\in W} \sum_{r\in R_w} f_{rw}\delta_{ar},\ a \in A \tag{9.4}$$

$$f_{rw} \geq 0,\ d_w \geq 0,\ r \in R_w,\ w \in W \tag{9.5}$$

The notation is as defined as before, particularly, $\bar{A} \subset A$ is a subset of candidate subject to toll charge; $t_a(v_a, u_a) = t_a(v_a) + u_a/\beta$, if $a \in \bar{A}$; and $t_a(v_a)$, if $a \in A$, $a \notin \bar{A}$. Link travel time $t_a(v_a)$ is a strictly increasing and continuous function of its link flow v_a, and benefit or inverse demand function $B_w(d_w)$ is a strictly decreasing and continuous function of OD demand d_w. U is the feasible set of link tolls, which could be defined by

$$U = \left\{\mathbf{u} \,\middle|\, u_a^{\min} \leq u_a \leq u_a^{\max},\ a \in \bar{A}\right\} \tag{9.6}$$

where $u_a^{\min}$ and $u_a^{\max}$ are the prespecified lower and upper bounds of link tolls u_a, $a \in \bar{A}$.

9.2.1 Genetic Algorithm for Determination of Optimal Tolling Links

From the bi-level model (9.1)-(9.6), we know that given a fixed set of toll links $\bar{A}$, a maximum social welfare $S(\mathbf{u}^*)$ associated with optimal tolls $\mathbf{u}^*$ on these links can be found with the solution methods developed in previous chapters. So the maximum social welfare

$S(\mathbf{u}^*)$ can be ... implicit function with the toll link set $\bar{A}$. Then, the problem is

... toll link set $\bar{A}$. Without doubt, we could always increase the ...dding toll links before it reaches its maximum if the pricing ... ignored. At least, social welfare can be maintained at the same ... additional links to be zero and keeping the tolls on the original ... here is that, when we add a new toll link to the network, the ...ll station should be taken into account. As a result, there is a ...he social welfare and minimizing the extra operating cost. This ... of toll links should be treated as a decision variable to be ... locations and charging levels.

...ticable, suppose a set of candidate toll links $\tilde{A} \subset A$ is ...d only the members in set $\tilde{A}$ can be selected. As a rule of ...ks (bottlenecks) can be chosen as the candidates for avoiding ...erceived travel cost on these links. Let $\bar{L}$ and $\tilde{L}$ denote the ... $\tilde{A}$, respectively. The combinations of choosing $\bar{L}$ members ... a practical problem. It may be very hard if not impossible to .... Therefore, we have to find a rational procedure to search for ...ntly. The genetic algorithm (GA) is able to do this, because of ...ural selection. It is one of the population evaluation-based ... useful for discrete optimization. For GA application to our ...h candidate link correspond to the parameter of describing a ...didates $\tilde{L}$ represent the length of chromosome. For each ... two alternatives, either to be charged or not. We define that ... selected

(9.7)

...tal number of toll links being equal to $\bar{L}$

(9.8)

1	0	1	1	1	0	1	0	0	0	1

7	34	39	45	53	59	64	69	73	82	93

...ter representation in a binary genetic algorithm

The candidates $\tilde{a}$ with $g_{\tilde{a}} = 1$ will constitute the set of tolling links, $\bar{A}$. Therefore, we can encode the parameters (genes) with the simplest binary variable, and 1 bit is enough for each gene, *i.e.* 0-1 integers. For example, in Figure 9.1, line (a) represents a chromosome. The length of the chromosome is $\tilde{L} = 15$, and the total number of toll links is $\overline{L} = 8$. Assuming that the corresponding link numbers of each candidate are given in line (b), then the toll link set is defined by $\overline{A} = \{6,11,27,39,45,53,64,93\}$.

We now introduce the detailed procedure of the binary genetic algorithm below:

Step 1. (*Initial population*) Randomly generate an initial population of the toll link combinations.

Step 2. (*Function evaluation*) Employ the bi-level model (9.1)-(9.6) to obtain the optimum tolls on each link for each combination of toll links.

Step 3. (*Natural selection*) Select part of the tolling link combinations with higher values of social welfare gains and discard the others.

Step 4. (*Crossover*) Pair the survivors and randomly exchange the tolling links between pairs.

Step 5. (*Mutation*) Randomly change some tolling links.

Step 6. (*Verification of stopping criterion*) If the convergence criterion has not been reached, go to Step 2 to continue the next generation; otherwise stop.

Note that constraint (9.8) must always be maintained during the whole process. Hence special treatment is needed in the operations of crossover and mutation.

The GA proposed above is able to search for the optimal subset of tolling links $\overline{A}$, the optimal toll pattern $\mathbf{u}^*$ and the corresponding maximal social welfare $S\left(\mathbf{u}^*, \overline{L}\right)$ for a given number of tolling links $\overline{L}$. In this sense, $S\left(\mathbf{u}^*\right)$ can be regarded as an implicit function of $\overline{L}$. However, social welfare does not include the extra operating cost of the tolling system up to date, hence it should be called gross social welfare. If the extra operating cost is taken into account, the net social welfare can be obtained by subtracting the extra cost from the gross social welfare. Obviously, the extra operating cost is highly dependent on the total number of tolling stations. If we further assume that every tolling station has identical extra operating cost, and hence the total extra operating cost is proportional to $\overline{L}$. Therefore, the maximal net social welfare for a given $\overline{L}$ takes the following form:

$$\overline{S}\left(\mathbf{u}^*, \overline{L}\right) = S\left(\mathbf{u}^*, \overline{L}\right) - \kappa \overline{L} \tag{9.9}$$

Here $\overline{S}\left(\mathbf{u}^*, \overline{L}\right)$ represents the maximal net social welfare among all the scenarios that have $\overline{L}$ tolling links, and κ is the operating cost of one tolling station.

As mentioned before, there is a tradeoff between increasing gross social welfare and decreasing implementation cost. Obviously, in (9.9) the term $S\left(\mathbf{u}^*, \overline{L}\right)$ is an increasing function in $\overline{L}$ while $(-\kappa\overline{L})$ is a decreasing function in $\overline{L}$. Now we have the following model to determine the optimal total number of tolling links.

$$\max_{0\le\overline{L}\le\tilde{L}} \overline{S}(\mathbf{u}^*,\overline{L}) = S(\mathbf{u}^*,\overline{L}) - \kappa\overline{L} \tag{9.10}$$

where $\tilde{L}$ is, as defined above, the number of candidate tolling links. Since there is only one variable in the model, a one dimension search method can suffice to search for the optimal solution of $\overline{L}$ in combination the GA algorithm described above.

9.2.2 Selection of Minimal Number and Locations of Tolling Links

As described in Section 6.2 of Chapter 6, we can obtain the maximal social welfare gain by the first-best or marginal cost pricing scheme with the corresponding social optimum OD demands and link traffic flows. However, apart from marginal cost pricing, there could be many toll patterns that can obtain the same maximal social welfare. It is thus interesting and meaningful to identify a second-best tolling scheme that can achieve the same system optimal flow pattern with a minimal number of tolling links. This can be easily done with the help of the model (9.10) as follows:

$$\min_{0\le\overline{L}\le\tilde{L}} \overline{L} + \rho\left[S^* - S(\mathbf{u}^*,\overline{L})\right] \tag{9.11}$$

where S^* refers to the maximum social welfare achieved under marginal-cost pricing; ρ is a a sufficiently large penalty parameter and the second term in (9.11) can be regarded as a penalty term. If $S^* > S$, the objective function value will be very large and hence not optimal; if, however, $S^* = S$, the objective function value becomes the number of tolling links $\overline{L}$. So the model is able to achieve system optimum and meanwhile minimize the number of tolling links. Therefore, only a minimum subset of tolling links resulting in a maximal social welfare gain will be chosen. Note that in this case the set of candidate toll links, $\tilde{A}$, in model (9.11) must be the whole set of links in the network (*i.e.*, $\tilde{A} = A$ and $\tilde{L}$ is the total number of network links). Otherwise there is no guarantee of always achieving the system optimum.

9.3 THE LINK-BASED PRICING: EXAMPLE

Consider the network shown in Figure 9.2, consisting of 43 links and 20 nodes. There is a single OD pair form node 1 to node 20 with the following demand function:

$$d_{1\to20} = 2.5\times10^3\exp(-0.02\mu_{1\to20}) \tag{9.12}$$

The following link travel time function is used:

$$t_a(v_a) = t_a^0\left\{1.0 + 0.15\left(\frac{v_a}{C_a}\right)^4\right\},\quad a \in A \tag{9.13}$$

where link capacity C_a and free-flow travel time t_a^0 are given in Table 9.1.

The standard UE traffic assignment is first conducted, giving rise to a social welfare value of 153,790 (HK$). At the un-tolled traffic equilibrium, there are 12 most congested links, {3, 4, 6, 9, 16, 19, 22, 25, 32, 35, 38 and 42}, with their flow/capacity ratios greater than 1.0. When the marginal-cost pricing scheme is implemented, a maximum social welfare value of 157,080 (HK$) is obtained.

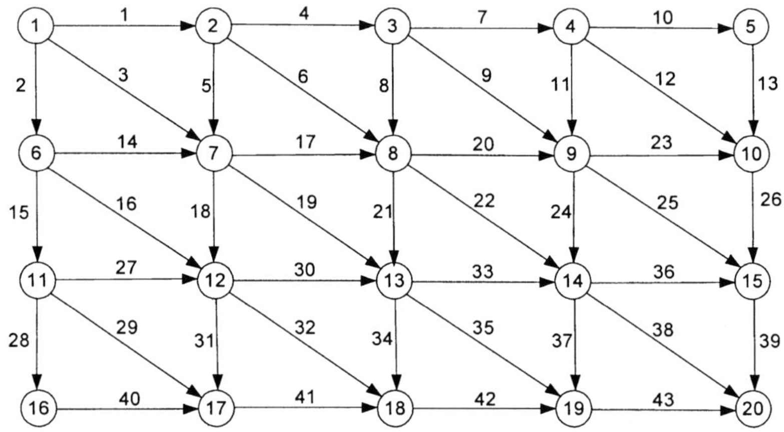

Figure 9.2 Example network for demonstrating link-based pricing scheme

Table 9.1 Input data for the Figure 9.2 network

Link No.	t_a^0 (min)	C_a (veh/h)	Link No.	t_a^0 (min)	C_a (veh/h)	Link No.	t_a^0 (min)	C_a (veh/h)
1	4.0	1000	16	5.0	300	31	3.0	800
2	3.0	1000	17	4.0	200	32	5.0	300
3	5.0	100	18	3.0	600	33	4.0	200
4	4.0	600	19	5.0	100	34	3.0	600
5	3.0	200	20	4.0	600	35	5.0	100
6	5.0	100	21	3.0	200	36	4.0	600
7	4.0	700	22	5.0	100	37	3.0	200
8	3.0	400	23	4.0	800	38	5.0	100
9	5.0	300	24	3.0	600	39	3.0	1000
10	4.0	800	25	5.0	300	40	4.0	600
11	3.0	600	26	3.0	600	41	4.0	700
12	5.0	400	27	4.0	600	42	4.0	600
13	3.0	600	28	3.0	800	43	4.0	1000
14	4.0	600	29	5.0	400			
15	3.0	600	30	4.0	600			

Now let us consider a second-best link-based pricing scheme. We regard the 12 most congested links as bottlenecks in the network, and take them as the candidate tolling links.

The GA in association with a simulated annealing (SA) method is used to seek optimal toll locations and toll levels. The GA is used to find the best toll link combination for a given number of toll links and the SA described in Section 7.5 of Chapter 7 is used to solve the bi-level program (9.1)-(9.6). A total of 10 cases are analyzed when the number of tolling links is increased from 1 to 10. In each case, the optimal tolling links and optimal toll levels are obtained together with the corresponding maximal social welfare. The overall results are given in Table 9.2. It is clear from the table that we can always increase social welfare by adding more tolling links. When we charge optimal tolls on 10 appropriate links, the social welfare reaches 157,010 (HK\$), which is sufficiently close to the maximal social welfare value of 157,080 (HK\$).

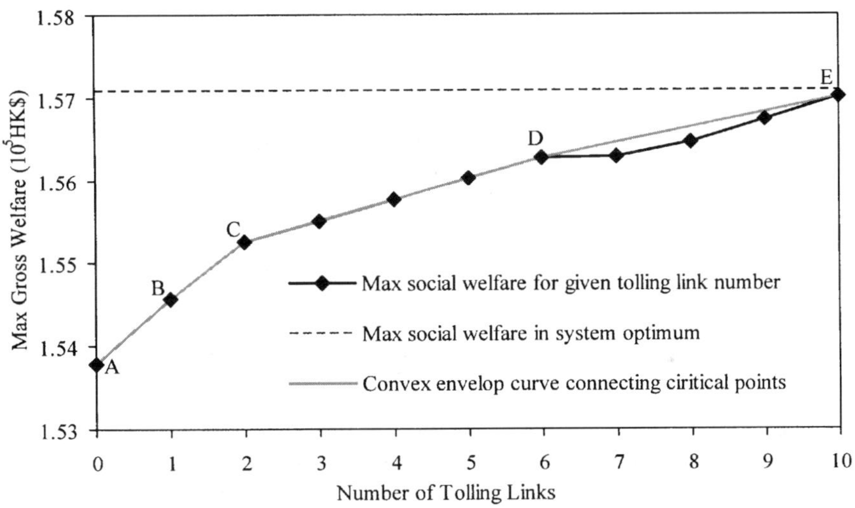

Figure 9.3 The maximal social welfare for a given number of toll links

In the above analysis, the implementation costs are ignored. We now consider the net social welfare by subtracting the total operating costs spent on all tolling stations from the gross social welfare. The result is shown in Figure 9.3, where the horizontal axis denotes number of tolling links and the vertical axis the corresponding maximal *gross* social welfare. If we connect 5 points of A, B, C, D and E with 4 line segments; these 5 points form a convex envelope curve. These 5 extreme points have special meanings: whatever the unit operating cost is, to maximize net social welfare the optimal number of toll links can only be their horizontal axis values, namely 0, 1, 2, 6 or 10. Furthermore, the slopes of the 4 line segments AB, BC, CD and DE are 772, 682, 258 and 184 (HK\$ per tolling station) respectively, which represent the critical unit operating costs for the selection of optimal toll locations. If the unit operating cost of each toll station is less than 184 (HK\$), we can enhance the net social welfare by charging on 10 links; if the unit operating cost falls in the intervals of (184, 258), (258, 682) or (682, 772), the optimal number of tolling links should be 6, 2 or 1, respectively;

if, however, the unit operating cost is greater than 772, no tolling link should be introduced as the net social welfare will be negative.

As we already mentioned, the maximum social welfare of 157,080 (HK$) is achieved through the first-best pricing scheme; the same amount of social welfare could be also achieved in the second-best pricing scheme with less number of tolling links. Now we apply model (9.11) to determine the minimal number of tolling links to decentralize the system optimum into user-optimal traffic equilibrium. In this case, the set of candidate tolling links is extended to cover the whole set of links in the network, and the number of tolling link constraints is removed. It is found that at least 14 tolling links are required to achieve a system optimum. The tolling links and the corresponding optimum link tolls are presented in Table 9.3.

Table 9.2 The selected links, toll levels and the corresponding maximal social welfare for each given number of tolling links ranging from 1 to 10

Link Num.	Subset of Tolling Links	Toll on Each Link (HK$)	Welfare (HK$)
1	9	3.206	154564
2	9,32	3.048,3.048	155246
3	3,9,32	3.214,3.156,2.984	155502
4	3,9,32,38	3.186,3.116,3.104,3.104	155762
5	3,6,9,32,38	3.230,3.322,3.242,3.128,3.312	156020
6	3,6,9,32,35,38	3.188,3.264,3.212,3.188,3.236,3.248	156276
7	3,4,6,9,32,35,38	3.244,0.206,3.238,3.022,3.212,3.284,3.198	156280
8	3,4,6,16,25,35,38,42	3.312,3.196,3.142,3.200,3.224,3.190,3.312,3.164	156458
9	3,4,6,16,19,25,35,38,42	3.164,3.276,3.260,3.204,3.230,3.204,3.300,3.280,3.242	156734
10	3,4,6,16,19,22,25,35,38,42	3.192,3.256,3.278,3.210,3.178,3.204,3.220,3.210,3.264,3.232	157010

Table 9.3 The minimal set of tolling links and toll levels to achieve a system optimum

Tolling Link	3	4	6	9	16	19	22
Toll (HK$)	3.202	3.212	3.202	0.006	3.196	3.210	3.208
Tolling Link	25	32	35	38	39	42	43
Toll (HK$)	3.196	0.006	3.208	6.020	2.884	3.194	2.884

9.4 THE CORDON-BASED PRICING: METHODOLOGY

As mentioned before, of a practical relevance and importance is the cordon-based second-best congestion pricing scheme that is being implemented in a number of urban areas. In this section, we present a systematic way for determination of various forms of tolling cordons and their toll levels in a general network, including the simplest single-layered cordon, multi-layered cordons and multi-centered cordons. It is self-evident that the standard mathematical programming method does not apply for this complex optimization problem involving both discrete and continuous variables. We thus propose to jointly use GA, *cutset* graph theory and direct grid search methods to tackle problems of interest. The GA generates an improved combination of toll nodes and then the cutset theory checks whether the candidate toll nodes are interconnected and thus forms a feasible cordon area, and finally using a grid search method ascertains the optimal toll levels on the selected cordons. The performance of a given toll cordon is evaluated in terms of the maximal social welfare that can be achieved with an appropriate toll charge.

9.4.1 Mathematical Properties of Toll Cordons

The simplest tolling cordon around a central business district (CBD) is made up of a minimal set of links to place tolls. These links divide the network into two areas, namely the tolling area and the non-tolling area. In some large cities, there are several separate CBD areas and then one cordon around each CBD can be designed. The properties of tolling cordons can be described by the concepts of cutset and/or cut in graph theory. To help readers understand these concepts, some preliminary knowledge about graph theory is given in this subsection.

A transportation network can be mathematically viewed as a directed graph, $G(N, A)$, consisting of a set of nodes N and a set of directed links (edges) A connecting these nodes. In the context of this section, the transportation network is a connected network (graph) without self-loop links. This means we can always find at least one path to travel from one node to another node; and all the links connect different nodes (*i.e.*, the two endpoints of each link or edge are different nodes). The node-link incidence matrix is frequently used in the analysis of graph theory. For a graph with $|N|$ nodes and $|A|$ links, this is a matrix with order $|N|\times|A|$, *i.e.*, $\mathbf{A}=\left[a_{ij}\right]$, where

$$a_{ij}=\begin{cases}1 & \text{if link } e_j \text{ is incident at node } n_i\text{, and directed from node } n_i\\ 0 & \text{if link } e_j \text{ is not incident at node } n_i\\ \text{-1} & \text{if link } e_j \text{ is incident at node } i\text{, and directed to node } n_i\end{cases} \tag{9.14}$$

Thus, in the node-link incidence matrix each row corresponds to a node and each column corresponds to an edge. In the graph theory, the rank of the incidence matrix of a graph is termed as the *rank* of the graph.

A *component* of a graph (connected or unconnected) is a connected subgraph containing the maximal number of edges in that graph. Certainly, a connected graph itself is the biggest component in this graph. According to the graph theory, the *rank* of a graph is given by the number of nodes minus the number of components, *i.e.*, $Rank = |N| - N_{\text{compt}}$, where $Rank$ and N_{compt} represent the rank of the graph and the number of components, respectively.

Example 9.1 As an illustration, consider an example road network shown in Figure 9.4. This network is a connected graph consisting of $|N| = 9$ nodes and $|A| = 20$ links. Since there is only $N_{\text{compt}} = 1$ component in the network, thus the rank of the graph is $Rank = 8$. The node-node-link incidence matrix is:

$$
\mathbf{A} = \begin{array}{c} \\ n_1 \\ n_2 \\ n_3 \\ n_4 \\ n_5 \\ n_6 \\ n_7 \\ n_8 \\ n_9 \end{array}
\begin{array}{c}
\begin{array}{cccccccccccccccccccc} e_1 & e_2 & e_3 & e_4 & e_5 & e_6 & e_7 & e_8 & e_9 & e_{10} & e_{11} & e_{12} & e_{13} & e_{14} & e_{15} & e_{16} & e_{17} & e_{18} & e_{19} & e_{20} \end{array} \\
\begin{bmatrix}
-1 & 0 & 0 & 1 & 1 & 0 & 0 & 0 & 0 & 0 & 0 & -1 & 0 & 0 & 0 & 0 & 0 & 0 & 0 & 0 \\
1 & -1 & 0 & 0 & 0 & -1 & 1 & 0 & 0 & 0 & 0 & 0 & 0 & 0 & 0 & 0 & 0 & 0 & 0 & 0 \\
0 & 1 & -1 & 0 & 0 & 0 & 0 & -1 & 1 & 0 & 0 & 0 & 0 & 0 & 0 & 0 & 0 & 0 & 0 & 0 \\
0 & 0 & 1 & -1 & 0 & 0 & 0 & 0 & 0 & -1 & 1 & 0 & 0 & 0 & 0 & 0 & 0 & 0 & 0 & 0 \\
0 & 0 & 0 & 0 & -1 & 1 & 0 & 0 & 0 & 0 & 0 & 0 & 1 & 0 & 0 & -1 & 1 & 0 & 0 & 0 \\
0 & 0 & 0 & 0 & 0 & 0 & -1 & 1 & 0 & 0 & 0 & 0 & 0 & 0 & -1 & 1 & 0 & 0 & 0 & -1 \\
0 & 0 & 0 & 0 & 0 & 0 & 0 & 0 & -1 & 1 & 0 & 0 & 0 & -1 & 1 & 0 & 0 & -1 & 0 & 0 \\
0 & 0 & 0 & 0 & 0 & 0 & 0 & 0 & 0 & 0 & -1 & 1 & -1 & 1 & 0 & 0 & 0 & 0 & 1 & 0 \\
0 & 0 & 0 & 0 & 0 & 0 & 0 & 0 & 0 & 0 & 0 & 0 & 0 & 0 & 0 & 0 & -1 & 1 & -1 & 1
\end{bmatrix}
\end{array}
$$

It is easy to verify that the rank of this matrix is $Rank = 8$.

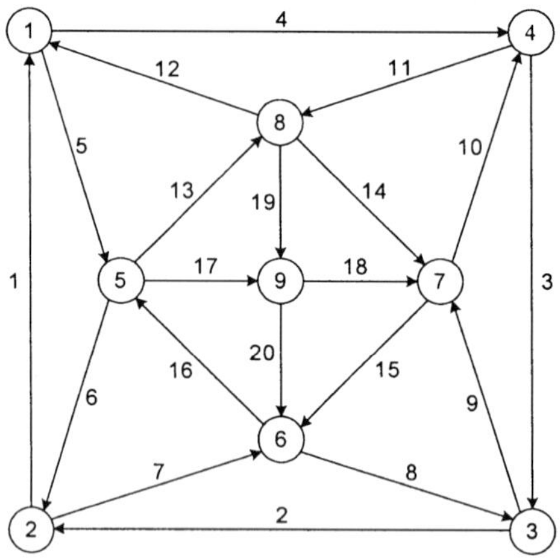

Figure 9.4 Network used in Example 9.1

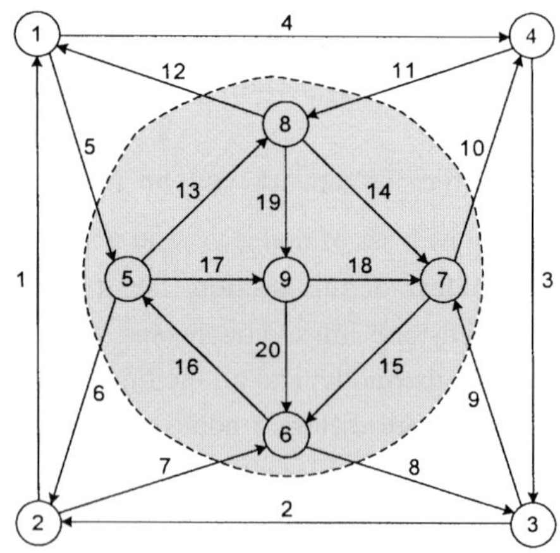

Figure 9.5 The cutset in Example 9.2

A *cutset* of a graph is defined as a minimal collection of links whose removal reduces the rank of the graph by one (and only one). A single cutset or edge-disjointed union of cutsets of a graph is called a *cut*. A cut can also be interpreted in another usual fashion. Let N_1 be a nonempty proper subset of the node set N of a graph G, and its complement is $N_2 = N - N_1$. Then, the set of some links of G, each link of which is incident with one of its two endpoints in N_1 and the other in N_2, is a cut of G. In particular, if the removal of these links from G increases the number of components by one (and no more than one), then the cut is also a cutset.

Example 9.2 Now we divide the 9 nodes of the network in Figure 9.4 into two subsets, namely, $N_1 = \{n_5,\ n_6,\ n_7,\ n_8,\ n_9\}$ and $N_2 = \{n_1,\ n_2,\ n_3,\ n_4\}$, then a cut will be defined uniquely as shown in Figure 9.5, which is given by the set of links of $\{e_5,\ e_6,\ e_7,\ e_8,\ e_9,\ e_{10},\ e_{11},\ e_{12}\}$. Intuitively, there will appear two components after the removal of these links from G, namely, the inner shaded part containing N_1 and the outer plain part containing N_2. Clearly, the number of components is increased by one exactly, and then the cut is also a cutset. Mathematically, this observation can be confirmed by checking the rank of the incidence matrix of the graph after cutting, which is given by

$$\mathbf{A} = \begin{array}{c} \\ n_1 \\ n_2 \\ n_3 \\ n_4 \\ n_5 \\ n_6 \\ n_7 \\ n_8 \\ n_9 \end{array} \begin{array}{c} \begin{array}{cccccccccccc} e_1 & e_2 & e_3 & e_4 & e_{13} & e_{14} & e_{15} & e_{16} & e_{17} & e_{18} & e_{19} & e_{20} \end{array} \\ \begin{bmatrix} -1 & 0 & 0 & 1 & 0 & 0 & 0 & 0 & 0 & 0 & 0 & 0 \\ 1 & -1 & 0 & 0 & 0 & 0 & 0 & 0 & 0 & 0 & 0 & 0 \\ 0 & 1 & -1 & 0 & 0 & 0 & 0 & 0 & 0 & 0 & 0 & 0 \\ 0 & 0 & 1 & -1 & 0 & 0 & 0 & 0 & 0 & 0 & 0 & 0 \\ 0 & 0 & 0 & 0 & 1 & 0 & 0 & -1 & 1 & 0 & 0 & 0 \\ 0 & 0 & 0 & 0 & 0 & 0 & -1 & 1 & 0 & 0 & 0 & -1 \\ 0 & 0 & 0 & 0 & 0 & -1 & 1 & 0 & 0 & -1 & 0 & 0 \\ 0 & 0 & 0 & 0 & -1 & 1 & 0 & 0 & 0 & 0 & 1 & 0 \\ 0 & 0 & 0 & 0 & 0 & 0 & 0 & 0 & -1 & 1 & -1 & 1 \end{bmatrix} \end{array}$$

The rank of this matrix is $Rank = 7$, then the number of components is $N_{\text{compt}} = 2$.

Example 9.3 Now we consider one more scenario with $N_1 = \{n_5,\ n_6,\ n_7,\ n_8\}$ and $N_2 = \{n_1,\ n_2,\ n_3,\ n_4,\ n_9\}$. As shown in Figure 9.6, the cut is given by the set of links $\{e_5,\ e_6,\ e_7,\ e_8,\ e_9,\ e_{10},\ e_{11},\ e_{12},\ e_{17},\ e_{18},\ e_{19},\ e_{20}\}$. There are also three components in the graph after removal of these edges from G. However, differing from the former example, here the plain area of N_2 is separated into two parts and the shaded area of N_1 is a ring, hence the node set N_2 is multi-layered. In this example, the number of components after cutting is increased by two, thus the cut is not a cutset. The incidence matrix of the graph after cutting is given by

$$\mathbf{A} = \begin{array}{c} \\ n_1 \\ n_2 \\ n_3 \\ n_4 \\ n_5 \\ n_6 \\ n_7 \\ n_8 \\ n_9 \end{array} \begin{array}{c} \begin{array}{cccccccc} e_1 & e_2 & e_3 & e_4 & e_{13} & e_{14} & e_{15} & e_{16} \end{array} \\ \begin{bmatrix} -1 & 0 & 0 & 1 & 0 & 0 & 0 & 0 \\ 1 & -1 & 0 & 0 & 0 & 0 & 0 & 0 \\ 0 & 1 & -1 & 0 & 0 & 0 & 0 & 0 \\ 0 & 0 & 1 & -1 & 0 & 0 & 0 & 0 \\ 0 & 0 & 0 & 0 & 1 & 0 & 0 & -1 \\ 0 & 0 & 0 & 0 & 0 & 0 & -1 & 1 \\ 0 & 0 & 0 & 0 & 0 & -1 & 1 & 0 \\ 0 & 0 & 0 & 0 & -1 & 1 & 0 & 0 \\ 0 & 0 & 0 & 0 & 0 & 0 & 0 & 0 \end{bmatrix} \end{array}$$

The rank of this matrix is $Rank = 6$, then we get the number of components $N_{\text{compt}} = 3$.

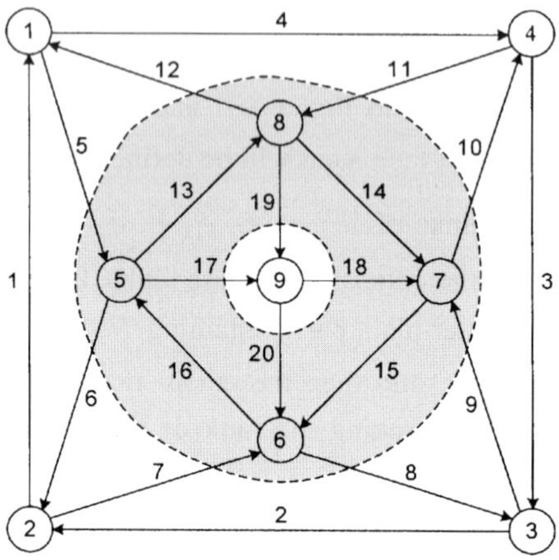

Figure 9.6 The cut in Example 9.3

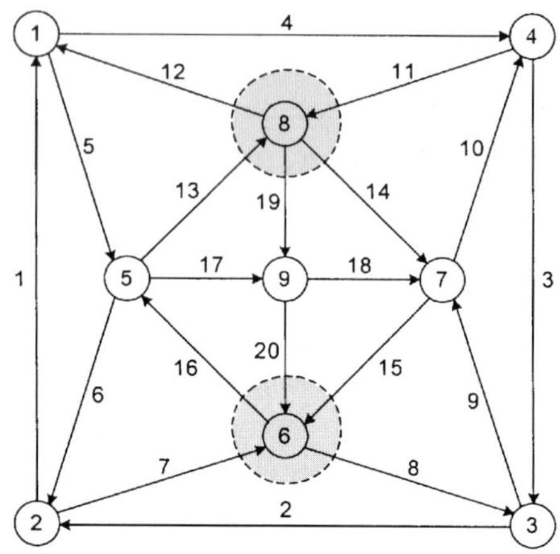

Figure 9.7 The cut in Example 9.4

Example 9.4 Set $N_1 = \{n_6, n_8\}$ and $N_2 = \{n_1, n_2, n_3, n_4, n_5, n_7, n_9\}$ as shown in Figure 9.7. The cut is given by the link set $\{e_7, e_8, e_{11}, e_{12}, e_{13}, e_{14}, e_{15}, e_{16}, e_{19}, e_{20}\}$. Intuitively, there appear three components after removal of these links from G, i.e. two disjointed shaded areas and one plain area, hence we say that the node set N_1 is multi-centered. In another way, since the number of components after cutting is increased by two, the cut is not a cutset. The incidence matrix of the graph after cutting is given by

$$
\mathbf{A} = \begin{array}{c} n_1 \\ n_2 \\ n_3 \\ n_4 \\ n_5 \\ n_6 \\ n_7 \\ n_8 \\ n_9 \end{array}
\overset{\begin{array}{cccccccccc} e_1 & e_2 & e_3 & e_4 & e_5 & e_6 & e_9 & e_{10} & e_{17} & e_{18} \end{array}}{\begin{bmatrix}
-1 & 0 & 0 & 1 & 1 & 0 & 0 & 0 & 0 & 0 \\
1 & -1 & 0 & 0 & 0 & -1 & 0 & 0 & 0 & 0 \\
0 & 1 & -1 & 0 & 0 & 0 & 1 & 0 & 0 & 0 \\
0 & 0 & 1 & -1 & 0 & 0 & 0 & -1 & 0 & 0 \\
0 & 0 & 0 & 0 & -1 & 1 & 0 & 0 & 1 & 0 \\
0 & 0 & 0 & 0 & 0 & 0 & 0 & 0 & 0 & 0 \\
0 & 0 & 0 & 0 & 0 & 0 & -1 & 1 & 0 & -1 \\
0 & 0 & 0 & 0 & 0 & 0 & 0 & 0 & 0 & 0 \\
0 & 0 & 0 & 0 & 0 & 0 & 0 & 0 & -1 & 1
\end{bmatrix}}
$$

It is easy to calculate that the rank of this matrix is $Rank = 6$ and then the number of components is $N_{\text{compt}} = 3$.

With the mathematical definition of cut and cutset in graph theory, we now introduce rigorous definition, classification and interpretation of various cordons for area-based congestion pricing with different geographical features.

9.4.2 Types of Cordon

Single-layered cordon. When an area-based pricing scheme is considered for a congested area such as the central business district, the subject area is cordoned off by a simple imaginary closed-loop; the area enclosed within this loop is defined as the cordon area subject to toll charge. The closed-loop C_1 and C_2 in Figure 9.8 are examples of such simplest complete cordons. Note that in the same figure, the screen line S divides the study area into two sections and can be considered as a special cordon as well. Differing from the closed-loop cordon that divides the whole area into an inner and an outer subarea, screen line S crosses the boundary of the study area. Both types of cordon may be adopted for area-based congestion pricing.

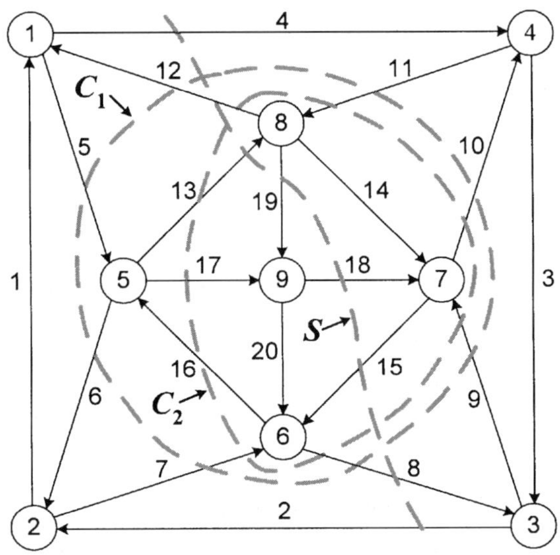

Figure 9.8 Examples of single-layered cordons and screen-lines

It is straightforward to see that the set of links crossing the cordon is a cutest, as defined before. Since the cordon divides the whole network into two parts, if we take the nodes in one part as set N_1, and the other nodes as N_2, the links crossing the cordon are exactly the set of links with one endpoint in N_1 and the other in N_2, which is a cutset by definition. Note that the single-layered cordon divides the whole network into two components; hence the rank of the graph will decrease from $(|N|-1)$ to $(|N|-2)$, where $|N|$ is the number of nodes. This was illustrated in Example 9.2.

Multi-layered cordons. Suppose there is one large city center, traffic becomes more congested on moving to the innermost part. In this case, multi-layered cordons may be more preferable in order to mitigate traffic congestion to a desirable level. Similarly, the multi-layered cordons are also a disjointed combination of multiple closed-loops and a non-cutset cut. In this case, one cordon contains the other and users have to pay money once crossing a closed-loop of the cordon. In general, for a m-layered cordon, totally there are $(m+1)$ components generated after the cutting. Again, the rank of the graph will decrease from $(|N|-1)$ to $(|N|-m-1)$ after removal of the links crossing the cordons. This was illustrated in Example 9.3.

Multi-centered cordons. A large city may contain more than one separate business centers, and an area-based toll charge may be desirable for each center to mitigate traffic congestion. Since the multi-centered cordons are a disjointed combination of individual simple closed-loops, it is a cut but not a cutset by definition. If there are m centers enclosed with closed-loops, then there are $(m+1)$ components generated after cutting, namely, the m city centers and the remainder. In other words, if the links crossing the cordons are removed, the rank of the graph will decrease from $(|N|-1)$ to $(|N|-m-1)$. This was illustrated in Example 9.4.

There might be more complex cordons consisting of a combination of the various aforementioned forms of cordons. Their properties can be discussed in a similar manner and are omitted here.

9.4.3 Determination of Tolling Cordons

Determination of optimal tolling cordons is one kind of location problem in networks. It is well known that solving the network location problem by traditional discrete optimization program is very hard. Here, we again apply the GA method used in previous sections, in which the populations refer to the feasible cordons and their performances are evaluated by the maximal social welfare that can be achieved with optimal toll charges on them. The general idea of using GA for selection of tolling cordons is given below.

General procedure for selection of tolling cordon

(i) Determine the type of cordon by examining the characteristics of the city.
(ii) Generate a set of feasible cordons of the selected cordon type randomly, and evaluate their performances with the bi-level model (9.1)-(9.6).
(iii) Discard the cordons with poor performance, and let those with better performance survive.
(iv) Pair and cross the surviving cordons, then give birth to new cordons of the next generation. Meanwhile, the mutation will generate other new cordons.

In step (ii) the bilevel model (9.1)-(9.6) can be simply applied to find the optimal tolls on predetermined tolling cordons. The single layered-cordon has one toll level and the multi-layered or multi-centered cordons have several toll levels (one toll level for each closed loop). All links crossing the same closed cordon loop are charged with the same level of toll. Links not crossing any cordon loops are free of charge. As discussed before, there are a couple of methods available to solve the bi-level toll optimization program, such as simulated annealing and grid search algorithm. Since in our problem there are very few variables (levels of cordon toll charge) in the upper level, the grid search method is employed for search of a global optimum. In this case, a traffic assignment has to be executed for each trial toll charge. The key problem in the above procedure is how to represent the cordons by chromosomes and how to generate feasible cordons. This problem is discussed in detail for different types of cordons below.

Single-layered cordon

The single-layered cordon divides the whole network into two sub-areas, namely the *tolling area* and the *non-tolling area*. Users have to pay when crossing the cordon from non-tolling area to the tolling area. Let us term the nodes in tolling area *tolling nodes* and those in non-tolling area *non-tolling nodes*. Of course, the area inside the cordon is the tolling area and the area outside the cordon is the non-tolling area.

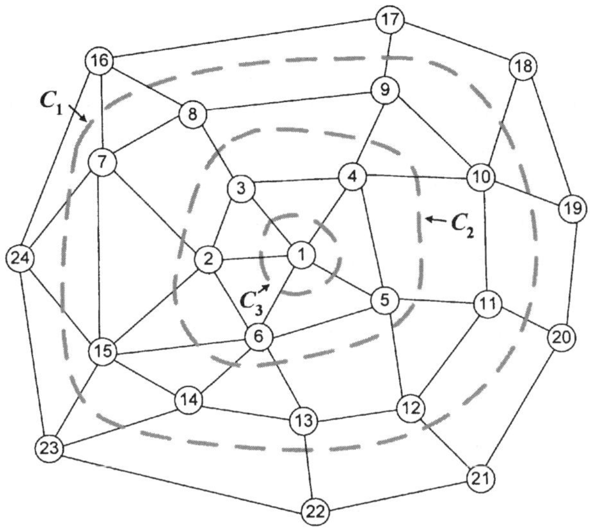

Figure 9.9 An example network used for illustration of selection of a single-layered cordon and parameter representation of genetic algorithm

Being the most fundamental and commonly used, the single-layered cordon is discussed in more detail, as it is also helpful to the understanding of other forms of cordons. Suppose a road network is given in Figure 9.9 and a single-layered tolling cordon is to be set around the CBD area. Instead of determining the optimal tolling links directly, we determine the optimal tolling nodes (tolling area), and thus the optimal tolling cordon is determined subsequently. Around the most congested CBD area, some nodes are predetermined as candidate tolling nodes, for example, in Figure 9.9 the nodes within the closed-loop C_1 are set to be candidates. Note that the tolling area containing the tolling nodes should be large enough to include the future optimal tolling cordon; otherwise an optimal tolling cordon may not be found. Then the GA is employed to search for the optimal tolling nodes (tolling cordon).

The procedure of searching for a feasible cordon is as follows. From the candidate set, some nodes are randomly picked up as a subset of tolling nodes, and then a cut is determined automatically, having the links with one endpoint in the tolling area and the other in the non-tolling area. Then the rank of the incidence matrix, after removal of the cut, is calculated. If the rank is equal to $\left(|N|-2\right)$, where $|N|$ is, as mentioned before, the number of nodes in the network, this cut is accepted as a cutset or a feasible cordon; otherwise, it is rejected and another set of nodes is randomly picked up until a new feasible cordon is found. For each given cordon (tolling links), the bi-level model (9.1)-(9.6) is applied to obtain the maximal social welfare and the corresponding optimum uniform toll. Through the process of natural selection in the GA, the cordon with best performance will be chosen in the end.

The GA parameter representation here is somewhat different from those in other applications. The parameter (gene) denotes the state of each candidate nodes, for each candidate node $\hat{n} \in \hat{N}$, where $\hat{N}$ is the set of pre-selected candidate nodes, it has only two alternatives, either to be charged or not. We define that

$$g_{\hat{n}} = \begin{cases} 1, & \text{if candidate node } \hat{n} \text{ is selected as a toll node} \\ 0, & \text{otherwise} \end{cases} \tag{9.15}$$

The candidate nodes $\hat{n}$ with $g_{\hat{n}} = 1$ constitute the set of tolling nods N^*. Therefore, we can encode the parameters (genes) with the simplest binary variable, and 1 bit is enough for each gene, *i.e.* 0-1 integers.

Example 9.5 Suppose that a single-layered cordon is to be installed in the network of Figure 9.9. In this network, every undirected line represents two opposite directed links. Parameter representation in a binary GA is given below.

(a)	1	2	3	4	5	6	7	8	9	10	11	12	13	14	15
(b)	1	1	1	1	1	1	0	0	0	0	0	0	0	0	0
(c)	0	1	1	1	1	1	0	0	0	0	0	0	0	0	0

The 15 nodes within the closed-loop C_1 is set as candidate tolling nodes, whose numbers are given by the above row (a). Row (b) represents a chromosome whose length is 15. Hence the tolling node set represented by this chromosome is $N^* = \{1,2,3,4,5,6\}$, which is given by the nodes within the closed-loop C_2 in Figure 9.9. The closed-loop C_2 is a cut, which is also a cutset and hence it is accepted as a feasible cordon. Row (c) represents another chromosome, where the tolling node set is $N^* = \{2,3,4,5,6\}$, which is given by the nodes between the closed-loops C_2 and C_3 in Figure 9.9. Since the cut given by the union of C_2 and C_3 is not a cutset and hence not a feasible single-layered cordon, and therefore it should be rejected. Actually, it is a two-layered cordon to be examined in next subsection.

The procedure of GA used for determining optimal single-layered cordon is stated as follows:

Step 1. (*Initial population*) Randomly generate the initial population of feasible single-layered tolling cordons, according to the above-mentioned method.

Step 2. (*Function evaluation*) Apply the bi-level model to obtain maximum social welfare for each given cordon.

Step 3. (*Natural selection*) Select those cordons with higher social welfare as survivors and discard the rest.

Step 4. (*Crossover*) Conduct pairing among survivors and exchange tolling nodes between pairs.

Step 5. (*Mutation*) Randomly modify the parameters of some nodes.

Step 6. (*Next generation*) For each new set of tolling nodes, determine the corresponding cut automatically. Maintain those cuts that are cutset (*i.e.* feasible cordon), and discard the rest. Randomly generate new cordons to complement the population.

Step 8. (*Verification of stopping criterion*) If the stopping criterion has not been reached, go to Step 2; otherwise stop.

If the cordon to be determined is a screen-line, then the candidate nodes along the predetermined boundary are pre-selected, and the above approach can be modified slightly to determine the optimal screen-line.

Multi-layered cordons

For multi-layered cordons, the genetic algorithm can be used in a similar manner; the difference lies in the generation of feasible cordons. Here, for simplicity, we use closed-loops to represent the candidate tolling and non-tolling areas without adding specific node-link structure of the network.

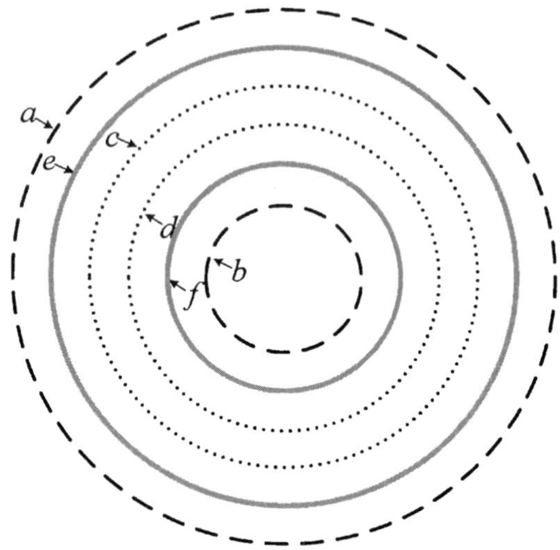

Figure 9.10 Generation of multi-layered cordons

In Figure 9.10, there is only one city center, but this center is to be cordoned in two layers. Hence there will be three components after cutting, namely the inner tolling area, the outer tolling area and the non-tolling area. The nodes in the region between curve a and curve b are set to be candidate tolling nodes between the outer and inner cordons, furthermore to keep the cordon to be layered, a set of nodes in the ring between loop c and loop d are pre-selected as compulsory tolling nodes. In this way, the tolling nodes between the outer and inner cordons are randomly generated in the candidate set, to construct feasible tolling cordons subject to the rank of the graph after cutting equal to $(|N|-3)$. In this way, the outer feasible cordon will be generated between loop a and loop c, such as loop e; and the inner feasible cordon will be generated between loop b and loop d, such as loop f. Then the GA is used to search for the optimal toll cordons.

Multi-centered cordons

As represented in Figure 9.11, the city has two centers, eastern and western, and one may consider area-based pricing with two disjoint cordons. The method is similar to the case of the single-layered cordon, where two sets of candidate nodes are predetermined, which are demarcated by loops a and b. Within the two loops, two disjoint single cordons are selected, such as loop c and loop d. The multi-centered cordons are a cut and can be determined by picking out two sets of nodes from the two candidate sets as tolling nodes. Since two disjointed sets of nodes are picked out, there should be at least three components after cutting, and the rank of the network must be less than or equal to $(|N|-3)$. If the rank is exactly

$(|N|-3)$, then the nodes in each candidate set are connected, implying that there is only one cordon around each center. In this case, one can claim that feasible two-centered cordons are found. Thus we can generate feasible cordons by randomly picking out the tolling nodes and then examining the resulting rank of the incidence matrix. In this manner, the GA can be readily used to search for the optimal multi-centered cordons.

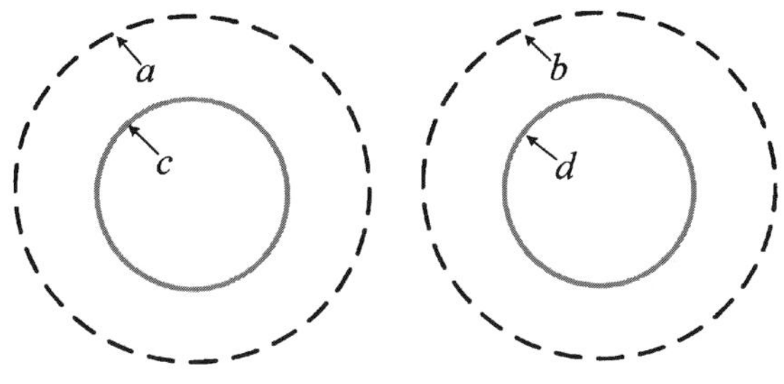

Figure 9.11 Generation of multi-centered cordons

Finally, we point out that in reality there might be various complex cordons consisting of a combination of the aforementioned three types of cordon, and the selection of optimal tolling nodes or tolling areas can be conducted in a similar manner by presetting appropriate candidate tolling nodes and applying the genetic algorithm and the cut/cutset concepts in graph theory.

9.5 THE CORDON-BASED PRICING: EXAMPLE

Figure 9.12 depicts the arterial road network of Shanghai metropolis, the largest city in China. The network consists of a total of 690 directional links (each line segment in the figure represents two opposite directed links) and 187 nodes, out of which there are 30 origin nodes and 30 destination nodes. Homogeneous users are considered with a mean time value of 60 (HK$/h). We consider the traffic condition of the morning peak hour during which most trips are generated in the suburban area and attracted to the CBD. The link travel time function (9.13)is used for all road links in the network. Elastic demand function is used here to describe the reaction of travelers to the travel disutility (inclusion of time and monetary costs), and the demand function takes the following form for each OD pair:

$$d_w = \hat{D}_w \exp\left[\rho\left(1.0 - \frac{\mu_w}{\mu_w^0}\right)\right], \quad w \in W \tag{9.16}$$

here d_w is the realized OD demand, $\hat{D}_w$ is the potential OD demand, μ_w is the present O-D travel disutility, and μ_w^0 is the free-flow O-D travel disutility between OD pair $w \in W$. The demand elasticity with respect to the OD travel disutility is given by $-\rho\mu_w/\mu_w^0$ where ρ is regarded as a dimensionless demand elasticity parameter.

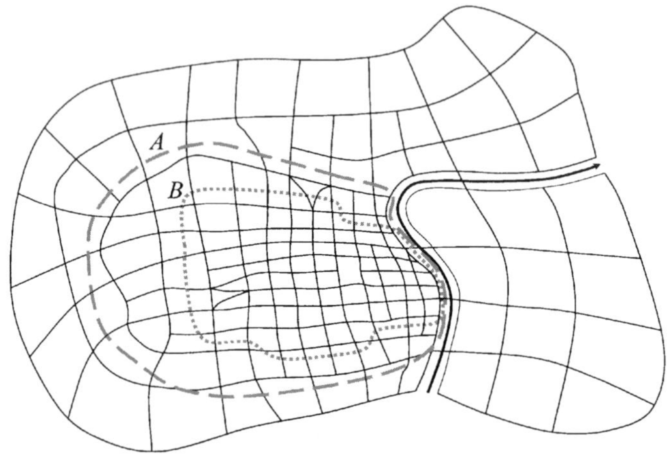

Figure 9.12 The optimal location (closed-loop *B*) of a single-layered cordon

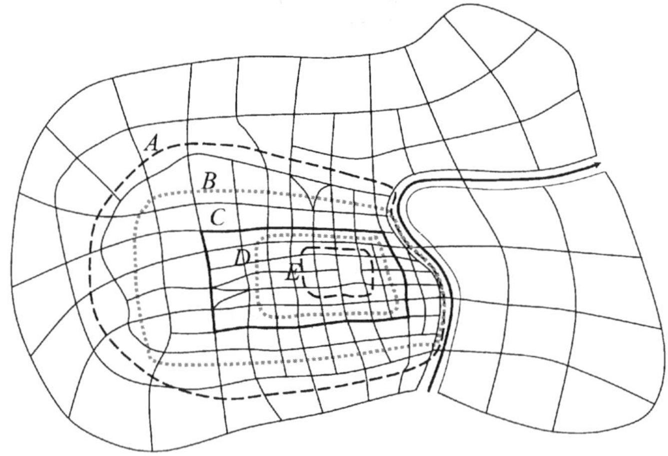

Figure 9.13 The optimal location (outer loop *B* and inner loop *D*) of a double-layered cordon

In this example, the elasticity parameter ρ is taken to be 0.25. The original social welfare in the absence of toll charge is 1.619×10^7 (HK$), and the maximal social welfare achieved under the first-best pricing is 1.672×10^7 (HK$), which implies a maximum percentage welfare gain of 3.27%. To mitigate network traffic congestion and air pollution problems during the morning peak hour, the cordon-based congestion pricing around the CBD area is considered. In the following, we investigate the various cordon-based pricing strategies for the network.

9.5.1 Determination of Location of a Single-layered Tolling Cordon

The genetic algorithm described in previous section is used to determine the optimal single cordon location. In Figure 9.12, the nodes within loop A are set to be candidate tolling nodes. By executing the GA, loop B is eventually selected to be the optimal tolling cordon. On this cordon the optimal toll level is 10.6 (HK\$), and the corresponding maximum social welfare is 1.634×10^7 (HK\$), which represents a welfare increase by 0.93% compared with the no-tolling equilibrium case, and a 2.27% gap from the maximum level of social welfare under the first-best pricing.

Table 9.4 Summary of the results for the single- and double-layered cordon pricing

Type of cordon	Cordon toll (HK\$)	Percentage social welfare gain over the non-tolling equilibrium	Percentage welfare gap from the first-best social optimum	Percentage welfare gain as a share of the max welfare gain
Single-layered cordon	10.60	0.93%	2.27%	28.30%
Double-layered cordons	Inner: 4.90 Outer: 8.50	1.35%	1.85%	41.51%

9.5.2 Determination of Location of Double-layered Tolling Cordons

The GA is again used to determine the optimal location of double-layered cordons. In Figure 9.13, the nodes in-between curve A and curve E are set to be candidate tolling nodes between the outer and inner cordons. The nodes on the closed-loop C (solid dark line) are pre-selected tolling nodes to keep the cordons being double-layered (this corresponds to the nodes in-between loops c and d in Figure 9.10). After the process of natural selection, eventually loop B and loop D are found to be the optimal outer and inner cordons. The optimal toll levels on the outer and inner cordons are found to be 8.50 and 4.90 (HK\$) respectively, and the maximal social welfare achieved is 1.641×10^7 (HK\$). This represents a 1.35% welfare increase over the non-tolling case and a 1.85% welfare gap from the first-best social optimum. Note that the reported percentage welfare gain is very marginal, which is largely due to the relatively high total consumer surplus realized (the type of demand function and the parameter values used also make a difference). Therefore, we now introduce the following more meaningful efficiency index to compare the performance of different pricing schemes:

$$\theta=\frac{S-S^0}{S^*-S^0} \tag{9.17}$$

where S represents the social welfare with a given cordon pricing scheme, S^0 is the original social welfare without pricing, and S^* is, as used before, the maximal social welfare under the first-best pricing scheme. Thus, this efficiency index measures the welfare gain as a share of the maximum gain under the first-best pricing. From the above numerical results with parameter $\rho = 0.25$, the efficiency index $\theta = 0.2830$ (or 28.30%) in single-layered cordon pricing, and $\theta = 0.4151$ (41.51%) in double-layered cordon pricing. Table 9.4 summarizes the above results for both the single-layered and double-layered cordon pricing cases.

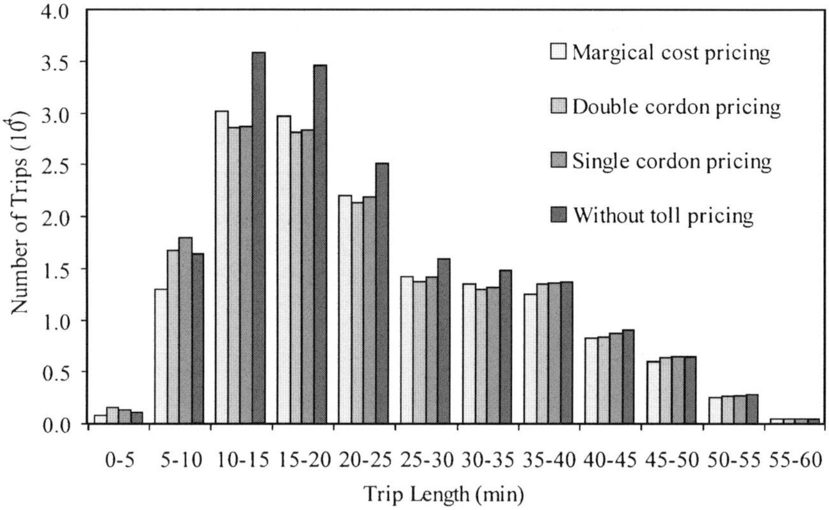

Figure 9.14 The impact of alternative toll pricing schemes on trip length distribution

9.5.3 Impact of the Cordon-based Pricing on Trip Length Distribution

Here we further investigate the impact of alternative pricing strategies on trips of different lengths. Figure 9.14 displays the trip length distribution for the following four cases: the marginal-cost or first-best pricing, the single- and double-layered cordon pricing and the no toll pricing. The length of a trip is measured with respect to the shortest *free-flow* travel time from its origin to destination, which is proportional to the actual physical distance. The discrepancy among the four trip length distributions reflect the impacts of the different pricing schemes on the users traveling between different O-D pairs with different trip lengths. As observed in Figure 9.14, for trip lengths less than 10 (min), the demand after introducing cordon-pricing increases, compared with the no tolling case, and is higher than that in the marginal cost pricing case. This is due to the simple fact that the users with short distance trips do not cross over the tolling cordon and thus avoid toll charges, but benefit from reduced traffic congestion on the network. For trip length between 10 and 35 (min), the demand after introducing cordon-pricing decreases compared with the no tolling case, and is lower than those in the marginal-cost pricing case. In addition, the demand under single-cordon pricing is slightly higher than that under double-cordon pricing. This implies that the cordon-based second-best pricing mainly causes medium-length travel demand to drop. For trip lengths greater than 35 (min), the demand after introducing cordon-pricing decreases, compared with the no tolling case, but is higher than that in the marginal-cost pricing case. This means that the long-distance travel demand, although dropped after introducing cordon pricing, still exceeds the socially optimal demand level. The above numerical results show that trips are under-priced in locations inside the cordon, over-priced just outside the cordon and under-priced on the fringe of the urban area.

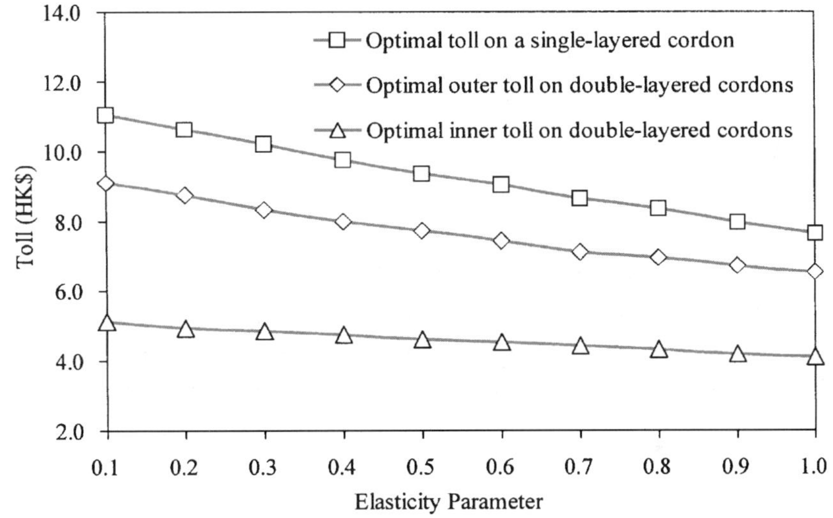

Figure 9.15 Sensitivity of optimal cordon tolls to demand elasticity parameter

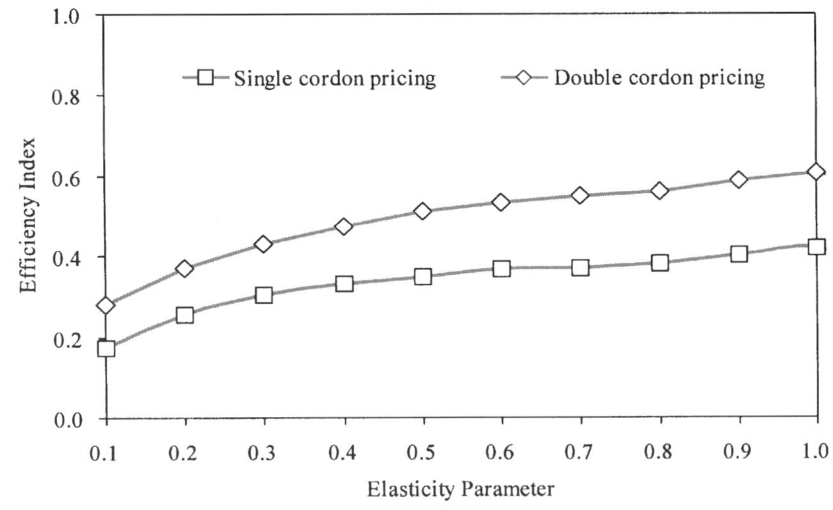

Figure 9.16 Sensitivity of social welfare efficiency index to demand elasticity parameter

9.5.4 Sensitivity Analysis of Demand Elasticity

Now we conduct a sensitivity analysis of the elasticity of demand by varying the elasticity parameter ρ in the demand function. In the following analysis, the cordon locations are fixed, as given in Figure 9.12 and Figure 9.13 for single-layered and double-layered pricing cordons. Figure 9.15 displays the change of optimal tolls as parameter ρ varies from 0.1 to 1.0. Clearly, as the value of ρ increases, optimal toll levels on all cordons decrease. This means that as travel demand is more elastic or more sensitive to travel cost, a lower toll will be enough to achieve social welfare maximization. Figure 9.16 shows the change of the social welfare efficiency index defined in eqn. (9.17) as parameter ρ varies from 0.1 to 1.0, for both the single-layered and double-layered cordon pricing schemes. Clearly, the efficiency index increases with ρ value, which means that the cordon-based pricing scheme is more effective when travel demand is more sensitive to travel disutility. Within the practical range of demand elasticity (-0.30 ~ 0.40), the welfare efficiency achieved through the cordon based pricing schemes is between 20-60%. There is still a large gap from the first-best social optimum. This result is different from the theoretical observation made in Mun et al. (2003) for a mono-centric city in which he found that a single cordon pricing scheme attains an economic welfare level nearly as good as the first-best optimum. One possible explanation for this discrepancy is given below. The first-best pricing in a network influences both trip rate and route choice in a socially optimal manner, and the cordon pricing scheme could effectively restrain the demand for travel but has very limited impact on users' route choice in a real network, as examined here. In contrast, the spatial model of traffic congestion for the mono-centric city does not entertain route choice behavior and thus may overestimate the actual social welfare gained through cordon pricing in a road network.

9.6 SUMMARY

In this chapter we have examined how to determine the toll levels and tolling locations simultaneously for the link-based and cordon-based second-best pricing schemes. In each scheme, optimal tolls can be determined by the methods developed in previous chapters for given charging locations; while the optimal charging locations can be identified effectively by a genetic algorithm. For a link-based pricing scheme, the optimal toll levels on given tolling links are determined using a simulated annealing algorithm. For the link-based pricing scheme, the model was slightly altered to determine the minimum number of tolling links required to achieve a system optimum with and without inclusion of implementation costs of toll collection.

For a cordon-based pricing scheme, the concepts of cutset and cut in graph theory were used to describe the mathematical properties of single-layered, multi-layered and multi-centered tolling cordons. We showed that each type of cordon corresponds to a certain kind of cut or cutset in a network. The node-link incidence matrix of a graph is applied to examine the rank of graphs, which can identify whether or not a given subset of candidate nodes forms a feasible cordon of a certain type. The genetic algorithm is employed to naturally select optimal tolling cordons by setting appropriate candidate tolling nodes and examining the resulting node-link incidence matrix. A case study was conducted with the urban arterial road network of Shanghai City. From our numerical experiment results, the cordon-based pricing schemes achieve about 20-60% welfare gain as a share of the maximum welfare gain by appropriate selection of (single or double) cordon locations and toll levels. For both the single- and double-layered cordon pricing schemes, there remains a substantial gap in social welfare from the first-best social optimum level. In addition, the cordon-based pricing generally causes the short- and long-distance trips to be under-priced and the medium-distance trips over-priced, in comparison with their respective first-best pricing toll levels.

9.7 SOURCES AND NOTES

A few authors considered the link-based and cordon-based second-best pricing problem. Hearn and Ramana (1998) proposed an approach to determine the minimal number of tolling links to achieve a system optimum. May and Milne (2000) tested and compared various kinds of road pricing schemes, including cordon-based charging. Shepherd et al. (2001) investigated the sensitivity of optimal toll charges with respect to pre-specified cordons of different sizes. Verhoef (2002) examined the link-based second-best pricing problem and proposed heuristic algorithms for finding second-best optimal toll levels and tolling points in networks. Mun et al. (2003) presented a theoretical analysis of cordon pricing in a mono-centric city. Shepherd and Sumalee (2004) and Sumalee (2004) applied genetic algorithm for optimal cordon design. Santos (2004) and Santos and Rojey (2004) simulated cordon tolls for eight English towns and assessed and examined the distributional effects and environmental impacts.

This chapter is developed mainly based on the works of Yang and Zhang (2002) and Zhang and Yang (2004). The background on graph theory used in this chapter is from Chen (1997). The genetic algorithm and its application are well documented in Haupt and Haupt (1998).

10

Sequential Pricing Experiments with Limited Information

10.1 Introduction

In previous chapters, we have introduced the significant advance that has been made towards better modeling and understanding of traffic congestion and possible impacts of congestion pricing. There remain, however, a few questions surrounding the actual design and implementation of road pricing schemes, for which policy makers and traffic engineers require answers. A fundamental question is how to choose the optimal charge level of congestion tolls in a simple yet practical manner. Previous analysis and discussion of optimal congestion pricing centered on three fundamental elements, namely, the speed-flow relationship, the demand function, and the generalized disutility (and hence the value of travel time savings). Among all these three elements of primary concern in actual implementation of a congestion pricing scheme, and analytical demand functions tailored for congestion pricing are, however, difficult to establish in practice, even with advanced transport modeling techniques.

In this chapter, we propose trial-and-error implementation methods for the various congestion pricing schemes examined in previous chapters, when particularly the demand functions (and/or value of time) are unknown. Three typical pricing policies are considered here including: the first-best pricing scheme, the second-best pricing scheme and the traffic restraint and road pricing scheme. The fundamental idea behind the methods is to adjust toll charges at frequent intervals as traffic patterns changes brought about by price change. Given a trial of a set of link tolls, the revealed aggregate link flows can be observed with ease, and based on the observed link flows, a new set of link tolls can be determined and used for the next trial. One can thus expect to identify the efficient toll rates through an iterative toll adjustment procedure, which would allow for a traffic planner to easily estimate the socially optimal congestion tolls in a network, without resort to the demand functions.

This chapter is organized as follows. We begin by proposing an iterative procedure for determining the socially optimal first-best link tolls based on the method of successive averages and give a rigorous theoretical justification for its convergence. Then, we develop a sequential experimental approach for analyzing the second-best pricing problem and describe the necessary bi-level programming models and algorithms for the sub-problems of Origin-Destination (OD) demand estimation and link toll selection. We move on to examine the traffic restraint and road pricing scheme and develop an iterative toll adjustment procedure derived from the dual formulation of the traffic equilibrium problem. The procedure updates link toll charges from observed link flows using a simple gradient projection method and its convergence is established under mild conditions. We conclude this chapter by highlighting a few behavioral and political issues in the implementation of the trial-and-error procedure.

10.2 IMPLEMENTATION OF THE FIRST-BEST PRICING SCHEME

The basic logic behind the iterative implementation procedure for the first-best or the marginal-cost pricing problem is given below.

"With information on the underlying speed-flow relationship on a highway and the generalized cost, the optimal congestion toll occurs if and only if the intended speed level or traffic volume that is used to calculate the theoretical congestion toll is exactly equal to the observed speed level or traffic volume after the imposition of the toll."

As a result, the exact knowledge of the demand function is not really necessary for identification of the optimal toll charge. We begin our exploration of the trial-and-error procedure by examining the simple standard case for a single highway, and then moving on to investigate the marginal-cost pricing problem on general networks.

10.2.1 An Iterative Toll Adjustment Procedure for a Single Road

Consider the demand-supply (performance) curve and the underlying theory of marginal cost pricing illustrated graphically in Figure 10.1. As examined in Section 3.1 in Chapter 3, this corresponds to the simplified but, in the literature, standard case of a homogenous traffic stream moving along a given uniform stretch of road. The optimal demand (or flow) is, as we can see, equal to d^{so}, where marginal cost (MC) and demand are equated, while the actual demand in the absence of toll charge tends to be d^{ue} (intersection between the average cost (AC) and the demand curve), because road users ignore the congestion that they impose on others. Therefore, the optimal toll to be charged is equal to u^{opt}. Nevertheless, the demand function is generally unknown and hence u^{opt} cannot be determined analytically. What we know is that the revealed demand or traffic flow d on the road is observable for a given level of toll charge. We are thus able to observe the responses of traffic flow to alternative toll charges, such collectable reaction data information is in fact sufficient to find the optimal toll for at least the simple demand-supply curve on a single highway.

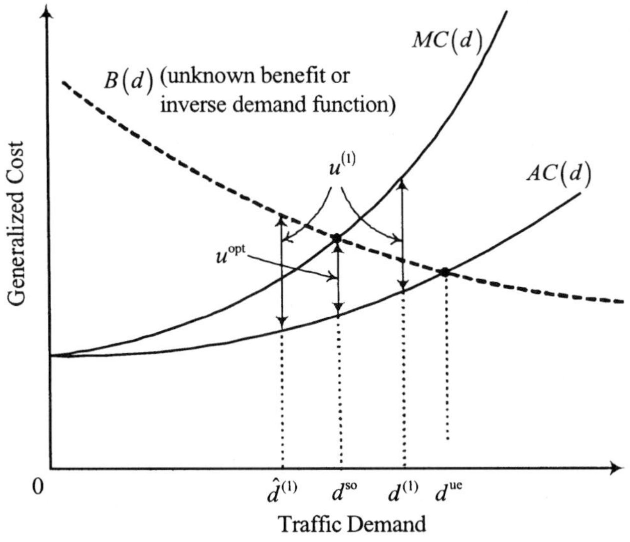

Figure 10.1 Demand-performance equilibrium on a single highway

The iterative trial and error procedure works as follows. Starting with an initial targeted flow (or a targeted speed according to the underlying speed-flow relationship) to be achieved by imposing a corresponding congestion toll. Let the initial target of flow be $d^{(1)}$ (of course, $d^{(1)} = d^{\text{ue}}$ is an acceptable initial choice; $d^{(1)}$ should be larger than d^{so}) and the corresponding toll to achieve this level of flow is estimated by $u^{(1)} = MC\left(d^{(1)}\right) - AC\left(d^{(1)}\right)$ without resort to the demand function. Once $u^{(1)}$ is imposed, the revealed or observed traffic flow becomes $\hat{d}^{(1)}$, which is an aggregate result of the users' willingness-to-pay (dictated by the demand or benefit function unknown to the planner) according to their marginal private cost (*AC* curve) and the amount of toll in place. From Figure 10.1, $\hat{d}^{(1)} < d^{(1)}$ or the observed level of flow (speed) is lower (higher) than the origin intended flow (speed) level. This in turn implies that the initial congestion toll charge is set too high, and thus triggers a revision of the congestion toll with a new flow level, say $d^{(2)}$, such that $\hat{d}^{(1)} < d^{(2)} < d^{(1)}$.

Now consider an appropriate one dimensional search method, the bisection method, to modify the intended traffic flow: $d^{(2)} = \left(d^{(1)} + \hat{d}^{(1)}\right)/2$. Given $d^{(2)}$, the new theoretical estimate of congestion toll is determined by $u^{(2)} = MC\left(d^{(2)}\right) - AC\left(d^{(2)}\right)$. Since $d^{(2)} < d^{(1)}$, we must have $u^{(2)} < u^{(1)}$. Once this new toll is imposed, there will be a new response from the market, which leads to a new revealed level of flow $\hat{d}^{(2)}$, corresponding to the users' willingness-to-pay of $\left(AC(\hat{d}^{(2)}) + u^{(2)}\right)$ by the same argument used above in deriving $\hat{d}^{(1)}$.

The above operations can be expressed by the following three equations:

$$B\left(\hat{d}^{(1)}\right) = AC\left(\hat{d}^{(1)}\right) + MC\left(d^{(1)}\right) - AC\left(d^{(1)}\right)$$

$$d^{(2)} = \frac{1}{2}\left(d^{(1)} + \hat{d}^{(1)}\right)$$

$$B\left(\hat{d}^{(2)}\right) = AC\left(\hat{d}^{(2)}\right) + MC\left(d^{(2)}\right) - AC\left(d^{(2)}\right)$$

where $B(\cdot) = D^{-1}(\cdot)$ is the inverse of the true but unknown demand function (or benefit function). Assume that AC is a convex, monotonically increasing function and $B(\cdot)$ is a convex, monotonically decreasing function. Then, the observed flow must be decreasing with respect to the intended flow since $MC(d) - AC(d)$ is monotonically increasing and $B\left(\hat{d}\right) - AC\left(\hat{d}\right)$ is monotonically decreasing. So, we can define a decreasing function, $\hat{d} = F(d)$, and have $\hat{d}^{(1)} = F\left(d^{(1)}\right)$ and $\hat{d}^{(2)} = F\left(d^{(2)}\right)$. Furthermore, we have

$$\begin{aligned} d^{(2)} - \hat{d}^{(2)} = \frac{d^{(1)} + \hat{d}^{(1)}}{2} - \hat{d}^{(2)} &= \frac{d^{(1)} - \hat{d}^{(1)}}{2} + \hat{d}^{(1)} - \hat{d}^{(2)} \\ &= \frac{d^{(1)} - \hat{d}^{(1)}}{2} + F\left(d^{(1)}\right) - F\left(d^{(2)}\right) \end{aligned}$$

Note that $F\left(d^1\right) < F\left(d^2\right)$ holds due to $d^1 > d^2$. Hence, we must have

$$\left|d^{(2)} - \hat{d}^{(2)}\right| < \frac{1}{2}\left(d^{(1)} - \hat{d}^{(1)}\right)$$

After k iterations, a sequence $\left\{d^{(k)}, u^{(k)}, \hat{d}^{(k)}\right\}$ is generated with the following properties:

$$u^{(k)} = MC\left(d^{(k)}\right) - AC\left(d^{(k)}\right), \quad k \geq 1$$

$$\left|d^{(k)} - \hat{d}^{(k)}\right| < \frac{1}{2^{k-1}}\left(d^{(1)} - \hat{d}^{(1)}\right), \quad \text{with } d^{(k)} = \frac{1}{2}\left(d^{(k-1)} + \hat{d}^{(k-1)}\right), \ k \geq 2$$

where $\hat{d}^{(k)}$ is the revealed flow level corresponding to congestion toll $u^{(k)}$. With the above properties, it can be concluded that

$$\lim_{k\to\infty} d^{(k)} = \lim_{k\to\infty} \hat{d}^{(k)}$$

This means that $B\left(d^{(\infty)}\right) = AC\left(d^{(\infty)}\right) + MC\left(d^{(\infty)}\right) - AC\left(d^{(\infty)}\right)$. In Figure 10.1 there is only one point, d^{so}, that satisfies this condition. So, we have

$$\lim_{k\to\infty} d^{(k)} = \lim_{k\to\infty} \hat{d}^{(k)} = d^{so}$$

and

$$\lim_{k\to\infty} u^{(k)} = u^{opt} = MC\left(d^{so}\right) - AC\left(d^{so}\right)$$

From the above analysis, one can easily see that the estimated congestion toll will converge (to the optimal value) only when the traffic flow is at the socially optimal level. Even without the full knowledge of the demand function, the planner is able to 'find' the correct amount of toll as long as there is an adjustment process in the toll charge.

10.2.2 An Iterative Toll Adjustment Procedure for a General Network

The above implementation mechanism applies for the standard demand-supply model, with which most existing theoretical arguments on road pricing are concerned. The analysis of convergence does hold for the convex, monotonic demand and supply curves for a single highway or for the aggregate demand-supply relationship for a congested area. The convergence is largely due to the *fact* that the socially optimal level of demand always lies in between the intended and the revealed flow levels at each trial, as long as the true but unknown demand function is monotonically decreasing and the supply or performance function is monotonically increasing. Furthermore, an *implicit assumption* actually adopted in the argument is that the revealed or observed flow is always equal to the origin to destination demand since only a single road is involved.

Once we move to a general road network, the problem is not so simple and a number of factors compound its complexity. First, given a complete set of observed link flows on the network, arising from a trial of a complete set of link tolls, the corresponding OD demands remain unknown. One may naturally consider identification of the OD matrix from link traffic counts by virtue of many available techniques. Unfortunately, the OD matrix that reproduces a given set of equilibrium link flows when user-optimally assigned to the network, is in general not unique. Second, when the toll on a given link (or a set of links) is altered, the demand between a specific OD pair and flow on a specific link could either increase or decrease or remain unchanged. In other words, the change of OD demands and link flows in response to link tolls is not as simple and obvious as the standard textbook demand-supply case examined above. These facts imply that the bisection trial scheme does not necessarily work on a general road network. This conjuncture is indeed true. As verified later by numerical examples, the bisection (or other fixed step size) trial scheme does not always converge on a general network.

We begin with restating the following assumptions required throughout the analysis.

Assumption 10.1 All users in the network are homogeneous in terms of their value of time and follow the deterministic UE behavior in their route choices.

Assumption 10.2 For each link $a \in A$, the corresponding link travel cost $t_a(v_a)$ is a strictly increasing, convex and twice-continuously differentiable function of link flow v_a.

Assumption 10.3 For each OD pair $w \in W$, the corresponding true, but unknown OD demand function $D_w(\mu_w)$ is nonnegative, strictly decreasing, bounded and continuously differentiable in OD travel cost μ_w, $0 \le D_w(\mu_w) \le \hat{D}_w$, where $\hat{D}_w$ is the upper bound of the demand function $D_w(\mu_w)$. For simplicity, we consider separable travel demand functions.

The net economic benefit or social welfare, S, is calculated by the following formula for a give set of link flows and OD demands:

$$S = \sum_{w \in W} \int_0^{d_w} B_w(\omega)\,d\omega - \sum_{a \in A} t_a(v_a) v_a \tag{10.1}$$

where $B(d_w) = D_w^{-1}(d_w)$ is the benefit function or the inverse of the demand function $D_w(\mu_w)$. The marginal-cost pricing problem is to maximize the above welfare function subject to the flow conservation equations. After changing the sign of the welfare function, the problem is formulated as the following minimization program:

$$\min_{(\mathbf{v},\mathbf{d}) \in \Omega} F_1(\mathbf{v},\mathbf{d}) = \sum_{a \in A} t_a(v_a) v_a - \sum_{w \in W} \int_0^{d_w} B_w(\omega)\,d\omega \tag{10.2}$$

where Ω is the feasible set of link flows and OD demands as defined before by

$$\Omega = \left\{ (\mathbf{v},\mathbf{d}) \mid v_a = \sum_{w \in W} \sum_{r \in R_w} f_{rw} \delta_{ar}, a \in A;\ f_{rw} \ge 0, r \in R_w, \sum_{r \in R_w} f_{rw} = d_w \le \bar{D}_w, w \in W \right\} \tag{10.3}$$

where f_{rw} is the flow on route $r \in R_w$ between OD pair $w \in W$, u_a denotes the toll charge expressed in equivalent time unit on link $a \in A$.

Because $t_a(v_a)v_a = \int_0^{v_a}(t_a(\omega)+\omega t_a'(\omega))\mathrm{d}\omega$, where $t_a'(v_a)=\mathrm{d}t_a(v_a)/\mathrm{d}v_a$, problem (10.2) can be solved by the user equilibrium traffic assignment procedure with elastic demand via setting a link travel cost function as the following marginal link cost function:

$$\tilde{t}_a(v_a)=t_a(v_a)+v_a t_a'(v_a),\ a\in A \tag{10.4}$$

Let $\mathbf{v}^*$ and $\mathbf{d}^*$ be the optimal solution of problem (10.2), then the optimal link tolls based on the marginal-cost pricing scheme, as shown in Chapter 3, are set as follows:

$$u_a^* = v_a^* t_a'(v_a^*),\ a\in A \tag{10.5}$$

On the other hand, given the above assumptions (10.1-10.3), the resulting equilibrium link flows and OD demands for any given link toll pattern $\mathbf{u}=(u_a, a\in A)^{\mathrm{T}}$ can be identified by solving the following typical elastic-demand traffic assignment problem:

$$\min_{(\mathbf{v},\mathbf{d})\in\Omega} \sum_{a\in A}\int_0^{v_a}(t_a(\omega)+u_a)\mathrm{d}\omega - \sum_{w\in W}\int_0^{d_w} B_w(\omega)\mathrm{d}\omega \tag{10.6}$$

Note that one can use a more general link travel cost function with flow interactions (see Chapter 3 for more details). With such a generalization, the subsequent discussion still holds as long as the link travel cost and OD demand functions meet appropriate monotonicity and differentiability assumptions.

As seen from above, obtaining optimal link tolls from the mathematical model (10.2) requires knowledge of the analytical demand functions. In reality, it is extremely difficult to know exactly users' willingness-to-pay for a journey and thus identify analytical demand functions tailored for congestion pricing. To circumvent this difficulty, we now propose the following trial-and-error iterative method to find the system-optimal link flows and link tolls defined in eqn. (10.5), which obviates the need of the OD demand functions. What is required is to observe traffic flow on each link after each trial of link toll pattern.

Trial-and-error procedure for the first-best pricing scheme

Step 0. (*Initialization*) Let $\{v_a^{(0)},\ a\in A\}$ be an initial set of feasible link flows. Set $k:=0$.

Step 1. (*Estimate link tolls*) For each link $a\in A$, calculate the current link toll charge by

$$u_a^{(k)} = v_a^{(k)} t_a'(v_a^{(k)}),\ a\in A. \tag{10.7}$$

Step 2. (*Observe link flow*) Observe the revealed link flows and denote them by $\{\hat{v}_a^{(k)},\ a\in A\}$ after imposition of the tolls given by eqn. (10.7).

Step 3. (*Check convergence*) If $\left\|\hat{\mathbf{v}}^{(k)}-\mathbf{v}^{(k)}\right\| / \left\|\mathbf{v}^{(k)}\right\| \leq \varepsilon$, then stop. Otherwise go to Step 4.

Step 4. (*Update link flows*) Set

$$v_a^{(k+1)} = v_a^{(k)} + \alpha^{(k)}\left(\hat{v}_a^{(k)} - v_a^{(k)}\right), \ a \in A \tag{10.8}$$

and let $k := k+1$, go to Step 1.

In the procedure, the vectors $\hat{\mathbf{v}}^{(k)} = \left(\hat{v}_a^{(k)}, a \in A\right)^{\mathrm{T}}$ and $\mathbf{v}^{(k)} = \left(v_a^{(k)}, a \in A\right)^{\mathrm{T}}$; '$\|\cdot\|$' is the Euclidean norm; ε is a positive number of convergence tolerance; $\left\{\alpha^{(k)}\right\}$ is a sequence of predetermined step sizes and it must satisfy the following three conditions.

$$0 < \alpha^{(k)} \leq 1; \quad \sum_{k=1}^{\infty} \alpha^{(k)} = +\infty; \quad \sum_{k=1}^{\infty} \left(\alpha^{(k)}\right)^2 < +\infty. \tag{10.9}$$

A typical sequence of $\alpha^{(k)}$ is $\alpha^{(k)} = 1/(k+1)$. Note that as the true objective function (10.2) is not precisely known, one cannot count on a gradient-based descent algorithm such as Newton's method, or conduct an exact line search in Step 4.

To execute the procedure, one can assume and assign an arbitrary OD matrix to the network to obtain an initial link flow solution, or use the observable, un-tolled UE link flows as an initial set of feasible link flows. The procedure will be terminated after the difference between two successive trial results are within a tolerance level. At the convergent point, the intended flow level that is used to calculate the theoretical congestion tolls is exactly equal to the observed flow level after the imposition of the calculated tolls, and thus the optimal congestion link tolls are identified.

10.2.3 Proof of Convergence

We now prove that the proposed procedure does converge and converges to the optimal solution. Denote the initial OD demands at Step 0 by $\left\{d_w^{(0)}, w \in W\right\}$, which can be arbitrarily assumed (which means that they are not necessarily accurate). Clearly, $\left\{\hat{v}_a^{(k)}, a \in A\right\}$ of Step 2 is the optimal link flow solution of the strictly convex minimization problem (10.6) with the link toll pattern $\left\{u_a = u_a^{(k)}, a \in A\right\}$ where $u_a^{(k)}$ is defined by (10.7). Let $\left\{\hat{d}_w^{(k)}, w \in W\right\}$ be the corresponding optimal OD demand solution of this problem. Similar to eqn. (10.8), here we add a virtual updating scheme for OD demands at Step 4 as follows:

$$d_w^{(k+1)} = d_w^{(k)} + \alpha^{(k)}\left(\hat{d}_w^{(k)} - d_w^{(k)}\right) \tag{10.10}$$

It should be particularly clarified that the OD demand and the updating formula (10.10) are purely employed to show the convergence of the solution method, and they are not required at all throughout the course of implementation of the above iterative trial-and-error procedure. In fact, the OD demand functions are assumed to be unknown, neither could they be determined uniquely from observed link flows. Since the predetermined step size $\alpha^{(k)}$ is equal to or smaller than one, the generated sequence $\left(\mathbf{v}^{(k)},\mathbf{d}^{(k)}\right)$ is guaranteed to be feasible, where $\mathbf{d}^{(k)}=\left(d_w^{(k)},w\in W\right)^{\mathrm{T}}$. This means that the link flows are consistent with the OD demands after each iteration operation, i.e., such path flows $f_{rw}\geq 0,\ r\in R_w,\ w\in W$, always exist such that $\left(\mathbf{v}^{(k)},\mathbf{d}^{(k)}\right)\in\Omega$. We now show that the proposed procedure is indeed correct even though we do not know the exact values of $\left\{d_w^{(k)},w\in W\right\}$ and $\left\{\hat{d}_w^{(k)},w\in W\right\}$.

Lemma 10.1 If $\left\|\hat{\mathbf{v}}^{(k)}-\mathbf{v}^{(k)}\right\|=0$ at the convergent point, then $\left\{v_a^{(k)}\right\}$ is the UE link flow pattern with the marginal link cost function (10.4) and $\left\{u_a^{(k)},a\in A\right\}$ is the corresponding optimal link toll pattern.

Proof Because $\left(\hat{\mathbf{v}}^{(k)},\hat{\mathbf{d}}^{(k)}\right)$ is the optimal solution of the strictly convex program (10.6) with toll pattern $\left\{u_a^{(k)},a\in A\right\}$, for any $(\mathbf{v},\mathbf{d})\in\Omega$, we have the following inequality by the necessary optimality conditions for a convex program:

$$\sum_{a\in A}\left(t_a\left(\hat{v}_a^{(k)}\right)+v_a^{(k)}t_a'\left(v_a^{(k)}\right)\right)\left(v_a-\hat{v}_a^{(k)}\right)-\sum_{w\in W}B_w\left(\hat{d}_w^{(k)}\right)\left(d_w-\hat{d}_w^{(k)}\right)\geq 0 \tag{10.11}$$

Note that $\left\|\hat{\mathbf{v}}^{(k)}-\mathbf{v}^{(k)}\right\|=0$ leads to $\hat{v}_a^{(k)}=v_a^{(k)},\ a\in A$, at the convergent point. From the feasibility conditions of $\left(\hat{\mathbf{v}}^{(k)},\hat{\mathbf{d}}^{(k)}\right)$, we have

$$\hat{v}_a^{(k)}=\sum_{w\in W}\sum_{r\in R_w}f_{rw}\delta_{ar}^{w},\quad a\in A;\quad \sum_{r\in R_w}f_{rw}=\hat{d}_w^{(k)}\leq\hat{D}_w,\quad w\in W.$$

When $\hat{v}_a^{(k)}=v_a^{(k)}$, $a\in A$, the iteration stops at this final stage and then $\hat{\mathbf{d}}^{(k)}$ can be set to equal $\mathbf{d}^{(k)}$ that satisfies $v_a^{(k)}=\sum_{w\in W}\sum_{r\in R_w}f_{rw}\delta_{ar}^{w}$ and $\sum_{r\in R_w}f_{rw}=d_w^{(k)}\leq\bar{D}_w$, $a\in A$, $w\in W$, although there may exist other OD matrices that are feasible too. Hence, eqn. (10.11) can be rewritten as follows:

$$\sum_{a\in A}\left(t_a\left(v_a^{(k)}\right)+v_a^{(k)}t_a'\left(v_a^{(k)}\right)\right)\left(v_a-v_a^{(k)}\right)-\sum_{w\in W}B_w\left(d_w^{(k)}\right)\left(d_w-d_w^{(k)}\right)\geq 0, \tag{10.12}$$

for any $(\mathbf{v},\mathbf{d})\in\Omega$. With assumptions on link travel cost and OD demand functions, we see that problem (10.2) is a strictly convex minimization problem with linear constraints. By the sufficient conditions for a convex program, eqn. (10.12) implies that $\left(\mathbf{v}^{(k)},\mathbf{d}^{(k)}\right)$ is the optimal solution of the optimal marginal cost-pricing problem (10.2). Thus, the proposition holds. ¦

Lemma 10.2 If the vector $\begin{pmatrix}\mathbf{t}(\mathbf{v})\\ -\mathbf{B}(\mathbf{d})\end{pmatrix}$ of the link travel cost and OD demand functions is strongly monotone on the set Ω, i.e., there exits a positive number ρ such that for any distinct $(\mathbf{v}_1,\mathbf{d}_1)\in\Omega$ and $(\mathbf{v}_2,\mathbf{d}_2)\in\Omega$ we have

$$\begin{pmatrix}\mathbf{t}(\mathbf{v}_1)-\mathbf{t}(\mathbf{v}_2)\\ -\mathbf{B}(\mathbf{d}_1)-(-\mathbf{B}(\mathbf{d}_2))\end{pmatrix}^{\mathrm{T}}\begin{pmatrix}\mathbf{v}_1-\mathbf{v}_2\\ \mathbf{d}_1-\mathbf{d}_2\end{pmatrix}\geq\rho\left\|\begin{matrix}\mathbf{v}_1-\mathbf{v}_2\\ \mathbf{d}_1-\mathbf{d}_2\end{matrix}\right\|^2 \tag{10.13}$$

then, the following inequality is true for the objective function (10.2):

$$\nabla F_1\left(\mathbf{v}^{(k)},\mathbf{d}^{(k)}\right)^{\mathrm{T}}\begin{pmatrix}\hat{\mathbf{v}}^{(k)}-\mathbf{v}^{(k)}\\ \hat{\mathbf{d}}^{(k)}-\mathbf{d}^{(k)}\end{pmatrix}\leq-\rho\left(\left\|\hat{\mathbf{v}}^{(k)}-\mathbf{v}^{(k)}\right\|^2+\left\|\hat{\mathbf{d}}^{(k)}-\mathbf{d}^{(k)}\right\|^2\right) \tag{10.14}$$

Proof Since

$$\nabla F_1\left(\mathbf{v}^{(k)},\mathbf{d}^{(k)}\right)=\left(\ldots,\left(t_a\left(v_a^{(k)}\right)+v_a^{(k)}t_a'\left(v_a^{(k)}\right)\right),\ldots,-B_w\left(d_w^{(k)}\right),\ldots\right)^{\mathrm{T}} \tag{10.15}$$

then we have

$$\nabla F_1\left(\mathbf{v}^{(k)},\mathbf{d}^{(k)}\right)^{\mathrm{T}}\begin{pmatrix}\hat{\mathbf{v}}^{(k)}-\mathbf{v}^{(k)}\\ \hat{\mathbf{d}}^{(k)}-\mathbf{d}^{(k)}\end{pmatrix}$$

$$=\begin{pmatrix}\mathbf{t}(\mathbf{v}^{(k)})-\mathbf{t}(\hat{\mathbf{v}}^{(k)})\\ -\mathbf{B}(\mathbf{d}^{(k)})-\left(-\mathbf{B}\left(\hat{\mathbf{d}}^{(k)}\right)\right)\end{pmatrix}^{\mathrm{T}}\begin{pmatrix}\hat{\mathbf{v}}^{(k)}-\mathbf{v}^{(k)}\\ \hat{\mathbf{d}}^{(k)}-\mathbf{d}^{(k)}\end{pmatrix}+\begin{pmatrix}\tilde{\mathbf{t}}\left(\hat{\mathbf{v}}^{(k)}\right)\\ -\mathbf{B}\left(\hat{\mathbf{d}}^{(k)}\right)\end{pmatrix}^{\mathrm{T}}\begin{pmatrix}\hat{\mathbf{v}}^{(k)}-\mathbf{v}^{(k)}\\ \hat{\mathbf{d}}^{(k)}-\mathbf{d}^{(k)}\end{pmatrix} \tag{10.16}$$

where

$$\tilde{t}_a\left(\hat{v}_a^{(k)}\right)=t_a\left(\hat{v}_a^{(k)}\right)+v_a^{(k)}t_a'\left(v_a^{(k)}\right)=t_a\left(\hat{v}_a^{(k)}\right)+u_a^{(k)},\ a\in A \tag{10.17}$$

Note that $\left(\hat{\mathbf{v}}^{(k)},\hat{\mathbf{d}}^{(k)}\right)$ is the unique optimal solution of the following strictly convex minimization problem:

$$\min_{(\mathbf{v},\mathbf{d})\in\Omega}F_2(\mathbf{v},\mathbf{d})=\sum_{a\in A}\int_0^{v_a}\left(t_a(\omega)+v_a^{(k)}t_a'\left(v_a^{(k)}\right)\right)d\omega-\sum_{w\in W}\int_0^{d_w}B_w(\omega)\,d\omega \tag{10.18}$$

so, from the necessary optimality conditions, we have

$$\sum_{a\in A}\left[t_a\left(\hat{v}_a^{(k)}\right)+\hat{v}_a^{(k)}t_a'\left(\hat{v}_a^{(k)}\right)\right]\left(v_a-\hat{v}_a^{(k)}\right)-\sum_{w\in W}B_w\left(\hat{d}_w^{(k)}\right)\left(d_w-\hat{d}_w^{(k)}\right)\geq 0$$

or

$$\begin{pmatrix} \tilde{\mathbf{t}}\left(\hat{\mathbf{v}}^{(k)}\right) \\ -\mathbf{B}\left(\hat{\mathbf{d}}^{(k)}\right) \end{pmatrix}^{\mathrm{T}} \begin{pmatrix} \mathbf{v}-\hat{\mathbf{v}}^{(k)} \\ \mathbf{d}-\hat{\mathbf{d}}^{(k)} \end{pmatrix} \geq 0 \tag{10.19}$$

for any $(\mathbf{v},\mathbf{d}) \in \Omega$. Inequality (10.19) tells us that the second term of the right-hand side of eqn. (10.16) is non-positive. By (10.13), the first term of the right-hand side of eqn. (10.16) is less than or equal to $-\rho\left(\left\|\hat{\mathbf{v}}^{(k)}-\mathbf{v}^{(k)}\right\|^{2}+\left\|\hat{\mathbf{d}}^{(k)}-\mathbf{d}^{(k)}\right\|^{2}\right)$. Therefore, we conclude that inequality (10.14) is true. ¦

In fact, Lemma 10.2 implies that vector $\begin{pmatrix} \hat{\mathbf{v}}^{(k)} \\ \hat{\mathbf{d}}^{(k)} \end{pmatrix}-\begin{pmatrix} \mathbf{v}^{(k)} \\ \mathbf{d}^{(k)} \end{pmatrix}$ is a feasible descent direction of the objective function at $\begin{pmatrix} \mathbf{v}^{(k)} \\ \mathbf{d}^{(k)} \end{pmatrix}$ for the minimization program (10.2) of the marginal cost pricing problem.

Theorem 10.1 The generated link flows and link tolls by the iterative procedure have the following convergence property:

$$v_a^{(k)} \underset{k\to\infty}{\to} v_a^{*},\ a \in A \tag{10.20}$$

$$u_a^{k} \underset{k\to\infty}{\to} u_a^{*},\ a \in A \tag{10.21}$$

$$\left|\hat{v}_a^{(k)}-v_a^{(k)}\right| \underset{k\to\infty}{\to} 0,\ a \in A \tag{10.22}$$

Proof For any $(\mathbf{v},\mathbf{d}) \in \Omega$, we have

$$\nabla^2 F_1(\mathbf{v},\mathbf{d})=\begin{bmatrix} \ddots & & & & \\ & \tilde{t}_a'(v_a) & & 0 & \\ & & \ddots & & \\ & & & \ddots & \\ & 0 & & -B_w'(d_w) & \\ & & & & \ddots \end{bmatrix} \tag{10.23}$$

where $\tilde{t}_a'(v_a)$ is the derivative of marginal link travel time function (10.4) with respect to link flow v_a, i.e., $\mathrm{d}\tilde{t}_a(v_a)/\mathrm{d}v_a = 2\,\mathrm{d}t_a(v_a)/\mathrm{d}v_a + v_a\,\mathrm{d}^2 t_a(v_a)/\mathrm{d}^2 v_a$ and $B_w'(d_w)$ is the derivative of benefit function with respect to OD demand d_w. Hence,

$$\left[\begin{pmatrix} \hat{\mathbf{v}}^{(k)} \\ \hat{\mathbf{d}}^{(k)} \end{pmatrix}-\begin{pmatrix} \mathbf{v}^{(k)} \\ \mathbf{d}^{(k)} \end{pmatrix}\right]^{\mathrm{T}} \nabla^2 F_1(\mathbf{v},\mathbf{d}) \left[\begin{pmatrix} \hat{\mathbf{v}}^{(k)} \\ \hat{\mathbf{d}}^{(k)} \end{pmatrix}-\begin{pmatrix} \mathbf{v}^{(k)} \\ \mathbf{d}^{(k)} \end{pmatrix}\right]$$

$$= \sum_{a\in A} \tilde{t}_a'(v_a)\left(\hat{v}_a^{(k)} - v_a^{(k)}\right)^2 - \sum_{w\in W} B_w'(d_w)\left(\hat{d}_w^{(k)} - d_w^{(k)}\right)^2 \qquad (10.24)$$

Because Ω is a compact set, it follows that the right hand side of eqn. (10.24) must be bounded by the assumptions on link travel cost and OD demand functions. In view of Lemma 10.2, all the necessary conditions for the proof of the convergence of the method of successive averages are satisfied. We thus conclude that $v_a^{(k)} \underset{k\to\infty}{\to} v_a^*,\ a\in A$ and $d_w^{(k)} \underset{k\to\infty}{\to} d_w^*,\ w\in W$, where $\{v_a^*,\ a\in A\}$ and $\{d_w^*,\ w\in W\}$ are the optimal solution of the minimization problem (10.2)-(10.3). This also implies that $\left|\hat{v}_a^{(k)} - v_a^{(k)}\right| \underset{k\to\infty}{\to} 0,\ a\in A$. By eqn. (10.7), it follows that $u_a^{(k)} \underset{k\to\infty}{\to} u_a^*,\ a\in A$. ¦

10.2.4 A Numerical Example

Example 10.1 We now illustrate the proposed iterative procedure with a simple example that was used in Section 4.4 in Chapter 4. Here for convenience, we present the network and input data again. The network, as shown in Figure 10.2, consists of 11 links, 7 nodes and 4 OD pairs (1→7, 2→7, 3→7 and 6→7). The true, but unknown demand functions are given below:

$$D_{1\to7}(\mu_{1\to7}) = 600\exp(-0.04\mu_{1\to7});\quad D_{2\to7}(\mu_{2\to7}) = 500\exp(-0.03\mu_{2\to7})$$
$$D_{3\to7}(\mu_{3\to7}) = 500\exp(-0.05\mu_{3\to7});\quad D_{6\to7}(\mu_{6\to7}) = 400\exp(-0.05\mu_{6\to7})$$

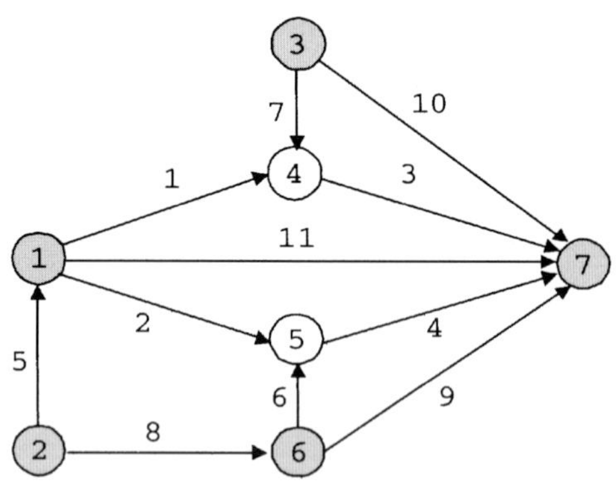

Figure 10.2 The network used for numerical example

The link travel time function:

$$t_a(v_a) = t_a^0\left(1 + 0.15\left(\frac{v_a}{C_a}\right)^4\right)$$

is used with link free-flow travel time, t_a^0, and link physical capacity, C_a, given in Table 10.1 ($\bar{C}_a$ in the table is the link environmental capacity to be used later). Here link toll is given in equivalent time unit.

Table 10.1 Input data for the example network

Link a	1	2	3	4	5	6	7	8	9	10	11
t_a^0	6	5	6	7	6	1	5	10	11	11	15
C_a	200	200	200	200	100	100	150	150	200	200	200
$\bar{C}_a$	160	150	200	150	100	100	150	100	160	160	150

With these demand functions, we have the true optimal link flows and link tolls shown in Table 10.2 by accurately solving the system-optimal marginal-cost pricing problem (10.2)-(10.3), using the Frank-Wolfe convex combination method (2000 Frank-Wolfe iterations are employed for a sufficiently accurate solution).

The initial link flows are not restrictive and are generated via an all-or-nothing traffic assignment with an initial predetermined OD matrix having an identical value for all elements. One can of course use an equilibrium traffic assignment procedure or use the observed, un-tolled link flows to obtain an initial set of link flows. The observed link flows at each trial are simulated by using an elastic-demand UE traffic assignment algorithm. Namely, for given toll pattern in eqn. (10.7) at iteration k, the observed link flows $\{\hat{v}_a^{(k)},\ a \in A\}$ are generated by solving the UE traffic assignment problem (10.6).

Table 10.2 System-optimal link flows and link tolls

Link Number	Link Flow	Link Toll
1	152.18	1.21
2	86.74	0.11
3	203.32	3.85
4	208.49	4.96
5	97.86	3.30
6	121.75	1.32
7	51.14	0.04
8	115.25	2.09
9	174.88	3.86
10	175.23	3.89
11	147.33	2.65

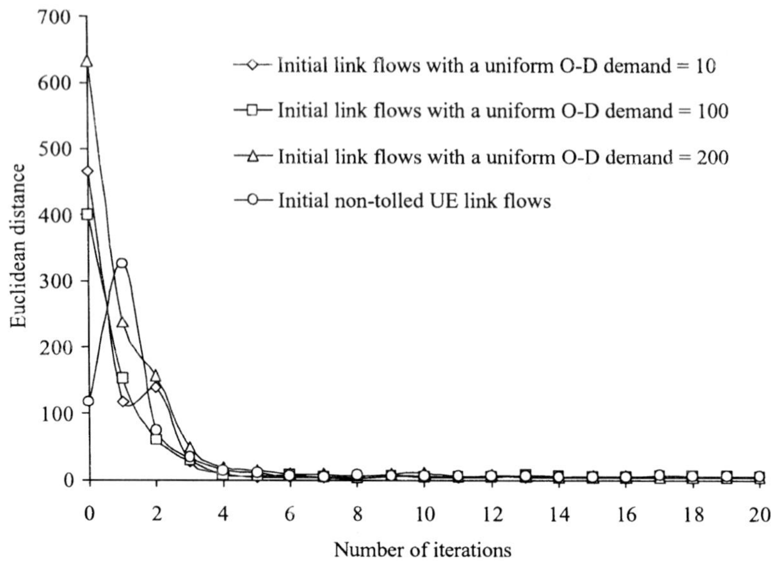

Figure 10.3 Change of the Euclidean distance with iterations for various initial flows

Table 10.3 Estimated optimal link flows and link tolls

Link Number	Link Flow	Link Toll
1	153.22	1.24
2	88.13	0.11
3	203.81	3.88
4	208.85	4.99
5	98.27	3.36
6	120.72	1.27
7	50.59	0.04
8	116.06	2.15
9	175.92	3.95
10	175.90	3.95
11	149.04	2.78

Using the true optimal link flow pattern shown in Table 10.2, we now use the following Euclidean distance from an intermediate estimated link flows to the optimal link flows to assess the convergence of the iterative procedure:

$$dis\left(\mathbf{v}^{(k)},\mathbf{v}^{*}\right)=\left\|\mathbf{v}^{(k)}-\mathbf{v}^{*}\right\|=\left(\sum_{a\in A}\left(v_a^{(k)}-v_a^{*}\right)^2\right)^{\frac{1}{2}} \tag{10.25}$$

For various initial link flows (including the observed, untolled UE link flows), Figure 10.3 plots the change of this Euclidean distance with iterations of the proposed procedure using a predetermined step size: $\alpha^{(k)} = 1/(k+1)$, where k is the number of iterations. As seen for the first 20 iterations, the procedure does converge and the final convergent point is independent of the initial link flows. When a uniform OD demand equal to 100 is used to generate the initial link flows, the proposed method terminates after 8 iterations with a stopping criterion of $\varepsilon = 0.05$. The estimated system-optimal link flows and optimal link tolls are given in Table 10.3, which are sufficiently close to the true value in Table 10.2.

Now we examine the convergence of a fixed step size in the link flow-updating scheme in (10.8). Here we consider two typical values of $\alpha^{(k)} \equiv 0.5$ and $\alpha^{(k)} \equiv 1.0$, leading to the following heuristic procedures. For $\alpha^{(k)} \equiv 0.5,\ k = 1,2,\cdots$, eqn. (10.8) yields:

$$v_a^{(k+1)} = \frac{v_a^{(k)} + \hat{v}_a^{(k)}}{2},\ a \in A \tag{10.26}$$

For $\alpha^{(k)} \equiv 1.0,\ k = 1,2,\cdots$, eqn. (10.8) results in:

$$v_a^{(k+1)} = \hat{v}_a^{(k)},\ \ a \in A \tag{10.27}$$

Equation (10.26) indicates an average updating procedure based on the current observed link flows and the latest iterative link flows. The bisection method for a single highway discussed in Sub-section 10.2.1 belongs to this scheme. Equation (10.27) indicates an iterative algorithm for finding a solution of a *fixed-point* problem. Namely, given a set of observed link flows, link tolls are calculated, and then after imposing the link tolls, a new set of link flows can be observed and used for the next iteration. Unfortunately, as demonstrated below, these two intuitive iterative procedures do not necessarily converge.

With the link flows generated with an initial uniform demand equal to 100, Figure 10.4 shows a comparison of the convergences in terms of the Euclidean distance measure (10.25) by the proposed method of successive averages and the other constant step size schemes. Clearly, the iterative procedure with a constant step size greater than or equal to 0.5 is not convergent. The iterative procedure with a constant step size less than 0.5 converges for this simple example (but such convergence is not guaranteed theoretically), and the proposed method of successive averages does perform better in terms of both initial quick convergence and iterative solution stability. This is practically meaningful because one cannot expect too many revisions in reality to obtain an estimate of the optimal congestion tolls. To provide further evidence of the convergence properties, Figure 10.5 shows the performance of the iterative procedure with the various step size schemes, when the un-tolled UE link flows are used as an initial solution. Once again, the different convergence properties of the various step sizes are confirmed from the figure.

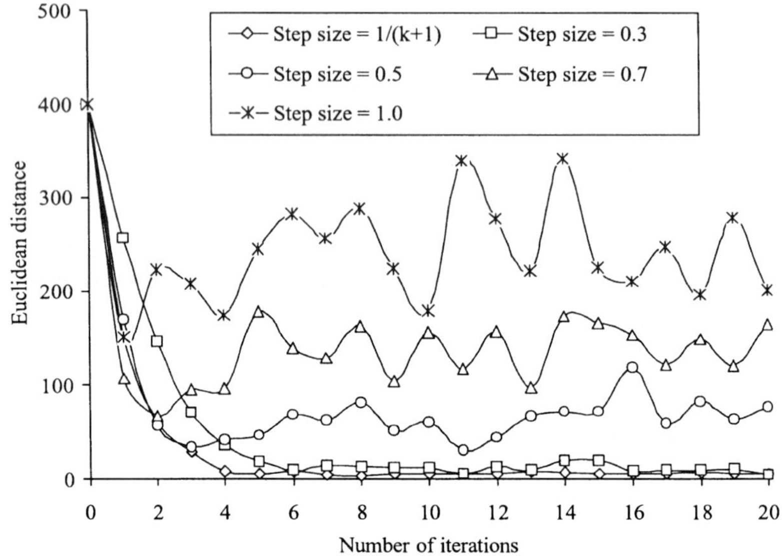

Figure 10.4 Convergence of the iterative procedure with various step size schemes for the initial link flows associated with a uniform OD demand equal to 100

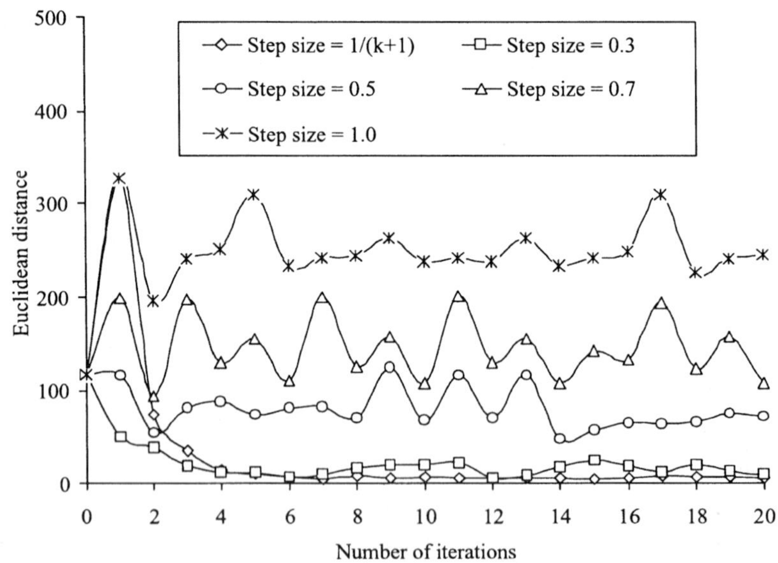

Figure 10.5 Convergence of the iterative procedure with various step size schemes from the initial un-tolled UE link flows

10.3 IMPLEMENTATION OF THE SECOND-BEST PRICING SCHEME

We now move on to develop a trial-and-error implementation procedure for the practical second-best pricing problem. In contrast to the previous straightforward iterative procedure for the first-best pricing, we deal with the price experimentation when only a subset of links is tolled and only a subset of link traffic counts is available in each trial. We aim at developing an effective and efficient procedure capable of at least working out a good estimation or approximation of the relevant congestion tolls with incomplete set of data derived from the limited number of trial experiments. Our objective is achieved by virtue of advanced bi-level programming techniques, which are applied alternately and sequentially for estimating the OD demands from link traffic counts and determining the optimal link tolls with user equilibrium constraints on general networks.

10.3.1 A Sequential Implementation Procedure

Let $\bar{A} \subseteq A$ denote a subset of links subjected to a toll charge and $\tilde{A} \subseteq A$ a subset of links whose flows are observed after a trial for each link toll pattern, $\bar{A}$ and $\tilde{A}$ are not necessarily identical. The basic iterative estimation and optimization procedure works as follows. Suppose that, after k trials of toll pricing on link $a \in \bar{A}$, we obtain a set of calibrated, approximate demand functions $\hat{D}_w^{(k)}(\mu_w, \theta)$, $w \in W$ where $\theta \in \Theta$ is a vector of parameters in the demand function and Θ is the feasible set of these parameters. Then based on the updated, approximate demand function, we can determine a new subset of link tolls $u_a^{(k+1)}$, $a \in \bar{A}$ for subsequent price experimentation by solving the following welfare-maximizing Bi-level Programming Problem (BLPP) with the approximate demand function:

$$\max_{\mathbf{u} \in U} \sum_{w \in W} \int_0^{d_w(\mathbf{u})} \hat{B}_w(\omega, \theta) d\omega - \sum_{a \in A} t_a(v_a(\mathbf{u})) v_a(\mathbf{u}) \tag{10.28}$$

where, $(\mathbf{v}(\mathbf{u}), \mathbf{d}(\mathbf{u}))$ solves the following UE problem for given $\mathbf{u} \in U$ and $\theta \in \Theta$:

$$\min_{(\mathbf{v}, \mathbf{d}) \in \Omega} \sum_{a \in \bar{A}} \int_0^{v_a} (t_a(\omega) + u_a) d\omega + \sum_{a \in A, a \notin \bar{A}} \int_0^{v_a} t_a(\omega) d\omega - \sum_{w \in W} \int_0^{d_w} \hat{B}_w(\omega, \theta) d\omega \tag{10.29}$$

where $\hat{B}_w(\cdot, \theta) = \hat{D}_w^{-1}(\cdot, \theta)$, being the inverse function of the currently calibrated, approximate demand function $\hat{D}_w(\mu_w, \theta)$ and U is the feasible set of toll vector $\mathbf{u} = (u_a, a \in \bar{A})$.

After imposition of the newly determined link tolls $u_a^{(k+1)}$, $a \in \bar{A}$, a subset of revealed link flows $\bar{v}_a^{(k+1)}$, $a \in \tilde{A}$ is observed. The observed link flows are the result of distribution of the realized OD demands on the network, and thus provide useful information about the true but unknown demand functions. Thus we can use the BLPP technique to estimate or update the OD matrix and the approximate demand functions from the newly available link traffic counts, thereby obtaining a new set of updated OD demand functions $\hat{D}_w\left(\mu_w, \theta^{(k+1)}\right)$, $w \in W$.

There are two ways to update the demand functions: one is the updating of the OD matrix obtained in the last iteration from the traffic counts, and then using the new OD matrix to tune the approximate OD demand functions; the other is calibrating and updating the parameters of the assumed OD demand functions directly from the observed new trial results.

The OD matrix-updating problem from traffic counts can be formulated as the following BLPP:

$$\min_{\mathbf{d} \in \Omega_{\mathbf{d}}} \gamma_1 F_1\left(\mathbf{v}(\mathbf{d}), \hat{\mathbf{v}}\right) + \gamma_2 F_2\left(\mathbf{d}, \hat{\mathbf{d}}\right) \tag{10.30}$$

where $\mathbf{v}(\mathbf{d})$ solves the following fixed-demand UE problem for given $\mathbf{d} \in \Omega_{\mathbf{d}}$ and $\mathbf{u} \in U$:

$$\min_{\mathbf{v} \in \Omega_{\mathbf{v}}(\mathbf{d})} \sum_{a \in \bar{A}} \int_0^{v_a} \left(t_a(\omega) + u_a\right) \mathrm{d}\omega + \sum_{a \in A, a \notin \bar{A}} \int_0^{v_a} t_a(\omega) \mathrm{d}\omega \tag{10.31}$$

where

$$\Omega_{\mathbf{d}} = \left\{ \left(d_w, w \in W\right) \middle| \, 0 \le d_w \le \hat{D}_w, w \in W \right\} \tag{10.32}$$

$$\Omega_{\mathbf{v}}(\mathbf{d}) = \left\{ \left(v_a, a \in A\right) \middle| \, v_a = \sum_{w \in W} \sum_{r \in R_w} f_{rw} \delta_{ar}, a \in A; f_{rw} \ge 0, r \in R_w, \sum_{r \in R_w} f_{rw} = d_w, w \in W \right\} \tag{10.33}$$

In this model, $\hat{\mathbf{v}} = \left(\hat{v}_a, a \in \tilde{A}\right)^{\mathrm{T}}$ represents the link flows vector observed in the last trial; $\hat{\mathbf{d}} = \left(\hat{d}_w, w \in W\right)^{\mathrm{T}}$ is the OD matrix (rearranged as a vector) obtained in the last trial; $F_1(\mathbf{v}, \hat{\mathbf{v}})$ and $F_2\left(\mathbf{d}, \hat{\mathbf{d}}\right)$ are functions of the generalized distance or error measurement between $\mathbf{v}$ and $\hat{\mathbf{v}}$, and $\mathbf{d}$ and $\hat{\mathbf{d}}$, respectively. The following Euclidean distance function is frequently used:

$$\gamma_1 F_1\left(\mathbf{v}(\mathbf{d}), \hat{\mathbf{v}}\right) + \gamma_2 F_2\left(\mathbf{d}, \hat{\mathbf{d}}\right) = \gamma_1 \sum_{a \in \tilde{A}} \left(v_a(\mathbf{d}) - \hat{v}_a\right)^2 + \gamma_2 \sum_{w \in W} \left(d_w - \hat{d}_w\right)^2 \tag{10.34}$$

where γ_1 and γ_2 are two weighting factors reflecting the relative confidence in $\hat{\mathbf{v}}$ and $\hat{\mathbf{d}}$ respectively. Because traffic counts are revealed and reliable information is collected with a good accuracy in the pricing experiment, a larger γ_1 $(> \gamma_2)$ may be preferred.

In the case that the approximate OD demand functions are tuned by updating a set of parameters $\theta \in \Theta$ directly, the problem is formulated as the following similar BLPP:

$$\min_{\theta\in\Theta} \gamma_1 F_1\left(\mathbf{v}(\theta),\hat{\mathbf{v}}\right)+\gamma_2 F_2\left(\mathbf{d}(\theta),\hat{\mathbf{d}}\right) \tag{10.35}$$

where $(\mathbf{v}(\theta),\mathbf{d}(\theta))$ solves the following elastic-demand UE problem for given $\theta\in\Theta$ and $\mathbf{u}\in U$

$$\min_{(\mathbf{v},\mathbf{d})\in\Omega} \sum_{a\in\bar{A}}\int_0^{v_a}\left(t_a(\omega)+u_a\right)\mathrm{d}\omega+\sum_{a\in A,a\notin\bar{A}}\int_0^{v_a}t_a(\omega)\mathrm{d}\omega-\sum_{w\in W}\int_0^{d_w}\hat{B}_w(\omega,\theta)\mathrm{d}\omega \tag{10.36}$$

The same quadratic function in (10.34) can be used for the objective function (10.35).

The above iterative bilevel OD demand function estimation and bilevel link toll optimization process is repeated until an appropriate convergence criterion is reached. To sum up, the general iterative trial-and-error procedure through sequential price experimentation for estimating the second-best link tolls is given below.

Trial-and-error procedure for the second-best pricing scheme

Step 0. (*Initialization*) Let $\left\{\hat{D}_w\left(\mu_w,\theta^{(0)}\right),\ w\in W\right\}$ be an initial set of approximate demand functions. Set $k:=0$.

Step 1. (*Estimate link tolls*) Solve the BLPP (10.28)-(10.29) to obtain a new set of link tolls $\left\{u_a^{(k)},\ a\in\bar{A}\right\}$.

Step 2. (*Observe link flows*) Observe the revealed link flows denoted by $\left\{\hat{v}_a^{(k)},\ a\in\tilde{A}\right\}$ after the imposition of the new link tolls $\left\{u_a^{(k)},\ a\in\bar{A}\right\}$.

Step 3. (*Check convergence*) If $\left\|\mathbf{u}^{(k+1)}-\mathbf{u}^{(k)}\right\|/\left\|\mathbf{u}^{(k)}\right\|\le\varepsilon$, then stop. Otherwise, go to Step 4.

Step 4. (*Update OD demand function*) Solve the BLPP (10.30)-(10.31) or (10.35)-(10.36) to obtain a new set of updated OD demand functions $\left(\hat{D}_w\left(\mu_w,\theta^{(k+1)}\right),\ w\in W\right)$. Let $k:=k+1$ and go to Step 1.

In the algorithm, ε is a positive number for convergence tolerance. The procedure will be terminated after the difference between two successive trial results is within a given tolerance.

Two remarks on the proposed procedures are appropriate here. First, to execute the procedure, one needs to assume a specific functional form as an approximation of the true but unknown demand functions, and an existing reference OD matrix, if available, could be helpful for estimating/updating the OD matrix and the approximate OD demand functions initially. Given a set of limited trial experiments around the optimum solution, the procedure is expected to derive the demand curve for a limited range of traffic levels that is relevant to road pricing together with the estimation of optimal link tolls. Second, as a special case of the general second-best pricing problem envisioned here, the proposed sequential linear demand function approximation (presented below) can of course be used to determine socially optimal tolls in a first-best pricing environment, without the demand functions considered in Section 10.2. We may reasonably expect that the secant-like algorithm based on successive approximations would zone in on the optimal price much faster than the painfully slow process of the method of successive averages. This is important in practice, since the price experiments are generally limited to a few trials. Thus the proposed approach has an added bonus for the first-best pricing problem studied in previous section, it involves fewer price changes and thus reduces the cost of implementing the pricing scheme, which is itself a social benefit.

10.3.2 Sequential Linear Approximation

As assumed throughout this study, we have to specify an approximate (but easily invertible and computable) function $\hat{D}_w(\mu_w,\theta)$, $w\in W$, $\theta\in\Theta$, to use in place of the true, *but unknown*, demand function in the neighborhood of the optimum point of the second-best pricing problem. One favorable choice is an interpolation and extrapolation scheme by a polynomial, including the simple linear and quadratic approximations. Here we adopt the following simplest sequential linear approximation scheme based on successively observed and estimated experimental data:

$$\hat{D}_w\left(\mu_w,\theta_w^{(k)}\right)=\hat{d}_w^{(k)}+z_w^{(k)}\left(\mu_w-\hat{\mu}_w^{(k)}\right),\ w\in W,\ k=1,2,\ldots \tag{10.37}$$

where $\theta_w^{(k)}=\left\{z_w^{(k)},\hat{d}_w^{(k)},\hat{\mu}_w^{(k)}\right\}, w\in W$ are the function parameters, $\left\{z_w^{(k)},w\in W\right\}$ are the slopes of the linear demand function approximations, $\left\{\hat{d}_w^{(k)},w\in W\right\}$ are the OD demands estimated from observed link flows at iteration k using the OD matrix updating model (10.30)-(10.31), and $\left\{\hat{\mu}_w^{(k)},w\in W\right\}$ are the corresponding equilibrium OD travel cost inclusive of toll charges if any.

By considering the straight line through the latest two experiment points, we have:

$$z_w^{(k)}=\frac{\hat{d}_w^{(k)}-\hat{d}_w^{(k-1)}}{\hat{\mu}_w^{(k)}-\hat{\mu}_w^{(k-1)}},\ w\in W,\ k=1,2,\ldots \tag{10.38}$$

The line slopes, $\{z_w^{(k)},\ w\in W\}$, are updated from iteration to iteration, based on the observed results in each trial. This successive linear approximation, if convergent, is expected to become a tangential approximation of the true demand functions and the tangent point is the resulting equilibrium point associated with the second-best optimum toll charge.

Note that, when estimating the current OD matrix $\hat{d}_w^{(k)}, w\in W$ by the model (10.30)-(10.31), the OD matrix $\hat{d}_w^{(k-1)}, w\in W$ obtained in the previous iteration is used as the reference matrix to ensure that the sequence of the OD matrices generated converges to the final optimum. In this regard an initial seed or reference OD matrix is used to estimate the initial OD matrix for the linear approximation and an old matrix from a previous study could be used for this purpose. The quality of the initial seed OD matrix is immaterial because its impact on the resulting OD matrix estimates will diminish as the OD matrix is successively converged. In addition, a rational linear approximation of the true demand curve requires that the slope $\{z_w^{(k)},\ w\in W\}$ calculated by (10.38) from the latest two experiment points be negative, a property of a demand function as mentioned in Assumption 10-3. Nonetheless, this requirement is not always ensured as the iteration continues, particularly when the trial solutions approach the real optimum. Because the OD demands, $\hat{d}_w^{(k)}$ and $\hat{d}_w^{(k-1)}$, are merely estimates from traffic counts, the slope $z_w^{(k)}$ may become unstable as $\hat{d}_w^{(k)}$ and $\hat{d}_w^{(k-1)}$ move closer to each other due to estimation inaccuracy. Thus, a correction has to be made whenever a positive slope emerges by, for example, resetting it to a small negative value.

10.3.3 Two Numerical Examples

We now present two simple numerical examples to elucidate the applications of the proposed sequential price experimental approach to the first-best and the second-best road pricing problems with unknown demand functions, respectively.

Example 10.2 In this example, we show that the algorithm based on successive linear approximations may involve fewer price changes than the method of successive averages does for the first-best pricing scheme. For simplicity, we consider the standard textbook case; a single OD pair connected by a single road, with the following true demand and link travel time functions:

$$D(\mu) = 600\exp(-0.05\mu) \tag{10.39}$$

$$t(v)=10\left(1+0.15\left(\frac{v}{200}\right)^4\right) \tag{10.40}$$

Since a single road is concerned, the revealed or observed flow, $\hat{v}$, is always equal to the OD demand, $\hat{d}$, and hence the OD demand estimation process is bypassed here.

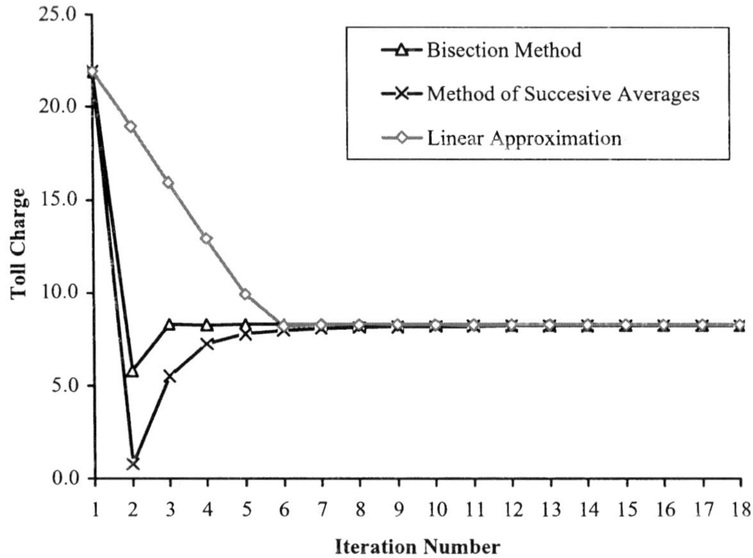

Figure 10.6 Comparison of the convergence rates by the bisection method, the method of successive averages and the sequential linear approximation method in Example 10.2

By equalizing the inverse of the true demand function and the following marginal-confunction denoted as $\tilde{t}(v)$

$$\tilde{t}(v)=t(v)+v\frac{\mathrm{d}t(v)}{\mathrm{d}v}=10\left(1+0.75\left(\frac{v}{200}\right)^4\right) \tag{10.41}$$

the socially optimal level of flow, full trip cost and toll charge can be identified to be:

$v^*=d^*=216.898$; $\mu^*=20.350$; $u^*=8.300$

The equilibrium flow and full trip cost without tolling are equal to $v^{(0)}=d^{(0)}=276.581$ and $\mu^{(0)}=15.489$. Starting with this observed flow with the corresponding initial toll charge $u^{(1)}=21.933$ calculated by (10.7), the results by three methods (the bisection method with $\alpha^{(k)}\equiv 1/2$ in (10.8); the method of successive averages with $\alpha^{(k)}\equiv 1/(k+1)$ in (10.8), and the linear approximation method proposed in this section) are shown below.

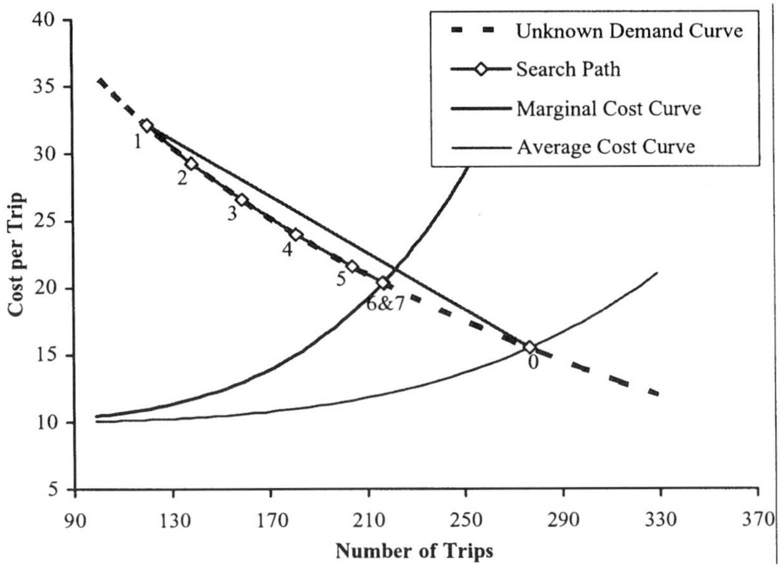

Figure 10.7 Convergence pattern of the sequential linear demand function approximation in Example 10.2

As already mentioned, the bisection method does converge for the simple single road case considered, and hence is applied here for a comparison. For a given tight convergence criterion $\varepsilon = 0.001$, the number of trials required by the bisection method, the method of successive averages and the linear approximation method are respectively 5, 18 and 7 (also refer to Figure 10.6). For this special example, the bisection method has the quickest convergence (but it does not work for a general network), the proposed sequential linear demand function approximation method outperforms the method of successive averages. Note that the relative convergence of the three methods depends on the curvature of the demand function. Clearly, if the true but unknown demand function is linear, the linear approximation method will arrive at the optimum with two iterations only.

The average private cost and the marginal social cost curves are plotted in Figure 10.7 together with the true but unknown demand curves (dashed). The linear extrapolation and interpolation lines are drawn through the two most recent experimental points (except the initial point which is the observed point without toll charge or in the do-nothing case). The points are numbered in the order that they are identified in the sequential price experimentation. For this simple single road example, the true OD demand and OD cost in each trial are observed directly without an estimation process and thus all trial points are located on the true demand curves. As observed from the figure, the sequence of experimental points converges to the social optimum (the intersection between the true demand curve and the marginal social cost curve).

Example 10.3 In this example we use a small but general network to illustrate the application of the trial-and-error procedure for the second-best pricing problem. The network, as shown in Figure 10.8, consists of 4 links, 3 nodes and 2 OD pairs (1→3, 2→3). The true demand functions are given below:

$$D_{1\to 3}(\mu_{1\to 3}) = 500\exp(-0.03\mu_{1\to 3}),\quad D_{2\to 3}(\mu_{2\to 3}) = 400\exp(-0.05\mu_{2\to 3})$$

The following link travel time functions are used for the 4 links respectively:

$$t_1(v_1) = 12\left(1+0.15\left(\frac{v_1}{200}\right)^4\right),\quad t_2(v_2) = 10\left(1+0.15\left(\frac{v_2}{150}\right)^4\right)$$

$$t_3(v_3) = 9\left(1+0.15\left(\frac{v_3}{150}\right)^4\right),\quad t_4(v_4) = 11\left(1+0.15\left(\frac{v_4}{200}\right)^4\right)$$

The set of tolled links and observed links are assumed to be identical with two links: $\overline{A} = \tilde{A} = \{3,4\}$.

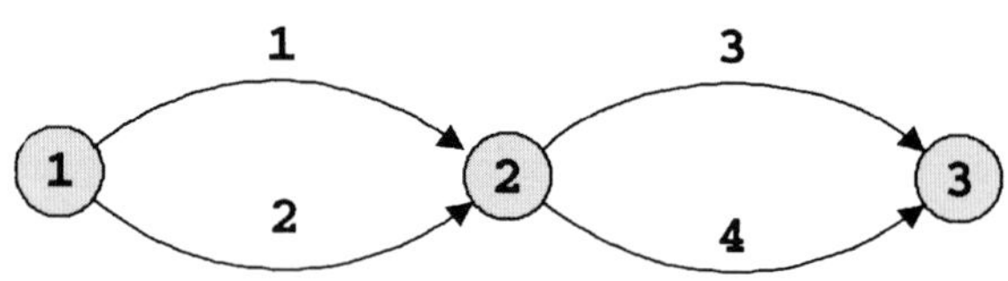

Figure 10.8 The network used for Example 10.3

For given toll charges in each trial experiment, the observed link flows are simulated (generated) by using the elastic-demand traffic assignment method with the true nonlinear demand functions. In view of the small size of the example network, we used an extensive direct search method without derivatives (Hooke-Jeeves pattern search method) for finding the global optimal solutions of both the bi-level OD estimation and toll optimization problems in each trial.

For the purpose of validation, we identified the true optimum (never known in reality without demand functions) by extensive direct search using the true OD demand functions. With the known optimum toll solution, we can test whether or not the sequential alternate bi-level OD estimation and toll optimization algorithm converges to the real optimum.

To start the iterative procedure, the initial observed link flows are given as the equilibrium link flows without toll charge (do-nothing case), and the initial OD demand and OD cost for the first linear approximation of the demand function are estimated from the initial observed flows with an initial seed OD matrix: $\hat{d}_{1\to3} = \hat{d}_{2\to3} = 200$. The starting point of the toll charge is $\left(u_3^{(0)}, u_4^{(0)}\right) = (4.0, 4.0)$. The two weighting factors for the OD matrix estimation problem (10.34) are set to be $(\gamma_1, \gamma_2) = (1000.0, 1.0)$, with the directly observed link flows carrying much higher weighting. The convergence tolerance is set to be $\varepsilon = 0.01$.

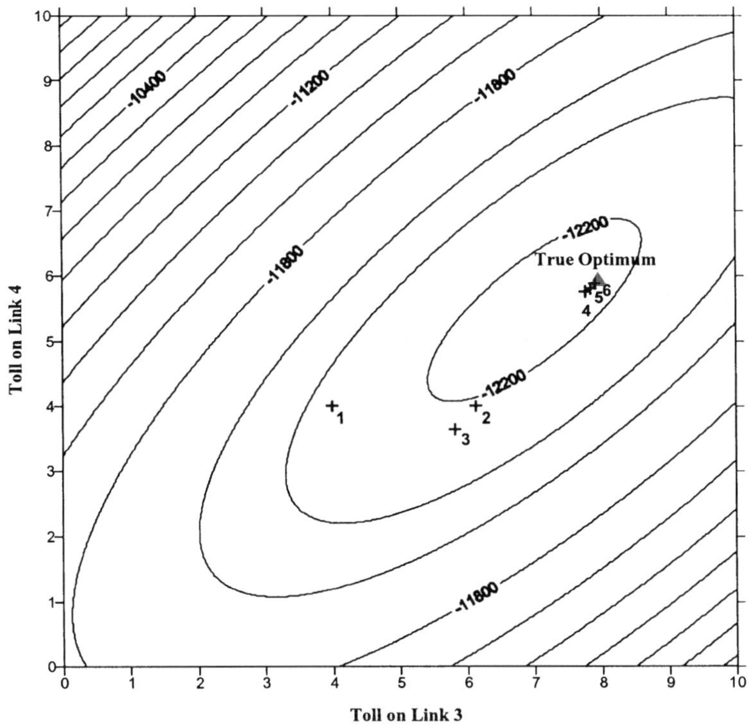

Figure 10.9 Convergence pattern of the sequential trial-and-error toll adjustment scheme for the second-best pricing problem in Example 10.3

Figure 10.9 plots the true optimum for the second-best pricing problem and the convergence pattern of the link tolls identified through the sequential price experimentation using the sequential BLPP methods. The true or exact optimum occurs at $\left(u_3^*, u_4^*\right) = (7.95, 5.95)$. The algorithm converges after 6 iterations with a convergent point $\left(u_3^{(6)}, u_4^{(6)}\right) = (7.84, 5.80)$ which is sufficiently close to the exact optimum.

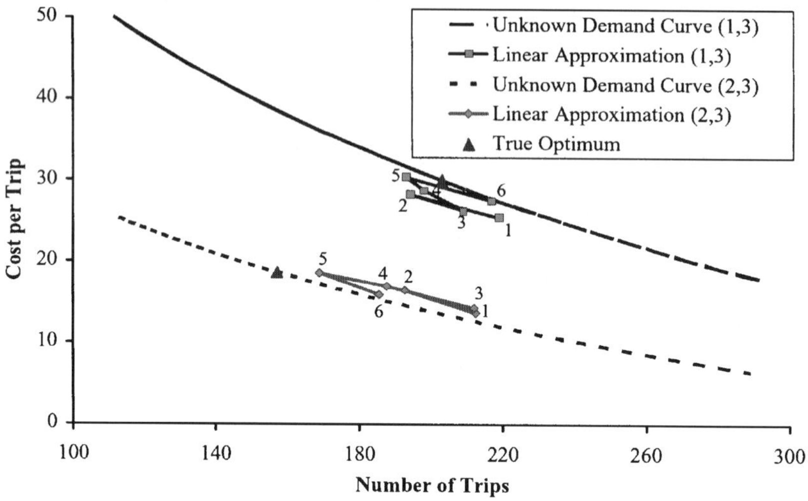

Figure 10.10 Convergence pattern of the sequential linear demand function approximation in Example 10.3

Figure 10.10 displays the successive linear approximation to the true, but unknown, nonlinear demand functions. It is observed that, as the trial experiment continues, the linear approximation does become more tangential to the true demand curve near the true optimum points on the demand curve. In contrast to Figure 10.7 in Example 10.2, it is observed in this figure that the trial points are not necessarily located on the true demand curves, which are the direct results of the imperfection of the OD demand estimation sub-problem, mainly arising from the incomplete set of link traffic counts. As acknowledged before, the instability problem, including the positive slope estimates of the linear demand function approximation, was indeed encountered when commencing the trial experiments with alternative initial toll charges. It is thus suggested that flow observations should be made on as many links as possible to enhance the accuracy and reliability of the OD demand estimation, thereby leading to better linear approximations of the true demand curves.

In the above examples, we have adopted the simplest functional approximation scheme: a successive linear demand function approximation, which may, as indeed observed in our study, encounter instability problems near the optimum point. It is expected to improve the stability and convergence of the successive function approximation by using a more accurate high-order polynomial with more observed experiment points. For example, it is straightforward to use a quadratic approximation function, which is unique through the latest three experiment points. From an alternative perspective, one may also consider the methods of the non-parametric curve estimation method, well established in econometrics, to derive the demands from the observed experiment results, without knowledge on the form of the demand function.

10.4 IMPLEMENTATION OF THE TRAFFIC RESTRAINT AND ROAD PRICING SCHEME

The traffic restraint and road pricing scheme belongs to a type of second-best pricing problems examined in Chapters 4. It aims to seek a set of link tolls so as to hold traffic demand within a desirable level such as an "environmental" capacity, which can be regarded as the maximum traffic volume that can be accommodated along the streets without exceeding a certain threshold of environmental damage. As shown in Chapter 4, the problem can be tackled by determining a set of optimal Lagrangian multipliers (shade costs or prices) for a special UE program with link (physical or environmental) capacity constraints. The values of the resulting Lagrangian multipliers associated with link capacity constraints give the desirable link tolls, in terms of time equivalents, for achieving the required capacity constraints. Here, we develop a trial-and-error procedure in the same spirit as in previous sections to identify the desirable optimal Lagrangian multipliers in the absence of OD demand functions.

10.4.1 The Primal and Dual Formulation

Let again $\bar{A} \subseteq A$ be a subset of links subjected to capacity constraints and hence toll charges in the network. The traffic restraint and road pricing problem seeks a set of tolls, $\mathbf{u}^* = \left(u_a^*,\ a \in \bar{A}\right)^{\mathrm{T}}$, such that the resultant UE traffic flow denoted by $v_a\left(\mathbf{u}^*\right)$ for a considered link $a \in \bar{A}$ does not exceed a desirable upper bound or an acceptable threshold level of link flow denoted by $\bar{C}_a$ after implementing the toll charge:

$$v_a\left(\mathbf{u}^*\right) \le \bar{C}_a,\ a \in \bar{A} \tag{10.42}$$

Note that the threshold for each tolled link in eqn. (10.42) is predetermined by the planner. Without over-implementing the traffic restraint scheme, we require that the chosen link toll pattern should be meaningful in the sense that a link is free of charge, if traffic flow on this link is less than its capacity; otherwise, it would be subjected to a toll charge to restrain its flow to its prescribed restraint level. That is

$$u_a^* = 0,\ \text{if}\ v_a\left(\mathbf{u}^*\right) < \bar{C}_a;\quad u_a^* \ge 0,\ \text{if}\ v_a\left(\mathbf{u}^*\right) = \bar{C}_a,\ a \in \bar{A} \tag{10.43}$$

As shown in Section 4.8 in Chapter 4, the UE conditions together with the complementary conditions (10.43) are equivalent to the first-order optimality conditions for the following elastic-demand UE program with link capacity constraints.

$$\min_{(\mathbf{v},\mathbf{d})\in\Omega} \sum_{a\in A}\int_0^{v_a} t_a(\omega)\,d\omega - \sum_{w\in W}\int_0^{d_w} B_w(\omega)\,d\omega \tag{10.44}$$

subject to

$$v_a \le \bar{C}_a,\ a\in \bar{A} \tag{10.45}$$

where Ω is again the set of feasible link flows and OD demands without including the additional link capacity constraints. The desired link tolls, $\mathbf{u}^* = \left(u_a^*,\ a\in \bar{A}\right)^{\mathrm{T}}$, correspond to the optimal Lagrangian multipliers associated with capacity constraints (10.45). One should note that, although model (10.44)-(10.45) is a strictly convex minimization problem, its optimal Lagrangian multiplier is not unique, depending on the linear dependence of the binding link capacity constraints at the optimum. Thus the optimal link toll for achieving the capacity constraint (10.43) is not unique.

Bearing in mind that the optimal Lagrangian multipliers for a strictly convex minimization problem is an optimal solution of its Lagrangian dual, we now consider the dual of the above convex program (10.44)-(10.45) by introducing the following partial Lagrangian function:

$$L(\mathbf{v},\mathbf{d},\mathbf{u}) = \sum_{a\in A}\int_0^{v_a} t_a(\omega)d\omega - \sum_{w\in W}\int_0^{d_w} B_w(\omega)d\omega + \sum_{a\in \bar{A}} u_a\left(v_a - \bar{C}_a\right) \tag{10.46}$$

where $u_a,\ a\in \bar{A}$ is the Lagrangian multiplier associated with constraint (10.45). The Lagrangian dual problem for the strictly convex program (10.44) can be formulated as:

$$\max_{\mathbf{u}\ge 0}\ \varphi(\mathbf{u}) \tag{10.47}$$

where $\mathbf{u} = \left(u_a,\ a\in \bar{A}\right)^{\mathrm{T}}$ and, according to the duality theory in nonlinear programming, the objective function $\varphi(\mathbf{u})$ is defined below

$$\varphi(\mathbf{u}) = \min_{(\mathbf{v},\mathbf{d})\in\Omega} L(\mathbf{v},\mathbf{d},\mathbf{u}) \tag{10.48}$$

By the property of the dual function for strictly convex programs, the following Lemma is applicable.

Lemma 10.3 $\varphi(\mathbf{u})$ *is a concave and continuously differentiable function with gradient:*

$$\frac{\partial\varphi(\mathbf{u})}{\partial u_a} = v_a(\mathbf{u}) - \bar{C}_a,\ a\in \bar{A} \tag{10.49}$$

where $\{v_a(\mathbf{u}),\ a\in\bar{A}\}$ *is the subset of traffic flows for the tolled links or part of the optimal solution* $(\mathbf{v}(\mathbf{u}),\mathbf{d}(\mathbf{u}))$ *for the strictly convex minimization problem (10.48) for any given non-negative multiplier* $\mathbf{u}$.

As the dual problem (10.47) is a concave but not a strictly concave maximization problem, its optimal solution is not unique. Let U^* be the set of all its optimal solutions, then we have the following theorem, from the duality theory in nonlinear programming.

Theorem 10.2 *Let* $\mathbf{u}^*\in U^*$, *then* $(\mathbf{v}(\mathbf{u}^*),\mathbf{d}(\mathbf{u}^*))$ *is the unique optimal solution for the elastic-demand UE program (10.44) with link capacity constraints (10.45), and* $\mathbf{u}^*$ *is its optimal Lagrangian multiplier associated with constraint (10.45).*

Theorem 10.2 shows that that the desirable tolls for the traffic restraint and road pricing problem can be obtained by solving the Lagrangian dual problem (10.47).

10.4.2 Trial-and-error Implementation Procedure

When the demand functions are unknown, existing algorithms for the UE traffic assignment problems with capacity constraints are no longer workable for the problem considered here, and thus are unable to find the optimal Lagrangian multipliers or tolls for the primal convex program (10.44)-(10.45). Nonetheless, as pointed out earlier, the UE traffic flow $\{v_a(\mathbf{u}),a\in\bar{A}\}$ on the concerned links can be easily observed in practice after implementing any given toll charges; the set of observed link flows is part of the unique optimal solution for the following UE problem with given toll charges $\mathbf{u}=\{u_a,\ a\in\bar{A}\}$:

$$\min_{(\mathbf{v},\mathbf{d})\in\Omega}\ \sum_{a\in A}\int_0^{v_a}t_a(\omega)d\omega-\sum_{w\in W}\int_0^{d_w}B_w(\omega)d\omega+\sum_{a\in\bar{A}}u_av_a \tag{10.50}$$

One can readily see that the Lagrangian function $L(\mathbf{v},\mathbf{d},\mathbf{u})$ given by eqn. (10.46) and the objective function (10.50) differ by a constant term $-\sum_{a\in\bar{A}}u_a\bar{C}_a$ for given toll charge $\mathbf{u}=\{u_a,a\in\bar{A}\}$, and the optimal solutions for the strictly convex minimization problems (10.48) and (10.50) are thus identical. Lemma 10.3 thus tells us that the derivative of the objective function for the Lagrangian dual problem (10.47) in a particular multiplier u_a in connection with a tolled link $a\in\bar{A}$ is equal to the relevant observed link flow minus its threshold capacity constraint. Namely, the gradient of the objective function for the Lagrangian dual problem (10.47) can be evaluated by using observed traffic flows on the tolled links. We are thus motivated to apply a gradient projection method to solve the dual problem (10.47). The step size sequence of this method should be, however, determined a priori, because the value of the objective function for the dual problem cannot be evaluated in the absence of OD demand functions. In summary, we have the following trial-and-error implementation procedure for the traffic restraint and road pricing scheme, when the demand functions are unknown.

Trial-and-error procedure for the traffic restraint and road pricing scheme

Step 0. (*Initialization*) Let $\{u_a^{(0)},\ a \in \bar{A}\}$ be an initial toll pattern. Set $k := 0$.

Step 1. (*Observe link flows*) Implementing toll pattern $\{u_a^{(k)},\ a \in \bar{A}\}$, and then observe traffic flows $\{\hat{v}_a^{(k)},\ a \in \bar{A}\}$ on the concerned links.

Step 2. (*Estimate link tolls*) Adjust the link toll charges by

$$u_a^{(k+1)} = \max\left\{u_a^{(k)} + \alpha^{(k)}\left(\hat{v}_a^{(k)} - \bar{C}_a\right),\ 0\right\},\ a \in \bar{A} \tag{10.51}$$

Step3. (*Check convergence*) If $\left\|\mathbf{u}^{(k+1)} - \mathbf{u}^{(k)}\right\| / \left\|\mathbf{u}^{(k)}\right\| \le \varepsilon$, then stop. Otherwise set $k := k+1$ and go to Step 1.

Here the predetermined step size sequence $\{\alpha^{(k)}\}$ must satisfy the condition (10.9). At iteration k of the above procedure, the implementing toll pattern $\mathbf{u}^{(k)}$ results in UE link flows and OD demands denoted by $\left(\mathbf{v}\left(\mathbf{u}^{(k)}\right), \mathbf{d}\left(\mathbf{u}^{(k)}\right)\right)$, which is the unique optimal solution for the standard traffic assignment problem (10.50) where $\mathbf{u} = \mathbf{u}^{(k)}$. The observed link flows in Step 1 are part of the UE link flow solution $\mathbf{v}\left(\mathbf{u}^{(k)}\right)$. Namely, $v_a^{(k)} = v_a\left(\mathbf{u}^{(k)}\right),\ a \in \bar{A}$. From eqn. (10.49) in Lemma 10.3, it can be readily verified that the right-hand-side of eqn. (10.51) amounts to a projection operation

$$\mathbf{u}^{(k+1)} = \mathrm{Proj}_{\Re^+}\left(\mathbf{u}^{(k)} + \alpha^{(k)} \nabla \varphi\left(\mathbf{u}^{(k)}\right)\right) \tag{10.52}$$

where $\Re^+ = \{\mathbf{u} \mid \mathbf{u} \ge 0\}$, $\nabla \varphi\left(\mathbf{u}^{(k)}\right) = \left(\partial \varphi\left(\mathbf{u}^{(k)}\right) / \partial u_a,\ a \in \bar{A}\right)^{\mathrm{T}}$ where the projection operator is defined by

$$\mathrm{Proj}_{\Re^+}(\mathbf{y}) = \underset{\mathbf{x} \in \Re^+}{\arg\min} \left\|\mathbf{y} - \mathbf{x}\right\|^2 \tag{10.53}$$

Hence, the iterative formula (10.52) is a gradient projection method with a step size $\alpha^{(k)}$ satisfying condition (10.9) for the dual problem (10.47). The following theorem shows the convergence of the iterative scheme (10.52) in finding an effective toll pattern for the traffic restraint and road pricing scheme.

Theorem 10.3 *If* $\mathbf{u}^{(k+1)} = \mathbf{u}^{(k)}$ *at iteration* k*, then* $\mathbf{u}^{(k)} \in U^*$*, being the set of optimal solutions for the dual problem (10.47). Otherwise,* $\lim_{k\to\infty} \mathbf{u}^{(k)} = \mathbf{u}^*$ *and* $\mathbf{u}^* \in U^*$.

As the gradient $\nabla\varphi(\mathbf{u})$ defined in (10.49) is a bounded function, then the sequence of vectors, $\{\mathbf{u}^{(k)}\}$, generated by iterative scheme (10.52), will be convergent to an optimal solution for the dual problem (10.47). The theorem comes from the fundamental property of projection operators and the (sub-)gradient algorithm for the Lagrangian dual formulation of a convex program.

We conclude this section with two remarks. First, unlike the trial-and-error method for the first-best and second-best pricing problems examined in Sections 10.2 and 10.3, the procedure proposed here for the traffic restraint and road pricing scheme updates the link tolls in a straightforward manner, based on the difference between the given flow restraint levels and the observed link flows only after each trial; neither link travel time nor demand functions and nor users' value of time are needed explicitly. Second, the trial-and-error procedure introduced in this section deals purely with the traffic restraint policy through pricing, and it can be simply altered to handle the marginal-cost pricing problem with link (physical or environmental) capacity constraints described in Section 3.3 in Chapter 3. In this case, the procedure given in this section and that developed in Section 10.2 should be combined or the primal and dual method for a convex program should be used to identify the optimal link tolls. Namely, the new trial tolls should be given as the sum of the tolls determined by eqns. (10.51) and (10.7). Clearly, in the joint implementation, step sizes used in eqns. (10.51) and (10.8) in the two procedures should be different, and the users' value of time is needed for determining the marginal-cost pricing link tolls.

10.4.3 A Numerical Example

Example 10.4 We consider the same network used in Example 10.1. The traffic restraint and road pricing scheme here is to find an efficient set of link tolls to hold the flow on *each* link in the network ($\bar{A} = A$) below or equal to its environmental capacity, that is already given in the bottom row of Table 10.1.

To test the proposed trial-and-error procedure, we apply two step size sequences satisfying condition (10.9): $\alpha^{(k)} = 1/(k+1)$ and $\alpha^{(k)} \in [0.5/(1+k),\ 2.5/(1+k)]$. For the second sequence, an appropriate step size at each iteration is given by randomly generating a number in the relevant interval. In both cases, the initial toll charge is zero and the observed, un-tolled UE link flows are used to obtain a first set of link tolls for the toll experiments After implementing the iterative trial-and-error scheme, the convergent link toll pattern (in equivalent time units) and the ratios of equilibrium link flow to link environmental capacity are together summarized in Table 10.4. It can be seen from Table 10.4 that the ratio of flow to environmental capacity for each link is less than or equal to one; a link is subjected to a toll charge only when its flow reaches its environmental capacity threshold; otherwise it is free of charge. This means that the objective of environmental capacity constraints is achieved perfectly through the effective link toll charge identified from the iterative trial-and-error implementation procedure.

Figure 10.11 shows the convergence of the iterative trial-and-error scheme in terms of the absolute difference of link tolls between two successive iterations: $\left\|\mathbf{u}^{(k+1)}-\mathbf{u}^{(k)}\right\|$. As expected from our theoretical proof, the proposed scheme does converge. These observations show that the proposed method is indeed feasible and useful for dealing with an important and practical problem of traffic restraint and road pricing when the available information in pricing implementation is limited.

Table 10.4 Link flow to link environmental capacity ratio and link toll for Example 10.4

Link No. a	$\alpha^{(k)}=\frac{1}{(k+1)}$		$\alpha^{(k)}\in\left[\frac{0.5}{k+1},\frac{2.5}{k+1}\right]$	
	Ratio $\frac{v_a^*}{\bar{C}_a}$	Toll u_a^*	Ratio $\frac{v_a^*}{\bar{C}_a}$	Toll u_a^*
1	1.00	1.19	1.00	1.18
2	0.34	0.00	0.34	0.00
3	1.00	6.39	1.00	6.43
4	1.00	8.52	1.00	8.55
5	1.00	2.74	1.00	2.75
6	1.00	1.33	1.00	1.30
7	0.27	0.00	0.27	0.00
8	1.00	1.86	1.00	1.91
9	1.00	6.65	1.00	6.66
10	1.00	6.62	1.00	6.66
11	1.00	5.14	1.00	5.17

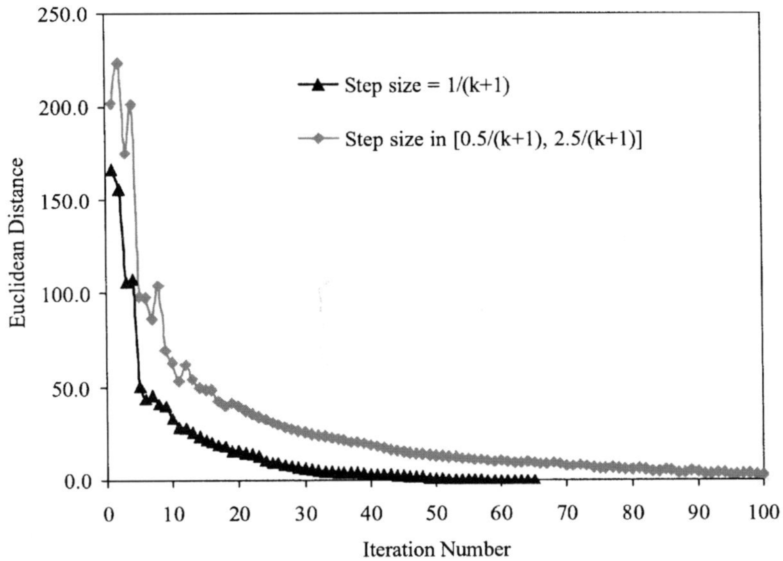

Figure 10.11 Change of the convergence error with number of iterations

10.5 Summary

In this chapter, we developed a class of trial-and-error implementation procedures for three typical pricing schemes: the first-best pricing, the second-best pricing and the traffic restraint and road pricing schemes in road networks. The procedure updates link tolls in a straightforward iterative manner for the first-best pricing scheme from observed link flows, without requiring the demand functions. For the second-best pricing scheme, the procedure involves sequential alternate solutions of the bi-level OD demand estimation and the bi-level toll optimization problems. In this case, the estimation of the demand functions is in itself meaningful if one wishes to tackle the welfare and the re-distributional effects, both of which are critical to resolve the political issues of congestion pricing. For the traffic restraint and road pricing problem, the procedure can identify a set of effective link tolls to hold the flow on relevant links within their threshold levels. It requires flow observation on the targeted links only rather than all links of the entire network, and obviates the use of link travel time functions, OD demand functions as well as users' value of time.

The techniques presented here allow a traffic planner to easily estimate the desirable link tolls without resort to the demand functions, and thus overcome the practical difficulty in congestion pricing. The framework presented in this chapter remains preliminary;

nevertheless, we have opened an important research path from both a practical and a theoretical perspective. A number of interesting issues are worthy of further exploration in terms of the scope of the applications. Here we provide a few examples and discussion of some behavioral and political issues in the actual implementation of the trial and error procedure.

In practical applications, one may wish to employ as few trials as possible to obtain an acceptable estimation of the optimal congestion tolls. In this respect, it is vital to establish an error bound of the current toll estimates by the iterative descent procedure. Note that the conventional error bounds in mathematical programming do not apply to the aforementioned optimization problem, because the gradient and the value of the objective function at a given trial point are not available.

The current procedure for the first-best and the second-best pricing policies obviates the explicit use of the demand functions, however, it does require an accurate estimate of the generalized travel cost and hence the users' value of travel time saving, which is important in calculating the toll amount in dollars. Even though the latter task is much easier than the estimation of the demand functions, it certainly deserves our attention to simultaneously estimate the optimal link tolls and the users' value of time, particularly on networks with heterogeneous users.

The trial-and-error procedure can be extended to handle the peak and off-peak differential congestion pricing problem. One may adopt a sequential approach that tackles the peak-congestion first, and then address the off-peak toll charge in the same spirit or make a synchronous toll adjustment of both peak and off-peak tolls. Such a sequential or synchronous, iterative scheme can be carried out without worrying about the demand shifts and price interdependence between peak and off-peak periods. Certainly, the proposed extension is not a mere academic exercise, but a real scheme presently being implemented in Singapore.

As observed from our numerical examples for all three pricing schemes examined, the proposed sequential experimental procedures involve both upward and downward adjustment of the starting and intermediate toll levels, which might be politically unacceptable. It is thus desirable to design a procedure that optimally considers some plausible bounds for the trajectory of realistic toll evolution over time.

Our sequential experimentation procedure to update link tolls or uncover the demand curve is built upon the assumption that changes in demand are provoked by short run changes in price along the same demand curve. The demand revelation mechanism thus requires a series of price changes to identify optimal link tolls or derive the demand functions properly. Politically speaking, it is clear that a series of quick changes to a toll system are an unlikely social event, as it would make the newly introduced system unsustainable. A plausible toll adjustment by a willing authority would be in annual, at most semi-annual intervals, like the situation in Singapore. Nevertheless, such a socially acceptable long inter-trial period could create a behavioral dilemma for the analysis envisioned here. On the one hand, it would allow travelers to have sufficient time to learn and adjust their trip-making decisions in a new pricing environment, although this might not be a critical issue, as advanced information technology is nowadays available and travelers can be quickly informed of altered toll charges. On the other hand, the background variables, such as the inflation and real income growth, are changing over such lengths of time.

The above issues suggest that the short run - long run differences in behavior, as well as the time lag of user responses, should be considered carefully in formulating a practical pricing mechanism. The political and behavioral limitations mentioned above could be mitigated in two different manners. First, although the price experiments are limited to a few trials and the inter-trial period could be considerably long, the traffic counts are relatively inexpensive to collect with automatic devices, even on a daily basis, with good accuracy. These readily and frequently available traffic counts can be utilized effectively to update OD demands and thus capture the long run demand shift prior to the next price trial. Second, apart from the actually observed behavioral changes, a set of stated preference experiments can be conducted to analyze the repeated reactions of a set of respondents to price changes, thereby complementing the limited revealed preference experiments.

10.6 SOURCES AND NOTES

Vickrey (1993) and Downs (1993) were the first to argue that congestion pricing could be implemented on a trial-and-error basis without the demand function, but they did not propose an actual mechanism on how to implement it. Only recently did Li (1999, 2002) make notable progress in exploring this conceptual proposal. He proposed the bisection method for the iterative toll adjustment based on observed flow for the simple standard case of a homogeneous traffic stream moving on a single link, connecting a single OD pair. The trial-and error procedures for the first-best pricing scheme, the second-best pricing scheme and the traffic restraint and road pricing scheme described in this chapter appear respectively in Yang, Meng and Lee (2004), Yang, Xu and Meng (2005) and Meng et al. (2005). Other references for the various tools used in this chapter are given below. Yang Iida and Sasaki

(1994) showed that the OD matrix that reproduces a given set of equilibrium link flows when user-optimally assigned to the network is in general not unique; Powell and Sheffi (1982) proved the convergence of the method of successive averages and established the conditions for such convergence; excellent references for the duality theory in nonlinear programming and the gradient projection methods are the books by Bazaraa et al. (1993) and Bertsekas and Tsitsiklis (1989). Larsson and Patriksson (1999) established the convergence in dual sub-gradient schemes for convex programming with application to the link capacity side constrained traffic assignment problems. The bi-level link toll optimization problems were discussed in detail in Chapters 4 and 5; readers may refer to Yang and Iida et al. (1992) and Yang (1995) for the bi-level OD demand estimation problem.

11

BOUNDING THE EFFICIENCY GAIN OR LOSS OF ROAD PRICING*

11.1 INTRODUCTION

In previous chapters, we have shown that the system optimum (SO) problem is a well defined optimization problem and can be decentralized as a Wardropian user equilibrium (UE) by charging tolls on all links according to the principle of marginal-cost pricing. The optimal toll on a link is equal to the difference between the marginal social cost and the marginal private cost, which can internalize the user externalities and thus achieve a system optimum flow pattern in the network. The SO problem is to minimize the total network travel time in the case of fixed demand, or maximize the total economic benefit in the case of elastic demand, with or without physical or environmental capacity constraints. In the presence of pricing constraints, we developed various second-best pricing schemes to determine the optimal tolls under given constraints for system travel time minimization or social welfare maximization. In particular, we have developed practical trial-and-error experiments of both the first-best and the second-best pricing schemes under limited information.

In this Chapter, we look into the following interesting questions for a general traffic network with pricing: what is the maximum efficiency gain that can be achieved through a marginal-cost pricing scheme? what is the maximum efficiency loss of an inexact marginal-cost pricing scheme, or a second-best pricing scheme due to pricing constraints. We seek an answer to the first question by bounding the inefficiency of un-tolled selfish user equilibrium using the recent concept of the price of anarchy, and deal with the second question by examining the gap between a current second-best flow pattern and the desirable system optimal one. Our analyses are first put on the first-best pricing problem and then the second-best one, with either fixed or elastic demand.

---

* Sections 11.3 to 11.5 (also part of Section 11.2) in this chapter contain the latest research results by the first author, with his colleagues and students. The analytical results presented are preliminary, subject to further rigorous analyses.

11.2 MAXIMUM EFFICIENCY GAIN OF FIRST-BEST PRICING SCHEMES

11.2.1 Efficiency Gain with Fixed Demand

Recall that a standard UE model with fixed demands and separable link cost functions is formulated as

$$\min_{\mathbf{v}\in\Omega_v} \sum_{a\in A} \int_0^{v_a} t_a(\omega)\mathrm{d}\omega \tag{11.1}$$

where Ω_v is given by

$$\Omega_v = \left\{\mathbf{v} \mid \mathbf{v} = \Delta\mathbf{f},\ \Lambda\mathbf{f} = \mathbf{d},\ \mathbf{f} \geq 0\right\} \tag{11.2}$$

with $\mathbf{v} = (v_a, a \in A)^{\mathrm{T}}$, $\mathbf{d} = (d_w, w \in W)^{\mathrm{T}}$ and $\mathbf{f} = (f_{rw}, r \in R_w, w \in W)^{\mathrm{T}}$ being the vectors of link flows, OD demands and path flows respectively, as defined before. Alternatively, the UE problem can be formulated as equivalent Variational Inequalities (VI) in terms of link flow variables. Find $\mathbf{v}^{\mathrm{ue}} \in \Omega_v$ such that

$$\mathbf{t}\left(\mathbf{v}^{\mathrm{ue}}\right)^{\mathrm{T}}\left(\mathbf{v} - \mathbf{v}^{\mathrm{ue}}\right) \geq 0, \text{ for any } \mathbf{v} \in \Omega_v \tag{11.3}$$

With the UE link flow solution $\mathbf{v}^{\mathrm{ue}}$, then the total system travel time is given by $T_{\mathrm{UE}} = T(\mathbf{v}^{\mathrm{ue}}) = \sum_{a\in A} t_a\left(v_a^{\mathrm{ue}}\right)v_a^{\mathrm{ue}}$. On the other hand, the standard SO model that minimizes the total system travel time is given by

$$\min_{\mathbf{v}\in\Omega_v} T(\mathbf{v}) = \sum_{a\in A} t_a\left(v_a\right)v_a \tag{11.4}$$

where, as shown in Chapter 2, if $t_a\left(v_a\right)$ is monotonically increasing and convex, then $t_a\left(v_a\right)v_a$ is convex and hence the solution to the SO problem (11.4) is unique. Let $\mathbf{v}^{\mathrm{so}}$ denote the link flow solution of the SO problem and define the following ratio

$$\rho_{\mathrm{fx}}^{\mathrm{ue}} = \frac{T_{\mathrm{UE}}}{T_{\mathrm{SO}}} = \frac{T\left(\mathbf{v}^{\mathrm{ue}}\right)}{T\left(\mathbf{v}^{\mathrm{so}}\right)} \tag{11.5}$$

where 'fx' denotes the case of *fixed* demand. Clearly, $\rho_{\mathrm{fx}}^{\mathrm{ue}} \geq 1$, this ratio is called the *inefficiency*, or *price of anarchy*, of the selfish user equilibria (Papadimitriou, 2002; Roughgarden, 2003). The ratio, $\rho_{\mathrm{fx}}^{\mathrm{ue}}$, can also be regarded as the efficiency gain of a marginal-cost pricing scheme, because it can drive a UE flow pattern to a system optimum or completely remove the inefficiency of selfish user equilibria. Here we introduce the following *relative efficiency gain* of a marginal-cost pricing scheme in terms of the ratio $\rho_{\mathrm{fx}}^{\mathrm{ue}}$:

$$\phi_{\mathrm{fx}}^{\mathrm{ue}} = \frac{T\left(\mathbf{v}^{\mathrm{ue}}\right) - T\left(\mathbf{v}^{\mathrm{so}}\right)}{T\left(\mathbf{v}^{\mathrm{so}}\right)} = \rho_{\mathrm{fx}}^{\mathrm{ue}} - 1 \tag{11.6}$$

Our purpose here is to find an upper bound of $\rho_{\text{fx}}^{\text{ue}}$, thereby quantifying the maximum efficiency gain of marginal-cost pricing schemes.

The case with linear cost functions

The following theorem quantifies the maximum inefficiency of the UE link flow pattern with linear link cost functions.

Theorem 11.1 *Let* $\mathbf{v}^{\text{ue}}$ *be the UE link flows with separable linear link cost functions, and let* $\mathbf{v}^{\text{so}}$ *be the SO link flows. Then* $\rho_{\text{fx}}^{\text{ue}} = T(\mathbf{v}^{\text{ue}})/T(\mathbf{v}^{\text{so}}) \le 4/3$.

Proof. Suppose that the linear cost function takes the form of $t_a(v_a) = a_a v_a + b_a$, $a \in A$, where $a_a \ge 0$, $b_a \ge 0$, $a \in A$. From VI (11.3) of the UE problem, we readily have

$$T(\mathbf{v}^{\text{ue}}) = \mathbf{t}(\mathbf{v}^{\text{ue}})^{\text{T}} \cdot \mathbf{v}^{\text{ue}} \le \mathbf{t}(\mathbf{v}^{\text{ue}})^{\text{T}} \cdot \mathbf{v} = \sum_{a \in A} (a_a v_a^{\text{ue}} + b_a) v_a$$
$$\le \sum_{a \in A} (a_a v_a + b_a) v_a + \frac{1}{4} \sum_{a \in A} a_a (v_a^{\text{ue}})^2 \le T(\mathbf{v}) + \frac{1}{4} T(\mathbf{v}^{\text{ue}}) \tag{11.7}$$

where the second inequality holds because $(v_a - 0.5 v_a^{\text{ue}})^2 \ge 0$, and the third inequality holds because $a_a (v_a^{\text{ue}})^2 \le (a_a v_a^{\text{ue}} + b_a) v_a^{\text{ue}}$. It follows that $\rho = T(\mathbf{v}^{\text{ue}})/T(\mathbf{v}) \le 4/3$ for any feasible $\mathbf{v} \in \Omega_v$ including $\mathbf{v}^{\text{so}} \in \Omega_v$. ■

Theorem 11.1 states that the maximum efficiency gain that can be achieved by a marginal-cost pricing scheme with linear cost functions is $\phi_{\text{fx}}^{\text{ue}} = \rho_{\text{fx}}^{\text{ue}} - 1 = 4/3 - 1 = 1/3$ or 33.3%.

We now present an alternative geometric proof. Let $\mathbf{v}$ be an arbitrary feasible link flow distribution $\mathbf{v} \in \Omega_v$. From VI (11.3), we have

$$T(\mathbf{v}^{\text{ue}}) \le \sum_{a \in A} t_a(v_a^{\text{ue}}) v_a = \sum_{a \in A} t_a(v_a) v_a + \sum_{a \in A} \left(t_a(v_a^{\text{ue}}) - t_a(v_a)\right) v_a \tag{11.8}$$

Consider the last term of the right-hand side of eqn. (11.8). Note that the link cost function is non-decreasing and thus $\left(t_a(v_a^{\text{ue}}) - t_a(v_a)\right) v_a \le 0$ for $v_a \ge v_a^{\text{ue}}$, we only need to focus on the term $\left(t_a(v_a^{\text{ue}}) - t_a(v_a)\right) v_a$ for which $v_a < v_a^{\text{ue}}$ to bound the last term in (11.8) from above. In this case, $\left(t_a(v_a^{\text{ue}}) - t_a(v_a)\right) v_a$ is equal to the area of the shaded rectangle in Figure 11.1. Note that the area of any rectangle located in a triangle, with the upper-left corner point at $\left(0, t_a(v_a^{\text{ue}})\right)$ and the lower-right corner point on the line of $t_a(v_a) = a_a v_a + b_a$, is, at most, half that of the triangle defined by the three points $\left(0, t_a\left(v_a^{\text{ue}}\right)\right)$, $\left(0, b_a\right)$ and $\left(v_a^{\text{ue}}, t_a\left(v_a^{\text{ue}}\right)\right)$, and the area of the latter triangle is at most half of the rectangle defined by the four points $(0,0)$, $\left(v_a^{\text{ue}}, 0\right)$, $\left(v_a^{\text{ue}}, t_a\left(v_a^{\text{ue}}\right)\right)$ and $\left(0, t_a\left(v_a^{\text{ue}}\right)\right)$, and because of $b_a \geq 0$, we thus arrive at

$$\left(t_a\left(v_a^{\text{ue}}\right) - t_a\left(v_a\right)\right) v_a \leq \frac{1}{4} t_a\left(v_a^{\text{ue}}\right) v_a^{\text{ue}} = \frac{1}{4} T\left(\mathbf{v}^{\text{ue}}\right)$$

This completes the proof. ■

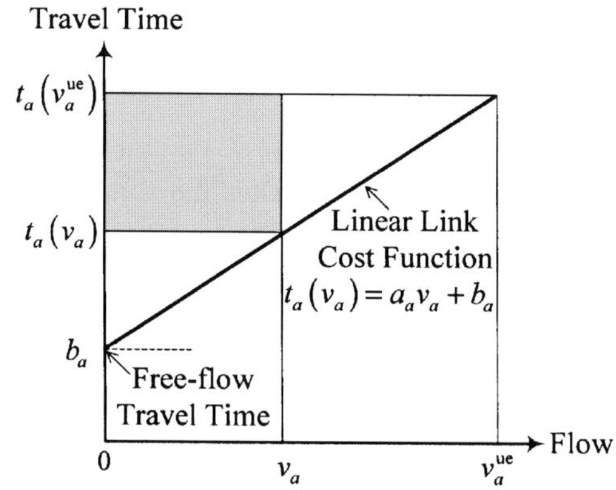

Figure 11.1 Geometric illustration of the proof of Theorem 11.1

From the above proof, we have the following immediate result of inequality for any nonnegative link flow vector $\mathbf{v} \geq 0$:

$$\sum_{a \in A} t_a\left(v_a^{\text{ue}}\right) v_a \leq T(\mathbf{v}) + \frac{1}{4} T\left(\mathbf{v}^{\text{ue}}\right) \tag{11.9}$$

The following theorem shows a pseudo-approximation result that upper bounds the social cost of a UE link flow pattern by that of an SO flow distribution with uniformly up-scaled OD demands.

Theorem 11.2 *Let* $\mathbf{v}^{\text{ue}}$ *be the UE link flows with separable linear link cost functions, and let* $\mathbf{v}_{(1+1/4)}^{\text{so}}$ *be an SO link flow solution with the uniformly scaled OD demand* $(1+1/4)\mathbf{d}$ *or* $5/4\,\mathbf{d}$, *then* $T\left(\mathbf{v}^{\text{ue}}\right) \leq T\left(\mathbf{v}_{(1+1/4)}^{\text{so}}\right)$.

Proof. Let $\mathbf{v}_{(1+1/4)}$ be a feasible link flow solution associated with uniformly up-scaled OD demand of $(1+1/4)\mathbf{d}$ or $5/4\,\mathbf{d}$. Then,

$$T\left(\mathbf{v}^{\text{ue}}\right) = \frac{5}{4} \sum_{a \in A} t_a\left(v_a^{\text{ue}}\right) v_a^{\text{ue}} - \frac{1}{4} T\left(\mathbf{v}^{\text{ue}}\right) \leq \sum_{a \in A} t_a\left(v_a^{\text{ue}}\right) v_{a,(1+1/4)} - \frac{1}{4} T\left(\mathbf{v}^{\text{ue}}\right) \leq T\left(\mathbf{v}_{(1+1/4)}\right)$$

The first inequality holds, because $4\mathbf{v}_{(1+1/4)}/5$ is a feasible link flow solution to the original VI (11.3) with OD demand $\mathbf{d}$, and as a result,

$$\frac{5}{4}\sum_{a\in A} t_a\left(v_a^{\text{ue}}\right)v_a^{\text{ue}} \le \frac{5}{4}\sum_{a\in A} t_a\left(v_a^{\text{ue}}\right)\frac{4}{5}v_{a,(1+1/4)} = \sum_{a\in A} t_a\left(v_a^{\text{ue}}\right)v_{a,(1+1/4)}$$

Whereas the second inequality follows from (11.9).

The case with nonlinear link cost functions

We now consider the case with general nonlinear separable link cost function. Like Figure 11.1 for the linear cost functions, Figure 11.2 depicts the situation for arbitrary, but still separable, link cost functions.

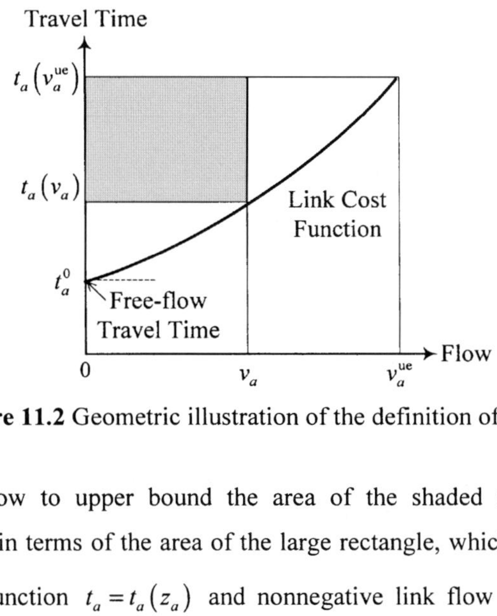

Figure 11.2 Geometric illustration of the definition of $\gamma(\mathcal{C})$

We now consider how to upper bound the area of the shaded rectangle, or the term $\left(t_a\left(v_a^{\text{ue}}\right)-t_a\left(v_a\right)\right)v_a$, in terms of the area of the large rectangle, which is of size $t_a\left(v_a^{\text{ue}}\right)v_a^{\text{ue}}$. For each link cost function $t_a = t_a\left(z_a\right)$ and nonnegative link flow $z_a \ge 0$, we define the following parameter

$$\gamma_a\left(t_a, z_a\right) = \max_{v_a \ge 0} \frac{\left(t_a\left(z_a\right)-t_a\left(v_a\right)\right)v_a}{t_a\left(z_a\right)z_a} \tag{11.10}$$

Here, $0/0=0$ by convention. Since $\left(t_a\left(z_a\right)-t_a\left(v_a\right)\right)v_a \le t_a\left(z_a\right)v_a$ if $0 \le v_a \le z_a$ and $\left(t_a\left(z_a\right)-t_a\left(v_a\right)\right)v_a \le 0$ if $v_a > z_a$, we have $0 \le \gamma_a\left(t_a, z_a\right) \le 1$. For a given class $\mathcal{C}$ of link cost function (for example, a family of linear cost function examined above, or polynomials of a certain degree), we let

$$\gamma(\mathcal{C}) = \max_{t_a\in\mathcal{C},\, z_a\ge 0} \gamma_a\left(t_a, z_a\right) \tag{11.11}$$

With this definition, we have the following Lemma.

Lemma 11.1 *Let* $\mathbf{v}^{\text{ue}}$ *be the UE link flows with separable link cost functions drawn from a given class* $\mathcal{C}$, *and let* $\mathbf{v}$ *be an arbitrary nonnegative feasible link flow vector. Then*

$$\sum_{a\in A} t_a\left(v_a^{\text{ue}}\right)v_a \le T(\mathbf{v}) + \gamma(\mathcal{C})T\left(\mathbf{v}^{\text{ue}}\right) \tag{11.12}$$

Proof. From definitions (11.10) and (11.11), with z_a replaced by v_a^{ue}, we have

$$\begin{aligned}\sum_{a\in A}\left(t_a\left(v_a^{\text{ue}}\right)-t_a(v_a)\right)v_a &\le \sum_{a\in A}\gamma_a\left(t_a, v_a^{\text{ue}}\right)t_a\left(v_a^{\text{ue}}\right)v_a^{\text{ue}} \\ &\le \sum_{a\in A}\gamma(\mathcal{C})t_a\left(v_a^{\text{ue}}\right)v_a^{\text{ue}} = \gamma(\mathcal{C})T\left(\mathbf{v}^{\text{ue}}\right)\end{aligned} \tag{11.13}$$

Substituting (11.13) into (11.8) yields (11.12). ■

From Lemma 11.1, we have the following generalization of Theorem 11.1 and Theorem 11.2.

Theorem 11.3 *Let* $\mathbf{v}^{\text{ue}}$ *be a UE link flow pattern with separable cost functions drawn from a given class* $\mathcal{C}$.

(i) *If* $\mathbf{v}^{\text{so}}$ *is an SO link flow solution, then*

$$T\left(\mathbf{v}^{\text{ue}}\right) \le \frac{1}{1-\gamma(\mathcal{C})}T\left(\mathbf{v}^{\text{so}}\right) \tag{11.14}$$

(ii) *If* $\mathbf{v}^{\text{so}}_{1+\gamma(\mathcal{C})}$ *is an SO link flow solution with the uniformly scaled OD demand* $(1+\gamma(\mathcal{C}))\mathbf{d}$, *with* $0 \le \gamma(\mathcal{C}) \le 1$ *defined in (11.11), then*

$$T\left(\mathbf{v}^{\text{ue}}\right) \le T\left(\mathbf{v}^{\text{so}}_{1+\gamma(\mathcal{C})}\right) \tag{11.15}$$

Proof. The proof follows immediately from previous derivations. Letting $\mathbf{v} = \mathbf{v}^{\text{so}}$ in (11.3) and (11.12), and combining the two inequalities yields (11.14). Part (ii) follows from the proof of Theorem 11.2 except for the replacement of (11.9) with Lemma 11.1. ■

Part (i) of Theorem 11.3 simply states that, for the traffic equilibrium with fixed demand

$$\rho_{\text{fx}}^{\text{ue}} \le \frac{1}{1-\gamma(\mathcal{C})} \tag{11.16}$$

$$\phi_{\text{fx}}^{\text{ue}} = \rho_{\text{fx}}^{\text{ue}} - 1 \le \frac{\gamma(\mathcal{C})}{1-\gamma(\mathcal{C})} \tag{11.17}$$

The special case of polynomial link cost functions

Amongst various classes of link cost functions, the set of polynomials with degree at most p

and nonnegative coefficients are of particular interest. In particular, the following type of link cost functions has been used so far and is examined here.

$$t_a(v_a) = t_a^0 + \alpha_a (v_a)^p, \; a \in A \tag{11.18}$$

where t_a^0 is a constant free-flow travel time, $\alpha_a \geq 0$ is a link-specific non-negative parameter and $p \geq 0$ is an integer. Substituting function (11.18) into (11.10) yields

$$\gamma_a(t_a, z_a) = \max_{v_a \geq 0} \frac{\alpha_a \left((z_a)^p - (v_a)^p \right) v_a}{t_a(z_a) z_a} \tag{11.19}$$

One can easily find the following optimal solution to the maximization problem (11.19):

$$v_a^* = \left(\frac{1}{p+1} \right)^{\frac{1}{p}} z_a, \quad \gamma_a(t_a, z_a) = \alpha_a \left(\frac{p}{p+1} \right) \left(\frac{1}{p+1} \right)^{\frac{1}{p}} \frac{(z_a)^p}{t_a(z_a)}$$

Thus,

$$\begin{aligned}
\gamma(C) &= \max_{t_a \in C,\, z_a \geq 0} \gamma_a(t_a, z_a) = \max_{t_a \in C,\, z_a \geq 0} \alpha_a \left(\frac{p}{p+1} \right) \left(\frac{1}{p+1} \right)^{\frac{1}{p}} \frac{(z_a)^p}{t_a(z_a)} \\
&= \max_{t_a \in C,\, z_a \geq 0} \alpha_a \left(\frac{p}{p+1} \right) \left(\frac{1}{p+1} \right)^{\frac{1}{p}} \frac{(z_a)^p}{t_a^0 + \alpha_a (z_a)^p} \\
&\leq \left(\frac{p}{p+1} \right) \left(\frac{1}{p+1} \right)^{\frac{1}{p}} \quad \left(\text{since } t_a^0 \geq 0 \text{ for any } a \in A \right)
\end{aligned} \tag{11.20}$$

As a result of eqn. (11.20) for the polynomial link cost functions, from (11.5), (11.6) and (11.14) we have

$$\rho_{\text{fx}}^{\text{ue}} = \frac{1}{1 - \gamma(C)} = \left(1 - \left(\frac{p}{p+1} \right) \left(\frac{1}{p+1} \right)^{\frac{1}{p}} \right)^{-1} \tag{11.21}$$

$$\phi_{\text{fx}}^{\text{ue}} = \rho_{\text{fx}}^{\text{ue}} - 1 = \left(\frac{p}{p+1} \right) \left(\frac{1}{p+1} \right)^{\frac{1}{p}} \left(1 - \left(\frac{p}{p+1} \right) \left(\frac{1}{p+1} \right)^{\frac{1}{p}} \right)^{-1} \tag{11.22}$$

In the special case of $p = 1$, we have $\gamma(C) = 1/4$, $\rho_{\text{fx}} = 4/3$ and $\phi_{\text{fx}}^{\text{ue}} = 1/3$, the same result as obtained before. For BPR type link cost functions with $p = 4$, we have $\gamma(C) = 4/5^{5/4} \approx 0.5350$, $\rho_{\text{fx}}^{\text{ue}} = 2.1505$ and $\phi_{\text{fx}}^{\text{ue}} = 1.1505$. In addition, $\rho_{\text{fx}}^{\text{ue}} \to 1$ and $\phi_{\text{fx}}^{\text{ue}} \to 0$ as $p \to 0$ (without traffic congestion), but $\rho_{\text{fx}}^{\text{ue}} \to \infty$ and $\phi_{\text{fx}}^{\text{ue}} \to \infty$ as $p \to +\infty$ (with severe congestion).

Example 11.1 (Network example of furnishing the maximum efficiency gain) Consider a network having one OD pair connected by two links. Link travel time functions are

$t_1(v_1)=1$ and $t_2(v_2)=(v_2)^p$, $p>0$, respectively. Let the OD demand be $d=v_1+v_2=1$. For any p, the UE solution is $v_1^{ue}=0$ and $v_2^{ue}=1$ with $T(\mathbf{v}^{ue})=1$. The SO solution is $v_1^{so}=1-(p+1)^{-1/p}$ and $v_2^{so}=(p+1)^{-1/p}$ with $T(\mathbf{v}^{so})=1-p(p+1)^{-(p+1)/p}<1$. Therefore,

$$\phi_{fx}^{ue}=\frac{T(\mathbf{v}^{ue})-T(\mathbf{v}^{so})}{T(\mathbf{v}^{so})}=\left(\frac{p}{p+1}\right)\left(\frac{1}{p+1}\right)^{\frac{1}{p}}\left(1-\left(\frac{p}{p+1}\right)\left(\frac{1}{p+1}\right)^{\frac{1}{p}}\right)^{-1} \tag{11.23}$$

From eqn. (11.23), we can see that this simple network example matches the maximum efficiency gain given in (11.22). In other words, the two parallel link network with the link cost functions, $t_1(v_1)=1$ and $t_2(v_2)=(v_2)^p$, $p>0$, represents the worst-case example of the inefficiency of selfish user equilibria, or the maximum efficiency gain of a marginal-cost pricing scheme for a class of polynomial link cost functions.

11.2.2. Efficiency Gain for Cost Functions with Limited Congestion Effects

We note that the inefficiency bound given in Theorem 11.3 for the standard traffic equilibrium problem is a worst-case measure, taken over all possible instances. The actual ratio of the UE total cost to the SO total cost in realistic instances could be substantially smaller. Indeed, in a traffic network, the free-flow travel time is usually not a negligible fraction, which is encountered in both UE and SO flow states. Here, we present a parameterized, improved bound on the inefficiency of equilibria introduced by Correa et al. (2005), where the ratio of fixed to total travel cost at equilibria come into play.

Lemma 11.2 *Let* $\mathbf{v}^{ue}$ *be a UE link flow pattern, with separable link cost functions drawn from a given class* $\mathcal{C}$, *such that* $t_a^0=t_a(0)\ge\eta(\mathbf{v}^{ue})t_a(v_a^{ue})$ *for all* $a\in A$, *for some positive constant* $0\le\eta(\mathbf{v}^{ue})\le 1$, *where* η *can depend on the UE link flow pattern* $\mathbf{v}^{ue}$. *Moreover, let* $\mathbf{v}$ *be an arbitrary nonnegative link flow vector. Then,*

$$\sum_{a\in A}t_a(v_a^{ue})v_a\le T(\mathbf{v})+(1-\eta(\mathbf{v}^{ue}))\gamma(\mathcal{C})T(\mathbf{v}^{ue}) \tag{11.24}$$

where $\gamma(\mathcal{C})$ *is defined in (11.11) and (11.10).*

Proof. We revisit (11.8), $\sum_{a\in A}t_a(v_a^{ue})v_a=\sum_{a\in A}t_a(v_a)v_a+\sum_{a\in A}(t_a(v_a^{ue})-t_a(v_a))v_a$. If $v_a\ge v_a^{ue}$ for all $a\in A$, eqn. (11.24) clearly holds. Now, we assume $v_a<v_a^{ue}$ for certain links, and consider Figure 11.3. Because $t_a^0=t_a(0)\ge\eta(\mathbf{v}^{ue})t_a(v_a^{ue})$, the area $(t_a(v_a^{ue})-t_a(v_a))v_a$ of the smaller shaded rectangle is at most $\gamma(\mathcal{C})$ times that of the

rectangle with upper-left corner point $\left(0, t_a\left(v_a^{\mathrm{ue}}\right)\right)$ and lower-right corner point $\left(v_a^{\mathrm{ue}}, t_a(0)\right)$, which is of size at most $\left(1-\eta\left(\mathbf{v}^{\mathrm{ue}}\right)\right)t_a\left(v_a^{\mathrm{ue}}\right)v_a^{\mathrm{ue}}$. The result follows. ■

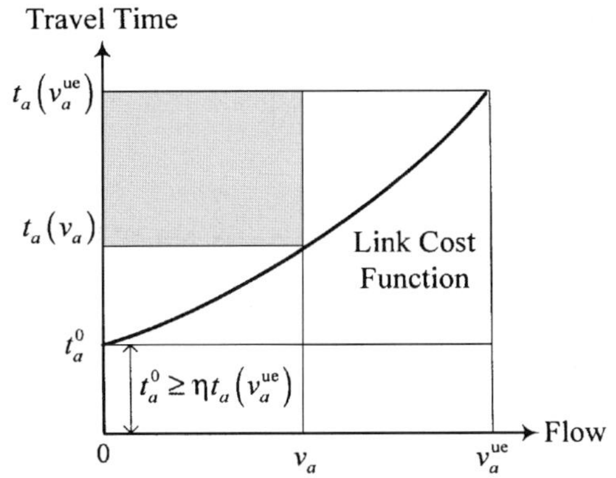

Figure 11.3 Geometric illustration of the proof of Lemma 11.2

The following theorem is a generalization of Theorem 11.3 as a direct result of Lemma 11.2.

Theorem 11.4 *Let* $\mathbf{v}^{\mathrm{ue}}$ *be a UE link flow pattern with separable cost function drawn from a given class* C, *such that* $t_a^0 = t_a(0) \geq \eta\left(\mathbf{v}^{\mathrm{ue}}\right)t_a\left(v_a^{\mathrm{ue}}\right)$ *for all* $a \in A$, *for some positive constant* $0 \leq \eta\left(\mathbf{v}^{\mathrm{ue}}\right) \leq 1$.

(i) *If* $\mathbf{v}^{\mathrm{so}}$ *is an SO link flow solution, then*

$$T\left(\mathbf{v}^{\mathrm{ue}}\right) \leq \frac{1}{1-\left(1-\eta\left(\mathbf{v}^{\mathrm{ue}}\right)\right)\gamma(C)} T\left(\mathbf{v}^{\mathrm{so}}\right) \tag{11.25}$$

(ii) *If* $\mathbf{v}^{\mathrm{so}}_{1+\left(1-\eta\left(\mathbf{v}^{\mathrm{ue}}\right)\right)\gamma(C)}$ *is an SO link flow solution with the uniformly scaled OD demand* $\left(1+\left(1-\eta\left(\mathbf{v}^{\mathrm{ue}}\right)\right)\gamma(C)\right)\mathbf{d}$, *with* $0 \leq \gamma(C) \leq 1$ *and* $0 \leq \eta\left(\mathbf{v}^{\mathrm{ue}}\right) \leq 1$, *then*

$$T\left(\mathbf{v}^{\mathrm{ue}}\right) \leq T\left(\mathbf{v}^{\mathrm{so}}_{1+\left(1-\eta\left(\mathbf{v}^{\mathrm{ue}}\right)\right)\gamma(C)}\right) \tag{11.26}$$

Example 11.2 Consider a traffic network with the BPR-type link cost function: $t_a\left(v_a\right) = t_a^0 + \alpha_a\left(v_a\right)^p$, $a \in A$. Let $\mathbf{v}^{\mathrm{ue}}$ be a UE link flow pattern on the network associated with certain OD demands, then we have

$$\eta\left(\mathbf{v}^{\mathrm{ue}}\right) = \min_{a \in A} \eta_a\left(\mathbf{v}_a^{\mathrm{ue}}\right) = \min_{a \in A}\left(\frac{t_a^0}{t_a^0 + \alpha_a\left(v_a^{\mathrm{ue}}\right)^p}\right)$$

From Theorem 11.4 and eqns. (11.21) and (11.22), we have

$$\rho_{\rm fx}^{\rm ue} = \frac{1}{1-\left(1-\eta\left(\mathbf{v}^{\rm ue}\right)\right)\gamma(\mathcal{C})} = \left(1-\left(1-\eta\left(\mathbf{v}^{\rm ue}\right)\right)\left(\frac{p}{p+1}\right)\left(\frac{1}{p+1}\right)^{\frac{1}{p}}\right)^{-1} \tag{11.27}$$

$$\phi_{\rm fx}^{\rm ue} = \rho_{\rm fx}^{\rm ue} - 1 = \left(1-\eta\left(\mathbf{v}^{\rm ue}\right)\right)\left(\frac{p}{p+1}\right)\left(\frac{1}{p+1}\right)^{\frac{1}{p}}\left(1-\left(1-\eta\left(\mathbf{v}^{\rm ue}\right)\right)\left(\frac{p}{p+1}\right)\left(\frac{1}{p+1}\right)^{\frac{1}{p}}\right)^{-1} \tag{11.28}$$

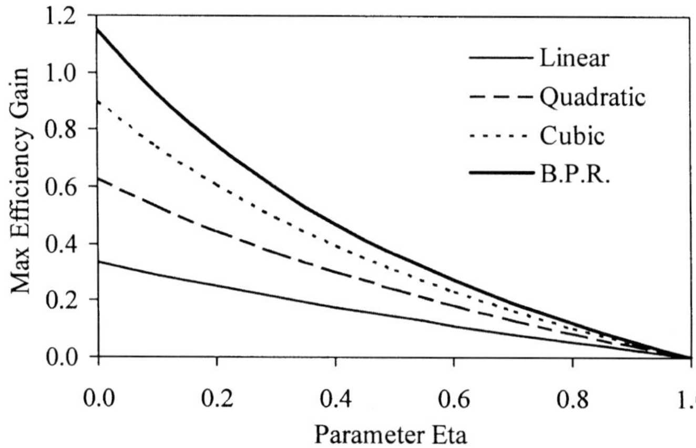

Figure 11.4 Maximum efficiency gain of a marginal-cost pricing scheme as a function of the ratio of fixed to total travel cost

Figure 11.4 plots the relationships between parameter η $(0 \le \eta \le 1)$ and the maximum efficiency gain $\phi_{\rm fx}^{\rm ue}$ for $p=1$ (linear), $p=2$ (quadratic), $p=3$ (cubic) and $p=4$ (BPR functions of degree 4).

11.2.3 Efficiency Gain with Elastic Demand

In the elastic demand case, the following social welfare (or net economic benefit), defined and used previously, can serve as a meaningful system performance measure.

$$S(\mathbf{v},\mathbf{d}) = \sum_{w\in W}\int_0^{d_w} B_w(\omega)\mathrm{d}\omega - \sum_{a\in A} t_a(v_a)v_a \tag{11.29}$$

where the benefit (or inverse demand) function $B_w(d_w)$, $w \in W$ is non-increasing. As explained in Chapter 2, we have the following UE and SO formulations with elastic demand. The elastic demand UE formulation is given as:

$$\max_{(\mathbf{v},\mathbf{d})\in\Omega} \sum_{w\in W} \int_0^{d_w} B_w(\omega)\mathrm{d}\omega - \sum_{a\in A} \int_0^{v_a} t_a(\omega)\,\mathrm{d}\omega \tag{11.30}$$

and the elastic demand SO formulation is given by:

$$\max_{(\mathbf{v},\mathbf{d})\in\Omega} \sum_{w\in W} \int_0^{d_w} B_w(\omega)\mathrm{d}\omega - \sum_{a\in A} t_a(v_a)v_a \tag{11.31}$$

where Ω is defined by:

$$\Omega = \left\{(\mathbf{v},\mathbf{d}) \middle| \mathbf{v} = \Delta\mathbf{f},\ \Lambda\mathbf{f} = \mathbf{d},\ \mathbf{f} \geq 0,\ \mathbf{d} \geq 0\right\}$$

Let the solutions of the UE and SO problems be $(\mathbf{v}^{\mathrm{ue}},\mathbf{d}^{\mathrm{ue}})$ and $(\mathbf{v}^{\mathrm{so}},\mathbf{d}^{\mathrm{so}})$, respectively. For the elastic-demand traffic equilibrium problem, we define the inefficiency of selfish user equilibria, or the efficiency gain of a marginal-cost pricing scheme, as follows:

$$\rho_{\mathrm{ec}}^{\mathrm{ue}} = \frac{S(\mathbf{v}^{\mathrm{so}},\mathbf{d}^{\mathrm{so}})}{S(\mathbf{v}^{\mathrm{ue}},\mathbf{d}^{\mathrm{ue}})} \quad (\geq 1) \tag{11.32}$$

$$\phi_{\mathrm{ec}}^{\mathrm{ue}} = \frac{S(\mathbf{v}^{\mathrm{so}},\mathbf{d}^{\mathrm{so}}) - S(\mathbf{v}^{\mathrm{ue}},\mathbf{d}^{\mathrm{ue}})}{S(\mathbf{v}^{\mathrm{so}},\mathbf{d}^{\mathrm{so}})} = 1 - \frac{1}{\rho_{\mathrm{ec}}^{\mathrm{ue}}} \quad (\geq 0) \tag{11.33}$$

where 'ec' denotes the case of *elastic* demand. Clearly, $\rho_{\mathrm{ec}}^{\mathrm{ue}} \geq 1$ holds since the UE does not maximize the objective function defined by (11.29). Again we attempt to seek the upper bound of $\rho_{\mathrm{ec}}^{\mathrm{ue}}$, or to quantify the maximum potential of raising the total social welfare by a marginal-cost pricing scheme.

We first use a simple example to show that finding the bound of $\rho_{\mathrm{ec}}^{\mathrm{ue}}$ in the elastic demand case is not as manageable as in the fixed demand case, even if all functions of the system are linear. Consider a network with one OD pair and one link, where the link travel time function is $t(v) = av + b,\ a \geq 0$ and the benefit function $B(d) = md + n,\ m < 0.$ The UE solution and the corresponding social welfare are

$$v^{\mathrm{ue}} = d^{\mathrm{ue}} = \frac{n-b}{a-m},\quad S(\mathbf{v}^{\mathrm{ue}},\mathbf{d}^{\mathrm{ue}}) = -\frac{m(n-b)^2}{2(a-m)^2}$$

The SO solution and the corresponding social welfare are

$$v^{\mathrm{so}} = d^{\mathrm{so}} = \frac{n-b}{2a-m},\quad S(\mathbf{v}^{\mathrm{so}},\mathbf{d}^{\mathrm{so}}) = \frac{(n-b)^2}{2(2a-m)}$$

Hence, we have

$$\rho_{\mathrm{ec}}^{\mathrm{ue}} = \frac{S(\mathbf{v}^{\mathrm{so}},\mathbf{d}^{\mathrm{so}})}{S(\mathbf{v}^{\mathrm{ue}},\mathbf{d}^{\mathrm{ue}})} = \frac{(m-a)^2}{m(m-2a)} = \left(1 - \left(\frac{a}{m-a}\right)^2\right)^{-1}$$

Unlike that bounded by 4/3 in Theorem 11.1 for the fixed demand case, there is no deterministic upper bound independent of $m.$ In the fixed demand case, the price of anarchy of the UE is not too severe since it is bounded, and thus the efficiency gain of the marginal-cost pricing is mild. However, in the presence of elastic demands, as considered in this simple example of a linear setting, the price of anarchy of an elastic-demand UE can be dramatic if $m \to 0$ (the demand is perfectly elastic).

In what follows, we attempt to derive a pseudo-approximation bound of ρ_{ec} in terms of the social welfare and user benefit at a given user optimum solution as well as the parameter $\gamma(C)$ established previously. We first introduce the following lemma.

Lemma 11.3 *If $B_w(d_w)$ is a non-increasing function of d_w for $d_w > 0$, then*

$$\sum_{w\in W}\int_0^{d_w} B_w(\omega)d\omega \le \sum_{w\in W}\int_0^{d_w^{ue}} B_w(\omega)d\omega + \sum_{w\in W} B_w(d_w^{ue})(d_w - d_w^{ue}) \tag{11.34}$$

Proof. Since $B_w(d_w)$ is non-increasing, we then have

$$(d_w - d_w^{ue})B_w(d_w^{ue}) \ge \int_{d_w^{ue}}^{d_w} B_w(\omega)d\omega,\ w\in W \tag{11.35}$$

which can be rewritten as

$$\int_0^{d_w} B_w(\omega)d\omega \le \int_0^{d_w^{ue}} B_w(\omega)d\omega + (d_w - d_w^{ue})B_w(d_w^{ue}),\ w\in W \tag{11.36}$$

Summing up over all OD pairs $w\in W$ leads to (11.34). ∎

Theorem 11.5 *Given general non-decreasing link cost functions, $t_a(v_a)$, $a\in A$, and non-increasing demand functions, $B_w(d_w)$, $w\in W$, then*

$$\rho_{ec}^{ue} \le 1 + \left(\omega(\mathbf{v}^{ue},\mathbf{d}^{ue}) - 1\right)\gamma(C) \tag{11.37}$$

$$\phi_{ec}^{ue} = 1 - \frac{1}{\rho_{ec}} \le \frac{\left(\omega(\mathbf{v}^{ue},\mathbf{d}^{ue}) - 1\right)\gamma(C)}{1 + \left(\omega(\mathbf{v}^{ue},\mathbf{d}^{ue}) - 1\right)\gamma(C)} \tag{11.38}$$

where $\gamma(C)$ is defined by eqn. (11.11) and $\omega(\mathbf{v}^{ue},\mathbf{d}^{ue})$ is the ratio of user benefit (denoted by U) to social welfare at user optimum:

$$\omega(\mathbf{v}^{ue},\mathbf{d}^{ue}) = \frac{U(\mathbf{d}^{ue})}{S(\mathbf{v}^{ue},\mathbf{d}^{ue})} = \frac{\sum_{w\in W}\int_0^{d_w^{ue}} B_w(\omega)d\omega}{\sum_{w\in W}\int_0^{d_w^{ue}} B_w(\omega)d\omega - \sum_{a\in A} v_a^{ue} t_a(v_a^{ue})} > 1 \tag{11.39}$$

Proof. Since $(\mathbf{v}^{ue},\mathbf{d}^{ue})$ is an equilibrium solution, from the VI formulation of the elastic-demand traffic equilibrium problem we have

$$\sum_{a\in A} t_a\left(v_a^{\text{ue}}\right)\left(v_a - v_a^{\text{ue}}\right) - \sum_{w\in W} B_w\left(d_w^{\text{ue}}\right)\left(d_w - d_w^{\text{ue}}\right) \geq 0, \text{ for any } (\mathbf{v},\mathbf{d}) \in \Omega \tag{11.40}$$

Substituting (11.34) into (11.40) yields

$$\sum_{a\in A} t_a\left(v_a^{\text{ue}}\right)\left(v_a - v_a^{\text{ue}}\right) + \sum_{w\in W} \int_0^{d_w^{\text{ue}}} B_w(\omega)\mathrm{d}\omega - \sum_{w\in W} \int_0^{d_w} B_w(\omega)\mathrm{d}\omega \geq 0$$

It can be rewritten as

$$\sum_{w\in W} \int_0^{d_w^{\text{ue}}} B_w(\omega)\mathrm{d}\omega - \sum_{a\in A} t_a\left(v_a^{\text{ue}}\right)v_a^{\text{ue}} - \left\{\sum_{w\in W} \int_0^{d_w} B_w(\omega)\mathrm{d}\omega - \sum_{a\in A} t_a(v_a)v_a\right\}$$
$$+\sum_{a\in A} \left(t_a\left(v_a^{\text{ue}}\right) - t_a(v_a)\right)v_a \geq 0$$

Using the definition (11.29) and Lemma (11.1), it follows that

$$S\left(\mathbf{v}^{\text{ue}},\mathbf{d}^{\text{ue}}\right) - S(\mathbf{v},\mathbf{d}) + \gamma(C)T\left(\mathbf{v}^{\text{ue}}\right) \geq 0 \tag{11.41}$$

Using the definition (11.32) and let $(\mathbf{v},\mathbf{d}) = \left(\mathbf{v}^{\text{so}},\mathbf{d}^{\text{so}}\right)$ in (11.41), we have

$$\rho_{\text{ec}}^{\text{ue}} \leq 1 + \gamma(C)\frac{T\left(\mathbf{v}^{\text{ue}}\right)}{S\left(\mathbf{v}^{\text{ue}},\mathbf{d}^{\text{ue}}\right)}$$

Using $T\left(\mathbf{v}^{\text{ue}}\right) = -S\left(\mathbf{v}^{\text{ue}},\mathbf{d}^{\text{ue}}\right) + U\left(\mathbf{d}^{\text{ue}}\right)$, we thus obtain eqn. (11.37). ■

Example 11.3 Consider the following negative exponential demand function used in previous chapters:

$$d = d_0 \exp\left[-\alpha\left(\frac{\mu}{\mu_0} - 1\right)\right] \tag{11.42}$$

where $\alpha > 0$ is a cost sensitivity parameter μ_0 is the minimum free-flow travel time and d_0 is the maximum demand when $\mu = \mu_0$.

The inverse demand function is given by

$$\mu = \mu_0\left(1 - \frac{1}{\alpha}\ln\left(\frac{d}{d_0}\right)\right)$$

The user benefit, U, is given by

$$U = \int_0^d \mu_0\left(1 - \frac{1}{\alpha}\ln\left(\frac{x}{d_0}\right)\right)\mathrm{d}x = \mu_0 d\left[1 - \frac{1}{\alpha}\left(\ln\left(\frac{d}{d_0}\right) - 1\right)\right]$$

and the social welfare, S, is

$$S = U - \mu d = \mu_0 d\left[1 - \frac{1}{\alpha}\left(\ln\left(\frac{d}{d_0}\right) - 1\right)\right] - \mu_0 d\left(1 - \frac{1}{\alpha}\ln\left(\frac{d}{d_0}\right)\right) = \frac{1}{\alpha}\mu_0 d$$

Therefore, from the definition (11.39)

$$\omega = \frac{U}{S} = \frac{\mu_0 d\left[1 - \frac{1}{\alpha}\left(\ln\left(\frac{d}{d_0}\right) - 1\right)\right]}{\frac{1}{\alpha}\mu_0 d} = 1 + \alpha - \ln\left(\frac{d}{d_0}\right) \tag{11.43}$$

11.3 INEFFICIENCY OF STOCHASTIC USER EQUILIBRIA

In Section 3.7, Chapter 3, we showed that the principle of marginal-cost pricing still holds for a network in a logit-based stochastic user equilibrium (SUE), where a system optimum in terms of economic benefit maximization can be established. The result makes sense from economic and behavioral perspectives of the variety-seeking discrete route choice model. In this context, the basic hypothesis of a SUE model should be interpreted as that where the preferences of users are dispersed, and in particular, may reflect considerations other than travel cost.

One alternative interpretation of the SUE in the literature is that it is an outcome of the users' route choice for minimizing their perceived travel costs. The perceived travel cost is regarded as a random variable due to travel time uncertainty and users' perception error of travel time. In this context one should focus on the Wardropian system optimum in terms of pure cost efficiency. In this section, we follow this latter line of thinking and investigate the bound of the cost inefficiency of a SUE flow pattern in relation to the Wardropian system optimum.

11.3.1 Determination of the Cost Inefficiency Bound

We begin our analysis by introducing the following Lemma.

Lemma 11.4 *If the separable link cost function, $t_a(v_a)$, $a \in A$, is monotonically increasing with link flow, a logit-based SUE problem with fixed OD demand is equivalent to the following variational inequality, i.e., find $\mathbf{f}^{\text{sue}} \in \Omega_f$, such that*

$$\sum_{w \in W} \sum_{r \in R_w} \left(c_{rw}\left(\mathbf{f}^{\text{sue}}\right) + \frac{1}{\theta} \ln f_{rw}^{\text{sue}} \right)\left(f_{rw} - f_{rw}^{\text{sue}}\right) \geq 0 \quad \text{for any } \mathbf{f} \in \Omega_f \tag{11.44}$$

where $\theta > 0$ is a travel time variability parameter and

$$\Omega_f = \left\{ \mathbf{f} \mid \Lambda \mathbf{f} = \mathbf{d}, \mathbf{f} \geq 0 \right\} \tag{11.45}$$

Proof. It is known that the logit-based SUE problem can be formulated as the following equivalent minimization program

$$\min\ Z(\mathbf{f}) = \frac{1}{\theta}\sum_{w\in W}\sum_{r\in R_w} f_{rw}\ln f_{rw} + \sum_{a\in A}\int_0^{v_a} t_a(\omega)\mathrm{d}\omega \tag{11.46}$$

subject to

$$\sum_{r\in R_w} f_{rw} = d_w,\quad w\in W \tag{11.47}$$

$$f_{rw}\geq 0,\quad r\in R_w,\quad w\in W \tag{11.48}$$

With the assumption of monotonically increasing link cost function, the above problem of minimizing a strictly convex function over a compact (closed and bounded) set guarantees the existence and uniqueness of a path flow solution $\mathbf{f}^{\text{sue}}\in\Omega_f$. In addition, the entropy-type function ensures that the optimum is achieved at an interior point. Using $v_a = \sum_{w\in W}\sum_{r\in R_w} f_{rw}\delta_{ar}$, a necessarily and sufficient condition for a unique optimum $\mathbf{f}^{\text{sue}}\in\Omega_f$ is that

$$\left[\nabla_{\mathbf{f}} Z\left(\mathbf{f}^{\text{sue}}\right)\right]^{\mathrm{T}}\left(\mathbf{f}-\mathbf{f}^{\text{sue}}\right)\geq 0\quad \text{for any }\ \mathbf{f}\in\Omega_f \tag{11.49}$$

Substituting

$$\left[\nabla_{\mathbf{f}} Z\left(\mathbf{f}^{\text{sue}}\right)\right]^{\mathrm{T}} = \left[\cdots,\frac{1}{\theta}+\frac{1}{\theta}\ln f_{rw}^{\text{sue}}+\sum_{a\in A} t_a\left(v_a^{\text{sue}}\right)\delta_{ar},\cdots\right]^{\mathrm{T}} = \left[\cdots,\frac{1}{\theta}+\frac{1}{\theta}\ln f_{rw}^{\text{sue}}+c_{rw}\left(\mathbf{f}^{\text{sue}}\right),\cdots\right]^{\mathrm{T}}$$

into (11.49) and in view of

$$\sum_{w\in W}\sum_{r\in R_w}\frac{1}{\theta}\left(f_{rw}-f_{rw}^{\text{sue}}\right) = \sum_{w\in W}\frac{1}{\theta}\left(d_w - d_w\right) = 0$$

we have VI (11.44). ■

Let $\mathbf{f}^{\text{so}}\in F$ be a system-optimal path flow vector. From eqn. (11.44) we have

$$\sum_{w\in W}\sum_{r\in R_w}\left(c_{rw}\left(\mathbf{f}^{\text{sue}}\right)+\frac{1}{\theta}\ln f_{rw}^{\text{sue}}\right)\left(f_{rw}^{\text{so}}-f_{rw}^{\text{sue}}\right)\geq 0 \tag{11.50}$$

This leads to

$$T_{\text{SUE}}\leq T_{\text{SO}}+\sum_{w\in W}\sum_{r\in R_w}\left(c_{rw}^{\text{sue}}-c_{rw}^{\text{so}}\right)f_{rw}^{\text{so}}+\frac{1}{\theta}\sum_{w\in W}\sum_{r\in R_w}\left(f_{rw}^{\text{so}}-f_{rw}^{\text{sue}}\right)\ln f_{rw}^{\text{sue}} \tag{11.51}$$

where $c_{rw}^{\text{sue}} = c_{rw}\left(\mathbf{f}^{\text{sue}}\right)$, $c_{rw}^{\text{so}} = c_{rw}\left(\mathbf{f}^{\text{so}}\right)$ and

$$T_{\text{SUE}} = \sum_{w\in W}\sum_{r\in R_w} c_{rw}^{\text{sue}} f_{rw}^{\text{sue}} = \sum_{a\in A} t_a\left(v_a^{\text{sue}}\right)v_a^{\text{sue}}$$

$$T_{\text{SO}} = \sum_{w\in W}\sum_{r\in R_w} c_{rw}^{\text{so}} f_{rw}^{\text{so}} = \sum_{a\in A} t_a\left(v_a^{\text{so}}\right)v_a^{\text{so}}$$

Note that

$$\sum_{w\in W}\sum_{r\in R_w}\left(c_{rw}^{\text{sue}}-c_{rw}^{\text{so}}\right)f_{rw}^{\text{so}} = \sum_{a\in A}\left(t_a\left(v_a^{\text{sue}}\right)-t_a\left(v_a^{\text{so}}\right)\right)v_a^{\text{so}}$$

Thus eqn. (11.51) becomes

$$T_{\text{SUE}} \le T_{\text{SO}} + \sum_{a\in A}\left(t_a\left(v_a^{\text{sue}}\right) - t_a\left(v_a^{\text{so}}\right)\right)v_a^{\text{so}} + \frac{1}{\theta}\sum_{w\in W}\sum_{r\in R_w}\left(f_{rw}^{\text{so}} - f_{rw}^{\text{sue}}\right)\ln f_{rw}^{\text{sue}} \tag{11.52}$$

As discussed before, the second term of the right-hand-side of (11.52) is bounded by

$$\sum_{a\in A}\left(t_a\left(v_a^{\text{sue}}\right) - t_a\left(v_a^{\text{so}}\right)\right)v_a^{\text{so}} \le \gamma(C)\sum_{a\in A} t_a\left(v_a^{\text{sue}}\right)v_a^{\text{sue}} = \gamma(C)T_{\text{SUE}} \tag{11.53}$$

Now we seek a bound of the third term of the right-hand-side of (11.52) and thereby bound the overall cost inefficiency of the SUE.

Lemma 11.5 *Consider the following maximization problem*

$$\max\ Z(\mathbf{x},\mathbf{y}) = \sum_{i=1}^{n}(y_i - x_i)\ln x_i \tag{11.54}$$

subject to

$$\sum_{i=1}^{n} x_i = d \tag{11.55}$$

$$\sum_{i=1}^{n} y_i = d \tag{11.56}$$

$$x_i, y_i \ge 0,\ i = 1,2,\cdots,n \tag{11.57}$$

where $d > 0$ *is a constant. The optimal value of this problem is* $Z_{\max} = kd$, *where* k *solves equation,* $ke^k = (n-1)/e$, *with* e *being the base of natural logarithm, or if it is defined that* $g(x) = xe^x$, *then* $k = g^{-1}((n-1)/e)$.

Proof: The KKT necessary conditions for optimality are

$$\frac{\partial Z}{\partial x_i} + \lambda_1 \le 0,\ x_i \ge 0,\ \left(\frac{\partial Z}{\partial x_i} + \lambda_1\right)x_i = 0,\quad i = 1,2,\ldots n$$

$$\frac{\partial Z}{\partial y_i} + \lambda_2 \le 0,\ y_i \ge 0,\ \left(\frac{\partial Z}{\partial y_i} + \lambda_2\right)y_i = 0,\quad i = 1,2,\ldots n$$

where λ_1 and λ_2 are the Lagrange multipliers associated with the equality constraints (11.55) and (11.56), respectively. Note that the entropy type of function ensures an interior point of positive solution: $x_i > 0,\ i = 1,2,\cdots,n$. Using $\partial Z/\partial x_i = y_i/x_i - \ln x_i - 1$ and $\partial Z/\partial y_i = \ln x_i$ for $i = 1,2,\ldots n$, the KKT conditions reduce to

$$\frac{y_i}{x_i} - \ln x_i - 1 + \lambda_1 = 0,\ x_i > 0,\ i = 1,2,\cdots,n \tag{11.58}$$

$$\ln x_i + \lambda_2 = 0,\ \text{if}\ y_i > 0,\quad i = 1,2,\ldots n \tag{11.59}$$

$$\ln x_i + \lambda_2 \le 0,\ \text{if}\ y_i = 0,\quad i = 1,2,\ldots n \tag{11.60}$$

From (11.58), (11.59) and (11.60), we have the following solutions: $(x_i, y_i) = \left(e^{-1+\lambda_1}, 0\right)$ or

$(x_i,y_i)=\left(e^{-\lambda_2},(1-\lambda_1-\lambda_2)e^{-\lambda_2}\right)$, $i=1,2,\cdots,n$, $1-\lambda_1-\lambda_2>0$. Let $k_1=-1+\lambda_1$ and $k_2=-\lambda_2$, the solutions become

$$(x_i,y_i)=\left(e^{k_1},0\right) \text{ or } (x_i,y_i)=\left(e^{k_2},(k_2-k_1)e^{k_2}\right),\ i=1,2,\cdots,n,\ k_2-k_1>0$$

Let m be the number of (x_i,y_i) taking value $\left(e^{k_2},(k_2-k_1)e^{k_2}\right)$ at optimum, then $(n-m)$ is the number of (x_i,y_i) taking value $\left(e^{k_1},0\right)$. Substituting these values of (x_i,y_i) into the objective function (11.54), we have

$$Z_{\text{opt}}=-(n-m)e^{k_1}k_1+m(k_2-k_1-1)e^{k_2}k_2 \tag{11.61}$$

Also, from constraints (11.55) and (11.56), we have

$$(n-m)e^{k_1}+me^{k_2}=d \tag{11.62}$$

$$m(k_2-k_1)e^{k_2}=d \tag{11.63}$$

With (11.62) and (11.63), Z_{opt} in (11.61) becomes

$$Z_{\text{opt}}=(k_2-k_1-1)d \tag{11.64}$$

Moreover, combining (11.62) and (11.63) yields

$$(k_2-k_1-1)e^{k_2-k_1}=\frac{n}{m}-1 \tag{11.65}$$

Let $k=k_2-k_1-1$, (11.64) becomes

$$Z_{\text{opt}}=kd \tag{11.66}$$

and (11.65) becomes

$$ke^k=\frac{1}{e}\left(\frac{n}{m}-1\right) \tag{11.67}$$

Define $g(x)=xe^x$, then (11.67) gives $k=g^{-1}\left((n/m-1)/e\right)$. From the definition of m as well as (11.63), we have $1\le m\le n$, thus k attains its maximum value when $m=1$, because $g^{-1}(x)$ is a monotonically increasing function of x. Therefore, the optimal value of problem (11.54)-(11.57) is given by $Z_{\max}=kd$, where k solves $ke^k=(n-1)/e$. ■

From Lemma 11.5, it follows immediately that

$$\sum_{r\in R_w}\left(f_{rw}^{\text{so}}-f_{rw}^{\text{sue}}\right)\ln f_{rw}^{\text{sue}}\le k_w d_w,\ w\in W \tag{11.68}$$

where $k_w=g^{-1}\left((|R_w|-1)/e\right)$, $w\in W$ and $|R_w|$ is the number of feasible paths between OD pair $w\in W$. Substituting (11.53) and (11.68) into (11.52) yields

$$T_{\text{SUE}}\le T_{\text{SO}}+\gamma(C)T_{\text{SUE}}+\frac{1}{\theta}\bar{k}D \tag{11.69}$$

where $D=\sum_{w\in W}d_w$ is the total traffic demand and $\bar{k}$ is the average of k_w, $w\in W$

weighted by OD demand:

$$\bar{k} = \sum_{w \in W} \left(\frac{d_w}{D} \right) k_w, \text{ where } k_w \text{ solves } k_w e^{k_w} = \frac{1}{e}\left(|R_w| - 1 \right) \tag{11.70}$$

Furthermore, define $\bar{c} = T_{SO}/D$ as the average travel time of all network users at system optimum. Then, we arrive at the following bounding result:

$$\rho_{fx}^{sue} = \frac{T_{SUE}}{T_{SO}} \le \left(\frac{1}{1-\gamma(\mathcal{C})} \right)\left(1 + \frac{\bar{k}}{\theta \bar{c}} \right) \tag{11.71}$$

We conclude this section by remarking that the above inefficiency bounding method can be extended to the SUE problem with elastic demand, based on the following VI formulation: find $\left(\mathbf{f}^{sue}, \mathbf{d}^{sue} \right) \in \Omega_{fd}$, such that

$$\begin{aligned} \sum_{w \in W} \sum_{r \in R_w} \left(c_{rw}\left(\mathbf{f}^{sue} \right) + \frac{1}{\theta} \ln f_{rw}^{sue} \right)\left(f_{rw} - f_{rw}^{sue} \right) \\ - \sum_{r \in R_w} \left(D_w^{-1}\left(d_w^{sue} \right) + \frac{1}{\theta} \ln d_w^{sue} \right)\left(d_w - d_w^{sue} \right) \ge 0 \end{aligned} \tag{11.72}$$

for any $(\mathbf{f}, \mathbf{d}) \in \Omega_{fd} = \left\{ (\mathbf{f}, \mathbf{d}) \middle| \Lambda \mathbf{f} = \mathbf{d},\ \mathbf{f} \ge 0,\ \mathbf{d} \ge 0 \right\}$, where D_w^{-1} is the inverse of the OD demand function, $d_w = D_w(S_w)$ and $S_w = S_w(c_w)$ is the expected perceived travel time between each OD pair: $S_w = -\theta^{-1} \ln \sum_{r \in R_w} \exp(-\theta c_{rw}),\ w \in W$.

11.3.2 Interpretation of the Cost Inefficiency Bound

As seen from eqn. (11.71), the cost inefficiency bound of the SUE depends on four parameters, namely $\gamma(\mathcal{C})$, $\bar{k}$, θ and $\bar{c}$. $\gamma(\mathcal{C})$ is a dimensionless number of the price of anarchy defined exclusively by the class of link cost functions. $\bar{k}$ is also a dimensionless coefficient defined by eqn. (11.70) that increases with the number of feasible paths and thus reflects the degree of network complexity. The logit model parameter θ, in its original meaning, is inversely proportional to the standard error of the distribution of the perceived path travel time, and the logit model further assumes that this random error has the same variance for all paths in the network. Specifically, $\theta = \pi / \left(\sqrt{6}\sigma \right)$, with a unit corresponding to the inverse of the unit for measuring the average travel time $\bar{c}$, where σ is the common standard deviation of the perceived path travel times. One may further relax equation (11.71) by replacing $\bar{c}$ with the average free-flow travel times for all OD pairs $\bar{c}_0$, $\bar{c}_0 \le \bar{c}$, and sensibly assume that the common standard deviation of the perceived path travel times is proportional to the network average free-flow travel times or path lengths, $\sigma = \varsigma \bar{c}_0$, where ς is a dimensionless proportionality constant. With these assumptions, we arrive at

$$\rho_{\text{fx}}^{\text{sue}} = \left(\frac{1}{1-\gamma(\mathcal{C})}\right)\left(1+\frac{\bar{k}}{\theta\bar{c}}\right) \le \left(\frac{1}{1-\gamma(\mathcal{C})}\right)\left(1+\frac{\bar{k}}{\theta\bar{c}_0}\right) = \left(\frac{1}{1-\gamma(\mathcal{C})}\right)\left(1+\frac{\varsigma\sqrt{6}}{\pi}\bar{k}\right) \tag{11.73}$$

Equation (11.73) simply states that the cost inefficiency bound depends on the degree of travel time uncertainty or perception error and the network complexity (number of available paths). If the travel time is deterministic, then $\varsigma = 0 \quad (\theta \to \infty)$ and thus $\rho_{\text{fx}}^{\text{sue}} = (1-\gamma(\mathcal{C}))^{-1}$, or we have the result of the price of anarchy of the standard deterministic UE problem. In addition, if $|R_w| = 1$ for all $w \in W$, or the perception error of travel time has no effect on route choice, we have $k_w = 0,\ w \in W$ from (11.70) and thus $\bar{k} = 0$. In this case, we have $\rho_{\text{fx}}^{\text{sue}} = (1-\gamma(\mathcal{C}))^{-1}$ as well.

Whenever $|R_w| > 1$, the value of k_w (and hence $\bar{k}$) is very limited. As seen below, k_w is only marginally larger than $\log_{10}^{|R_w|}$. For a sufficiently complex network with the number of paths between each OD pair, $100 \le |R_w| \le 1000$, k_w takes only a limited value between 2.63 and 4.42. This observation shows that the network topology, or the network size and complexity, has very limited effects on the cost inefficiency bound of stochastic user equilibrium.

$\lvert R_w \rvert$	1	10	10^2	10^3	10^4	10^5
k_w	0	1.10	2.63	4.42	6.36	8.39

11.4 Inefficiency of Cournot-Nash Equilibria

The foregoing discussion of the inefficiency of selfish traffic equilibria has been limited to the deterministic and stochastic traffic equilibria with an infinite number of infinitesimal players or users, each controlling a negligible fraction of the overall traffic. In this section, we investigate the inefficiency in the case of a finite number of Cournot-Nash (CN) players such as self-optimizing oligopoly Cournot firms examined in Chapter 6, each of whom controls a strictly positive amount of flow.

11.4.1 CN Equilibrium with a Finite Number of Players

Instead of the multiple or mixed equilibrium behaviors by both UE and CN players sharing the same network examined in Chapter 6, here we consider CN players only. As defined in Chapter 6, let K be the set of CN players on the network, W^k be the set of OD pairs of which users or flows are controlled by CN player $k \in K$, and $W = \bigcup_{k\in K} W^k$. Furthermore, let v_a^k be the flow of link a arising out of player k or the OD flows from the set W^k, $k \in K$, $\mathbf{v}^k = \left(v_a^k, a \in A\right)^{\mathrm{T}}$, $v_a = \sum_{k\in K} v_a^k$ and $\mathbf{v} = \left(v_a, a \in A\right)^{\mathrm{T}}$. Assume that the OD demand d_w between each OD pair $w \in W$ is given and fixed. Then, the feasible sets for the CN players, Ω^k, $k \in K$, are given below.

$$\Omega^k = \left\{ \mathbf{v}^k \middle| v_a^k = \sum_{w\in W^k} \sum_{r\in R_w} f_{rw} \delta_{ar}, a \in A; \sum_{r\in R_w} f_{rw} = d_w, f_{rw} \geq 0, r \in R_w, w \in W^k \right\},\ k \in K \quad (11.74)$$

Suppose all players aim to optimize their own objective functions by routing flows under their control, given knowledge of the other players' flows, but without realizing how the other players will react to their routing decisions. Assuming each player can split the flow along any feasible paths, then, for a CN player $k \in K$, the total travel time of the users under this specific player is minimized, based on the current routing decisions of other players:

$$\min_{\mathbf{v}^k \in \Omega^k} \sum_{a\in A} v_a^k t_a\left(v_a^{-k} + v_a^k\right) \quad \left(= \sum_{a\in A} v_a^k t_a\left(v_a\right) \right),\ k \in K \quad (11.75)$$

where

$$v_a^{-k} = \sum_{i\in K, i\neq k} v_a^i = v_a - v_a^k,\ a \in A,\ k \in K \quad (11.76)$$

is taken as fixed. Under the assumption of strictly increasing and convex link cost functions, the above minimization problems (11.75) have unique solutions in their own arguments while other variables are fixed. Let $\mathbf{v}^{\mathrm{cn},k}$, $k \in K$ be the CN equilibrium solution satisfying the simultaneous optimization of the problems (11.75) for all $k \in K$. As shown in Chapter 6, $\mathbf{v}^{\mathrm{cn},k}$, $k \in K$ is an equilibrium solution if and only if it solves the following VI:

$$\sum_{a\in A} \sum_{k\in K} \left(t_a\left(v_a^{\mathrm{cn}}\right) + v_a^{\mathrm{cn},k} t_a'\left(v_a^{\mathrm{cn}}\right)\right)\left(v_a^k - v_a^{\mathrm{cn},k}\right) \geq 0 \text{ for any } \mathbf{v}^k \in \Omega^k,\ k \in K \quad (11.77)$$

where $t_a'\left(v_a\right) = \mathrm{d}t_a\left(v_a\right)/\mathrm{d}v_a$, $a \in A$ is the derivative of link cost function with respect to link flow. This VI equilibrium condition means that, at equilibrium, the link cost perceived by a CN player $k \in K$ is the 'partial' marginal social cost given by $t_a\left(v_a\right) + v_a^k t_a'\left(v_a\right)$, $a \in A$.

For analytical tractability, from now on we limit our analysis to the polynomial link cost function (11.18) and introduce the following quantity:

$$p^* := \frac{3|K| - 1}{|K| - 1} \quad (11.78)$$

where $|K|$ denotes the number of CN players on the network or the cardinality of set K. The following theorem states the uniqueness of the CN equilibrium solution to VI (11.77).

Theorem 11.6 *For a general network with polynomial link cost functions (11.18), with* $0<p<p^*$, *the player-specific link flow solution of VI (11.77),* $\mathbf{v}^{\mathrm{cn},k}$, $k\in K$, *is unique.*

A detailed proof of the theorem can be found in Altman et al. (2002). One may note that $p^*>3$ for all $|K|\geq 2$.

11.4.2 Upper-bound of the Inefficiency of CN Equilibria

Again let $\mathbf{v}^{\mathrm{so}}=\left(v_a^{\mathrm{so}},a\in A\right)^{\mathrm{T}}=\left(\sum_{k\in K}v_a^{\mathrm{so},k},a\in A\right)^{\mathrm{T}}$ be the system-optimal link flow solution to the SO problem (11.4). From VI (11.77) and the fact that $\mathbf{v}^{\mathrm{so},k}\in\Omega^k$, $k\in K$, we have

$$\begin{aligned}
T\left(\mathbf{v}^{\mathrm{cn}}\right)&\leq\sum_{a\in A}\sum_{k\in K}t_a\left(v_a^{\mathrm{cn}}\right)v_a^{\mathrm{so},k}+\sum_{a\in A}\sum_{k\in K}v_a^{\mathrm{cn},k}t_a'\left(v_a^{\mathrm{cn}}\right)\left(v_a^{\mathrm{so},k}-v_a^{\mathrm{cn},k}\right)\\
&=\sum_{a\in A}\sum_{k\in K}t_a\left(v_a^{\mathrm{so}}\right)v_a^{\mathrm{so},k}+\sum_{a\in A}\sum_{k\in K}v_a^{\mathrm{cn},k}t_a'\left(v_a^{\mathrm{cn}}\right)\left(v_a^{\mathrm{so},k}-v_a^{\mathrm{cn},k}\right)\\
&\quad+\sum_{a\in A}\sum_{k\in K}\left(t_a\left(v_a^{\mathrm{cn}}\right)-t_a\left(v_a^{\mathrm{so}}\right)\right)v_a^{\mathrm{so},k}
\end{aligned}$$

Since $v_a=\sum_{k\in K}v_a^k$, $t_a\left(v_a\right)=t_a^0+\alpha_a\left(v_a\right)^p$ and $t_a'\left(v_a\right)=\alpha_a p\left(v_a\right)^{p-1}$,

$$\begin{aligned}
T\left(\mathbf{v}^{\mathrm{cn}}\right)&\leq T\left(\mathbf{v}^{\mathrm{so}}\right)+\sum_{a\in A}\alpha_a p\left(v_a^{\mathrm{cn}}\right)^{p-1}\sum_{k\in K}v_a^{\mathrm{cn},k}\left(v_a^{\mathrm{so},k}-v_a^{\mathrm{cn},k}\right)+\sum_{a\in A}\alpha_a\left(\left(v_a^{\mathrm{cn}}\right)^p-\left(v_a^{\mathrm{so}}\right)^p\right)v_a^{\mathrm{so}}\\
&\leq T\left(\mathbf{v}^{\mathrm{so}}\right)+\max_{\mathbf{v}^k\in\Omega^k,k\in K}\left\{\sum_{a\in A}\alpha_a p\left(v_a^{\mathrm{cn}}\right)^{p-1}\sum_{k\in K}v_a^{\mathrm{cn},k}\left(v_a^k-v_a^{\mathrm{cn},k}\right)+\sum_{a\in A}\alpha_a\left(\left(v_a^{\mathrm{cn}}\right)^p-\left(v_a\right)^p\right)v_a\right\}\\
&\leq T\left(\mathbf{v}^{\mathrm{so}}\right)+\max_{\mathbf{v}^k\geq 0,k\in K}\left\{\sum_{a\in A}\alpha_a p\left(v_a^{\mathrm{cn}}\right)^{p-1}\sum_{k\in K}v_a^{\mathrm{cn},k}\left(v_a^k-v_a^{\mathrm{cn},k}\right)+\sum_{a\in A}\alpha_a\left(\left(v_a^{\mathrm{cn}}\right)^p-\left(v_a\right)^p\right)v_a\right\}
\end{aligned}\tag{11.79}$$

The last inequality is due to the fact that the constraint $\mathbf{v}^k\in\Omega^k$ is relaxed into $\mathbf{v}^k\geq 0$, $k\in K$. Now we introduce the following theorem to establish the upper-bound of the inefficiency of the CN equilibria.

Theorem 11.7 *Let* $\mathbf{v}^{\mathrm{cn},k}$, $k\in K$ *be a solution of the CN equilibrium problem (11.77) and let* $\mathbf{v}^{\mathrm{so}}$ *be a solution of the SO problem (11.4), with polynomial link cost function (11.18). Then,*

$$1\leq\rho_{\mathrm{fx}}^{\mathrm{cn}}=\frac{T\left(\mathbf{v}^{\mathrm{cn}}\right)}{T\left(\mathbf{v}^{\mathrm{so}}\right)}\leq\frac{1}{1-\xi}\tag{11.80}$$

for $|K|\geq 2$ *and* $\rho_{\mathrm{fx}}^{\mathrm{cn}}=T\left(\mathbf{v}^{\mathrm{cn}}\right)/T\left(\mathbf{v}^{\mathrm{so}}\right)=1$ *for* $|K|=1$, *where* ξ *is defined by (11.90) and (11.89) given below.*

Proof. The task here is to find a solution of the second term of the right-hand side of (11.79), i.e.,

$$\max_{v^k \geq 0, k\in K} \left\{ \sum_{a\in A} \alpha_a p \left(v_a^{\text{cn}}\right)^{p-1} \sum_{k\in K} v_a^{\text{cn},k} \left(v_a^k - v_a^{\text{cn},k}\right) + \sum_{a\in A} \alpha_a \left[\left(v_a^{\text{cn}}\right)^p - \left(v_a\right)^p\right] v_a \right\} \tag{11.81}$$

Introducing the Lagrange multiplier for the constraint $v_a^k \geq 0,\ k\in K,\ a\in A,$ we can write down the first-order optimality conditions for (11.81) as:

$$\alpha_a p v_a^{\text{cn},k} \left(v_a^{\text{cn}}\right)^{p-1} + \alpha_a \left[\left(v_a^{\text{cn}}\right)^p - \left(v_a\right)^p\right] - \alpha_a p \left(v_a\right)^p + \lambda_a^k = 0,\ k\in K \tag{11.82}$$

$$\lambda_a^k \geq 0,\ v_a^k \geq 0,\ \lambda_a^k v_a^k = 0,\ k\in K \tag{11.83}$$

From (11.82) and (11.83), we conclude that if $v_a^{\text{cn},1} > v_a^{\text{cn},2}$, then $v_a^1 > v_a^2 = 0$. Thus, let

$$v_a^{\text{cn},\bar{k}} = \arg\max_{k\in K} v_a^{\text{cn},k},\ a\in A \tag{11.84}$$

and

$$\zeta_a = \frac{v_a^{\text{cn},\bar{k}}}{v_a^{\text{cn}}},\ a\in A \tag{11.85}$$

Clearly, $0 \leq \zeta_a \leq 1,\ a\in A.$ Then, from (11.82), we obtain

$$v_a = \left(\frac{p\zeta_a + 1}{1+p}\right)^{\frac{1}{p}} v_a^{\text{cn}},\ a\in A \tag{11.86}$$

and

$$v_a^{\bar{k}} = v_a = \left(\frac{p\zeta_a + 1}{1+p}\right)^{\frac{1}{p}} v_a^{\text{cn}},\ v_a^k = 0, \text{ for any } k\in K,\ k\neq \bar{k}$$

Therefore,

$$\begin{aligned}
&\max_{v^k \geq 0, k\in K} \left\{ \sum_{a\in A} \alpha_a p \left(v_a^{\text{cn}}\right)^{p-1} \sum_{k\in K} v_a^{\text{cn},k} \left(v_a^k - v_a^{\text{cn},k}\right) + \sum_{a\in A} \alpha_a \left[\left(v_a^{\text{cn}}\right)^p - \left(v_a\right)^p\right] v_a \right\} \\
&\quad = \sum_{a\in A} \alpha_a p \left[\left(\frac{p\zeta_a + 1}{1+p}\right)^{\frac{1}{p}} - \zeta_a\right] \zeta_a \left(v_a^{\text{cn}}\right)^{p+1} - \sum_{a\in A} \alpha_a p \left(v_a^{\text{cn}}\right)^{p-1} \sum_{k\in K, k\neq \bar{k}} \left(v_a^{\text{cn},k}\right)^2 \\
&\qquad + \sum_{a\in A} \alpha_a \left(1 - \zeta_a\right) \left(\frac{p}{1+p}\right) \left(\frac{p\zeta_a + 1}{1+p}\right)^{\frac{1}{p}} \left(v_a^{\text{cn}}\right)^{p+1} \\
&\quad \leq \sum_{a\in A} \alpha_a \xi_a \left(v_a^{\text{cn}}\right)^{p+1} \qquad (11.87) \\
&\quad \leq \sum_{a\in A} \xi_a t_a \left(v_a^{\text{cn}}\right) v_a^{\text{cn}} \qquad (11.88)
\end{aligned}$$

where

$$\xi_a := p \left[\left(\frac{p\zeta_a + 1}{1+p}\right)^{\frac{1}{p}} - \zeta_a\right] \zeta_a - p \frac{\left(1-\zeta_a\right)^2}{|K| - 1} + \left(1 - \zeta_a\right) \frac{p}{1+p} \left(\frac{p\zeta_a + 1}{1+p}\right)^{\frac{1}{p}} \tag{11.89}$$

Inequality (11.87) follows from the fact that

$$\sum_{k\in K,k\neq\bar{k}}\left(v_a^{\mathrm{cn},k}\right)^2 \geq \frac{1}{|K|-1}\left(\sum_{k\in K,k\neq\bar{k}} v_a^{\mathrm{cn},k}\right)^2 = \frac{(1-\zeta_a)^2}{|K|-1}\left(v_a^{\mathrm{cn}}\right)^2$$

and (11.88) follows from the fact that $t_a^0 \geq 0$ for any $a\in A$. Define

$$\xi = \max_{a\in A}\ \xi_a \tag{11.90}$$

Then it follows from (11.79) and (11.88) that

$$T\left(\mathbf{v}^{\mathrm{cn}}\right) \leq T\left(\mathbf{v}^{\mathrm{so}}\right) + \xi T\left(\mathbf{v}^{\mathrm{cn}}\right)$$

Hence, the assertion (11.80) follows immediately. ■

Note that, in the proof of the above theorem, we assume that there is a unique $\bar{k}\in K$, such that $v_a^{\mathrm{cn},\bar{k}} > v_a^{\mathrm{cn},k}$ for all $k\in K,\ k\neq\bar{k}$. If there are $k_1,\ k_2,\ \cdots,\ k_m$, such that $v_a^{\mathrm{cn},k_1} = v_a^{\mathrm{cn},k_2} = \cdots = v_a^{\mathrm{cn},k_m} > v_a^{\mathrm{cn},k}$ for all $k\in K,\ k\neq k_i,\ i=1,2,\cdots,m,$ then in this case, eqn. (11.86) still holds, but v_a^k is not unique. We can take any $v_a^k\geq 0,\ k\in K$ such that $\sum_{i=1}^m v_a^{k_i} = v_a$ and $v_a^k = 0$ for any $k\neq k_i,\ i=1,2,\cdots,m,$ and the assertion (11.80) also holds.

11.4.3 Upper-bound of Special Cases and a Numerical Example

If there is only one CN player, i.e., $|K|=1$, then the CN equilibrium problem of interest reduces to the standard system optimum problem. Indeed, in this case, $\zeta_a=1$ in eqn. (11.85) and $\xi_a=0$ in (11.89) for all $a\in A$, and as a result, the inefficiency bound is $\rho_{\mathrm{fx}}^{\mathrm{cn}}=1$, which simply implies that there is no efficiency loss.

For the linear cost function with $p=1$, from (11.89) we have

$$\xi_a = \frac{(1-\zeta_a)\left[(3|K|+1)\zeta_a + |K|-5\right]}{4(|K|-1)},\ a\in A \tag{11.91}$$

It is obvious that when $|K|\to\infty$ or when there are an infinite number of infinitesimal players, then $\zeta_a\to 0$ and $\xi_a\to 1/4$ in eqn. (11.91) for all $a\in A$, we thus have $1/(1-\xi)=4/3$, a bound obtained and given previously in Theorem 11.1 for the Wardropian user equilibrium. Note that one can interpret this extreme case in the following manner. In a network with a certain number of OD pairs $w\in W$ and demand d_w, suppose there are m_w players in OD pair w, each controlling a positive amount of demand $d_w^j,\ j=1,2,\cdots,m_w$ and $\sum_{j=1}^{m_w} d_w^j = d_w,\ w\in W$. One may assume m_w identical players and thus $d_w^j = d_w/m_w$.

Then, as $m_w \to \infty$ (hence $|K| \to \infty$), the behavior of the CN equilibrium yields a total link flow vector corresponding to a Wardrop equilibrium (Haurie and Marcotte, 1985).

For the general case where $p > 1$, if there are infinite number of players competing on the network and $\zeta_a \to 0,\ a \in A$

$$\xi_a \to \left(\frac{p}{1+p}\right)\left(\frac{1}{1+p}\right)^{\frac{1}{p}} \tag{11.92}$$

and the bound of the CN equilibria becomes

$$\rho_{\text{fx}}^{\text{cn}} = \left\{1 - \left(\frac{p}{1+p}\right)\left(\frac{1}{1+p}\right)^{\frac{1}{p}}\right\}^{-1} \tag{11.93}$$

which is identical with the upper bound result (11.21) obtained previously for the deterministic Wardropian user equilibrium problem.

Example 11.4 Consider a simple network shown in Figure 11.5, consisting of 3 nodes and 4 directed links, used in Section 6.4 of Chapter 6. Link cost functions are given by

$$t_1 = 6 + 2v_1,\ \ t_2 = 20 + v_2,\ \ t_3 = 8 + v_3,\ \ t_4 = v_4$$

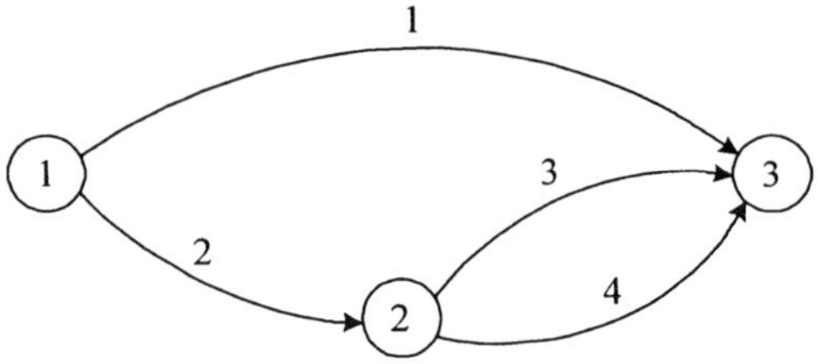

Figure 11.5 The simple network used in Example 11.4

There are two OD pairs ($1 \to 3$ and $2 \to 3$) in the network, and the demands are assumed to be fixed with $d_{1\to3} = 20$ and $d_{2\to3} = 20$. There are three paths connecting OD pair $1 \to 3$: path 1 with a single link 1, path 2 with link 2 and link 3, and path 3 with link 2 and link 4. There are two paths connecting OD pair $2 \to 3$: path 4 with a single link 3, and path 5 with a single link 4.

The unique link flows at the system optimum are $v_1^{\text{so}} = 14$, $v_2^{\text{so}} = 6$, $v_3^{\text{so}} = 11$ and $v_4^{\text{so}} = 15$, with the corresponding link travel times $t_1\left(v_1^{\text{so}}\right) = 34$, $t_2\left(v_2^{\text{so}}\right) = 26$, $t_3\left(v_3^{\text{so}}\right) = 19$ and $t_4\left(v_4^{\text{so}}\right) = 15$. The total travel time at system optimum is 1066.

Suppose that the two OD pairs are controlled by two distinct CN players, with OD pair $1 \rightarrow 3$ by player 1 and OD pair $2 \rightarrow 3$ by player 2. At the CN equilibrium, the player-specific link flows are unique and are given by $v_1^{\text{cn},1} = 88/7$, $v_2^{\text{cn},1} = 52/7$, $v_3^{\text{cn},1} = 50/21$ and $v_4^{\text{cn},1} = 106/21$; $v_1^{\text{cn},2} = 0$, $v_2^{\text{cn},2} = 0$, $v_3^{\text{cn},2} = 26/3$ and $v_4^{\text{cn},2} = 34/3$. The total travel time is $67664/63$. The ratio of inefficiency is $\rho_{\text{fx}}^{\text{cn}} = 67664/63/1066 = 1.007534$.

In our notation, $\zeta_1 = \zeta_2 = 1$, $\zeta_3 \approx 0.7845$ and $\zeta_4 \approx 0.6919$. $\xi_1 = \xi_2 = 0$, $\xi_3 = 0.1342$ and $\xi_4 = 0.1420$. Thus, $\xi = \max\{\xi_1, \xi_2, \xi_3, \xi_4\} = 0.1420$ and our bound is $\rho_{\text{fx}}^{\text{cn}} = (1-\xi)^{-1}$ $= (1-0.1420)^{-1} \approx 1.1655$.

11.5 MAXIMUM EFFICIENCY LOSS OF SECOND-BEST PRICING SCHEMES

As pointed out before, due to the imperfection of the first-best pricing from a political and technical implementation perspective, the second-best charging schemes are more practically relevant, and indeed have received ample attention recently. A second best pricing scheme, if introduced, is expected to lead to system efficiency in between those of the un-tolled UE and SO flow patterns. Therefore, we are interested in establishing the efficiency loss of a second-best pricing scheme in comparison with the first-best one, and determining the room or potential for further improvement of the second-best pricing scheme per se.

11.5.1 Measure of Efficiency Loss

We now consider measuring the efficiency loss of a second-best pricing scheme by the (absolute and relative) gap between the performance measures under the current second-best pricing scheme and the system-optimal one. As before, the total system travel time for the fixed demand case or the total social welfare for the elastic demand case can be used as the system performance measure. Let $T(\mathbf{v}^{\text{ue}}(\mathbf{u}))$ be the total system travel time under a second-best pricing scheme $\mathbf{u}$, where $\mathbf{v}^{\text{ue}}(\mathbf{u})$ is the corresponding UE link flows with pricing scheme $\mathbf{u}$. Again let $T(\mathbf{v}^{\text{so}})$ be the minimum system travel time associated with SO link flows $\mathbf{v}^{\text{so}}$. Again we define

$$\rho_{\text{fx}}^{\text{ue}}(\mathbf{u}) = \frac{T(\mathbf{v}^{\text{ue}}(\mathbf{u}))}{T(\mathbf{v}^{\text{so}})} \tag{11.94}$$

Again, $\rho_{\text{fx}}^{\text{ue}}(\mathbf{u}) \geq 1$, by definition of $\mathbf{u}$, being a second-best pricing scheme. We can thus have the following *relative efficiency loss* associated with a second-best pricing scheme in terms of the ratio $\rho_{\mathrm{fx}}^{\mathrm{ue}}(\mathbf{u})$:

$$\varphi_{\mathrm{fx}}^{\mathrm{ue}}(\mathbf{u})=\frac{T\left(\mathbf{v}^{\mathrm{ue}}(\mathbf{u})\right)-T\left(\mathbf{v}^{\mathrm{so}}\right)}{T\left(\mathbf{v}^{\mathrm{so}}\right)}=\rho_{\mathrm{fx}}^{\mathrm{ue}}(\mathbf{u})-1 \tag{11.95}$$

Similarly, in the case of elastic demand, we have the following counterparts:

$$\rho_{\mathrm{ec}}^{\mathrm{ue}}(\mathbf{u})=\frac{S\left(\mathbf{v}^{\mathrm{so}},\mathbf{d}^{\mathrm{so}}\right)}{S\left(\mathbf{v}^{\mathrm{ue}}(\mathbf{u}),\mathbf{d}^{\mathrm{ue}}(\mathbf{u})\right)} \tag{11.96}$$

$$\varphi_{\mathrm{ec}}^{\mathrm{ue}}(\mathbf{u})=\frac{S\left(\mathbf{v}^{\mathrm{so}},\mathbf{d}^{\mathrm{so}}\right)-S\left(\mathbf{v}^{\mathrm{ue}}(\mathbf{u}),\mathbf{d}^{\mathrm{ue}}(\mathbf{u})\right)}{S\left(\mathbf{v}^{\mathrm{so}},\mathbf{d}^{\mathrm{so}}\right)}=1-\frac{1}{\rho_{\mathrm{ec}}^{\mathrm{ue}}(\mathbf{u})} \tag{11.97}$$

Therefore, determining the maximum efficiency loss of a second-best pricing scheme is equivalent to establishing an upper bound of the inefficiency index $\rho_{\mathrm{fx}}^{\mathrm{ue}}(\mathbf{u})$ in (11.94) or $\rho_{\mathrm{ec}}^{\mathrm{ue}}(\mathbf{u})$ in (11.96), associated with a given second-best pricing scheme, $\mathbf{u}$, with fixed or elastic demand.

11.5.2 Bound for Traffic Equilibria with Fixed Demands

Consider a second-best pricing scheme $\mathbf{u}=(u_a,a\in A)^{\mathrm{T}}\geq 0$, with the modified link cost function $t_a(v_a)+u_a$, the VI formulation (11.3) of the UE problem can then be rewritten as:

$$\left(\mathbf{t}\left(\mathbf{v}^{\mathrm{ue}}\right)+\mathbf{u}\right)^{\mathrm{T}}\left(\mathbf{v}-\mathbf{v}^{\mathrm{ue}}\right)\geq 0,\ \text{for any } \mathbf{v}\in\Omega_{\mathrm{v}} \tag{11.98}$$

which leads to

$$T\left(\mathbf{v}^{\mathrm{ue}}\right)\leq\sum_{a\in A}t_a(v_a)v_a+\sum_{a\in A}\left(t_a\left(v_a^{\mathrm{ue}}\right)-t_a(v_a)\right)v_a+\sum_{a\in A}\left(v_a-v_a^{\mathrm{ue}}\right)u_a \tag{11.99}$$

For each link cost function $t_a=t_a(v_a)$ and nonnegative user equilibrium link flow $v_a^{\mathrm{ue}}\geq 0$, we define the following parameter for each link $a\in A$, associated with link toll charge u_a:

$$\gamma_a\left(t_a,v_a^{\mathrm{ue}},u_a\right)=\max_{v_a\geq 0}\frac{\left(t_a\left(v_a^{\mathrm{ue}}\right)-t_a(v_a)\right)v_a+\left(v_a-v_a^{\mathrm{ue}}\right)u_a}{t_a\left(v_a^{\mathrm{ue}}\right)v_a^{\mathrm{ue}}},\ \text{if } 0\leq u_a\leq v_a^{\mathrm{ue}}t_a'\left(v_a^{\mathrm{ue}}\right) \tag{11.100}$$

$$\gamma_a\left(t_a,v_a^{\mathrm{ue}},u_a\right)=\max_{v_a\geq 0}\frac{\left(t_a\left(v_a^{\mathrm{ue}}\right)-t_a(v_a)\right)v_a+\left(v_a-v_a^{\mathrm{ue}}\right)u_a}{t_a(v_a)v_a},\ \text{if } u_a\geq v_a^{\mathrm{ue}}t_a'\left(v_a^{\mathrm{ue}}\right) \tag{11.101}$$

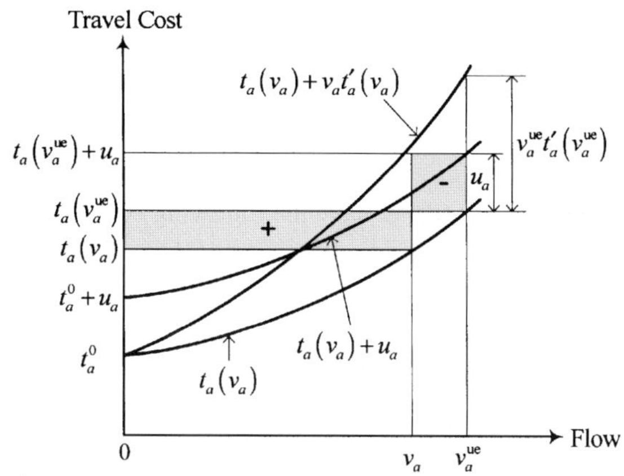

Figure 11.6 Geometric illustration of the numerator of eqn.(11.100) for $0 \le u_a \le v_a^{ue} t_a'(v_a^{ue})$

We first consider the case of $0 \le u_a \le v_a^{ue} t_a'(v_a^{ue})$. Because the denominator in (11.100) is fixed, our task here is to solve the following one-dimensional maximization problem for v_a

$$\max_{v_a \ge 0} F(v_a) = \left(t_a(v_a^{ue}) - t_a(v_a)\right) v_a + \left(v_a - v_a^{ue}\right) u_a \tag{11.102}$$

Note that it is assumed that $t_a(v_a)$ is monotonically increasing and convex and hence $F(v_a)$ is concave. Figures 11.6 plots the area corresponding to the numerator of eqn.(11.100) for $0 \le u_a \le v_a^{ue} t_a'(v_a^{ue})$.

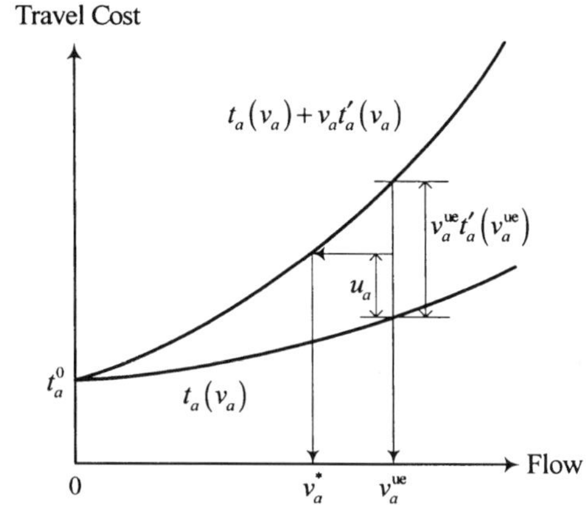

Figure 11.7 Geometric illustration of the solution to equation (11.103)

Let $\mathrm{d}F(v_a)/\mathrm{d}v_a = 0$, we have

$$t_a(v_a)+v_a t'_a(v_a)=t_a(v_a^{ue})+u_a \tag{11.103}$$

As shown in Figure 11.7, a unique solution $v_a^* \le v_a^{ue}$ is obtained for $0 \le u_a \le v_a^{ue} t'_a(v_a^{ue})$.

Next we briefly examine the case of $u_a \ge v_a^{ue} t'_a(v_a^{ue})$. Define again

$$F(v_a)=\frac{\left(t_a(v_a^{ue})-t_a(v_a)\right)v_a+\left(v_a-v_a^{ue}\right)u_a}{t_a(v_a)v_a}=-1+\frac{\left(t_a(v_a^{ue})+u_a\right)v_a-v_a^{ue}u_a}{t_a(v_a)v_a} \tag{11.104}$$

Clearly, $\lim_{v_a\to+\infty}F(v_a)=-1$ and $\lim_{v_a\to 0}F(v_a)=-\infty$, the curve of $F(v_a)$ generally takes the shape shown in Figure 11.8, where the curves are plotted for $t(v)=6.0+0.9(v/200)^p$ with $u=9$, $v^{ue}=85$ and $p=1,2,3,4$. Without much difficulty, one can show that there is one positive solution v_a^* only.

Again let $\mathrm{d}F(v_a)/\mathrm{d}v_a=0$, we have

$$\left[t_a(v_a^{ue})+u_a\right]v_a t(v_a)-\left[\left(t_a(v_a^{ue})+u_a\right)v_a-v_a^{ue}u_a\right]\left(t(v_a)+v_a t'(v_a)\right)=0$$

It simplifies into:

$$\frac{t_a(v_a^{ue})+u_a}{v_a^{ue}u_a}=\frac{t(v_a)+v_a t'_a(v_a)}{(v_a)^2 t'_a(v_a)} \tag{11.105}$$

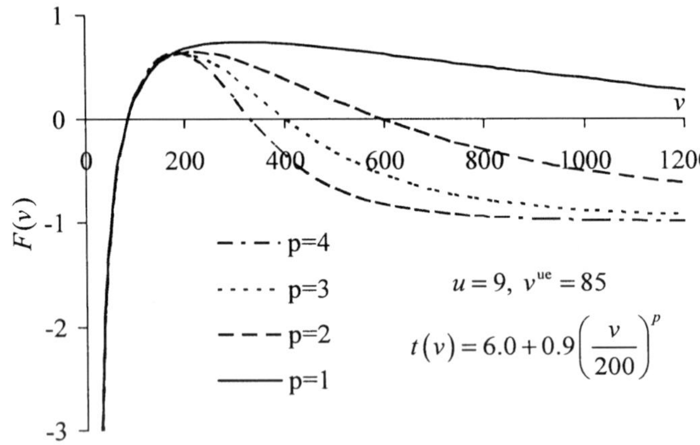

Figure 11.8 The general shape and unique maximum of function (11.104)

Let v_a^* be the solution of eqn. (11.105), substituting eqn. (11.105) into (11.104) yields:

$$\gamma_a(t_a,v_a^{ue},u_a)=F(v_a^*)=-1+\frac{v_a^{ue}u_a}{(v_a^*)^2 t'_a(v_a^*)} \tag{11.106}$$

As before, for a given class $\mathcal{C}$ of link cost functions and a pricing scheme $\mathbf{u}$ with $\mathbf{v}^{\text{ue}} = \mathbf{v}^{\text{ue}}(\mathbf{u})$, we define

$$\gamma(\mathcal{C},\mathbf{u}) = \max_{t_a \in \mathcal{C},\ a \in A} \gamma_a\left(t_a, v_a^{\text{ue}}, u_a\right) \tag{11.107}$$

With this definition, the following theorem follows immediately.

Theorem 11.8 *Let* $\mathbf{v}^{\text{ue}}(\mathbf{u})$ *be a UE link flow pattern associated with a pricing scheme* $\mathbf{u}$, *with separable cost functions drawn from a given class* $\mathcal{C}$, *and let* $\mathbf{v}^{\text{so}}$ *be an SO link flow solution, then*

$$T\left(\mathbf{v}^{\text{ue}}(\mathbf{u})\right) \le \frac{1}{1-\gamma(\mathcal{C},\mathbf{u})} T\left(\mathbf{v}^{\text{so}}\right) \ \text{ if } 0 \le u_a \le v_a^{\text{ue}} t_a'\left(v_a^{\text{ue}}\right) \text{ for all } a \in A \tag{11.108}$$

$$T\left(\mathbf{v}^{\text{ue}}(\mathbf{u})\right) \le \left(1+\gamma(\mathcal{C},\mathbf{u})\right) T\left(\mathbf{v}^{\text{so}}\right) \ \text{ if } u_a \ge v_a^{\text{ue}} t_a'\left(v_a^{\text{ue}}\right) \text{ for all } a \in A \tag{11.109}$$

Remark 11.1 Depending on the given pricing scheme $\mathbf{u}$, eqn. (11.108) shows that $\rho_{\text{fx}}^{\text{ue}}(\mathbf{u}) \le \left(1-\gamma(\mathcal{C},\mathbf{u})\right)^{-1}$ for all $0 \le u_a \le v_a^{\text{ue}} t_a'\left(v_a^{\text{ue}}\right)$, $a \in A$ and $\rho_{\text{fx}}^{\text{ue}}(\mathbf{u}) \le 1+\gamma(\mathcal{C},\mathbf{u})$ for all $u_a \ge v_a^{\text{ue}} t_a'\left(v_a^{\text{ue}}\right)$, $a \in A$. In the special case of marginal-cost pricing, we have $u_a = v_a^{\text{ue}} t_a'\left(v_a^{\text{ue}}\right)$ for all $a \in A$. Then, it follows that $v_a^* = v_a^{\text{ue}}$ from (11.103), and $\gamma_a\left(t_a, v_a^{\text{ue}}, u_a\right) = 0$ from (11.100). As a result, $\gamma(\mathcal{C},\mathbf{u}) = 0$, $\rho_{\text{fx}}^{\text{ue}}(\mathbf{u}) = 1$ and $\varphi_{\text{fx}}^{\text{ue}}(\mathbf{u}) = 0$, which simply implies that there is no efficiency loss in the system under a marginal-cost pricing scheme. Similarly, we can apply eqn. (11.101) for $u_a = v_a^{\text{ue}} t_a'\left(v_a^{\text{ue}}\right)$, $a \in A$. In this case, from (11.105) we have

$$\frac{t_a\left(v_a^{\text{ue}}\right) + v_a^{\text{ue}} t_a'\left(v_a^{\text{ue}}\right)}{\left(v_a^{\text{ue}}\right)^2 t_a'\left(v_a^{\text{ue}}\right)} = \frac{t\left(v_a\right) + v_a t_a'\left(v_a\right)}{\left(v_a\right)^2 t_a'\left(v_a\right)} \tag{11.110}$$

A unique solution of the equation is given by $v_a^* = v_a^{\text{ue}}$, $a \in A$. Then, from eqn. (11.106), $\gamma_a\left(t_a, v_a^{\text{ue}}, u_a\right) = 0$. Hence we obtain the same results: $\gamma(\mathcal{C},\mathbf{u}) = 0$, $\rho_{\text{fx}}^{\text{ue}}(\mathbf{u}) = 1$ and $\varphi_{\text{fx}}^{\text{ue}}(\mathbf{u}) = 0$.

Remark 11.2 We have adopted two different definitions of $\gamma_a\left(t_a, v_a^{\text{ue}}, u_a\right)$ given in (11.100) and (11.101) respectively for the two cases of $0 \le u_a \le v_a^{\text{ue}} t_a'\left(v_a^{\text{ue}}\right)$ and $u_a \ge v_a^{\text{ue}} t_a'\left(v_a^{\text{ue}}\right)$, which, as pointed out in Remark 11.1, give rise to consistent values of $\gamma_a\left(t_a, v_a^{\text{ue}}, u_a\right) = 0$ at a marginal-cost pricing scheme: $u_a = v_a^{\text{ue}} t_a'\left(v_a^{\text{ue}}\right)$, $a \in A$. Two separate definitions for the two cases are necessary. First, from (11.108), the bound is meaningful only if $0 \le \gamma(\mathcal{C},\mathbf{u}) \le 1$, which indeed holds for the current definition. If, however, we extend the definition (11.100) to the case of $u_a \geq v_a^{\text{ue}} t_a'(v_a^{\text{ue}})$, then it is possible that $\gamma_a(t_a, v_a^{\text{ue}}, u_a) > 1$, when u_a is sufficiently large. To see this, we can choose a constant v_a slightly greater than v_a^{ue}, then the term $(v_a - v_a^{\text{ue}})u_a$ in (11.100) is positive and always increases with u_a. Because the negative term $(t_a(v_a^{\text{ue}}) - t_a(v_a))v_a$ is limited and $t_a(v_a^{\text{ue}})v_a^{\text{ue}}$ is a positive constant in (11.100), $\gamma_a(t_a, v_a^{\text{ue}}, u_a)$ becomes much greater than 1 as u_a becomes large. Also, from (11.109), $\gamma(C, \mathbf{u})$ should not always go to positive infinity for meaningful $\mathbf{u}$, otherwise, the presented bound becomes ineffective. If we still use definition (11.101) for $0 \leq u_a \leq v_a^{\text{ue}} t_a'(v_a^{\text{ue}})$, then the value of $\gamma_a(t_a, v_a^{\text{ue}}, u_a)$ may become huge if u_a is sufficiently small. This can be seen in the extreme case of $u_a = 0$ and zero free-flow travel time because $\gamma_a(t_a, v_a^{\text{ue}}, u_a) \to \infty$ as $v_a \to 0$ in this case.

Note that the bounding equations (11.108) and (11.109) assume that the toll charge is either uniformly less (or greater) than the congestion externality for *all* links in the network. It is obviously unrealistic in practice. In particular, for the trial-and-error pricing scheme developed in Chapter 10, the toll charge in each trial for each link can be either less or greater than the congestion externality. It is therefore necessary to establish an inefficiency bound for general second-best pricing schemes that can accommodate both possibilities. This can be done by the following relaxation.

Let set A_1 consist of those links whose toll charges are less than their congestion externalities, i.e., $0 \leq u_a < v_a^{\text{ue}} t_a'(v_a^{\text{ue}})$, $a \in A_1$, and set A_2 consist of those links with $u_a > v_a^{\text{ue}} t_a'(v_a^{\text{ue}})$, $a \in A_2$. If $u_a = v_a^{\text{ue}} t_a'(v_a^{\text{ue}})$ then a can be classified into either A_1 or A_2. With this classification, we denote

$$\gamma_1(C, \mathbf{u}) = \max_{t_a \in C,\, a \in A_1} \gamma_a(t_a, v_a^{\text{ue}}, u_a) \quad \text{for } 0 \leq u_a \leq v_a^{\text{ue}} t_a'(v_a^{\text{ue}}),\ a \in A_1$$

$$\gamma_2(C, \mathbf{u}) = \max_{t_a \in C,\, a \in A_2} \gamma_a(t_a, v_a^{\text{ue}}, u_a) \quad \text{for } u_a \geq v_a^{\text{ue}} t_a'(v_a^{\text{ue}}),\ a \in A_2$$

where $\gamma_a(t_a, v_a^{\text{ue}}, u_a)$ are defined respectively by (11.100) and (11.101) for $a \in A_1$ and $a \in A_2$. Then from the basic inequality (11.99), it follows that

$$\begin{aligned} T(\mathbf{v}^{\text{ue}}) &\leq \sum_{a \in A} t_a(v_a) v_a + \gamma_1(C, \mathbf{u}) \sum_{a \in A_1} t_a(v_a^{\text{ue}}) v_a^{\text{ue}} + \gamma_2(C, \mathbf{u}) \sum_{a \in A_2} t_a(v_a) v_a \\ &\leq \sum_{a \in A} t_a(v_a) v_a + \gamma_1(C, \mathbf{u}) T(\mathbf{v}^{\text{ue}}) + \gamma_2(C, \mathbf{u}) \sum_{a \in A} t_a(v_a) v_a \end{aligned} \tag{11.111}$$

As before, using the definition (11.94) and let $v_a = v_a^{\text{so}}$, we have

$$T\left(\mathbf{v}^{\mathrm{ue}}\right) \le \frac{1+\gamma_2(\mathcal{C},\mathbf{u})}{1-\gamma_1(\mathcal{C},\mathbf{u})} T\left(\mathbf{v}^{\mathrm{so}}\right)$$

that is

$$\rho_{\mathrm{fx}}^{\mathrm{ue}}(\mathbf{u}) \le \frac{1+\gamma_2(\mathcal{C},\mathbf{u})}{1-\gamma_1(\mathcal{C},\mathbf{u})} \tag{11.112}$$

To sum up, we state the following Theorem.

Theorem 11.9 *Let* $\mathbf{v}^{\mathrm{ue}}(\mathbf{u})$ *be a UE link flow pattern associated with a pricing scheme* $\mathbf{u}$, *with separable cost functions drawn from a given class* $\mathcal{C}$, *and let* $\mathbf{v}^{\mathrm{so}}$ *be an SO link flow solution, then*

$$T\left(\mathbf{v}^{\mathrm{ue}}(\mathbf{u})\right) \le \frac{1+\gamma_2(\mathcal{C},\mathbf{u})}{1-\gamma_1(\mathcal{C},\mathbf{u})} T\left(\mathbf{v}^{\mathrm{so}}\right) \tag{11.113}$$

11.5.3 Bound with Polynomial Cost Functions

Consider the convex polynomial cost function (11.18), $t_a(v_a) = t_a^0 + \alpha_a (v_a)^p$, $a \in A$, $t_a^0 \ge 0$, $\alpha_a \ge 0$ and $p \ge 1$. Let u_a be the toll charge on link $a \in A$. For the case where $0 \le u_a \le v_a^{\mathrm{ue}} t_a'\left(v_a^{\mathrm{ue}}\right)$, $a \in A_1$, eqn. (11.103) with this specific cost function becomes

$$t_a^0 + \alpha_a (v_a)^p + v_a \alpha_a p (v_a)^{p-1} = t_a^0 + \alpha_a \left(v_a^{\mathrm{ue}}\right)^p + u_a \tag{11.114}$$

and

$$v_a = \left(\frac{\alpha_a \left(v_a^{\mathrm{ue}}\right)^p + u_a}{\alpha_a (1+p)} \right)^{\frac{1}{p}} \tag{11.115}$$

Let

$$u_a = \kappa_a \left[v_a^{\mathrm{ue}} t_a'\left(v_a^{\mathrm{ue}}\right) \right] = \kappa_a \alpha_a p \left(v_a^{\mathrm{ue}}\right)^p \tag{11.116}$$

where the term $v_a^{\mathrm{ue}} t_a'\left(v_a^{\mathrm{ue}}\right)$ is the link congestion externality at UE link flow v_a^{ue} and κ_a is a link-specific proportionality constant. With eqn. (11.116), eqn. (11.115) is simplified to

$$v_a = \left(\frac{(1+\kappa_a p)}{(1+p)} \right)^{\frac{1}{p}} v_a^{\mathrm{ue}} \tag{11.117}$$

where $0 \le \kappa_a \le 1$, $a \in A_1$. Thus, it follows from (11.100) that

$$\gamma_a\left(t_a, v_a^{\text{ue}}, u_a\right) = \frac{\left(t_a\left(v_a^{\text{ue}}\right) - t_a\left(v_a\right)\right)v_a + \left(v_a - v_a^{\text{ue}}\right)u_a}{t_a\left(v_a^{\text{ue}}\right)v_a^{\text{ue}}}$$

$$= \frac{\left(1 - \frac{(1+\kappa_a p)}{(1+p)}\right)\alpha_a\left(v_a^{\text{ue}}\right)^p\left(\left(\frac{(1+\kappa_a p)}{(1+p)}\right)^{\frac{1}{p}} v_a^{\text{ue}}\right) + \left(\left(\frac{(1+\kappa_a p)}{(1+p)}\right)^{\frac{1}{p}} - 1\right)v_a^{\text{ue}}\kappa_a\alpha_a p\left(v_a^{\text{ue}}\right)^p}{v_a^{\text{ue}}\left(t_a^0 + \alpha_a\left(v_a^{\text{ue}}\right)^p\right)}$$

$$= \frac{\frac{(1+\kappa_a p)p}{1+p}\left(\frac{(1+\kappa_a p)}{(1+p)}\right)^{\frac{1}{p}} - \kappa_a p}{t_a^0 + \alpha_a\left(v_a^{\text{ue}}\right)^p}\alpha_a\left(v_a^{\text{ue}}\right)^p$$

and

$$\gamma_1(C, \mathbf{u}) = \max_{t_a \in C,\, a \in A_1} \gamma_a\left(t_a, v_a^{\text{ue}}, u_a\right)$$

$$= \max_{t_a \in C,\, a \in A_1} \frac{\frac{(1+\kappa_a p)p}{1+p}\left(\frac{(1+\kappa_a p)}{(1+p)}\right)^{\frac{1}{p}} - \kappa_a p}{t_a^0 + \alpha_a\left(v_a^{\text{ue}}\right)^p}\alpha_a\left(v_a^{\text{ue}}\right)^p$$

$$\leq \max_{a \in A_1} \frac{(1+\kappa_a p)p}{1+p}\left(\frac{(1+\kappa_a p)}{(1+p)}\right)^{\frac{1}{p}} - \kappa_a p \tag{11.118}$$

because $t_a^0 \geq 0$ for all $a \in A$.

Next we consider the case where $u_a \geq v_a^{\text{ue}} t_a'\left(v_a^{\text{ue}}\right)$ or $\kappa_a \geq 1$, $a \in A_2$. By definition,

$$\gamma_a\left(t_a, v_a^{\text{ue}}, u_a\right) = \max_{v_a \geq 0} \frac{\alpha_a\left(\left(v_a^{\text{ue}}\right)^p - \left(v_a\right)^p\right)v_a + \left(v_a - v_a^{\text{ue}}\right)u_a}{\left(t_a^0 + \alpha_a\left(v_a\right)^p\right)v_a}$$

$$\leq \max_{v_a \geq 0} \frac{\alpha_a\left(\left(v_a^{\text{ue}}\right)^p - \left(v_a\right)^p\right)v_a + \left(v_a - v_a^{\text{ue}}\right)u_a}{\left(\alpha_a\left(v_a\right)^p\right)v_a} \tag{11.119}$$

where the inequality holds for positive value of numerator and $t_a^0 \geq 0$ for all $a \in A$. This is true because, for the maximization of $\gamma_a\left(t_a, v_a^{\text{ue}}, u_a\right)$ and the bounding inequality (11.99), we only need to consider v_a, for which $\alpha_a\left(\left(v_a^{\text{ue}}\right)^p - \left(v_a\right)^p\right)v_a + \left(v_a - v_a^{\text{ue}}\right)u_a > 0$. This means that the maximum value of $\gamma_a\left(t_a, v_a^{\text{ue}}, u_a\right)$ can be obtained by taking $t_a^0 = 0$ for the specific polynomial cost function.

Now we are at the stage to find the optimal v_a^* for the maximization problem (11.119). Define

$$F(v_a)=\frac{\alpha_a\left(\left(v_a^{\text{ue}}\right)^p-\left(v_a\right)^p\right)v_a+\left(v_a-v_a^{\text{ue}}\right)u_a}{\left(\alpha_a\left(v_a\right)^p\right)v_a} \tag{11.120}$$

Let $\mathrm{d}F(v_a)/\mathrm{d}v_a=0,$ we have

$$\frac{\alpha_a\left(v_a^{\text{ue}}\right)^p+\kappa_a\alpha_a p\left(v_a^{\text{ue}}\right)^p}{\kappa_a\alpha_a p\left(v_a^{\text{ue}}\right)^{p+1}}=\frac{\alpha_a\left(v_a\right)^p+\alpha_a p\left(v_a\right)^p}{\alpha_a p\left(v_a\right)^{p+1}} \tag{11.121}$$

Where κ_a is defined in (11.116). Solving the equation yields

$$v_a^*=\left(\frac{1+p}{p}\right)\left(\frac{\kappa_a p}{1+\kappa_a p}\right)v_a^{\text{ue}}$$

Then from eqn. (11.119), we have

$$\gamma_a\left(t_a,v_a^{\text{ue}},u_a\right)\le\kappa_a\left(\frac{v_a^{\text{ue}}}{v_a^*}\right)^{p+1}-1=\kappa_a\left[\left(\frac{p}{1+p}\right)\left(\frac{1+\kappa_a p}{\kappa_a p}\right)\right]^{p+1}-1$$

and

$$\gamma_2(C,\mathbf{u})=\max_{t_a\in C,\,a\in A_2}\gamma_a\left(t_a,v_a^{\text{ue}},u_a\right)=\max_{a\in A_2}\kappa_a\left[\left(\frac{p}{1+p}\right)\left(\frac{1+\kappa_a p}{\kappa_a p}\right)\right]^{p+1}-1 \tag{11.122}$$

If we further assume that the second-best pricing scheme, $\mathbf{u}$, is chosen such that $\kappa_a\equiv\kappa$ for all $a\in A,$ then finally we arrive at

$$\gamma(C,\mathbf{u})=\begin{cases}\dfrac{(1+\kappa p)p}{1+p}\left(\dfrac{(1+\kappa p)}{(1+p)}\right)^{\frac{1}{p}}-\kappa p, & \text{if } 0\le\kappa\le1\\[2ex] \kappa\left[\left(\dfrac{p}{1+p}\right)\left(\dfrac{1+\kappa p}{\kappa p}\right)\right]^{p+1}-1, & \text{if } \kappa\ge1\end{cases} \tag{11.123}$$

Clearly, if $\kappa=0$ $(\mathbf{u}=0)$, we have $\gamma(C,\mathbf{u}=0)=p(1+p)^{-(p+1)/p}$. As expected, we have the same result given in (11.20), in the absence of pricing. In contrast, if $\kappa_a\equiv\kappa\equiv1$ for all $a\in A$ or in the case of a perfect marginal-cost pricing scheme, we obtain $\gamma(C,\mathbf{u})=0$. This result simply implies that "there is no efficiency loss" or "the UE flow pattern is also system-optimal" under the marginal-cost pricing scheme.

Example 11.5 Consider a traffic network with the polynomial link cost function, $t_a(v_a)=t_a^0+\alpha_a(v_a)^p,\ a\in A.$ Let $\mathbf{v}^{\text{ue}}(\mathbf{u})$ be a UE link flow pattern on the network associated with a pricing scheme $\mathbf{u}$. If we assume that $u_a = \kappa\left[\alpha_a v_a^{\text{ue}} t_a\left(v_a^{\text{ue}}\right)\right] = \kappa\alpha_a p\left(v_a^{\text{ue}}\right)^p$ for each link $a \in A$, then, by definition, (11.94) and (11.95), the *relative efficiency loss* in relation to the system optimum, associated with a pricing scheme, $\mathbf{u}$, is given by

$$\varphi_{\text{fx}}^{\text{ue}}(\mathbf{u}) = \begin{cases} \left(1-\gamma(C,\mathbf{u})\right)^{-1} - 1, & \text{if } 0 \le \kappa \le 1 \\ \gamma(C,\mathbf{u}), & \text{if } \kappa \ge 1 \end{cases} \tag{11.124}$$

where $\gamma(C,\mathbf{u})$ is given by (11.123).

Figure 11.9 plots the relationships between parameter κ in the interval $0 \le \kappa \le 3.0$ and the maximum efficiency loss $\varphi_{\text{fx}}^{\text{ue}}(\mathbf{u})$ for $p=1$ (linear), $p=2$ (quadratic), $p=3$ (cubic) and $p=4$ (BPR functions of degree 4). In this figure, the values of efficiency loss at $u=0$ corresponds to the early bounding results without pricing (refer to Figure 11.4 with $\eta = 0$).

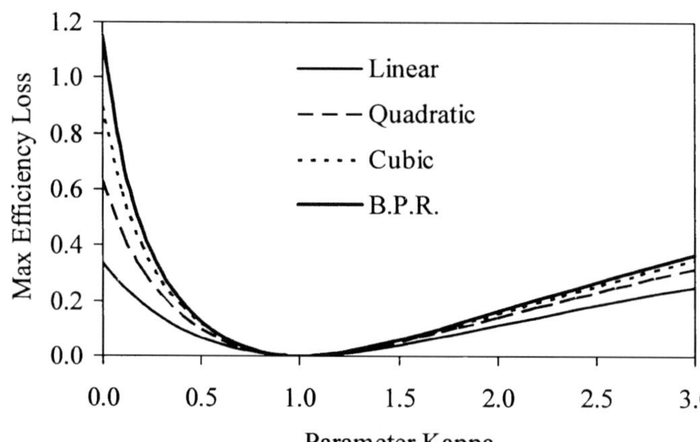

Figure 11.9 The maximum inefficiency loss associated with a second-best pricing scheme for polynomial cost functions

11.5.4 Bound for Traffic Equilibria with Elastic Demands

Now we move on to deal with the bounds of efficiency loss of a pricing scheme for the case with elastic demand. We begin our analysis with the second-best toll charge being uniformly less (or greater) than the congestion externality for all network links, and then present our results for the general mixed situation. The following theorem follows immediately.

Theorem 11.10 *Let* $\mathbf{v}^{\text{ue}}(\mathbf{u})$ *be an elastic-demand UE link flow pattern associated with a pricing scheme* $\mathbf{u}$, *with separable cost functions drawn from a given class* C, *and let* $\mathbf{v}^{\text{so}}$

be an SO link flow solution, then

$$\rho_{\text{ec}}^{\text{ue}}(\mathbf{u}) \le \begin{cases} 1+(\omega(\mathbf{u})-1)\gamma(C,\mathbf{u}) & \text{if } 0 \le u_a \le v_a^{\text{ue}} t_a'(v_a^{\text{ue}}) \text{ for all } a \in A \\ \dfrac{1+\omega(\mathbf{u})\gamma(C,\mathbf{u})}{1+\gamma(C,\mathbf{u})} & \text{if } u_a \ge v_a^{\text{ue}} t_a'(v_a^{\text{ue}}) \text{ for all } a \in A \end{cases} \tag{11.125}$$

where

$$\omega(\mathbf{u}) = \begin{cases} \omega_1(\mathbf{u}) = \dfrac{U^{\text{ue}}(\mathbf{u})}{S^{\text{ue}}(\mathbf{u})} & \text{if } 0 \le u_a \le v_a^{\text{ue}} t_a'(v_a^{\text{ue}}) \text{ for all } a \in A \\ \omega_2(\mathbf{u}) = \dfrac{U^{\text{so}}}{S^{\text{ue}}(\mathbf{u})} & \text{if } u_a \ge v_a^{\text{ue}} t_a'(v_a^{\text{ue}}) \text{ for all } a \in A \end{cases} \tag{11.126}$$

$U^{\text{ue}}(\mathbf{u}) = U(\mathbf{d}^{\text{ue}}(\mathbf{u}))$ *and* $S^{\text{ue}}(\mathbf{u}) = S(\mathbf{v}^{\text{ue}}(\mathbf{u}), \mathbf{d}^{\text{ue}}(\mathbf{u}))$ *are the user benefit and social welfare at user equilibrium associated with pricing scheme* $\mathbf{u}$, *and* $U^{\text{so}} = U(\mathbf{d}^{\text{so}})$ *is the user benefit at the social optimum.*

Proof. If $0 \le u_a \le v_a^{\text{ue}} t_a'(v_a^{\text{ue}})$ for all $a \in A$, we have the definition (11.100), then eqn. (11.108) holds, and clearly Lemma 11.3 and Theorem 11.5 still apply in this case. Thus we obtain the first case result in (11.125). If, however, $u_a \ge v_a^{\text{ue}} t_a'(v_a^{\text{ue}})$ for all $a \in A$, we have to establish the bounding result according to definition (11.101). In this case, the counterpart of eqn. (11.41) in the proof of Theorem 11.5 becomes

$$S(\mathbf{v}^{\text{ue}}(\mathbf{u}), \mathbf{d}^{\text{ue}}(\mathbf{u})) - S(\mathbf{v}, \mathbf{d}) + \gamma(C,\mathbf{u}) T(\mathbf{v}) \ge 0 \tag{11.127}$$

Using the definition (11.96) and let $(\mathbf{v}, \mathbf{d}) = (\mathbf{v}^{\text{so}}, \mathbf{d}^{\text{so}})$ in (11.127), we have

$$\rho_{\text{ec}}^{\text{ue}}(\mathbf{u}) \le 1 + \gamma(C,\mathbf{u}) \frac{T(\mathbf{v}^{\text{so}})}{S(\mathbf{v}^{\text{ue}}(\mathbf{u}), \mathbf{d}^{\text{ue}}(\mathbf{u}))} = 1 + \gamma(C,\mathbf{u}) \frac{U(\mathbf{d}^{\text{so}}) - S(\mathbf{v}^{\text{so}}, \mathbf{d}^{\text{so}})}{S(\mathbf{v}^{\text{ue}}(\mathbf{u}), \mathbf{d}^{\text{ue}}(\mathbf{u}))}$$

$$= 1 + \gamma(C,\mathbf{u}) \left(-\rho_{\text{ec}}^{\text{ue}}(\mathbf{u}) + \frac{U(\mathbf{d}^{\text{so}})}{S(\mathbf{v}^{\text{ue}}(\mathbf{u}), \mathbf{d}^{\text{ue}}(\mathbf{u}))} \right)$$

$$= 1 + \gamma(C,\mathbf{u}) \left(-\rho_{\text{ec}}^{\text{ue}}(\mathbf{u}) + \omega_2(\mathbf{u}) \right)$$

This leads to the second-case result given in the lower part of eqn. (11.125), with the definition of $\omega_2(\mathbf{u})$ in the lower part of eqn. (11.126). ■

Next, we eliminate the uniformity magnitude assumption of link toll charges $\mathbf{u}$ to include both possibilities of $0 \le u_a \le v_a^{\text{ue}} t_a'(v_a^{\text{ue}})$ and $u_a \ge v_a^{\text{ue}} t_a'(v_a^{\text{ue}})$ in a single bound. Using the same definitions of A_1, A_2, $\gamma_1(C,\mathbf{u})$ and $\gamma_2(C,\mathbf{u})$ as in the fixed demand case, we now have the following Theorem.

Theorem 11.11 *Let* $\mathbf{v}^{ue}(\mathbf{u})$ *be an elastic-demand UE link flow pattern associated with a pricing scheme* $\mathbf{u}$, *with separable cost functions drawn from a given class* $\mathcal{C}$, *and let* $\mathbf{v}^{so}$ *be an SO link flow solution, then*

$$\rho_{ec}^{ue}(\mathbf{u}) \le \frac{1-\gamma_1(\mathcal{C},\mathbf{u})}{1+\gamma_2(\mathcal{C},\mathbf{u})} + \frac{\gamma_1(\mathcal{C},\mathbf{u})\omega_1(\mathbf{u}) + \gamma_2(\mathcal{C},\mathbf{u})\omega_2(\mathbf{u})}{1+\gamma_2(\mathcal{C},\mathbf{u})} \tag{11.128}$$

where

$$\omega_1(\mathbf{u}) = \frac{U^{ue}(\mathbf{u})}{S^{ue}(\mathbf{u})}, \quad \omega_2(\mathbf{u}) = \frac{U^{so}}{S^{ue}(\mathbf{u})} \tag{11.129}$$

$U^{ue}(\mathbf{u}) = U(\mathbf{d}^{ue}(\mathbf{u}))$ *and* $S^{ue}(\mathbf{u}) = S(\mathbf{v}^{ue}(\mathbf{u}), \mathbf{d}^{ue}(\mathbf{u}))$ *are the user benefit and social welfare at user equilibrium associated with pricing scheme* $\mathbf{u}$, *and* $U^{so} = U(\mathbf{d}^{so})$ *is the user benefit at the social optimum.*

Proof. Like the proof of Theorem 11.5, the counterpart of eqn. (11.41) becomes

$$S(\mathbf{v}^{ue}(\mathbf{u}), \mathbf{d}^{ue}(\mathbf{u})) - S(\mathbf{v},\mathbf{d}) + \gamma_1(\mathcal{C},\mathbf{u})T(\mathbf{v}^{ue}(\mathbf{u})) + \gamma_2(\mathcal{C},\mathbf{u})T(\mathbf{v}) \ge 0 \tag{11.130}$$

Substituting $T(\mathbf{v}^{ue}(\mathbf{u})) = -S(\mathbf{v}^{ue}(\mathbf{u}), \mathbf{d}^{ue}(\mathbf{u})) + U(\mathbf{d}^{ue}(\mathbf{u}))$ and $T(\mathbf{v}) = -S(\mathbf{v},\mathbf{d}) + U(\mathbf{d})$ into (11.130) yields

$$\begin{aligned}(1-\gamma_1(\mathcal{C},\mathbf{u}))S(\mathbf{v}^{ue}(\mathbf{u}), \mathbf{d}^{ue}(\mathbf{u})) - (1+\gamma_2(\mathcal{C},\mathbf{u}))S(\mathbf{v},\mathbf{d}) \\ + (\gamma_1(\mathcal{C},\mathbf{u})U(\mathbf{d}^{ue}(\mathbf{u})) + \gamma_2(\mathcal{C},\mathbf{u})U(\mathbf{d})) \ge 0\end{aligned} \tag{11.131}$$

Using the definition (11.96) and let $(\mathbf{v},\mathbf{d}) = (\mathbf{v}^{so}, \mathbf{d}^{so})$ in (11.131), we have

$$\rho_{ec}^{ue}(\mathbf{u}) \le \frac{1-\gamma_1(\mathcal{C},\mathbf{u})}{1+\gamma_2(\mathcal{C},\mathbf{u})} + \frac{\gamma_1(\mathcal{C},\mathbf{u})\dfrac{U^{ue}(\mathbf{u})}{S^{ue}(\mathbf{u})} + \gamma_2(\mathcal{C},\mathbf{u})\dfrac{U^{so}}{S^{ue}(\mathbf{u})}}{1+\gamma_2(\mathcal{C},\mathbf{u})}$$

By the definitions of $\omega_1(\mathbf{u})$ and $\omega_2(\mathbf{u})$, we obtain eqn. (11.128). ■

Theorem 11.11 is particularly useful to establish the inefficiency bound or efficiency loss for practical second-best pricing schemes with elastic demands. Once $\rho_{ec}^{ue}(\mathbf{u})$ is determined, we can calculate the efficiency loss, $\varphi_{ec}^{ue}(\mathbf{u})$, of the second-best pricing scheme straightforwardly using the definition (11.97). Nevertheless, for such calculations, parameter $\omega(\mathbf{u})$, defined in eqn. (11.126) and (11.129), have to be ascertained. If the demand function is known, it is straightforward to calculate $\omega(\mathbf{u})$, based on the known demand function and the relevant SO and UE solutions with pricing. If the demand function is unknown, which is the case in practice as discussed in Chapter 10, the value of $\omega(\mathbf{u})$ is limited and its approximate value should suffice to serve the bounding purpose. This is due to the fact that

$$1+(\omega(\mathbf{u})-1)\gamma(C,\mathbf{u})\to 1.0;\quad \frac{1+\omega(\mathbf{u})\gamma(C,\mathbf{u})}{1+\gamma(C,\mathbf{u})}\to 1.0$$

as $\gamma(C,\mathbf{u})\to 0$ for any limited value of $\omega(\mathbf{u})$. Moreover,

$$\frac{1-\gamma_1(C,\mathbf{u})}{1+\gamma_2(C,\mathbf{u})}+\frac{\gamma_1(C,\mathbf{u})\omega_1(\mathbf{u})+\gamma_2(C,\mathbf{u})\omega_2(\mathbf{u})}{1+\gamma_2(C,\mathbf{u})}\to 1.0$$

as $\gamma_1(C,\mathbf{u})\to 0$ and $\gamma_2(C,\mathbf{u})\to 0$ for any limited values of $\omega_1(\mathbf{u})$ and $\omega_2(\mathbf{u})$. To put it differently, with an approximate value of $\omega(\mathbf{u})$, the convergence of a sequential experimental pricing scheme or the nearness of a given current second-best pricing scheme to the first-best one in its neighborhood, can still be well understood. The following lemma is useful for gauging a practical value of ω.

Lemma 11.6 *If the demand function* $d=D(\mu)$, *where* μ *is the generalized travel cost, inclusive of toll charge, if any, is monotonically decreasing and convex, then*

$$\omega=\frac{U}{S}\le 1-2E_d^{\mu} \tag{11.132}$$

where U *and* S *denotes the user benefit and social welfare for any realized* (μ,d) *and* E_d^{μ} *is the price elasticity of demand at* (μ,d), *defined by*

$$E_d^{\mu}=\frac{\mathrm{d}D(\mu)}{\mathrm{d}\mu}\frac{\mu}{d}=D'(\mu)\frac{\mu}{d}\quad(\le 0) \tag{11.133}$$

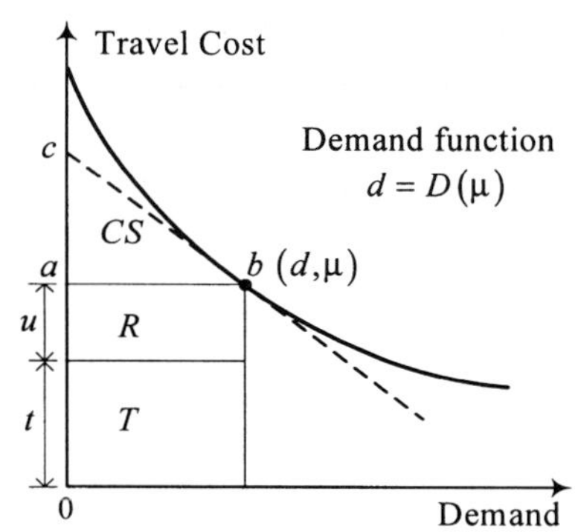

Figure 11.10 Geometric illustration of the proof of Lemma 11.6

Proof. Consider Figure 11.10, where $T=td$ denotes the total travel time cost with t being the travel time, $R=ud$ denotes the toll revenue with u being the toll charge, and CS denotes the consumer surplus (or net user benefit) given by the area under the demand curve and above the line segment $\overline{ab}$.

By definition

$$\omega = \frac{U}{S} = \frac{U}{U-T} = \frac{CS+R+T}{CS+R} = 1 + \frac{T}{CS+R} \le 1 + \frac{T}{CS}$$

since $R \ge 0$. Because the demand function, $d = D(\mu)$, is monotonically decreasing and convex, clearly we have $CS \ge \Delta_{abc}$, where Δ_{abc} is the area of the triangle $\overline{abc}$ with $\overline{bc}$ being the tangent line of the demand curve at point (d,μ). One can easily find that

$$\Delta_{abc} = -\frac{1}{2}\frac{d^2}{D'(\mu)} \quad \text{where } D'(\mu) < 0$$

Hence,

$$1 < \omega \le 1 + \frac{T}{CS} \le 1 + td\left(-\frac{1}{2}\frac{d^2}{D'(\mu)}\right)^{-1} = 1 - 2\left(\frac{t}{t+u}\right)E_d^\mu \le 1 - 2E_d^\mu$$

since $\mu = t + u \ge t$ with $u \ge 0$. Thus, eqn. (11.132) is true. ■

Lemma 11.6 shows that $\omega(\mathbf{u}) = U^{\text{ue}}(\mathbf{u})/S^{\text{ue}}(\mathbf{u}) > 1$ is upper-bounded by $(1 - 2E_d^\mu)$ for any demand function and any pricing scheme $\mathbf{u}$. The equality of the bound holds for linear demand functions. Since users have to pay their full social cost (private cost plus congestion externality) at the system optimum, it is *generally* true that $U^{\text{so}} \le U^{\text{ue}}(0)$ at $\mathbf{u} = 0$ (user benefit at un-tolled user equilibrium). This is equivalent to the assumption that the realized user demand is reduced at system optimum after introducing a marginal-cost pricing scheme. One may also reasonably assume that the pricing scheme of interest does improve the system performance in comparison with the non-tolling traffic equilibrium, namely $S^{\text{ue}}(\mathbf{u}) \ge S^{\text{ue}}(0)$. These observations together imply that

$$\omega(\mathbf{u}) = \frac{U^{\text{so}}}{S^{\text{ue}}(\mathbf{u})} \le \frac{U^{\text{ue}}(0)}{S^{\text{ue}}(0)} \le 1 - 2E_d^\mu(\mathbf{u} = 0)$$

For the case of multiple OD pairs, because the user benefit and social welfare are OD pair additive, we have immediately that

$$\omega = \frac{\sum_{w\in W} U_w}{\sum_{w\in W} S_w} \le \frac{\sum_{w\in W}\left(1 - 2E_{d_w}^{\mu_w}\right)S_w}{\sum_{w\in W} S_w} \le \frac{\sum_{w\in W} S_w}{\sum_{w\in W} S_w}\max_{w\in W}\left(1 - 2E_{d_w}^{\mu_w}\right) = \max_{w\in W}\left(1 - 2E_{d_w}^{\mu_w}\right)$$

If the realized demand at equilibrium is in the inelastic range, then $-1 \le E_d^\mu < 0$ and hence $1 < \omega \le 3$. The practical value of elasticity is approximately in the range between -0.3 and -0.5 (see, Oum et al., 1992, and Goodwin, 1992, for surveys of travel demand elasticity), and one may thus choose a practical value of ω within the range of $1.0 < \omega \le 2.0$.

Example 11.6 Consider again Example 11.3, with negative exponential demand function $d = d_0 \exp\left[-\alpha(\mu/\mu_0 - 1)\right]$. From eqn. (11.43), we know

$$\omega = 1 + \alpha - \ln\left(\frac{d}{d_0}\right)$$

Applying the formula of elasticity to the demand function yields

$$E_d^{\mu} = \frac{\mathrm{d}D(\mu)}{\mathrm{d}\mu}\frac{\mu}{d} = d\left(-\frac{\alpha}{\mu_0}\right)\frac{\mu}{d} = -\alpha\frac{\mu}{\mu_0} = \ln\left(\frac{d}{d_0}\right) - \alpha$$

Therefore, for the negative exponential demand function, we have $\omega = 1 - E_d^{\mu}$.

11.5.5 Alternative Approach for Bounding Efficiency Loss

In the previous analysis, we defined $\gamma_a\left(t_a, v_a^{\text{ue}}, u_a\right)$ differently for the two cases where $0 \le u_a \le v_a^{\text{ue}} t_a'\left(v_a^{\text{ue}}\right)$ and $u_a \ge v_a^{\text{ue}} t_a'\left(v_a^{\text{ue}}\right)$, and then reached a bound of the efficiency loss by introducing the following relaxation in (11.111):

$$\sum_{a \in A_1} t_a\left(v_a^{\text{ue}}\right)v_a^{\text{ue}} \le T\left(\mathbf{v}^{\text{ue}}\right) = \sum_{a \in A} t_a\left(v_a^{\text{ue}}\right)v_a^{\text{ue}}; \quad \sum_{a \in A_2} t_a\left(v_a\right)v_a \le T(\mathbf{v}) = \sum_{a \in A} t_a\left(v_a\right)v_a$$

This relaxation, however, may potentially make the inefficiency bound loose. To avoid this relaxation, we now propose an alternative approach that is subject to further analysis.

Redefine a unified $\gamma_a\left(t_a, v_a^{\text{ue}}, u_a\right)$ for all links, irrespective of their levels of toll charge:

$$\gamma_a\left(t_a, v_a^{\text{ue}}, u_a\right) = \max_{v_a \ge 0} \frac{\left(t_a\left(v_a^{\text{ue}}\right) - t_a\left(v_a\right)\right)v_a + \left(v_a - v_a^{\text{ue}}\right)u_a}{t_a\left(v_a^{\text{ue}}\right)v_a^{\text{ue}} + t_a\left(v_a\right)v_a} \tag{11.134}$$

and

$$\gamma(C, \mathbf{u}) = \max_{t_a \in C,\, a \in A} \gamma_a\left(t_a, v_a^{\text{ue}}, u_a\right) \tag{11.135}$$

Then we do not need to do further relaxation as previously in (11.111). Instead, in the same spirit, we have the following straightforward results, with reference to Theorem 11.9 and Theorem 11.11.

i) The bound for traffic equilibria with fixed demand:

$$\rho_{\text{fx}}^{\text{ue}}(\mathbf{u}) \le \frac{1 + \gamma(C, \mathbf{u})}{1 - \gamma(C, \mathbf{u})} \tag{11.136}$$

ii) The bound for traffic equilibria with elastic demand

$$\rho_{\text{ec}}^{\text{ue}}(\mathbf{u}) \le \frac{1 - \gamma(C, \mathbf{u})}{1 + \gamma(C, \mathbf{u})} + \frac{\gamma(C, \mathbf{u})\left(\omega_1(\mathbf{u}) + \omega_2(\mathbf{u})\right)}{1 + \gamma(C, \mathbf{u})} \tag{11.137}$$

Here, to find the value of $\gamma(\mathcal{C},\mathbf{u})$, the key problem is still to determine the maximum of the following function:

$$F(v_a)=\frac{\left(t_a\left(v_a^{\mathrm{ue}}\right)-t_a\left(v_a\right)\right)v_a+\left(v_a-v_a^{\mathrm{ue}}\right)u_a}{t_a\left(v_a^{\mathrm{ue}}\right)v_a^{\mathrm{ue}}+t_a\left(v_a\right)v_a} \tag{11.138}$$

Any analytical solution for $\max F(v_a)$ is difficult, if not impossible, even for the specific polynomial cost functions examined in the previous section.

11.5.6 Determination of the Inefficiency Bound for Actual Pricing Schemes

As investigated in Chapter 10, an approximate first-best or second-best pricing scheme can be developed, with limited information (e.g., with unknown demand functions), through a sequential experimental pricing scheme. The central idea of the trial-and-error pricing scheme is to adjust the link toll charges by observing and comparing the users' responses (observed aggregate link flows) and the intended or targeted flow levels adopted for estimation of the toll charges. An exact first-best or marginal-cost pricing scheme is ensured if the observed and targeted link flows match each other. Nevertheless, because the actual number of pricing trials could be very limited, one could end up with an inexact marginal-cost, or a second-best, pricing scheme. In this case, it is vital to determine the bound of the inefficiency or welfare loss of the current pricing scheme, thereby assessing whether or not further pricing experiments are needed.

The desirable inefficiency bound can be easily established using the bounding method developed in previous sections, with no more than the information needed for the pricing experiments. What are needed are the individual link cost functions, the current link toll charges and the easily available link flows observed after implementing the pricing scheme. Let $\hat{\mathbf{u}}=\left(\hat{u}_a, a\in A\right)^{\mathrm{T}}$ be the current estimated toll charge, and $\hat{\mathbf{v}}(\hat{\mathbf{u}})$ be the observed link flow after implementing $\hat{\mathbf{u}}$. Because the observed link flow pattern is in user equilibrium, then from eqn. (11.116), for each link $a\in A$, one can calculate

$$\hat{\kappa}_a=\frac{\hat{u}_a}{\hat{v}_a t_a'\left(\hat{v}_a\right)},\quad a\in A$$

In the case of the BPR link cost function, $t_a(v_a)=t_a^0\left(1+0.15\left(v_a/C_a\right)^4\right)$, where t_a^0 and C_a are respectively the link free-flow travel time and link capacity, we have

$$\hat{\kappa}_a=\frac{\hat{u}_a}{0.6t_a^0}\left(\frac{C_a}{\hat{v}_a}\right)^4,\quad a\in A \tag{11.139}$$

From (11.118) with $p=4$, $0\le\hat{\kappa}_a\le 1$, $a\in A_1$, we obtain

$$\gamma_1(\text{BPR},\hat{\mathbf{u}}) \le \frac{(1+\hat{\kappa}_a p)p}{1+p}\left(\frac{(1+\hat{\kappa}_a p)}{(1+p)}\right)^{\frac{1}{p}} - \hat{\kappa}_a p$$

$$= \frac{(1+4\hat{\kappa}_a)4}{1+4}\left(\frac{(1+4\hat{\kappa}_a)}{(1+4)}\right)^{\frac{1}{4}} - 4\hat{\kappa}_a \tag{11.140}$$

$$= 4\left(\frac{1+4\hat{\kappa}_a}{5}\right)^{\frac{5}{4}} - 4\hat{\kappa}_a$$

From (11.122) with $p=4$, $\hat{\kappa}_a \ge 1$, $a \in A_2$, we obtain

$$\gamma_2(\text{BPR},\hat{\mathbf{u}}) \le \kappa_a\left[\left(\frac{p}{1+p}\right)\left(\frac{1+\kappa_a p}{\kappa_a p}\right)\right]^{p+1} - 1$$

$$= \kappa_a\left[\left(\frac{4}{1+4}\right)\left(\frac{1+4\kappa_a}{4\kappa_a}\right)\right]^{4+1} - 1 \tag{11.141}$$

$$= \kappa_a\left[\frac{4}{5}\left(\frac{1+4\kappa_a}{4\kappa_a}\right)\right]^{5} - 1$$

Note that, if the demand is fixed, we obtain the maximum inefficiency given by (11.112), with γ_1 and γ_2 provided by (11.140) and (11.141) and $\hat{\kappa}_a$ as in (11.139), based on the observed link flows. Then the estimated bound of the relative efficiency loss is followed by eqn. (11.95). If the demand is elastic, we have to use eqn. (11.128) to determine the maximum inefficiency with the above γ_1 and γ_2. The estimated bound of the relative efficiency loss is then readily calculated by eqn. (11.97).

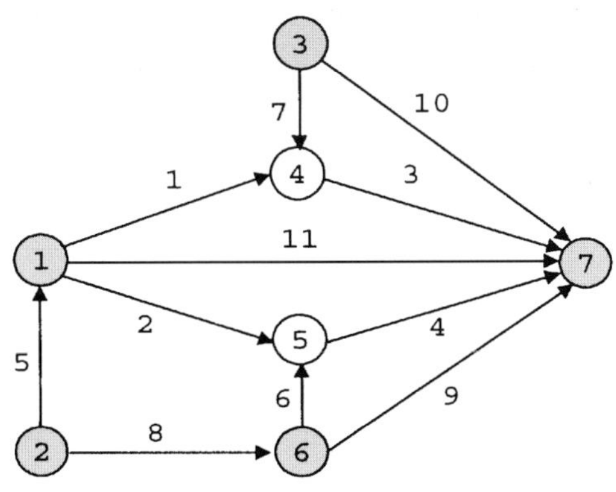

Figure 11.11 The network used for Example 10.7

Example 10.7 We now illustrate application of the inefficiency bounding methods for the trial-and-error pricing scheme with unknown demand functions developed in Chapter 10. Consider again Example 10.1 used in Chapter 10. For convenience, here the network in Figure 10.7, link cost and OD demand functions are presented again, but the input data are available in Table 10.1 in Chapter 10.

$$D_{1\to7}(\mu_{1\to7}) = 600\exp(-0.04\mu_{1\to7}); \quad D_{2\to7}(\mu_{2\to7}) = 500\exp(-0.03\mu_{2\to7})$$

$$D_{3\to7}(\mu_{3\to7}) = 500\exp(-0.05\mu_{3\to7}); \quad D_{6\to7}(\mu_{6\to7}) = 400\exp(-0.05\mu_{6\to7})$$

$$t_a(v_a) = t_a^0\left(1+0.15\left(\frac{v_a}{C_a}\right)^4\right)$$

We consider bounding the efficiency loss for the inexact marginal-cost pricing schemes in the sequential experimental pricing process for the elastic demand case with the above demand functions. Four levels of parameter ω are chosen: $\omega = 1.5,\ 2.0,\ 2.5,\ 3.0$.

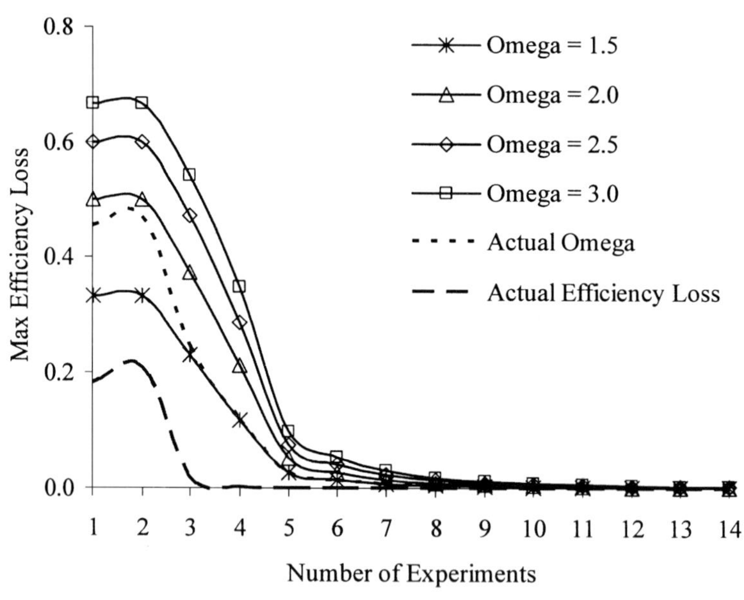

Figure 11.12 The upper bound of the relative efficiency loss in the sequential experimental pricing process with elastic demands

The bounding results are shown in Figure 11.12, together with the actual inefficiency loss. Note that the actual inefficiency loss and the bound with the actual value of ω becomes known only if the demand functions are known and they are presented in the figure for comparative analysis. With appropriate a priori values of ω, one can see the bounds established with unknown demand functions are effective and indeed useful. It tells us whether a sufficiently good approximate marginal-cost pricing scheme is already found, without resorting to demand functions. It is worthwhile to note that the bound with the actual ω is located in between the bounds for $\omega = 1.5$ and $\omega = 2.0$. This confirms our early observation that the practical ω value is with the range of $1.0 \leq \omega \leq 2.0$.

11.6 Summary

In this chapter we introduced the notion of the *price of anarchy* that was used recently to quantify the inefficiency between user and system optimal solutions for non-atomic congestion games. The theory of price of anarchy has been well developed so far for the traffic equilibria problem with fixed demand, however, bounding the inefficiency for the elastic-demand traffic equilibrium problem is still in its infancy. The concept of price of anarchy can be used to determine the maximum efficiency gain achieved by a marginal-cost pricing scheme to drive a UE flow pattern to a SO state. In the case of polynomial link cost functions, extension of the price of anarchy or cost inefficiency bound was successfully extended to the stochastic user equilibrium problem, and to the Cournot-Nash equilibria with a finite number of players, which includes the Wardropian equilibrium with an infinite number of infinitesimal players as a special case. In this chapter, we have also successfully established the maximum efficiency loss of a given second-best pricing scheme in relation to the first-best one, with either fixed or elastic demand. Like the trial-and-error pricing scheme with unknown demand function, the inefficiency bound can be established with limited information. It is applied to assess the accuracy of inexact marginal-cost pricing in the sequential experimental pricing process developed in previous chapters.

11.7 Sources and Notes

The term coined as the price of anarchy is a new concept used to quantify the inefficiency of Nash equilibrium by looking for the worst possible ratio between the total cost incurred by players in an equilibrium situation and in an outcome of minimum-possible total cost. This term was first dubbed "the price of anarchy" by Papadimitriou (2002). Roughgarden (2003) proved that the worst-case inefficiency due to selfish routing (*i.e.*, the non-toll UE) is independent of the network topology. Roughgarden and Tardos (2004) proved that the total time of a non-toll UE is at most that of the SO with doubled demand in the same network. Moreover, the total time of a non-toll UE is at most 4/3 times that of the SO when all the link travel time functions are linear. Correa et al. (2004, 2005) provided a simple geometric proof for the price of anarchy described in Section 11.2.1 for the equilibria with fixed demand, using a VI expression of UE conditions. They also showed that the addition of link capacity constraints does not change the worst ratio between the best UE and the SO. The pseudo-approximation bound for the equilibria with elastic demand is drawn from Chau and Sim (2003), who also proved that the price of anarchy result also holds for systems with symmetric non-separable link travel time functions. It is suggested that readers refer to Roughgarden (2005) for a recent comprehensive summary of the research subject. The inefficiency bound for the Cournot-Nash equilibria with polynomial cost functions and the bounding method for the stochastic user equilibrium problem are newly developed. The bounding methods for the efficiency loss or gain of the general second-best pricing problems are newly proposed by the first author, and should prove to be very important and meaningful for evaluation of actual pricing schemes. Nevertheless, the analytical results presented in this chapter are quite preliminary and are subject to further careful and rigorous analysis.

12

Dynamic Road Pricing: Single and Parallel Bottleneck Models*

12.1 Introduction

Up to now we have dealt extensively with the various theoretical and practical issues of traffic congestion and road pricing in a static context involving their space (network) dimensions. It is common that traffic congestion occurs over space but exhibits substantial time-of-day variation, and thus, it can not be overemphasized, a successful pricing scheme must take into account the time dimension of traffic congestion, together with its spatial features. From a practical prospective, electronic road pricing schemes have been proposed, tested or implemented successfully worldwide, for example, in such cities as London, Singapore and Hong Kong. It is conceivable that the current generation of road pricing technologies already offers efficient tools ready to implement variable road-use pricing for traffic management. Alongside this background are the greatest needs for the development of a variable tolling system that enables co-ordination of road tolls in both time and space.

In this and subsequent chapters we continue our analysis of road pricing by explicitly including its time dimension in simple and general spatial settings. We start with analysis and formulation of basic bottleneck models, and make an extension to the simple network of parallel routes with elastic demand. We further our study to a competitive two-mode transportation system in which an alternative mass commuting mode, such as a railway or a subway exists, in parallel to the road with a bottleneck.

12.2 Single Bottleneck Models

In the basic traffic bottleneck model, we study the commuting congestion on a highway with a single bottleneck between a residential area and a workplace, and investigate the effects of various road tolls to alleviate the queue behind the bottleneck. Since the capacity of the bottleneck is finite, each commuter is confronted with a trade-off between travel time cost

* Notation is used in this chapter independently of the previous chapters.

relating to queue length and schedule delay cost of arriving early or late at work. The travel cost experienced by a commuter will be determined by his/her departure time from home. Using the deterministic queuing theory, we can develop an endogenous departure time choice model which leads to an equilibrium of costs for all commuters.

There are two types of bottleneck models, dealing with the cases having homogeneous and heterogeneous commuters, respectively. Both of these are to rationally decide the departure times of commuters over a time horizon from a residential area based on the private travel cost minimization principle, but the latter allows commuters to differ in marginal disutility parameters of their travel times and schedule delay times, as well as their preferred work starting times. In what follows, we treat the bottleneck equilibrium problem using a deterministic queuing approach with a vertical queue. The models based on fluid or wave theory, optimal control theory, or a simulation approach can be applied to study the problem of interest, but are not considered here, because they are analytically intractable and their complexity tends to obscure the basic insights of the problem.

12.2.1 The Case with Homogeneous Commuters

Consider a simplified network with one OD pair connected by a highway. The origin may be a residential area or home; the destination is a workplace. There is a bottleneck facility such as a bridge or a tunnel on the highway; without loss generality, the bottleneck is assumed to be located at the entering point of highway and has a deterministic capacity of s commuters per unit time. The other parts of the highway have sufficient capacity so that no congestion occurs on them.

Assume that every morning there are N identical commuters who have to travel on highway by car (one person per car) from the origin to the destination. Let $r(t)$ be the departure rate of auto users from origin at time t. Queuing will develop when the arrival rate of flow at the bottleneck, i.e., the departure rate $r(t)$, exceeds its capacity s. The queue length, $q(t)$, evolves according to the following equation:

$$\frac{\mathrm{d}q(t)}{\mathrm{d}t} = r(t) - s \text{, for } q(t) > 0 \tag{12.1}$$

Then, the travel time by a commuter from origin to destination is $t_f + q(t)/s$, where $q(t)/s$ is the waiting time in the queue, constant t_f is the uncongested travel time from origin to destination (it is referred to as moving time hereinafter).

A commuter's total travel cost depends on his/her travel time, schedule delay (time-early or time-late in arriving at the destination) and road toll. For simplicity, we assume a linear travel cost function

$$C(t)=\begin{cases}\alpha\left[t_f+\dfrac{q(t)}{s}\right]+\beta\left[t^*-\left(t+t_f+\dfrac{q(t)}{s}\right)\right]+u(t), & \text{for } t\in[t_s,t_o]\\ \alpha\left[t_f+\dfrac{q(t)}{s}\right]+\gamma\left[\left(t+t_f+\dfrac{q(t)}{s}\right)-t^*\right]+u(t), & \text{for } t\in[t_o,t_e]\end{cases} \tag{12.2}$$

where α is the unit cost of travel time, β is the unit cost of schedule delay time-early, γ is the unit cost of schedule delay time-late, t^* is the official work start time (assumed to be identical to all commuters here), $u(t)$ is the road toll at time t, t_s is the departure time at which the queue begins, t_e is the departure time at which the queue ends, and t_o is the departure time at which an individual arrives at the destination on time t^*, i.e.,

$$t_o+t_f+\frac{q(t_o)}{s}=t^* \tag{12.3}$$

In accordance with empirical results, the relation $\gamma>\alpha>\beta$ must hold. In fact, $\alpha>\beta$ is the necessary condition for the existence and uniqueness of the equilibrium considered. In place of the linear function (12.2), one may adopt a nonlinear or any other more flexible form to study the bottleneck models.

In equilibrium, any commuter is unable to find a departure time to reduce his/her travel cost. In other words, $\mathrm{d}C(t)/\mathrm{d}t=0$. Hence, for the no-toll equilibrium (i.e., $u(t)=0$) we have

$$\frac{\mathrm{d}q(t)}{\mathrm{d}t}=\begin{cases}\dfrac{\beta}{\alpha-\beta}s, & \text{for } t\in[t_s,t_o]\\ \dfrac{-\gamma}{\alpha+\gamma}s, & \text{for } t\in[t_o,t_e]\end{cases} \tag{12.4}$$

and

$$r(t)=\begin{cases}\dfrac{\alpha}{\alpha-\beta}s, & \text{for } t\in[t_s,t_o]\\ \dfrac{\alpha}{\alpha+\gamma}s, & \text{for } t\in[t_o,t_e]\end{cases} \tag{12.5}$$

Integrating $\mathrm{d}q(t)/\mathrm{d}t=0$ leads to:

$$q(t)=\begin{cases}\dfrac{\beta}{\alpha-\beta}(t-t_s)s, & \text{for } t\in[t_s,t_o]\\ -\dfrac{\gamma}{\alpha+\gamma}(t-t_o)s+\dfrac{\beta}{\alpha-\beta}(t_o-t_s)s, & \text{for } t\in[t_o,t_e]\end{cases} \tag{12.6}$$

The first and last persons face no queue, and have the same travel cost. Note that the exiting rate from the bottleneck during $[t_s,t_e]$ is s, hence we have

$$\alpha t_f + \beta\left[t^* - (t_s + t_f)\right] = \alpha t_f + \gamma\left[(t_e + t_f) - t^*\right] \quad (12.7)$$

$$N = s(t_e - t_s) \quad (12.8)$$

Combining these two equations and the definition of t_o in (12.3), we can determine the three unknowns related to time, i.e.,

$$t_s = t^* - \frac{\delta}{\beta} \times \frac{N}{s} - t_f;\ t_e = t^* + \frac{\delta}{\gamma} \times \frac{N}{s} - t_f;\ t_o = t^* - \frac{\delta}{\alpha} \times \frac{N}{s} - t_f \quad (12.9)$$

where $\delta = \beta\gamma/(\beta+\gamma)$. As a result, the total travel cost perceived by each auto commuter without tolling during $[t_s, t_e]$ is

$$C = \delta\frac{N}{s} + \alpha t_f \quad (12.10)$$

which is independent of their departure time. The maximum queue length occurs at time t_o :

$$q^* = q(t_o) = \frac{\delta}{\alpha} N \quad (12.11)$$

The total social cost of the system comprises three parts, i.e., total schedule delay cost (t.s.d.c.), total queuing time cost (t.q.t.c.) and total moving time cost (t.m.t.c.). The sum of these three parts is given below:

$$\underset{\text{(t.s.d.c.)}}{\frac{\delta N^2}{2s}} + \underset{\text{(t.q.t.c.)}}{\frac{\delta N^2}{2s}} + \underset{\text{(t.m.t.c.)}}{\alpha t_f N} = N\left(\frac{\delta N}{s} + \alpha t_f\right) \quad (12.12)$$

It is interesting to observe that both (t.s.d.c.) and (t.q.t.c.) are all independent of α. An explanation of this result is given below: The length of the rush hour is independent of α. Since the first and last individuals to depart experience only schedule delay, identical moving time and no queuing time, and since their trip costs are the same in equilibrium, their schedule delay costs must be identical (see (12.7)). It follows that the start and end of the rush hour are independent of α (see (12.9)). With knowledge of the start and end of the rush hour, (t.s.d.c.) and (t.q.t.c.) can be calculated independently of α.

The time-unvarying road-use toll, i.e., $u(t) = \text{constant}$, will not change the distribution of commuters' departure time choices and their costs relating to moving and waiting times, so from (12.10), the individual cost in equilibrium becomes: $C = \delta N/s + \alpha t_f + \text{constant toll}$.

Dynamic Pricing

It is well known that there exists a time-varying road-use toll (beginning and ending at zero) which can eliminate any queue and then reduce the total social cost. To eliminate queuing while minimizing schedule delay costs, the departure rate from the origin and the exiting rate from the bottleneck must equal the bottleneck capacity s throughout the rush hour $[t_s, t_e]$

where t_s and t_e are the first and last departure times, respectively. The first and last commuters face no toll and have the same travel cost, so the timing of the rush hour is the same as in the no-tolling case, see (12.9); and the individual cost in equilibrium is also the same as in the no-tolling case, i.e., $C = \delta N/s + \alpha t_f$. The individual cost remains unchanged because the waiting time cost incurred by a commuter departing at time t is just replaced by an equivalent amount of toll that he/she has to pay at that time.

So, for holding the equilibrium of individual cost over the whole rush hour, the toll $u(t)$ at any time should be given bt:

$$u(t) = \begin{cases} 0, \text{ for } t < t_s \\ C - \left[\beta\left(t^* - (t + t_f)\right) + \alpha t_f\right], \text{ for } t \in \left[t_s, t^* - t_f\right] \\ C - \left[\gamma\left((t + t_f) - t^*\right) + \alpha t_f\right], \text{ for } t \in \left[t^* - t_f, t_e\right] \\ 0, \text{ for } t > t_e \end{cases} \tag{12.13}$$

where C is given by eqn. (12.10), t_s and t_e are given by (12.9). The tolls are null outside the peak period because high schedule delay costs impose restrictions on commuting at any times outside this period.

The total social cost of the current system, after eliminating the queue, comprises two parts only, i.e., total schedule delay cost and total moving time cost. The total social cost can be derived from its definition as follows:

$$TSC = \int_{t_s}^{t^*-t_f} \beta s\left[t^* - (t + t_f)\right]\mathrm{d}t + \int_{t^*-t_f}^{t_e} \gamma s\left[(t + t_f) - t^*\right]\mathrm{d}t + \alpha t_f N = N\left(\frac{\delta N}{2s} + \alpha t_f\right) \tag{12.14}$$

Hence, in relation to the no-toll equilibrium, application of the optimal dynamic toll does not change the total schedule delay cost but eliminates queuing time, resulting in a social cost reduction of (t.q.t.c.) given by eqn. (12.12).

Dynamic bottleneck pricing is capable of eliminating queuing time completely, but such pricing scheme has practical difficulties because it requires continuously changeable charges. A step-toll scheme can be considered as an alternative to reduce (but not completely remove) the queue. It can be shown that at most $n/(n+1)$ of the total queuing time can be reduced with an optimal n-step toll scheme (Laih, 1994).

Elastic Demand Case

Let $B(N)$ be the benefit (or inverse demand) function. The optimal use of a highway with a bottleneck is achieved when the social welfare (or net economic benefit) is maximized. The social welfare is given by

$$S=\int_{0}^{N}B(\omega)\mathrm{d}\omega-\int_{t_s}^{t_e}r(t)C(t)\mathrm{d}t \tag{12.15}$$

where $C(t)$ is given by eqn. (12.2), but excludes the term representing tolls. $C(t)$ in (12.15) thus covers three parts only: the moving time cost, waiting time cost and schedule delay cost. It is assumed that the optimal dynamic toll eliminates any queuing, hence, the waiting time cost becomes zero. In addition, after eliminating any queue, both the exiting rate across and arriving rate at the bottleneck equal the bottleneck capacity s, during the peak period, so, $r(t)=s$, $t\in[t_s, t_e]$ and $N=s(t_e-t_s)$. Then, (12.15) can be rewritten as

$$\begin{aligned}S=&\int_{0}^{s(t_e-t_s)}B(\omega)\mathrm{d}\omega-\int_{t_s}^{t^*-t_f}\beta s\left[t^*-(t+t_f)\right]\mathrm{d}t\\&-\int_{t^*-t_f}^{t_e}\gamma s\left[(t+t_f)-t^*\right]\mathrm{d}t-\alpha t_f\left[s(t_e-t_s)\right]\end{aligned} \tag{12.16}$$

For maximizing the social welfare, setting the partial derivatives of S with respect to t_s and t_e equal to zero and using $N=s(t_e-t_s)$, we obtain:

$$\begin{cases}B(N)=\alpha t_f+\beta\left[t^*-(t_s+t_f)\right]\\B(N)=\alpha t_f+\gamma\left[(t_e+t_f)-t^*\right]\end{cases} \tag{12.17}$$

From (12.17) and $\tilde{N}=s(t_e-t_s)$, we can solve the two unknown time variables, see (12.9).

Using (12.9) to replace the two unknown time variables and letting the right hand sides of (12.17) equal $\delta N/s+\alpha t_f$. Then, (12.17) becomes

$$B(N)=\delta\frac{N}{s}+\alpha t_f \tag{12.18}$$

Therefore, for a given demand function, we can determine t_s and t_e, and the total number of commuters N by solving the group of equations (12.17)-(12.18). Equation (12.18) represents the equilibration between the individual travel costs and the marginal benefit from trip making. To hold this equilibrium over the whole period, a dynamic toll given by (12.13) should be imposed.

Up to this point, the derivation of an optimal dynamic toll presumes that the queuing delay at a bottleneck is considered to be pure deadweight loss and can be eliminated by a well-designed time-varying toll. By using optimal control theory, Yang and Huang (1997) showed that this assumption is suitable to the case where the bottleneck capacities are fixed, but it does not hold in other cases. In their numerical experiments, queuing still exists during the optimal use of road bottlenecks, where the state-varying exit capacity functions are adopted.

12.2.2 The Case with Heterogeneous Commuters

To more precisely evaluate the welfare effects of congestion pricing on different commuting populations and to enhance the accuracy of cost-benefit analysis of a congestion pricing scheme, it is necessary to develop bottleneck models which can incorporate commuters of different types. In a general way, professional and self-employed workers have high values of times but relatively flexible work hours, assembly-line workers have high values of schedule delay times-late in arriving at work, as they have rigid work schedules. In addition, higher-income commuters may be willing to pay more to avoid queuing than the lower-income ones.

In this subsection, we divide all commuters into two groups, who have different unit costs of travel time (α_1, α_2) and schedule delay time (β_1 and β_2 for time-early, γ_1 and γ_2 for time-late). In addition to the early assumption that $\beta_i < \alpha_i < \gamma_i$, $i = 1,2$, we further assume that $\alpha_1/\beta_1 > \alpha_2/\beta_2$, $\gamma_1/\beta_1 > \gamma_2/\beta_2 = \eta$, and all commuters have the same official work start time. These assumptions indicate that group 1 has higher ratio of travel time cost to schedule delay cost than group 2. Hence, group 1 is more likely to comprise relatively highly paid white-collar workers, with flexible work hours but higher values of time; group 2 likely consists of blue-collar workers and clerks or support staff in white-collar jobs, with rigid work schedules but relatively lower values of time.

We first give a succinct introduction to the basic no-tolling bottleneck model with two groups of commuters. For the sake of simplicity, we set the moving time t_f to be zero. Let the numbers of commuters of group 1 and group 2 be N_1 and N_2, respectively, and set $\delta_1 = \beta_1\gamma_1/(\beta_1 + \gamma_1) = \beta_1\eta/(1+\eta)$, $\delta_2 = \beta_2\gamma_2/(\beta_2 + \gamma_2) = \beta_2\eta/(1+\eta)$. The individual travel cost of group i, without tolling, can be expressed as:

$$C_i(t) = \begin{cases} \alpha_i\left[\dfrac{q(t)}{s}\right] + \beta_i\left[t^* - \left(t + \dfrac{q(t)}{s}\right)\right], & \text{for } t \in [t_s, t_o] \\ \alpha_i\left[\dfrac{q(t)}{s}\right] + \gamma_i\left[\left(t + \dfrac{q(t)}{s}\right) - t^*\right], & \text{for } t \in [t_o, t_e] \end{cases} \tag{12.19}$$

where $i = 1,2$. An equilibrium means that the individuals in the same group, no matter when he or she leaves home, must experience identical travel cost, hence $\mathrm{d}C_i(t)/\mathrm{d}t = 0$. This yields:

$$\frac{\mathrm{d}q(t)}{\mathrm{d}t} = \begin{cases} \dfrac{\beta_i}{\alpha_i - \beta_i} s, & \text{for } t \in [t_s, t_o] \\ \dfrac{-\gamma_i}{\alpha_i + \gamma_i} s, & \text{for } t \in [t_o, t_e] \end{cases} \tag{12.20}$$

where $i = 1, 2$.

From (12.20), we know that the queue length is a piecewise linear function of departure time t. There exist *three* slope turning points between t_s and t_e, one in $[t_s, t_o]$, one in $[t_o, t_e]$ and one at t_o, since $s\beta_1/(\alpha_1-\beta_1)\neq s\beta_2/(\alpha_2-\beta_2)$, $-s\gamma_1/(\alpha_1+\gamma_1)\neq -s\gamma_2/(\alpha_2+\gamma_2)$ and $s\beta_i/(\alpha_i-\beta_i)\neq -s\gamma_i/(\alpha_i+\gamma_i)$, $i=1,2$. In view of $s\beta_1/(\alpha_1-\beta_1)< s\beta_2/(\alpha_2-\beta_2)$ and $-s\gamma_1/(\alpha_1+\gamma_1)<-s\gamma_2/(\alpha_2+\gamma_2)$, which stem from the assumptions $\alpha_1/\beta_1>\alpha_2/\beta_2$ and $\gamma_1/\beta_1>\gamma_2/\beta_2=\eta$, minimizing the individual costs requires the following order of commuting: Namely, group 1 should have commuting at the beginning of the rush hour and again at the end, while group 2 should travel in the middle of the rush hour. Otherwise, commuters will experience more waiting times. Denote t_{12} and t_{21} as the slope turning points of the queue length curve in $[t_s, t_o]$ and $[t_o, t_e]$, respectively, thus group 1 leaves the origin during $[t_s, t_{12}]$ and $[t_{21}, t_e]$, and group 2 during $[t_{12}, t_{21}]$.

Recall that the first and last individuals of group 1 face no queuing time and have the same schedule delay costs, i.e., $\beta_1(t^*-t_s)=\gamma_1(t_e-t^*)$. The bottleneck operates at capacity s during rush hour, so, $t_e-t_s=(N_1+N_2)/s$. These facts lead to:

$$\begin{cases} t_s = t^* - \dfrac{\delta_1(N_1+N_2)}{\beta_1 s} = t^* - \dfrac{\eta(N_1+N_2)}{(1+\eta)s} \\ t_e = t^* - \dfrac{\delta_1(N_1+N_2)}{\gamma_1 s} = t^* + \dfrac{(N_1+N_2)}{(1+\eta)s} \end{cases} \tag{12.21}$$

and the individual cost of group 1:

$$C_1 = \delta_1 \frac{N_1+N_2}{s} \tag{12.22}$$

It remains to find the values of t_{12} and t_{21}, and the individual cost of group 2.

Let the queue lengths at time t_{12} and t_{21} be $q(t_{12})$ and $q(t_{21})$, respectively. An individual of group 1 leaving origin at time t_{12} and t_{21} has the costs as follows:

$$\begin{cases} C_1(t_{12}) = \alpha_1\left[\dfrac{q(t_{12})}{s}\right] + \beta_1\left[t^* - t_{12} - \dfrac{q(t_{12})}{s}\right] \\ C_1(t_{21}) = \alpha_1\left[\dfrac{q(t_{21})}{s}\right] + \gamma_1\left[t_{21} + \dfrac{q(t_{21})}{s} - t^*\right] = C_1(t_{12}) \end{cases} \tag{12.23}$$

Similarly, for individuals of group 2 leaving the origin at time t_{12} and time t_{21}, they have the following costs:

$$\begin{cases} C_2(t_{12}) = \alpha_2\left[\dfrac{q(t_{12})}{s}\right] + \beta_2\left[t^* - t_{12} - \dfrac{q(t_{12})}{s}\right] \\ C_2(t_{21}) = \alpha_2\left[\dfrac{q(t_{21})}{s}\right] + \lambda_2\left[t_{21} + \dfrac{q(t_{21})}{s} - t^*\right] = C_2(t_{12}) \end{cases} \quad (12.24)$$

Subtracting equation $C_1(t_{12})/\beta_1 = C_1(t_{21})/\beta_1$ from equation $C_2(t_{12})/\beta_2 = C_2(t_{21})/\beta_2$ leads to $q(t_{12}) = q(t_{21})$. The number of commuters in group 1 leaving origin between t_s and t_{12} is $(t_{12} - t_s)s + q(t_{12})$, and that between t_{21} and t_e is $(t_e - t_{21})s - q(t_{21})$, the summation of these equals N_1, which leads to $(t_{21} - t_{12}) = N_2/s$. Utilizing the slopes of the queue length curve given by eqn. (11.20), we have

$$q(t_{12}) = \frac{\beta_1}{\alpha_1 - \beta_1}(t_{12} - t_s)s = q(t_{21}) = \frac{\gamma_1}{\alpha_1 + \gamma_1}(t_e - t_{21})s \quad (12.25)$$

Combining these relations and the definition of t_o, i.e., $t_o + q(t_o)/s = t^*$, we obtain:

$$\begin{cases} t_{12} = t^* - \dfrac{\eta}{1+\eta} \times \dfrac{N_2}{s} - \dfrac{\beta_1}{\alpha_1} \times \dfrac{\eta}{1+\eta} \times \dfrac{N_1}{s} \\ t_{21} = t^* + \dfrac{1}{1+\eta} \times \dfrac{N_2}{s} - \dfrac{\beta_1}{\alpha_1} \times \dfrac{\eta}{1+\eta} \times \dfrac{N_1}{s} \\ t_o = t^* - \dfrac{\beta_2}{\alpha_2} \times \dfrac{\eta}{1+\eta} \times \dfrac{N_2}{s} - \dfrac{\beta_1}{\alpha_1} \times \dfrac{\eta}{1+\eta} \times \dfrac{N_1}{s} \end{cases} \quad (12.26)$$

and the individual cost of group 2 at equilibrium:

$$C_2 = \delta_2 \frac{N_2}{s} + \frac{\alpha_2}{\alpha_1}\delta_1 \frac{N_1}{s} \quad (12.27)$$

As in the case with identical commuters, the time-unvarying road-use toll, i.e., $u(t) = \text{constant}$, will not change the distribution of departure time choices and the waiting times for commuters of both groups, so the individual costs in equilibrium become C_1 + constant toll and C_2 + constant toll, for group 1 and group 2, respectively.

There also exists a time-varying tolling which can eliminate any queue behind the bottleneck. However, once a time-varying tolling scheme is carried out, the groups would be rationally allocated to departure time slots so as to minimize their schedule delay costs. The group with larger β-value travels closer to t^*, and the group with smaller β-value departs in adjacent time intervals, earlier and later.

Note that after implementing the time-varying tolling scheme, the timing of the rush hours, t_s and t_e, are the same as given in eqn. (12.21) regardless of the departure orders of the groups, since the two groups have the same ratio of $\gamma_i/\beta_i = \eta$, $i = 1, 2$. The original queue formed in no-tolling equilibrium is eliminated and replaced by a fine toll, and the toll curve is a piecewise linear function with four slopes β_1, β_2, γ_1, and γ_2. As mentioned above, the order in which groups depart from the origin under time-varying tolling may differ from the order under no-tolling equilibrium because of their different β-values, then the individual costs of both groups and the total social costs will change consequently. We show the main outputs by dividing the problem into two cases of $\beta_2 > \beta_1$ and $\beta_2 \le \beta_1$, respectively.

Dynamic Pricing When $\beta_2 > \beta_1$

When $\beta_2 > \beta_1$ holds, group 2 makes commuting in the middle of the rush hour, i.e., during $[t_{12}, t_{21}]$, and group 1 departs from the origin during $[t_s, t_{12}]$ and $[t_{21}, t_e]$, where

$$\begin{cases} t_{12} = t^* - \dfrac{\eta}{1+\eta} \times \dfrac{N_2}{s} \\ t_{21} = t^* + \dfrac{1}{1+\eta} \times \dfrac{N_2}{s} \end{cases} \tag{12.28}$$

The individual cost of group 1, which equals the schedule delay cost incurred by the first or last commuter of this group, is

$$\overline{C}_1 = \delta_1 \frac{N_1}{s} + \delta_1 \frac{N_2}{s} \tag{12.29}$$

which is identical with that generated in the non-tolling case, see eqn. (12.22). The individual cost of group 2, which equals the sum of the schedule delay cost and the toll imposed on this group, is

$$\overline{C}_2 = \delta_1 \frac{N_1}{s} + \delta_2 \frac{N_2}{s} \tag{12.30}$$

By comparing (12.30) and (12.27), we find that $\overline{C}_2 < C_2$ if and only if $\alpha_1 < \alpha_2$. Hence, group 2 is worse off with a fine dynamic toll in most situations, since the probability of having $\alpha_1 < \alpha_2$ is very small with reference to the condition $\alpha_1/\beta_1 > \alpha_2/\beta_2$. In addition, from (12.29) and (12.30) we know that $\overline{C}_2 > \overline{C}_1$ since $\delta_2 > \delta_1$ (note that $\delta = \beta\gamma/(\beta+\lambda)$ by definition).

The fine dynamic (time-varying) road-use toll, $u(t)$, for holding the equilibrium of the individual cost over the whole rush hour, is:

$$u(t)=\begin{cases}0, \text{ for } t<t_s \\ \bar{C}_1-\beta_1\left(t^*-t\right), \text{ for } t\in\left[t_s,t_{12}\right] \\ \bar{C}_2-\beta_2\left(t^*-t\right), \text{ for } t\in\left[t_{12},t^*\right] \\ \bar{C}_2-\gamma_2\left(t-t^*\right), \text{ for } t\in\left[t^*,t_{21}\right] \\ \bar{C}_1-\gamma_1\left(t-t^*\right), \text{ for } t\in\left[t_{21},t_e\right] \\ 0, \text{ for } t>t_e\end{cases} \tag{12.31}$$

where t_{12}, t_{21}, $\bar{C}_1$ and $\bar{C}_2$ are given by (12.28), (12.29) and (12.30), respectively. It is easy to verify that at times t_{12} and t_{21}, $u\left(t_{12}\right)=u\left(t_{21}\right)=\delta_1 N_1/s$. The total social cost of the highway (excluding toll revenue) is

$$\begin{aligned}TSC&=\int_{t_s}^{t_{12}}\beta_1\left(t^*-t\right)s\mathrm{d}t+\int_{t_{12}}^{t^*}\beta_2\left(t^*-t\right)s\mathrm{d}t+\int_{t^*}^{t_{21}}\gamma_2\left(t-t^*\right)s\mathrm{d}t+\int_{t_{21}}^{t_e}\gamma_1\left(t-t^*\right)s\mathrm{d}t\\&=\frac{\delta_1}{2s}\left(N_1\right)^2+\frac{\delta_1}{s}N_1N_2+\frac{\delta_2}{2s}\left(N_2\right)^2\end{aligned} \tag{12.32}$$

By comparing (12.32) with the following total social cost generated in the non-tolling case:

$$C_1N_1+C_2N_2=\frac{\delta_1}{s}\left(N_1\right)^2+\left(1+\frac{\alpha_2}{\alpha_1}\right)\frac{\delta_1}{s}N_1N_2+\frac{\delta_2}{s}\left(N_2\right)^2 \tag{12.33}$$

we find that the time-varying tolling scheme reduces the total social cost (TSC) by:

$$\Delta TSC=\frac{\delta_1}{2s}\left(N_1\right)^2+\frac{\alpha_2}{\alpha_1}\frac{\delta_1}{s}N_1N_2+\frac{\delta_2}{2s}\left(N_2\right)^2$$

Dynamic Pricing When $\beta_2\le\beta_1$

We now consider the second case with $\beta_2\le\beta_1$. In this case, the fine dynamic toll induces group 1 to travel in the middle of the rush hour, $\left[t_{21},t_{12}\right]$, and group 2 at the tails, i.e., $\left[t_s,t_{21}\right]$ and $\left[t_{12},t_e\right]$. We can prove

$$\begin{cases}t_{21}=t^*-\dfrac{\eta}{1+\eta}\times\dfrac{N_1}{s} \\ t_{12}=t^*+\dfrac{1}{1+\eta}\times\dfrac{N_1}{s}\end{cases} \tag{12.34}$$

The individual cost of group 1, which equals the sum of the schedule delay cost and the toll levied on an individual of this group at time t_{21}, is

$$\tilde{C}_1=\delta_1\frac{N_1}{s}+\delta_2\frac{N_2}{s} \tag{12.35}$$

It can be seen that $\tilde{C}_1<C_1$ due to $\delta_2<\delta_1$, which says group 1 is better off with the fine toll. The individual cost of group 2, which equals the schedule delay cost incurred by the first or last commuter, is:

$$\tilde{C}_2 = \frac{\beta_2}{\beta_1}\delta_1\frac{N_1}{s} + \delta_2\frac{N_2}{s} = \delta_2\frac{N_1+N_2}{s} \tag{12.36}$$

Since $\beta_2/\beta_1 > \alpha_2/\alpha_1$, then, $\tilde{C}_2 > C_2$, hence, group 2 is worse off with a fine dynamic toll. From eqns. (12.36) and (12.35), we know $\tilde{C}_2 \le \tilde{C}_1$ since $\delta_2 \le \delta_1$.

The fine dynamic (time-varying) toll, $u(t)$, for holding the equilibrium of individual cost over the whole rush hour, is:

$$u(t) = \begin{cases} 0, \text{ for } t < t_s \\ \tilde{C}_2 - \beta_2\left(t^* - t\right), \text{ for } t \in [t_s, t_{21}] \\ \tilde{C}_1 - \beta_1\left(t^* - t\right), \text{ for } t \in \left[t_{21}, t^*\right] \\ \tilde{C}_1 - \gamma_1\left(t - t^*\right), \text{ for } t \in \left[t^*, t_{12}\right] \\ \tilde{C}_2 - \gamma_2\left(t - t^*\right), \text{ for } t \in [t_{12}, t_e] \\ 0, \text{ for } t > t_e \end{cases} \tag{12.37}$$

where t_{21}, t_{12}, $\tilde{C}_1$ and $\tilde{C}_2$ are given by (12.34), (12.35) and (12.36), respectively. It is easy to verify that at times t_{21} and t_{12}, $u\left(t_{21}\right) = u\left(t_{12}\right) = \delta_2 N_2/s$. The total social cost of the system, excluding toll revenue, is:

$$TSC = \frac{\delta_1}{2s}(N_1)^2 + \frac{\delta_2}{s}N_1N_2 + \frac{\delta_2}{2s}(N_2)^2 \tag{12.38}$$

12.3 Parallel Bottleneck Models

In this section, we study the dynamic tolls in a simple congested network of parallel bottleneck routes connecting a single OD pair with elastic demand. In this case, a certain number of potential homogeneous commuters decide whether to make a trip, and, if affirmed, decide their departure times and routes rationally, based on their private trip-cost minimization principle. The following assumptions are made: 1) one bottleneck per route and the capacity of each bottleneck is a finite constant, s_r for route r; 2) the moving time on each route from origin to destination is zero for simplicity; 3) the time horizon of the study is large enough not to affect the departure time choices of individuals; 4) the benefit function is $B(N)$, where N is again the total demand, $N = \sum_{r\in R} N_r$ and R is a set of parallel routes and N_r is the number of commuters choosing route r. We first consider the case where optimal dynamic tolls are imposed on all routes.

12.3.1 Dynamic Tolls on All Routes

As stated before, it is assumed that the optimal dynamic toll designed for each route eliminates any queuing, so that the total social cost of the network, after implementing the tolling scheme, contains schedule delay costs only. In addition, after eliminating the queue, both the exiting rate across and arriving rate at each bottleneck equal the bottleneck capacity s_r, during the rush hour of this route; hence, $N_r = s_r\left(t_e^r - t_s^r\right)$ where t_s^r and t_e^r are the first and last departure times on route r, respectively.

The optimal use of the network is achieved when the social welfare is maximized. The social welfare is defined as the following total trip benefit minus the total social cost:

$$S = \int_0^N B(\omega)\mathrm{d}\omega - \left(\sum_{r\in R} \int_{t_s^r}^{t^*} \beta\left(t^* - t\right) s_r \mathrm{d}t + \sum_{r\in R} \int_{t^*}^{t_e^r} \gamma\left(t - t^*\right) s_r \mathrm{d}t \right) \tag{12.39}$$

where β, γ and t^* are as defined before. Let the partial derivatives of S with respect to t_s^r and t_e^r equal zero for maximizing the social welfare, and using $N_r = s_r\left(t_e^r - t_s^r\right)$, we obtain

$$\begin{cases} B(N) = \beta\left(t^* - t_s^r\right) \\ B(N) = \gamma\left(t_e^r - t^*\right) \end{cases}, \ r \in R \tag{12.40}$$

together with

$$N = \sum_{r\in R} N_r \tag{12.41}$$

$$N_r = s_r\left(t_e^r - t_s^r\right),\ r \in R \tag{12.42}$$

Note that (12.40) describes an equilibrium among marginal trip benefit and individual travel costs regardless of the actually used routes and departure times. The values of all variables, t_s^r, t_e^r, N_r, $r \in R$ and N can be obtained by solving the group of equations (12.40)-(12.42).

The dynamic toll $u_r(t)$ on route $r \in R$ is given by

$$u_r(t) = \begin{cases} 0, \ \text{for } t < t_s^r \\ B(N) - \beta\left(t^* - t\right), \ \text{for } t \in \left[t_s^r, t^*\right] \\ B(N) - \gamma\left(t - t^*\right), \ \text{for } t \in \left[t^*, t_e^r\right] \\ 0, \ \text{for } t > t_e^r \end{cases} \tag{12.43}$$

In the above analyses, the moving time on each route is assumed to be zero, so that all routes are actually used at equilibrium state, i.e., $N_r > 0$, $r \in R$. However, if some routes have relatively large moving times, i.e., the equivalent cost to moving time is larger than $B\left(N^*\right)$ where N^* is the sum of numbers of commuters on the used routes in equilibrium, they may not be chosen by commuters, even without toll charges on them. We can make an ascending order for all routes according to their values of moving times, and try to find such a route that the routes with lower moving times will be more likely used at equilibrium.

12.3.2 Dynamic Tolls on Partial Routes

Now we consider a typical example of the second-best pricing in a network of parallel routes where some un-tolled alternatives exist. A simple two-route network is used to highlight this kind of pricing problems. We assume that an optimal dynamic toll is designed to eliminate any queuing on one route and the alternative route is free of charge.

Let t_s^1 and t_e^1 be the first and last departure times on the tolled route, respectively; and let t_s^2 and t_e^2 be the beginning and ending times of queues on the un-tolled route, respectively. In equilibrium, if there are N_1 and N_2 commuters choosing the tolled and un-tolled routes, respectively, we then have $N_1 = s_1\left(t_e^1 - t_s^1\right)$ and $N_2 = s_2\left(t_e^2 - t_s^2\right)$.

We know that for the tolled route, the equilibrium travel cost (including toll) is $\delta N_1/s_1$; for the non-tolled route, the equilibrium travel cost is $\delta N_2/s_2$. From the following equilibrium relationships between individual costs and marginal trip benefit, we can solve for N_1 and N_2:

$$B\left(N_1 + N_2\right) = B(N) = \frac{\delta}{s_1}N_1 = \frac{\delta}{s_2}N_2 \tag{12.44}$$

Then, the four departure times can be solved from equations: $N_r = s_r\left(t_e^r - t_s^r\right)$ and $\beta\left(t^* - t_s^r\right) = \gamma\left(t_e^r - t^*\right)$, $r = 1, 2$. The dynamic toll for the tolled road is

$$u_1(t) = \begin{cases} 0, \text{ for } t < t_s^1 \\ B(N) - \beta\left(t^* - t\right), \text{ for } t \in \left[t_s^1, t^*\right] \\ B(N) - \gamma\left(t - t^*\right), \text{ for } t \in \left[t^*, t_e^1\right] \\ 0, \text{ for } t > t_e^1 \end{cases} \tag{12.45}$$

Note that the total social cost of the tolled route consists of schedule delay costs only, and is given by $\delta\left(N_1\right)^2/2s_1$ with reference to eqn. (12.14); the total social cost of the un-tolled route that includes schedule delay and queuing costs is valued as $\delta\left(N_2\right)^2/s_2$ with reference to (12.12). Hence, the total social cost of the two-route network is $\delta\left(N_1\right)^2/2s_1 + \delta\left(N_2\right)^2/s_2$.

However, the route use given by (12.44) is not the optimum. The optimal use of the network is achieved when the social welfare is maximized. The social welfare is defined as total trip benefit minus the total social cost given by:

$$S = \int_0^N B(\omega)\mathrm{d}\omega - \left(\frac{\delta}{2s_1}(N_1)^2 + \frac{\delta}{s_2}(N_2)^2 \right) \tag{12.46}$$

where $\delta = \beta\gamma/(\beta+\gamma)$, $N_1 = s_1(t_e^1 - t_s^1)$, $N_2 = s_2(t_e^2 - t_s^2)$, and $N = N_1 + N_2$. By setting the partial derivatives of S with respect to t_s^1, t_e^1, t_s^2 and t_e^2 equal to zero, we obtain:

$$\begin{cases} B(N) = \delta\left(t_e^1 - t_s^1\right) = \dfrac{\delta}{s_1} N_1 \\ B(N) = 2\delta\left(t_e^2 - t_s^2\right) = \dfrac{2\delta}{s_2} N_2 \end{cases} \tag{12.47}$$

From (12.47), we can obtain the optimal road use. Besides a dynamic toll is charged on route 1, however, the second equation in (12.47) requires that route 2 should be charged a time-invarying toll equal to the congestion externality $\delta N_2/s_2$.

So far, we have studied various bottleneck pricing schemes using the deterministic queuing theory. A particularly important feature of the time-varying tolls is that queuing is eliminated without increasing user costs. Considering the difficulty of implementing a fine time-varying toll in reality, one may further consider an optimal coarse toll which is a fixed fee paid at the front of the queue over a time interval and is expected to significantly reduce queuing congestion as well.

12.4 Bottleneck Pricing and Modal Split

In many cities, there usually exists an alternative mass commuting mode such as a railway or subway parallel to the road with a bottleneck. For example, in Hong Kong, there are three cross-harbor road tunnels and subways connecting Hong Kong Island and the Kowloon Peninsula. In such a competitive system with parallel transit and highway modes, road pricing can be regarded as a measure for restraining auto use and providing revenue for mass transport improvement. Unlike the road, the generalized cost by a mass transit mode mainly depends on its fare level and service quality, such as station and in-vehicle crowding, and its generally constant journey time. Obviously, analysis of this bi-modal system differs from dealing with the above-mentioned parallel road bottleneck system in the sense that the mode heterogeneity should be considered in attracting commuters, but has commonality in the sense that both systems provide commuters two or more substitutable choices. In this section we extend our early analysis by dealing with bottleneck congestion pricing and mode split jointly. In particular, we pay attention to the crowding/discomfort effects of mass transit and travel time difference between the transit and road modes. The logit-based modal split is introduced for the elastic total commuting demand.

12.4.1 Competition between Mass Transit and Highway

Consider a simplified corridor network which comprises two types of modes to provide transportation service between H (a residential area or home) and W (a workplace). Mode R represents a mass transit (*e.g.*, railway) with an assumed infinite capacity and mode A represents a highway with a single bottleneck which is located at the entering point of highway and has a deterministic capacity of s commuters per unit time. There are N identical commuters who can either travel on the highway by car (auto mode, one person per car) or on a railway by transit from H to W daily each morning. Assume that in equilibrium, there are N_A commuters who choose auto mode and N_R commuters choosing the mass transit mode, $N = N_A + N_R$.

Per bottleneck model study presented earlier, the individual travel cost of auto commuters in a departure time choice equilibrium in the absence of toll charge is given by:

$$C_A = \alpha t_A + \delta \frac{N_A}{s} \tag{12.48}$$

where t_A is the constant moving time by auto mode from H to W. The individual cost of transit commuters is defined as:

$$C_R = \theta g\left(N_R\right) + u_R + \alpha t_R \tag{12.49}$$

where u_R is the transit fare which is assumed to be time-invariant, θ is the unit cost of discomfort, $g\left(N_R\right)$ describes the discomfort experienced by a transit commuter, and t_R is the constant travel time by railway. The travel time by railway includes in-carriage time and access (egress) time from H to the railway station and from the railway station to W. The waiting time for a train at the station, which depends on the transit service frequency, is assumed to be constant and incorporated into t_R. The body congestion function $g\left(N_R\right)$ in (12.49) takes explicit account of the crowding effects at a railway station and inside a train on the commuters' mode and departure time choice (Lam et al., 1999). To facilitate our analytical investigation, we use a linear crowding function $g\left(N_R\right) = N_R$.

In the case of no-tolling on the highway bottleneck, equilibrium modal split is characterized by:

$$C_R = C_A \text{ if } N_R > 0 \text{ and } N_A > 0; \quad C_R \le C_A \text{ if } N_A = 0; \quad C_R \ge C_A \text{ if } N_R = 0 \tag{12.50}$$

subject to $N_R + N_A = N$. The total social cost of the system is

$$TSC = N_A C_A + N_R\left(\alpha t_R + \theta N_R + c\right) + F \tag{12.51}$$

where c represents the marginal (variable) cost of transit service, F is the fixed cost of the transit mode, consisting of facility costs and fixed operating costs. The marginal cost mainly comprises the daily expenses on labor, fuel and electricity per commuter being burdened by the transit operator. The fare and toll revenues are excluded from the total social cost.

Pricing on Transit versus No-tolling on Road

Assume that the public authority sets the railway fare u_R equal to the marginal (variable) cost, average cost and an optimum of minimizing the total social cost, respectively, while the road toll charge is not implemented for certain technical or political reasons. In this case, the railway fare becomes the unique means to adjust traffic flow distribution between the two modes. Our objective is to derive the modal split, evaluate the individual travel cost and the total social cost at an equilibrium state of the system.

In the following analyses we further assume that the total number of commuters, N, is sufficiently large to lead to both $N_A > 0$ and $N_R > 0$. It is easy to show that, when N is less than a certain number, there exists the case where only the auto mode is preferable and the railway would not be worth building.

(i) Setting $u_R = c$

This means that the mass transit operates at a deficit since it can not cover its fixed cost F. We can readily obtain the modal split in equilibrium by using eqn. (11.48) as follows:

$$\begin{cases} N_R^m = \dfrac{\delta}{\delta + \theta s} N + \dfrac{s}{\delta + \theta s}\left[\alpha(t_A - t_R) - c\right] \\ N_A^m = \dfrac{\theta s}{\delta + \theta s} N - \dfrac{s}{\delta + \theta s}\left[\alpha(t_A - t_R) - c\right] \end{cases} \tag{12.52}$$

where superscript 'm' represents solution of 'marginal' cost pricing on the transit mode. From (12.52), we can see that the number of transit commuters is proportional to $(t_A - t_R)$ if $t_R < t_A$ but inversely proportional to θ. This simply says that the transit patronage will increase if the railway sector improves its service quality while keeping its fare unchanged. The service-enhancing measures can include, for example, improving ventilation at stations and inside trains (lowering the θ-value); increasing the service frequency and thus shortening travel time t_R.

As N_R^m increases (by decreasing the value of θ or t_R), N_A^m will decrease, which results in a decline of all commuters' travel costs regardless of their travel modes, as seen from the following result in equilibrium:

$$C_R^m = C_A^m = \alpha t_R + \theta N_R^m + c = \alpha t_A + \frac{\delta N_A^m}{s} \tag{12.53}$$

Therefore, under the marginal-cost transport pricing policy for the transit mode, both transit and auto commuters can benefit from reducing the value of (θ, t_R), which of course needs additional investment.

By definition (12.51) and relation (12.53), the total social cost becomes:

$$TSC^m = N_A^m\left(\alpha t_A + \frac{\delta N_A^m}{s}\right) + N_R^m\left(\alpha t_R + \theta N_R^m + c\right) + F = N\left(\alpha t_A + \frac{\delta N_A^m}{s}\right) + F$$
$$= N\left(\alpha t_R + \theta N_R^m + c\right) + F \tag{12.54}$$

(ii) Setting $u_R = c + F/N_R$

This represent an average cost pricing policy for the transit mode, under which the fare revenue just covers the fixed and variable operating cost of the transit mode (break-even). Solving for N_R and N_A from equilibrium conditions (12.50), we obtain two candidate solutions: one is unstable and the other is stable against small perturbations. The stable solution is given by:

$$\begin{cases} N_R^a = \dfrac{N_R^m}{2} + \sqrt{\left(\dfrac{N_R^m}{2}\right)^2 - F\dfrac{s}{\delta + \theta s}} \\ N_A^a = \dfrac{N}{2} + \dfrac{N_A^m}{2} - \sqrt{\left(\dfrac{N_R^m}{2}\right)^2 - F\dfrac{s}{\delta + \theta s}} \end{cases} \tag{12.55}$$

where the superscript 'a' represents the solution of 'average' cost pricing on the transit mode; N_R^m and N_A^m are given by (12.52). It can be seen that $N_R^a < N_R^m$ as $F > 0$ and then $N_A^a > N_A^m$ since $N_R^a + N_A^a = N$. This simply stems from the fact that the transit patronage decreases with increase in fare. It is worthwhile to mention here that the transit patronage is still inversely proportional to the θ-value under average cost-based fare policy, but it is not reflected in (12.55) explicitly. To see this, we consider two distinct θ-values: $0 < \theta' < \theta$. Using eqn. (12.55), we have

$$\frac{N_R^{a'}}{N_R^a} = \frac{N_R^{m'}}{N_R^m} \times \frac{1 + \sqrt{1 - \dfrac{4Fs}{\left(N_R^{m'}\right)^2(\delta + \theta' s)}}}{1 + \sqrt{1 - \dfrac{4Fs}{\left(N_R^m\right)^2(\delta + \theta s)}}} \tag{12.56}$$

From eqn. (12.52) we know $N_R^{m'} > N_R^m$. From $\theta' < \theta$, we have

$$\frac{\left[\delta N + s\left(\alpha(t_A - t_R) - c\right)\right]^2}{\delta + \theta' s} > \frac{\left[\delta N + s\left(\alpha(t_A - t_R) - c\right)\right]^2}{\delta + \theta s} \tag{12.57}$$

This means that $\left(N_R^{m'}\right)^2(\delta+\theta' s)>\left(N_R^m\right)^2(\delta+\theta s)$ in view of (12.52). Combining (12.56)-(12.57), we conclude that $N_R^{a'}>N_R^a$. $N_R^{a'}$ remains larger than N_R^a if the fixed cost F rises to F' as long as $F'/F<(\delta+\theta s)/(\delta+\theta' s)$ or $\Delta F<Fs\left[(\theta-\theta')/(\delta+\theta' s)\right]$ holds, where ΔF represent additional investment cost for improving transit service quality. This is an important point that verifies the possibility of attracting more commuters by making certain additional investment for enhancing service quality even though the investment cost is covered in fare revenue.

The travel cost perceived by each commuter in equilibrium is

$$C_R^a=C_A^a=\alpha t_R+\theta N_R^a+c+\frac{F}{N_R^a}=\alpha t_A+\delta\frac{N_A^a}{s} \tag{12.58}$$

Comparing (12.58) with (12.53), we know that the individual cost increases since $N_A^a>N_A^m$. From (12.51) and (12.58), the total social cost is:

$$\begin{aligned} TSC^a &= N_A^a\left(\alpha t_A+\frac{\delta N_A^a}{s}\right)+N_R^a\left(\alpha t_R+\theta N_R^a+c\right)+F=N\left(\alpha t_A+\frac{\delta N_A^a}{s}\right) \\ &= N\left(\alpha t_R+\theta N_R^a+c+\frac{F}{N_R^a}\right) \end{aligned} \tag{12.59}$$

Subtracting (12.54) from (12.59) yields

$$TSC^a-TSC^m=F\left(\frac{N}{N_R^a}-1\right)-N\theta\left(N_R^m-N_R^a\right) \tag{12.60}$$

Since $N_R^a<N$, the first term of the right hand side is positive, which indicates an increase in total social cost associated with the average cost-based fare policy, but the second term represents an reduction in commuter discomfort cost due to $N_R^a<N_R^m$. The sign of $\left(TSC^a-TSC^m\right)$ depends on the counterbalance of the two terms.

(iii) Setting socially optimal transit fare.

We seek an optimal transit fare to minimize total social cost. This is done here by first finding the optimal modal split giving rise to the minimum total social cost and then the optimal transit fare is determined. From eqn. (12.51), we have

$$TSC^o=N_A^o\left(\alpha t_A+\frac{\delta N_A^o}{s}\right)+N_R^o\left(\alpha t_R+\theta N_R^o+c\right)+F \Rightarrow \min$$

where superscript 'o' represents solution of social 'optimal' pricing on the transit mode. Substituting $N_A^o=N-N_R^o$ into the above equation and letting the first-order derivative with respect to N_R^o be zero, we obtain the following optimal modal split:

$$\begin{cases} N_R^o = \dfrac{\delta}{\delta+\theta s}N + \dfrac{s}{2(\delta+\theta s)}\left[\alpha(t_A - t_R) - c\right] \\ N_A^o = \dfrac{\theta s}{\delta+\theta s}N - \dfrac{s}{2(\delta+\theta s)}\left[\alpha(t_A - t_R) - c\right] \end{cases} \tag{12.61}$$

Comparing (12.61) with (12.52), we find that, if $\alpha(t_A - t_R) < c$, then $N_R^o > N_R^m$ and $N_A^o < N_A^m$, and the individual cost will decrease; otherwise, $N_R^o \le N_R^m$ and $N_A^o \ge N_A^m$.

Substituting (12.61) into equilibrium conditions (12.50), we get the optimal transit fare of minimizing the total social cost as follows:

$$u_R^o = \frac{1}{2}\left[c + \alpha(t_A - t_R)\right] \tag{12.62}$$

Of particular note is that u_R^o is independent of θ. If $\alpha(t_A - t_R) < c$ (very likely case in reality), then $u_R^o < c$, which implies that railway sector suffers a higher deficit beyond F. Since the optimal fare is less than marginal cost, the number of transit commuters is certainly larger than that under marginal cost-based fare policy, as understood by comparing (12.61) and (12.52). Clearly, this optimal fare policy is beneficial to all commuters due to the decline in individual cost. The total social cost, of course, declines as given by

$$TSC^o - TSC^m = -\frac{s}{4(\delta+\theta s)}\left[\alpha(t_A - t_R) - c\right]^2 < 0 \tag{12.63}$$

Time-invariant Tolling on Road

As stated before, the time-invariant road toll does not alter the departure time, and the moving and queuing times of auto commuters, so the individual cost of auto commuters in equilibrium is $C_A = \alpha t_A + \delta N_A/s + u_A$, where u_A is the fixed toll on road.

(i) Average cost-based transit fare versus optimal constant road toll

Keeping the optimal modal split (12.61), setting the transit fare equal to the average cost, and using the equilibrium conditions (12.50) in which C_A is given by $\delta N_A/s + \alpha t_A + u_A$, we obtain the optimal road toll of minimizing total social cost as follows:

$$u_A^o = \frac{c}{2} - \frac{\alpha}{2}(t_A - t_R) + \frac{F}{N_R^o} \tag{12.64}$$

Therefore, the average cost-based fare policy together with constant optimal road toll (12.64) gives rise to the same optimal modal split (12.61) as achieved by the socially optimal transit fare in the absence of road tolling.

From (12.64), if $\alpha(t_A - t_R) < c$, then $u_A^o > F/N_R^o$ (average-shared fixed cost by all transit commuters). The individual cost in equilibrium is $\delta N_A^o/s + \alpha t_A + u_A^o$, which is higher than that in the case of adopting the socially optimal transit fare only (i.e., $\delta N_A^o/s + \alpha t_A$). The reason for this result is that the railway sector now incurs no deficit whilst road tolling generates certain revenue. Hence, the policy will be well received by the railway sector and road tolling authority but not by commuters. It would be preferable if the revenue generated from the road toll charge can be used to subsidize mass transit while the railway sector chooses a marginal cost-based transit fare policy.

(ii) Marginal cost-based transit fare versus a road toll with a transit subsidy

We set the transit fare equal to the marginal cost and try to find a road toll charge which generates revenue just covering the fixed cost F as a subsidy to the transit mode. For this purpose, we have to solve the following equilibrium equation across the two modes:

$$\alpha t_R + \theta N_R^s + c = \alpha t_A + \frac{\delta N_A^s}{s} + u_A^s \tag{12.65}$$

where $u_A^s N_A^s = F$, $N_R^s + N_A^s = N$, and superscript 's' represents solution with a 'subsidy' policy. The stable solution is given by:

$$\begin{cases} N_R^s = \dfrac{N}{2} + \dfrac{N_R^m}{2} - \sqrt{\left(\dfrac{N_A^m}{2}\right)^2 - F\dfrac{s}{\delta + \theta s}} \\[2ex] N_A^s = \dfrac{N_A^m}{2} + \sqrt{\left(\dfrac{N_A^m}{2}\right)^2 - F\dfrac{s}{\delta + \theta s}} \end{cases} \tag{12.66}$$

$$u_A^s = \frac{F}{N_A^s} \tag{12.67}$$

where N_R^m and N_A^m are given by (12.52). The differences between (12.66) and (12.55) should be noticed carefully.

From (12.66), we know that $N_A^s < N_A^m$, hence the maximum queue length on the highway is less than that in the case of using marginal cost-based fare *versus* no-tolling on road. However, the equilibrium individual cost rises as $N_A^s < N_A^m$ yields $N_R^s > N_R^m$ and $\alpha t_R + \theta N_R^s + c > \alpha t_R + \theta N_R^m + c$. The comparison between (N_R^s, N_A^s) and (N_R^o, N_A^o) is case-dependent. The equilibrium individual cost under a transit subsidy policy is higher than that under optimal transit fare policy if $\alpha(t_A - t_R) < c$. But its comparison with that in the case of average cost-based fare versus socially optimal road toll can be made only case by case. Nothing is definite either as to the comparison in terms of the total social costs among the different cases.

Optimal Time-varying Tolling on Road

It is already known in previous sections that there exists a time-varying toll which can eliminate any queue without changing the rush hour commuting pattern and increasing the equilibrium individual costs. The total social cost of commuting on the highway, which comprises the total schedule delay cost and the total moving time cost, is $N_A\left(\alpha t_A + \delta N_A/2s\right)$. It is clear that the total social cost of the transit mode is $N_R\left(\alpha t_R + \theta N_R + c\right) + F$. We now investigate two situations: (i) average cost-based transit fare versus time-varying road toll, and (ii) marginal cost-based fare versus time-varying toll with a transit subsidy.

(i) Average cost-based transit fare versus time-varying road toll

The optimal modal split can be obtained by minimizing the total social cost of the whole system as follows:

$$TC^d = N_A^d\left(\alpha t_A + \frac{\delta N_A^d}{2s}\right) + N_R^d\left(\alpha t_R + \theta N_R^d + c\right) + F \;\Rightarrow\; \min$$

subject to $N_R^d + N_A^d = N$, where superscript d represents the case of 'dynamic tolling' on the road. The solution is

$$\begin{cases} N_R^d = \dfrac{\delta}{\delta + 2\theta s}N + \dfrac{s}{\delta + 2\theta s}\left[\alpha\left(t_A - t_R\right) - c\right] \\ N_A^d = \dfrac{2\theta s}{\delta + 2\theta s}N - \dfrac{s}{\delta + 2\theta s}\left[\alpha\left(t_A - t_R\right) - c\right] \end{cases} \tag{12.68}$$

The individual cost of transit commuters at equilibrium is

$$C_R^d = \alpha t_R + \theta N_R^d + c + \frac{F}{N_R^d} \tag{12.69}$$

which should equal the individual cost of auto commuters below:

$$C_A^d\left(t\right) = \alpha t_A + \text{schedule delay cost} + \text{road toll} = C_R^d \tag{12.70}$$

To sustain the equilibrium of departure time choice, the optimal dynamic or time-varying road toll, $u(t)$, should be given by:

$$u\left(t\right)\begin{cases} > u\left(t_s\right), \text{ for } t < t_s \\ = C_R^d - \left[\alpha t_A + \beta\left(t^* - \left(t + t_A\right)\right)\right], \text{ for } t \in \left[t_s, t^* - t_A\right] \\ = C_R^d - \left[\alpha t_A + \gamma\left(\left(t + t_A\right) - t^*\right)\right], \text{ for } t \in \left[t^* - t_A, t_e\right] \\ > u(t_e), \text{ for } t > t_e \end{cases} \tag{12.71}$$

where t_s and t_e are given by (12.9) with the number of auto commuters given by (12.68), and

$$u(t_s) = u(t_s) = \frac{F}{N_R^d} - \frac{\theta s}{\delta + 2\theta s}\left[\frac{\delta N}{s} + \alpha(t_A - t_R) - c\right] \tag{12.72}$$

Note that (12.9) still holds although the first and last commuters now are charged by $u(t_s)$ and $u(t_e)$, respectively, because all conditions for obtaining (12.9) are not affected due to $u(t_s) = u(t_e)$. In (12.71), setting tolls higher than $u(t_s) = u(t_e)$ outside the rush hour is for the purpose of forcing auto commuters to leave home during $[t_s, t_e]$. An efficient road tolling scheme should be such that $u(t_s) = u(t_e) \geq 0$. Otherwise, a subsidy (negative toll) must be made to some individuals who leave home at the tails of the rush hours.

Comparing (12.68) with (12.52), we find that $N_R^d < N_R^m$. Note that N_R^a approaches N_R^m when F becomes zero as seen from (12.55), but $N_R^d < N_R^m$ always holds except $\theta = 0$.

The travel cost incurred by the first or the last auto commuter, which is of course subject to the equilibrium consequence of all auto and transit commuters is $\alpha t_A + \delta N_A^d / s + u(t_s)$. Since $N_A^d > N_A^m$, so the individual cost in equilibrium under optimal time-varying toll is higher than that under marginal cost-based transit fare versus no-tolling, if the time-varying toll is positive: $u(t_s) \geq 0$.

In a hope that the first and last auto commuters are not charged, and hence the individual cost of auto commuters is $\alpha t_A + \delta N_A^d / s$ (including the fine dynamic toll), then the resulting modal split is identical with that under the policy of average cost-based transit fare versus no-tolling, as seen in (12.55), because the same equilibrium conditions are based in determining travel costs. The corresponding tolling scheme is a standard time-varying road tolling with beginning and ending zero-toll at times t_s and t_e, respectively. In fact, here the queuing costs for auto commuters under average cost-based transit fare policy versus no-tolling are already substituted by the tolls charged under this new policy. However, the total social cost resulting from such a new policy (policy of having $u(t_s) = u(t_e) = 0$) may not be equal to the minimum.

In addition, in the case of the marginal cost-based transit fare versus optimal time-varying road toll, the modal split can still be the optimal one as given in (12.68) through excluding the term F/N_R^d in C_R^d and also this term in (12.71). As a result, the equilibrium individual cost declines, but the railway sector suffers a deficit F. Note that this policy is practicable only when the beginning and ending tolls given by (12.72), with the exclusion of F/N_R^d, are still positive.

(ii) Marginal cost-based fare versus time-varying toll with a transit subsidy

Suppose that the transit fare is set equal to marginal cost c. In equilibrium, the individual cost for transit commuters is $C_R^{ds} = \alpha t_R + \theta N_R^{ds} + c$, where superscript '$ds$' represents the case of 'dynamic-tolling and subsidizing transit'. All auto commuters experience the same cost, so the *total travel cost* incurred can be expressed as $\left(\alpha t_R + \theta N_R^{ds} + c\right) N_A^{ds}$. Since the *total social cost* on the highway is $\left(\alpha t_A + \delta N_A^{ds}/2s\right) N_A^{ds}$, then the revenue generated from road tolling equals $\left(\alpha t_R + \theta N_R^{ds} + c\right) N_A^{ds} - \left(\alpha t_A + \delta N_A^{ds}/2s\right) N_A^{ds}$. This revenue can be used to subsidize the fixed cost F of transit. Therefore, the modal split can be obtained by solving the following equation for its stable solution:

$$\left(\alpha t_R + \theta N_R^{ds} + c\right) N_A^{ds} - \left(\alpha t_A + \frac{\delta N_A^{ds}}{2s}\right) N_A^{ds} = F \qquad (12.73)$$

with $N_R^{ds} + N_A^{ds} = N$. The stable solution is

$$\begin{cases} N_R^{ds} = N_R^d + \dfrac{\theta s}{\delta + 2\theta s} - \sqrt{\left(N_A^d - \dfrac{\theta s}{\delta + 2\theta s}\right)^2 - \dfrac{2Fs}{\delta + 2\theta s}} \\ N_A^{ds} = N_A^d - \dfrac{\theta s}{\delta + 2\theta s} + \sqrt{\left(N_A^d - \dfrac{\theta s}{\delta + 2\theta s}\right)^2 - \dfrac{2Fs}{\delta + 2\theta s}} \end{cases} \qquad (12.74)$$

where N_R^d and N_A^d are given by (12.68). Then, the time-varying road toll can be obtained using (12.71) in which C_R^d must be replaced by C_R^{ds}, t_s and t_e should be computed based on N_A^{ds}, and the beginning and ending tolls are

$$\begin{aligned} u(t_s) = u(t_e) &= \left[\alpha t_R + \theta N_R^{ds} + c\right] - \beta\left[t^* - \left(t_q + t_A\right)\right] - \alpha t_A \\ &= \frac{1}{N_A^{ds}}\left(F + \alpha t_A N_A^{ds} + \frac{\delta\left(N_A^{ds}\right)^2}{2s}\right) - \left(\alpha t_A + \frac{\delta}{s} N_A^{ds}\right) \\ &= \frac{F}{N_A^{ds}} - \delta\frac{N_A^{ds}}{2s} \end{aligned} \qquad (12.75)$$

For a practical tolling scheme, tolls should be non-negative. Thus, from (12.75), we have

$$N_A^{ds} \leq \sqrt{\frac{2Fs}{\delta}} \qquad (12.76)$$

The above condition indicates that the revenue generated from road tolling is enough to cover the fixed cost when the number of auto commuters reaches $\sqrt{2Fs/\delta}$. If this number goes up further, the road toll revenue will become in excess of a tolling target revenue of F. Therefore, when the N_A^{ds} computed by (12.74) is greater than $\sqrt{2Fs/\delta}$, there are two pricing alternatives worthy of perusal: 1) the policy of marginal cost-based fare versus the time-varying tolling (12.71) with the optimal modal split (12.68), and 2) the policy of marginal cost-based fare versus standard time-vary tolling with the modal split (12.52). Selection between the two policies can be made on the basis of excess revenue, total social cost, individual cost and modal split.

Table 12.1 Simulation results under various pricing policies

	No-tolling			Constant Tolling		Dynamic Tolling	
	Marginal Cost	Average Cost	Optimal Fare	Average Cost	Marginal Cost*	Average Cost	Marginal Cost#
Number of Transit Commuters	104	85	141	141	125	94	104
Number of Auto Commuters	96	115	59	59	75	106	96
Individual Cost in Equilibrium	46.1	49.2	39.8	49.0	46.5	49.1	46.1
Total Social Cost	9514.3	9847.8	9251.8	9251.8	9364.3	8729.0	8739.4
Revenue from Road Tolling	0	0	0	537.8	300.0	1086.5	774.9
Maximum Queue Length	40	48	25	25	31	0	0
t_s	48.21	42.94	58.63	58.63	54.17	45.43	48.21
t_e	80.36	81.41	78.27	78.27	79.17	80.91	80.36
Transit Fare	20.00	23.55	13.00	22.13	20.00	23.21	20.00
Constant Road Toll				9.13	4.00		
$u(t_s)=u(t_e)$						1.34	0

*The policy with transit fare equal to marginal cost and a transit subsidy; the revenue generated from time-invariant road tolling equals the fixed cost of transit (or constant subsidy needed).

#The policy with a transit subsidy. Because the beginning and ending tolls computed by (12.75) are negative, the policy of marginal cost-based fare versus standard time-varying tolling is adopted.

Simulation Results

The above analyses show that the moving time difference between mass transit and highway should not be neglected because of its direct influence on mode choice. Mass transit can better ensure commuters arrive at work on time, but meanwhile it may bring commuters discomfort due to crowding at railway stations and inside trains. Under all types of transit fare policies, improving transit service quality (reducing θ -value) and increasing service frequency can of course attract more commuters to use transit mode. It is worthwhile to do so when the additional investment cost for this improvement is counted against the benefit of increased transit patronage from a social perspective.

As noted above, in certain cases the analytical results derived earlier are obscure for making comparisons between the various pricing policies in terms of flow patterns, individual costs and total social costs. Herein, we present some simulation results for a simple comparison. The input data are: $N = 200$, $s = 3$, $F = 300$, $c = 20$, $\gamma = 3.0$, $\alpha = 1.2$, , $\beta = 0.6$, $\theta = 0.02$, $t_A = 25$, $t_R = 20$ and $t^* = 100$. We have $\delta = \beta\gamma/(\beta+\gamma) = 0.5$. Table 12.1 provides the simulation results, from which a qualitative comparison can be made.

12.4.2 Pricing and Logit-based Mode Choice with Elastic Demand

In practice, the above assumption of deterministic mode choice by equalizing travel costs in (12.50) between the two transit and highway modes may be inappropriate, because a number of qualitative and quantitative factors contribute the mode choice decision of commuters. In addition, whilst the demands by modes are treated variables but the overall number of commuters is fixed. This means that only the internal demand elasticity which reflects the extent to which commuters divide themselves between auto and transit modes is taken into account, but the external (or overall) system demand elasticity is ignored. In this subsection, we present a more general and realistic model by incorporating the overall system demand elasticity and employ the popular logit-based mode choice model. The model is then applied to derive and compare various time-invariant pricing schemes.

Logit-based Mode Choice

We use the generalized utility function to characterize each mode as below

$$U_i = U - C_i + \xi_i, \quad i = A, R \tag{12.77}$$

where U is a constant term representing the utility received through a working trip, and it could be related to individual's daily income; ξ_i represents the unobservable or unmeasurable factors of utility in specifying the utility of selecting mode i. Suppose the random terms ξ_i be identically and independently distributed Gumbel variables with mean zero, then at equilibrium, the modal split at aggregate demand level is governed by a logit formula specified below:

$$N_i = N\frac{\exp(-\mu C_i)}{\exp(-\mu C_A)+\exp(-\mu C_R)}, \quad i = A,\ R \tag{12.78}$$

where μ is a positive parameter relating to the standard deviation of the random term and measures the sensitivity of mode choices to travel cost. Clearly, the modal split (12.78) is not affected by adding a constant into the utility function (12.77). Hereinafter, we thus assume $U = 0$ for simplicity.

Alternative Pricing Schemes

With the logit-based mode choice, we now investigate the following pricing schemes: i) the non-optimized pricing, ii) the first-best pricing for a social optimum use of the system, and iii) the second-best pricing in the case of incapability of road tolling. We show that the first-best pricing requires simultaneous implementation of a road toll and a transit fare, and the optimal transit fare for the second-best solution should be set to be a weighted sum of the marginal external costs between auto and transit commuters.

(i) The non-optimized pricing model

Let u_A and u_R be the arbitrarily fixed road toll and transit fare, respectively, and by our early definition of mode-specific travel cost, we have: $C_R = \alpha t_R + \theta g(N_R) + u_R$ and $C_A = \alpha t_A + \delta N_A/s + u_A$, where $\delta = \beta\gamma/(\beta+\gamma)$ as defined before. To take account of overall demand elasticity, let $B(N)$ denote the marginal trip benefit or the inverse of the demand function with the property of $dB(N)/dN < 0$. The equilibrium conditions for the logit-based model choice with elastic demand require, apart from eqn. (12.78), the following demand-supply equilibration:

$$\hat{U} = E\left[\max\ \{U_A, U_R\}\right] = \frac{1}{\mu}\ln\left[\exp(-\mu C_A) + \exp(-\mu C_R)\right] = B(N) \tag{12.79}$$

Conditions (12.78) and (12.79) are equivalent to

$$\frac{1}{\mu}\ln N_A + C_A = \frac{1}{\mu}\ln N_R + C_R = B(N) + \frac{1}{\mu}\ln N \tag{12.80}$$

with $N_A + N_R = N$. The logit equilibrium solution $\left(N_A^*, N_R^*, N^*\right)$ can be uniquely obtained from solving (12.80) once all parameters together with the marginal benefit function $B(N)$ are specified.

(ii) The first-best pricing model

Here we derive the optimal constant road toll and transit fare through maximizing the net social benefit or the social welfare of the system at an expected aggregate level and determine the corresponding socially optimal modal split. The optimization problem is formulated as follows:

$$\max\ S=\int_0^N B(\omega)\,d\omega+\left[\frac{N\ln N}{\mu}-\frac{N_A\ln N_A+N_R\ln N_R}{\mu}\right]$$
$$-\left[N_A\left(\alpha t_A+\frac{\delta N_A}{s}\right)+N_R\left(\alpha t_R+\theta g\left(N_R\right)\right)+\left(N_R c+F\right)\right] \tag{12.81}$$

where $N_A+N_R=N$ and $N_A\geq 0, N_R\geq 0$. In (12.81), the integration term represents the total gross benefit of all commuters from trip-making; the term in the first square bracket represents the additional gross direct utility of commuters enjoyed from mode choice due to their different tastes and preferences for diversity; the term in the second square bracket is the total social cost of the bi-modal system, including the total travel cost by each mode and the total transit mode operating cost.

The first-order optimality conditions of the optimization problem (12.81) are:

$$\frac{1}{\mu}\ln N_A+\left(\alpha t_A+\frac{\delta N_A}{s}\right)+\left(\frac{\delta N_A}{s}\right)=B(N)+\frac{1}{\mu}\ln N \tag{12.82}$$

$$\frac{1}{\mu}\ln N_R+\left[\alpha t_R+\theta g\left(N_R\right)\right]+\left[c+\theta N_R g'\left(N_R\right)\right]=B(N)+\frac{1}{\mu}\ln N \tag{12.83}$$

and $N_A+N_R=N$ and $g'(\cdot)=dg'(\cdot)/dx$. Equations (12.82) and (12.83) represent the conditions for a socially optimal logit-based mode choice and trip-making. By comparing these conditions with the equilibrium conditions (12.80), one can easily see that the social optimum can be decentralized as a user equilibrium with a logit-based mode choice by implementing the following trans-modal transport pricing scheme: each auto commuter traveling on highway should be charged a toll amounting to $u_A=\delta N_A/s$, which is the third term of the left-hand side in eqn. (12.82) and is the queuing externality generated by an additional auto commuter; each transit commuter should pay a mount of $u_R=c+\theta N_R g'\left(N_R\right)$, the third term of the left-hand side in eqn. (12.83), where $\theta N_R g'\left(N_R\right)$ is the crowding externality and c is the marginal transit operating cost caused by an additional transit commuter. These first-best road toll and transit fare can internalize the externality of each commuter using each mode and therefore a social optimum is established.

(iii) The second-best pricing model

Suppose that the public authority can set the transit fare maximizing the net social benefit, while the road toll can not be implemented for certain technical or political reasons. In this second-best pricing case, the transit fare is the unique tool to adjust traffic flow distribution between the two modes and affect the trip-making of commuters. Let u_R be the transit fare, the logit-based equilibrium conditions can then be written as:

$$\frac{1}{\mu}\ln N_A+\left(\alpha t_A+\frac{\delta N_A}{s}\right)=B(N)+\frac{1}{\mu}\ln N \tag{12.84}$$

$$\frac{1}{\mu}\ln N_R + \left(\alpha t_R + \theta g\left(N_R\right)\right) + u_R = B\left(N\right) + \frac{1}{\mu}\ln N \tag{12.85}$$

Hence, the second-best pricing model is to maximize the objective function (12.81) subject to constraints (12.84) and (12.85). Let λ_A and λ_R be the multipliers associated with (12.84) and (12.85) respectively, the following Lagrangian can be formed:

$$\begin{aligned} L = \int_0^N B(\omega)\,d\omega + &\left[\frac{N\ln N}{\mu} - \frac{N_A\ln N_A + N_R\ln N_R}{\mu}\right] \\ &- \left[N_A\left(\alpha t_A + \frac{\delta N_A}{s}\right) + N_R\left(\alpha t_R + \theta g\left(N_R\right)\right) + \left(N_R c + F\right)\right] \\ &+ \lambda_A\left[B(N) + \frac{1}{\mu}\ln N - \frac{1}{\mu}\ln N_A - \left(\alpha t_A + \frac{\delta N_A}{s}\right)\right] \\ &+ \lambda_R\left[B(N) + \frac{1}{\mu}\ln N - \frac{1}{\mu}\ln N_R - \left(\alpha t_R + \theta g\left(N_R\right)\right) - u_R\right] \end{aligned} \tag{12.86}$$

where $N = N_A + N_R$ again. Maximizing L with respect to N_A, N_R and u_R yields:

$$\begin{aligned} 0 = &\left[B(N) + \frac{1}{\mu}\ln N\right] - \left[\alpha t_A + \frac{\delta N_A}{s} + \frac{1}{\mu}\ln N_A\right] - \frac{\delta N_A}{s} \\ &+ \lambda_A\left[B'(N) + \frac{1}{\mu N} - \frac{1}{\mu N_A} - \frac{\delta}{s}\right] + \lambda_R\left[B'(N) + \frac{1}{\mu N}\right] \end{aligned} \tag{12.87}$$

$$\begin{aligned} 0 = &\left[B(N) + \frac{1}{\mu}\ln N\right] - \left[\alpha t_R + \theta g(N_R) + \frac{1}{\mu}\ln N_R\right] - \left[c + \theta N_R g'\left(N_R\right)\right] \\ &+ \lambda_A\left[B'(N) + \frac{1}{\mu N}\right] + \lambda_R\left[B'(N) + \frac{1}{\mu N} - \frac{1}{\mu N_R} - \theta g'\left(N_R\right)\right] \end{aligned} \tag{12.88}$$

$$0 = -\lambda_R \tag{12.89}$$

Substituting (12.84)-(12.85) and (12.89) into (12.87)-(12.88) yields:

$$\frac{\delta N_A}{s} = \lambda_A\left[B'(N) + \frac{1}{\mu N} - \frac{1}{\mu N_A} - \frac{\delta}{s}\right] \tag{12.90}$$

$$c + \theta N_R g'\left(N_R\right) = u_R + \lambda_A\left[B'(N) + \frac{1}{\mu N}\right] \tag{12.91}$$

Solving equations (12.90)-(12.91) for u_R, we obtain

$$u_R = \left[c + \theta N_R g'\left(N_R\right)\right] + \frac{B'(N) + \left(\dfrac{N}{\mu}\right)}{\left(\dfrac{\delta}{s}\right) + \left(\dfrac{N_A}{\mu}\right) - B'(N) - \left(\dfrac{N}{\mu}\right)}\left(\frac{\delta N_A}{s}\right) \tag{12.92}$$

In (12.92), the terms $c + \theta N_R g'\left(N_R\right)$ and $\delta N_A/s$ are the marginal external costs of a transit commuter and a highway commuter, respectively, as explained before. Consequently, the optimal transit fare in the second best case is a weighted sum of the marginal external costs associated with the two classes of commuters. The first weighting factor equals 1.0 and the second one can be either positive or negative, because $B'(N) = \mathrm{d}B(N)/\mathrm{d}N < 0$. This says that the optimal transit fare in this pricing scheme should consider the full marginal external cost caused by transit commuters, and then plus or minus a fraction of the marginal external cost of highway commuters. If overall demand is perfectly inelastic: $B'(N) = -\infty$, then the second weighting factor becomes -1.0, and thus the resultant transit fare should be set at the difference between the two pricing levels designed for the two modes in the first-best case. This implies that in the case of fixed demand if the automobile does not pay its marginal external cost, the correct policy is to adjust the fare on transit commuters downwards so that the split of travel demand between these two modes will be adjusted toward its socially optimal level.

It is easy to verify that if let $B'(N) = -\infty$, $\mu = +\infty$ and $g(N_R) = N_R$, the above second-best pricing results become identical with those in the case of optimal fare versus non-tolling scheme presented in Subsection 12.4.1, or the modal split and optimal fare given by the solution of group of eqns. (12.84)-(12.85) and (12.92) are the same as those by eqns. (12.61) and (12.62).

A Numerical Example

Note that the groups of nonlinear equations formulated for each model must be numerically solved, it is then difficult to check the properties of the solutions analytically. Here, we present a simple example to compare the first-best and the second-best pricing models. The parameters of our numerical example are: $(\gamma,\alpha,\beta) = (2.0,1.0,0.5)$ (\$/min), $s = 4$ (veh/min), $F = 300$ (\$), $c = 15$ (\$/commuter), $\theta = 0.01$ (\$/discomfort), $t_A = 25$ (min), $t_R = 20$ (min), $t^* = 100$ (min), $\mu = 0.5$. We adopt the following benefit (or inverse demand) function: $B(N) = -\omega \ln(N/N_{\max})$ where $N_{\max} = 10^3$. A larger value of ω in the function implies a less sensitivity of demand to marginal trip benefit and thus the final realized demand will be higher. The crowding discomfort function takes the form of $g(N_R) = 0.05(N_R)^2 + 0.25N_R$. We focus on the solution sensitivity with respect to parameter ω, it is of course straightforward to do so with other parameters such as c, θ and μ.

We consider three scenario, 1) we simply set $u_A = 0$ and $u_R = c$ in model (12.80) for the non-optimized pricing case, or the road toll is null and the transit fare equals the variable cost, 2) the first-best pricing, and 3) the second-best pricing with road toll equal to zero. The optimal toll (case 2) and fares (cases 2 and 3) are plotted in Figure 12.1.

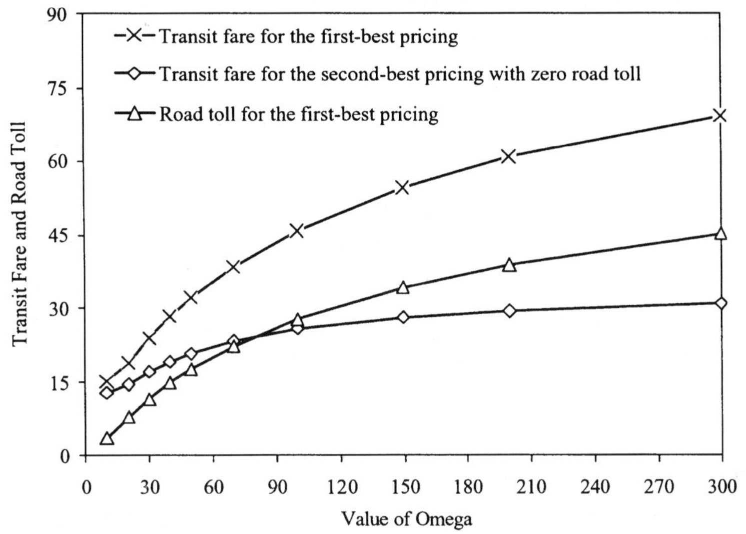

Figure 12.1 Toll and fare levels of the first-best and second-best pricing schemes

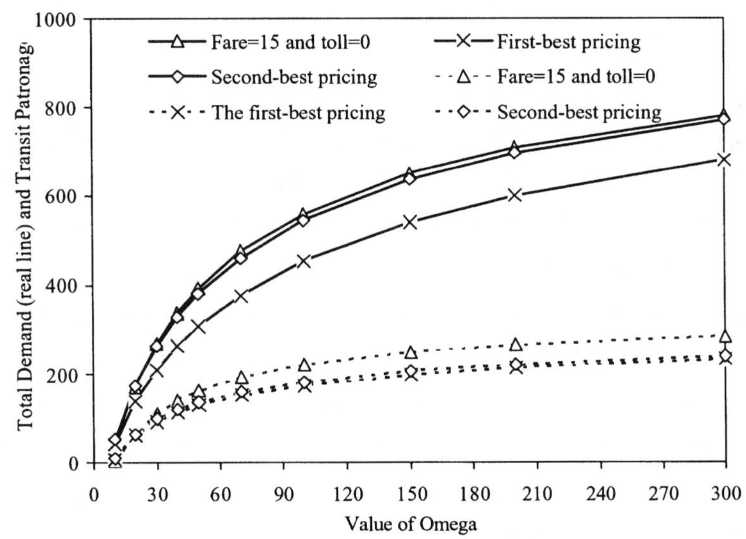

Figure 12.2 Impact of pricing on total demand and modal split

Figure 12.2 shows the total demand and number of transit commuters generated by the three pricing policies. The first policy with null toll and fare equal to the variable cost generates the largest number of commuters, then followed by the second-best pricing and the first-best pricing policies. It is found that the difference in transit patronage among the three cases is insignificant, but the total demand exhibits much big disparity and hence is more sensitive to the pricing policies adopted.

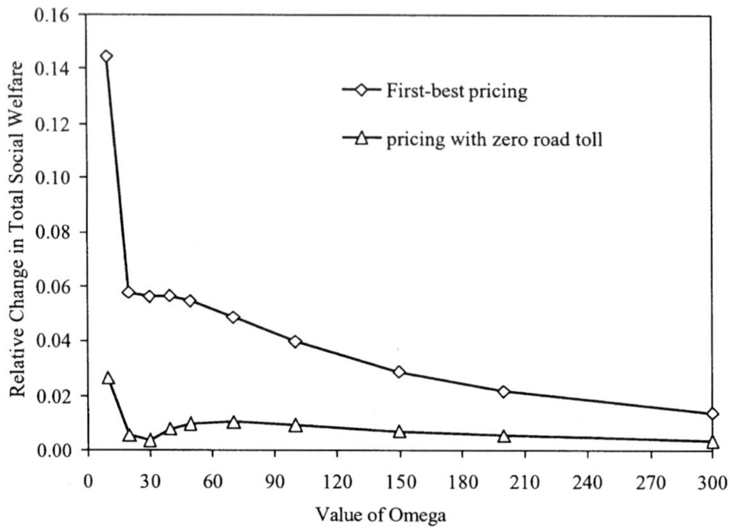

Figure 12.3 Impact of pricing on relative change in total social welfare

Figure 12.3 displays the relative change in total social welfare. The relative change is defined as the ratio of the overall welfare gain in comparison with the first case with $u_A = 0$ and $u_R = c$ in model (12.80). As expected, the first-best pricing yields higher social welfare improvement than the second-best pricing.

12.5 SUMMARY

In this chapter, we provided a thorough analysis and review of dynamic road pricing which is of great importance due to ever-increasing traffic congestion. Albeit limited to a simple spatial setting with either a single or parallel bottleneck routes, the analysis presented in this chapter does offer interesting insights into the dynamic nature of traffic congestion and congestion pricing. Our analysis added realism by including user heterogeneity, demand elasticity and mode split into the dynamic bottleneck pricing models. In the case of a single bottleneck, analytical solutions of time-varying tolls and departure rates can be obtained. Demand elasticity can be easily incorporated in both the single and parallel bottleneck models. Further meaningful results are obtained from a competitive two-mode transportation system, in which an alternative mass commuting mode, such as railway or subway, exists in parallel to the road with a bottleneck.

The models and analyses in this chapter explored some essential elements of dynamic or time-varying pricing and provided important references for further investigations, but they are limited in the spatial context. In the subsequent and also the last chapter, we make one more significant step forward by developing a numerically tractable dynamic road pricing model with bottlenecks in a general road network.

12.6 SOURCES AND NOTES

There is a vast body of literature geared toward bottleneck congestion pricing mainly by well-known economists. Vickrey (1969), Braid (1989) and Arnott *et al.* (1993a,b) and others presented analysis of a pure road bottleneck. Henderson (1974), Agnew (1977) and Chu (1995) determined time-varying tolls by applying a speed-flow function for a congested road. Ben-Akiva *et al.* (1986), Arnott *et al.* (1993a) and Braid (1989) and Mun (1994) conducted equilibrium analyses of bottlenecks with elastic demand. Laih (1994) examined queuing at a bottleneck with single- and multi-step tolls. Henderson (1974, 1981) incorporated two groups of commuters differing in value of time and schedule delay penalty into a dynamic model. Cohen (1987), Newbery (1988) and Evans (1992) investigated the welfare effects of tolls on two groups of commuters. Arnott *et al.* (1987, 1988, 1992, 1994) studied various aspects of the bottleneck problem with general group-specific heterogeneous commuters. Newell (1987) dealt with a general case where commuters are continuously distributed in their work start times, costs of travel time and costs of schedule delay. Yang and Huang (1997) and Huang and Yang (1996, 1999) applied the optimal control theory to develop a general time-varying road-use pricing model for a state-varying exit capacity bottleneck or Hyper-congesion (Herman, 1982) with elastic demand. Bottleneck road congestion pricing with a competing railroad service were investigated by Tabuchi (1993), Huang (2000) and Huang (2002) and Danielis and Marcucci (2002). An excellent early review was given by Arnott *et al.* (1998). For most recent developments of the bottleneck models, readers may refer to Van der Zijpp and Koolstra (2002), de Palma and Lindsey (2002), Marvin (2003), Verhoef (2003), Konishi (2004), Lindsey (2004) and Zhang et al. (2005).

For more details about Section 12.2, readers may consult works by Arnott *et al.* (1990a, 1990b, 1993, 1994, 1995), Braid (1986), Yang and Huang (1997), Lindsey and Verhoef (2001). Relevant studies in Section 12.3 can be found in Arnott *et al.* (1990a, 1992), Braid (1996) and Huang and Yang (1996). Section 12.4 is based on Tabuchi (1993), Huang and Yang (1999), Huang (2000) and Huang (2002). Readers can also consult Huang *et al.* (2000) for extension to the logit-based models in carpooling and pricing problems. Empirical results about $\gamma > \alpha > \beta$ were first reported in Small (1982). In fact, $\alpha > \beta$ is also the condition required for existence and uniqueness of no-toll equilibrium (Smith, 1984 and Daganzo,

1985). The bottleneck models with an un-tolled substitute were discussed in Braid (1996), Verhoef *et al.* (1996), Liu and McDonald (1999).

13

DYNAMIC ROAD PRICING: GENERAL NETWORK MODELS*

13.1 INTRODUCTION

In Chapter 11, we examined dynamic pricing models with a single bottleneck by seeking time-varying tolls to remove queues with or without elastic demand, and investigating the welfare effects of tolls on different groups of commuters. Extensions to parallel bottlenecks or a bottleneck parallel to a mass transit line were made as well. In this chapter, we make one major step ahead by dealing jointly with the time and space dimensions of road pricing in a general network with bottleneck congestion. The problem becomes much more difficult because of the complexions of dynamic traffic assignment and the network structure, and indeed only very limited studies of dynamic pricing in general networks are available in the literature.

This Chapter deals with the modeling of peak-period congestion and optimal pricing in a queuing network with elastic travel demand. The approach employed here is a combined application of the space-time expanded network (STEN) representation of time-varying traffic flow and the conventional network equilibrium modeling techniques. Given the elastic demand function for trips between each Origin-Destination (OD) pair and the schedule delay cost associated with each destination (workplace), the departure time and route choice of commuters and the optimal variable tolls of bottlenecks will be determined jointly by solving a system optimization problem over the STEN. The STEN approach can deal with a general queuing network with elastic demand, and allow for treatment of commuter heterogeneity in their work start time and schedule delay cost, and hence make a significant advance over the previous simple bottleneck models of peak-period congestion.

This chapter is organized as follows. We give a general description of the departure time and route choice problem with schedule delay costs, and then present a space-time expanded network where commuter's behavioral decision on departure time and route choice can be described explicitly. We develop a dynamic traffic flow model, followed by the derivation of

* Notation is used in this chapter independently of the previous Chapters 1-10

the optimal congestion tolls for each link over the space-time expanded network, which aims to maximize the social benefit over the whole study horizon. Simple and general numerical examples are provided to evidence the potential application of the dynamic traffic congestion and pricing network model in practice.

13.2 Problem Description

The notation used in this chapter is independent of previous chapters. Let $G=(N,A)$ be a network with P being the set of origin nodes and Q the set of destination nodes, a typical origin and destination node is denoted by p and q respectively. Let R_{pq} denote the set of routes between Origin-Destination (OD) pair (p,q).

Let the overall time horizon of study $[0,T]$ be divided into equally spaced discrete time periods sequentially numbered $t=1,2,\cdots,T$. Suppose the time horizon $[0,T]$ is chosen to be large enough such that it does not affect the results of analysis (*i.e.*, it covers the whole time period within which commuter's departure time may be adjusted and all commuters arrive at their destinations). Let $d_{pq}(t)$ be the demand for travel from origin p to destination q in time period t, and d_{pq} be the total demand over the whole study horizon between OD pair (p,q). Obviously,

$$d_{pq}=\sum_{t=0}^{T}d_{pq}(t),\ p\in P,\ q\in Q \tag{13.1}$$

Here we suppose commuters have a free choice of their departure time from home, and thus, $d_{pq}(t)$ are endogenous variables in our model. Furthermore, in the medium to long run, demand may be reasonably elastic, since commuters can change residences, jobs, trip frequency, transport mode and so on to avoid bottleneck congestion and tolls. We thus suppose the total demand between each OD pair over the whole time horizon is determined by a demand function:

$$d_{pq}=D_{pq}(\mu_{pq}),\ p\in P,\ q\in Q \tag{13.2}$$

where μ_{pq} is the generalized cost for each commuter which includes travel and waiting time cost, schedule delay cost and toll at the equilibrium state of the system. The assumption that the total demand over the whole study horizon $[0,T]$ is elastic with respect to the equilibrium generalized cost, is in accordance with the conventional treatment of bottleneck analysis. This assumption of demand function could allow adjustment of trip departure time over the entire time study horizon, which is a significant characteristic different from the instantaneous demand function adopted by previous researchers. Instantaneous demand function is simply defined as a decreasing function of the travel cost associated with *each instant* of departure. This type of demand function is difficult to establish in practice and is difficult to capture the adjustment of departure time.

Because travel demand is time-dependent, traffic flow and travel time along a route will also be time-dependent. Let $T_{pq}^{r}(t)$ be the travel time incurred by a commuter who departs from origin p, in time period t, and travels on route $r \in R_{pq}$, to destination q. $T_{pq}^{r}(t)$ also depends on the demand and supply characteristics of the queuing network.

Suppose the destination q, represents the workplace of a group of homogeneous auto-commuters who have the same preferred arrival time or common work start time. This is specified by an interval $\left[t_q^* - \Delta_q, t_q^* + \Delta_q\right] \subset [0, T]$ where $\left(t_q^* - \Delta_q\right)$ is the commuters' desired earliest time of arrival at the destination, and $\left(t_q^* + \Delta_q\right)$ is the desired latest arrival time at the destination. Commuters whose workplace is q incur no schedule delay cost if they arrive at the destination inside the time interval $\left[t_q^* - \Delta_q, t_q^* + \Delta_q\right]$.

Commuters may arrive at the destination earlier or later compared to the time period $\left[t_q^* - \Delta_q, t_q^* + \Delta_q\right]$ in order to avoid long queues or high toll at road bottlenecks. Consequently, there will be three possible arrival patterns at work, with the corresponding schedule delay costs for each individual. The schedule delay costs can be expressed mathematically as

$$c_q^s(t) = \begin{cases} \beta_q\left\{\left(t_q^* - \Delta_q\right) - \left[t + T_{pq}^r(t)\right]\right\}, & \text{if } t + T_{pq}^r(t) < \left(t_q^* - \Delta_q\right) \\ 0, & \text{if } t_q^* - \Delta_q \leq t + T_{pq}^r(t) \leq \left(t_q^* + \Delta_q\right) \\ \gamma_q\left\{\left[t + T_{pq}^r(t)\right] - \left(t_q^* + \Delta_q\right)\right\}, & \text{if } t + T_{pq}^r(t) > \left(t_q^* + \Delta_q\right) \end{cases} \tag{13.3}$$

where β_q $\left(\gamma_q\right)$ is the unit cost of schedule delay early (late) at the destination q.

Note that we assume that all commuters designated to the same destination have the same preferred arrival time and the same marginal disutility parameters of schedule delay time, which are independent of their origins. This assumption is reasonable because these commuters could be considered to be in the same working group. If they have different preferred arrival times at work, we can always divide these commuters into several groups and set their corresponding destination nodes so that each group consists of only the identical commuters with the same preferred arrival schedule. This representation could allow for driver heterogeneity in our model.

Therefore, the cost of a trip from home p to workplace q on route r for a commuter leaving home at time t is:

$$\varphi_{pq}^{r}(t) = \alpha T_{pq}^{r}(t) + \beta_q(\text{time early}) + \gamma_q(\text{time late}) = c_{pq}^{r}(t) + c_q^{s}(t) \tag{13.4}$$

where α is a convention factor (the cost of one unit of travel time) to transform travel time $T_{pq}^{r}(t)$ into travel cost $c_{pq}^{r}(t)$. In accordance with empirical results, we assume that $\gamma > \alpha > \beta$. Note that we can also set different values of parameter α for commuters designated to different destinations to allow for different commuter types having different costs per minute delay or travel on a link. The resultant model will involve traffic assignment with multi-user classes.

In deciding when to leave home, each commuter trades off travel time, schedule delay, and the toll (if any) by minimizing his or her generalized travel cost (13.4). Equilibrium is obtained when no individual can decrease his or her travel cost by altering departure time and travel routes.

13.3 SPACE-TIME EXPANDED NETWORK

12.3.1 Basic Assumptions

We now show that the space-time extended network (STEN) approach can be used to describe commuter's departure time and route choice in a queuing network with schedule delay cost. Before this, we first present some assumptions as follows.

Assumption 13.1 The dynamic flow problem is described by a store-and-forward transportation network. There exist a certain number of bottleneck links in the network and vehicle queues may build up behind these bottlenecks due to their limited exit capacities. Traversal time of vehicles from bottleneck to bottleneck is assumed to be constant (flow-independent).

Assumpton 13.2 According to Assumption 13.1, the total time spent by a vehicle on a bottleneck link $a \in A$ may be decomposed into a fixed travel time t_a^0, which is the free (uncongested) travel time on link a, and a queuing time, which is the time spent in the exit queue of the link.

Assumption 13.3 Queuing time for an individual depends on the number of vehicles in the queue at the time the commuter joins the queue, but not on the physical length of the queue (vertical queue assumption is used).

Assumption 13.4 The free traversal time t_a^0, $a \in A$ is measured in numbers of time periods.

Assumptions (13.1)-(13.3) are in line with those in the standard single bottleneck models, but concerned with a general queuing network. We can also associate a finite link storage capacity with the queue volume, but this would not be further sought in our study, because the number of vehicles which are prevented from leaving a link in each period will usually be zero under optimal congestion tolls.

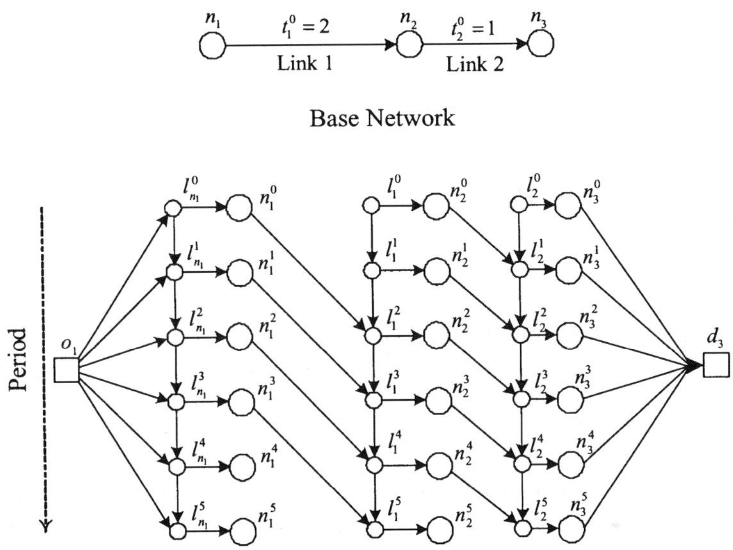

Expansion of Base Network

Figure 13.1 A simple network and its space-time expansion

13.3.2 Static Temporal Expanded Network

According to the above assumptions, a vehicle that enters a link $a \in A$ at period t, must travel during t_a^0 periods of time, and then it may either exit the link or join the exit queue of the link at period $t+t_a^0$; in the later case, after one period of time, it will have again a choice of exiting the link or joining the exit queue of the link corresponding to the time period $t+t_a^0+1$, and the process is repeated until the vehicle exits the link. For a given base traffic network $G=(N,A)$, this process may be described as path following in the space-time network to be constructed in the following ways.

Nodes: Each transshipment node n_k $(k \in N)$ of the base network is expanded to $T+1$ nodes n_k^t, $t=0,1,\cdots,T$, of the expanded network.

Links: For each link $a = (n_i,\ n_j) \in A$, we construct, for each $t = 0,1,\cdots,T$

- one node l_a^t
- one link $\left(n_i^{t-t_a^0},\ l_a^t\right)$ if $t - t_a^0 \geq 0$
- one link $\left(l_a^t,\ n_j^t\right)$
- one link $\left(l_a^t,\ l_a^{t+1}\right)$ if $t+1 \leq T$

These three links correspond respectively to the fixed travel time on the original link, the exit part of the process and the queue at the given time period t.

In order to prohibit more vehicles than possible entering the network at the origin nodes, and to allow for commuters to have a free choice of departure time, we implement the following expansion at the origin nodes.

Origin nodes: For each origin node n_k $(k \in P)$, we construct

- one single origin node o_k; and, for each $t = 0,1,\cdots,T$
- one node $l_{n_k}^t$
- one link $\left(l_{n_k}^t,\ n_k^t\right)$
- one link $\left(l_{n_k}^t,\ l_{n_k}^{t+1}\right)$ if $t+1 \leq T$
- one link $\left(o_k,\ l_{n_k}^t\right)$

The first two links correspond respectively to the entry of traffic into the network and the waiting queue at the origin node n_k during the time period t. The third link with zero travel time implies the free choice of departure period of commuters from home.

Destination nodes: For each destination node n_k $(k \in Q)$, we construct

- one single destination node d_k
- one link $\left(n_k^t,\ d_k\right)$ for each $t = 0,1,\cdots,T$

This link corresponds to the exit of traffic of the network at destination node n_k during period t, $t = 0,1,\cdots,T$.

Now we consider a simple network of Figure 13.1 to illustrate the network expansion process. Suppose that n_1 is an origin node, n_3 a destination node and n_2 a regular node, the corresponding expanded network (for five periods) is shown in the same figure. Note that the aforementioned expansion procedure may produce some unnecessary nodes and links, which could be removed to reduce the size of the expanded network.

13.3.3 Traffic on the STEN

For each link $a \in A$ and each time period t, $t = 0,1,\cdots,T$ in the original network, we let $u^a_{pq}(t)$ be the number of OD pair (p,q) 's vehicles entering link a at period t and $u_a(t) = \sum_{(p,q)} u^a_{pq}(t)$, $g^a_{pq}(t)$ be the number of OD pair (p,q)'s vehicles exiting link a at period t and $g_a(t) = \sum_{(p,q)} g^a_{pq}(t)$, $q^a_{pq}(t)$ be the number of OD pair (p,q) 's vehicles waiting on link a at period t and $q_a(t) = \sum_{(p,q)} q^a_{pq}(t)$. The measure unit for these quantities is 'veh', which represents the number of vehicles.

The relations that express the dynamic process of transfer of vehicles within a link of the original network are the simple static traffic conservation constraints at the nodes $l^t_a, a \in A, t = 0,1,\cdots,T$, of the STEN, for each pair (p,q), $p \in P$, $q \in Q$:

$$q^a_{pq}(t) = q^a_{pq}(t-1) + u^a_{pq}(t - t^0_a) - g^a_{pq}(t),\ a \in A,\ t = 0,1,\cdots,T \tag{13.5}$$

The transfer of vehicles between the links (*e.g.*, at the nodes) is such that the number of pair (p,q)'s arriving vehicles to a node at a given time period, is equal to the number of exiting vehicles of that pair, from that node at the same period; this is expressed by the static traffic conservation constraint at the nodes n^t_k of the STEN:

$$b^k_{pq}(t) + \sum_{a \in B_k} g^a_{pq}(t) = \sum_{a \in A_k} u^a_{pq}(t) + e^k_{pq}(t),\ k \in N,\ t = 0,1,\cdots,T \tag{13.6}$$

where B_k is the set of links arriving to node k, A_k is the set of links exiting from node k, $b^k_{pq}(t)$ is the entry traffic in the network at node n^t_k designated to q (zero if $k \neq p$), and $e^k_{pq}(t)$ is the exit traffic of the network at node n^t_k designated to q (zero if $k \neq q$).

The last equations are relative to the origin and destination nodes that are o_p and d_p in the STEN, for each OD pair (p,q):

$$\sum_{t=0}^{T} d_{pq}(t) = \sum_{t=0}^{T} e_{pq}(t) = d_{pq},\ p \in P,\ q \in Q \tag{13.7}$$

where d_{pq} is the total demand over the whole study horizon between OD pair (p,q), $d_{pq}(t)$ and $e_{pq}(t)$ are departing and arriving vehicles from p to q in time period t, respectively.

Therefore, all the dynamic traffic moves in the original network may be seen as static traffic moves in the STEN.

13.3.4 Link Exit Capacity and Travel Cost on the STEN

Here we only consider the capacity relative to a link exit. The link exit capacity plays a key role in the queuing process and, therefore, on the waiting times on the link, which when added to the fixed free flow travel time gives the total travel time of the corresponding vehicles on the link. In addition, exit capacities of individual bottlenecks will jointly control the throughput of the whole queuing network.

Suppose each link of the original network has an exit capacity, thus for each link $a \in A$, and for each period $t = 0,1,\cdots,T$, we set:

$$g_a(t) \le s_a,\ a \in A,\ t = 0,1,\cdots,T \tag{13.8}$$

where s_a is the exit capacity (vehicles/period) of link $a \in A$ and $g_a(t)$ is the number of vehicles exiting link a in period t. Here for simplicity, we have assumed exit capacity of a link is constant (or we can assume that a link has a different constant exit capacity in a different time period, or a time-dependent exit capacity), but in general, the exit capacity depends on the traffic conditions of other links at the same intersection, as well as on the geometric and signalization conditions at the intersection. In addition, as the queue grows at a bottleneck when inflow exceeds its capacity, the existing flow rate may be reduced — the so-called hyper-congestion. In these situations, the exit capacity of a link must not be constant, but rather a function of the vector of exit traffic flow.

Now we define the travel time for each link in the STEN. In our model, the constant part of a link unit cost function is associated with the fixed travel time on the travel link (namely, t_a^0 periods), whereas the waiting time spent by a vehicle in the link queues $q_a(t)$, $t = 0,1,\cdots,T$, is exactly one period of time, after which it either exits the link, or joins the next link queue $q_a(t+1)$ in which another period of time will be spent, and so on. Therefore, the link travel times in the STEN are: for a travel link with $u_a(t)$, t_a^0 periods; for an exit link with $g_a(t)$, 0 period; for a waiting link with $q_a(t)$, 1 period.

The travel cost will then be obtained by the travel times multiplied by the conversion factors α appearing in (13.4).

For the link at the entry of the network, namely, the departure link $(o_k,\ l_{n_k}^t)$ from origin o_k, $k \in P$, the capacities are taken to be infinite, and the costs zero. The zero cost and infinite capacity for departure links mean that commuters have a free choice of the period of departure from their homes.

For the link at the exit of the network, namely, the arrival link (n_k^t, d_k) to destination d_k, $k \in Q$, a period-dependent cost will be associated to represent the schedule delay cost. This cost depends on the individual destination (working group) to account for the commuter heterogeneity, and is already defined by (13.3) for all $t = 0,1,\cdots,T$.

13.4 System Optimum, Externality and Congestion Toll

13.4.1 Model Formulation

Now we consider a system optimum in terms of the maximization of economic benefit and derive the optimal tolls over the STEN. Hereinafter, we regard STEN as a general network as used elsewhere in the book and denote the set of nodes in STEN by $\underline{N}$, the set of links in STEN by $\underline{A}$. The notations of origins and destinations remain unchanged because each such node in STEN corresponds to the original one in the base network $G = (N, A)$.

Let $B_{pq}(d_{pq})$ be the benefit or the inverse demand function: $B_{pq}(d_{pq}) = D_{pq}^{-1}(d_{pq})$. Then the total gross commuter benefit from travel between all OD pairs over the whole study horizon is evaluated as

$$GCB = \sum_{(p,q)} \int_0^{d_{pq}} B_{pq}(\omega)d\omega$$

Given the link costs of STEN defined in preceding subsection, a path cost in the STEN is defined to be the sum of the costs of the links that belong to that path:

$$c_r(\mathbf{f}) = \sum_{a \in \underline{A}} \delta_{ar} c_a(v_a),\ r \in \underline{R}_{pq},\ p \in P,\ q \in Q \tag{13.9}$$

where $\delta_{ar} = 1$ if link a is in path r and 0 otherwise, $\underline{R}_{pq}$ is the set of paths between OD pair (p,q) in the STEN. The flow on a given link (including queuing links) is the sum of all those assigned to the paths passing on this link; this is expressed mathematically as

$$v_a = \sum_{(p,q)} \sum_{r \in \underline{R}_{pq}} \delta_{ar} f_r,\ a \in \underline{A} \tag{13.10}$$

The total social cost incurred by all commuters is thus given by

$$TSC = \sum_{a \in \underline{A}} v_a c_a \tag{13.11}$$

It is assumed that the optimal use of the network capacity is achieved when the net economic benefit (total commuters benefit minus total social cost) is maximized. Therefore, the problem can be formulated as:

$$\max \sum_{(p,q)} \int_0^{d_{pq}} B_{pq}(\omega)d\omega - \sum_{a\in \underline{A}} c_a v_a \tag{13.12}$$

subject to

$$\sum_{t=0}^{T} d_{pq}(t) = d_{pq}, p\in P,\ q\in Q \tag{13.13}$$

$$\sum_{r\in \underline{R}_{pq}^{t}} f_r = d_{pq}(t), p\in P,\ q\in Q,\ t=0,1,\cdots,T \tag{13.14}$$

$$v_b \le s_a, b\in \underline{A}_a^{e}, a\in A \tag{13.15}$$

$$f_r \ge 0,\ r\in \underline{R}_{pq}, p\in P,\ q\in Q \tag{13.16}$$

where $\underline{R}_{pq}^{t}$ is the set of paths available between OD pair (p,q) during time period t in the STEN, and $\underline{A}_a^{e}$ is the set of exit links in the STEN corresponding to link $a\in A$ of the base network.

13.4.2 Optimality Conditions

To derive the necessary conditions for an optimal solution of the above optimization problem, we construct the Lagrangian function:

$$L(\mathbf{d},\mathbf{f},\mu,\varphi,\lambda) = -\sum_{(p,q)} \int_0^{d_{pq}} B_{pq}(\omega)d\omega + \sum_{a\in \underline{A}} c_a v_a + \sum_{t=0}^{T}\sum_{(p,q)} \mu_{pq}(t)\left(d_{pq}(t) - \sum_{r\in \underline{R}_{pq}^{t}} f_r\right)$$
$$+\sum_{(p,q)} \varphi_{pq}\left(d_{pq} - \sum_{t=0}^{T} d_{pq}(t)\right) + \sum_{a\in A}\sum_{b\in \underline{A}_a^{e}} u_b(v_b - s_a) \tag{13.17}$$

where φ_{pq} and $\mu_{pq}(t)$ are the Lagrange multipliers associated with the flow conservation constraints (13.13) and (13.14), respectively, u_b is the Lagrange multiplier associated with the link exit capacity constraints (13.15), and v_a is again defined by (13.10).

The Lagrangian should be minimized with respect to the flow variables (and maximized with respect to the dual variables) and subject to the following constraints:

$$f_r \ge 0,\ r\in \underline{R}_{pq}, p\in P,\ q\in Q \tag{13.18}$$

$$d_{pq}(t) \ge 0, p\in P,\ q\in Q,\ t=0,1,\cdots,T \tag{13.19}$$

$$d_{pq} \ge 0, p\in P,\ q\in Q \tag{13.20}$$

The first-order conditions for a stationary point of the program (13.12)-(13.16) with constraints (13.18)-(13.20) are given below:

$$f_r\left[\bar{c}_{pq}^{r}(t) - \mu_{pq}(t)\right] = 0,\ r\in \underline{R}_{pq}^{t}, p\in P,\ q\in Q,\ t=0,1,\cdots,T \tag{13.21}$$

$$\bar{c}_{pq}^{r}(t) - \mu_{pq}(t) \ge 0,\ r\in \underline{R}_{pq}^{t}, p\in P,\ q\in Q,\ t=0,1,\cdots,T \tag{13.22}$$

$$u_b(v_b - s_a) = 0, b \in \underline{A}_a^e, a \in A \tag{13.23}$$

$$d_{pq}(t)\left[\mu_{pq}(t) - \varphi_{pq}\right] = 0, p \in P, q \in Q, t = 0,1,\cdots,T \tag{13.24}$$

$$\mu_{pq}(t) - \varphi_{pq} \geq 0, p \in P, q \in Q, t = 0,1,\cdots,T \tag{13.25}$$

$$d_{pq}\left[\varphi_{pq} - B_{pq}(d_{pq})\right] = 0, p \in P, q \in Q \tag{13.26}$$

$$\varphi_{pq} - B_{pq}(d_{pq}) \geq 0, p \in P, q \in Q \tag{13.27}$$

$$u_b \geq 0, b \in \underline{A}_a^e, a \in A \tag{13.28}$$

and (13.13)-(13.15) and (13.18)-(13.20), where

$$\bar{c}_{pq}^r(t) = \sum_{b \in \underline{A}} \delta_{br} \bar{c}_b, r \in \underline{R}_{pq}^t, p \in P, q \in Q, t = 0,1,\cdots,T \tag{13.29}$$

$$\bar{c}_b = c_b + u_b \text{ if } b \in \underline{A}_a^e, a \in A \text{ and } \bar{c}_b = c_b \text{ otherwise}. \tag{13.30}$$

For the moment, we view $u_b, b \in \underline{A}_a^e, a \in A$ in (13.30) as an "additional cost" incurred by commuters besides the usual cost c_b in the STEN, and thus view $\bar{c}_{pq}^r(t)$ in (13.29) as the travel cost of path $r \in \underline{R}_{pq}^t$, $p \in P$, $q \in Q$, $t = 0,1,\cdots,T$. It is easy to understand that the set of the first-order conditions describe the commuters' equilibrium choice of departure time and route in the queuing network with schedule delay cost. The Lagrange multiplier $\mu_{pq}(t)$ is the minimum path travel cost between OD pair (p,q) during time period t. The OD specific Lagrange multiplier φ_{pq} is the minimum travel cost between OD pair (p,q) during any used period.

From conditions (13.15), (13.23) and (13.28), we can see that for any exit link $b \in \underline{A}_a^e$ in the STEN corresponding to the original link $a \in A$, if $v_b < s_a$ then $u_b = 0$; and if $v_b = s_a$ then $u_b \geq 0$. These conditions indicate that the "additional cost" on an exit link of the STEN should be charged only when flow on this link reaches its exit capacity. Therefore, if u_b, $b \in \underline{A}_a^e$, $a \in A$ in (13.30) is regarded as a special cost, an equilibrium is achieved, where the generalized costs (including the special term u_b for all departure times and routes that are actually used are identical and smaller than those for any time periods and routes not in use. Namely, no individual has an incentive to change his or her departure time and route for reducing the generalized cost in equilibrium.

Note that the traversal times on all links are constant, and the system optimization problem (13.12)-(13.16) can be actually regarded as a variable-demand network equilibrium assignment problem with explicit capacity constraints on link $b \in \underline{A}_a^e$, $a \in A$ in the STEN. The algorithm presented in Section 2.3 of Chapter 2 can be used to solve this problem.

13.4.3 Externality and Congestion Toll

Now we investigate the "additional cost" u_b, $b \in \underline{A}_a^e$, $a \in A$ in (13.30). Recall that $\underline{A}_a^e$ is the set of exit links in the STEN corresponding to the original link $a \in A$ for any periods $t = 0,1,\cdots,T$, and we rewrite these additional cost as $u_a(t)$, $a \in A$, $t = 0,1,\cdots,T$. We already understand that the set of the first-order necessary conditions for an optimum of the economic benefit maximization problem (13.12)-(13.16)is also the condition that governs the dynamic user equilibrium if the link cost and path cost are given by (13.30) and (13.29) respectively (we will say $\overline{c}_{pq}^r(t)$ and $\overline{c}_b$ are the generalized cost). The term c_b, $b \in \underline{A}$ of (13.30) is the constant free travel cost. This is the commuter's perceived trip -cost on this link. Theoretically, each additional commuter of a congested bottleneck imposes a congestion cost (known as an *externality*) on other commuters, by increasing the length of the queue and consequently the delay to later arrival commuters. However, in deciding when to depart, each commuter normally considers only his or her own cost (*i.e.* the perceived trip-cost) and does not consider the cost which he or she imposes on others. By imposing a toll exactly equal to the externality, we can ensure that the commuters' optimal private choices will also be optimal social choices. In our queuing network, the externality is just the special term in (13.30), namely the term $u_a(t)$, $a \in A$, $t = 0,1,\cdots,T$ which acts to drive a user-optimal flow pattern toward a system optimum. Therefore, this special term is nothing but the optimal toll to be charged for each original link during each time period. When these additional costs are charged, in deciding when and whether to travel, each commuter has to take account of the full social cost of his or her trip; consequently, a system optimum in terms of the maximization of net economic benefit is achieved.

We should point out that we are unable to provide a reduced-form expression and intuitive interpretation of the commuter's congestion externality or optimal congestion toll $u_a(t)$, $a \in A$, $t = 0,1,\cdots,T$ as in the standard static congestion pricing model or simple analytical dynamic tolling models. The reason is that we have already divided the whole study horizon (rush hour) into a number of inter-related periods and adopted an extended network representation of the dynamics of traffic congestion in the original network, and the contemporaneous (static) component and intertemporal (dynamic) component of a marginal commuter are thus hidden.

Finally, we spend few minutes to discuss the first-in-first-out (FIFO) property. It is well-known that the FIFO property of road traffic tends to be a problem in mathematical programming models for dynamic traffic assignment. The FIFO requirement states that if there is traffic in a queue and this traffic entered over a few time periods, one should ensure that the traffic which exits first is the traffic which entered first. The FIFO question does arise in the STEN. However, in the current context of system optimum, queues will be generally removed or replaced by the time-dependent tolls, and thus there would not be a serious FIFO problem in our model. The reason is that in the case of constant exit capacities for all bottlenecks, the system throughput is governed by the bottleneck capacities irrespective of the presence of queues. If there was a queue behind a bottleneck, we could always use a toll to replace (remove) it by affecting commuters' departure time from their home, thereby reducing the objective value at the system optimum. Therefore, queuing is not socially-optimal and the FIFO question is not existent. Note that these assertions generally hold under certain (realistic) conditions (*e.g.*, $\gamma > \alpha > \beta$ and constant exit capacity), but may not hold in some special situations.

13.5 NUMERICAL EXAMPLES

We present two numerical examples. The first example is concerned with only one bottleneck where optimal departure time and congestion toll can be obtained analytically and hence can be used to validate our model. In the second example, we apply our model to a general bottleneck network with elastic demand. This example demonstrates the potential application of the model to analyze the temporal and spatial evolution of traffic congestion and the optimal variable tolls to remove traffic queue.

13.5.1 A Single Bottleneck Network

Consider one origin-destination pair connected by one route with a bottleneck. The road on each side of the bottleneck (*e.g.* a bridge) has sufficient capacity that no congestion occurs. The bottleneck, whose capacity is s (vehicles/period), is subject to pure queuing congestion. Because the traveling time other than waiting in the queue is constant for this single route, we can simply assume this constant is zero without affecting results of interest. The O-D demand function is assumed to be $D(\mu) = \hat{D}\exp(-0.01\mu)$, where $\hat{D}$ represents the potential level of travel demand over the whole study horizon of time. The basic input data are: $T = 200$, $\hat{D} = 2000$, $s = 10$, $t^* = 100$, $\Delta = 10$, $\alpha = 0.7$, $\beta = 0.5$, $\gamma = 1.1$. Note that the time used here is measured in terms of period. For example, the first period ($t = 1$) may represent "7:00am - 7:01am" where each period is 1 minute long.

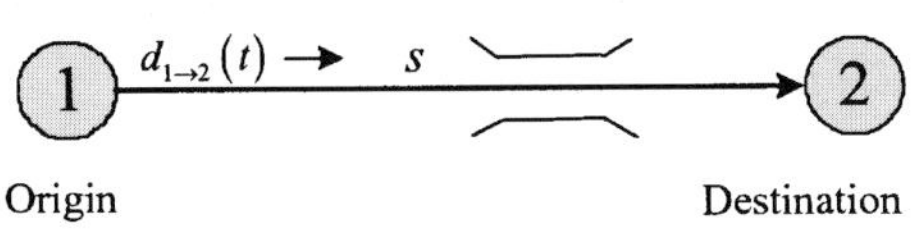

Figure 13.2 A single bottleneck route connecting an O-D pair

Table 13.1 Comparison of STEN results with analytical solutions

	STEN Method	Analytical Solution
Total traffic	1294.70	1347.90
Earliest departure period	13.00	11.08
Latest departure period	145.00	145.87
Equilibrium trip cost	39.39	39.46
Total schedule delay cost	21099.62	22651.47
Total waiting cost	0.00	0.00
Net benefit	164672.78	165326.57

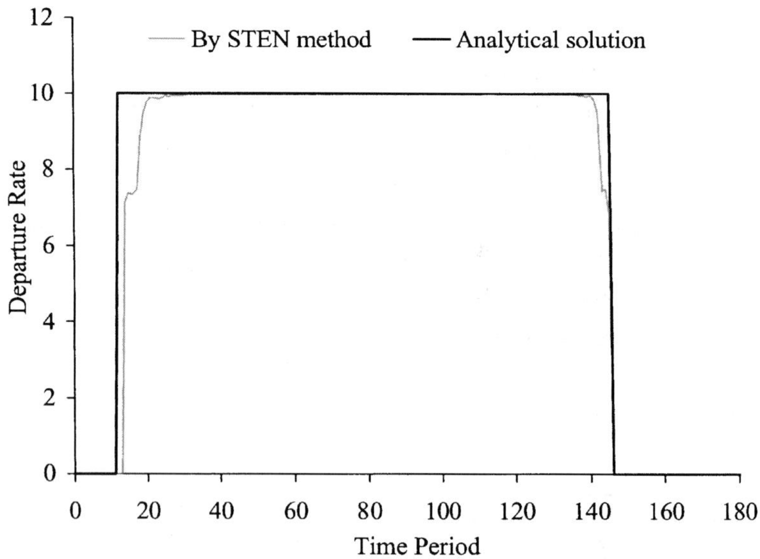

Figure 13.3 Comparison of departure flow rates (vehicles/period) for example 1 obtained by STEN method with analytical solution

The solution obtained with the STEN method is compared with the exact solution which can be obtained by analytical method (see, the elastic demand case in Subsection 11.2.1 in Chapter 11). The main results are summarized in Table 13.1. Figures 13.3 and 13.4 show comparisons of the toll and departure flow rate in each period obtained by the STEN method with the analytical solution. From these figures, it can be seen that the numerical results obtained by STEN method almost coincide with the exact solutions. This simple example validates that our STEN model works well.

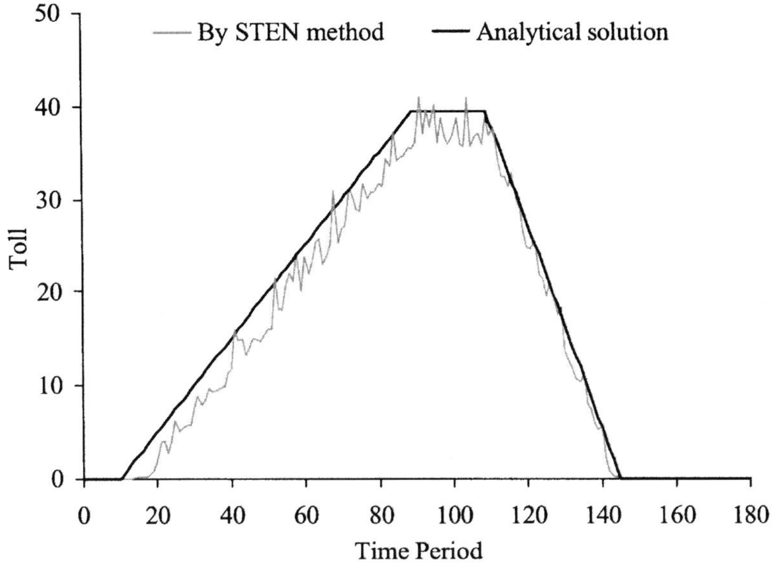

Figure 13.4 Comparison of bottleneck tolls for example 1 obtained by STEN method with analytical solution.

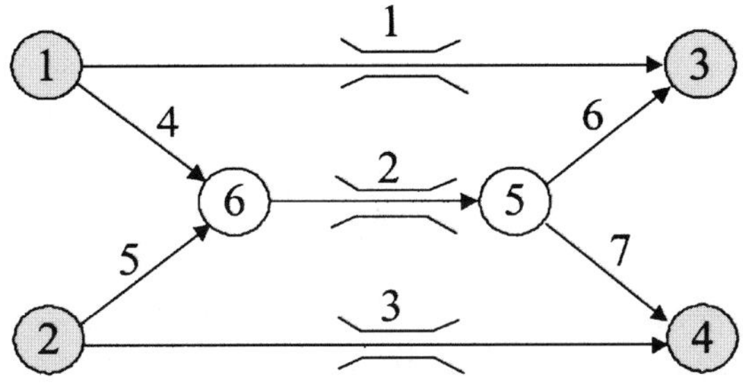

Figure 13.5 A general network with four OD pairs and three bottlenecks

Table 13.2 Link travel time and capacity for the general network

Link	1	2	3	4	5	6	7
Travel time	2.0	2.0	3.0	1.0	2.0	1.0	1.0
Capacity	50	150	80	9999	9999	9999	9999

Table 13.3 Group-specific work start time and schedule delay cost

	Commuters with common workplace at destination 3	Commuters with common workplace at destination 4
Preferred work starting time	$\left[t_3^* - \Delta_3, t_3^* + \Delta_3\right] = [12,13]$	$\left[t_4^* - \Delta_4, t_4^* + \Delta_4\right] = [10,11]$
Early arrival penalty	$c_3^s(t) = 0.9 \times (12 - t)$ for $t<12$ $(\beta_3 = 0.9)$	$c_4^s(t) = 0.8 \times (10 - t)$ for $t<10$ $(\beta_4 = 0.8)$
Late arrival penalty	$c_3^s(t) = 1.8 \times (t - 13)$ for $t > 13$ $(\gamma_3 = 1.8)$	$c_4^s(t) = 1.6 \times (t - 11)$ for $t > 11$ $(\gamma_4 = 1.6)$

13.5.2 A General Bottleneck Network

Figure 13.5 shows a general network with three bottlenecks. The bottleneck capacities and link free travel times are presented in Table 13.2 where a large number '9999' means no capacity constraint. It is assumed there are 4 OD pairs ($1\to3$, $1\to4$, $2\to3$, $2\to4$) with the following demand functions:

$$D_{1\to3}(\mu_{1\to3}) = 600\exp(-0.042\mu_{1\to3}),\ D_{1\to4}(\mu_{1\to4}) = 1200\exp(-0.050\mu_{1\to4}),$$

$$D_{2\to3}(\mu_{2\to3}) = 1500\exp(-0.040\mu_{2\to3}),\ D_{2\to4}(\mu_{2\to4}) = 700\exp(-0.043\mu_{2\to4}).$$

Note that all commuters must pass one of the three bottlenecks in order to reach their workplaces. We suppose there are two different groups of commuters whose working places are located at destinations 3 and 4, respectively. Each group has its own work start times and marginal disutility parameters of schedule delay. We represent the clock time by 20 time periods ($T = 20$) and set a common parameter value $\alpha = 1.0$. The group-specific work start times and schedule delay parameters are given in Table 13.3. The base network shown in Figure 13.5 is expanded over the 20 time periods, which leads to an expanded network of 479 links and 264 nodes (among which are 56 toll links).

The resultant realized travel demand between each OD pair are, respectively, $d_{1\to3}$=453.10, $d_{1\to4}$=811.95, $d_{2\to3}$=1046.12, $d_{2\to4}$=512.67 with the corresponding equilibrium generalized cost given by $\varphi_{1\to3}$=6.68, $\varphi_{1\to4}$=7.81, $\varphi_{2\to3}$=9.01, $\varphi_{2\to4}$=7.27.

Figure 13.6 depicts the departure rates (vehicles/period) of commuters between all four OD pairs. We can see that commuters between different OD pairs have different time periods of departure, and the departure rates over the used periods are almost constant except for the first one or two starting periods and the last one or two ending periods. The time period of departure for commuters between a particular OD pair depends on the work start time and the distance from homes (origins) to workplaces (destinations) and the demand to capacity ratios.

The constant (or saturated) departure rates are controlled by the limited exit capacities of bottlenecks.

Figure 13.7 plots the time trajectories of exit flows at the three bottlenecks. The exit flow at each bottleneck during its used periods equals its capacity except for the first and last one or two periods, which are due to discretization of time and error of numerical computation. Note that under the optimal time-dependent toll, which leads to a system optimum, queues at bottlenecks will be completely removed. Our numerical results, although not presented here, indeed demonstrate this conclusion, which are reflected by the fact that the flows on all waiting links in the STEN are almost zero.

Figure 13.8 depicts the toll during each period at each bottleneck. It is evident that the variable toll exhibits a similar pattern as in a single bottleneck situation. The toll at each bottleneck increases continuously from zero at the beginning to a maximum value, and then decreases continuously to zero. The starting and ending times and the maximum values of tolls for different bottlenecks are different.

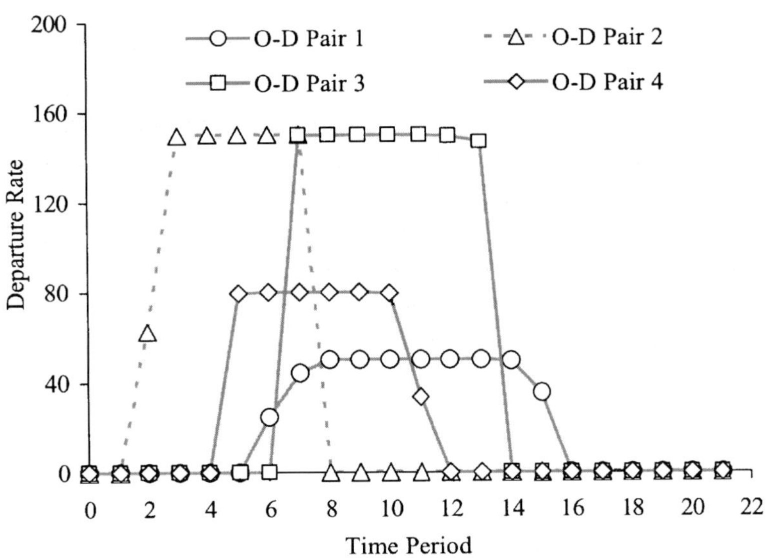

Figure 13.6 Departure distribution (veh/period) of trips between all OD pairs

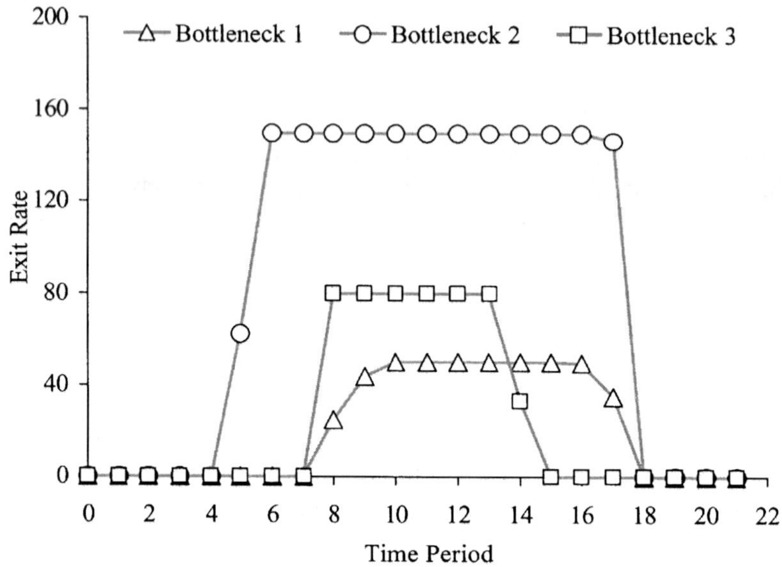

Figure 13.7 Exit flow rates (veh/period) at the three bottlenecks

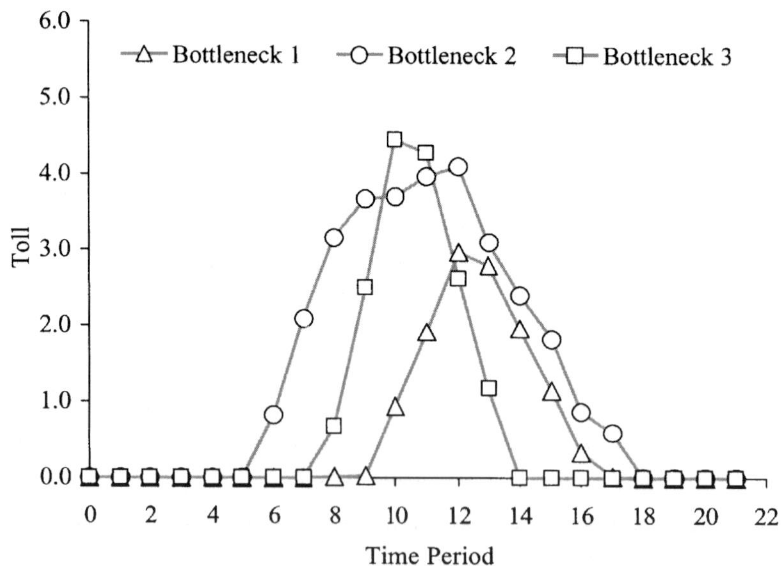

Figure 13.8 Tolls for the three bottlenecks over period

13.6 SUMMARY

In this chapter, we have extended the simple bottleneck models to general queuing networks. Our approach involves representation of the dynamics and interactions of commuter departure time and road traffic congestion by a space-time expanded network, over which the conventional network modeling techniques can readily be applied. The model takes into account the commuter heterogeneity in terms of their work start times and marginal utility parameters of schedule delays. A commuter's departure time and route choice are determined jointly together with the optimal time-varying tolls to achieve a system optimum. The expansion procedure of the base network can easily be fulfilled, and the computer implementation of the numerical algorithm involves nothing but a simple static capacity-constrained traffic assignment with elastic demand examined in previous chapters. The model can provide the planner with important information on traffic congestion: the evolution of traffic congestion over both space and time and the optimal tolls to remove queues.

13.7 SOURCES AND NOTES

Several studies have been developed in the literature to deal with traffic congestion and pricing in general networks. Carey and Srinivasan (1993) and Carey (1995) derived system marginal costs, user perceived costs, user externality costs and a set of optimal congestion tolls on general congested networks by using the Kuhn-Tucker necessary conditions. Ghali and Smith (1993) made an attempt to combine marginal-cost pricing with traffic control in a dynamic traffic assignment context for given dynamic demand. Wie (1993, 1995) examined the dynamic mixed behavior traffic equilibrium problem by applying the optimal control theory and non-cooperative N-person non-zero-sum differential game theory. Wie and Tobin (1998) determined time-varying congestion tolls by solving a convex control formulation of the dynamic system optimal traffic assignment problem on a network in the context of both day-to-day and instantaneous dynamic user equilibrium problems.

The STEN approach was originally proposed by Ford and Fulkerson (1962) for study of the dynamic maximal flow problem, where each link has a capacity and a fixed traversal time, and for any period of time, at each node vehicles can either be transshipped on exiting links or wait until the next period. Zawack and Thompson (1987) adapted the STEN approach for the dynamic traffic assignment on transportation networks with the terminology of green links for the travel links and red links for the queues. Afterwards, Drissi and Hameda (1992) and Drissi (1993) brought improvements to the STEN of Ford and Fulkerson (1962) by setting queues on the links, so that the vehicles in the queue of a link share the physical space with the other vehicles on the link. The material presented in the current chapter is drawn from Yang and Meng (1998), who further generalized the early STEN model to the analysis of departure time, route choice and congestion tolls with heterogeneous and elastic demand.

REFERENCES

Aarts, E.H.L. and Korst, J., 1989. *Simulated Annealing and Boltzmann Machines: A Stochastic Approach to Combinatorial Optimization and Neural Computing*. John Wiley & Sons.

Adler, J.L. and Cetin, M., 2001. A direct redistribution model of congestion pricing. *Transportation Research* 35B, 447-460.

Agnew, C.E., 1977. The theory of congestion tolls. *Journal of Regional Science* 17, 381-393.

Akamatsu, T., 1997. Decomposition of path choice entropy in general transport networks. *Transportation Science* 31, 349-362.

Akamatsu, T. and Kuwahara, M. 1989. Optimal toll pattern on a road network under stochastic user equilibrium with elastic demand. *Proceedings of the 5th WCTR*, Vol.I, pp.259-273.

Akamatsu, T. and Kuwahara, M., 1988. Optimal road pricing under stochastic user equilibrium. *Proceedings of the Japan Society of Civil Engineers* No.389/IV-8, 121-129.

Altman, E., Basar, T., Jimenez, T. and Shimkin, N., 2002. Competitive routing in networks with polynomial costs. *IEEE Transactions on Automatic Control* 47, 92-96.

Anderson, S.P., De Palma, A. and Thisse, J.F., 1992. *A Discrete Choice Theory of Imperfect Competition*. MIT Press, Cambridge.

Arnott, R., De Palma, A. and Lindsey, R., 1998. Recent developments in the bottleneck model. In: *Road Pricing, Traffic Congestion and the Environment: Issues of Efficiency and Social Feasibility* (eds., Button, K. and Verhoef, E.), Edward Elgar.

Arnott, R., De Palma, A. and Lindsey, R., 1994. The welfare effects of congestion tolls with heterogeneous commuters. *Journal of Transport Economics and Policy* 28, 139-161.

Arnott, R., De Palma, A. and Lindsey, R., 1993a. A structural model of peak-period congestion: A traffic bottleneck with elastic demand. *American Economic Review* 83, 161-179.

Arnott, R., De Palma, A. and Lindsey, R., 1993b. Properties of dynamic traffic equilibrium involving bottlenecks, including a paradox and metering. *Transportation Science* 27, 148-160.

Arnott, R., De Palma, A. and Lindsey, R., 1992. Route choice with heterogeneous drivers and group-specific congestion costs. *Regional Science and Urban Economics* 22, 71-102.

Arnott, R., De Palma, A. and Lindsey, R., 1990a. Departure time and route choice for the morning commute. *Transportation Research* 24B, 209-228.

Arnott, R., De Palma, A. and Lindsey, R., 1990b. Economics of a bottleneck. *Journal of Urban Economics* 27, 111-130.

Arnott, R., De Palma, A. and Lindsey, R., 1988. Schedule delay and departure time decisions with heterogeneous commuters. *Transportation Research Record* 1197, 56-67.

Arnott, R. and Kraus, M., 1998. When are anonymous congestion charges consistent with marginal cost pricing? *Journal of Public Economics* 67, 45-64.

Arnott, R. and Kraus, M., 1995. Financing capacity in the bottleneck model. *Journal of Urban Economics* 38, 272-290.

Bai, L., Hearn, D.W. and Lawphongpanich, S., 2004. Decomposition technique for the minimum toll revenue problem. *Networks* 44, 142-150,

Banister, D., Andersen, B. and Barrett, S., 1993. Private sector investments in transport infrastructure in Europe. In: *European Transport and Communication Networks* (eds., Banister D., Capello R. and Nijkamp P.), John Wiley & Sons, pp.191-219.

Bard, J.F., 1998. *Practical Bilevel Optimization: Algorithm and Applications*. Kluwer Academic Publishers.

Bazaraa, M., Sherali, H.D. and Shetty, C.M., 1993. *Nonlinear Programming: Theory and Algorithms* (2nd edn). John Wiley & Sons, New York.

Beckmann, M.J., 1965. On optimal tolls for highways, tunnels and bridges. In: *Vehicular Traffic Science* (eds., Herman L.C. and Rothery R.). Elsevier, New York, pp.331-341.

Beckmann, M.J., McGuire, C.B. and Winsten, C.B., 1956. *Studies in the Economics of Transportation*. Yale University Press, New Haven, CT.

Bell, M.G.H., 1995. Stochastic user equilibrium assignment in networks with queues. *Transportation Research* 29B, 125-137.

Bell, M.G.H. and Iida, Y., 1997. *Transportation Network Analysis*. John Wiley and Sons.

Bellei, G. Gentile, G. and Papola, N., 2002, Network pricing optimization in multi-user and multimodal context with elastic demand. *Transportation Research* 36B, 779-798.

Ben-Akiva, M., De Palma, A. and Kanaroglou, P., 1986. Dynamic model of peak period traffic congestion with elastic arrival rates. *Transportation Science* 20, 164-181.

Ben-Akiva, M. and Lerman, S.R., 1985. *Discrete Choice Analysis: Theory and Application to Travel Demand*. The MIT Press, Cambridge.

Bergendorff, P., Hearn, D.W. and Ramana, M.V., 1997. Congestion toll pricing of traffic networks. In: *Network Optimization* (eds., Pardalos P.M., Hearn D.W. and Hager W.W.), *Lecture Notes in Economics and Mathematical Systems*. Springer-Verlag Series, pp.51-71.

Bernstein, D. and Gabriel, S., 1997. Solving the non-additive traffic equilibrium problem. In: *Network Optimization* (eds., Pardalos P.M., Hearn D.W. and Hager W.W.), *Lecture Notes in Economics and Mathematical Systems*. Springer-Verlag Series, pp.72-102.

Bernstein, D., 1993. Congestion pricing with tolls and subsidies. In: *Proceedings of the Pacific Rim Transportation Technology Conference*, Vol.2, pp.145-151

Bertsekas, D.P., 1982. *Constrained Optimization and Lagrange Multiplier Methods*. Academic Press, New York.

Bertsekas, D.P., 1999. *Nonlinear Programming*. Athena Scientific, Belmont, Mass.

Bertsekas, D.P. and Tsitsiklis, J.N., 1989. *Parallel and Distributed Computation: Numerical Methods*. Prentice-Hall, Englewood Cliffs, NJ, 1989

Boyce, D.E., LeBlanc, L.J. and Chon, K.S., 1988. Network equilibrium models of urban location and travel choices: a retrospective survey. *Journal of Regional Science* 28, 159-183.

Braess, D., 1968. Uber ein paradoxen der verkehrsplaning. *Unternehmensforschung* 12, 258-268.

Braid, R.M., 1996. Peak-load pricing of a transport facility with an unpriced substitute. *Journal of Urban Economics* 40, 179-197.

Braid, R.M., 1989. Uniform versus peal-load pricing of a bottleneck with elastic demand. *Journal of Urban Economics* 26, 320-327.

Brotcorne, L., Labbe, M., Marcotte, P. and Savard, G., 2001. A bilevel model for toll optimization on a multicommodity transportation network. *Transportation Science* 35, 345-358.

Bruynooghe, M., Gilbert, A., Sakarovitch, M., 1968. Une mèthode d'affectation du trafic. In: *Proceedings of the 4th International Symposium on the Theory of Road Traffic Flow*. Karlsruhe, Germany, pp.198-204.

Button, K.J., 1993. *Transport Economics* (2nd Edition). Edward Elgar, England.

Button, K.J. and Verhoef, E.T., (eds.) 1998. *Road Pricing, Traffic Congestion and the Environment: Issues of Efficiency and Social Feasibility*. Edward Elgar.

Carey, M., 1995. Dynamic congestion pricing and the price of FIFO. In: *Urban Transportation Networks: Dynamic Flow Modeling and Control* (eds., Gartner N.H. and Improta G.). Springer-Verlag, pp.233-250.

Carey, M. and Srinivasan, S., 1993. Externalities, average and marginal costs and tolls on congested networks with time-varying flows. *Operations Research* 41, 217-231.

Ceylan, H. and Bell, M.G.H., 2004. Sensitivity analysis on stochastic equilibrium transportation networks using genetic algorithm. *Journal of Advanced Transportation* 38, 291-321.

Chau, C.K. and Sim, K.M., 2003. The price of anarchy for non-atomic congestion games with symmetric cost maps and elastic demands. *Operations Research Letters* 31, 327-334.

Chen, A., Lo, H.K. and Yang, H., 2001. A self-adaptive projection and contraction algorithm for the traffic equilibrium problem with path-specific costs. *European Journal of Operational Research Society* 135, 27-41.

Chen, M., Bernstein, D.H. and Spasovic, L.N., 2004. Toll-design problem with stochastic route choice. *Environmental and Planning* 31B, 731-742.

Chen, M. and Bernstein, D.H., 2004. Solving the toll design problem with multiple user groups. *Transportation Research* 38B, 61-79.

Chen, W.K., 1997. *Graph Theory and Its Engineering Applications*. World Scientific, Singapore.

Chen, Y. and Florian, M., 1995. The nonlinear bilevel programming problem: formulations, regularity and optimality conditions. *Optimization* 32, 193-209.

Cho, H.J., Smith, T.E. and Friesz, T.L., 2000. A reduction method for local sensitivity analyses of network equilibrium arc flows. *Transportation Research* 34B, 31-51.

Chu, X., 1995. Endogenous trip scheduling: The Henderson approach reformulated and compared with the Vickrey approach. *Journal of Urban Economics* 37, 324-343.

Clark, S.D. and Watling, D.P., 2002. Sensitivity analysis of the probit-based stochastic user equilibrium assignment model. *Transportation Research* 36B, 617-635.

Clark, S.D. and Watling, D.P., 2000. Probit-based sensitivity analysis for general traffic networks. *Transportation Research Record* 1733, 88-95.

Clegg, J., Smith, M.J., Xiang, Y.L. and Yarrow, R., 2001. Bilevel programming applied to optimizing urban transportation. *Transportation Research* 35B, 41-70.

Cohen, Y., 1987. Commuter welfare under peak-load congestion tolls: Who gains and who loses? *International Journal of Transport Economics* 14, 239-266.

Correa, J.R., Schulz, A.S., and Stier-Moses, N.E., 2004. Selfish routing in capacitated networks. *Mathematics of Operations Research* 29, 961–976.

Correa, J.R., Schulz, A.S., and Stier Moses, N.E., 2005. On the inefficiency of equilibria in congestion games. In: *Proceedings of the 11th Conference on Integer Programming and Combinatorial Optimization* (IPCO 2005), to appear.

Dafermos, S.C., 1971. An extended traffic assignment model with applications to two-way traffic. *Transportation Science* 5, 366-389.

Dafermos, S.C. and Sparrow, F.T., 1971. Optimal resource allocation and toll patterns in user-optimized transport network. *Journal of Transport Economics and Policy* 5, 198-200.

Dafermos, S.C., 1972. The traffic assignment problem for multi-class user transportation networks. *Transportation Science* 6, 73-87.

Dafermos, S.C., 1973. Toll patterns for multiclass-user transportation networks. *Transportation Sciences* 7, 211-223.

Dafermos, S.C., 1980. Traffic equilibrium and variational ineqalities. *Transportation Science* 14, 42-54.

Dafermos, S.C., 1982. Relaxation algorithms for the general asymmetric traffic equilibrium problem. *Transportation Science* 16, 231-240.

Dafermos, S.C. and Sparrow, F.T., 1969. The traffic assignment problem for a general network. *Journal of Research of the National Bureau of Standards* 73B, 91-118.

Dafermos, S.C. and Sparrow, F.T., 1971. Optimal resource allocation and toll patterns in user-optimized transport network. *Journal of Transport Economics and Policy* 5, 198-200.

Dafermos, S.C. and Nagurney, A., 1984. Sensitivity analysis for the asymmetric network equilibrium problem. *Mathematical Programming* 28, 174-184.

Daganzo, C.F., 1983. Stochastic network equilibrium with multiple vehicle types and asymmetric, indefinite link cost Jacobians. *Transportation Science* 17, 282-300.

Daganzo, C.F., 1985. The uniqueness of a time-dependent equilibrium distribution of arrivals at a single bottleneck. *Transportation Science* 19, 29-37.

Danielis, R. and Marcucci, E., 2002. Bottleneck road congestion pricing with a competing railroad service. *Transportation Research* 38E, 379-388.

David, A.K. and Fernando, P.N., 1995. The BOT option: conflicts and compromises. *Energy Policy* 23, 669-675.

DeCorla-Souza, P., 1994. Applying the cashing out approach to congestion pricing. *Transportation Research Record* 1450, 34-37.

Dekkers, A. and Aarts, E., 1991. Global optimization and simulated annealing. *Mathematical Programming* 50, 367-393.

Dempe, S., 2002. *Foundation of Bilevel Programming.* Klumer Academic Publishers.

Dempe, S., 2000. A bundle algorithm applied to bilevel programming problems with non-unique lower level solutions. *Computational Optimization and Applications* 15, 145-166.

De Palma, A., 1992. A game-theoretic approach to the analysis of simple congested networks. *American Economic Review* 82, 494-500.

De Palma, A. and Arnott, R., 1986. Usage dependent peak-load pricing. *Economics Letters* 20, 101-105.

De Palma A. and Lindsey, R., 2004. Congestion pricing with heterogeneous travelers: A general-equilibrium welfare analysis. *Networks and Spatial Economics* 4, 135-160.

De Palma, A. and Lindsey, R., 2002. Comparison of morning and evening commutes in the Vickrey bottleneck model. *Transportation research Record* 1807, 26-33.

De Palma, A. and Lindsey, R., 2000. Private toll roads: Competition under various ownership regimes. *Annals of Regional Science* 34, 13-35.

De Palma, A. and Lindsey, R., 2002. Private roads, competition, and incentives to adopt time-based congestion tolling. *Journal of Urban Economics* 52, 217–241.

De Palma A and Nesterov, Y., 1998. Optimization formulations and static equilibrium in congested transportation networks. CORE Discussion Paper 9861.

De Rus, G. and Romero, M., 2004. Private financing of roads and optimal pricing: Is it possible to get both? *Annals of Regional Science* 38, 485-497.

De vany, A. and Saving, T., 1980. Competition and highway pricing for stochastic traffic. *Journal of Business* 53, 45-60.

Devarajan, S., 1981. A note on network equilibrium and non-cooperative games. *Transportation Research* 15B, 421-426.

Dial, R.B., 2000. Minimal-revenue congestion pricing Part II: an efficient algorithm for the general case. *Transportation Research* 34B, 645-665.

Dial, R.B., 1999a. Network-optimized road pricing Part 1: a parable and a model. *Transportation Science* 47, 54-64.

Dial, R.B., 1999b. Network-optimized road pricing Part 2: algorithms and examples. *Transportation Science* 47, 327-336.

Dial, R.B., 1999c. Minimal-revenue congestion pricing Part I: a fast algorithm for the single-origin case. *Transportation Research* 33B, 189-202.

Dial, R.B., 1997. Bi-criterion traffic assignment: Efficient algorithms plus examples. *Transportation Research* 31B, 357-379.

Dial, R.B., 1996. Bicriterion traffic assignment: Basic theory and elementary algorithms. *Transportation Science* 30, 93-111.

Downs, A., 1993. Point of view: implementing peak-hour road pricing at full scale: finding solution to practical problems. *TR News* 167, 7-9.

Drissa-Kaïtouni, O., 1993. A variational inequality formulation of the dynamic traffic assignment problem. *European Journal of Operational Research* 71, 188-204.

Drissa-Kaïtouni, O. and Hameda-Benchekroun, A., 1992. A dynamic traffic assignment model and a solution algorithm. *Transportation Science* 26, 119-128.

Eliasson, J., 2001. Road pricing with limited information and heterogeneous users: A successful case. *Annals of Regional Science* 35, 595-604.

Else, P.K., 1981. A reformulation of the theory of optimal congestion taxes. *Journal of Transport Economics and Policy* 16, 217-232.

Else, P.K., 1982. A reformulation of the theory of optimal congestion taxes, A rejoinder. *Journal of Transport Economics and Policy* 17, 299-304.

Erlander, S. and Stewart, N.F., 1990. *The Gravity Model in Transportation Analysis: Theory and Extensions*, VSP, Utrecht, The Netherlands.

Evans, A.W., 1992. Road congestion pricing: when is it a good policy? *Journal of Transport Economics and Policy* 26, 213-243.

Evans, A.W., 1993. Road congestion pricing: When is it a good policy? A rejoinder. *Journal of Transport Economics and Policy* 27, 99-105.

Facchinei, F. and Pang, J.S., 2003. *Finite-dimensional Variational Inequalities and Complementarity Problems*. Springer-Verlag.

Ferrari, P., 1999. A model of urban transport management. *Transportation Research* 33B, 43-61.

Ferrari, P., 1997. Capacity constraints in urban transport networks. *Transportation Research* 31B, 291-301.

Ferrari, P., 1995. Road pricing and network equilibrium. *Transportation Research* 29B, 357-372.

Fiacco, A.V., 1983. *Introduction to Sensitivity and Stability Analysis in Nonlinear Programming*. Academic Press, New York.

Fisk, C.S., 1980. Some developments in equilibrium traffic assignment. *Transportation Research* 14B, 243-255.

Fisk, C. and Nguyen, S., 1982. Solution algorithms for network equilibrium models with asymmetric user costs. *Transportation Science* 16, 361-381.

Florian, M., 1998. Network equilibrium models for analyzing toll highways. In: *Proceedings of the International Conference on Transportation into the Next Millennium*. Singapore.

Florian, M. and Spiess, H., 1982. The convergence of diagonalization algorithms for asymmetric network equilibrium problems. *Transportation Research* 16B, 447-483.

Ford, L.R. and Fulkerson, D.R., 1962. *Flows in Networks*. Princeton University Press, Princeton, N.J.

Foster, C., 1975. A note on the distributional effects of road pricing: A comment. *Journal of Transport Economics and Policy* 9, 186-187.

Frank, M. and Wolfe, P., 1956. An algorithm for quadratic programming. *Naval Research Logistic* Quarterly 3, 95-110.

Friesz, T.L., Bernstein, D. and Kydes, N., 2004. Dynamic congestion pricing in disequilibrium. *Networks and Spatial Economics* 4, 181-202.

Friesz, T.L., Cho, H.J., Mehta, N.J., Tobin, R.L. and Anandalinggam, G., 1992. A simulated annealing approach to the network design problem with variational inequality constraints. *Transportation Science* 26, 18-26.

Friesz, T.L., Tobin, R.L., Cho, H.J. and Mehta, N.J., 1990. Sensitivity analysis based heuristic algorithms for mathematical programs with variational inequality constraints. *Mathematical Programming* 48, 265-284.

Fukushima, M., 1992. Equivalent differentiable optimization problems and descent methods for asymmetric variational inequality problems. *Mathematical Programming* 53, 99-110.

Fukushima, M., 1984. A modified Frank-Wolfe algorithm for solving the traffic equilibrium problem. *Transportation Research* 18B, 169-177.

Gabriel, S. and Bernstein, D., 1997. The traffic equilibrium problem with non-additive path costs. *Transportation Science* 31, 337-348.

Gauvin, J. and Dubeau, F., 1982. Differential properties of the marginal function in mathematical programming. *Mathematical Programming Study* 9, 101-119.

Geltner, D. and Moavenzadeh, F., 1987. An economic argument for privatization of highway ownership. *Transportation Research Record* 1107, 14-20.

Ghali, M.O. and Smith, M.J., 1993. Traffic assignment, traffic control and road pricing. In: *Transportation and Traffic Theory* (ed., Daganzo C.F.). Elsevier Science Publishers, 147-169.

Giuliano, G., 1992. An assessment of the political acceptability of congestion pricing. *Transportation* 19, 335-358.

Glazer, A., 1981. Congestion tolls and consumer welfare. *Public Finance* 36, 77-83.

Gomez-Ibanez, J., Meyer, J.R. and Luberoff, D.E., 1991. The prospects for privatizing infrastructure. *Journal of Transport Economics and Policy* 25, 259-278.

Goodwin, P.B., 1992. A review of new demand elasticities with special reference to short and long run effects of price changes. *Journal of Transport Economics and Policy* 26, 155-169.

Goodwin, P.B., 1989. The rule of three: a possible solution to the political problem of competing objectives for road pricing. *Traffic Engineering and Control* 29, 495-497.

Harker, P.T., 1988. Multiple equilibrium behaviors on networks. *Transportation Science* 22 39-46.

Hall, M.A., 1978. Properties of the equilibrium state in transportation networks. *Transportation Science* 12, 208-216.

Hau, T.D., 1992. *Economic Fundamentals of Road Pricing: A Diagrammatic Analysis.* Transport Division, The World Bank.

Hau, T.D., 1998. Congestion pricing and road investment. In: *Road Pricing, Traffic Congestion and the Environment—Issues of Efficiency and Social Feasibility* (eds., Button K.J. and Verhoef E.T.). Edward Elgar, pp. 39-78.

Haupt, R.L. and Haupt, S.E., 1998. *Practical Genetic Algorithms*. John Wiley & Sons.

Haurie, A. and Marcotte, P., 1985. On the relationship between Nash-Cournot and Wardrop equilibria. *Networks* 15, 295-308.

Hearn, D.W. and Ramana, M.V., 1998. Solving congestion toll pricing models. In: *Equilibrium and Advanced Transportation Modeling* (eds., Marcotte P. and Nguyen S.). Kluwer Academic Publishers, pp.109-124.

Hearn, D.W. and Yildirim, M.B., 2002. A toll pricing framework for traffic assignment problem with elastic demand. In: *Current Trends in Transportation and Network Analysis* (eds., Gendreau M. and Marcotte P.). Kluwer Academic Publishers, pp.135-145.

Henderson, J.V., 1974. Road congestion: A reconsideration of pricing theory. *Journal of Urban Economics* 1, 346-365.

Henderson, J.V., 1981. The economics of staggered work hours. *Journal of Urban Economics* 9, 349-364.

Henderson, J.V., 1985. *Economic Theory and the Cities* (2nd Edition). Academic Press, NY.

Hensher, D.A. and Button, K.J., (eds.) 2000. *Handbook of Transport Modeling*. Elsevier Science.

Hensher, D.A. and Truong, T.P., 1985. Valuation of travel times savings. *Journal of Transport Economics and Policy* 19, 237-260.

Herman, A., 1982. Remarks on traffic flow theories and the characterization of traffic in cities. In: *Self-Organization and Dissipative Structures* (eds., Schieve C. and Allen P.M.). University of Texas Press, Austin.

Hills, P., 1993, Road congestion pricing: When is it a good policy? A comment. *Journal of Transport Economics and Policy* 27, 91-99.

Huang, H.J., 1995. A combined algorithm for solving and calibrating the stochastic traffic equilibrium model. *Journal of the Operational Research* Society 46, 977-987.

Huang, H.J., 2000. Fares and tolls in a competitive system with transit and highway: the case with two groups of commuters. *Transportation Research* 36E, 267-284.

Huang, H.J., 2002. Pricing and logit-based mode choice models of a transit and highway system with elastic demand. *European Journal of Operational Research* 140, 562-570.

Huang H.J. and Bell, M.G.H., 1998. Continuous equilibrium network design problem with elastic demand: Derivative-free solution methods. In: *Transportation Networks: Recent Methodological Advances* (ed., Bell M.G.H.). Elsevier Science, pp.175-193.

Huang, H.J. and Yang, H., 1996. Optimal variable road-use pricing on a congested network of parallel routes with elastic demand. In: *Transportation and Traffic Theory* (ed., Lessort J.B.). Elsevier Science, pp.479-500.

Huang, H.J. and Yang, H., 1999. Optimal utilization of a transport system with auto/transit parallel modes. *Optimal Control Applications and Methods* 20, 297-313.

Huang H.J., Yang, H. and Bell, M.G.H., 2000. The models and economics of carpools. *Annals of Regional Science* 34, 55-68.

Johansson, B. and Mattsson, L., (eds.) 1995. *Road Pricing: Theory, Empirical Assessment and Policy*. Kluwer Academic Publishers.

Josefsson, M. and Patriksson, M., 2003. Sensitivity analysis of separable traffic euilibria, with applcation to bilevel optimization in network design. http://www.md.chalmers.se /~mipat/traffic.html.

Kalmanje, S. and Kockelman K.M., 2004. Credit-based congestion pricing: travel, land value, & welfare impacts. *Transportation Research Record* 1864, 45-53.

Kawakami, S., Hirobata, Y. and Zu, Z., 1989. A study of the multi-class traffic assignment method with separation of car and truck link flows. *Review of Infrastructure Planning* 7, 243-250 (in Japanese).

Keeler, T.E. and Small, K.A., 1977. Optimal peak-load pricing, investment, and service levels on urban expressways. *Journal of Political Economy* 85, 1-25.

Kinderlehrer, D. and Stampacchia, G., 1980. *An Introduction to Variational Inequalities and Their Applications*. Academic Press, New York.

Knight, F.H., 1924. Some fallacies in the interpretation of social costs. *Quarterly Journal of Economics* 38, 582-606.

Konishi, H., 2004. Uniqueness of user equilibrium in transportation networks with heterogeneous commuters. *Transportation Science* 38, 315-330.

Labbe, M., Marcotte, P. and Savard, G., 1998. A bilevel model of taxation and its application to optimal highway pricing. *Management Science* 44, 1608-1622.

Laih, C.H., 1994. Queuing at a bottleneck with single- and multi-step tolls. *Transportation Research* 28A, 197-208.

Lam, W.H.K., Cheung, C.Y. and Lam, C.F., 1999. A study of crowding effects at the Hong Kong light rail transit stations. *Transportation Research* 33A, 401-415.

Larsson, T., Lindberg, P.O., Patriksson, M. and Rydergren, C., 2002. On traffic equilibrium models with a nonlinear time/money relation. In: *Transportation Planning: State of the Art* (eds., Patriksson M and Labbé M). Kluwer Academic Publishers, pp.19-31.

Larsson, T. and Patriksson, M., 1995. An augmented Lagrangean dual algorithm for link capacity side constrained traffic assignment problems. *Transportation Research* 29B, 433-455.

Larsson, T. and Patriksson, M., 1999. Ergodic, primal convergence in dual subgradient schemes for convex programming. *Mathematical Programming* 86, 283-312.

Lawphongpanich, S. and Hearn, D.W., 2004. An MPEC approach to second-best toll pricing. *Mathematical Programming* 101, 33-55.

Layard, R., 1977. The distributional effects of congestion taxes. *Economica* 44, 297-304.

LeBlanc, L.J., Helgason, R.V. and Boyce, D.E., 1985. Improved efficiency of the Frank-Wolfe algorithm for convex network programs. *Transportation Science* 19, 445-462.

LeBlanc, L.J., Morlok, E.K. and Pierskalla, W., 1975. An efficient approach to solving the road network equilibrium traffic assignment problem. *Transportation Research* 9, 309-318.

Leurent, F., 1993. Cost versus time equilibrium over a network. *European Journal of Operational Research* 71, 205-221.

Leurent, F., 1996. The theory and practice of a dual criteria assignment model with a continuously distributed value-of-time. In: *Transportation and Traffic Theory* (ed., Lesort JB). Elsevier Science, pp.455-477.

Leurent, F., 1998. Sensitivity and error analysis of the dual criteria traffic assignment model. *Transportation Research* 32B,189-204.

Levinson, D.M., 2002. *Financing Transportation Networks*. Edward Elgar.

Levy-Lambert, H., 1968. Tarification des services a qualite variable: application aux peages decirculation. *Econometrica* 36, 564-574.

Lewis, N.C., 1993. *Road Pricing: Theory and Practice*. Thomas Telford, London.

Li, M.Z.F., 2002. The role of speed-flow relationship in congestion pricing implementation with an application to Singapore. *Transportation Research* 36B, 731-754.

Li, M.Z.F., 1999. Estimating congestion toll by using traffic count data – Singapore's area licensing scheme. *Transportation Research* 35E, 1-10.

Lindsey, R. and Verhoef, E.T., 2001. Traffic congestion and congestion pricing. In: *Handbook of Transport Systems and Traffic Control* (eds., Button K.J. and Hensher D.A.). Elsevier Science, pp.77-105.

Lindsey, R., 2004. Existence, uniqueness, and trip cost function properties of user equilibrium in the bottleneck model with multiple user classes. *Transportation Science* 38, 293-314.

Litman, T., 1996. Using road pricing revenue: economic efficiency and equity considerations. *Transportation Research Record* 1558, 24-28.

Liu, L.N. and Boyce, D.E., 2002. Variational inequality formulation of the system-optimal travel choice problem and efficient congestion tolls for a general transportation network with multiple time periods. *Regional Science and Urban Economics* 32: 627-650.

Liu, L.N. and McDonald, F., 1999. Economic efficiency of second-best congestion pricing schemes in urban highway systems. *Transportation Research* 33B, 157-188.

Lo, H.K. and Chen, A., 2000a. Traffic equilibrium problem with route-specific costs: formulation and algorithms. *Transportation Research* 34B, 493-513.

Lo, H.K. and Chen, A., 2000b. Reformulating the traffic equilibrium problem via a smooth gap function. *Mathematical and Computer Modeling* 31, 179-195.

Lo, H.K. and Hickman, M.D., 1997. Toward an evaluation framework for road pricing. *Journal of Transportation Engineering* ASCE 123, 316-324.

Luo, Z.Q., Pang, J.S. and Ralph, D., 1996. *Mathematical Programs with Equilibrium Constraints.* Cambridge University Press.

Maher, M. Stewart, K. and Rosa, A., 2005. Stochastic social optimum traffic assignment. *Transportation Research* 39B, 753-767.

Marchand, M., 1968. A note on optimal tolls in an imperfect environment. *Econometrica* 36, 575-581.

Marcotte, P. and Wynter, L., 2004. A new look at the multiclass network equilibrium problem. *Transportation Science* 38, 282-292.

Marcotte, P. and Zhu, D.L., 2000. Equilibria with infinitely many differentiated classes of customers. In: *Complementarity and Variational Problems—State of the* Art (eds., Ferris M.C. and Pang J.S.). SIAM, Philadelphia, PA.

Marcotte, M. and Zhu, D.L., 1996. Exact and inexact penality methods for the generalized bilevel programming problems. *Mathematical Programming* 74, 141-157.

Marvin, K., 2003. A new look at the two-mode problem. *Journal of Urban Economics* 54, 511-530.

May, A.D. and Milne, D.S., 2000. Effects of alternative road pricing systems on network performance. *Transportation Research* 34A, 407-436.

May, A.D., Milne, D.S., Shepherd, S.P. and Sumalee, A., 2002. Specification of optimal cordon pricing locations and charges. *Transportation Research Record* 1812, 60-68.

May, A.D., Liu, R., Shepherd, S.P. and Sumalee, A., 2002. The impact of cordon design on the performance of road pricing schemes. *Transport Policy 9, 209-220.*

Mayet, J. and Hansen, M., 2000. Congestion pricing with continuously distributed values of time. *Journal of Transport Economics and Policy* 34, 359-370.

McDoland, J.F., 1995. Urban highway congestion. *Transportation* 22, 353-369.

McDonald, J.F., d'Ouville, E.L. and Liu, L.N., 1999. *Economics of Urban Highway Congestion and Pricing.* Kluwer Academic Publishers.

Meng, Q., Lee, D.H., Cheu, R.L. and Yang, H., 2004. Logit-based stochastic user equilibrium problem for entry-exit toll scheme. *Journal of Transportation Engineering* 130, ASCE, 805-813.

Meng, Q., Xu, W. and Yang, H., 2005. A trial-and-error procedure for implementing a road-pricing scheme. *Transportation Research Record* (in press).

Meng, Q. and Yang, H., 2002. Benefit distribution and equity in road network design. *Transportation Research* 36B, 19-35.

Meng, Q., Yang, H. and Bell, M.G.H., 2001. An equivalent continuously differentiable model and a locally convergent algorithm for the continuous network design problem. *Transportation Research* 35B, 83-105.

Mills, G., 1995. Welfare and profit divergence for a tolled link in a road network. *Journal of Transport Economics and Policy* 29, 137-146.

Mohring, H., 1970. The peak load problem with increasing returns and pricing constraints. *American Economic Review* 60, 693-705.

Mohring, H., 1976. *Transportation Economics*. Cambridge.

Mohring, H., and Harwitz, M., 1962. *Highway Benefits: An Analytical Framework.* Northwestern University Press, Evanston, IL.

Mun, S., Konishi, K. and Yoshikawa, K., 2003. Optimal cordon pricing. *Journal of Urban Economics* 54, 21-38.

Mun, S., 1994. Traffic jams and the congestion toll. *Transportation Research* 28B, 365-375.

Nagurney, A., 2000. A multiclass, multicriteria traffic network equilibrium model. *Mathematical and Computer Modeling* 32, 393-411.

Nagurney, A., 1999. *Network Economics: A Variational Inequality Approach.* Second and revised edition, Kluwer Academic Publishers.

Nagurney, A. and Dong, J., 2002. A multiclass, multicriteria traffic network equilibrium model with elastic demand. *Transportation Research* 36B, 445-469.

Nash, C.A., 1982. A reformulation of the theory of optimal congestion taxes, a comment and a rejoinder. *Journal of Transport Economics and Policy* 17, 299-304.

Netter, M., 1971. Equilibrium and marginal cost pricing on a road network with several traffic flow types. In: *Proceedings of 5th International Symposium on the Theory of Traffic Flow and Transportation.* Berkeley, pp.155-163.

Newbery, D.M., 1988. Road damage externalities and road user charges. *Econometrica* 56, 295-316.

Newbery, D.M., 1989. Cost recovery from optimally designed roads. *Economica* 56, 165-185.

Newell, G.F., 1987. The morning commute for non-identical travelers. *Transportation Science* 21, 74-88.

Newell, G.F., 1988. Traffic flow for the morning commute. *Transportation Science* 22, 47-58.

Nijkamp, P. and Rienstra, S.A., 1995. Private sector involvement in financing and operating transport infrastructure. *Annals of Regional Science* 29, 221-235.

Oppenheim, N., 1995. *Urban Travel Demand Modeling: From Individual Choices to General Equilibrium.* John Wiley & Sons.

Oum, T.H. and Zhang, Y., 1990. Airport pricing: congestion tolls, lumpy investment, and cost recovery. *Journal of Public Economics* 48, 353-374.

Oum, T.H., Waters, W.G. and Yong, J.S., 1992. Concepts of price elasticities of transport demand and recent empirical estimates. *Journal of Transport Economics and Policy* 26, 139-154.

Parry, I.W.H. and Bento, Q., 2001. Revenue recycling and the welfare effects of road pricing. *Scandinavian Journal of Economics* 103, 645-671.

Paulley, N., 2002. Recent studies on key issues in road pricing. *Transport Policy* 9, 175-177.

Papadimitriou, C.H., 2001. Algorithms, games, and the internet. In: *Proceedings of the 33rd Annual ACM Symposium on the Theory of Computing*, pp. 749-753.

Patriksson, M. and Rockafellar, R.T., 2003. Sensitivity analysis of aggregated variational in equality problems, with application to traffic equilibria. *Transportation Science* 37, 56-68.

Patriksson, M., 2004. Sensitivity analysis of traffic equilibria. *Transportation Science* 38, 258-281.

Patriksson, M., 1994. The *Traffic Assignment Problem: Models and Methods*. VSP BV, Utrecht, Netherlands.

Patriksson, M. and Rockafellar, R.T., 2003. Sensitivity analysis of aggregated variational inequality problems, with application to traffic equilibria. *Transportation Science* 37, 56-68.

Penchina, C.M., 2004. A minimal-revenue congestion pricing: some more good-news and bad-news. *Transportation Research* 38B, 559-570.

Perakis, G., 2004. The "price of anarchy" under nonlinear and asymmetric costs. *Lecture Notes in Computer Science* 3064, pp. 46–58. Springer.

Pigou, A.C., 1920. *The Economics of Welfare*. MacMillan, London.

Poole, R.W., 1992. Introducing congestion pricing on a new toll road. *Transportation* 19, 383-396.

Qui, Y. and Magnanti, T.L., 1989. Sensitivity analysis for variational inequalities defined on polyhedral sets. *Mathematics of Operations Research* 14, 410-432.

Powell, W.B. and Sheffi, Y., 1982. The convergence of equilibrium algorithms with predetermined step size. *Transportation Science* 16, 45-55.

Raux, C. and Souche, S., 2004. The acceptability of urban road pricing - a theoretical analysis applied to experience in Lyon. *Journal of Transport Economics and Policy* 38, 191-215.

Richardson, H.W. and Bae, C.H.C., 1998. The equity impacts of road congestion pricing. In: *Road Pricing, Traffic Congestion, and the Environment* (eds., Button K.J. and Verhoef E.T.). Edward Elgar, pp. 247-262.

Romeijin, H.E. and Smith, R.L., 1994. Simulated annealing for constrained global optimization. *Journal of Global Optimization* 5, 101-126.

Roth, G., 1996. *Roads in a Market Economy*. Avebury Technical, Ashgate Publishing Limited.

Roughgarden, T., 2005. *Selfish Routing and the Price of Anarchy*. The MIT Press, Cambridge.

Roughgarden, T., 2003. The price of anarchy is independent of the network topology. *Journal of Computer and System Sciences* 67, 341–364.

Roughgarden, T. and Tardos, E., 2002. How bad is selfish routing? *Journal of the ACM* 49, 236–259.

Roughgarden, T. and Tardos, E., 2004. Bounding the inefficiency of equilibria in non-atomic congestion games. *Games and Economic Behavior* 47, 389-403.

Santos, G. (ed.), 2004. *Road Pricing: Theory and Evidence*. Elsevier Science.

Santos, G. and Rojey, L., 2004. Distributional impacts of road pricing: the truth behind the myth. *Transportation* 31, 21-42.

Santos, G., 2004. Urban congestion charging - a second-best alternative. *Journal of Transport Economics and Policy* 38, 345-369.

Santos, G., 2002. Double cordon tolls in urban areas to increase social welfare. *Transportation Research Record* 1812, 49-55.

Santos, G., Newbery, D. and Rojey, L., 2001. Static vs. demand sensitive models and the estimation of efficient cordon tolls: an exercise for eight English towns. *Transportation Research Record* 1747, 44-50

Segal, D. and Steinmeier, T.L., 1980. The incidence of congestion and congestion tolls. *Journal of Urban Economics* 7, 42-62.

Sheffi, Y., 1985. *Urban Transportation Networks: Equilibrium Analysis with Mathematical Programming Methods*. Prentice-Hall, Inc., Englewood Cliffs, NJ.

Shepherd, S. and Sumalee, A., 2004. A genetic algorithm based approach to optimal toll level and location problems. *Networks & Spatial Economics* 4, 161-179.

Shimizu, K., Ishizuka, Y. and Bard, F., 1997. *Non-differentiable and Two-Level Mathematical Programming*. Kluwer Academic Publishers.

Small, K.A., 1982. The scheduling of consumer activities: Work trips. *American Economic Review* 72, 467-479.

Small, K.A., 1983. The incidence of congestion tolls on urban highways. *Journal of Urban Economics* 13, 90-110.

Small, K.A., (ed.) 1992a. Congestion pricing, a special issue. *Transportation* 19, 287-291.

Small, K.A., 1992b. *Urban Transportation Economics*. Harwood Academic.

Small, K.A., 1992c. Using the revenues from congestion pricing. *Transportation* 19, 359-381.

Small, K.A., 1999. Economies of scale and self-financing rules with non-competitive factor markets. *Journal of Public Economics* 74, 431-450.

Small, K.A., and Rosen, H.S., 1981. Applied welfare economics with discrete choice models. *Econometrica* 49, 105-130.

Smith, M.J., 1979a. The existence, uniqueness and stability of traffic equilibrium. *Transportation Research* 13B, 295-304.

Smith, M.J., 1979b. The marginal cost taxation of a transportation network. *Transportation Research* 13B, 237-242.

Smith, M.J., 1984. The existence of a time-dependent equilibrium distribution of arrivals at a single bottleneck. *Transportation Science* 18, 385-393.

Smith, T.E., Eriksson, A. and Lindberg, P.O., 1994. Existence of optimal tolls under conditions of stochastic user-equilibria. In: *Road Pricing: Theory, Empirical Assessment and Policy* (eds. Johansson B. and Mattsson, L.G.), Kluwer Academic Publishers, pp.65-87.

Starkie, D., 1986. Efficient and politic congestion tolls. *Transportation Research* 20A, 169-173.

Strotz, R.H., 1964. Urban transportation parables. In: *The Public Economy of Urban Communities, Resources for the Future* (ed., Margolis J.). Johns Hopkins University Press, Baltimore, MD, pp.127-169.

Sumalee, A., 2004. Optimal road user charging cordon design: A heuristic optimization approach. *Computer-aided Civil and Infrastructure Engineering* 19, 377-392.

Tabuchi, T., 1993. Bottleneck congestion and modal split. *Journal of Urban Economics* 34, 414-431.

Tam, A., 1998. Developing toll roads in China. *Asia Engineer* 26, 9-10.

Tobin, R.L. and Friesz, T.L., 1988. Sensitivity analysis for equilibrium network flow. *Transportation Science* 22, 242-250.

Toint, P. and Wynter, L., 1996. Asymmetric multiclass traffic assignment: A coherent formulation. In: *Proceedings of the 13th International Symposium on Transportation and Traffic Theory* (ed., Lesort, J.B.). Pergamon, Exeter, U.K., pp.237-260.

Tsai, J.F. and Chu, C.P., 2003. The analysis of regulation on private highway investment under a build-operate-transfer scheme. *Transportation* 30, 221-243.

Van der Zijpp N. and Koolstra, K., 2002. Multiclass continuous-time equilibrium model for departure time choice on single-bottleneck network. *Transportation Research Record*, 1783, 134-141.

Verhoef, E.T., 2003. Inside the queue: hyper-congestion and road pricing in a continuous time-continuous place model of traffic congestion. *Journal of Urban Economics* 54, 531-565.

Verhoef, E.T., 2002. Second-best congestion pricing in general networks: heuristic algorithms for finding second-best optimal toll levels and toll points. *Transportation Research* 36B, 707-729.

Verhoef, E.T., 1996. *The Economics of Regulating Road Transport*. Cheltenham, U.K.

Verhoef, E.T., Nijkamp, P. and Rietveld, P., 1996. Second-best congestion pricing: The case of an untolled alternative. *Journal of Urban Economics* 40, 279-302.

Verhoef, E.T. and Rouwendal, J., 2004. Pricing, capacity choice, and financing in transportation networks. *Journal of Regional Science* 44, 405-435.

Verhoef, E.T. and Small, K.A., 2004. Product differentiation on roads - Constrained congestion pricing with heterogeneous users. *Journal of Transport Economics and Policy* 38, 127-156.

Vickrey, W.S., 1969. Congestion theory and transport investment. *American Economic Review* (Papers and Proceedings) 59, 251-261.

Vickrey, W., 1993. Point of view: principles and applications of congestion pricing. *TR News* 167, 4-5.

Viegas, J.M., 2001. Making urban road pricing acceptable and effective: searching for quality and equity in urban mobility. *Transport Policy* 8, 289-294.

Viton, P.A., 1995. Private roads. *Journal of Urban Economics* 37, 260-289.

Walters, A.A., 1961. The theory and measurement of private and social cost of highway congestion. *Econometrica* 29, 676-699.

Wang, J.Y.T., Yang, H. and Verhoef, E.T., 2004. Strategic interactions of bilateral monopoly on a private highway. *Networks and Spatial Economics* 4, 203-235.

Wardrop, J.G., 1952. Some theoretical aspects of road traffic research. *Proceedings of Institution of Civil Engineers*-Part II, 1, 325-378.

Wie, B.W., 1995. A differential game approach to the dynamic mixed behavior traffic network equilibrium problem. *European Journals of Operations Research* 83, 117-136.

Wie, B.W., 1993. A differential game model of Nash equilibrium on a congested traffic network. *Networks* 23, 557-565.

Wie, B.W. and Tobin, R.L., 1998. Dynamic congestion pricing models for general traffic networks. *Transportation Research* 32B, 313-327.

Williams, H.C.W.L., 1977. On the formation of travel demand models and economic evaluation measures of user benefits. *Environment and Planning* 9A, 285-344.

Yang, H., 1999. System optimum, stochastic user equilibrium, and optimal link tolls. *Transportation Science* 33, 354-360.

Yang, H., 1997. Sensitivity analysis for the elastic demand network equilibrium problem with applications. *Transportation Research* 31B, 55-70.

Yang, H., 1995. Sensitivity analysis for queuing equilibrium network flow and its application to traffic control. *Mathematical and Computer Modeling* 22, 247-258.

Yang, H. and Bell, M.G.H., 2005. Sensitivity analysis of network traffic equilibria revisted: the corrected approach. *The Hong Kong University of Science and Technology*. Working Paper.

Yang, H, and Bell, M.G.H., 2001. Transport bilevel programming problems: recent methodological advances. *Transportation Research* 35B, 1-4.

Yang, H. and Bell, M.G.H., 1997. Traffic restraint, road pricing and network equilibrium. *Transportation Research* 31B, 303-314.

Yang, H. and Guo, X.L., 2005. Pareto-improving road pricing and revenue refunding schemes. *The Hong Kong University of Science and Technology*. Working Paper.

Yang, H. and Huang, H.J., 2004. The multiclass, multicriteria traffic network equilibrium and system optimum problem. *Transportation Research* 38B, 1-15.

Yang, H. and Huang, H.J., 1999. Carpooling and congestion pricing in a multilane highway with high-occupancy-vehicle lanes. *Transportation Research* 33A, 139-155.

Yang, H. and Huang, H.J., 1998. Principle of marginal-cost pricing: How does it work in a general network? *Transportation Research* 32A, 45-54.

Yang, H. and Huang, H.J., 1997. Analysis of the time-varying pricing of a bottleneck with elastic demand using optimal control theory. *Transportation Research* 31B, 425-440.

Yang, H. and Lam, W.H.K., 1996. Optimal road tolls under conditions of queuing and congestion. *Transportation Research* 30A, 319-332.

Yang, H. and Meng, Q., 2002. A note on highway pricing and capacity choice in a road network under a build-operate-transfer scheme. *Transportation Research* 36A, 659-663.

Yang, H. and Meng, H., 2000. Highway pricing and capacity choice in a road network under a build-operate-transfer scheme. *Transportation Research* 34A, 207-222.

Yang, H. and Meng, Q., 1998. Departure time, route choice and congestion toll in a general queuing network with elastic demand. *Transportation Research* 32B, 247-260.

Yang, H., Meng, Q. and Hau, T.D., 2004. Optimal integrated pricing in a bi-modal transportation network. Book Chapter in "*Urban and Regional Transportation Modeling: Essays in Honor of David Boyce*" (ed., Lee, D.H.), pp.134-156.

Yang, H., Meng, Q. and Lee, D.H., 2004. Trial-and-error implementation of marginal-cost pricing on networks in the absence of demand functions. *Transportation Research* 38B, 477-493.

Yang, H., Tang, W.H., Cheung, W.M. and Meng, Q., 2002. Profitability and welfare gain of private toll roads in a network with heterogeneous users. *Transportation Research* 36A, 537-554.

Yang, H. and Verhoef, E.T., 2004. Guest Editorial: Road Pricing Problems: Recent Methodological Advances. *Networks and Spatial Economics* 4, 131-133.

Yang, H. and Woo, K.K., 2000. Competition and equilibria of private toll roads in a traffic network. *Transportation Research Record* 1733, 15-22.

Yang, H., Iida, Y. and Sasaki, T., 1994. The equilibrium-based origin-destination matrix estimation problem. *Transportation Research* 28B, 23-33.

Yang, H., Sasaki, T., Iida, Y. and Asakura, Y., 1992. Estimation of origin-destination matrices from link traffic counts on congested networks. *Transportation Research* 26B, 1-18.

Yang, H., Xu, W. and Meng, Q., 2005. Trial-and-error implementation of the second-best congestion pricing problem with unknown demand function. In: Proceeding of the *16th International Symposium on Transportation and Traffic Theory (ISTTT15*), 19-21 July 2005, University of Maryland, College Park, USA (in press).

Yang, H. and Yagar, S., 1994. Traffic assignment and traffic control in general freeway-arterial corridor systems. *Transportation Research* 28B, 463-486.

Yang, H., Yagar, S., Iida, Y. and Asakura, Y., 1994. An algorithm for the inflow control problem on urban freeway networks with user-optimal flows. *Transportation Research* 28B, 123-139.

Yang, H. and Zhang, X.N., 2003. Existence of anonymous link tolls for system optimum on networks with multiple equilibrium behaviors. Working paper, Hong Kong University of Science and Technology.

Yang, H. and Zhang, X.N., 2002a. Determination of optimal toll levels and toll locations of alternative congestion pricing schemes. In: *Proceedings of the 15th International Symposium on Transportation and Traffic Theory* (ed., Taylor, M.A.P.), Pergamon, pp.519-540.

Yang, H. and Zhang, X.N., 2002b. Multiclass network toll design problem with social and spatial equity constraints. *Journal of Transportation Engineering* 128, ASCE, 420-428.

Yang, H., Zhang, X.N., and Meng, Q., 2004. Modeling private highways in networks with entry-exit based toll charges. *Transportation Research* 38B, 191-2113.

Yang, H., Zhang, X.N., and Meng Q., 2003. Stackelberg game and multiple equilibrium behaviors on networks. *The Hong Kong University of Science and Technology*. Working Paper.

Ye, J.J., Zhu, D.L. and Zhu, Q.J., 1997. Exact penalization and necessary optimality conditions for generalized bilevel programming problems. *SIAM Journal on Optimization* 7, 481-507.

Yildirim, M.B. and Hearn, D.W., 2005. A first-best toll pricing framework for variable demand traffic assignment problems. *Transportation Research* 39B, 659-678.

Yin, Y. and Yang, H., 2004. Optimal tolls with a multiclass, bicriteria traffic network equilibrium. *Transportation Research Record* 1882, 45-52.

Ying, J.Q., 2005. Sensitivity analysis based method for optimal road network pricing. *Annals of Operations Research* 133, 303-317.

Ying, J.Q. and Miyagi, T., 2001. Sensitivity analysis for stochastic user equilibrium network flows - A dual approach. *Transportation Science* 35, 124-133.

Ying, J.Q. and Yang, H., 2005. Sensitivity analysis of stochastic user equilibrium flow in a bi-modal network with application to optimal pricing. *Transportation Research* 39B, 769-795.

Zawack, D.J., Thompson, G.L., 1987. A dynamic space-time network flow model for city traffic congestion. *Transportation Science* 21, 153-162.

Zhang, H.M. and Ge, Y. E., 2004. Modeling variable demand equilibrium under second-best road pricing. *Transportation Research* 38B, 733-749.

Zhang, X.N., 2003. *Optimal Road Pricing in Transportation Networks. The Hong Kong University of Science and Technology*. PhD Thesis.

Zhang, X.N and Yang, H., 2004. The optimal cordon-based network congestion pricing problem. *Transportation Research* 38B, 517-537.

Zhang, X.N., Yang, H., Huang, H.J. and Zhang H.M., 2005. Integrated scheduling of daily work activities and morning-evening commutes with bottleneck congestion. *Transportation Research* 39A, 41-60.

SUBJECT INDEX